Software Development
Case Studies in Java

Davide Brugali
Università degli Studi di Bergamo, Italy

Marco Torchiano
Politecnico di Torino, Italy

 ADDISON-WESLEY

Harlow, England • London • New York • Boston • San Francisco • Toronto • Sydney • Singapore • Hong Kong
Tokyo • Seoul • Taipei • New Delhi • Cape Town • Madrid • Mexico City • Amsterdam • Munich • Paris • Milan

Pearson Education Limited
Edinburgh Gate
Harlow
Essex CM20 2JE
England

and Associated Companies throughout the world

Visit us on the World Wide Web at:
www.pearsoned.co.uk

First published 2005

ISBN 0 321 11783 2

British Library Cataloguing-in-Publication Data
A catalogue record for this book is available from the British Library

Library of Congress Cataloging-in-Publication Data
Brugali, Davide
   Software development : case studies in Java / Davide Brugali, Marco Torchiano.
      p. cm,
   Includes bibliographical references and index.
   ISBN 0-321-11783-2
     1. Computer software--Development. 2. Java (Computer program language) I.
Torchiano, Marco. II. Title

   QA76.76.D47B78 2005
   005.1--dc22

                                                                    2004060103

10 9 8 7 6 5 4 3 2 1
09 08 07 06 05

Typeset by 25
Printed in Great Britain by Henry Ling Ltd, at the Dorset Press, Dorchester, Dorset

The publisher's policy is to use paper manufactured from sustainable forests.

PARK LEARNING CENTRE

The Park Cheltenham

Gloucestershire GL50 2RH

Telephone: 01242 714333

UNIVERSITY OF
GLOUCESTERSHIRE

at Cheltenham and Gloucester

Visit the *Software* _____ *n Java*
Companion Website at www.pearsoned.co.uk/brugali
to find valuable **student** learning material including:

- Source code for every case study
- Collection of sidebars illustrating techniques and
  technologies used in the case studies
- Collection of idioms and patterns demonstrating
  good development practice

To Giovanna e Giacomo

D. Brugali

To Silvia e Sara

M. Torchiano

Contents

20 Negotiation-based service configuration   538

21 Workflow management system   576

Supporting resources

Visit **www.pearsoned.co.uk/brugali** to find valuable online resources

Companion Website for students

- Source code for every case study
- Collection of sidebars illustrating techniques and technologies used in the case studies
- Collection of idioms and patterns demonstrating good development practice

For more information please contact your local Pearson Education sales representative or visit **www.pearsoned.co.uk/brugali**

Preface

Conceptual software development is the art of crafting software in an engineering way. This craft's tools are software processes, development methodologies, programming techniques and, most of all, a critical analysis attitude, creative synthesis ability and problem-solving experience. It is both an art and an engineering discipline.

Software engineering offers principles, theories and technologies that aim to standardize software product development. The effective programmer translates the general principles into good practice. Mastering general principles requires good skills; exercising good practice requires extensive experience. Teaching by example is the approach of this book. The goal is to distil the best practice of an experienced software engineer and to make it available to the reader in order to shape his or her ability to master the development of concrete applications.

The result is a conceptual roadmap that the reader can follow in his or her own personal software process to develop any kind of application, from standalone applications such as a computer simulator, to distributed systems such as a messaging server, and up to complex object frameworks such as a workflow management system.

This book addresses single programmers or small teams of programmers. Case studies reproduce small projects that may last no longer than a few days or weeks and guide the reader step by step throughout the whole life cycle of concrete applications, from problem formulation and requirements analysis, through component and system design, down to Java coding and testing.

The case studies exploit object-oriented concepts and techniques incrementally: structures of classes, design patterns, system architectures and frameworks. Each case study explores alternative design approaches, explains the rationale of each choice, demonstrates the consequences, and provides concrete advice useful in the subsequent case studies.

Whom this book is for

The book emphasizes the object-oriented methodology and exemplifies the object-oriented software process in a pedagogically sound and careful way by discussing many case studies from which readers can easily generalize.

This book is appropriate for senior level courses on object-oriented programming, intermediate or advanced Java programming in departments of computer science, CIS, MIS, IT, business and continuing education.

It is also appropriate for upper-level courses where the instructor wants an exercise book. This text assumes readers have completed a previous course in programming that covers the basic concepts of the Java language, an introduction to object-oriented analysis and design, and to UML notation. It includes sidebars that give a working knowledge of advanced topics such as design patterns, networking, multithreading and databases applied in specific case studies.

Structure of this book

The first chapter of the book is a reading guide that defines the presentation structure of each case study. The rest of the book is divided into four parts: Part I, Objects and Classes, exploits the basic concepts of the object-oriented technology, such as information hiding, polymorphism and design patterns. Part II, Object Architectures, stresses the concept of separation of concerns and focuses on the construction of complex applications such as composition of basic building blocks. Part III, Distributed Architectures, addresses the design and construction of large distributed software systems. Part IV, Object Frameworks, shows how the object-oriented technology supports the concept of frameworks for the development of families of similar applications.

Each part includes an introductory chapter and four case studies. Each case study describes the development of a concrete application and in particular:

- Illustrates the entire object-oriented development process from conception and design, to programming and implementation. Alternative solutions emphasize the importance of good design practice, alert readers to potential design pitfalls and offer important tips and guidance for avoiding such mistakes.
- Adopts the UML notation and emphasizes the role of documentation in the development process.
- Adopts innovative object-oriented techniques. Several case studies exemplify and motivate the use of well-known design patterns and exploit advanced reuse-oriented techniques, such as components and frameworks. Each case study highlights the reuse of off-the-shelf solutions (domain models, design solution, code fragments) that are derived from previous case studies or from the literature.
- Presents fully implemented and thoroughly documented applications. Complete programming examples enable readers to verify that programs run as expected and to manipulate their code.
- Covers advanced Java-related technologies: JDBC, RMI, Sockets, Applets, Servlets, JavaScript, XML and Swing GUI.
- Has an assessment section that indicates possible extensions, revisions and programming exercises.

Acknowledgements

Many of the case studies presented in this book were developed as a result of the teaching activities of Davide Brugali at the University of Bergamo and of Marco Torchiano at the Politecnico di Torino. Several of our students contributed a considerable amount of their time to implement an initial version of each case study.

Hundreds of students have elaborated variants to the solutions presented in the case studies, which in many cases have been documented as extensions at the end of each chapter. We wish to thank all of these students for their precious criticism which helped us to illustrate the case studies in a sound pedagogical style.

We would like to offer a special vote of thanks to Professor Joan Lukas, of the University of Massachusetts, Boston, whose insights and guidance in the preparation of the manuscript proved invaluable.

Finally, we wish to express our gratitude to the publisher and in particular to Kate Brewin, Owen Knight, Mary Lince, Robert Chaundy and Ruth Freestone King for their valuable support throughout the whole editorial process.

Reading guide

1

1.1 ■ Key concepts

The book is organized as a set of increasingly complex case studies, which are presented according to a simplified development process. Such a process is intended to keep track of all the activities that are involved in the development of the case study and builds on the following concepts:

- flow of thought;
- refine and evolve;
- incremental approach;
- development vocabulary.

Each of these concepts forms a sort of guide line that the reader may follow through each case study and across the book's chapters. As far as possible the flow of thoughts is "serialized" in order to make it easy to read. However, since thought is not linear by nature, possible alternative branches that were explored during the solution-discovery process will be presented in the form of "decision points".

Each step in the solution process is the result of the refinement of ideas present in previous steps. Starting from analysis and throughout the design, earlier and simpler solutions are evolved into solutions that are more complex and closer to a working system.

The experience of the readers builds up incrementally. As they encounter new problems and find the relative solutions, they adds new terms to their solutions vocabulary, which they will be able to use in the solution of future problems.

Each case study is self-contained. The initial synthesis enumerates the concepts that will be presented in the case study and the required background. Some initial assumptions might come from the final assessment of previous case studies.

The book supports multiple reading approaches:

- *Process oriented*. Each case study represents an instance of an object-oriented development process. The reader is invited to follow the straightforward structure of the book from the first to the last case study, that is, from the simplest to the most complex and complete case study.
- *Scope oriented*. Each part of the book covers a specific sector of the object-oriented technology (simple standalone applications, complex multi-threaded applications, concurrent and distributed systems, application

frameworks). Most readers will read the parts sequentially and return to specific parts as reference materials.

■ *Domain oriented.* The case studies document the development of applications in three broad software domains: computer simulation of control systems (Chapters 5, 9, 10, 11, 13), data processing (Chapters 3, 4, 6, 8, 18, 21) and information systems (Chapters 14, 15, 16, 19, 20). The reader can browse the book according to his or her interest in specific domains.

1.2 ■ The process

Our intent is not to propose a new software development process, but to present the reader with a consistent approach throughout the book. We will define a set of lightweight process guidelines that form a unifying framework through all the case studies. The process that will be adopted is based on incremental development. The structure of each case study chapter will follow this development process, since we want to repeat, together with the reader, the process of devising and implementing a solution for a problem. Table 1.1 shows the phases of the development process.

1.2.1 □ Specification

The first section of each case study presents the description of the problem from the customer's point of view.

1.2.2 □ Problem analysis

The information available during this phase consists of the requirements specification. That artifact is mainly an unstructured document in natural language containing the description of the system. This phase is made up of three activities:

■ *Analysis of the domain of the problem.* Often a system encompasses several topics that fall into well-defined areas in which there are widely accepted domain models or theoretical background. Such models must be taken into account in order to solve the problem in the most effective way.

■ *Identification of main features.* The main features that the system is required to exhibit are identified in the problem analysis phase. They are tracked back to the issues presented in the requirement specification and are described at a shallow level of detail. Features usually consist of functional requirements, but if some other decomposition criteria are obvious they can be adopted to define the features. If use cases can provide clarity, they can supplement the textual description of the requirements. An initial priority can be assigned to the features, possibly based on some knowledge of the domain.

Table 1.1 The phases of the development process

Phase		Description	Artifacts
Specifications		Description of the problem	A natural language text describing the problem as it would appear during an interview with the customer. Examples can be used to make the description of the problem clearer. Informal drawings can be used to better explain complex concepts or to provide examples
Problem analysis		Analysis of the specifications in order to identify the main features of the system. Domain analysis	A natural language text that explains step by step the main features of the system, how they can be traced in the specifications and their relationship to each other. Use cases can be used to identify the stakeholders and the main functionalities of the system. System-level test cases are defined at this point
Architecture		Definition of the software architecture of the system and planning of development steps	A natural language text that describes the architecture of the system with its rationale. UML diagrams are used to describe architectural views. A natural language text that shows the plan of the increments and the allocation of components to them
Increment	Analysis	Detailed analysis of the system for this iteration and selection of available technologies	Detailed analysis model (class diagrams) together with the rationale of analysis process and choices
	Design	Detailed design of the system for this iteration, with evaluation of different solutions	UML diagrams accompanied by rationale for design decisions
	Implementation	Implementation of the design	Code
	Test	Identification of test cases in order to assess the correct behaviour of the prototype	Test cases for the modules developed in the iteration
Assessment		Definition of reusable elements and summary of new terms in the "design vocabulary"	A list of the positive and reusable issues that emerged during the solution. Patterns are presented in tabular form

■ *Definition of system level acceptance tests*. Based on the findings of the problem analysis and on the main features of the system, a suite of test cases is defined. These tests can be applied at the system level. It is important to build the test cases in a modular way and to relate them to features. This is intended to make it easy to apply the tests to intermediate software artifacts produced during the incremental development.

1.2.3 ☐ **Architecture**

During this phase two main activities are performed:

- the conception/selection of the system's software architecture, and
- the planning of the development.

The increments are defined as a consequence of the problem analysis and based on the architecture defined for the system. Each increment consists of the analysis and design of a set of architectural components and leads to the implementation of a prototype that tests their functionalities.

1.2.4 ☐ **Iterative development**

A new iteration is started with every increment. The rationale for the choices made during the definition of models is provided and a generic approach is used whenever possible (i.e. in analysis, identification of nouns and verbs is important).

The models are developed incrementally and evolve from a simple intuitive solution to a pattern-oriented, smart, optimal solution.

Assessment of the design is performed at each iteration. Such assessment represents the rationale for design evolution in the next iterations.

Each iteration is a sequence of four activities:

- *Analysis*. This consists in the identification of classes and relationships. The process is described and motivated step by step. When a large model is considered, it is allowed to "skip some low-level step". The artifacts of the analysis are mainly: object diagrams, class diagrams and detailed use cases.
- *Design*. We adopt a flow of thoughts approach: we start with an initial solution that is the most obvious and intuitive and is defined using only the "design vocabulary" that the reader has acquired so far. The "design vocabulary" is the one provided by the preceding parts of the book or the initial knowledge of the reader, who is required to know the basic concepts of generic object-oriented analysis, design and Java programming. Then the solution is evolved into a smarter and better one: new development techniques and design models are introduced, which have proven to be effective in solving similar problems.
- *Implementation*. We adopt the Java coding conventions described in Sun Microsystems (see References at the end of the chapter). Getter and setter methods have a "get" or "set" prefix respectively. Parameters which are intended to be copied into attributes should have the same name. Exceptions to these rules are admitted when appropriate.
- *Test*. Test cases are defined in order to exercise the components' functionalities.

1.2.5 ☐ **Assessment**

Each chapter ends with a summary of the relevant issues encountered in the development process of the case study application. The assessment section is structured around those development aspects that are common to all the chapters of the same book part, as listed in Table 1.2. The goal of the assessment section is to review the milestones of the development path from the problem specification to the final implementation, in order to assess the knowledge that the reader has acquired.

The art of solving problems often consists of reapplying known solutions to new problems. Reusable solutions to recurring problems are called patterns. We present the knowledge gained about solutions, and techniques emerge from the case study development in the form of patterns.

The most general definition of a pattern is a literary form, which describes an application *Context*, a design *Problem*, which occurs in that context, and a *Solution* to the problem, which has been shown by experience to be effective.

Some authors extend the description of their patterns by including other paragraphs: the opposing *Forces* and tradeoffs, which the pattern resolves; an *Example*, which shows how the pattern has been applied in a specific case; the *Implementation* which describes techniques for implementing the pattern.

Table 1.2 The key aspects of the development process in the case studies of each part of the book

Book part	Focus on	Key aspects
Part I **Objects and Classes**	The focus is on the transition from the problem specification to the implementation, which is made up of a sequence of refinement steps. Reusable patterns are identified and applied when appropriate	Analysis technique Modelling notation Design approach Reusable patterns
Part II **Object Architectures**	The focus is no longer on individual objects but on the whole architecture of an application. More importance is given to the fundamental role that relationships between the elements have in any design	Architectural styles Generic components Communication Concurrency
Part III **Distributed Architectures**	The focus is on reuse-based development. Developing large distributed architectures is complex. Middleware infrastructures are a promising technology for reifying proven software designs and implementations in order to reduce development costs and improve software quality	Architecture model Distribution paradigm Middleware technology
Part IV **Object Frameworks**	The focus is on reuse-oriented development. Frameworks are a powerful developing approach as they consist of both reusable code (the component library) and reusable design (the architecture)	Domain analysis Framework scope Framework customization

A pattern documents a concrete reusable solution to a recurrent architectural problem. Several "pattern libraries" have already been defined (Gamma *et al.* 1995); by "library" we mean a document (e.g. a book or a paper) that describes one or more design patterns. The developer selects the design pattern which is most applicable to the problem in question, and reuses the corresponding solution. The context and problem sections of the pattern make it easy for the developer to retrieve the right pattern.

Patterns cover the range from analysis and overall program architecture (architectural patterns), to class and component design (design patterns), up to very specific details of physical design or implementation (idioms).

Since patterns are concrete representations of domain expertise, they greatly raise the level of communication between designers working together. Each pattern is given a name, capturing its essence; the pattern name becomes part of the designers' vocabulary allowing them to refer to complex problems and solutions with a single word, with no possibility of misunderstanding. Patterns are applicable not only to design but also to analysis.

Unfortunately, design patterns do not support code reuse in a systematic way as class libraries: the *Implementation* paragraph is very often missing or it just sketches a description in a high-level language.

Patterns will be presented according the following schema:

Pattern type	Pattern name
Context	The context where a design problem has emerged
Problem	The design problem to solve
Forces or tradeoffs	The forces in action that cause the problem and define the context
Solution	An operational description of how to solve the problem
Examples	An example showing how to apply the solution
Force resolution	The effect of applying the solution, in terms of both new resulting forces and modified context
Design rationale	The motivation for using the techniques adopted in the solution

1.3 ■ References

Gamma, E., Helm, R., Johnson, R. and Vlissides, J. (1995) *Design Patterns: Elements of Reusable Object-Oriented Software*, Addison-Wesley.

Sun Microsystems, *Code Conventions for the Java Programming Language* available at http://java.sun.com/docs/codeconv/.

PART I

Objects and Classes

Objects and classes

2

Synthesis

The object-oriented (OO) approach to software development consists of a set of techniques and mechanisms to be used in structuring models and program code according to the concepts and the relative relationships found in the problem domain. Classes represent abstract concepts, which are made concrete by objects. Classes are related to each other by means of associations that define the semantics of their links.

The strength of the OO approach is the capability of using the same basic tools and constructs throughout the whole development process. The formalization of the problem, the design solution, and the structure of the executable code are based on the same foundations: objects and classes. Through a process of progressive refinement a model of the problem evolves into the executable Java code that is able to solve it.

Objects and classes make the OO programming paradigm different from procedural and functional paradigms: a piece of information and the code that accesses and modifies it form a bundle; they are confined to one location in the program and not spread, uncontrollably, throughout the program. Classes define the data structure and the interface through which data can be accessed; objects contain the data and operate on it.

The first part of this book is dedicated to the understanding of the OO paradigm and how it is possible to map real-world problems onto it by means of models.

2.1 ■ Development approach

The focus in this first part of the book will be on building the basic knowledge that supports the transition from the problem specification to the solution implementation. The transition is made up of a sequence of refinement steps: the analysis of the user requirements, the definition of an object-oriented analysis model, the evolution of this model into a design model, the implementation of this model in Java, and the test of the application functionalities against the initial requirements.

Object-oriented analysis is about identifying the basic concepts underpinning the problem under study and their inter-relationships. They can be described by means of classes and relationships in the OO paradigm. The analysis model expresses a problem-oriented view; it provides entities and relationships that capture everything of importance in the system to be developed. OO methods encourage analysts to represent a system the way it is perceived, without being constrained by how it will be implemented.

Domain models play an important role any time we address a new application domain (e.g. enterprise information systems, simulation environments, text editors). The requirements that we are likely to analyse have often been studied and are well understood. Therefore, it is important to refer to the related literature and to find hints and help from it.

Object-oriented design is concerned with the transformation of analysis models into design models with desirable functional (e.g. browsing a catalogue in alphabetic order) and non-functional (e.g. high performance and safety) properties.

An important step is the transition from the design model to the implementation code. This process must meet the capabilities of the implementation language, which we begin to explore in this first part of the book. Here we assume a working knowledge of the basic constructs of the Java language. The case studies will focus on basic design and implementation techniques such as many-to-one associations, generalization and collections. These techniques will be coded in a reusable format and form the base of the reader's development vocabulary.

2.2 ■ Basic building blocks

In the OO paradigm objects are characterized by state, behaviour and identity. Each object has a state, i.e. the data it contains. The behaviour consists in the set of operations that the object can perform on its data. Finally, each object has an identity that identifies it univocally within the application.

Classes define the common data structure (i.e. the data types that are used to represent the state), and behaviour (i.e. the set of operations that can be performed by an object) of a family of objects. Objects with similar properties belong to the same class. They are program units, which encapsulate both data and algorithms.

The OO paradigm supports the development of software applications by offering three basic techniques. (1) *Encapsulation*, which consists in constructing new classes around data. (2) *Inheritance*, which consists in deriving new classes as specializations of other classes. (3) *Polymorphism*, which allows two or more subclasses of the same class to respond to the same message (the invocation of an operation) in different ways.

New classes can be defined on the basis of existing ones by means of inheritance. This technique allows both reusing characteristics defined in already existing classes and to factor common characteristics of several classes within a single class. The latter options leads to two advantages: first it reduces development effort, second it simplifies maintenance by providing a single point of change.

OO technology has the advantage of facilitating the development of highly modular systems. The behaviour of a composite object is the result of the collaboration among its component objects. The basic mechanism of collaboration is *delegation*. The composite object implements a complex algorithm by delegating to the component objects the execution of part of the algorithm's steps. The component objects hold the data (encapsulation) that are required to execute the delegated operations.

2.3 ■ Modelling notations

The notation adopted throughout this part of the book ranges from informal problem description, to UML diagrams and Java source code. We will demonstrate the use of several UML diagrams:

- class diagrams,
- object diagrams,
- sequence diagrams,
- collaboration diagrams,
- state transition diagrams, and
- use cases.

Table 2.1 summarizes the notations covered during the development of the case studies.

Table 2.1 OO modelling notations adopted in each case study

Case study	Class	Object	Sequence	Collaboration	State transition	Use case
3 Scheduler	✗					
4 Classifier	✗	✗	✗			
5 HDL	✗				✗	
6 Multi-format calculator	✗			✗		✗

We will also explain how the Java language supports the OO concepts and general programming principles such as modularity, abstract data types and code robustness.

2.4 ■ Part overview

The first part of this book presents the foundations of OO software development, the basic development techniques vocabulary, and its representation in the Java programming language.

Chapter 3 (Scheduler) deals with the development of a tool that supports interactive scheduling of project activities. This case study emphasizes the separation of concerns between the problem description, the scheduling algorithm, and the user interface. The tool is tested in two different scheduling scenarios: a mail delivery service and a fitness club.

Chapter 4 (Classifier) deals with the development of a classification system that partitions items into categories according to their characteristics; such a system can be used for example by an insurance company to define risk categories for new car models. The case study presents the basic techniques used to represent in Java generic OO concepts such as associations and attributes.

Chapter 5 (Hardware description language) deals with the use of Java as a general-purpose hardware description and simulation language. It leverages the capability of the object-oriented approach to model physical components interacting with each other. This case study focuses on state-based behaviour, which can be described by means of state transition diagrams.

Chapter 6 (Multi-format calculator) deals with the development of a multi-format calculator that is able to convert operand and results between different numbering bases and representation formats. The main OO concept that is applied in this case study is polymorphism. In addition, the handling of abnormal conditions through exception is exemplified.

2.5 ■ References

Fowler, M. (2000) *UML Distilled*, Addison-Wesley.

Liskov, Barbara (1988) "Data Abstraction and Hierarchy", *SIGPLAN Notices*, Vol. 23, No. 5, May.

Scheduler

3

Synthesis

This chapter addresses the problem of building a tool for activities scheduling. The scheduling tool offers essential functionalities, such as creating activities and tasks, assigning resources to activities, devising a time plan that enforces temporal and resource constraints, and displaying the results in a graphical interface.

- Focus: this case study emphasizes the role of domain models and the mapping between entities of the problem and objects of the solution.
- OO techniques: inclusion and separation of concerns.
- Java features: Collections, AWT and Swing components.
- Background: the reader is required to know the basic OO concepts and fundamental Java programming techniques.

3.1 ■ Specifications

To illustrate the capabilities of the collaborative scheduling tool, we consider two scenarios that depict how the tool can be used to solve different scheduling problems. In both scenarios, the concepts of project, project manager and team members are used in a broad sense. Roughly speaking, a project is a coherent set of tasks related to one another by the use of common resources in a given time frame corresponding to the duration of the project. The first scenario is about mail delivery in a city, where the distribution clerk of the central post office plays the role of project manager. He or she sorts mail and delegates its distribution to the carriers. The second scenario is about a fitness club where the trainer schedules workouts for the athletes. In both scenarios, the project manager has the responsibility to elaborate a time plan and the team members to revise it while carrying out their activities.

3.1.1 □ Mail delivery service

The post office employs a number of carriers for daily mail delivery. The city is partitioned into delivery areas and every area is assigned to only one carrier. Each carrier is in charge of delivering mail within the assigned area following a predefined set of delivery routes. Each route starts and ends at the post office where the carrier racks and ties the mail before delivering it. Delivery routes are executed according to a preferred (but not fixed) order.

For each route the average delivery time is known. This information allows the distribution clerk at the post office to sort mail for each carrier at the right time. Since the mail sorting process is complex and time consuming, it is important to schedule the delivery activities appropriately. The goal is to minimize delays and to avoid confusion at the post office.

The delivery time plan defines for each carrier the start time of each delivery route. Since delivery times depend on variable parameters (traffic conditions, quantity of mail, etc.), each carrier revises the time plan before starting any new delivery route.

3.1.2 □ Fitness club

A fitness club organizes training courses for its member athletes. The fitness room is equipped with a comprehensive range of training machines including bikes, leg extension machines, rowing machines and weight machines. The fitness club employs a qualified trainer who designs personalized routines suited for the club members according to their problems and needs, their goals (losing weight, strengthening muscles, etc.), and current condition. For example, three athletes repeat the following routine programmes:

- Athlete, A1: 15 min. bike, 15 min. leg extension, 10 min. rowing.
- Athlete, A2: 20 min. bike, 15 min. leg extension, 10 min. weight.
- Athlete, A3: 20 min. bike, 15 min. leg extension, 10 min. rowing, 10 min. weight.

Exercises are executed according to a preferred (but not fixed) order. The workout of an athlete consists of a temporal sequence of exercises each one requiring the exclusive use of a training machine for the entire duration of his or her exercise. The daily plan defines the usage constraints of each training machine: the sequence of athletes using a given machine and the start and end time of each exercise on that machine.

The fitness plan should take into account the individual routines of each athlete and the duration and sequence of their exercises. The trainer must pay special attention to minimize the delay between two consecutive exercises performed by the same athlete in order to prevent his or her muscles from getting cold. In any case, a minimum delay is recommended for the athlete to rest (this delay might be accounted for in the duration of the exercise).

During the execution of their training workouts the athletes can revise the time plan to update the actual duration of each exercise: sometimes athletes may need additional time to rest or feel able to carry on an exercise (beyond the time specified by the trainer).

3.1.3 □ The scheduling tool

The project manager uses the scheduling tool to formulate the time plan for the project at hand. The tool should provide the user with three fundamental functionalities: (1) to define a new scheduling problem, (2) to elaborate a time plan, and (3) to revise the time plan.

For example, the definition of a scheduling problem requires the distribution clerk to specify how many carriers are available, how many areas each carrier serves, the average duration of the delivery service in each area, the preferred start time for each service. Similarly, the trainer should define the equipment of the fitness club, the number of athletes who attend the course on a given day, the sequence of exercises for each athlete, the duration of each exercise, and the preferred start time of each exercise.

The tool should have a user friendly interface that allows the project manager and the team members to set the temporal parameters of each activity and to view the time plan in a graphical representation. The tool might offer common functionalities such as saving/loading the time plan to/from a permanent storage medium.

3.2 ■ Problem analysis

The scenarios outlined in the previous section describe two situations where a project manager uses a scheduling tool to define a time plan for a set of tasks carried on by the team members. Complex tasks are broken down into activities that represent the units of work of a resource.

In the first scenario, carriers play the role of team members and correspond to the available resources. Every day each carrier is responsible of the execution of a mail delivery task. A task is made up of a sequence of activities corresponding to the delivery routes. It is important to note that there is a temporal constraint between the activities of a task. An activity can start only after the completion of the previous one. On the other hand, there is no temporal dependency between different tasks, since different carriers execute them.

In the second scenario, the tasks are the workouts of the members of the fitness club, the activities are the exercises of the training programme, and the resources are the machines needed for their execution. We assume that the number of training machines is limited (this is reasonable, although it is not specified in the scenario description) and that the number of athletes that attend the fitness club simultaneously is bigger than the number of training machines of the same type. It is clear that some conflicts might arise in the allocation of training machines to the athletes, and that the tasks carried on by the athletes are interrelated and dependent on one another.

The scheduler records the scheduling problem in terms of tasks, activities, and resources as specified by the user and elaborates a time plan on demand. It takes into account the dependencies among the resources, the tasks and their component activities (*which* activity is assigned to a resource, *when* does a resource perform an activity). The user (the project manager or the team members) revises the time plan iteratively by modifying the temporal parameters of each activity. Figure 3.1 shows the UML analysis model.

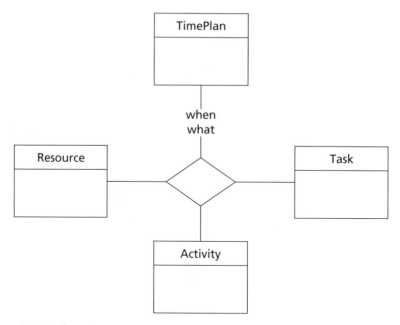

Figure 3.1 Analysis diagram

3.2.1 □ Domain models

Both scenarios resemble typical job-shop scheduling problems that are well known in the operational research field. This kind of problem is characterized by the exclusive use of finite-capacity resources for the execution of process activities and tasks. Common examples can be found in the factory automation domain, where the resources are the manufacturing facilities (robots, machines, transports, etc.), the tasks are production jobs (e.g. painting a car body), and the activities represent specific steps of the production process (e.g. polishing).

An activity is characterized by five parameters.

- The *type* determines the association between an activity and the resources that can perform it as a service on demand.
- The *release time* indicates the instant when the activity might start to be executed if a resource is available.
- The *activation time* is the actual instant to start the activity.
- The *termination time* is the instant when the activity will complete its execution according to the resource performance and the type of activity.
- The *due time* represents the deadline when the activity is to be completed.

A task represents a chain of related activities. It maintains the temporal dependencies (Figure 3.2) between activities through their release time and due time. In reality, this definition applies to those application scenarios where tasks are made up of activities that cannot be executed concurrently. For example, a car body cannot be painted and polished simultaneously.

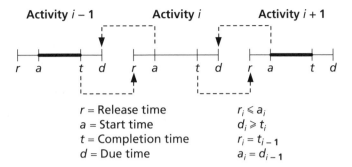

Figure 3.2 The relationship between task and activity

A resource represents a physical entity (e.g. a piece of manufacturing equipment) that receives requests for an activity of proper types to be delivered over a certain time interval.

Two types of constraint characterize a job-shop scheduling problem: temporal consistency constraints and resource consistency constraints.

- A temporal consistency constraint states that within a given task each activity can only start when the previous one is finished.
- A resource consistency constraint states that a given resource can process only one activity at a time. In fact, it is assumed that each activity requires the exclusive use of a resource.

The solution of a job-shop problem consists of the set values for the activation time and termination time variables of each activity. Such values must respect all the temporal and resource consistency constraints and guarantee that all the activities are processed after their release time and within their due times.

A variety of scheduling algorithms are documented in the literature. From an architectural point of view, they can be divided in two categories: centralized and decentralized.

Centralized algorithms require the model of the system to be expressed in terms of global state variables (the temporal parameters of each activity) and global constraints (the temporal and resource dependencies between activities). Usually, they are customized for the specific problem at hand in order to compute the optimal solution that maximizes or minimizes the target parameters (e.g. the total mail delivery time, or the total delay between two exercises). These algorithms compute all the possible permutations between activities and evaluate the target parameter for each of them. The main drawback is that both the system model identification and the consequent ad hoc algorithm design are complex tasks even for trivial problems. In addition, centralized algorithms have to be designed with "ad hoc" techniques. Every new problem must be solved from scratch.

Decentralized algorithms exploit the natural decomposition of the problem into sub-problems according to the physical system organization in subsystems and allow the system designer to tackle each sub-problem individually. For example, scheduling the time plan for a single mail carrier represents a sub-problem of the scheduling problem for the entire post office. The decentralized approach prevents the algorithm from finding the optimal solution of a given scheduling problem (the algorithm does not have global visibility of the state variables) but simplifies the system model identification and solution evaluation. The solution emerges as the result of the interactions between the subsystems: each subsystem optimizes its own objective but coordinates with the other subsystems when conflicts arise.

For a wide class of problem, scheduling algorithms try to minimize earliness and tardiness. This means that an activity should not start before its release time and should not complete after its due time. The earliness and tardiness constraints might be strong or weak. In the former case the constraints cannot be violated, while in the latter case they can be violated to the prejudice of the scheduling performance. For the sake of simplicity, we consider only weak constraints. This guarantees that the scheduling problem always has a solution, no matter how bad. The performance of the scheduling algorithm measures the quality of the solution, i.e. how much the solution enforces the temporal constraints.

The performance of an activity is computed as illustrated in Equation 3.1 as a function the parameters r, a, t and d, which have the meaning defined in Figure 3.2. The lower is the value of performance the better is the solution. The pe is the earliness performance, the pt is the tardiness performance, we and wt are the weights on pe and pt, and P is the activity performance. We define the performance of the entire system as the sum of the performances of all the activities.

$$pe = \begin{cases} we * (r-a) & r > a \\ 0 & r \leqslant a \end{cases} \qquad pt = \begin{cases} wt * (t-d) & t > d \\ 0 & t \leqslant d \end{cases}$$

$$P = pe + pt$$

Equation 3.1 Earliness, tardiness and task overall performance

The values of we and wt depend on the problem at hand. For example, we can give more importance to the tardiness constraint if we want the activities to complete as soon as possible.

The scheduling algorithm has the goal of minimizing the value of P while looking for a solution to the scheduling problem (assignment of new values to the activity parameters) that satisfies the temporal and resource constraints. The algorithm enforces these constraints by sequencing the activities executed by a resource. This implies shifting values of the temporal parameters of each activity forwards or backwards. It is clear that the performance of the result depends on the specific order imposed on the activities processed by all the resources.

In order to find the optimal solution (the one that corresponds to the minimum value of P), the algorithm would have to permute all the possible sequences of activities for each resource. This is the typical centralized approach, where the algorithm has visibility of the entire model of the scheduling problem.

On the other hand, the decentralized approach assigns to each resource the responsibility to schedule its activities. The resource applies a three-step procedure that does not require evaluating all the possible permutations of activities.

- First, the resource orders the activities by their activation time.
- Second, the resource enforces resource and temporal constraints. This requires shifting the activities' activation time and termination time forward in order to avoid temporal overlapping between consecutive activities.
- Third, each activity evaluates its performance and proposes a new activation time that tries to minimize earliness and tardiness. The new activation time is evaluated according to Equation 3.2. Parameter g (gain) represents the strength of the activity's preferences. The greater this value, the stronger is the ability of the activity to enforce its preferences. The resource repeats the above procedure for all the tasks until the global performance or the number of iterations (indicated by k) reaches a desired threshold.

$$a[k+1] = a[k] + g * (d - t)$$

Equation 3.2 Earliness, tardiness and task overall performance

This approach is actually one of dynamic scheduling and implements a strict separation of concerns between resource and activity. The former knows its availability and is simply the bookkeeper that orders the list of activities temporally in order to avoid overlapping; the latter takes the initiative proposing its preferred activation time based on its constraints (release time and due date) and the estimated termination time received as a response from the resource.

This algorithm resembles a discrete time control feedback loop that minimizes earliness and tardiness (see Figure 3.3). It has been shown that the emerging behaviour, which results from the unconscious interaction between activities on a resource, as previously described, has good stability and performance properties (Prabhu and Duffie 1999).

3.2.2 □ Main features

We are now able to summarize all the main features emerging from the problem analysis.

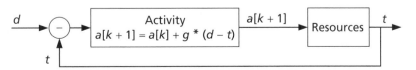

Figure 3.3 Discrete time control feedback loop

- *Scheduler architecture*. This is the central topic of this case study. We have to define the basic components of the scheduling tool that allow the representation of a scheduling problem and its sub-problems.
- *Scheduling algorithm*. We have to define how the algorithm computes a solution and how it identifies the best solution.
- *Graphical user interface*. The scheduling tool is an interactive application that requires a graphical user interface. We will consider a Gantt-like representation.

3.2.3 ☐ Test

One suite of test cases will be defined for each scenario. They consist in the representation of resources, activities and tasks and in the evaluation of a time plan that enforces the resource and temporal constraints among their temporal parameters.

3.3 ■ Architecture and planning

In order to ensure scalability and reusability of the scheduling tool, we have to factor out the stable parts and to isolate the variable parts. The stable parts are the basic components needed to build a model of the problem (task, activities, resources) and the scheduling algorithm. It is important to pay attention to avoid dependencies between the structure of the scheduling algorithm and the actual size of the problem to hand. The variable part is the model of the problem. We address these issues with an iterative development process that is organized in two phases. The result of each phase is a prototype of the scheduling tool. Possible extensions of the final prototype will be identified.

- *Prototype 1: Decentralized scheduling*. This consists of a command line application that implements the basic components of the decentralized scheduler and the scheduling algorithm. It will be tested in the two application scenarios outlined in Section 3.1.
- *Prototype 2: User interaction*. This adds a graphical user interface to Prototype 1. It will allow the user to modify the temporal parameters of each activity and will display the performance of the algorithm during the scheduling process.

3.4 ■ Prototype 1: Decentralized scheduling

The first prototype is an application that solves problems similar to the mail delivery; i.e. problems where resources are independent from each other. The resulting time plan is printed out on the screen in textual format.

3.4.1 ☐ **Analysis**

According to the domain models presented in Section 3.3, a task is made up of a temporal sequence of activities. The temporal consistency constraint states that, for a given task, each activity can only start when the previous one is finished. In order to process an activity, a resource should be available. The kind of resource depends on the type of activity. The resource consistency constraint states that a resource can process only one activity at a time. In a give period of time, a resource can process a sequence of activities belonging to different tasks.

In the first scenario, each carrier represents a resource. The city is partitioned into delivery areas and each area is assigned to only one carrier. A delivery area corresponds to a mail delivery task. A delivery task is made up of a sequence of delivery activities corresponding to different delivery routes. Each carrier performs the activities of a single task.

The scenario set in the fitness club brings an additional complexity to the scheduling problem. The scheduler tool should model and manage interdependent resources. This is the case of several athletes using the same set of training machines for their exercises. Both athletes and machines are resources that perform activities (i.e. the exercises). Each athlete is assigned a predefined set of workouts (the training task). The temporal and resource constraints apply both to the athletes and to the training machines.

Figure 3.4 depicts the revised analysis model. Relationship nextOf indicates that a resource executes sequences of non-overlapping activities.

Let's consider the situation before the execution of the scheduling algorithm:

- Each activity records the temporal parameters as specified by the user. They represent the preferences of the user and thus the scheduler should try to satisfy them as much as possible.

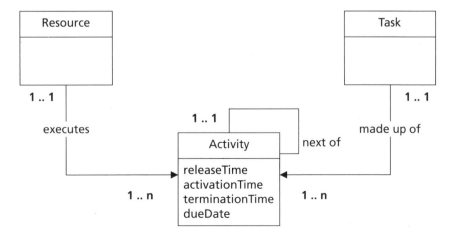

Figure 3.4 The revised analysis model

- These temporal parameters do not (usually) satisfy the temporal and resource constraints of the entire scheduling problem.

The scheduling algorithm computes new values of the temporal parameters of each activity in order to satisfy all the temporal and resource constraints and to maximize satisfaction of the user preferences.

3.4.2 ☐ Design

We need to transform the analysis diagram depicted in Figure 3.4 into a Design class diagram. This requires defining the attributes of each class, identifying their responsibilities and specifying the relationships between the classes. A set of decisions must be taken and the result is depicted in Figure 3.5.

Decision point

How do we represent Activity, Task and Resource?

Class Activity has a simple data structure that records the temporal parameters introduced in Figure 3.2. It implements a method for evaluating the performance value as defined in Equation 3.1 and a method for updating the temporal parameters according to Equation 3.2.

Class Task is a simple collection (see Sidebar 3.1) of Activity objects. It is used mainly to keep track of which activity is part of which task.

Class Resource is an ordered collection of Activity objects. It implements the scheduling algorithm presented in Section 3.3.1. In particular, it serializes the

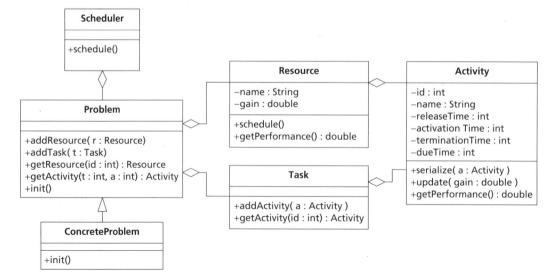

Figure 3.5 The class diagram of the scheduling tool

Sidebar 3.1 Collections

Collections are objects that encapsulate other objects, which are called items. Collections are commonly classified in three categories:

- A list is just a group of items.
- A set is a list that contains no duplicates.
- A map is a set of key–value pairs.

The Java Collections Framework provides a set of interfaces for storing and manipulating groups of data as depicted in the figure below.

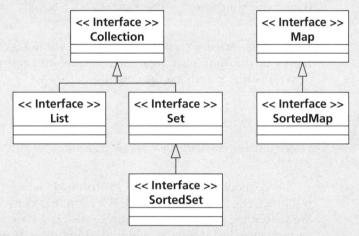

SortedSet and SortedMap represent collections of items ordered according to criteria defined in the items' classes. For this purpose, item classes must implement the comparable interface.

The Java Collections Framework also provides a set of concrete classes that implement the collection interfaces, as summarized in the table below.

Interface	Class	Description
Set	HashSet	The set is implemented as a hash table
SortedSet	TreeSet	The sorted set is implemented as a balanced binary tree
List	ArrayList	The list is implemented as a resizable array
List	LinkedList	The list is implemented as a doubly linked list
Map	HashMap	The map is implemented as a hash table
SortedMap	TreeMap	The sorted map is implemented as a balanced binary tree

set of activities to be processed over a certain period of time, evaluates their activation and termination time, and measures their performance.

Decision point

How do we model a scheduling problem?

A scheduling problem is described in terms of resources and tasks and is represented by the abstract class Problem. Specific problems are described by concrete subclasses of Problem. During the initialization phase, activities are assigned to resources. The preferred order of execution is indicated by the activation time of each activity. This order might change during the time plan generation.

Decision point

How do we represent the Time Plan?

Since every Activity records its temporal parameters, we do not need to represent the time plan explicitly. The information that creates the time plan is distributed among the activities.

Decision point

Where is the scheduling algorithm implemented?

The scheduling algorithm is distributed among the resources. Each resource schedules its activities. We introduce class Scheduler to initialize the scheduling process and to activate the resources. It computes the global performance and evaluates when the iterative scheduling process of each resource should terminate.

Decision point

How do we represent the dependencies between resources?

In the fitness club scenario, each athlete works out on one exercise (activity) at a time. Similarly, each training machine can be used to perform only one exercise at a time. According to the analysis, each machine is dedicated to a single athlete at a time. This means that, at a given point in time, an athlete performs an exercise using a machine exclusively.

Thus, we decide to represent both athletes and machines as instances of class Resource and the exercises as instances of class Activity. Every activity is simultaneously assigned to a machine and to an athlete. Machines and athletes schedule their activities according to their temporal preferences and constraints.

3.4.3 □ Implementation

We start the implementation with class Activity since it is the basic component of the architecture. The data structure records the name of an activity and the temporal parameters as defined in Figure 3.5. Two more member variables are needed to store the values of the activation and termination times corresponding to the best performance of the scheduling algorithm.

The constructor initializes the temporal parameters and computes the activity's duration. During the execution of the scheduling algorithm, only the activation time and the termination time will be updated. The reset() method initializes the activation time and termination time before any new run of the scheduling algorithm.

```java
package scheduler;
public class Activity {
  private int id = 0;
  private String name;
  private double releaseTime;
  private double activationTime;
  private double terminationTime;
  private double dueTime;
  private double duration;
  private double tempActivationTime = 0.0;
  private double tempTerminationTime = 0.0;
  public Activity(String name, double r, double a,
                                 double t, double d) {
    this.name = name;
    this.releaseTime = r;
    this.activationTime = a;
    this.terminationTime = t;
    this.dueTime = d;
    this.duration = t - a;
  }

  public int getID() { return id; }
  public String getName() { return name; }
  public double getActivation() { return activationTime; }
  public double getRelease() { return releaseTime; }
  public double getTermination() { return terminationTime; }
  public double getDueTime() { return dueTime; }
  public double getDuration() { return duration; }
  public void setID(int id) { this.id = id; }
  // The next two methods set the values of release time and
  // due date. If necessary, they change the values of
  // termination time and activation time consistently
  public void setReleaseTime(double time) {
    if (time < 0.0)
      return;
    if (time < activationTime || (time + duration) < dueTime)
      releaseTime = time;
    if (releaseTime > activationTime) {
```

```
      activationTime = releaseTime;
      terminationTime = activationTime + duration;
    }
  }
  public void setDueTime(double time) {
    if (time < 0.0) return;
    if (time > dueTime || (time - duration) > releaseTime)
      dueTime = time;
    if (dueTime < terminationTime) {
      terminationTime = dueTime;
      activationTime = terminationTime - duration;
    }
  }
  public void reset() {
    activationTime = 0.0;
    terminationTime = activationTime + duration;
  }
  // The next two methods update the temporal parameters of
  // the activity. The serialize() method enforces the
  // resource and temporal constraints. The update() method
  // takes into account the activity preferences; in
  // particular, it updates the activation time in order to
  // start the activity after the release time and to
  // complete it as close as possible to the due date. The
  // parameter gain represents the strength of an activity's
  // preferences.
  public void serialize(Activity previous) {
    if (previous.terminationTime > activationTime)
      activationTime = previous.terminationTime;
    terminationTime = activationTime + duration;
  }
  public void update(double gain) {
    activationTime += gain * (dueTime - terminationTime);
    if (activationTime < releaseTime)
      activationTime += gain * (releaseTime-activationTime);
    terminationTime = activationTime + duration;
  }
  // The getPerformance() method implements the formula
  // described in Equation 3.1, where the weights of
  // the earliness and tardiness performance parameters
  // are set to 1.0.
  public double getPerformance() {
    double pe = 0.0;
    double pt = 0.0;
    if (terminationTime > dueTime)
      pt = (terminationTime - dueTime);
```

```
    if (activationTime < releaseTime)
      pe = (releaseTime - activationTime);
    return pe + pt;
  }
  // The store() method is used to store an activity's
  // temporal parameters that correspond to the best
  // performance solution found by the scheduling algorithm
  // during a given iteration step.
  public void store() {
    tempActivationTime = activationTime;
    tempTerminationTime = terminationTime;
  }
  // The restore() method is invoked at the end of the
  // scheduling process to copy into an activity's
  // temporal parameters the values corresponding to the
  // best performance solution.
  public void restore() {
    activationTime = tempActivationTime;
    terminationTime = tempTerminationTime;
  }
}
```

Class **Resource** aggregates **Activity** objects. We use class **ArrayList** to implement the containment relationship. Since the **Resource** needs to sort the list of activities according to their activation time, we define the inner class **CompareActivities** that implements the **Comparator** interface.

The core of class **Resource** is the **schedule()** method that enforces the temporal and resource constraints of the scheduling problem. The method executes three basic operations. First, it requests its activities to update their temporal parameters. They could have been modified by the previous iteration of the scheduling algorithm. As a consequence, the activities do not necessarily enforce the temporal and resource constraints of this resource. Thus, the **schedule()** method re-orders the activities according to their new activation time. Finally, the method sequences the activities in such a way that they do not overlap. This operation requires modifying the temporal parameters of the activities.

Since the **schedule()** method modifies the values of the activities' temporal parameters, it is important to evaluate how these values enforce the temporal constraints represented by the release time and the due time of each activity. The **getPerformance()** method computes the performance of the scheduling algorithm with regard to all the activities.

```
package scheduler;
import java.util.*;
public class Resource {
  class CompareActivity implements Comparator {
    public int compare(Object o1, Object o2) {
```

```
        Activity t1 = (Activity) o1;
        Activity t2 = (Activity) o2;
        if(t1.getActivation() > t2.getActivation())
        return 1;
        if(t1.getActivation() < t2.getActivation())
        return -1;
        return t1.getName().compareTo(t2.getName());
    }
  }
  private String name;
  private ArrayList activities = new ArrayList();
  private double gain = 0.0;
  public Resource(String name) { this.name = name; }
  public String getName() { return name; }
  public void addActivity(Activity activity) {
    activities.add(activity);
  }
  public void addTask(Task task) {
    Iterator iterator = task.getActivities();
    Activity activity;
    while(iterator.hasNext())
      activities.add( (Activity) iterator.next() );
  }
  public void setGain(double gain) { this.gain = gain; }
  public void reset() {
    Iterator iterator = activities.iterator();
    Activity activity;
    while(iterator.hasNext()) {
      activity = (Activity) iterator.next();
      activity.reset();
    }
  }
  public void schedule() {
    // updates the activationTime of each activity
    for(int i=0; i < activities.size(); i++)
      ((Activity) activities.get(i)).update(gain);
    // sorts the list of activities for activationTime
    Collections.sort(activities, new CompareActivity());
    // evaluates the new completionTime of each activity
    Activity previous = (Activity) activities.get(0);
    for(int i=1; i < activities.size(); i++) {
      Activity activity = (Activity) activities.get(i);
      activity.serialize(previous);
      previous = activity;
    }
  }
```

```java
public double getPerformance() {
  double performance = 0.0;
  for(int i=0; i < activities.size(); i++) {
    Activity activity = (Activity) activities.get(i);
    performance += activity.getPerformance();
  }
  return performance;
}
public void store() {
  for(int i=0; i < activities.size(); i++) {
    Activity activity = (Activity) activities.get(i);
    activity.store();
  }
}
public void restore() {
  for(int i=0; i < activities.size(); i++) {
    Activity activity = (Activity) activities.get(i);
    activity.restore();
  }
}
}
```

Class Task is a simple container that aggregates activities as specified by the problem at hand.

```java
package scheduler;
import java.util.*;
public class Task {
  private ArrayList activities = new ArrayList();
  public int addActivity(Activity activity) {
    activity.setID(activities.size());
    activities.add(activity);
    return activity.getID();
  }
  public Iterator getActivities() {
    return activities.iterator();
  }
  public Activity getActivity(int id) {
    Iterator iterator = activities.iterator();
    Activity activity;
    while(iterator.hasNext()) {
      activity = (Activity) iterator.next();
      if(activity.getID() == id)
        return activity;
    }
    return null;
  }
}
```

Class **Problem** describes the scheduling problem in terms of tasks and resources. It is an abstract class that must be specialized in order to describe specific problems. Every subclass must implement method init().

```java
package scheduler;
import java.util.*;
public abstract class Problem {
  private ArrayList tasks = new ArrayList();
  private ArrayList resources = new ArrayList();
  public Resource getResource(int i) {
    return (Resource) resources.get(i);
  }
  public Iterator getResources() {
    return resources.iterator();
  }
  public void addTask(Task task) {
    tasks.add(task);
  }
  public void addResource(Resource resource) {
    resources.add(resource);
  }
  public void clear() {
    tasks.removeAll(tasks);
    resources.removeAll(resources);
  }
  public Activity getActivity(int taskID, int activityID) {
    Task task = (Task) tasks.get(taskID);
    if(task == null) return null;
    Activity activity =
                  (Activity) task.getActivity(activityID);
    return activity;
  }
  public abstract void init();
}
```

Class **Scheduler** is the main class of the architecture. It is initialized with an instance of a concrete problem and supervises the execution of the scheduling algorithm by the resources.

The schedule() method simply iterates the basic scheduling step, which requests the resources to schedule their activities, evaluates the performance at each step, and stores the solution corresponding to the best performance computed so far. The algorithm terminates after a predefined number of iterations (80 in this case). A better implementation of this method could define a more general termination clause. At the end of the algorithm's execution, the method restores the solution corresponding to the best performance value, which is the final values of the activities' temporal parameters.

```java
package scheduler;
import java.util.*;
public class Scheduler {
  public static int STEPS = 80;
  private Problem problem = null;
  private int bestStep; // the index of the best performance
  private double bestValue; // the best performance value
  public void setProblem(Problem problem) {
    this.problem = problem;
    bestStep = 0;
    bestValue = 1e9;
    problem.init();
  }
  public double bestValue() { return bestValue; }
  public void schedule(double gain) {
    Iterator iterator = problem.getResources();
    Resource resource;
    while(iterator.hasNext()) {
      resource = (Resource) iterator.next();
      resource.reset();
      resource.setGain(gain);
    }
    // repeats the scheduling step 80 times
    for (int step = 0; step < STEPS; step++) {
      double totPerformance = 0.0;
      // every resource schedules its activities
      iterator = problem.getResources();
      while(iterator.hasNext())
        ((Resource) iterator.next()).schedule();
      // evaluates the total performance
      iterator = problem.getResources();
      while(iterator.hasNext())
        totPerformance +=
            ((Resource) iterator.next()).getPerformance();
      // evaluates the performance of this scheduling step
      if (totPerformance < bestValue) {
        bestValue = totPerformance;
        // this is the best performance up to now
        iterator = problem.getResources();
        while(iterator.hasNext())
          ((Resource) iterator.next()).store();
        bestStep = step;
      }
    }
    // restores the the best performance values
    iterator = problem.getResources();
```

```
        while(iterator.hasNext())
          ((Resource) iterator.next()).restore();
    }
  }
```

3.4.4 □ Test

As an example we implement class **PostOfficeProblem** that extends class **Problem** and specifies the temporal parameters of each mail delivery activity. We can assume that the values are expressed in minutes, but it is not relevant for testing the scheduler.

```
import scheduler.*;
public class PostOfficeProblem extends Problem {
  public void init() {
    super.clear();
    Task task1 = new Task();
    Activity a;
    a = new Activity("Zone11",  5.0, 10.0, 15.0, 20.0);
    task1.addActivity(a);
    a = new Activity("Zone12",  5.0, 10.0, 15.0, 20.0);
    task1.addActivity(a);
    a = new Activity("Zone13", 15.0, 17.0, 22.0, 25.0);
    task1.addActivity(a);
    a = new Activity("Zone14", 20.0, 22.0, 27.0, 35.0);
    task1.addActivity(a);
    a = new Activity("Zone15", 20.0, 30.0, 35.0, 40.0);
    task1.addActivity(a);
    a = new Activity("Zone16", 20.0, 30.0, 35.0, 45.0);
    task1.addActivity(a);
    a = new Activity("Zone17", 25.0, 30.0, 35.0, 50.0);
    task1.addActivity(a);
    this.addTask(task1);
    Resource carrier1 = new Resource("Carrier1");
    carrier1.addTask(task1);
    this.addResource(carrier1);
    Task task2 = new Task();
    Activity a;
    a = new Activity("Zone21",  5.0,  7.0, 12.0, 15.0);
    task2.addActivity(a);
    a = new Activity("Zone22", 10.0, 15.0, 20.0, 30.0);
    task2.addActivity(a);
    a = new Activity("Zone23", 15.0, 25.0, 30.0, 40.0);
    task2.addActivity(a);
    a = new Activity("Zone24", 25.0, 30.0, 35.0, 55.0);
    task2.addActivity(a);
    a = new Activity("Zone25", 20.0, 30.0, 35.0, 45.0);
```

```
      task2.addActivity(a);
      a = new Activity("Zone26", 15.0, 30.0, 35.0, 45.0);
      task2.addActivity(a);
      a = new Activity("Zone27", 10.0, 30.0, 35.0, 45.0);
      task2.addActivity(a);
      this.addTask(task2);

      Resource carrier2 = new Resource("Carrier2");
      carrier2.addTask(task2);
      this.addResource(carrier2);
   }
```

We developed the test within the JUnit automatic test framework (see Sidebar 3.2). Accordingly, the test case is implemented in class TestScheduler.

```
import scheduler.*;
import java.util.*;
import junit.framework.*;
public class TestScheduler extends TestCase {
   Scheduler scheduler = new Scheduler();
   public TestScheduler(String name) { super(name); }
   public void testPostOffice() {
      Problem problem = new PostOfficeProblem();
      double gain = 0.1;
      scheduler.setProblem(problem);
      scheduler.schedule(gain);
      // verifies the expected performance value
      assertEquals(0.0, scheduler.bestValue(), 0.1);
      HashMap expectedResults = new HashMap();
      expectedResults.put("Zone11", new Double(8.0));
      expectedResults.put("Zone12", new Double(13.0));
      expectedResults.put("Zone13", new Double(18.0));
      expectedResults.put("Zone14", new Double(23.0));
      expectedResults.put("Zone15", new Double(28.0));
      expectedResults.put("Zone16", new Double(33.0));
      expectedResults.put("Zone17", new Double(38.0));
      expectedResults.put("Zone21", new Double(5.0));
      expectedResults.put("Zone22", new Double(14.0));
      expectedResults.put("Zone23", new Double(28.0));
      expectedResults.put("Zone24", new Double(43.0));
      expectedResults.put("Zone25", new Double(38.0));
      expectedResults.put("Zone26", new Double(33.0));
      expectedResults.put("Zone27", new Double(23.0));
      // verifies the expected values for the temporal
parameters
      Activity activity;
      Double value;
```

```
      for(int taskID = 0; taskID < 2; taskID++)
        for(int activityID = 0; activityID < 7; activityID++){
          activity = (Activity) problem.getActivity(
                                    taskID, activityID);
          value = (Double) expectedResults.get(
                                    activity.getName());
          assertEquals(value.doubleValue(),
                              activity.getActivation(), 1.0);
        }
    }
  public static Test suite() {
    return new TestSuite(TestScheduler.class);
  }
  public static void main (String[] args) {
    junit.textui.TestRunner.run (suite());
  }
}
```

Sidebar 3.2 JUnit test framework

JUnit is an automated testing framework for Java programs (www.junit.org). More precisely, JUnit is a regression testing framework written by Erich Gamma and Kent Beck. It is used by the developer who implements unit tests in Java. There are plugins for several IDEs to make it easy the development and execution of tests.

To test a Java program using JUnit is very easy. It is sufficient to define a class that extends the class **TestCase** (defined in the framework), add public test methods that check that the program behaves as expected, and run the test.

The JUnit framework is made up of three essential elements that can be used by the programmer:

- the assert methods,
- class **TestCase**, and
- class **TestSuite**.

The assert methods are used to check whether the results obtained from the program are as expected; they can be used in the test methods. Class **TestCase** is the container of a set of test methods, its test methods are executed by the JUnit framework. Finally, class **TestSuite** is a collection of test cases, it can be used to run in a single shot all the tests for a program.

For instance, to test a stack class, we can write the following test case:

```
// first we import the base class TestCase
import junit.framework.TestCase;
public class StackTester // the test case class must
       extends TestCase {        // extend class TestCase
  // a constructor like this is required by
  // JUnit framework to work properly
  public void StackTester(String name) { super(name);  }
    // test methods must be "public void" and start with "test"
```

```
    public void testStack() {
      // first we set up the object(s) to be tested
      Stack aStack = new Stack();
      // we check if a condition (at creation the stack should
      // be empty) is met. If not an error message is shown
      assertTrue("Stack should be empty at creation",
                 aStack.isEmpty());
      // we perform some operations
      aStack.push(10);
      aStack.push(-4);
      // we check some conditions are met
      assertEquals(-4,aStack.pop());
      assertEquals(10,aStack.pop());
    }
  }
}
```

The assert methods are public methods that are inherited from the TestCase class. These methods start with "assert" and can be used in the test methods.

The simplest assert method is assertTrue whose syntax is: assertTrue(" message", condition). If the condition is false the test fails, the message is printed, and the rest of the test method is skipped. Otherwise the assertion is considered passed and the test methods proceed.

For instance:

```
assertTrue("Stack should be empty at creation",
                                   // error message
           aStack.isEmpty());      // condition to check
```

For integers, longs, bytes, chars and objects it is possible to use assertEquals whose syntax is: assertEquals(expectedValue, actualValue). For floating point values a variation of this method can be used, the syntax is: assertEquals(expectedValue, actualValue, error). If the comparison is successful the test methods proceed, otherwise the assert fails and the remaining test methods are skipped.

```
assertEquals(-4,aStack.pop());
assertEquals(1.0, Math.cos(3.14), 0.01);
```

For each test case JUnit executes all of its public test methods and ignores all the rest. If all the assert statements (invocations to assert methods) in a test method have success the test is considered passed, otherwise if only one assert statement fails the test fails.

Usually a test case class contains, in addition to the test methods, a set of helper methods that are either private or have names not starting with "test". These methods are used to factorize pieces of code that are common to several test methods.

3.5 ■ Prototype 2: User interaction

The second prototype implements a graphical user interface (GUI) that supports sophisticated patterns of interaction between the user and the scheduler: the user will be able to see a graphical representation of the time plan, to edit and revise the time plan, to evaluate the performance of the scheduling algorithm, and to modify the gain parameter.

3.5.1 □ Analysis

The graphical interface plays an important role since it allows the user to edit and revise the time plan gracefully. In fact, as we pointed out in Section 3.3.2, the decentralized scheduling algorithm does not guarantee finding the optimal solution, thus the direct intervention of the user is extremely important to guide the scheduler tool towards a solution that takes into account his or her preferences. For this purpose, the graphical interface should display a graphic that represents the behaviour of the scheduling algorithm and gives a measure of its performance. In summary, the graphical interface should support the following functionalities:

- Edit the temporal parameters of the activities.
- Modify the gain of the scheduling algorithm.
- Reschedule activities.
- Visualize the time plan and the performance values.

Figure 3.6 is a snapshot of the graphical user interface that we want to develop for the scheduling tool. It is organized in three parts. The upper part is the toolbar. It is made up of a menu for selecting a scheduling problem, two buttons ("Reset" and "Schedule"), a set of text areas that display the temporal parameters of a selected activity, and two text areas that display the gain and the performance values of the scheduling algorithm.

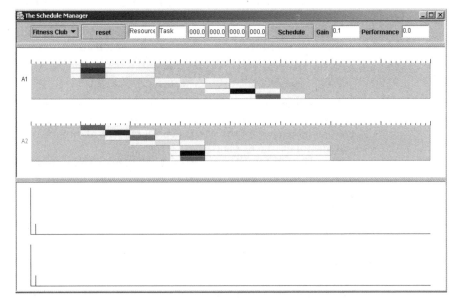

Figure 3.6 GUI before the execution of the scheduling process.

The middle part is a panel for drawing the time plan. The activities are represented as coloured rectangles (red, blue, etc; shown here in shades of grey). The left and right extremes of a rectangle represent the activation and termination time. Each activity is placed over a yellow (here, light grey) rectangle whose left and right extremes represent the release time and due date of the task. When the user moves the mouse pointer over an activity rectangle, its temporal parameters are displayed in the corresponding areas of the toolbar. The user can adjust the release time and due time parameters of an activity by dragging the extremes of the corresponding yellow rectangle. Figure 3.6 represents two groups of seven activities; each one is executed by a resource ("R0" and "R1"). If we consider the scenario set in the fitness club, the two resources might correspond to two athletes. Figure 3.6 does not depict the training machines explicitly. This would require a more complex and flexible GUI. Activities represented by rectangles of the same colour are performed by the same machine. Thus, every machine is assigned a different colour. Note that the figure represents the time plan as specified in the problem formulation, that is the temporal and resource constraints are not enforced yet. Finally, the lower part of the GUI draws the performance graphics. Since the figure represents the situation before the execution of the scheduling algorithm, the performance graphics are empty.

3.5.2 □ Design

The classical architecture of a GUI is structured in three layers: the model, the view and the controller. The model includes the classes that manage the data to be displayed. The view includes the visual components that make up the GUI. The controller represents the top-level component that coordinates the exchange of data between the model layer and the view layer.

The class diagram depicted in Figure 3.7 includes four new classes: ScheduleManager, ScheduleCommand, ScheduleSheet and Schedule Performance. Class ScheduleManager is the main class of the scheduler tool. The other three represent the three parts of the graphical interface described in Section 3.5.1.

3.5.3 □ Implementation

The implementation of the second prototype requires the definition of new classes that implement the graphical user interface depicted in Figure 3.6 and a few changes in the implementation of class Scheduler and Activity.

ScheduleManager is a container class that represents the structure of the graphical user interface and initializes the three graphical panels: ScheduleCommand, SchedulePerformance and ScheduleSheet.

```
public class ScheduleManager extends JFrame {
    HashMap problemList;
    Scheduler scheduler = new Scheduler();
    ScheduleSheet scheduleSheet;
```

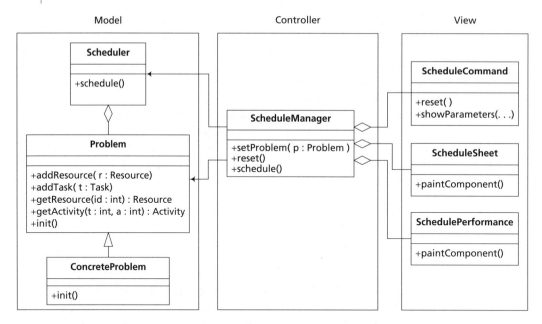

Figure 3.7 The model–view–controller architecture of the scheduling tool

```
ScheduleCommand scheduleCommand;
SchedulePerformance schedulePerformance;
Problem problem = null;
/**Construct the application*/
public ScheduleManager(HashMap problemList) {
  this.problemList = problemList;
  scheduleSheet = new ScheduleSheet(this);
  scheduleCommand = new ScheduleCommand(this);
  schedulePerformance = new SchedulePerformance(this);
  enableEvents(AWTEvent.WINDOW_EVENT_MASK);
  this.getContentPane().setLayout(new BorderLayout());
  this.setSize(new Dimension(870, 550));
  this.setTitle("The Schedule Manager");
  JSplitPane hSplit = new JSplitPane
                    (JSplitPane.VERTICAL_SPLIT,
                     scheduleCommand, scheduleSheet);
  JSplitPane hSplit2 = new JSplitPane
                    (JSplitPane.VERTICAL_SPLIT,
                     hSplit, schedulePerformance);
  this.getContentPane().add(hSplit2);
  this.validate();
  this.setVisible(true);
}
```

```java
void setProblem(String name) {
  problem = (Problem) problemList.get(name);
  if(problem != null) {
    scheduler.setProblem(problem);
    scheduleSheet.repaint();
  }
}
void reset() {
  if(problem != null) {
    problem.reset();
    scheduler.reset();
    scheduleSheet.repaint();
    scheduleCommand.reset();
    scheduleCommand.repaint();
  }
}
double schedule(double gain) {
  scheduler.schedule(gain);
  scheduleSheet.repaint();
  schedulePerformance.repaint();
  return scheduler.bestValue();
}
```

Three main functionalities should be addressed:

- The Scheduler must keep track of the performance values during the iterations of the scheduling algorithm. This allows the representation of the performance trend in the bottom part of the graphical interface.
- The user should be allowed to reset the scheduler and to execute the scheduling algorithm again. This means that every Activity object must keep a copy of the original values of the temporal parameters in order to restore them when the user resets the scheduler.
- The user should be allowed to modify the temporal parameters of each Activity object through the graphical interface and to execute the scheduling algorithm with the new temporal values.

The first and second functionalities require the following changes to class Activity and class Scheduler.

```java
public class Activity {
  . . .
  public Activity getClone() {
    Activity clone = new Activity(name, releaseTime,
                 activationTime, terminationTime, dueTime);
    clone.id = id;
    return clone;
  }
```

```java
    public void copy(Activity clone) {
      this.name = clone.name;
      this.releaseTime = clone.releaseTime;
      this.activationTime = clone.activationTime;
      this.terminationTime = clone.terminationTime;
      this.dueTime = clone.dueTime;
      this.duration = terminationTime - activationTime;
    }
  }


  public class Scheduler {
    . . .
    private ArrayList performances = new ArrayList();
    public void setProblem(Problem problem) {
      . . .
      performances.removeAll(performances);
      Iterator iterator = problem.getResources();
      Resource resource;
      while(iterator.hasNext()) {
        iterator.next();
        double perf[] = new double[STEPS];
        performances.add(perf);
      }
    }
    public void schedule(double gain) {
      // repeats the scheduling step 80 times
      for (int step = 0; step < STEPS; step++) {
        double totPerformance = 0.0;
        // every resource schedules its activities
        iterator = problem.getResources();
        while(iterator.hasNext())
          ((Resource) iterator.next()).schedule();
        // evaluates the total performance
        iterator = problem.getResources();
        int i = 0;
        while(iterator.hasNext()) {
          double p[] = (double[]) performances.get(i++);
          p[step] =
                  ((Resource) iterator.next()).getPerformance();
          totPerformance += p[step];
        }
        // evaluates the performance of this scheduling step
        if (totPerformance < bestValue) {
          bestValue = totPerformance;
          // this is the best performance up to now
          iterator = problem.getResources();
```

```
      while(iterator.hasNext())
        ((Resource) iterator.next()).store();
      bestStep = step;
    }
  }
  // restores the solution corresponding to the best
  // performance step
  iterator = problem.getResources();
  while(iterator.hasNext())
    ((Resource) iterator.next()).restore();
  }
}
```

The third functionality requires the use definition of two inner classes that are nested in class ScheduleSheet, i.e. class MouseHandler and class MouseMotionHandler.

MouseHandler extends class MouseAdapter of package java.awt.event by redefining method mousePressed(MouseEvent e) and method mouseReleased (MouseEvent e). These methods are executed when the corresponding input events are notified and are used to select an activity using the mouse pointer.

MouseMotionHandler extends class MouseMotionAdapter of package java.awt.event by redefining method mouseMoved(MouseEvent e) and mouse Dragged(MouseEvent e). These methods are used to change the temporal parameters of the selected activity.

```java
public class ScheduleSheet extends JPanel {
  ScheduleManager manager = null;
  Color colors[] = new Color[7];
  Activity selectedActivity = null;
  boolean dueDateSelected = false;
  public ScheduleSheet(ScheduleManager manager) {
    colors[0] = Color.red;
    colors[1] = Color.blue;
    colors[2] = Color.magenta;
    colors[3] = Color.cyan;
    colors[4] = Color.green;
    colors[5] = Color.black;
    colors[6] = Color.gray;
    this.manager = manager;
    this.setBackground(Color.white);
    this.addMouseListener(new MouseHandler());
    this.addMouseMotionListener(new MouseMotionHandler());
    this.setPreferredSize(new Dimension(50, 250));
  }
  public void paintComponent(Graphics graphics) {
    super.paintComponent(graphics);
```

```
if(manager.problem == null)
  return;
Graphics2D g = (Graphics2D) graphics;
int yPos;
for(int r=0; r<2; r++) {
  yPos = 30+r*120;
  Resource resource = manager.problem.getResource(r);
  g.drawString(resource.getName(), 10, yPos+35);
  g.setColor(Color.orange);
  g.fill3DRect(30, yPos, 800, 70, true);
  g.setColor(Color.black);
  for(int i=0; i <= 80; i++)
    g.drawLine(30+10*i, yPos, 30+10*i, yPos-3);
  for(int i=0; i <= 80; i+=10)
    g.drawLine(30+10*i, yPos, 30+10*i, yPos-7);

  // draws the tasks
  Activity activity;
  int release, activation, termination, due, duration;
  Iterator iterActivity = resource.getActivities();
  while(iterActivity.hasNext()) {
    activity = (Activity) iterActivity.next();
    release = (int) Math.round(activity.getRelease());
    activation = (int) Math.round
                            (activity.getActivation());
    termination = (int) Math.round
                            (activity.getTermination());
    due = (int) Math.round(activity.getDueTime());
    duration = (int) Math.round(activity.getDuration());

    if(release >= 0 && release <= 100 &&
                                  activation >= 0 &&
        activation <= 100 && termination >= 0 &&
        termination <= 100 && due >= 0 && due <= 100) {
      g.setColor(Color.yellow);
      g.fill3DRect(30+release*10, yPos+activity.
                                      getID()*10,
            (due-release)*10, 10, true);
      g.setColor(colors[activity.getID()]);
      g.fill3DRect(30+activation*10, yPos+activity.
                                      getID()*10,
            duration*10, 10, true);
    }
  }
  yPos+=80;
}
}
```

```
// inner class MouseHandler
class MouseHandler extends MouseAdapter {
  public void mousePressed ( MouseEvent e) {
    if(manager.problem == null)
      return;
    int posX = (int) e.getPoint().getX();
    posX = (posX-30)/10;
    int posY = (int) e.getPoint().getY();

    // verify if the mouse is over an activity of Resource 1
    for(int i=0; i<2; i++) {
      Resource resource = manager.problem.getResource(i);
      if(posY >= 30+i*120 && posY < 120*(i+1)) {
        Iterator iterActivity = resource.getActivities();
        Activity activity = null;
        int release, activation, termination, due;
        while(iterActivity.hasNext()) {
          activity = (Activity) iterActivity.next();
          if(posY >= 30+activity.getID()*10+i*120 &&
               posY < 40+activity.getID()*10+i*120) {
            release = (int) Math.round
                               (activity.getRelease());
            activation = (int) Math.round
                               (activity.getActivation());
            termination = (int) Math.round
                               (activity.getTermination());
            due = (int) Math.round(activity.getDueTime());
            selectedActivity = activity;
            if(posX < due+3 && posX > due-3)
              dueDateSelected = true;
            else
              dueDateSelected = false;
            return;
          }
        }
      }
    }
  }
  public void mouseReleased(MouseEvent e) {
    selectedActivity = null;
  }
}
class MouseMotionHandler extends MouseMotionAdapter {
  public void mouseMoved(MouseEvent e) {
    if(manager.problem == null)
      return;
    int posX = (int) e.getPoint().getX();
```

```java
      int posY = (int) e.getPoint().getY();
      // verify if the mouse is over a task of Resource 1
      for(int i=0; i<2; i++) {
        Resource resource = manager.problem.getResource(i);
        if(posY >= 30+i*120 && posY < 120*(i+1)) {
          Iterator iterActivity = resource.getActivities();
          Activity activity = null;
          int release, activation, termination, due;
          while(iterActivity.hasNext()) {
            activity = (Activity) iterActivity.next();
            if(posY >= 30+i*120+activity.getID()*10 &&
                posY < 40+i*120+activity.getID()*10) {
              release = (int) Math.round
                                (activity.getRelease());
              activation = (int) Math.round
                                (activity.getActivation());
              termination = (int) Math.round
                                (activity.getTermination());
              due = (int) Math.round(activity.getDueTime());
              manager.scheduleCommand.showParameters
                                        (resource.getName(),
                activity.getName(), release, activation,
                termination, due);
              return;
            }
          }
        }
      }
    }
    public void mouseDragged(MouseEvent e) {
      if(manager.problem == null)
        return;
      int posX = (int) e.getPoint().getX();
      posX = (posX-30)/10;
      if(selectedActivity != null) {
        if(dueDateSelected == true)
          selectedActivity.setDueTime(posX);
        else
          selectedActivity.setReleaseTime(posX);
        repaint();
      }
    }
  }
}
```

The graphical user interface can be implemented on top of the Swing library (see Sidebar 3.3).

Sidebar 3.3 AWT and Swing

Java provides an extensive framework for building graphical user interfaces (GUIs), which includes several important packages such as *Abstract Windows Toolkit* (AWT), Swing, Java Beans, and Java3D.

The Java AWT and Swing packages consist of four main categories of classes: components, containers, events and event listeners. Components and containers are the visual building blocks of graphical user interfaces. They define the visual characteristics of the GUI. Events, event listeners and event handlers represent user inputs and define the GUI behaviour in response to them.

- *Components*. Commonly used Swing classes are JButton and JCheckBox, JComboBox, JLabel, JList, JScrollbar, JtextField and JTextArea. All of these classes are customizable by defining specific values for their properties, such as the displayed label, the position, the dimension, the background colour, the border shape, etc. Usually, these classes do not need to be extended by inheritance.
- *Containers*. Commonly used Swing classes are JPanel, JApplet, JFrame and JDialog. Usually these classes need to be customized by deriving problem-specific subclasses. Concrete subclasses define which visual components build up the GUI, how they interact and how they respond to user inputs. For most programs, the top-level Swing container is a subclass of JFrame or JApplet. Both of them implement a single main window.
- *Events*. Commonly used AWT classes are ActionEvent, ItemEvent, KeyEvent and MouseEvent. These classes represent user inputs and usually do not need to be customized at all.
- *Event listeners*. The AWT package offers a variety of event listener interfaces, such as ActionListener, MouseListener, MouseMotionListener, etc. Every class that is interested in processing an event has to implement the corresponding event listener interface. Instances of this class must be registered with a component (e.g. a button). When the event occurs, the relevant method in the listener object is invoked. The AWT package implements a number of abstract classes that implement event listener interfaces, such as the classes MouseAdapter and MouseMotionAdapter. These classes define common methods for handling typical input events. Concrete subclasses overload these methods in order to express the desired behaviours.

3.5.4 ☐ Test

Two major aspects of the scheduling tool need to be tested: the scheduling algorithm and the graphical user interface. We adopt the following strategy:

- First we test the graphical interface in order to verify the correct correspondence between the data that are visualized and the actual temporal and performance values of the time plan. This can be done by inserting in the code above a few debug commands that display on the screen the textual representation of task and resource parameters. Thus, the test might consist in a set of experiments that verifies all the edit and revise functionalities of the graphical interface.
- Then we test the scheduling algorithm with data that represent the fitness club scenario.

Figure 3.8 shows the result of the scheduling algorithm when the gain parameter is set to 0.01. The resulting performance value is equal to 9.61116. Note that the resource constraints are enforced for all the resources (athletes and machines). In fact, the activities of athlete "A1" do not overlap one another. The same is true for athlete "A2". Similarly, activities of the same

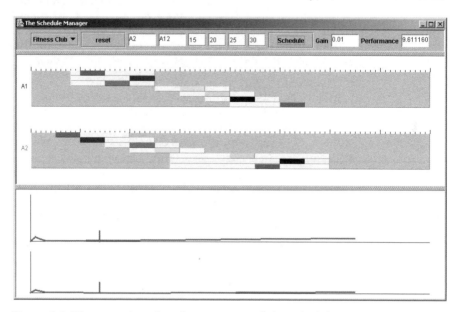

Figure 3.8 The time plan after the execution of the scheduling process. Copyright © 2005 Sun Microsystems, Inc. All rights reserved. Reproduced by permission of Sun Microsystems, Inc.

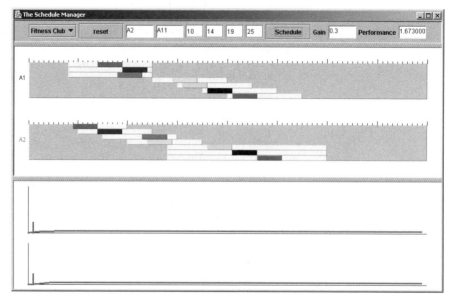

Figure 3.9 The time plan after the revision of the algorithm's gain. Copyright © 2005 Sun Microsystems, Inc. All rights reserved. Reproduced by permission of Sun Microsystems, Inc.

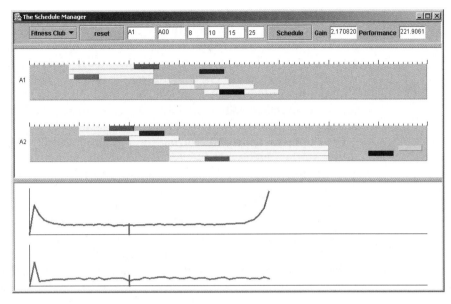

Figure 3.10 The system becomes unstable.

colour (one colour for each machine) performed by different athletes do not overlap one another. The result is not satisfactory because the temporal constraints are not enforced for all of the activities.

In order to improve the result, we raise the gain of the scheduling algorithm to the value of 0.3. The result is shown in Figure 3.9: the temporal constraints are better enforced. In fact, the new performance value is equal to 1.673. The drawback is that the resource constraints are not completely enforced. If the gain value is raised over 2.073 the system becomes unstable as depicted in Figure 3.10.

3.6 ■ Extensions

The second prototype allows users to modify the release time and due date parameters of each task and to shift the activation and termination time backwards and forwards. It does not allow the user to modify the duration of the tasks. The introduction of this functionality does not affect the scheduler architecture. It just requires the extension of the graphical user interface.

Another possible extension that would be useful is the introduction of the concept of user session. This basically consists in the possibility of loading and saving the problem description and the time plan from/to a stable storage medium, e.g. the file system.

3.7 ■ Assessment

The case study exemplified the development of a tool for activities scheduling.

Analysis technique. During the analysis phase, we used abstraction to find the commonalities between two apparently different application scenarios and we recognize they fall into a well-known problem. The literature in the field, together with our experience and knowledge of the domain, helps us in identifying the basic concepts that form the analysis model.

Modelling notation. We used the cornerstone notation of object-oriented development: class diagrams. They present the classes and the relationships among them.

Development approach. During the design phase we assigned responsibilities to the classes previously identified during analysis. We decided to split all the computation related to the scheduling algorithm among the classes Scheduler, Resource and Activity.

The two, apparently different, application scenarios show several similarities, which have been captured in the first prototype. Its implementation highlights the use of collections of objects. Pattern *Iterator* (Gamma *et al.* 1995) represents a common design practice when dealing with collections.

The second prototype has shown the basic features of the AWT and Swing component library for building graphical interfaces. Pattern *Model–View–Controller* describes the common architecture of graphical interfaces.

Pattern	Iterator
Context	Visiting the objects of a container class.
Problem	Decoupling the visiting algorithm from the container data structure.
Forces or tradeoffs	In order to enhance reusability, visiting algorithms (e.g. sorting or searching algorithms) must not worry about the particular sequence of objects they are operating on. Container classes cannot be abstract and generic. Container class implements different data structures to optimize specific performance criteria, e.g. memory occupancy, access speed, etc.
Solution	Visiting algorithms do not have direct access to the component objects through the container class. Instead they use iterator objects. An iterator is an instance of a class that implements the Iterator interface. Its methods are used by the visiting algorithm to navigate inside the container class. Using the Iterator, any container is seen as an ordered sequence of objects. Every container class is associated to a concrete iterator class that implements the Iterator interface as shown in the following class diagram.

| Examples | ```
import java.util.*;
class SampleClass {
  private ArrayList names = new Arraylist();
  public SampleClass(){
    names.add(new String("James"));
    names.add(new String("Maria"));
  }
  public void printNames(){
    Iterator iterator = names.iterator();
    while (iterator.hasNext()) {
      String name = (String) iterator.next();
      System.out.println(name);
    }
  }
}
``` |
| Force resolution | The visiting algorithms access the component objects through a standard interface. The implementation of concrete container classes and of specific visiting algorithms can vary independently. |
| Design rationale | This architectural solution keeps the method for creating the collection separate from the method for visiting the collection. Several iterator objects can visit the same collection simultaneously and independently. |

Pattern type	Model–view–controller
Context	The system architecture of a graphical user interface.
Problem	Often a GUI offers multiple views of the same data. Application data could be displayed as a table, as a graph, as a chart, etc.
Forces or tradeoffs	The user must be allowed to choose how to display the application data, i.e. how many and which views must be active simultaneously for the same data. The user must be allowed to input data in a view and see the updated values in all the other views.
Solution	The architecture of the graphical interface should separate the objects that hold the application data (the model) from the objects that present these data to the user (the views).
	The user inputs data using the standard I/O devices, i.e. the mouse and the keyboard. The objects that listen to the input events (the controller) should be kept separated from the model and the views. The controller has the responsibility to update the model with the input data and to refresh all the views. The resulting architecture is structured as in the following diagram.
```

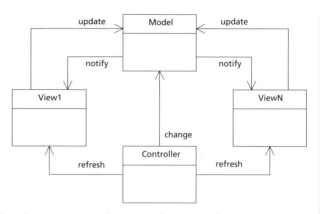

Force resolution   Data are stored in data structures that are independent from the graphical components. Graphical components can be added and removed dynamically (opening or closing a window). The controller has visibility of the application data structures and of the graphical views. It registers input data, updates the model and refreshes the views.

Design rationale   The architecture of this pattern often builds on another classical design pattern, i.e. pattern *Observer*.

3.8 ■ References

Gamma, E., Helm, R., Johnson, R. and Vlissides, J. (1995) *Design Patterns: Elements of Reusable Object-Oriented Software*, Addison-Wesley.

Pinedo, M. (1995). *Scheduling: Theory, Algorithms and Systems*, Prentice-Hall.

Prabhu, V.V. and Duffie, N.A. (1999) "Nonlinear Dynamics in Distributed Arrival Time Control of Heterarchical Manufacturing Systems", *IEEE Transactions on Control Systems Technology*, Vol. 7, No. 6.

Classifier

4

Synthesis

This chapter presents the development of a classifier tool, which assigns a category label to items based on their characteristics. The application developed here is intended to support decision making at insurance companies. The categories in this case are the risk levels and the items are insured objects, such as cars.

- Focus: this case study exemplifies the mapping between entities of the problem and objects of the solution, and the use of UML class diagrams.
- OO techniques: inclusion and inheritance.
- Java features: collections.
- Background: the reader is required to know the basic OO concepts and fundamental Java programming techniques.

4.1 ■ Specifications

One of the main problems in insurance companies is the calculation of insurance premiums. While for existing items the premiums can be based on statistics, it is more difficult to define them for new items.

To perform this task, insurance companies must identify the criteria that they used in the past and apply them to new items. In particular they should identify how the characteristics of the insured items are related to their risk category.

Let's consider, for instance, the car accident and theft insurances. We can assume that the engine power, maximum speed and type of braking system influence the probability of a car accident. Likewise, the presence and type of options installed on a car influence the rate of theft for that model.

An insurance company needs a tool that is able to capture the rules and criteria used in the past to assign the risk category, and apply them to new items. In particular it wants to be able to predict the risk associated with new car models and therefore associate them to an insurance premium category.

An important feature of the required system is the ability to represent in a human-readable way the criteria that are used to classify the items. This is useful as a form of control over the automatic procedure of assigning the premium category. It is obviously intended to avoid major mistakes.

The tool will be tested in a car insurance scenario, but it has to be generic enough to be useful for classifying other kinds of insured items.

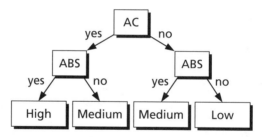

Figure 4.1 Decision tree

4.1.1 □ Classification criteria

As an example, we consider two characteristics of cars: AC (air conditioning) and ABS (automatic braking system). Both characteristics can assume one of the two values "yes" and "no", indicating whether the option is present.

Based on these two characteristics we classify the cars in three price categories: "high", "medium", "low". A car belongs to the "high" category if it has both AC and ABS, i.e. both characteristics have the value "yes". If both characteristics have the value "no" then the car belongs to the "low" category. In the other cases the car belongs to category "medium". From the above criteria it is possible to devise several classification criteria such as the one shown in Figure 4.1. It is a decision tree: it is possible to follow a path, based on the values of the characteristics, reaching a leaf that represents the category of the car.

4.2 ■ Problem analysis

In our application we have an initial set of existing car models that have been assigned to an existing category by the experts of the insurance company. We want to build a classifier that captures the criteria used so far and applies them to new car models. Our problem consists of two separate issues. First of all we need a tool to automatically analyse and capture the criteria applied by human experts to assign cars to their risk category in the past. Second, we need a tool that can evaluate the risk category of new car models.

Typically there are two kinds of classifier: expert-based and example-based. An expert-based classifier elaborates a set of rules defined by an expert and tells how to assign a category to an item. An example-based classifier identifies that set of rules by looking at a set of example items which have been previously labelled with a category tag.

Since insurance companies have a large set of examples we can start from, the obvious choice is to adopt an example-based classifier. The classifier must capture the correlation between the characteristics of the cars (e.g. ABS, AC, engine power).

The classifier must be as generic as possible in order to be applicable also to similar problems. It has to take into account extensions such as new characteristics of the items and different items described by a brand new set of characteristics. During the development of the classifier the reference will be the car accident and theft insurances problem but we will keep the system open to extensions.

4.2.1 ☐ **Domain models**

In artificial intelligence and data-mining literature it is possible to find many works dealing with classification and the construction of classifiers. The essential concepts involved in building and using a classifier are:

- *Item*: is the element that is or has to be assigned to a category. It is described by a set of features.
- *Feature*: consists of a name and a value. It is used to describe an item.
- *Category*: is a tag that is applied to an item based on its features.
- *Classifier*: is the tool that automatically assigns an item to a category.
- *Training set*: is a set of items that have already been assigned to a category. It is used to capture the assignment criteria.

We will assume that all features are of nominal type. That is, the features can assume value only in a finite set whose elements are defined completely by enumerating them. This assumption makes all the algorithms, both for identifying the classification rules and for classifying items, simpler.

There are several kinds of classifier models. The decision tree is one of the simplest (Cherkassky and Mulier 1998). It can easily represent hierarchies of concepts and has the great advantage of being easy to understand. In a decision tree both nodes and arcs have a label. Each non-leaf node is associated with a split feature. The arcs to the children nodes are associated with all the possible values of the parent feature. Each leaf is labelled with the name of a category.

The algorithm to assign a category to a new item is described below (Algorithm 4.1). The idea behind the algorithm is to find a path that describes the features of the item, starting from the root. At each node the path corresponding to the value of the feature is followed.

Input: an item, a decision tree
Output: a category for the item

1 start setting the root node as the current
2 repeat while the current node is not a leaf
    (a) the node label is the name of the feature to be considered
    (b) consider the value of the item's feature
    (c) follow the arc corresponding to the value
    (d) the node reached becomes the current node
3 the label of the leaf node is the category of the item

Algorithm 4.1 Categorization

The algorithm to build the decision tree is slightly more complex (see Algorithm 4.2). This task is called training. Each node is associated with a set of items (which is a subset of the training set), and a label, which is either the split feature (intermediate node) or the category name (leaf node). The tree is built incrementally starting from the root node.

The algorithm is presented in its recursive form, which is in our view more understandable.

Input: a training set of items T, a set of features F
Output: (the root node of) a decision tree

1 if all items in T belong to the same category return a leaf node labelled according to such a category
2 if F is empty
   (a) if T is empty return a leaf node labelled "unknown"
   (b) else return a leaf node labelled "uncertain"
3 select the "best" split feature s ∈ F
4 create a node n labelled s.name
5 for each possible value vi of the feature s
   (a) let ni be the result of a recursive execution of this algorithm where the first input is: Ti = {item ∈ T | item.s == vi} and the second input is: F – {s}
   (b) set ni as child node of n and label the connecting arc vi and
6 n is the resulting root node of the decision tree

Algorithm 4.2 Build the decision tree

Step 3 of Algorithm 4.2 leaves a detail unspecified. A criterion to identify which is the best split feature has to be defined. In the literature (see for instance Cherkassky and Mulier (1998)) several methods to select a split feature have been proposed. We select the simplest, which is based on information theory. We split on the feature that contains most information. According to information theory it is possible to assign to a sequence of symbols an information content, which is measured in bits.

Given an alphabet A containing N symbols, the information content of a sequence of symbols taken from that alphabet can be defined as follows:

$$I = \sum_{i=1}^{N_{symbols}} f_i \log_2(f_i)$$

Equation 4.1 Information content

where f_i is the frequency of ith symbol. In our case the alphabet is the set of categories. The sequence of symbols is generated taking each item of a set of items and looking at its category. Therefore f_i is the frequency of category i; it is calculated on set T as the number of items in T belonging to category i divided by the number of items in T. In symbols:

$$f_i = \frac{|\{item \in T \,|\, category(item) = category_i\}|}{|T|}$$

Equation 4.2 Symbol frequency

Note that if we have a sequence containing only one symbol, its information content is zero. Actually in Equation 4.1 the frequency f_i is exactly 1 and the number of symbols, N, is 1. Substituting these values in Equation 4.1 we obtain 0:

$$I = \sum_{i=1}^{1} 1 \cdot \log_2(1) = 1 \cdot \log_2(1) = 1 \cdot 0 = 0$$

Equation 4.3 Information content for the limit case

Given a test set of items T, the selection of s as splitting feature generates a group of subsets of T: $T_{s,1}, ..., T_{s,M}$, where M is the number of possible values of feature s. We define the information content of feature s for the set T as:

$$I_{s,T} = I_T - \sum_{i=1}^{M} \frac{|T_{s,i}|}{|T|} \cdot I_{T_{s,i}}$$

Equation 4.4 Information gain

That is, the information of the split feature s is the difference between the information of the initial set of items (I_T) and the weighted sum of the information of the sets of items induced by the split feature.

4.2.2 □ Main features

We are now able to summarize all the main features emerging from the problem analysis.

- *Classification*. This is the main goal of the system: the system must be able to assign a category to an item based on some criteria.
- *Classifier training*. To fulfil the previous goal, the system must be able to capture a set of criteria from an existing set of items.
- *Problem representation*. The tool is problem-independent; this means that the user should be allowed to represent the specific problem in terms of items, features and categories.
- *Criteria representation*. The outcome of the training must be represented in a human-readable format, which can be checked by experts.

4.2.3 □ Test

The following functionalities need to be tested carefully:

- The most important is the correct construction of the classifier from a set of items. The correctness of the classifier can be tested checking whether it assigns the expected category to items whose category is known.
- It is also important to check that the internal representation of the classifier is implemented correctly and that it can be represented in a readable way.

4.3 ■ Architecture and planning

The system is very simple. It is based on low-level or algorithmic details that will be addressed at the design level. The most relevant architectural issue is the separation of the generic problem solution algorithms from the visualization and interaction with the user. The overall architecture of the system should be the one depicted in Figure 4.2. There are two main components: the user interface and the classifier.

The algorithmic part of the system is confined in the Classifier component, while the interaction with the user is the responsibility of the User Interface component.

The system will be developed in an iterative and incremental fashion. In particular we plan to develop the system according to the following iterations, which produce three running prototypes.

- *Prototype 1: Classification*. The essential classes for the classifier are developed and the classification algorithm is implemented.
- *Prototype 2: Criteria representation*. The representation of the decision tree is addressed.
- *Prototype 3: Training*. The tree construction algorithm is implemented, so that a tree can be built based on a training set of items.

4.4 ■ Prototype 1: Classification

This prototype is able to assign a category to an item based on the information contained in a decision tree. We assume that someone has computed the decision tree such as the one shown in Figure 4.1.

4.4.1 □ Analysis

We will exploit the classification algorithms defined in the literature to develop a generic solution that can be applied both to the problem under study (cars) and to possible extensions to other types of items.

We face two main features: first the representation of the domain, i.e. of the items, their characteristics, and the categories they belong to; second the definition of the classification rules.

Figure 4.2 Component architecture

The main concepts that define the domain of the application are:

- item;
- feature;
- category.

These concepts and their relationships can be described using a UML class diagram as shown in Figure 4.3.

Class Item represents the core concept of our application domain; it is used to represent a car. The characteristics of an item are defined by means of a set of Feature objects. The defined_by association represents the relationships between an item and the features that define it. In addition an Item belongs to a Category.

The main concepts related to a classifier are described in the class diagram in Figure 4.4. Class Node represents the nodes of a tree; they are connected to each other through the parent–child association. Since the links also have a label, class Arc further specifies this association type: it adds a label.

The made_up_of association is an aggregation, this expresses the close connection between the concept of a decision tree and its constituent nodes. Among all the nodes that make up a decision tree, the root node is identified by a dedicated association.

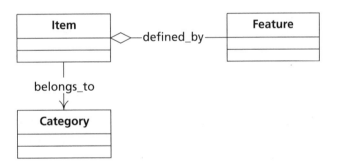

Figure 4.3 Classifier analysis

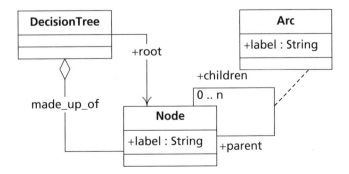

Figure 4.4 Decision tree analysis

4.4.2 □ **Design**

The design of the domain representation is straightforward, starting from the analysis. The classifier is responsible for assigning a category to an item. Each item (class Item) is related to a set of features that characterize it. Each feature has a name and a value; the value is taken from a limited set of possible values.

Decision point

How do we express the concept that features can assume only a limited set of values?

We must define the set of possible (or allowed) values; the easiest way is to provide an array containing them. There are two possible solutions: first we can provide the array to the constructor of the feature, second we encapsulate the array of allowed values into a "type" class. While the former solution is simpler, the latter is easier to understand and allows us to create a single object type that is common to all features that have the same type (i.e. can assume the same set of values).

To adopt the second solution, as shown in Figure 4.5, we define the FeatureType class that defines the type of the features by providing the set of allowed values. The features are represented by the class Feature that has a name and a value. To assign a new value to a feature, the value must be included in those allowed by the type.

Decision point

How do we represent values of features and categories?

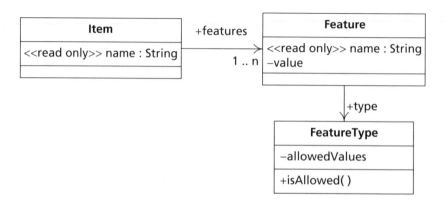

Figure 4.5 Item and feature classes

The values of the features and the categories can be represented in different ways. A generic solution could use Object to represent them. In practice the use of String is flexible enough for most uses and has the advantage of providing an immediate representation.

In our survey of the literature we focused on a simple kind of classifier: decision trees. There are several other types of classifiers, the system should be open to use on of them.

Decision point

How do we accommodate different types of classifiers?

Instead of providing a single classifier class we define the interface Classifier, which defines the method assignCategory. This method can be implemented in different ways by different types of classifiers. In this chapter we will develop only a decision tree classifier that is implemented by the DecisionTree class.

As far as the decision tree classifier is concerned, we keep the same classes, identified during the analysis phase, but we change the associations between them. The design of these classes is shown in Figure 4.6.

Decision point

How can we implement the typed association Arc?

Instead of having a Node object directly connected to its children we insert an Arc object in between. This object is intended to contain the label of the link. Also, class Node contains an attribute that represents the label of the node. Since the tree is basically a static structure that remains stable after it has been built, both label attributes are read-only.

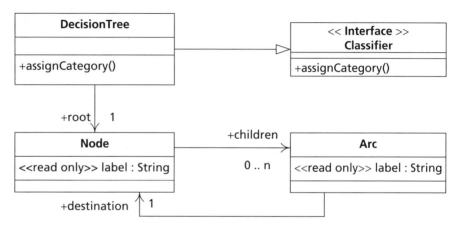

Figure 4.6 Decision tree classes

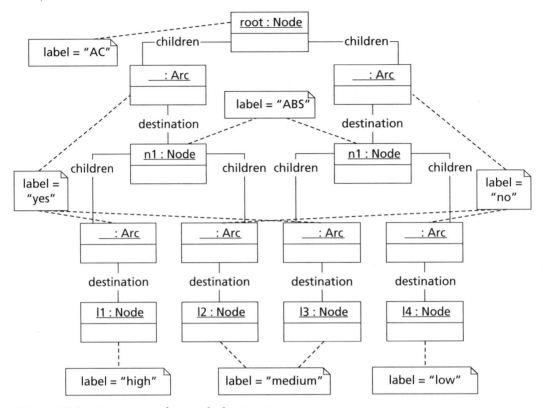

Figure 4.7 Static structure of a sample decision tree

Using this class structure, the test decision tree, which is shown in Figure 4.1, can be represented by a set of linked objects as shown in the object diagram depicted in Figure 4.7.

A Node object, called root in the figure, whose label is "AC", represents the root node. Since the links from a node to its children have been objectified into Arc objects, the root node is connected to its children, n1 and n2, through two Arc objects that have labels "yes" and "no" respectively. The other nodes and arcs of the test tree are represented likewise using the class structure shown in Figure 4.7.

4.4.3 ☐ Implementation

```
public class FeatureType {
  private String[] allowedValues;
  public FeatureType(String[] allowedValues) {
    this.allowedValues = allowedValues;
  }
  public boolean isAllowed(String value) {
    for(int i=0; i<allowedValues.length; ++i){
```

```
        if(value.equals(allowedValues[i]))
           return true;
    }
    return false;
  }
}
```

Class **Feature** has two basic attribute: **name** and **value**. The association between the feature and its type can be implemented by means of an attribute (**type**) that contains the reference to a **FeatureType** object (Sidebar 4.1). This is a standard approach to implement one-to-one and many-to-one associations.

Sidebar 4.1 Object variables

Java provides only one way of dealing with objects, i.e. through objects references (while C++ provides three different ways, i.e. objects, objects pointers and object references). The object variables in Java (i.e. variables not referencing primitive types such as int, float, etc.) are not objects: they are just references to objects. This has several consequences:

- when an object variable is declared it refers to no object and cannot be used;
- objects can be created only by means of the new operator;
- a single object can be referenced by any number of object variables;
- the equal operator (==) compares object variables, not objects, therefore it is true only if the object variables refer to the same object (or they are both null);
- to compare objects instead of references the method equals() should be used, not ==;
- an assignment between object variables only changes the reference. It does not touch the object.

Therefore in the following examples all the print statements are executed:

```
String someText; //just a reference NOT an object
//if(someText == null) System.out.println("1 TRUE");
// If the previous line is not commented,
// the compiler generates the following error:
// ...: variable someText might not have been initialized
someText = new String("some text"); // now an object exists
if(someText != null)
  System.out.println("2 TRUE");
String theSameObject = someText;
                   // they both refer to the same object
if(someText == theSameObject)
  System.out.println("3 TRUE");
String theSameText = new String("some text");
                   // another object containing the same text
if(someText != theSameText)
  System.out.println("4 TRUE");
```

▶

```
if(someText.equals(theSameText))
  System.out.println("5 TRUE");
someText = new String("another text");
                      // only changes the reference
if(theSameObject.equals(theSameText))
  System.out.println("6 TRUE");
```

While variables' lifetimes are linked to that of the method where they are defined, this is not true for the objects created in a method and referenced by object variables defined in it. A variable of a method exists only while a thread of control traverses the method. Attributes are used to store values of references that must be kept beyond the end of a method. Object attributes have the same characteristics as object variables.

The name attribute is initialized once and for ever by the constructor; its value can be read by means of the name() method (Sidebar 4.2). Such an approach can be generalized in the form of an idiom: read-only attribute. Value is a public attribute, but there are constraints on the values it can assume, in particular it can assume only the values allowed by the type. To ensure that only allowed values can be assigned, it is implemented as a private attribute. Two methods are provided to get and set its value. The getter method is analogous to the one used for the name read-only attribute. The setter method checks with the type if the new value is allowed; if it is not then an IllegalArgumentException is raised. This approach can be generalized as the constrained attribute idiom.

```
public class Feature {
  private String name;
  private String value;
  private FeatureType type;
  public Feature(String name, String value, FeatureType
type){
    this.name = name;
    this.value = value;
    this.type = type;
  }
  public String name() { return name; }
  public String value() { return value; }
  public void value(String newValue){
    if(type.isAllowed(newValue))
      value = newValue;
    else
      throw new IllegalArgumentException
            ("value" + newValue +
             " not valid for attribute " + name);
  }
}
```

Sidebar 4.2 Read-only attributes

The OO purists say that all attributes should be private; getter and setter methods that handle reading and writing the attributes should be provided as needed. In practice, when an attribute is meant to be read-only it can be implemented in two possible ways, depending on the context in which it will be used. The first is setting it private and providing a public method that returns its value. This ensures that no client of the class is allowed to change the attribute value. For instance:

```
private String readOnlyAttribute;
public String readonlyAttribute () {
  return readonlyAttribute;
}
```

Another option is to use an attribute that is public (or package public). In this case the clients of the class must know that the attribute is intended to be read-only and conform to this implicit assumption. It is a good practice to associate a comment that reminds of the assumption. For instance:

```
public String readOnlyAttribute; // Read-Only!!!
```

These two solutions provide different *safety* levels. While the first solution works in every context, the second is acceptable only where the class clients know very well the intended use of the attribute (e.g. the class is used only inside a package and its clients are written by the same developer as wrote the class). In addition to the above considerations, there are three other issues that should be taken into account: ease of use, efficiency and flexibility.

The *ease of use* of the two solutions is almost the same for a client that needs to access the attribute. The syntax required by the first solution involves a method invocation, while the syntax corresponding to the second solution is a simple access to the public variable.

When it comes to *efficiency* the first solution is clearly worse than the second one. The difference is marked by the method invocation; it is far less efficient than direct attribute access.

Finally, the *flexibility* of the first solution becomes evident when considering the following scenario: several alternative implementations are required; the common characteristics are defined in an interface that can be implemented by different classes.

Class **Item** represents the items. The name is implemented as in class **Feature**. In addition it has a one-to-many association to class **Feature**; since the number of the linked elements is known at the time the item is built, the association can be implemented as an array of Feature elements (**features**). The **value()** method returns the value of a feature, while the **setValue()** method sets a new value for a feature.

```
public class Item {
  private Feature[] features;
  private String name;
  private Feature category;
  public Item(String name, Feature[] features){
    this.name = name;
```

```
    this.features = features;
  }
  public String name() { return name; }
  public String value(String featureName){
  // iterates over the features to find the value of the
  // given one
    for(int i=0; i<features.length; ++i){
      if(featureName.equals(features[i].name())){
        return features[i].value();
      }
    }
    return null;
  }
  public void setValue(String featureName, String newValue){
    for(int i=0; i<features.length; ++i){
      if(featureName.equals(features[i].name())){
        features[i].value(newValue);
        return;
      }
    }
  }
}
```

The structure of the decision tree is described by means of the classes Node and Arc. Class Node has a read-only attribute (label) and is involved in the one-to-many association children. Since the number of objects is not known *a priori* it is not possible to use an array. We can implement the association applying the transformation shown in Figure 4.8. The transformed association can be easily implemented with a reference in the class One plus a reference in the Many class: in total one attribute per class. This is a standard way of implementing such associations and can be coded into an idiom. This transformation is made during the implementation phase

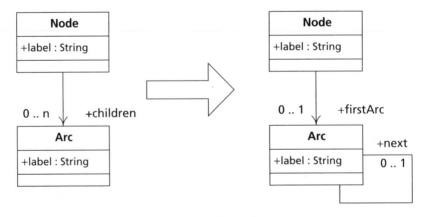

Figure 4.8 One-to-many association transformation

because it is very low level; as a result we keep the design simpler and easier to understand.

The isLeaf() method checks if the node is a leaf node, i.e. that it has no children. The addChild() method adds a new child node: it can be used to build the tree. The follow() method returns the child node which is linked through the arc with the given label.

```java
public class Node {
  private String label;
  private Arc firstArc;
  public Node(String label) {
    this.label = label;
  }
  public String label() { return label; }
  public void addChild(String arcLabel, Node child){
    firstArc = new Arc(arcLabel,child,firstArc);
  }
  public boolean isLeaf() { return firstArc==null; }
  public Node follow(String arcLabel) {
    for(Arc arc=firstArc; arc!=null; arc=arc.nextArc())
      if(arcLabel.equals(arc.label()))
        return arc.destination();
    return null;
  }
}
```

Class Arc is very simple: it has a read-only attribute (label) and a navigable many-to-one association (destination) with the class Node. It can be straightforwardly implemented as follows:

```java
public class Arc {
  private Node destination;
  private String label;
  private Arc nextArc;
  public Arc(String label, Node destination, Arc nextArc) {
    this.label = label;
    this.destination = destination;
    this.nextArc = nextArc;
  }
  public String label() {
    return label;
  }
  public Node destination() {
    return destination;
  }
  public Arc nextArc(){
    return nextArc;
  }
}
```

The class DecisionTree provides the access point for using a decision tree, in particular it embeds the structural representation of the decision tree (made up of Node and Arc objects) and provides the assignCategory() method which performs the classification task on an item. The association to the root node is implemented, as usual, by a private attribute (root); since it has to be navigated only by methods defined inside the class, there is no getter method. The assignCategory() method implements Algorithm 4.1. The algorithm requires two input arguments: an item to be classified and the root of the decision tree. The second input for this algorithm is implicit, it can be found through the root association, and thus it does not appear as an argument of the method.

```
public class DecisionTree
implements Classifier {
  private Node root;
  public DecisionTree(Node tree){
    root = tree;
  }
  // Assign a category to an item.
  // The algorithm takes as input an item and a decision tree.
  // The output is the name of the category.
  public String assignCategory(Item item){
    Node current;
    // 1) start at the root node
    current= root;
    // 2) repeat while the current node is not a leaf
    while(! current.isLeaf() ){
      // a) the node label is the name of the feature to be
      // considered
      String featureName = current.label();
      // b) consider the value of the item's feature
      String value = item.value(featureName);
      // c) follow the arc corresponding to the value
      Node reached = current.follow(value);
      // d) the node reached becomes the current node
      current = reached;
    }
    // 3) the label of the leaf node is the class of the item
    return current.label();
  }
}
```

4.4.4 □ Test

We break up the test into three test cases: one (TestItem) to test the class Item and the related classes, another (TestTree) to test the classes used to represent the tree, and finally one (TestClassifier) to verify the algorithm that

assigns a category to an item. The TestItem test case tests the basic functionalities of the classes FeatureType, Feature and Item.

```java
public class TestItem extends TestCase {
  public TestItem(String arg0) {
    super(arg0);
  }
  public void testFeatureType(){
    String featureTypeName="YesNo";
    String[] allowedValues = new String[] {"yes","no"};
    FeatureType type = new FeatureType(
      featureTypeName,allowedValues);
    for(int i=0; i< allowedValues.length; ++i)
      assertTrue(type.isAllowed(allowedValues[i]));
  }
  public void testFeature(){
    String featureTypeName="YesNo";
    String[] allowedValues = new String[] {"yes","no"};
    FeatureType type = new FeatureType(
      featureTypeName,allowedValues);
    String value = "yes";
    Feature feature = new Feature("name","yes",type);
      assertEquals(value,feature.value());
    try{
      feature.value("no");
      assertTrue(true);
    }catch(IllegalArgumentException e){
      fail("cannot set a valid value");
    }
    try{
      feature.value("invalid");
      fail("could set an invalid value");
    }catch(IllegalArgumentException e){
      assertTrue(true);
    }
  }
  public void testItem(){
    FeatureType yn = new FeatureType("YesNo",
                    new String[]{"yes","no"});
    Feature[] features = new Feature[]{
     new Feature("f1","yes",yn), new Feature("f2","no",yn)};
    Item item = new Item("name",features);
    assertEquals("yes",item.value("f1"));
    assertEquals("no",item.value("f2"));
    item.setValue("f1","no");
    assertEquals("no",item.value("f1"));
  }
}
```

The **TestTree** test case checks the functionalities of the classes **Node** and indirectly **Arc**.

```
public class TestTree extends TestCase {
  public void testLeaf(){
    String label = "leaf label";
    Node leaf = new Node(label);
    assertTrue("Should be a leaf",leaf.isLeaf());
    assertEquals(label,leaf.label());
  }
  public void testOneLevel(){
    Node leftLeaf = new Node("left");
    Node rightLeaf = new Node("right");
    String toLeft="to the left";
    String toRight="to the right";
    Node root = new Node("root");
    root.addChild(toLeft,leftLeaf);
    root.addChild(toRight,rightLeaf);
    assertFalse("root shouldn't be a leaf", root.isLeaf());
    assertSame(leftLeaf,root.follow(toLeft));
    assertSame(rightLeaf,root.follow(toRight));
  }
}
```

Finally the **TestClassifier** test case checks whether the classifier assigns the category correctly to an item. To test this functionality, four main steps are required:

■ define the type of item, i.e. its features;
■ build a decision tree;
■ apply it to some items;
■ check if the assigned categories are correct.

Given the classification tree shown in Figure 4.1, we have to define which items will be used to test the classifier. Since the classification algorithm follows a path through the decision tree, we will use items that force it to traverse all the paths in the test tree. There are four possible paths in the decision tree as described in Figure 4.1.

The **TestClassifier** test case has only one test method and a helper method that builds the decision tree. The test method applies the classifier to the four items described in Table 4.1.

Table 4.1 Test items

Item	AC	ABS	Expected category
1	Yes	Yes	High
2	Yes	No	Medium
3	No	Yes	Medium
4	No	No	Low

```
public class TestClassifier extends TestCase {
  private DecisionTree buildTree(){
    Node root = new Node("AC");
    Node n1 = new Node("ABS");
    Node n2 = new Node("ABS");
    root.addChild("yes",n1);
    root.addChild("no",n2);
    Node l1 = new Node("high");
    Node l2 = new Node("medium");
    Node l3 = new Node("medium");
    Node l4 = new Node("low");
    n1.addChild("yes",l1);
    n1.addChild("no",l2);
    n2.addChild("yes",l3);
    n2.addChild("no",l4);
    return new DecisionTree(root);
  }
  public void testCategory(){
    DecisionTree dt = buildTree();
    FeatureType yn = new FeatureType("YesNo",
        new String[]{"yes","no"});
    Feature[] features = new Feature[] {
        new Feature("AC","yes",yn),
        new Feature("ABS","yes",yn) };
    Item item = new Item("car",features);
    String category = dt.assignCategory(item);
    assertEquals("high",category);
    item.setValue("AC","no");
    category = dt.assignCategory(item);
    assertEquals("medium",category);
    item.setValue("AC","yes");
    item.setValue("ABS","no");
    category = dt.assignCategory(item);
    assertEquals("medium",category);
    item.setValue("AC","no");
    category = dt.assignCategory(item);
    assertEquals("low",category);
  }
}
```

4.5 ■ Prototype 2: Criteria representation

The prototype developed in this iteration provides a textual representation of the decision tree. The representation has the goal of being easy to understand, so it can be used as feedback to the problem expert.

4.5.1 □ Analysis

The tree that is described by means of nodes and arcs is a complex data structure. The goal here is to find an easy-to-understand representation. It has to be textual and must contain the same information originally present in the decision tree. For instance, the decision tree shown in Figure 4.1 can be represented as shown in Figure 4.9.

4.5.2 □ Design

The standard way of generating a textual representation of an object (or group of objects) is through the **toString()** method. Since we are interested in representing the whole tree, a recursive version of such a method is required.

Figure 4.10 shows how to extend the class structure defined in the previous iteration. Two methods are provided: one is private (**toString(String indent)**) and implements the recursive algorithm which is executed for each indent level, the other is public (**toString()**) and returns a representation of the whole tree rooted in the node.

The behaviour of the recursive algorithm can be depicted using a sequence diagram, as shown in Figure 4.11. The sequence diagram is based on the static structure described in Figure 4.7.

A client of class **Node** invokes the public **toString()** method, which in turn calls the *private* **toString()** recursive method on the same node, passing string " " as argument corresponding to the first indent level. Then the recursive method invokes itself on the node's children; child node *n*1 is shown in the figure. The recursion proceeds until the method is invoked on leaves, such as *l*1 and *l*2 in the figure, which just represent themselves and return control.

4.5.3 □ Implementation

The implementation of the **toString()** method for class **Item** requires the concatenation of strings. Since **String** objects are non-modifiable, every

```
[AC
  (yes) --> [ABS
               (yes) --> [high]
               (no)  --> [medium]
             ]
  (no)  --> [ABS
               (yes) --> [medium]
               (no)  --> [low]
             ]
]
```

Figure 4.9 Textual representation of a decision tree

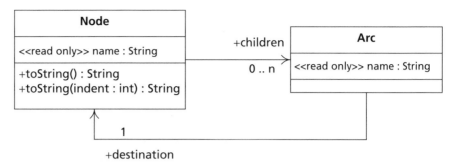

Figure 4.10 Class diagram for tree representation

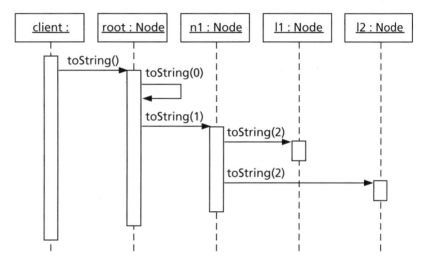

Figure 4.11 Sequence diagram for Node.toString() methods

concatenation makes it necessary to create a new object, which is highly inefficient. A better way of building a concatenation of strings is to use the StringBuffer class and its append() method (JDC 1998).

The implementation of the toString() method for class Node is a recursive method that prints all the nodes of a sub-tree; nodes are printed indented according to their level in the tree. To keep track of the indentation level a String argument is used. At each recursive call the indent argument is concatenated with the constant string indentStep in order to increase the indentation level. The recursion termination condition is met when the current node is a leaf.

We provide a toString() method that conforms to the one defined in the base class Object. This method has no argument and invokes the recursive toString() method passing an empty string as argument.

```
public String toString(){ return toString(""); }
private static final String indentStep="    ";
```

```
private String toString(String indent){
  StringBuffer buffer=new StringBuffer();
  buffer.append("[").append(label);
  if(!isLeaf()){
    buffer.append("\n");
    int i;
    for(Arc current=firstArc; current!=null;
                        current=current.nextArc()){
      String arcLabel = current.label();
      Node dest = current.destination();
      buffer.append(indent)
            .append("  (")
            .append(arcLabel)
            .append(")--> ")
            .append(dest.toString(indent+indentStep));
    }
    buffer.append(indent);
  }
  buffer.append("]\n");
  return buffer.toString();
}
```

We define a toString() method also for class DecisionTree; the implementation is straightforward, since it just invokes the toString() method of the root node.

```
public String toString(){
  return "Decision tree: \n" + root.toString();
}
```

4.5.4 ☐ Test

The test for the representation of the tree can address two main issues: the representation of a single node (a leaf) and the representation of a whole three. We introduce a degree of flexibility by testing the presence of substrings rather than a perfect match. Actually we test if the representation contains the labels of the node and arcs in the proper order. This approach allows us to modify the width of indentation and extra white spaces.

The first test method (testSingleNode()) checks if the representation of a leaf node contains the label of the node. The second test method (testSimpleTree()) checks if the first label is the label of the root node and if each node label is preceded by the label of the arc to that node.

```
public class TestRepresentation extends TestCase {
  public void testSingleNode(){
    String label="the label";
    Node node = new Node(label);
```

```
            String repres = node.toString();
            assertTrue(repres + " doesn't include " + label,
                    repres.indexOf(label)>-1);
        }
    public void testSimpleTree(){
        String leftLabel = "left";
        String rightLable = "right";
        Node leftLeaf = new Node(leftLabel);
        Node rightLeaf = new Node(rightLable);
        String toLeft="to the left";
        String toRight="to the right";
        String rootLabel="root";
        Node root = new Node(rootLabel);
        root.addChild(toLeft,leftLeaf);
        root.addChild(toRight,rightLeaf);
        String repres = root.toString();
        int index = repres.indexOf("root");
        assertTrue("root not found",index>0);
        int indexToL = repres.indexOf(toLeft,index);
        int indexToR = repres.indexOf(toRight,index);
        assertTrue("left arc not found",indexToL>index);
        assertTrue("right arc not found",indexToR>index);
        int indexL = repres.indexOf("left",indexToL);
        int indexR = repres.indexOf("right",indexToR);
        assertTrue("left node not found",indexL>index);
        assertTrue("right node not found",indexR>index);
    }
}
```

4.6 ■ Prototype 3: Training

In this iteration the decision tree construction algorithm is used to build a classifier starting from a training set of items.

4.6.1 □ Analysis

The class structure remains basically unchanged; the increment is essentially algorithmic. We have to implement Algorithm 4.2 that takes as input a set of features that are already assigned to categories and builds a decision tree that captures the criteria adopted to assign the categories.

4.6.2 □ Design

The main problem in the design of this prototype lies in the definition of the data structures used for the implementation of the training algorithm

(Algorithm 4.2). Essentially the algorithm is based on the manipulation of sets of items and sets of features.

Decision point

How do we represent the sets manipulated by the algorithm?

The simplest choice would be to use arrays that contain the elements of the set; in this case we would have to implement all the operations for manipulating such arrays. An alternative would be to use the standard collection classes of Java (Sidebar 4.3). We choose the latter option because it makes use of already defined operations and lets us focus on the algorithm.

Sidebar 4.3 Arrays vs collections

Collections were introduced in version 1.2 of Java. The main collection interface is Collection. It is a container of elements that can be added to or removed from the collection. Elements can be iterated on by means of an Iterator object. When compared with an array, a collection does not exhibit a specific implementation, its elements are not ordered, and it does not have a fixed size.

Another important difference between collections and arrays is that the former treat their elements as Object, while the latter can have different types of elements. The fact that collections deal with Object has two main consequences:

- they cannot contain primitive type (e.g. int);
- a cast is necessary when accessing their elements.

Since primitive types are not allowed, wrapper classes (e.g. Integer) should be used instead. Using casts brings a minor decrease in readability. We can compare arrays and collections looking at how simple operations can be performed.

```
Iterator it = items.iterator();
while(it.hasNext()){
  String item = (String)it.next();
  // do something with the item
}
```

Using an array the same iteration code can be written as follows:

```
for(int i=0; i < items.length; ++i){
  String item = items[i];
  // do something with the item
}
```

The two variations of iteration are almost equally complex. The main weakness of the former is the necessity of using casts to adapt the Object, manipulated by the collections, and the effective classes manipulated by the program. Manipulating Object instead of specific classes, gives great flexibility, because it is possible to write algorithms that are independent of details.

Up to now we have looked at the advantages of using the elements of a collection; collections provide several advantages also in populating the set. When using an array the number of elements must be known in advance, while the number of elements in a collection is not defined *a priori*.

Filling a set with two strings:

```
Collection items = new Vector();
items.add(new String("first"));
items.add(new String("second"));
```

Using an array the same population code can be written as follows:

```
String [] items = new String[2];
items[0] = new String("first");
items[1] = new String("first");
```

The use of arrays poses several problems: the number of elements must be known in advance, an index must be used to address elements.

Another important interface is Map. It represents the association of a set of keys to a set of values. The main methods of interface Map are void put(Object key, Object value) and Object get(Object key). The former stores an association between the key and the value, the latter retrieves the value associated with a key (or null if no value is present).

4.6.3 ☐ Implementation

We will have a method (buildDecisionTree()) that implements the main features of the algorithm, and several auxiliary methods that implement the details. The root node of the decision tree is computed according to Algorithm 4.2. Since the algorithm is generic and does not require accessing any extra information in addition to its arguments, we decide to implement is using static methods. The method buildDecisionTree is as close an implementation of the original algorithm as possible.

The method receives two parameters; the first is a map that associates each item with its category; the second is a map that associates the names of the features with their types. The collection of items can be obtained getting the key set from the map items (using the method keySet()).

```
//Input: a training set of items T, a set of attributes A
//Output: a decision tree (the root of it)
private static Node buildDecisionTree
                                (Map items, Map features){
  // 0) if the attribute set is empty or the items
  //    belong to a single class
  if(features.size()==0 || information(items)==0.0){
    // a) create a leaf node labelled according to the class
    //    of the item
    return new Node(findCategory(items));
  }
  // 1) select the "best" split attribute s in A
  String splitFeature = selectSplit(items,features);
  // 2) create a node n with label s.name
```

```
Node n = new Node(splitFeature);
// 3) for each possible value vi of s
FeatureType splitType =
                (FeatureType)features.get(splitFeature);
Map partitions=performSplit(items,splitFeature,
                splitType.allowedValues());
for (Iterator iter = partitions.keySet().iterator();
                                iter.hasNext();) {
  String value = (String) iter.next();
  // a) be ni the result of a recursive execution of this
  //    algorithm where:
  //    the fist input is: Ti = { item in T | item.s == vi }
  //    the second input is: A - { s }
  Map partition=(Map)partitions.get(value);
  Map remaining = new HashMap(features);
  remaining.remove(splitFeature);
  Node child = buildDecisionTree(partition,remaining);
  // b) set ni as child node of n and label the
  //    connecting arc vi
  n.addChild(value,child);
  }
  // 4) n is the resulting root node of the decision tree
  return n;
}
```

In step 0 to determine whether all the items in a set belong to the same category we check if the information content is null (see Equation 4.3).

In step 3, the loop operates on each of the sets of items resulting from the split. It is more efficient to generate all these sets in a single step instead of generating them separately. To keep the link between each value of the split feature and the relative split-set a Map is used. A map stores associations between a key (the possible value) and a value (the corresponding set of items), making it very easy to obtain the set of items given the value.

To keep the method buildDecisionTree as close as possible to the original algorithm (Algorithm 4.2), several details are missing:

- how to determine the category of a set of items,
- how to find the "best" split feature,
- how to split a set of items,
- how to calculate information content (in terms of number of bits) of a set of items,
- how to calculate the information gain deriving from a split.

The findCategory() method determines which is the category of a set of items. This is not as easy as it seems, since the set can be empty or it can contain items from several categories. If the set is empty then the category is unknown, otherwise the frequency of the categories must be computed.

If there is only one category, that is the category of the set, otherwise the category of the set cannot be determined.

```java
private static String findCategory(Map items){
  // no category if the set is empty
  if(items.size()==0)
    return "?";
  // computes the frequency of each category
  Map catFreq = new HashMap();
  Iterator it = items.keySet().iterator();
  String category = "";
  while(it.hasNext()){
    Item item = (Item)it.next();
    category = (String)items.get(item);
    Integer count = (Integer)catFreq.get(category);
    if(count==null)
      catFreq.put(category, new Integer(1));
    else
      catFreq.put(category, new Integer(1+count.intValue()));
  }
  // if only one category is present it is the set's category
  if(catFreq.keySet().size() == 1)
    return category;
  // otherwise it is not possible to assign a category
  return "?";
}
```

The selectSplit() method determines the best split feature for a set of items. The best split feature is the one implying the highest information gain.

```java
private static String selectSplit(Map items,Map features){
  Iterator attr=features.keySet().iterator();
  String split=null;
  double maxGain = 0.0;
  while(attr.hasNext()){
    String candidate = (String)attr.next();
    FeatureType type = (FeatureType)features.get(candidate);
    double gain = evaluateSplitGain(items,
                          candidate,type.allowedValues());
    if(gain>maxGain){
      maxGain = gain;
      split = candidate;
    }
  }
  return split;
}
```

The performSplit() method executes the split of a set of items according to a split feature. It returns the resulting sets of items, each of them being labelled with the relative feature value.

```
private static Map performSplit(Map items, String split,
                                Collection possibleValues){
  Map partitions=new HashMap();
  for (Iterator iter = possibleValues.iterator();
                                       iter.hasNext();) {
    String value = (String) iter.next();
    partitions.put(value,new HashMap());
  }
  Iterator it=items.keySet().iterator();
  while(it.hasNext()){
    Item item=(Item)it.next();
    String splitValue = item.value(split);
    Map partition=(Map)partitions.get(splitValue);
    partition.put(item,items.get(item));
  }
  return partitions;
}
```

The evaluateSplitGain() evaluates the information gain that would derive from splitting a set of items according to a given split feature; it computes Equation 4.4.

```
private static double evaluateSplitGain(Map items,
            String split, Collection possibleValues){
  double origInfo = information(items);
  double splitInfo = 0;
  Map partitions=performSplit(items,split,possibleValues);
  double size=items.size();
  for (Iterator iter = possibleValues.iterator();
                                     iter.hasNext();) {
    String value = (String) iter.next();
    Map partition = (Map)partitions.get(value);
    double partitionSize = partition.size();
    double partitionInfo = information(partition);
    splitInfo += partitionSize/size*partitionInfo;
  }
  return origInfo - splitInfo;
}
```

The information() method computes the information content of a set of items. The categories represent the symbols of the alphabet. As described in Equation 4.1, the information can be computed from the frequency of each symbol. Thus first of all we need to count the number of occurrences of each symbol, then we can apply the equation to compute the information content.

```
private static double information(Map items){
  Map frequencies = new HashMap();
  // compute number of occurrences of classes
  Iterator it=items.keySet().iterator();
  while(it.hasNext()){
    Item item=(Item)it.next();
    String category=(String)items.get(item);
    Long num_occur = (Long)frequencies.get(category);
    if(num_occur == null)
      frequencies.put(category,new Long(1));
    else
      frequencies.put(category,
                  new Long(num_occur.longValue()+1));
  }
  // compute information
  double info=0;
  double numItems = items.size();
  it = frequencies.values().iterator();
  while(it.hasNext()){
    Long num_occurr = (Long)it.next();
    double freq= num_occurr.doubleValue() / numItems;
    info += freq * Math.log(freq) / Math.log(2.0);
  }
  return -info;
}
```

Finally, we define a constructor for the DecisionTree class that invokes the buildDecisionTree() method to build the decision tree; the parameters of the constructor must be the same as those of the method.

```
public DecisionTree(Map items, Map features) {
  root = buildDecisionTree(items,features);
}
```

4.6.4 □ Test

To test the decision tree construction algorithm we need to:

- define a training set of items;
- instantiate the decision tree based on this set; and
- check if it classifies correctly some items.

If the training algorithm works correctly then a decision tree equivalent to the one used in previous testing should be generated, therefore the same test items can be used to check if the tree is correct. We will use the training set of items described in Table 4.2.

The test method testExample() is made up the following steps:

- create the set of features ("AC" and "ABS" both of type yn);

Table 4.2 Training set

Item	AC	ABS	Expected category
1	Yes	Yes	High
2	No	No	Low
3	Yes	No	Medium
4	No	Yes	Medium

- create the items, by means of the createItem() method, and add them to the training set mapping them to their categories;
- create a decision tree classifier based on the training set; and
- check if the classifier classifies correctly the test set element.

```java
public class TestTraining extends TestCase {
  public TestTraining(String arg0) {
    super(arg0);
  }
  private Item createItem(String ac, String abs){
    Feature[] features = new Feature[] {
      new Feature("AC",ac,yn),
      new Feature("ABS",abs,yn)
    };
    return new Item("car",features);
  }
  private FeatureType yn = new FeatureType("YesNo",
                            new String[]{"yes","no"});
  public void testExample(){
    Map items = new HashMap();
    Map features = new HashMap();
    features.put("AC",yn);
    features.put("ABS",yn);
    Item item1 = createItem("yes","yes");
    items.put(item1,"high");
    Item item2 = createItem("yes","no");
    items.put(item2,"medium");
    Item item3 = createItem("no","yes");
    items.put(item3,"medium");
    Item item4 = createItem("no","no");
    items.put(item4,"low");
    DecisionTree dc = new DecisionTree(items,features);
    assertEquals("high",dc.assignCategory(item1));
    assertEquals("medium",dc.assignCategory(item2));
    assertEquals("medium",dc.assignCategory(item3));
    assertEquals("low",dc.assignCategory(item4));
  }
}
```

The test, like those developed for the previous prototypes, is not complete but clearly defines the line that can be followed to make them more complete.

4.7 ■ Extensions

The classification criteria adopted in Prototypes 1 and 2 are quite simple. For each item they specify only whether a given feature is present or not. For example, they specify that a car has the airbag option. A straightforward extension could provide the ability to classify items based on the some characteristics of a given feature. For example, a car might have two airbags, four airbags or no airbags.

A more complex and interesting extension requires dealing with the theory of fuzzy sets (Klir and Yuan 1995). A fuzzy set differs from traditional mathematical sets in the form of the membership function. Items are not just said to belong (or not) to a given set. The membership function specifies for each item the percentage membership of that item in a given set. For example, a car with zero airbags belongs 100 per cent to the low risk category; a car with two airbags belongs 60 per cent to the low risk category and 40 per cent to the medium risk category; a car with four airbags belongs 10 per cent to the low risk category, 70 per cent to the medium risk category and 20 per cent to the high risk category. Using the fuzzy set theory, it is more easy to classify items that are not in only one category.

4.8 ■ Assessment

Analysis technique. We recognized in the problem statement a well-known domain, whose literature provides us with the main concepts that make up the analysis model.

Modelling technique. The analysis of this problem used, in addition to the class diagrams, the object diagrams to represent static structures and sequence diagrams to describe interactions among objects in typical scenarios.

Development approach. We divided the problem into two sub-problems: the representation of the classification information and its processing. The processing deals both with the use of the information to classify an item and the construction of a classification schema starting from a training set.

Attributes of classes may have different features. In particular, read-only attributes are initialized once and never modified; they can be implemented according to the read-only attribute idiom. When there are constraints on the values that an attribute can assume, the constrained-value attribute idiom provides a good implementation solution.

Associations between classes play an important role in object-oriented analysis and design. Associations exist to be navigated; this issue drives the implementation of *n*-to-1 (or 1-to-1) associations using the many-to-one association idiom.

Testing the implementation is an essential aspect of the development. There are several strategies and methodologies; two very simple approaches are described by the equals method testing and toString method testing design patterns.

Idiom	Read-only attribute
Context	A class has a read-only attribute.
Problem	It must be ensured that nobody can modify the attribute.
Forces or tradeoffs	It must be easy to read the attribute. It must be impossible to write it.
Solution	The attribute is implemented as a private member attribute of the class. A getter method with the same name as the attribute provides read access to the attribute. If the type of the attribute is a primitive type (e.g. **int**) or a non-modifiable class (e.g. String) the attribute can be directly returned by the method, otherwise a copy of the attribute should be returned. Since the attribute must be initialized at some point, the constructor is responsible for this.
| **Examples** | ```java
class SampleClass {
  private String name;
  public SampleClass(String name){
    this.name = name;
  }
  public String name() { return name; }
}
``` |
| **Force resolution** | Access to the attribute is easily achieved through the method with the same name. Since the attribute is private, it is not possible to modify it. |
| **Design rationale** | The getter method returns the value of the attribute avoiding direct manipulation of the attribute by the class clients. The simplest form of the getter method is just a return statement having the attribute as argument. If the attribute is a primitive type then it is passed "by value" to the method caller. Otherwise, if it is an object, the caller obtains a reference. In the latter case a problem arises: since the client obtains a reference to the object, nothing can avoid modification. Therefore a simple return statement is suitable only for non-modifiable classes. When a modifiable class is concerned, the getter method must return a copy of the attribute. |
```

Idiom	Constrained-value attribute
Context	A class has an attribute that has constraints on what values it can assume.
Problem	Ensure that only allowed values can be assigned to the attribute.
Forces or tradeoffs	It must be possible to easily read and write the attribute. Forbidden values must be avoided.
Solution	This idiom is an extension of the "read-only attribute" idiom. The attribute is implemented as a private member attribute of the class. A getter method with the same name as the attribute provides read access to the attribute. A setter method with the same name as the attribute provides write access to the attribute. The setter method checks if the new value is allowed; if it is, the attribute is updated. Otherwise an exception is thrown. The attribute must be initialized at some point; usually it is the constructor that is responsible for initialization.

Examples	`private` String value;
	// getter method
	`public` String value() { `return` value; }
	// setter method
	`public void` value(String newValue)
	        `throws` IllegalArgumentException {
	  `if`(satisfiesConstraints(newValue)){
	   value = newValue;
	   `return`;
	  }
	  `throw new` IllegalArgumentException(
	   "value '" + newValue +
	   "' not valid for attribute " + name);
	}

Force resolution	Access to the attribute is easily achieved through the method with the same name. Since the attribute is private, it is not possible to modify it.
Design rationale	The "read-only attribute" idiom avoids direct access to the attribute, thus a new value can be assigned only through the setter method that checks for conformance to constraints.

Idiom	Many-to-one association
Context	An $n : 1$ association between two classes navigable from the many role to the one role. Note that a $1 : 1$ association is just a special case of an $n : 1$ association.
Problem	Implement the association enabling navigation.
Forces or tradeoffs	A link to the object must be stored. It must be navigable.
Solution	An attribute contains a reference to the linked object; this attribute is implemented according to the "read-only attribute" idiom.
| Examples | ```
private Attribute category;
public Attribute category() { return category }
``` |
| Design rationale | Since, in Java, object variables (and attributes) are references to objects and not effective object storage, this kind of variable lends itself to implementing links. |

Idiom	One-to-many association decomposition
Context	A $1 : n$ association between two classes navigable from the one role to the many role. The exact cardinality of the association is not known in advance.
Problem	Implement the association enabling navigation.
Forces or tradeoffs	A link to the object must be stored. It must be navigable. Arrays require knowledge of the cardinality.
Solution	The transformed association can be easily implemented with a reference in the class One plus a reference in the Many class: in total one attribute per class.

Forces resolution	Knowledge of cardinality is not required. We need to implement two one-to-one associations.
Design rationale	Since we know how to implement one-to-one (and many-to-one) associations we decompose the original association into simpler and easily implementable associations.
```

4.9 ■ References

Cherkassky, V. and Mulier, F. (1998) *Learning From Data*, John Wiley & Sons.

Klir, G. J. and Yuan, B. (1995) *Fuzzy Sets and Fuzzy Logic: Theory and Applications*, Pearson Education.

Sun Microsystems (1998) JDC TechTips: January 20, 1998; available at http://java.sun.com/developer/TechTips/1998/tt0120.html

Hardware description language

5

Synthesis

This chapter investigates the use of Java as a hardware description language (HDL). The program simulates a typical computer that adopts the Von Neumann architecture. The basic components are the RAM memory that stores the programs and the data, the keyboard that reads input data from the command-line, the monitor that displays the results, the CPU that processes the elementary operations (load, store, add, jump, etc.), and the bus that interconnects the basic components.

- Focus: this case study exemplifies the exchange of data between objects and the use of state transition diagrams to describe the behaviour of the CPU.
- OO techniques: inclusion.
- Java features: Vectors, Files.
- Background: the reader is required to know the basic OO concepts and fundamental Java programming techniques.

5.1 ■ Specifications

Hardware description languages (HDLs) have been very popular in the last decade. They allow a hardware engineer to describe the system he or she wants to build in terms of the functionalities that it must provide.

The key success factor of HDLs is that they give the opportunity to simulate and test a high-level description of the system, which can be defined with a relatively little effort when compared with gate-level or even transistor-level descriptions.

HDLs usually incorporate most of the features that are used in general-purpose programming languages: namely structured programming constructs and OO concepts. Usually, HDLs build on a rich set of libraries that support the automatic generation of low-level system descriptions that can be easily synthesized in hardware components.

The aim of this case study is to use the Java language as HDL. The focus is on the simulation of common hardware components, such as the RAM, the I/O devices, the CPU and the bus. These components interact accordingly with the Von Neumann architecture, as indicated in Figure 5.1.

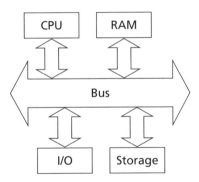

Figure 5.1 The Von Neumann architecture

The goal is to develop a simulation tool that allows monitoring of the behaviour of individual components during the execution of test programs written in an assembly-like programming language. Test programs are stored in the form of textual files and loaded by the simulation tool at start-up.

The simulation must emphasize the behavioural properties over temporal ones. Thus, time and performance will not be a concern.

5.1.1 □ The instruction set

We consider an architecture based on the simple instruction set defined in Table 5.1. Instructions are made up of two parts: the code and the argument. The code describes the type of operation to be performed (e.g. moving data from the memory to a register). The argument, when present, is the index of a memory location; it is used to perform the operation.

Table 5.1 Instruction set

Code	Argument	Description
HALT		Halts the CPU
JUMP	address	Jumps to the instruction at the given address
JUMPZ	address	Jumps to the instruction at the given address if register A contains zero
LOADA	address	Load register A with the content of the cell at address
LOADB	address	Load register B with the content of the cell at address
STOREA	address	Store the content of register A in the cell at address
STOREB	address	Store the content of register B in the cell at address
MOVEAB		Store the content of register A in the memory whose address is contained in register B
ADD		Add the content of register A to the content of register B and put the result into register A
INPUT	address	Read information from the I/O and store it in the cell at address
OUTPUT	address	Read information from the cell at address and send it to I/O
FOPEN	address	Open a file whose name is found in the cell at address
FREAD	address	Read information from the currently open file into the cell at address
FCLOSE		Close the previously opened file

Table 5.2 Simple program to sum two numbers

Address	Content	Description
0:	LOADA 5	Loads into register A the content of the cell with address 5
1:	LOADB 6	Loads into register B the content of the cell with address 6
2:	ADD	Sums registers A and B, the result goes into register A
3:	STOREA 7	Stores content of register A in the cell with address 7
4:	HALT	Stops the execution
5:	123	Cell containing the first number to sum
6:	432	Cell containing the second number to sum
7:	0	Cell that will contain the result of the sum

Table 5.2 presents a simple program and its position in memory. The program sums two integer numbers.

5.2 ■ Problem analysis

The system that must be described and simulated is a computer. The computer is made up of dynamic components that interact with each other through the bus.

The CPU is the master of the system: it executes the instructions defined in the assembler-like program and coordinates the functioning of all the other components. The RAM component represents the temporary memory which persists only while the computer is in operation. The I/O device is made up of two components: the keyboard takes input data from the user; the display shows output data to the user. The storage device can be identified with the hard disk: it holds information even when the computer is not in operation.

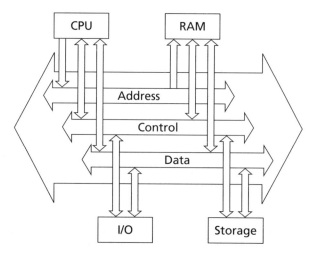

Figure 5.2 Detailed Von Neumann architecture

5.2.1 ☐ **Domain models**

The theory behind computer architectures is quite well understood (see, for instance, Hayes (1998)). The common structure for a computer is depicted in Figure 5.2. This is a more detailed description than the one provided in Figure 5.1.

CPU

The CPU is made up of the arithmetic logic unit (ALU) that executes elemental operations on byte data and the following set of registers to store operands, results, data and instructions:

- A and B: general-purpose registers;
- PC, program counter;
- IR, instruction register: holds the current instruction.

The general-purpose registers are used to hold information; their contents can be loaded from and stored to the RAM. They can be manipulated directly by instructions. The program counter register holds the location of the next instruction to be executed. It can be modified indirectly by means of jump instructions. The instruction register (IR) contains the instruction that is currently being executed.

The behaviour of the CPU can be described by means of a finite state automaton (FSA). A simple CPU behaves as described in Figure 5.3. The CPU elaborates each instruction of the assembler-like program following a three-step process:

- Fetch. The CPU copies the next instruction into the instruction register from the memory location indicated by the PC register.
- Decode. The CPU examines the IR and identifies the instruction to be executed.
- Execute. The CPU executes the operations required by the decoded instruction.

In addition, the CPU has a HALT state that indicates that the execution is terminated.

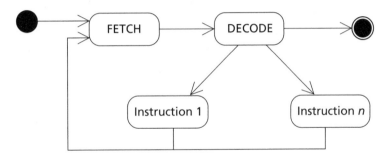

Figure 5.3 Finite state machine for the CPU

Bus

The CPU communicates with the other components of the system through the system bus. The bus is made up of three components:

- Command bus. It contains the commands issued by the CPU and the confirmation messages from the other components of the computer.
- Data bus. It contains the data exchanged between the CPU and the other components.
- Address bus. It contains the addresses of the memory cells to be read or written.

The three buses hold data permanently and allow the components of the system to read and write such data.

RAM

The RAM copies data from specific memory locations to the data bus when a "read" request is found on the command bus. Similarly, it copies data from the data bus into specific memory locations when a "write" request is found on the command bus. The address of the memory location to be read or written is retrieved from the address bus.

When the RAM has completed a read or write operation it sets the control bus to the ACK value in order to acknowledge the CPU.

I/O devices

The keyboard, the display and the hard disk behave like the RAM. They read or write data on the data bus when the corresponding commands are found on the command bus. In particular, the keyboard writes on the data bus the input received from the user. The display reads from the data bus the output to be shown to the user. The hard disk stores data persistently even when the computer is turned off.

5.2.2 ☐ Main features

We summarize here the main features emerging from the problem analysis.

- *Computer architecture*. The simulation tool must simulate the functionalities of the basic components of the Von Neumann architecture.
- *Assembler-like programs*. The simulation tool executes programs written in an assembler-like language. Programs are loaded from textual files into the RAM and processed by the CPU.
- *Input/output interactions*. The computer interacts with the user through simulated input/output devices.

5.2.3 ☐ Test

The main characteristics of the application to be tested are:

- The interaction of the CPU with the RAM over the bus.

- The capability of running programs made up of instructions.
- The interaction with the user through the keyboard and the display.
- The access to the file system.

5.3 ■ Architecture and planning

The development of the system will be carried out in three phases, each providing a working prototype.

- *Prototype 1: Hard-wired program*. This is a simplified version of the Von Neumann architecture: the CPU executes a predefined set of instructions that are hard-wired in the code and not loaded from the RAM.
- *Prototype 2: Volatile programs*. The CPU fetches the instructions loaded from the RAM.
- *Prototype 3: Persistent programs*. The CPU loads the program from the hard disk.

5.4 ■ Prototype 1: Hard-wired program

This prototype reflects a simplified Von Neumann architecture. The difference with respect to a full architecture is that the CPU does not fetch the instructions from the memory; instead it executes a fixed hard-wired program.

5.4.1 □ Analysis

The computer architecture we want to implement is depicted in Figure 5.2. The largest grained concept we want to represent is the computer (see Figure 5.4).

A computer is made up of a CPU, a bus and a RAM. This is represented by the composition relationship. The semantics of such a relationship are that a computer exists as long as its components exist, and the components cannot stand by themselves. While this strong assumption may seem too

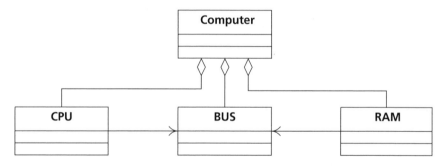

Figure 5.4 Analysis diagram of the simplified Von Neumann architecture

restrictive in reality, it makes perfect sense when we think of the purpose of our system. We are interested in simulating Von Neumann architecture as a whole, not the single components by themselves.

The computer provides a unitary view of the system. It is used to instantiate the whole system and it represents the interface for starting and controlling the simulation. The computer must provide a method for advancing the simulation of a given number of steps.

5.4.2 □ Design

The classes that we use to model the computer architecture are the same as those identified at the analysis level. The class diagram is shown in Figure 5.5. The Computer class aggregates the other components, i.e. the CPU, the Bus, and the RAM. Both the CPU and the RAM are connected to the Bus.

Decision point

How does the simulation evolve?

The simulation evolves in terms of computer steps. A step corresponds to an atomic operation, e.g. the CPU reading data from the bus.

We want to be able to specify the number of steps of simulation that must be executed. Thus, we need a way to trigger a single step of simulation for each component. The method execute() of CPU and RAM serves this purpose. Simulation can be performed as shown in the sequence diagram of Figure 5.6. The Computer class provides the user with a single functionality represented by method simulate(), which starts and controls the simulation.

The user requests the computer to perform one step of simulation, which determines one step of simulation for each of the components, i.e. the CPU and the RAM. The order of execution is also important. Since the CPU is the master of the system it must execute its simulation step before the other

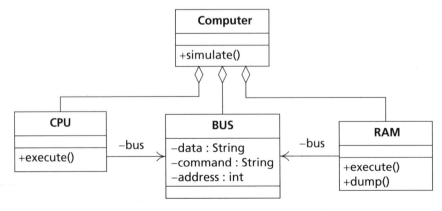

Figure 5.5 Class diagram of the simulated Von Neumann architecture

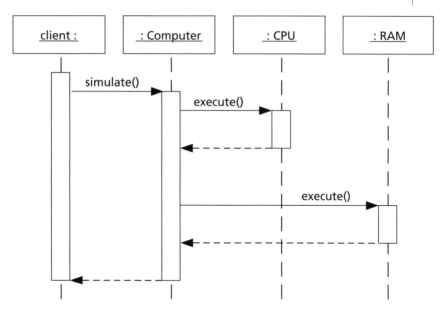

Figure 5.6 Single simulation step

components. If the simulation of the CPU were performed after the others, then the command issued by the CPU in a given simulation step would be executed by the other components in the next simulation step.

Decision point

> What format have data stored in the RAM and exchanged through the bus?

The memory of a real computer is organized in words, which are made up of a varying number of bits, usually multiples of 8 (i.e. bytes). The most common values are 32 and 64 bits per word; old computers also use 8 and 16 bits words.

For the sake of the simplicity and clarity, the simulated RAM is structured as an array of string cells. This solution makes it easier to understand the evolution of the simulation.

Consequently, the command bus and the data have to be structured as buffers that hold string values, while the address bus contains an integer number.

The RAM should be initialized with a given number of cells and with some content in each cell.

Decision point

> How does the CPU read and write data from/to the RAM?

The read and write operations are based on a command-acknowledge protocol. First the CPU issues a command, then it waits for the RAM to perform the operation; the RAM notifies the CPU that the operation has been completed by issuing an acknowledge message.

In particular, the read operation involves the following steps:

1 The CPU writes the address of the cell to be read on the address bus and writes the read command on the command bus.
2 The RAM senses the read command on the command bus, takes the cell address from the address bus, writes the cell content on the data bus, and writes the acknowledge message on the command bus.
3 The CPU senses the acknowledge message on the command bus and reads the content of the cell from the data bus.

The write operation is similar and involves the following steps:

1 The CPU writes the address of the destination cell on the address bus, the content on the data bus, and the write command on the command bus.
2 The RAM finds the write command on the command bus, takes the cell address from the address bus, reads the content from the data bus, writes it into the memory cell, and writes the acknowledge message on the command bus.
3 The CPU finds the acknowledge on the command bus.

This latter step of the write operation is required to avoid the possibility that the CPU changes the information on the bus before the RAM has read it.

Decision point

How do we describe the CPU behaviour?

In this prototype we develop a CPU that executes a fixed program, in particular we consider a simple program that loads two numbers from the RAM (cell 0 and cell 1) into the CPU registries (register A and register B), sums their values, and writes the result into the RAM (cell 2). The operations performed by the CPU to execute this program are the following:

1 Read RAM cell 0 into register A.
2 Read RAM cell 1 into register B.
3 Sum A and B, and put the result into register A.
4 Write register A into RAM cell 2.
5 Go to HALT state.

The behaviour of the CPU can be described by means of the state machine shown in Figure 5.7. Operation 1 is carried on in states READ_MEM0 and READ_A; operation 2 is carried on in states READ_MEM1 and READ_B; operation 3 is performed in state ADD; operation 4 is carried on in states WRITE_MEM2 and HALT.

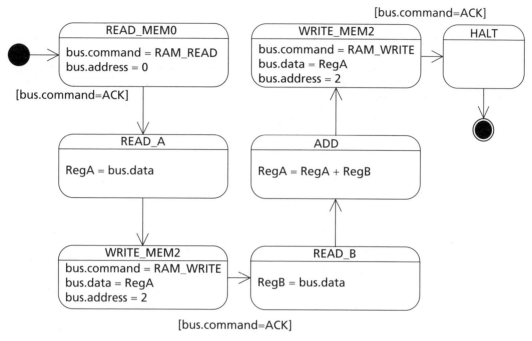

Figure 5.7 CPU state machine

5.4.3 □ **Implementation**

Since the elements that make up the system are interdependent, we start by implementing the parts that are not dependent on other elements and leave undetermined some features of other elements that are not yet known. Afterwards we will return to these features to complete the classes.

We start from the top class, Computer. The semantics of the aggregation associations between the computer and its component can be expressed by using the keyword "final" and initializing the attribute inline (see Sidebar 5.1). Since we have not defined the classes Bus, CPU and RAM we do not yet know the parameters required by their constructor.

```
public class Computer {
    final Bus bus = new Bus( ? );
    final CPU cpu = new CPU( ? );
    final RAM ram = new RAM( ? );
    void simulate(int numSteps){
        for(int step=0; step<numSteps; ++step){
            cpu.execute();
            ram.execute();
        }
    }
}
```

Sidebar 5.1 Aggregate association

Aggregation can be implemented as a normal one-to-one association, using attributes of the container that represent the links to the components. The semantics of aggregation require the lifetime of the components to be bound by the lifetime of the container; when the container is created the components are also created. There are two main solutions:

- initialization in the constructor; and
- inline initialization.

The first solution can be written as follows:

```
bus = new Bus();
```

This technique has a couple of drawbacks. First, it is error prone: it is easy to forget to write the creation instructions, resulting in uninitialized attributes. Second, it is not readable: when looking at the attributes it is impossible to understand that they represent aggregation without looking at the constructor too. The second alternative, the inline initialization can be implemented as follows:

```
public Bus bus = new Bus();
```

This approach overcomes the drawbacks of the previous one. It is less error prone: it is difficult to forget to create the objects because they are created in the same place as where they are defined. It is more readable: the final keyword together with the inline initialization clearly states that these objects are created once and their lifetime is linked to the lifetime of the compound object.

```
public final Bus bus = new Bus();
```

With the above declaration the bus attribute will refer to the same object for all its lifetime.

The bus is made up of three attributes holding persistently the information that components communicate to each other. These attributes are accessible through getter and setter methods.

```
public class Bus {
  private String data; // the data bus
  private String command; // the command bus
  private int address; // the address bus
  // getter and setter for data bus
  public void setData(String data) { this.data = data; }
  public String getData() { return data; }
  // getter and setter for command bus
  public void setCommand(String command)
                                 { this.command = command; }
  public String getCommand() { return command; }
  // getter and setter for address bus
  public void setAddress(int address)
                                 { this.address = address; }
  public int getAddress() { return address; }
}
```

The class **RAM** is connected to the **Bus**. The relationship can be implemented as usual with an attribute. Since it is a mandatory link, which is established at the creation of the computer and never changed, we initialize it in the constructor, which will have a parameter of type **Bus**.

The main feature of the RAM is to contain cells of data. The cells must be addressable by an integer index (taken from the address bus). The obvious implementation is an array of **String** objects. The default size is defined by the constant value **DEFAULT_SIZE**. A constant is implemented as a static final attribute; the **static** qualifier ensures that only one copy of the constant is seen by everyone; the **final** qualifier ensures that the attribute cannot be changed at run time (see idiom *Constant Attribute*, p. 120).

In addition it can be useful to have the capability of specifying the size as a parameter of a constructor. The constructors have two responsibilities: initialize the reference to the bus and create the memory cells.

```
public class RAM {
  final static int DEFAULT_SIZE = 256;
  private String [] cells;  // the sequence of memory cells
  private Bus bus;
  RAM(Bus bus) {
    this.bus = bus;
    cells = new String[DEFAULT_SIZE];
  }

  RAM(Bus bus, size) {
    this.bus = bus;
    cells = new String[size];
  }
```

The initialize() method receives a **String** array that is used to initialize the RAM. The size of the initial values array must be less than or equal to the size of the memory.

```
public void initialize(String [] initValues){
  // check precondition
  if(initValues.length > cells.length){
    System.err.println("Error initializing RAM: " +
                "initial values array bigger than RAM.");
    System.exit(0);
  }
  // initialized memory cells
  for(int i=0; i<initValues.length; ++i){
    cells[i]=initValues[i];
  }
}
```

An important feature of the RAM concerning the monitoring of the simulation is the capability of reading the contents of the memory cells.

A simple method can be used for this purpose.

```
public String cell(int i) {
  return cells[i];
}
```

The read and write commands issued by the CPU and the acknowledge command from the RAM are messages that must be codified in a common way shared by the two components. They are strings that are written to and read from the command bus. It would be very easy to misspell one of the commands exchanged between the CPU and the RAM. For instance, consider the case if the CPU sends a RAM-READ instead of RAM_READ (a hyphen character instead of an underscore). The RAM does not recognize the command and stays idle, while the CPU sits waiting for an ACK that will never arrive: a deadlock. In order to avoid this risk, command strings are defined in a single place as constants in order to allow the compiler to catch a spelling error.

```
final static String RAM_READ="RAM_READ";
final static String RAM_WRITE="RAM_WRITE";
final static String ACK="ACK";
```

The execute() method performs a single simulation step. It looks at the command bus, if it contains the RAM_READ or RAM_WRITE command then executes it and puts an ACK on the command bus.

```
boolean execute() {
  // Reads the command and the data from the bus
  if(bus.getCommand().equals(RAM_READ)) {
    // Writes the content of the selected cell in the
    // data bus
    bus.setData(cells[bus.getAddress()]);
    // Acknowledge the CPU of the command execution
    bus.setCommand(ACK);
    return true;
  }
  else if(bus.getCommand().equals(RAM_WRITE)) {
    // Write the content of the data bus into the
    // cell whose address is on the address bus
    cells[bus.getAddress()] = bus.getData();
    // Acknowledge the CPU of the command execution
    bus.setCommand(ACK);
    return true;
  }
  return false;
}
```

The association between the CPU and the bus is implemented as a private attribute initialized in the constructor. The registers of the CPU can be

Sidebar 5.2 FSA implementation

This procedure translates a FSA into Java code. The procedure can handle only:

- State machines, i.e. non-hierarchical states.
- States with only entry actions.
- Transitions having only the guard, i.e. without action.

Procedure for implementing a state machine:

1 For each state S define two constant integers: S and S_entry, where:
   - all S_entry variables have odd values
   - $S = S\_entry + 1$
2 Define an integer state attribute *state*.
3 Initialize state to I_entry, where I is the initial state.
4 Define the state evolution method with a switch construct having *state* as the index variable.
5 For each state S add the following code to the switch:
   - a case branch having index S_entry:
     ```
     case S_entry:
     ```
   - the entry action code
   - an instruction incrementing the state attribute
   - a case branch having index S:
     ```
     case S:
     ```
   - for each transition T from the current state to a state *Snext*, add the code:
     ```
     if( G ) state = Snext_entry;
     ```
     where G is the guard of the transition
   - add the break statement:
     ```
     break;
     ```

implemented as String attributes.

```
public class CPU {
  private Bus     bus;
  private String  RegA;
  private String  RegB;
  CPU(Bus bus) { this.bus = bus; }
```

The CPU must execute a sequence of operations as specified in the test. Using the automatic procedure, the state machine described in Figure 5.7 can be implemented in Java using the algorithm described in Sidebar 5.2. The detailed steps of the algorithm applied to the given FSA are described below.

Step 1. Define the integer constants:

```
private final static int READ_MEM0_entry=1;
private final static int READ_MEM0=2;
private final static int READ_A_entry=3;
private final static int READ_A=4;
private final static int READ_MEM1_entry=5;
private final static int READ_MEM1=6;
```

```
private final static int READ_B_entry=7;
private final static int READ_B=8;
private final static int ADD_entry=9;
private final static int ADD=10;
private final static int WRITE_MEM2_entry=11;
private final static int WRITE_MEM2=12;
private final static int HALT_entry=13;
private final static int HALT=14;
```

Step 2. Define an integer state attribute:

```
private int state;
```

Step 3. Initialize the state attribute. Here we initialize the state in the constructor; in particular we have to add a statement in the constructor that was defined above.

```
CPU(Bus bus) {
  this.bus = bus;
  state = READ_MEM0_entry;
}
```

Steps 4 and 5. Define the state evolution method.

```
void execute() {
  switch(state) {
  case READ_MEM0_entry:
            bus.setCommand(RAM.RAM_READ);
            bus.setAddress(0);
            state++;
  case READ_MEM0:
            if( bus.getCommand().equals(RAM.ACK))
                                        state = READ_A_entry;
            break;
  case READ_A_entry:
            RegA = bus.getData();
            state++;
  case READ_A:
            state = READ_MEM1_entry;
            break;
  case READ_MEM1_entry:
            bus.setCommand(RAM.RAM_READ);
            bus.setAddress(1);
            state++;
  case READ_MEM1:
            if(bus.getCommand().equals(RAM.ACK))
                                        state = READ_B_entry;
            break;
```

```
case READ_B_entry:
        RegB = bus.getData();
        state++;
case READ_B:
        state = ADD_entry;
        break;
case ADD_entry:
        RegA = Integer.toString(
                    Integer.parseInt(RegA)
                    + Integer.parseInt(RegB)
                    );
        state++;
case ADD:
        state = WRITE_MEM2_entry;
        break;
case WRITE_MEM2_entry:
        bus.setCommand(RAM.RAM_WRITE);
        bus.setData(RegA);
        bus.setAddress(2);
        state++;
case WRITE_MEM2:
        if(bus.getCommand().equals(RAM.ACK))
                            state = HALT_entry;
        break;
case HALT_entry:
        state++;
case HALT:
        break;
    }
}
```

It is important to detect when the CPU enters the halt state, because after this step the simulation stops. Since the state attribute must remain private, a function can be used to this purpose.

```
public boolean halted() { return state == HALT; }
```

Let's now refine the implementation of class **Computer**. The halted method of the CPU class should be checked in the simulate method in order to stop the simulation when the CPU enters the HALT state. In addition we define a constructor that takes as argument the initial content of the memory.

```
public class Computer {
  final Bus bus = new Bus();
  final CPU cpu = new CPU(bus);
  final RAM ram = new RAM(bus,3);
  public Computer(String[] initialMemory){
    ram.initialize(initialMemory);
  }
```

```
public void simulate(int numSteps){
  int step;
  for(step=0; step<numSteps && !cpu.halted(); ++step){
    cpu.execute();
    ram.execute();
  }
}
}
```

5.4.4 □ Test

The test of this prototype has to check the behaviour of the components of
the computer. The RAM can be tested for the initialization and for the interaction with the CPU through the bus. The CPU can be tested by executing
the simulation. In particular the CPU behaviour is correct if:

- the CPU terminates the program in a finite time;
- the memory contains the correct result of the operations.

The termination is an important test since it ensures that the system
has not entered some deadlock, i.e. for bad synchronization among the
elements. It can be tested checking the halted() method.

The correct result in the RAM ensures that the information has been
correctly transferred between the components and that it has been correctly
computed. It can be checked comparing the RAM at the end of the simulation with the expected memory contents.

The test case TestComputer performs these basic tests.

```
public class TestComputer extends TestCase {
  private void compareMemory(RAM ram, String[] expected){
    for(int i=0; i<expected.length; ++i)
      assertEquals(expected[i],ram.cell(i));
  }
  public void testMemoryInitialization() {
    String initialMemory[]={"123","432","555"};
    Computer computer = new Computer(initialMemory);
    compareMemory(computer.ram,initialMemory);
  }
  public void testExecution() {
    String initialMemory[]={"123","432","0"};
    Computer computer = new Computer(initialMemory);
    computer.simulate(10);
    assertTrue("CPU not halted",computer.cpu.halted());
    String expectedMemory[]={"123","432","555"};
    compareMemory(computer.ram,expectedMemory);
  }
}
```

5.5 ■ Prototype 2: Volatile programs

The goal of this prototype is to refine the design and implementation of the CPU in order to load instructions from the RAM and to fetch them in the CPU. Assembler-like programs are thus hard-coded in the constructor of class RAM and contain both data and instructions.

5.5.1 ☐ Analysis

The system must be able to execute programs described using a simple instruction set. The CPU processes instructions according to the fetch–decode–execute sequence as described by the FSA depicted in Figure 5.3. The instruction set that will be implemented in this prototype is set out in Table 5.3.

5.5.2 ☐ Design

The class structure for this iteration is the same as the one defined in the previous phase. The main difference lies in the behaviour of the CPU, which now executes instructions taken from the memory instead of a hard-wired program.

We define the behaviour of the CPU as described by the FSA depicted in Figure 5.8. It is based on the instructions described in Table 5.3. This FSA implements the fetch–decode–execute cycle. Actually this is an extension of the schematic FSA presented in Figure 5.3.

During the FETCH state the CPU issues a command to read the memory cell addressed by the program counter (PC). When the RAM reads the memory and issues an acknowledge command, the CPU enters the DECODE state. During this state the CPU copies the instruction into the IR and examines it. According to the instruction code, the CPU jumps to the appropriate state in order to execute the instruction. Most instructions require just one state

Table 5.3 Instruction set of the second prototype

Code	Argument	Description
HALT		Halts the CPU
JUMP	address	Jumps to the instruction at the given address
JUMPZ	address	Jumps to the instruction at the given address if register A contains zero
LOADA	address	Load register A with the content of the cell at address
LOADB	address	Load register B with the content of the cell at address
STOREA	address	Store the content of register A in the cell at address
STOREB	address	Store the content of register B in the cell at address
MOVEB		Store the content of register A in the memory cell whose address is contained in register B
ADD		Add the content of register A to the content of register B and put the result into register A

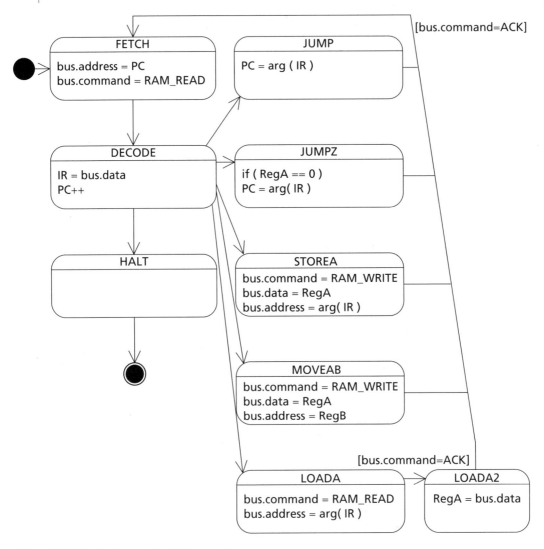

Figure 5.8 FSA for the basic CPU instructions

transition. A few instructions (i.e. LOADA, LOADB and MOVEAB) are more complex and involve two states.

5.5.3 ☐ Implementation

In this prototype we define a package, HDL, which contains all the classes used for the simulation. The user interface and the test classes are put outside this package.

The only class that is changed with respect to the previous prototype is the CPU. In particular we have to implement the execution of instructions as described in the FSA of Figure 5.8. The instructions are codified as string constants. They are public in order also to be visible outside the package; this allows their use to define the programs.

```java
public class CPU {
  public final static String HALT="HALT";
  public final static String JUMP="JUMP";
  public final static String JUMPZ="JUMPZ";
  public final static String LOADA="LOADA";
  public final static String LOADB="LOADB";
  public final static String STOREA="STOREA";
  public final static String STOREB="STOREB";
  public final static String MOVEAB="MOVEAB";
  public final static String ADD="ADD";
  public final static String INPUT="INPUT";
  public final static String OUTPUT="OUTPUT";
  public final static String FOPEN="FOPEN";
  public final static String FREAD="FREAD";
  public final static String FCLOSE="FCLOSE";
```

In order to support these instructions the CPU requires a set of registers:

```java
private int PC = 0;    // Program counter
private String  IR;    // Instruction register
private String  RegA; // Register A
private String  RegB; // Register B
```

It is important to notice that since the PC is initialized with the value 0 the execution of the programs will always start from that location. In other words, the first instruction executed by the CPU is the one in memory cell 0.

To execute instructions it is important to separate the two components of the instruction contained in the instruction register: the code and the argument. This can be achieved by means of two methods that return each part of the IR.

```java
private String code(String instruction){
  int separator = instruction.indexOf(' ');
  if( separator > 0)
    return instruction.substring(0,separator);
  else
    return instruction;
}
private int arg(String instruction){
  int separator = instruction.indexOf(' ');
  if( separator > 0)
    return Integer.parseInt(instruction.substring
                    (separator+1,instruction.length()));
  else
    return 0;
}
```

The method **execute()** derives from the straightforward application of the procedure presented in Sidebar 5.2 to the FSA shown in Figure 5.8.

```
public void execute() {
  switch(state){
    case FETCH_entry:
                bus.command = RAM.RAM_READ;
                bus.address = PC;
                state++;
    case FETCH:
                if(bus.command.equals(RAM.ACK))
                        state = DECODE_entry;
                break;
    case DECODE_entry:
                IR = bus.data;
                PC++;
                state++;
    case DECODE:
                if(code(IR).equals(HALT))
                                        state=EXEC_HALT_entry;
                if(code(IR).equals(JUMP))
                                        state=EXEC_JUMP_entry;
                if(code(IR).equals(JUMPZ))
                                        state=EXEC_JUMPZ_entry;
                if(code(IR).equals(LOADA))
                                        state=EXEC_LOADA_entry;
                if(code(IR).equals(LOADB))
                                        state=EXEC_LOADB_entry;
                if(code(IR).equals(STOREA))
                                        state=EXEC_STOREA_entry;
                if(code(IR).equals(STOREB))
                                        state=EXEC_STOREB_entry;
                if(code(IR).equals(MOVEAB))
                                        state=EXEC_MOVEAB_entry;
                if(code(IR).equals(ADD))
                                        state=EXEC_ADD_entry;
                break;
    case EXEC_HALT_entry:
                state++;
    case EXEC_HALT:
                break;
    case EXEC_JUMP_entry:
                PC = arg(IR);
                state++;
    case EXEC_JUMP:
                state = FETCH_entry;
                break;
```

```
case EXEC_JUMPZ_entry:
        if(RegA.equals("0")) PC = arg(IR);
        state++;
case EXEC_JUMPZ:
        state = FETCH_entry;
        break;
case EXEC_LOADA_entry:
        bus.command = RAM.RAM_READ;
        bus.address = arg(IR);
        state++;
case EXEC_LOADA:
        if(bus.command.equals(RAM.ACK))
                        state=EXEC_LOADA2_entry;
        break;
case EXEC_LOADA2_entry:
        RegA = bus.data;
        state++;
case EXEC_LOADA2:
        state = FETCH_entry;
        break;
case EXEC_LOADB_entry:
        bus.command = RAM.RAM_READ;
        bus.address = arg(IR);
        state++;
case EXEC_LOADB:
        if(bus.command.equals(RAM.ACK))
                        state=EXEC_LOADB2_entry;
        break;
case EXEC_LOADB2_entry:
        RegB = bus.data;
        state++;
case EXEC_LOADB2:
        state = FETCH_entry;
        break;
case EXEC_STOREA_entry:
        bus.command = RAM.RAM_WRITE;
        bus.data = RegA;
        bus.address = arg(IR);
        state++;
case EXEC_STOREA:
        if(bus.command.equals(RAM.ACK))
                        state=FETCH_entry;
        break;
case EXEC_STOREB_entry:
        bus.command = RAM.RAM_WRITE;
        bus.data = RegB;
```

```
                                      bus.address = arg(IR);
                                      state++;
                 case EXEC_STOREB:
                                      if(bus.command.equals(RAM.ACK))
                                                           state=FETCH_entry;
                                      break;
                 case EXEC_MOVEAB_entry:
                                      bus.command = RAM.RAM_WRITE;
                                      bus.data = RegA;
                                      bus.address = Integer.parseInt(RegB);
                                      state++;
                 case EXEC_MOVEAB:
                                      if(bus.command.equals(RAM.ACK))
                                                           state=FETCH_entry;
                                      break;
                 case EXEC_ADD_entry:
                                      RegA= Integer.toString(Integer.parseInt
                                      (RegA) + Integer.parseInt(RegB)); state++;
                 case EXEC_ADD:
                                      state = FETCH_entry;
                                      break;
             }
         }
```

5.5.4 □ Test

We can identify two different test cases. The first is a sort of regression test; we want to be able to implement the functionality of the hard-wired program developed in the previous phase using the CPU instructions. The second is a more complex test that exercises the features of all the instructions in the instruction set.

Sum program

The program shown in Table 5.4 sums the contents of memory locations 5 and 6, and puts the result into memory location 6. The difference between this program and the hard-wired program executed by the CPU in the previous phase lies in the location used to store data: here we cannot use location 0 since it must contain the first instruction that is executed by the CPU.

Test program 2

The program shown in Table 5.5 consists of a loop that fills memory locations from 20 to 31 with a fixed value (99). This program is structured as a "for" loop. Instructions 0 and 1 check the loop termination condition

Table 5.4 Sum program

Loc.	Content	Type	Description
0	LOADA 5	code	Load the content of location 5 into register A
1	LOADB 6	code	Load the content of location 6 into register B
2	ADD	code	Sum the two registers and put the result into register A
3	STOREA 7	code	Store the value of register A in memory location 7
4	HALT	code	Terminate the program
5	123	data	The first number to be summed
6	432	data	The second number to be summed
7	0	data	This cell will contain the result of the sum

Table 5.5 Test program 2

Loc.	Content	Type	Description
0	LOADA 13	code	Load content of location 13 (loop index) into register A
1	JUMPZ 12	code	If register A is zero jump to location 12 (end)
2	LOADB 14	code	Load content of location 14 (loop index increment) into register B
3	ADD	code	Add register A and register B (loop increment)
4	STOREA 13	code	Store the contents of register A in location 13
5	LOADB 15	code	Load content of location 15 (base address) into register B
6	ADD	code	Sum register A and register B
7	STOREA 16	code	Store the content of register A in location 16
8	LOADA 17	code	Load the content of location 17 (fixed value) into register A
9	LOADB 16	code	Load location 16 (address of location to be filled in) into register B
10	MOVEAB	code	Store value in register A in location whose address is in register B
11	JUMP 0	code	Jump to location 0 (the first of the program)
12	HALT	code	Terminate execution
13	12	data	Loop index
14	−1	data	Loop increment
15	20	data	The lower address to fill in with fixed value
16	0	data	Contains the current address of the location to be filled in
17	99	data	The fixed value with which to fill in the locations
18	0	data	Empty cell
19	0	data	Empty cell
20	0	data	Will be filled in with the fixed value
21	0	data	Will be filled in with the fixed value
22	0	data	Will be filled in with the fixed value
23	0	data	Will be filled in with the fixed value
24	0	data	Will be filled in with the fixed value
25	0	data	Will be filled in with the fixed value
26	0	data	Will be filled in with the fixed value
27	0	data	Will be filled in with the fixed value
28	0	data	Will be filled in with the fixed value
29	0	data	Will be filled in with the fixed value
30	0	data	Will be filled in with the fixed value
31	0	data	Will be filled in with the fixed value

(i.e. the loop variable is equal to 0); if the condition is met the execution proceeds to instruction 12 which is a HALT (i.e. program termination). Instructions 3, 4 and 5 increment the loop variable. Then instructions 5, 6 and 7 add the loop variable to the base address of the locations to be filled in; the result is used as an index to access all the locations by instructions 8, 9 and 10. Finally instruction 11 jumps to the beginning of the loop again.

The test case class **TestPrograms** tests that the execution of the two programs above produces the correct results.

```
import junit.framework.TestCase;
import HDL.*;
public class TestPrograms extends TestCase {
  public void testSum(){
    Computer computer = new Computer(sumProgram);
    computer.simulate(1000);
    // checks that memory location 7 contains the result:
    // "555"
    assertEquals("555",computer.ram.cell(7));
  }
  public void testLoop(){
    Computer computer = new Computer(loopProgram);
    computer.simulate(1000);
    // checks that memory locations from 20 to 31 are filled
    // with "99"
    for(int i=20; i>31; ++i)
      assertEquals("99",computer.ram.cell(i));
  }
  private final static String sumProgram[]={
    /*  0 */ CPU.LOADA + " 5",
    /*  1 */ CPU.LOADB + " 6",
    /*  2 */ CPU.ADD,
    /*  3 */ CPU.STOREA + " 7",
    /*  4 */ CPU.HALT,
    /*  5 */ "123",
    /*  6 */ "432",
    /*  7 */ "0",
  };
  private static final String[] loopProgram = {
    /*  0 */ CPU.LOADA + " 13",
    /*  1 */ CPU.JUMPZ + " 12",
    /*  2 */ CPU.LOADB + " 14",
    /*  3 */ CPU.ADD,
    /*  4 */ CPU.STOREA + " 13",
    /*  5 */ CPU.LOADB + " 15",
    /*  6 */ CPU.ADD,
    /*  7 */ CPU.STOREA + " 16",
```

```
/*  8 */ CPU.LOADA + " 17",
/*  9 */ CPU.LOADB + " 16",
/* 10 */ CPU.MOVEAB,
/* 11 */ CPU.JUMP + " 0",
/* 12 */ CPU.HALT,
/* 13 */ "12",
/* 14 */ "-1",
/* 15 */ "20",
/* 16 */ "0",
/* 17 */ "99",
/* 18 */ "0",
/* 19 */ "0",
/* 20 */ "0",
/* 21 */ "0",
/* 22 */ "0",
/* 23 */ "0",
/* 24 */ "0",
/* 25 */ "0",
/* 26 */ "0",
/* 27 */ "0",
/* 28 */ "0",
/* 29 */ "0",
/* 30 */ "0",
/* 31 */ "0",
    };
}
```

5.6 ■ Prototype 3: Persistent programs

The goal of the third prototype is to extend the simulator with the capability of simulating input, output and storage devices. Once a storage device is available, it is possible to load programs from it.

5.6.1 □ Analysis

The simulator is extended with three new components: keyboard, display and hard disk. The keyboard enables the CPU to receive input from the user. Actually it reads character strings that are entered through the keyboard and writes them on the bus when requested by the CPU. The display prints on the screen the character strings that are on the data bus when requested by the CPU. The hard disk device is able to open a file and to read it line by line. Accordingly, the instruction set is extended with the instructions set out in Table 5.6.

Table 5.6 I/O instructions for the CPU

Code	Argument	Description
INPUT	address	Read information from the I/O and store it in the cell at address
OUTPUT	address	Read information from the cell at address and send it to I/O
FOPEN	address	Open a file whose name is found in the cell at address
FREAD	address	Read information from the currently open file into the cell at address
FCLOSE		Close the previously opened file

5.6.2 ☐ Design

The new devices are represented by three classes: Display, Keyboard and HardDisk. They have characteristics similar to the other components of the system (i.e. CPU and RAM). The structure of the HDL package with the addition of the new classes is shown in Figure 5.9.

The main issue that we need to address in the development of the three new components concerns the level of abstraction of their functionalities.

Decision point

How do the keyboard and the display simulate the interaction with the user?

The keyboard and the display are complex devices. We adopt a simplified model of them: we assume that all the information read from the keyboard and written on the display is represented by strings. The information goes directly from the keyboard to the RAM and from the RAM to the display.

When the instruction INPUT is executed the CPU asks the keyboard to read a line of input from the user. Then, the CPU waits for the user to insert

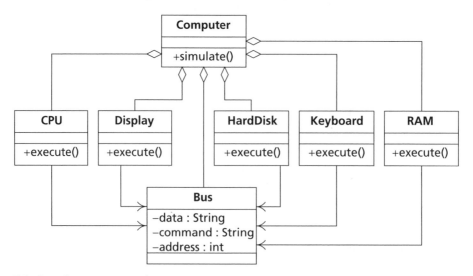

Figure 5.9 Complete computer classes

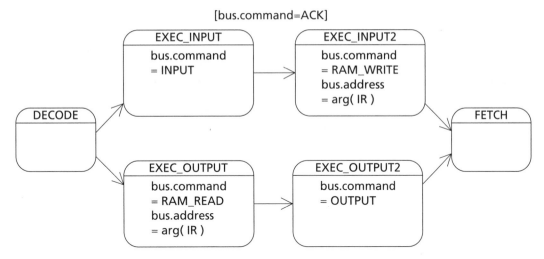

Figure 5.10 FSA for I/O instructions

the data. Clearly this approach simulates the high-level functionalities without taking into account the low-level details such as temporization.

The INPUT and OUTPUT instructions can be executed by the CPU introducing into the FSA the new states presented in Figure 5.10.

Decision point

How does the hard disk simulate the interaction with the file system?

In real computer systems the high-level operations of opening, closing and reading from file are implemented by the operating system. The hard disk component emulates the combination of both a hardware device and operating system.

The FREAD instruction is similar to the INPUT instruction: it reads a line from a text file and copies it into a memory cell.

The instructions FOPEN, FCLOSE and FREAD can be executed by the CPU introducing into the FSA the new states presented in Figure 5.11.

5.6.3 □ Implementation

The CPU new instructions can be easily implemented using the algorithm described in Sidebar 5.2. The lengthy code resulting from the application of the algorithm is not shown here.

Since all the classes must access information on the BUS it is important that they share a common codification for such information. The initial version of such information is contained in the RAM class. Since all the devices must share this codification a better place to define it is the class

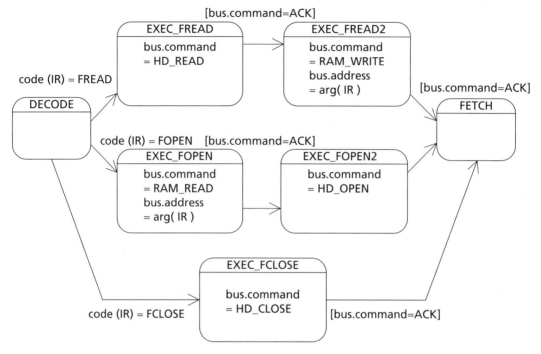

Figure 5.11 FSA for file system instructions

Bus, the constants must have package visibility and be accessible by all the components.

```
class Bus {
    final static String RAM_READ="RAM_READ";
    final static String RAM_WRITE="RAM_WRITE";
    final static String ACK="ACK";
    final static String INPUT="INPUT";
    final static String OUTPUT="OUTPUT";
    final static String FOPEN="FOPEN";
    final static String FREAD="FREAD";
    final static String FCLOSE="FCLOSE";
}
```

The new classes added in this prototype are the device classes Keyboard, HardDisk and Display. They are all components of the computer and interact through the Bus, thus they have an attribute bus implementing this association, which is initialized by the constructor.

The Keyboard class is based on a BufferedReader that is used to read line by line from the default input. The execute() method checks whether the command bus contains the INPUT command, then reads a line from the input and puts the string on the data bus; finally it acknowledges the command.

```
public class Keyboard {
  Bus bus;
  public Keyboard(Bus bus) {
    this.bus = bus;
  }
  BufferedReader lineReader = new  BufferedReader(
                    new InputStreamReader( System.in ) );
  void execute() {
    if(bus.command.equals(Bus.INPUT)) {
      try {
        System.out.print("> ");
        bus.data = lineReader.readLine();
      }
      catch(IOException ioe) {
        ioe.printStackTrace();
        bus.data = "";
      }
      bus.command = Bus.ACK;
    }
  }
}
```

The simplest class is Display. Its execute() method waits for the OUTPUT command, then prints the string lying on the data bus to the default output and acknowledges the command.

```
public class Display {
  Bus bus;
  public Display(Bus bus) {
    this.bus = bus;
  }
  void execute() {
    if(bus.command.equals(Bus.OUTPUT)) {
      System.out.println("\n> " + bus.data);
      bus.command = Bus.ACK;
    }
  }
}
```

The HardDisk class is similar to the Keyboard class in that it is based on a BufferedReader. In addition to a command to read a line from the reader, it recognizes two other commands: one initializes the reader to read from a file, the other closes the file. The execute() method recognizes the commands FOPEN, FCLOSE and FREAD. At each operation it checks for exceptions; if an exception is caught it prints an error message and acknowledges the command to avoid deadlocks.

```
public class HardDisk {
  Bus bus;
```

```java
    public HardDisk(Bus bus) {
      this.bus = bus;
    }
    BufferedReader lineReader;  // the line reader of the file
    void execute() {
      if(bus.command.equals(Bus.FOPEN)) {
        try {
          lineReader = new BufferedReader(
          new InputStreamReader
                              (new FileInputStream(bus.data)));
        }
        catch(FileNotFoundException fnfe) {
          fnfe.printStackTrace();
        }
        catch(IOException ioe) { ioe.printStackTrace(); }
        bus.command = Bus.ACK;
      }
      else if(bus.command.equals(Bus.FCLOSE)) {
        try {
          lineReader.close();
        }
        catch(IOException ioe) { ioe.printStackTrace(); }
        bus.command = Bus.ACK;
      }
      if(bus.command.equals(Bus.FREAD)) {
        try {
          String line;
          if((line = lineReader.readLine()) != null)
            bus.data = line;
          else
            bus.data = "";
        }
        catch(IOException ioe) { ioe.printStackTrace(); }
        bus.command = Bus.ACK;
      }
    }
  }
```

5.6.4 □ Test

We define two tests. The first test exercises only the I/O related instructions. The second test also exercises the storage instructions. The first test asks for two numbers on the display and reads them from the keyboard, then sums them and prints the result onto the display. The instructions of the program are described in Table 5.7.

The second test simulates the bootstrap program of a computer. It is the first program executed when the computer is turned on and has the purpose

Table 5.7 Test program 3

Loc.	Content	Type	Description
0	OUTPUT 11	code	Output the request for the first number
1	INPUT 14	code	Read the first number from keyboard
2	OUTPUT 12	code	Output the request for the second number
3	INPUT 15	code	Read the second number from keyboard
4	LOADA 14	code	Load into register A the first number read
5	LOADB 15	code	Load into register B the second number read
6	ADD	code	Add the two numbers
7	STOREA 16	code	Store the result in a memory location
8	OUTPUT 13	code	Output the announcement of a result
9	OUTPUT 16	code	Output the result
10	HALT	code	Terminate execution
11	Insert 1st number:	data	First message
12	Insert 2nd number:	data	Second message
13	Sum is	data	Result announcement message
14	0	data	Will contain the first number
15	0	data	Will contain the second number
16	0	data	Will contain the result

of loading the operating system from the file system. This program reads the name of a program file from a configuration file on the hard disk, then loads that program file and executes it. The test is made up of three parts:

- the bootstrap program described in Table 5.8;
- the configuration file; and
- the program file, described in Table 5.9.

The bootstrap program above makes two assumptions:

- the configuration file is called "boot.ini";
- the first line of the executable file contains the number of instructions to be read.

The executable file's instructions are loaded into RAM starting from location 100.

The rest of this test is equal to the previous test with the big difference that it will be loaded from a file through the storage device. The "boot.ini" file contains a single line with the name of the executable file:

```
test_sum.prg
```

The executable file ("test_sum.prg") will contain the lines shown in Table 5.9.

5.7 ■ Extension

The simulator can be extended in a number of different ways. For example, new I/O devices can be simulated and integrated within the proposed

Table 5.8 Bootstrap program

Loc.	Content	Type	Description
1	FOPEN 22	Code	Open the configuration file
2	FREAD 26	Code	Read the name of the executable file
3	FCLOSE	Code	Close the configuration file
4	FOPEN 26	Code	Open the executable file
5	FREAD 27	Code	Read the number of instructions of the executable file
6	LOADA 27	Code	Load into register A the number of instructions (yet to be read)
7	JUMPZ 20	Code	If it is zero then end the loop
8	LOADB 25	Code	Load into register B the address of the location for the next instruction
9	FREAD 28	Code	Read the next instruction
0	LOADA 28	Code	Load it into register A
10	MOVEAB	Code	Move the instruction into the location (in register B)
11	LOADA 25	Code	Load the address of the current instructions
12	LOADB 23	Code	Load the increment (1)
13	ADD	Code	Increment the address of the current instructions
14	STOREA 25	Code	Store it
15	LOADA 27	Code	Load the number of instructions yet to be read
16	LOADB 24	Code	Load the increment (−1)
17	ADD	Code	Decrement the number of instructions yet to be read
18	STOREA 27	Code	Store it
19	JUMP 6	Code	Jump to the beginning of the loop
20	FCLOSE	Code	Close the executable file
21	JUMP 100	Code	Jump to the first loaded instructions
22	boot.ini	Data	Name of the configuration file
23	1	Data	Increment for address of instructions
24	−1	Data	Decrement for number of instructions yet to be read
25	100	Data	Location of the next instruction: the first instruction is loaded at location 100
26	0	Data	Will contain the name of the executable file
27	0	Data	Will contain the number of instructions of the executable file
28	0	Data	Will contain the last instruction read

architecture, such as the printer or the mouse. The CPU could be extended by implementing internal components, such as the cache memory, the arithmetic logic unit (ALU), and the read only memory (ROM).

It would be interesting to develop a graphical user interface that depicts and animates the finite state machines describing the behaviour of the simulator components.

5.8 ■ Assessment

Analysis techniques. We analysed the description of a problem domain and mapped the domain entities (the components of computer architecture) into classes; then we described their associations and their behaviour.

Table 5.9 Test program file

Line	Content	Destination location
1	17	None: is the number of instructions to read
2	OUTPUT 114	100
3	INPUT 111	101
4	LOADA 111	102
5	OUTPUT 115	103
6	INPUT 112	104
7	LOADB 112	105
8	ADD	106
9	STOREA 113	107
10	OUTPUT 116	108
11	OUTPUT 113	109
12	HALT	110
13	0	111
14	0	112
15	0	113
16	Insert first number:	114
17	Insert second number:	115
18	Result:	116

Modelling techniques. In this case study we introduced the notation of state charts, that are used to describe finite state automata.

Development approach. During development we faced two features of the system separately: first, the structural representation of computer architectures; second, the behaviour of the components and in particular of the CPU.

The finite state automata are a well-defined formalism that describe a state-based behaviour. FSA can be translated into Java code that implements the required behaviour (see Sidebar 5.2).

Aggregation associations can be used to express a strong part–whole relationship between classes. Transferring most of the aggregation semantics into the code results in better traceability and improved readability of the code. The aggregate association idiom can be used to implement aggregation associations in the most expressive way.

When a constant value is used in several places, either in a single class or in multiple classes, there are problems of consistency and ease of update. These issues, among others, are addressed by the constant member idiom.

Idiom	Aggregate association
Context	An aggregation association between two classes.
Problem	How to implement the association preserving the semantics of aggregation and maximizing readability and ease of use.
Forces or tradeoffs	It must be navigable. The aggregation link remains unchanged for the entire lifetime of the container. The syntax must be readable. It is easy to forget to instantiate the components.

Idiom	Constant attribute
Solution	The attributes that refer to the component object are initialized inline and are declared final.

Examples	```class Container {
	    //...
	    final Component component = new Component();
	}```

Force resolution	The attribute can be used to navigate to the component. The component creation is automatic at container creation. The Java language ensures that the link cannot be modified. The syntax is compact and readable.
Design rationale	The advantages of this approach are discussed in Sidebar 5.1.
Context	A constant value is used in multiple places inside a class and/or across several classes.
Problem	How to ensure a consistent and easily updatable use of the constant.
Forces or tradeoffs	The constant value must be the same in all places. Changing the value has effects in several places. A misspelling in the constant value is difficult to identify and can have dramatic effects. The meaning of the constant should be clear. The value of the constant must remain the same (as opposed to a variable value).
Solution	Constant attributes can be defined. The attribute must be qualified as final static. The attribute must be initialized inline. The name of the attribute is all upper case, with words separated by the underscore character "_".
Examples	`final static String READ_COMMAND = "RAM_READ";`
Force resolution	Using the same attribute ensures that the same value is used in all the places. There is a single point of change that is automatically reflected in all the places where the constant is used. It is impossible to misspell the constant. The name of the attribute provides the meaning of the constant. The attribute value cannot be changed.
Design rationale	The static qualifier ensures that all the references to the attribute share the same value. The final qualifier ensures that the attribute cannot be changed at run time. The value of the constant is defined at a single point; this value is used through a reference to the final static attribute. It is not possible to misspell the value because it is written only once, and any misspelling of the attribute name is found by the compiler. The naming convention is part of the Java coding convention and helps to distinguish constants from variables.

5.9 ■ Reference

Hayes, J. P. (1998) *Computer Architecture and Organization*, 3rd edn, McGraw-Hill Education, ISE Editions.

Multi-format calculator

6

Synthesis

This standalone application is a mathematical calculator that supports multiple number bases (binary, decimal, hexadecimal) and formats (fixed point, floating point, rational). The application converts operands and results into/from the current base and format upon user requests.

- Focus: this case study exemplifies the use of UML interaction diagrams and use cases to describe the exchange of messages among objects representing different bases and formats.
- OO techniques: inheritance and polymorphism.
- Java features: exception handling.
- Background: the reader is required to know the basic OO techniques, which are exemplified in previous chapters.

6.1 ■ Specifications

In an educational setting the capability of switching from one type of representation of numbers to another is important. When making calculations on paper it is common to use a wide range of notations. On the other hand, common electronic calculators possess only limited capability in this respect.

In particular, a number representation format that is often neglected in calculators is the fractional format, used to represent rational numbers. What is required is a calculator that is able to manipulate rational numbers in their fractional format.

Such a calculator can be used as a teaching tool to help understand the relationship between different notations. In particular the calculator should handle the following representation formats:

- fixed point;
- floating point;
- fractional.

The number base represents another important issue. The most common base used by people is the decimal base, but in the digital era two other bases play an important role: binary and hexadecimal. Therefore the calculator must handle the following bases:

- binary;

- decimal;
- hexadecimal.

The calculator must be able to read numbers entered in any combination of base and representation format, and convert them into any other possible base and/or format.

Operands and operators are entered according to the postfix notation: first the operands, then the operation. For instance, to sum the values 1 and 2 the following steps are required:

1 enter first operand: 1
2 enter second operand: 2
3 specify operation: +
4 result: 3

For the sake of simplicity, the calculator is able to perform only the four basic arithmetic operations. The program must provide a simple and intuitive interface that allows experimenting with different formats and basis.

6.2 ■ Problem analysis

The most important feature of the calculator is the capability to handle different number bases and formats. Table 6.1 summarizes all the possible combinations of bases and formats.

The program can be used according to different modalities as described in the use case presented in Figure 6.1. First of all the calculator is a tool used to perform calculations; in this mode the user provides the operands, the operations to be performed and receives the results. In addition it must be possible to change the representation format and the number base; when the user selects a new format and/or base the calculator visualizes the values accordingly. These two modalities interact closely. The result of the calculation is provided using the most recently selected pair of representation format and number base.

When either the representation format or the number base is changed the calculator should visualize the result of the most recent calculation accordingly.

6.2.1 □ Domain models

The two main issues, i.e. the number bases and the representation formats,

Table 6.1 Instruction set

	Binary	Decimal	Hexadecimal
Fixed point	0.11	0.75	0.C
Floating point	$1.1 * 10^{-1}$	$7.5 * 10^{-1}$	$C.0 * 10^{-1}$
Fractional	11/100	3/4	3/4

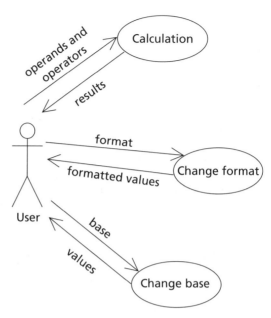

Figure 6.1 Calculator use cases

are well known and have a coded mathematical foundation. A summary of these concepts is presented below.

Number bases

Currently in most cultures people learn mathematics using the decimal base, but several other bases are possible. For instance, computer science utilizes the binary base.

The number base defines how many different digits can be used to represent a number. Table 6.2 shows a summary of the most important bases. For instance, the binary base uses two symbols: "0" and "1". For the hexadecimal base, since the decimal digits are not sufficient, by convention the letters of the alphabet are used; so "A" stands for 10, "B" for 11 and so on.

We are considering the *positional* representation of numbers, i.e. the value represented by a digit depends not only on the digit itself but also on its position inside the number.

A positional representation system, whose base is B, is represented as follows:

$$c_n \ldots c_2\, c_1\, c_0 \,.\, c_{-1}\, c_{-2} \ldots c_{-m}$$

Table 6.2 Bases and digits

Name	Base	Digits
binary	2	0, 1
decimal	10	0, 1, 2, 3, 4, 5, 6, 7, 8, 9
hexadecimal	16	0, 1, 2, 3, 4, 5, 6, 7, 8, 9, A, B, C, D, E, F

Each cipher c_i can be any of the digits allowed for the base B (e.g. 0 or 1 for the binary base). The value represented by the number above can be calculated with the following formula:

$$\sum_{-m}^{i=n} c_i \cdot B^i$$

Equation 6.1 Value of a number in base B

The initial and final indices of the ciphers (n and $-m$ in Equation 6.1) are determined on the basis of the position of the dot that separates the integer part from the fractional part. The cipher immediately preceding it has index 0 (i.e. will be multiplied for the base raised to the power of 0 that is equivalent to 1 for any base). The ciphers preceding the "." assume increasing indices as they move away from it. The opposite holds for the ciphers following the decimal point.

For instance, we can calculate as follows the value represented by a number in base 10:

$$12.5_{decimal} = 1 \cdot 10^1 + 2 \cdot 10^0 + 5 \cdot 10^{-1} = 10 + 2 + \frac{1}{2}$$

And for a base 2 number:

$$1100.1_{binary} = 1 \cdot 2^3 + 1 \cdot 2^2 + 0 \cdot 2^1 + 0 \cdot 2^0 + 1 \cdot 2^{-1} = 8 + 4 + \frac{1}{2}$$

And for a base 16 number:

$$C.8_{hexadecimal} = 12 \cdot 16^0 + 8 \cdot 16^{-1} = 12 + \frac{1}{2}$$

To find the representation of a given number according to a base B we have to find the initial and final indices and compute all the ciphers corresponding to such a range of indices.

Since the decimal point is essential in defining the value of a number, it must always be included in the representation. As a consequence the initial index cannot be lower than 0 and the final index cannot be greater than -1. The only exception to this rule is when there is only a "0" after the decimal point; in this case both the decimal point and the "0" can be omitted. This is the case of integer numbers.

The initial index n for a *number* can be found as:

$$n = \lfloor \log_B(number) \rfloor$$

Equation 6.2 Initial cipher index for representation in base B

while the final index m can be found as:

$$m = -\left\lceil \log_B \left(\frac{1}{number} \right) \right\rceil$$

Equation 6.3 Final cipher index for representation in base B

The ciphers representing the number can be found iteratively using the following equations:

$$value_n = number; \quad c_i = \left\lfloor \frac{value_i}{B^i} \right\rfloor; \quad value_i = value_{i+1} - c_{i+1} \cdot B^{i+1}$$

Equation 6.4 Ciphers for representation in base B

Representation format

The most used format is the fixed point format: it is the basic positional format described above. The other two formats are based on the fixed point format. According to the floating point format a number is represented as:

$$number = mantissa \cdot B^{exponent}$$

Equation 6.5 Floating point format

Here *mantissa* is a fixed point number that has a single cipher before the decimal point, *B* is the base, and *exponent* is an integer number (i.e. a fixed point with no cipher after the decimal point). The conversion between a fixed point and a floating point format can be performed using the following formula, where c_i is a cipher of the fixed point format while f_i is a cipher of the mantissa of the floating point number.

$$c_n \ldots c_2 \, c_1 \, c_0 \cdot c_{-1} \, c_{-2} \ldots c_{-m} = f_0 \cdot f_{-1} f_{-2} \ldots f_{-(n+m-1)} * B^{n-1}$$

Equation 6.6 Equivalence between fixed point and floating point

The fractional format is the most common way of representing rational numbers. A number is represented as the division of numerator and denominator:

$$number = \frac{numerator}{denominator}$$

Equation 6.7 Fractional format

6.2.2 □ Main features

We are now able to summarize all the main features emerging from the problem analysis.

- *Arithmetic operations*. The calculator should be able to perform binary arithmetic operations.
- *Multi-format representation*. The calculator should allow the user to insert operands in different number formats, to switch between formats, and to convert results from one format to another.
- *Multi-base representation*. Similarly, the calculator should allow the user to insert operands in different number bases, to switch between bases, and to convert results from one base to another.

6.2.3 ☐ **Test**

The main characteristics of the application to be tested are:

- the capability of performing arithmetic operations;
- the correct representation in the different representation formats;
- the correct representation in the different number bases.

6.3 ■ **Architecture and planning**

The system architecture shown in Figure 6.2 is very simple. It is made up of two main components: the multi-format calculator that provides all the basic functionalities and the user interface.

Figure 6.2 Architecture

The benefit stemming from such a structure is that it is possible to change independently the implementation of the calculator and the interface provided to its user.

The development of the system will be carried out in two phases, each providing a working prototype.

- *Prototype 1: Representation formats*. The first prototype will implement the basic features of the calculator, i.e. perform operations; in addition it will deal with multiple representation formats. The interface of this prototype will be a text-based command line interpreter.
- *Prototype 2: Number bases*. The second prototype will add the management of multiple number bases. In addition to performing more extensive testing it should be able to read commands from a file.

6.4 ■ **Prototype 1: Representation formats**

The focus of this prototype is on the execution of basic operations and on multiple representation formats. As required in the specification of the problem, priority is given to the fractional format.

6.4.1 ☐ **Analysis**

The problem at hand can be split into two sub-problems: the calculator and the user interface. The former problem deals with defining the computational model, i.e. how the calculator internally represents operands and results, how it supports multiple format conversions, and how it performs arithmetic operations. The latter problem is related to the definition of the commands that the user of the calculator can use to interact with it.

The calculator must be able to execute the four operations (+, −, *, /) on two operands. For this purpose, the calculator has two registers. The first register always stores the last operand inserted by the user or the result of an operation. The second register stores the previous operand inserted by the user and it is empty after the execution of an operation.

Some of the operations of the calculator can generate an error, e.g. wrong format for a number. The operations must be atomic, in the sense that they preserve the coherence of the state. In case of error, the previous value of the registers must be restored.

The essential feature of the calculator is the capability to switch from one representation format to another. The representation format is a generic concept, which can be separated into three specific formats (see Figure 6.3): fractional, fixed point and floating point. The format determines how the numbers entered by the user are parsed and how the numbers stored in the calculator are printed.

The user interface that is developed in this iteration is a text-based command line. Available commands are described in Table 6.3. After each command the user interface must report to the user the result and the status of the calculator, i.e. the value of the registers according to the current representation format, and the indication of the current selected format.

6.4.2 □ Design

We consider first the problem of changing format. It must be possible to change the behaviour of the calculator in terms of operand parsing and result printing.

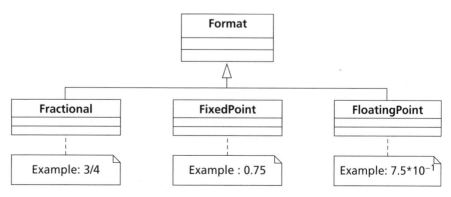

Figure 6.3 Analysis of representation format issues

Table 6.3 Command of the textual interface

Command	Description
Op <number>	Store an operand
+	Sum the last two operands
−	Subtract the last operand from the previous one
*	Multiply the last two operands
/	Divide the last two operands
fixed	Switch to fixed point format
Float	Switch to floating point format
Rat	Switch to rational format
help	Print the list of commands
exit	Terminate execution

Decision point

How does the calculator handle format conversion?

According to the problem specification, the calculator must handle three number formats: fixed point, floating point and fractional. Apparently, the simplest solution to format conversion consists in mapping each format to the other two. This is not a viable solution, if we think that the calculator might require maintenance, e.g. the introduction of a new number format (say, the Roman number format). In that case, the number of mapping relations between formats would grow exponentially.

A better solution consists in defining an internal number format that is used to store operands and results in the calculator registers. Conversion mapping is thus required only among the user-selected format and the internal format, and vice versa. The number of mapping relations between formats grows linearly with the number of number formats.

Decision point

How does the calculator modify the operand parsing and result printing behaviour according to the current selected format?

There are two possible ways to change behaviour dynamically (Sidebar 6.1). We decide to choose the one that enforces reusability and easy maintenance. This approach leads to the classes shown in the class diagram of Figure 6.4. Class Command implements the command interpreter that parses the user commands and invokes the corresponding methods of class Calculator.

According to Figure 6.4 number formats are represented by three classes: FloatingPointFormat, FixedPointFormat, FractionalFormat. These classes extend the abstract class Format. Class Command has the responsibility to create an

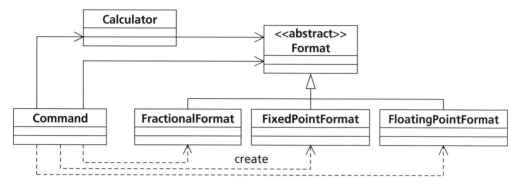

Figure 6.4 The classes that handle number format conversions

Sidebar 6.1 Dynamic behaviour

The problem of changing the behaviour of a program (or some of its parts) at run time is very common.

Let's focus on a simplified version of this problem. We consider a class (Changing) that has an entry method (public void perform()) whose behaviour can vary during the execution of the program, and method public void setBehavior() used to switch from one behaviour to the other. There are two possible solutions:

- to implement all the possible behaviours inside method perform() using a big switch construct that selects the code to be executed;
- to encapsulate every specific behaviour in a different object to be passed to class Changing.

The first solution requires a status attribute that keeps track of the current behaviour. The entry method contains a switch (or chain of else–if) to select the appropriate behaviour.

This solution is quite simple: class Changing contains the entry method and the behaviour selection method.

```
public class Changing {
  int behavior = 0;
  public static final int FIRST_BEHAVIOR=1;
  public static final int SECOND_BEHAVIOR=2;
  public void setBehavior(int newBehavior){ behavior=newBehavior; }
  public void perform(){
    switch(behavior){
    case 1: /* B1 */
    case 2: /* B2 */
    }
  }
}
```

The following code fragment shows the use of this solution:

```
Changing chObject = new Changing(;
chObject.setBehavior(Changing.FIRST_BEHAVIOR);
chObject.perform();
```

▶

The main advantage of this solution is that it requires only one class, and thus it is very compact. On the other hand, adding a new behaviour requires modification in several points of the class: a new constant and a new case in the switch construct. As a result the code is more difficult to understand and to maintain.

The second solution embeds each behaviour in a different class. The main class must have an attribute that refers to the object implementing the currently selected behaviour. All the different behaviour classes implement the common interface Behavior. In other words, the main class can be linked to any object that conforms to the contract in the Behavior interface.

The binding of the interface to a specific behaviour is carried out at run time. This is in the nature of polymorphism.

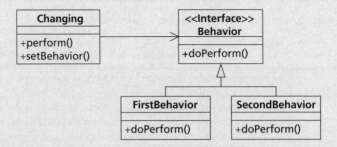

The above classes can be implemented as follows:

```
public class Changing {
  Behavior behavior = null;
  public void setBehavior(Behavior newBehavior)
                                      { behavior=newBehavior; }
  public void perform(){
    if (behavior != null)
      behavior.doPerform();
  }
}
public interface Behavior{
  void doPerform();
}
public class FirstBehavior implements Behavior {
  public doPerform(){/* B1 */ }
}
public class SecondBehavior implements Behavior {
  public doPerform(){/* B2 */ }
}
```

The following code fragment shows the use of this solution:

```
Changing chObject = new Changing(;
chObject.setBehavior(new FirstBehavior());
chObject.perform();
```

The main advantage of this approach is that adding a new behaviour is just a matter of defining a new class; this means that the main class is independent of the different behaviours. On the other hand, this approach uses many more classes making it more complex.

instance of these classes and to pass them to class Calculator according to the user-selected format.

Decision point

Which format is best suited to internal representation of operands and results?

Since the specification of the problem insists on the importance of the fractional format, top priority is given to the accuracy of representation of rational numbers (i.e. those represented by fractions). To simplify the conversion procedure we decide to adopt a unique internal representation format. Consequently, we decide to store the numbers internally using the fractional format.

The internal structure of the calculator component is shown in Figure 6.5. The main class is Calculator, which implements the main feature of the calculator, i.e. the four operations and the management of the operands.

The operands are implemented by the Rational class. This class represents a number as a fraction, i.e. it stores a numerator and a denominator. It provides methods to add, subtract, multiply and divide two Rational objects. The Calculator class has two associations to class Rational to represent the first and second operand. Since at initialization time there are no assigned values for the operands we decide to adopt zero as the default value of Rational.

In this prototype we assume that the standard base is the decimal base.

Decision point

How do the abstract class Format and its subclasses express the format conversion behaviour?

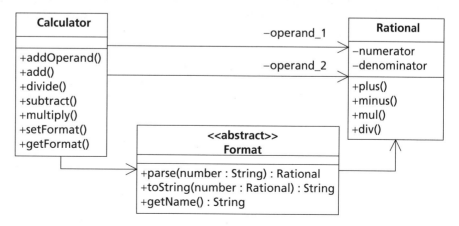

Figure 6.5 Class relations for format conversion

At this point we can also better define the responsibility of the class Format and its derived classes. It must provide two main functionalities:

■ parsing: convert a string representation of a number to the internal representation, i.e. to a Rational object; this is performed by method parse();
■ printing: convert a number from the internal representation to a string format; this is done by method toString().

Class Format is abstract therefore it only defines these methods and delegates their implementation to its derived classes. A relevant feature of the format classes is to provide the name of the format. This makes it possible to know which the current format is.

To better understand how the polymorphic implementation of the format works, we can observe a simple scenario that involves the parsing of an operand provided by the command line interpreter. The collaboration diagram of Figure 6.6 describes this scenario.

The sequence of operations is as follows. The command interpreter inserts a new operand in the calculator by means of the addOperand method (1). This method delegates the task of parsing the string to the current format (i.e. to the object currently connected through the format relationship). In this case it is an instance of the FixedPoint class; this is done invoking the method parse() (2). The method parse creates a new Rational object, which will contain the value, and returns it. Before terminating, the addOperand() method links the value returned by parse() as the second operand of the calculator, i.e. it is linked to the operand in the role operand_1.

6.4.3 □ Implementation

In order to have well-structured code, all the calculator-related classes are put into the multi-format package. Therefore all the classes are preceded by the package declaration:

```
package multiformat;
```

Class Rational implements the internal representation of operands and results. It represents rational numbers by means of a numerator and a denominator.

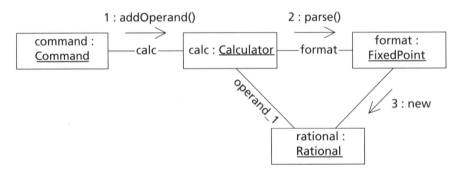

Figure 6.6 Collaboration of calculator classes

```java
public class Rational {
  static final double PRECISION=10;
  static final double EPSILON = Math.pow(10,-PRECISION);
  double numerator = 0.0;
  double denominator = 1.0;
  public Rational(double num, double den) {
    numerator = num;
    denominator = den;
    simplify();
  }
  public Rational(double number) {
    numerator = number;
    denominator = 1.0;
    canonical();
    simplify();
  }
```

The constructors make use of two methods: canonical() and simplify(). The former ensures that numerator and denominator are both integers, with an approximation of ten decimal figures. The latter simplifies the fraction by dividing both numerator and denominator by their common divisors.

```java
  void canonical() {
    double num = Math.abs(numerator);
    double decimal = num - Math.floor(num);
    int num_digits = 0;
    while (decimal > EPSILON && num_digits < PRECISION) {
      num = num * 10;
      decimal = num - Math.floor(num);
      num_digits++;
    }
    numerator = numerator * Math.pow(10.0, num_digits);
    denominator = denominator * Math.pow(10.0, num_digits);
  }
  public void simplify() {
    double divisor = Math.min(Math.abs(numerator),
                              denominator);
    for (; divisor > 1.0; divisor -= 1.0) {
      double rn = Math.abs(Math.IEEEremainder(
                  Math.abs(numerator), divisor));
      double rd = Math.abs(Math.IEEEremainder
                          (denominator, divisor));
      if (rn < EPSILON && rd < EPSILON) {
        numerator /= divisor;
        denominator /= divisor;
        divisor = Math.min(Math.abs(numerator),
                           denominator);
      }
    }
  }
}
```

The other methods of class **Rational** perform the arithmetic operations.

```
public Rational plus(Rational other) {
  if (denominator == other.denominator)
    return new Rational(numerator + other.numerator,
                        other.denominator);
  else
    return new Rational(numerator * other.denominator +
                        denominator * other.numerator,
                        denominator * other.denominator);
}
public Rational minus(Rational other) {
  if (denominator == other.denominator)
    return new Rational(numerator - other.numerator,
                        denominator);
  else
    return new Rational(numerator * other.denominator -
                        denominator * other.numerator,
                        denominator * other.denominator);
}
public Rational mul(Rational other) {
  return new Rational(numerator * other.numerator,
                      denominator * other.denominator);
}
public Rational div(Rational other) {
  return new Rational(numerator * other.denominator,
                      denominator * other.numerator);
}
public void copyOf(Rational other) {
  this.numerator = other.numerator;
  this.denominator = other.denominator;
}
}
```

Class **Format** implements the generic representation format. It is declared public in order to be visible from outside the package (e.g. from the command line interpreter). The method **getName()** is public and is therefore visible from outside the package, while the other two methods are visible only from other classes belonging to the same package. These choices about visibility are dictated by the information hiding principle, i.e. show only what is necessary, hide all the rest. The immediate benefit of this approach is that the interactions between the classes are clear.

```
public abstract class Format {
  // public members
  public abstract String getName();
  // package visible member
  abstract String toString(Rational number);
```

```
abstract Rational parse(String number) throws
                                       FormatException;
}
```

When method **parse()** receives a string representing a number, it is possible that an error occurs, the reason being the incorrect format of the string. To handle the possibility of errors in the **parse()** method we declare that this method can throw an exception. The reasons and consideration behind this choice are discussed in Sidebar 6.2.

Since the cause of the error in parsing is very specific we define a new class that represents this exceptional condition: **FormatException**. This class extends the **Exception** class, which is part of the core Java classes (in package **java.lang**). The only method implemented is the constructor that simply passes the message string to the superclass's constructor.

```
public class FormatException extends Exception {
  public FormatException(String msg) {
    super(msg);
  }
}
```

Sidebar 6.2 Error handling

When an error is found in a method there are two possible solutions:

- returning an error code, or
- throwing an exception.

The first solution is particularly complex when the method has a return value that represents the result of the execution; in this case a special value of the return value (e.g. null) is returned to signal the presence of an error.

Let's consider the two solutions in term of the code required to implement them. In the first case the class that signals the error looks like the following one:

```
public class C {
  Object method(){
  /* .. */
    if(some_error_condition) return null;
  /* .. */
  }
}
```

When using exceptions the code is the following:

```
public class C {
  Object method() throws MyErrorException(){
  /* .. */
    if(some_error_condition) throw new MyErrorException();
  /* .. */
  }
}
public class MyErrorException extends Exception {
}
```

▶

From the point of view of complexity the former solution is simpler since it consists of a single class. But the latter solution has several advantages. First, it is more readable since it declares explicitly that the method can generate an error. Second, the name of the exception provides further information about what kind of error has occurred. Exception classes on the one hand introduce complexity, but on the other hand they can be reused for similar errors, thus providing a uniform approach throughout the system.

We can further compare the two approaches from the point of view of the error handler.

In the first case the code must check the return value against the error condition:

```
Object result = c.method();
if(result == null){
  // handle error
}
// normal processing
```

In the second case we have to use the try–catch construct:

```
try{
  Object result = c.method();
  // normal processing
}catch(MyErrorException exception){
  // handle error
}
```

The main advantage of the latter solution is the separation of the normal processing code from the error handling code, which are intermingled in the former solution.

Another great advantage is the compiler enforcement. When exceptions are declared the programmer is forced to handle them, otherwise the compiler signals an error. In the former case if the programmer forgets to check the return value for errors the program can be compiled seamlessly.

Every subclass of Format must implement the three abstract methods getName(), toString() and parse().

The FixedPointFormat class represents the fixed point format. The toString() method simply performs the division of numerator and denominator and uses the standard Double.toString() method to convert the result into a string. Likewise the parse() method uses the standard Double.parseDouble() method.

```
public class FixedPointFormat extends Format {
  public String getName() { return "fixed"; }

  String toString(Rational number) {
    double value = (double)number.numerator
                              / (double)number.denominator;
    String result = Double.toString(value);
    if(value<0) result = result + "-";
    return result;
  }
```

```java
  public Rational parse(String number) {
    return new Rational(Double.parseDouble(number));
  }
}
```

The FractionalFormat class represents the fractional format. The toString() is straightforward since the internal representation format is already expressed in terms of numerator and denominator. The parse() method first identifies numerator and denominator, then uses the standard Double.parseDouble() method. If the "/" is not found, it means that the format of the number is not correct, therefore an exception is thrown.

```java
public class FractionalFormat extends Format {
  public String getName() { return "fract"; }
  String toString(Rational number) {
    return Double.toString(number.numerator) +
           "/" + Double.toString(number.denominator);
  }
  Rational parse(String number) throws FormatException {
    int index = number.indexOf('/');
    if(index >= 0)
      return new Rational(Double.parseDouble(
                  number.substring(0, index).trim()),
                  Double.parseDouble(number.substring
                                (index+1).trim())));
    else {
      throw new FormatException("Error!
                                Not a rational format");
    }
  }
}
```

The FloatingPointFormat class, which represents the floating point format, is the most complex of the three. The toString() method calculates the number as a double performing the division between numerator and denominator, then the simple case of 0 is skipped. The exponent of the number is the logarithm in base 10 of the number, while the mantissa equals the number divided by 10 raised to the exponent. The parse() method first identifies mantissa and exponent by means of the characters "*" and "^". If these characters are not found the format of the number is not correct, therefore an exception is thrown. Otherwise the value is computed according to Equation 6.5.

Since the mathematical package only provides the natural logarithm method we have to use Equation 6.8 to compute the base 10 logarithm:

$$\log_A x = \frac{\log_B x}{\log_B A}$$

Equation 6.8 Equivalence of logarithms

```
public class FloatingPointFormat extends Format {
  public String getName() { return "float"; }
  public String toString(Rational number) {
    double value = number.numerator / number.denominator;
    if(value == 0.0){
      return "0.0*10^1";
    }else{
      double exponent = Math.floor(Math.log
                         (Math.abs(value))/Math.log(10));
      double mantissa = Math.abs(value)
                                  / Math.pow(10,exponent);
      String result="";
      result = Double.toString(mantissa) +
               "*10^" + Double.toString(exponent);
      if(value < 0){
        result = "-" + result;
      }
      return result;
    }
  }
  public Rational parse(String number) throws
                                      FormatException {
    int indexMul = number.indexOf('*');
    int indexPow = number.indexOf('^');
    if(indexMul <= 0 || indexPow <= 0) {
      throw new FormatException("Error!
                        Not a floating point format");
    }
    double mantissa = Double.parseDouble
                        (number.substring(0,indexMul));
    double power = Double.parseDouble
                        (number.substring(indexPow+1));
    double value = mantissa*Math.pow(10,power);
    return new Rational(value);
  }
}
```

Class **Calculator** implements the basic functionalities of the calculator. The two operands are initialized with the default value of **Rational**. The format is initialized as fixed point.

Method **addOperand()** accepts a new operand, parses it and stores it as the second operand, while the previous value of the second operand is copied to the first operand. The exception thrown by the **parse()** method of class **Format** is simply propagated. In fact this method is declared to throw the **Format Exception**. The order of the statements in this method is arranged to preserve the coherence of the calculator if an exception is thrown: the `operand_1` attribute is overwritten only if the parse is successful (see Sidebar 6.3).

Sidebar 6.3 Dealing with exceptions

When dealing with exceptions it is important to remember that when an exception is thrown a whole set of statements are skipped between the throw statement and the matching catch statement. This is relatively easy to consider if the throw and catch statements are quite close, but it can be easily overlooked, becoming a serious problem, when the exception propagates through several methods.

If a method propagates an exception (generated either by the method itself or by some method it calls), all the statements from the point where it is generated to the end of the method are skipped.

Let's consider some examples of methods operating on bank accounts.

```
void withdrawal(double amount){
  try{
    subtract(amount); // can throw exception
    // in the case of an exception the following statement is skipped
    printConfirmation();
  }catch(AmountNotAvailableException e){ //.. }
}
void subtract(double amount)() throws AmountNotAvailableException {
  if(amount < available)
    throw new AmountNotAvailableException();
  available -= amount;
  //..
}
```

In the previous example the subtract() method throws an exception if amount is less than available, therefore the subtraction of amount from available is skipped.

The withdrawal() method calls subtract(), if subtract terminates normally then it prints a confirmation, otherwise the call to printConfirmation() is skipped.

This use of exceptions allows us to write the sequence of operations in the ideal case and to separate the handling of exceptional cases. It is important to consider carefully the order of operations. Let's consider the following example:

```
void transfer(double amount) throws AmountNotAvailableException {
  destinationBankAccount.add(amount);
  sourceBankAccount.subtract(amount); // can throw exception
}
```

If no exception is thrown, the above code appears to be correct. But the subtract() method can throw an exception that is propagated to the caller of the transfer() method. When this happens the amount is credited to the destination account, but no amount is withdrawn from the source account: some money has magically appeared! The overall coherence of the accounts is lost.

To solve this problem the following code should be used instead:

```
void transfer(double amount) throws AmountNotAvailableException {
  sourceBankAccount.subtract(amount); // can throw exception
  destinationBankAccount.add(amount);
}
```

In the absence of exceptions the overall effect of the method is the same, but if an exception is thrown the add() method is skipped, preserving the overall coherence of the accounts.

As a general rule, extra attention must be paid when exceptions can be thrown in order to preserve the coherence of the data.

The methods implementing the arithmetic operations are similar: they store in operand_2 the result and replace operand_1 with the default value of Rational.

```java
public class Calculator {
  private Rational operand_1 = new Rational();
  private Rational operand_2 = new Rational();
  private Format format = new FixedPointFormat();
  public void addOperand(String newOperand) throws
                                            FormatException {
      Rational previous = operand_2;
      operand_2 = format.parse(newOperand);
                                    // can throw exception
      operand_1 = previous;
  }
  public void add()
    operand_2 = operand_1.plus(operand_2);
    operand_1 = new Rational();
  }
  public void subtract() {
    operand_2 = operand_1.minus(operand_2);
    operand_1 = new Rational();
  }
  public void multiply() {
    operand_2 = operand_1.mul(operand_2);
    operand_1 = new Rational();
  }
  public void divide() {
    operand_2 = operand_1.div(operand_2);
    operand_1 = new Rational();
  }
  public void delete() {
    operand_2 = operand_1;
    operand_1 = new Rational();
  }
  public String firstOperand(){
    return format.toString(operand_1);
  }
  public String secondOperand(){
    return format.toString(operand_2);
  }
  public void setFormat(Format newFormat){
    format = newFormat;
  }
  public Format getFormat(){
    return format;
  }
}
```

Class **Command** implements the command line interpreter. It has an attribute (calc) that links the interpreter to an instance of the **Calculator** class. The method **nextCommand()** reads a command and process it. If a valid command is recognized the corresponding method of the calculator is invoked. The **readLine()** method of the **BufferedReader** class can throw an IOException when some problem with the input stream occurs. We handle this exception enclosing all the method's statements in a try–catch block. When an IOException is thrown we assume that there is no command to process, therefore all the statements are skipped and the method returns.

```java
public class Command {
  Calculator calc = new Calculator();
  BufferedReader lineReader = new BufferedReader(
                             new InputStreamReader
                                        ( System.in ) );
  boolean nextCommand() {
    System.out.print("\n[" + calc.getFormat().getName()+","
                          + calc.firstOperand() + ", "
                          + calc.secondOperand() + "] >");
    try {
      // reads the command from the keyboard
      String command = lineReader.readLine();
      // executes an arithmetical operation
      if(command.equals("+")) calc.add();
      else if(command.equals("-")) calc.subtract();
      else if(command.equals("*")) calc.multiply();
      else if(command.equals("/")) calc.divide();

      else if(command.equals("rat"))
        calc.setFormat(Format.rational);
      else if(command.equals("fixed"))
        calc.setFormat(Format.fixedPoint);
      else if(command.equals("float"))
        calc.setFormat(Format.floatingPoint);

      else if(command.equals("del"))
        calc.delete();
      else if(command.indexOf("op") >= 0)
        try{
          calc.addOperand(command.substring(2).trim());
        }
        catch(FormatException e){
          System.out.println("Wrong operand: " +
                            e.toString());
        }

      else if(command.equals("help"))
        printHelp();
```

```java
          else if(command.equals("exit"))
            return false;
          else
            System.out.println("Error! Not a valid command");
        }
      catch(IOException ioe) { ioe.printStackTrace(); }
      return true;
    }
  void printHelp() {
    System.out.println();
    System.out.println
      ("Insert one of the following commands:");
    System.out.println
      ("  op <number> (store an operand)");
    System.out.println
      ("  +          (sum the last two operands)");
    System.out.println
      ("  -          (subtract the last  two operands)");
    System.out.println
      ("  *          (multiply the last two operands)");
    System.out.println
      ("  /          (divide the last two operands)");
    System.out.println
      ("  dec        (switch to base 10)");
    System.out.println
      ("  bin        (switch to binary base)");
    System.out.println
      ("  hex        (switch to hexadecimal base)");
    System.out.println
      ("  fixed      (switch to fixed point format)");
    System.out.println
      ("  float      (switch to floating point format)");
    System.out.println
      ("  rat        (switch to rational format)");
    System.out.println
      ("  del        (remove last operand)");
    System.out.println
      ("  help       (print this command list)");
    System.out.println
      ("  exit       (terminate execution)");
    System.out.println();
  }
  public static void main(String[] args) {
    Command command = new Command();
    while(command.nextCommand());
  }
 }
}
```

6.4.4 □ Test

We have two main components in the architecture and we test them separately. Table 6.4 describes a test case; it presents a list of commands issued to the calculator, the resulting values of the first and second operands and the format being used.

First we test the calculator component invoking the methods of class Calculator directly. The following test method implements the first three lines of Table 6.4.

```java
public class TestCalculator extends TestCase {
  //...
  public void testOperations(){
    Calculator calc = new Calculator();
    try{
      calc.addOperand("3.2");
      assertEquals("0.0",calc.firstOperand());
      assertEquals("3.2",calc.secondOperand());
      calc.addOperand("2.8");
      assertEquals("3.2",calc.firstOperand());
      assertEquals("2.8",calc.secondOperand());
      calc.add();
      assertEquals("0.0",calc.firstOperand());
      assertEquals("6.0",calc.secondOperand());
    }catch(FormatException e){
      fail("Unexpected format exception");
    }
  }
}
```

The same test case is used to test the command line component. There are two significant differences from the previous test: first, the command line component takes the input from the standard input and writes the

Table 6.4 Test case

Command	First operand	Second operand	Format
Op 3.2	0.0	3.2	Fixed point
Op 2.8	3.2	2.8	Fixed point
+	0.0	6.0	Fixed point
Op 1	6.0	1.0	Fixed point
−	0.0	5.0	Fixed point
Op 2	5.0	2.0	Fixed point
*	0.0	10.0	Fixed point
Op 111	10.0	111.0	Fixed point
/	0.0	0.09009009009009009	Fixed point
Rat	0.0/1.0	10.0/111.0	Rational
Float	$0.0 * 10^1$	$9.009009009009008 * 10^{-2.0}$	Floating point

output to the standard output; second, the output may contain extra spaces or text in addition to the values of the operands.

How is it possible to test a program that uses standard input and output?

The simplest solution is to redirect the standard input and output streams (System.in and System.out). The input can be read from a string by means of class **StringBufferInputStream**. The output produced by the program can be recorded into a string buffer by means of class **ByteArrayOutputStream**.

How can we check an output containing extra blanks or text?

The option of performing an exact string match is not feasible because a minor change in the output (addition of a single white space) would break the test. A better option is to check the output for the presence of specific substrings. In addition it is useful to verify that the substrings appear in a given order within the output. In the test class **TestCommand** the purpose of the method **assertContainsInOrder()** is to verify that the output string contains all the elements of a string array in the correct order.

The following test class implements the first three lines of the test case described in Table 6.4. It is the text-oriented version of the **TestCalculator** test presented before.

```
public class TestCommand extends TestCase {
  //...
  public void testCommand(){
    String input = "op 3.2\n" + "op 2.8\n" +
                    "+\n" + "exit\n";
    // redirect the standard input to read
    // from the input string
    InputStream oldIn = System.in;
    System.setIn(new StringBufferInputStream(input));
    // redirect the standard output to write
    // into a string buffer
    PrintStream oldOut = System.out;
    ByteArrayOutputStream buffer =
                            new ByteArrayOutputStream();
    System.setOut(new PrintStream(buffer));
    // create a command object and run it
    Command c = new Command();
    c.run();
```

```
      // restore original standard input and output
      System.setOut(oldOut);
      System.setIn(oldIn);
      // copy the output into a string
      String output = buffer.toString();
      String[] expected={ "0.0","3.2","3.2",
                                    "2.8","0.0","6.0" };
      // verify the output contains the expected strings
      assertContainsInOrder(output,expected);
   }
   protected void assertContainsInOrder(String output,
                                        String[] strings){
      int lastIndex = -1;
      int currentIndex = -1;
      for (int i = 0; i < strings.length; i++) {
        currentIndex = output.indexOf(strings[i],lastIndex+1);
        assertTrue("Couldn't find [" + i + "]:"+ strings[i],
                   currentIndex>-1);
        lastIndex = currentIndex;
      }
   }
}
```

6.5 ■ Prototype 2: Number bases

The focus of this prototype is on the introduction of different number bases to the calculator.

6.5.1 □ Analysis

The main feature that is added in this development iteration is the capability of handling different number bases. Analogous with what we've done with the representation formats, we can represent the concepts involved in this issue as a set of related classes. The result of this analysis is presented in Figure 6.7 as a class diagram.

We start from the generic concept of number base; it involves the capability of parsing operands in a given base and printing the result in a given base. This abstract concept can be separated into three concrete number bases: decimal, binary and hexadecimal. Each number base is characterized by the base in the proper sense (e.g. 2 for the binary base) and by the set of digits that can be used (e.g. 0 and 1 for the binary base).

The command line must therefore accommodate new commands: to manage number bases and to read commands from a file. The new commands are described in Table 6.5.

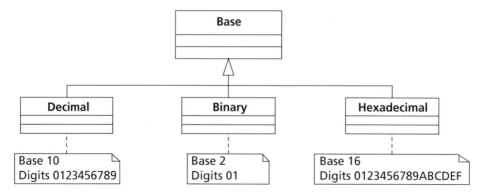

Figure 6.7 Analysis of number bases

The command line interpreter must provide the user with information about the current base and representation format. This is a simple extension of the information provided by the interpreter in the previous prototype.

6.5.2 □ Design

The design of this prototype is basically an extension of the previous one with the addition of the classes required to handle multiple number bases.

The structure of the classes identified during analysis is quite similar to the classes identified in the previous prototype, which were related to representation formats. Because of this analogy we decide to adopt a similar approach and to represent the base in use by the calculator through an object of type Base. The resulting class diagram is shown in Figure 6.8.

The class Base defines the interface and basic behaviour, which are common to all the concrete base classes, DecimalBase, BinartyBase and HexBase.

There is an important difference between the number base related class hierarchy and the representation format related one. Class Base can use generic algorithms to convert between a string and a number; therefore the subclasses need only define the parameters for such algorithms. In the case of format the separation is achieved by defining a specific behaviour in the concrete subclasses. In the case of the base, it is achieved by customizing the generic algorithms defined in the abstract class.

The sequence of calls to add a new operand to the calculator is described in Figure 6.9. The command class calls the addOperand() method to add a

Table 6.5 Additional commands

Command	Description
Dec	Switch to base 10
Bin	Switch to binary base
Hex	Switch to hexadecimal base

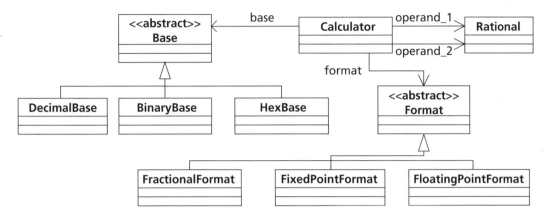

Figure 6.8 Calculator with format and base classes

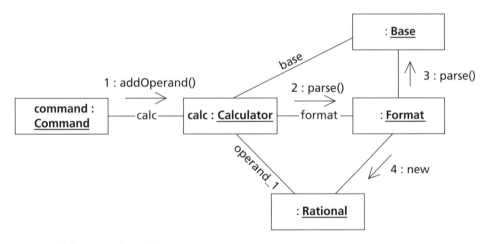

Figure 6.9 Collaboration for adding a new operand

new operand (1). The Calculator invokes the parse() method on the Format object and passes the Base object as a parameter (2). Thus Format is able to call the parse() method on the base to convert the number using the given number base (3). Finally the method parse() of Format creates a new Rational object.

6.5.3 ☐ Implementation

Class Base implements the generic concept of number base, it provides two essential methods: parse() converts a string representation of a number into a double, toString() does the opposite. The former is based on Equation 6.1, while the latter uses Equation 6.2 and Equation 6.4. These methods can be customized using two parameters: the base and the digits; they are stored in the homonymous attributes and are initialized through the constructor.

```java
public abstract class Base {
  private String name;
  private int base;
  private String digits;
  static final int MAX_PRECISION = 10;
                          // max number of decimal ciphers
  double EPSILON;         // smallest representable number
  Base(String name, int base, String digits){
    this.name = name;
    this.base = base;
    this.digits = digits;
    EPSILON = Math.pow(base,-MAX_PRECISION);
  }
  public String getName() { return name; }
  public int getBase() { return base; }
  double parse(String number) {
    // decodes the sign
    double sign = 1.0;
    if(number.charAt(0) == '-'){
      sign = -1.0;
      number = number.substring(1).trim();
    }else if(number.charAt(0) == '+'){
      sign = 1.0;
      number = number.substring(1).trim();
    }
    // parses the integer part and the decimal part
    int power;
    int index = number.indexOf('.');
    if(index >= 0)
      power = index-1;
    else
      power = number.length()-1;
    double result = 0.0;
    double mult = Math.pow(base,power);
    // decodes the integer part
    for(int i = 0; i < number.length(); i++)
      if(number.charAt(i)!='.'){
        result += mult * digits.indexOf(number.charAt(i));
        mult /= base;
      }
    return result * sign;
  }
  String toString(double number) {
    if(number == 0.0) return "0";
    StringBuffer result=new StringBuffer();
    if(number<0){
```

```
        result.append('-');
        number = -number;
    }
    int i;
    int power = (int)Math.floor(Math.log(number+EPSILON/2)
                                        /Math.log(base));

    if(power<0) power = 0;
    double divider = Math.pow(base,power);
    int num_digits = 0;
    double divResult, cipher;
    for(int i = power;
              (number>EPSILON && num_digits<MAX_PRECISION) ||
               i >= -1;  −i){
      divResult = number / divider;
      cipher = Math.floor((number+EPSILON/2) / divider);
      if(divider < 1.0){
        num_digits++;
        if(num_digits==1) result.append('.');
      }
      result.append(digits.charAt((int)cipher));
      number -= cipher * divider;
      divider /= base;
    }
    return result.toString();
  }
}
```

The Base class provides almost everything required to define a number base. The only thing left to be specified is the base together with the digits. The concrete number bases have only to provide these two parameters in addition to the name of the base.

```
public class BinaryBase extends Base{
  public BinaryBase() {
    super("bin", 2 ,"01");
  }
}
public class DecimalBase extends Base {
  public DecimalBase() {
    super("dec", 10 ,"0123456789");
  }
}
public class HexBase extends Base {
  public HexBase() {
    super("hex", 16 ,"0123456789ABCDEF");
  }
}
```

In the Command class it is sufficient to introduce three new elements in the command selection chain in order to handle the three different bases:

```java
public class Command {
  boolean nextCommand() {
    // ...
    try {
      // reads the command from the keyboard
      if(command.equals("+") || command.equals("-") ...
      ...
      else if(command.equals("dec"))
                          calc.setBase(new DecimalBase());
      else if(command.equals("bin"))
                          calc.setBase(new BinaryBase());
      else if(command.equals("hex"))
                          calc.setBase(new HexBase());
    }
    catch(IOException ioe) { ioe.printStackTrace(); }
    return true;
  }
}
```

6.5.4 □ Test

The test of the multiple number bases must be conducted together with the test of the representation format. The goal of the test is to check whether numbers are represented correctly using all possible combinations of base and format.

Class TestFormat is a simple test that verifies the conformance of the program with the example presented in Table 6.2.

```java
public class TestFormat extends TestCase {
  //...
  public void testFormatBase(){
    Calculator calc = new Calculator();
    try {
      calc.addOperand("0.75");
      assertEquals("0.75",calc.secondOperand());
      calc.setBase(new BinaryBase());
      assertEquals("0.11",calc.secondOperand());
      calc.setBase(new HexBase());
      assertEquals("0.C",calc.secondOperand());
      calc.setFormat(new FloatingPointFormat());
      assertEquals("C.0*10^-1.0",calc.secondOperand());
      calc.setBase(new BinaryBase());
      assertEquals("1.1*10^-1.0",calc.secondOperand());
      calc.setBase(new DecimalBase());
      assertEquals("7.5*10^-1.0",calc.secondOperand());
```

```
        calc.setFormat(new RationalFormat());
        assertEquals("3.0/4.0",calc.secondOperand());
        calc.setBase(new BinaryBase());
        assertEquals("11.0/100.0",calc.secondOperand());
        calc.setBase(new HexBase());
        assertEquals("3.0/4.0",calc.secondOperand());
    } catch (FormatException e)
                        { fail("Unexpected exception"); }
  }
}
```

6.6 ■ Extension

The reader can extend the application presented in this chapter in several
ways:

■ The use of only two operands in the calculator represents a limitation
   when complex expressions are needed. A more general solution consists
   of using a stack: each time an operand is added it is pushed onto the stack;
   when an operation is selected the operands are popped from the stack and
   the result is pushed back onto the stack.
■ The calculator described here is able to handle only constant numeric
   values. A powerful extension consists of adding the capability of dealing
   with variables. In this case the calculator must manage symbolic expressions: expressions must be stored using an internal format (an abstract
   syntax tree). In addition a table must contain the values of the variables
   that are used to compute the value of symbolic expressions.
■ A graphical user interface can be developed to provide a user friendly
   interaction with the calculator.

6.7 ■ Assessment

Analysis techniques. We analysed the problem domain and identified the
main concepts; since they are correlated we abstracted concepts into more
general ones.

Modelling techniques. In this chapter we introduced use case diagrams
and collaboration diagrams. In addition we used inheritance to factorize
common characteristics into base classes.

Development approach. The development of the multi-format calculator
highlighted two important issues:

■ dynamic behaviour and polymorphism; and
■ exception handling.

Handling a dynamic behaviour is a common problem and the solution
adopted in this system is largely reusable. Actually it is an instance of the

well-known *Strategy* pattern (Gamma *et al.* 1995). In addition, we have seen how exceptions can help in dealing with abnormal situations and how they allow a more readable and clean handling of errors.

Idiom	Class generalization
Context	Many classes have common features.
Problem	The replication of the same features makes classes less understandable and maintainable.
Forces or tradeoffs	The same attribute or method is repeated many times in different classes. Some operations are common to many classes.
Solution	Create a superclass of all the existing similar classes. Migrate the common characteristics into the superclass.
Force resolution	Common features are not replicated. The superclass becomes the single point of change. Derived classes are simpler. Code reuse is enforced. Gathering common features makes the structure more comprehensible.
Design rationale	We find commonalities among existing classes and make them into a single class.

Pattern	Strategy
Context	A class embeds a behaviour that can be chosen and/or changed at run time.
Problem	Switching the behaviour dynamically. Lets the behaviour vary independently from clients that use it.
Forces or tradeoffs	The clients need a stable interface. The behaviour must be changeable. The multiple behaviours must be evident from the structure of the classes.
Solution	Define a common interface for all the different behaviours (Strategy). For each behaviour define a class that implements the interface (ConcreteStrategyA, ConcreteStrategyB, ...). The behaviours are used by a client that defines the context within which they operate (Context). To select a behaviour an object of one of the behaviour classes can be linked to the Context.

Examples	To implement different representation formats for numbers an abstract interface can be declared. It defines two methods that can be used to convert between String and double:

```
interface Format {
  String toString(double number);
  double parse(String number);
}
```

Then we can define as many concrete behaviours as there are formats. For instance the concrete behaviour for the floating point format can be implemented as:

```
class FloatingPointFormat implements
                                  Format {
  String toString(double number){
    // convert to a floating point
    // formatted string
  }
  double toDouble(String number) {
    // parse a floating point formatted
    // string
  }
}
```

The client that wants to perform a conversion uses the abstract interface:

```
void printNumber(double number, Format
                                  format){
  System.out.println
              (format.toString(number));
}
```

The format actually adopted depends on the effective class of the object passed as argument format.

Force resolution	The clients always access the behaviour through the same invariable interface. The behaviour varies according to the effective class of the format object. The inheritance hierarchy makes the different behaviours explicit.
Design rationale	This pattern leverages the polymorphism and dynamic binding. The Context can be linked to any class that implements the Strategy interface; when it invokes one of the operations, the one defined in the actual class of the object is activated.

6.8 ■ Reference

Gamma, E., Helm, R., Johnson, R. and Vlissides, J. (1995) *Design Patterns: Elements of Reusable Object-Oriented Software*, Addison-Wesley.

PART

Object architectures

Object architectures **7**

Synthesis

The object-oriented (OO) paradigm claims to promote reuse, reduce development time and improve software quality. Originally these properties were considered at the level of single objects, and were achieved using libraries of reusable classes organized in hierarchies of inheritance. However, attention is now being shifted from individual objects to the whole architecture by giving more importance to the fundamental role that relationships between the elements have in any design. As software systems grow in size and complexity, the design and architecture of a software program represent an increasingly large part of the development effort.

In Part I of this book, we focused on the basic building blocks of object-oriented analysis and design. The transition from problem specification to application design was quite seamless: most of the entities found in the problem domain were mapped into classes in the solution domain.

When dealing with more complex applications (e.g. concurrent applications), we observe that simple analysis models (e.g. identification of nouns and verbs in the problem specification) are not suitable for implementation. We need to turn them into design models that take into consideration not only functional requirements (what the application does), but non-functional requirements as well; in particular we have to consider feasibility and reuse.

First of all the design must be feasible, i.e. it must be relatively easy to implement in a programming language. It is important to reduce the effort required to implement a system, therefore issues such as the number of classes and their complexity are very important. Second, the design must promote reuse of architectural models and code.

The second part of this book focuses on the exploitation of architectural models of object-oriented applications.

7.1 ■ Architectural styles

In recent years there has been a growing interest in software architectures (Shaw and Garlan 1996); an architecture is described in terms of identified system components, how they are connected, and the nature of these connections (protocols for communication, synchronization, data access).

This has led to the identification of a number of general-purpose architectures that frequently occur in software programs, e.g. pipes/filters, blackboard, data-centred, event-driven, client–server and layered architectures.

Software architecture reuse is based on the definition of "architectural styles", that is the recurring organizational and structural patterns and idioms used in architectural design (Abowd *et al*. 1993; Garlan 1995). An architectural style provides a specialized component vocabulary (e.g. the terms client, server, application server, etc.), a connector vocabulary (e.g. pipes, data stream, etc.) and a set of rules to build a specific topology using components and connectors.

Architectural styles improve the communication between designers, which can refer to a shared terminology for reusing design solutions. Unfortunately, systematic reuse of concrete architectures and designs is more difficult than code-level reuse, since a design is not worth much in itself as a reusable artifact; the design, with its tradeoffs and consequences, must be understood by the software developer so that the necessary adaptations and changes can be performed. Since software architectures are usually domain independent, no guidance is given to the developer for choosing the right architecture for the specific application to be developed.

7.2 ■ Communication mechanisms

The components of an object-oriented architecture interact with each other to carry on the function of the system. An important step in the definition of the architecture is the selection of the communication mechanism. In this part of the book we consider three main mechanisms.

1 **Method invocation**. It is the basic communication mechanism offered by all programming languages. According to this mechanism, a single functionality is performed by a method. Whenever that functionality is required the method is invoked. The method behaves like a subroutine: it delivers the functionality and eventually returns the result. The invoker and the invoked components are closely coupled.

2 **Event-driven**. With this approach a component receives notification that an event has occurred within the system. In response to the event notification, the component can perform some actions. This approach decouples the component that notifies an event and the one that receives the event notification and allows the components to evolve independently.

3 **Message-based**. According to this communication paradigm a component requiring a service sends a message to the component that provides that service. The provider component receives the message, parses the message, performs the corresponding service, and sends back a message with the result. This approach allows the components to evolve independently but forces them to adopt a common communication language and protocol.

7.3 ■ Control flow models

We identify three types of control flow models.

1 **Single-threaded**. This is the basic model where no concurrency is present; at any time there is only one instruction that is being executed. Only one component at a time is active and it has to yield control to other components (usually by method invocation).

2 **Virtual processes**. This is based on a single threaded model but gives the appearance of concurrent execution. In this approach a controller component schedules the execution of the other components and gives them control. The scheduling can be performed periodically or based on events. The components whose execution is scheduled are responsible for performing the scheduled activity and returning the control back to the controller. This model is based on a logical decomposition of activities in simple steps whose execution requires only short intervals of time. The programmer has the responsibility of decomposing the components' activities according to the application requirements.

3 **Multithreaded**. This approach allows real concurrency; it is based on the concurrency mechanisms of the operating system. Several threads can be running at the same time in an application. Even in this case, only one component has control over the application execution. In contrast to the virtual processes approach, the decomposition of components' activities in simple steps is performed by the operating system at a lower granularity. The main disadvantage is that the threads management raises the computational load.

7.4 ■ Part overview

The second part of this book is organized in four case studies. They present object architectures that implement different architectural styles, communication mechanisms and concurrency models. The case studies use different methods to synthesize generic components (see Table 7.1).

The case study presented in Chapter 8 (Code documentation) deals with the development of a graphical application that parses a source Java code

Table 7.1 Architectures adopted in the case studies

Case study	Architectural style	Communication mechanism	Concurrency models
8 Code documentation	Data-centred	Method invocation	Single-thread
9 Work cell	Virtual machine	Event-driven	Virtual processes
10 Mobile robot	Master–slave	Message-oriented	Multithread
11 Car Parking	Layered	Method invocation and event-driven	Multithread

file and formats the code structure in HTML. It emphasizes the role of association and relationships between application components.

The other three case studies discuss three different software control architectures that model the interaction between controller and controlled system.

Chapter 9 (Manufacturing work cell) deals with prototyping and simulation of a manufacturing work cell. The control system is simulated as a discrete event dynamic system, where system components are modelled as finite state automata. A centralized event clock schedules events that trigger state transitions. The control behaviour emerges from the event-based interaction among the simulated devices. The architecture is single threaded and supports the broadcaster–listener communication model.

Chapter 10 (Mobile robot exploration) deals with simulation of a robotic system. The system is structured according to the master–slave architecture. A software controller plays the role of master and sends commands (e.g. "move forward" or "get sensor measurements") to a mobile robot. The mobile robot is a multithreaded component made up of independent modules that simulate sensors and actuators and play the role of slaves. The communication between master and slaves is asynchronous and message-based and is implemented using the pipe mechanism.

Chapter 11 (Car parking) deals with simulation of an access control system for car parking. The software architecture is multithreaded and event-based. The system is organized in a client–server hierarchy of control modules. The clients send commands to the servers according to the caller–provider paradigm. The servers notify state changes using the observer–observable mechanism offered by the java.util package.

7.5 ■ References

Abowd, G., Allen, R. and Garlan, D. (1993) "Using Style to Give Meaning to Software Architecture", in *Proc. of SIGSOFT '93: Foundations of Software Engineering*, *Software Engineering Notes*, Vol. 118, No. 3, 9–20, ACM Press.

Garlan, D. (1995) "What is Style?", in *Proceedings of Dagshtul Workshop on Software Architecture*, February.

Shaw, M. and Garlan, D. (1996) *Software Architecture: Perspectives on an Emerging Discipline*, Prentice-Hall.

Code documentation

8

Synthesis

The application developed throughout this chapter is aimed at generating customizable documentation for source code. The format chosen for the documentation is HTML (HyperText Markup Language). The architecture of the application mainly addresses extensibility requirements.

- Focus: this case study exemplifies the application of the *Composite* design pattern which is widely used when representation of hierarchical structure is required.
- OO techniques: separation of concerns and delegation.
- Java features: a graphical user interface is developed to provide ease of use for the application. The GUI is developed by means of the swing set of components; in particular a component that is able to render HTML code is used.
- Background: the reader is required to know the basic OO concepts and fundamental Java programming techniques and to have a basic knowledge of HTML.

8.1 ■ Specifications

Understanding programs written in a high-level programming language is one of the main problems arising when maintenance and reuse are concerned. While some pretty printing programs are available on the marketplace, they are often not customizable and it is difficult to fine-tune their output.

We want to develop an application that is able automatically to produce the documentation of a program in source code. The documentation generated by the application must use a standard and widely adopted format. A documentation schema specifies both the information to be extracted from the source code and how it should be presented.

In summary, the application must be able to read one or more source code files and generate an HTML file for each of them containing formatted documentation. The application should initially be able to analyse and document Java code. The application must be easily extensible in order to accommodate new documentation schemas and possibly new languages.

8.1.1 ☐ **Example of Java documentation**

As a first proof of concept implementation, we choose Java as the source code programming language. We will consider a simple documentation that simply lists the public members of the program classes.

In particular, for each Java class an HTML page should be generated with the following characteristics: the title of the page should be the name of the class, the name of the class should also appear as a level 1 heading at the top of the page, then the page should contain a list of the public members.

The public members of the class conform to the following guidelines:

- public attributes will appear as they are written in the class, without the terminating ";";
- for each public method only the signature will be presented;
- in both cases, the keyword "public" will be omitted.

An additional requirement is on the fonts used in the page. The list of public members should use a Courier-like mono-spaced font. The heading at the top of the page and the rest of the text in the page should use a sans-serif font. Figure 8.1 shows an example of source code and the corresponding documentation.

```java
class Example {
  public int a_public_attribute;
  public void a_method (int a_parameter){
    //...
  }
}
```

Example
Public members:
- `a_public_attribute`
- `void int a_method(int a_parameter)`

Figure 8.1 An example of code documentation

8.2 ■ **Problem analysis**

The problem of generating the documentation for a program is very complex if considered in the most general setting. Fortunately the specification of the application introduces several assumptions that make the problem much easier.

We can identify three main elements, which are addressed throughout the specification: the source code, the documentation and the transformation of one into the other (i.e. the core functionality of the application). The overall functionality of the system can be described by the use case diagram, shown in Figure 8.2.

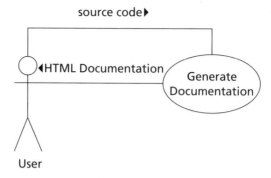

Figure 8.2 Use case of the application

When analysing the specification, two main issues arise concerning the input language: first we have to parse source code written in a high-level programming language (Java in the example), second the application should be easily adaptable to new languages. The parsing of a programming language is usually a non-trivial task, but many tools are available that simplify this task. In addition, from the reference example we can note that a very simple analysis of the source code is required, Therefore the implementation of the proof of concept does not require a fully fledged parser. The adaptability issue must be carefully addressed by the architecture of the application, since no simplification can be found reading the specification.

The selection of HTML as the format for the documentation has a twofold advantage: first we have to take into consideration only one output language, second HTML is based on a hierarchical structure, which helps in assembling several pieces of information in a single document. The example provides a good overview of the features of HTML that should be used for generating the documentation.

8.2.1 □ Domain models

The application exhibits a set of functionalities that are similar to the ones provided by the javadoc program, which is part of the Sun JDK, but javadoc requires the programmer to furnish the code with additional comments.

The approach taken with this application is more general and it is intended to be more customizable; moreover it is applicable to languages other than Java.

The system we want to develop is in essence a translator from an input language (the source code language) to output language (the documentation language). We can borrow many ideas regarding the architecture of such a system from the mature toolbox of compilers and formal languages.

The structure of a compiler, or more generally a translator, can be split into three main components:

■ a front end, responsible for the lexical and syntactical analysis of the input language (the programming language);

- an intermediate representation, with related processing modules;
- a back end, which is in charge of generating the output in the final language (documentation language).

This architecture provides a high degree of flexibility, since the internal processing components are independent of both the input and output languages. If the input language changes only the front-end component needs to be modified. If a different output language is required, changes are confined to the back-end component.

8.2.2 □ Main Features

We can now summarize the main features that the system shall exhibit:

- *Intermediate representation*. Support an object-oriented intermediate representation of HTML pages; this representation enables an easy manipulation and construction of the pages.
- *Source code parsing*. Parse the source language, focusing on the identification of the basic syntactic elements of the language such as class declaration and member definition.
- *HTML documentation*. Generate the HTML documentation for the source code. This is a bridge between the previous two features, since it is about relating the elements of the programming language to the operations required to generate the corresponding HTML documentation.

8.2.3 □ Test

For the test case at system level we use a simple class derived from the one presented as an example in the requirements specifications. This class represents the input code that will be documented with the application under development. In order to make the test case significant, we need to add other elements to the example class in order to test if the application picks up only the required parts and correctly ignores the rest.

Moreover the application must allow the selection of text colour and style, and the colour of the background. In this example we will adopt a colour schema, which is not mandatory; its purpose is to demonstrate how colours and other features can be used.

```
// this is a test class...
class TestClass {
  String an_attribute;
  public int a_public_attribute;
  public void a_method(int a_parameter){
    String s;
    s = "string content";
  }
  abstract private int another_method();
}
```

The class TestClass contains a total of four members, two attributes and two methods. Two attributes are public: the attribute an_attribute and the method a_method.

The application should produce an HTML page that looks like that shown in Figure 8.3. It is what a web browser shows (in colour) when we process the HTML code shown in Figure 8.4.

The title of the page, defined in the second line of Figure 8.4, is Class: followed by the name of the class. Then we see the body of the page that specifies a cyan background colour. The heading consisting of the name of the class is decorated with some extra attributes: the size of the font is increased by two points, the colour of the characters will be navy (dark blue), and the font is "Tahoma", which is a common sans-serif font. The list of the public members is preceded by the plain text Public members:, which is formatted in "Arial", navy colour and increased size. The list of public members is presented using an increased size, green, "Courier New" font. At the bottom of the page there is a link to the home page for the Java language. This last line is inserted in order to provide an example of an HTML item that can be useful when representing complex documentation.

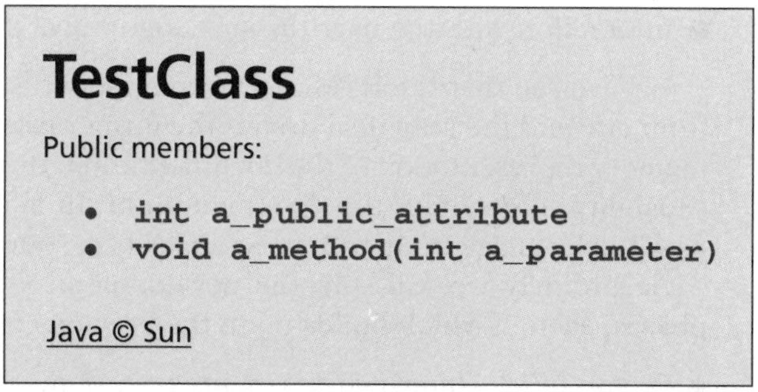

Figure 8.3 An example of HTML page. Copyright © 2005 Sun Microsystems, Inc. All rights reserved. Reproduced by permission of Sun Microsystems, Inc.

```
<HTML>
<head><title>Class: TestClass</title></head>
<BODY bgcolor="cyan" >
<H1><FONT size="+2" color="navy" face="Tahoma" >TestClass </FONT>
</H1><FONT size="+2" color="navy" face="Arial" >Public members:
<BR> </FONT><FONT size="+2" color="green" face="Courier New" >
  <UL>
    <LI>int a_public_attribute <BR> </LI>
    <LI>void a_method(int a_parameter) <BR></LI>
  </UL>
</FONT>
<A href="http://java.sun.com" >Java &copy; Sun </A>
</BODY></HTML>
```

Figure 8.4 An example of HTML code

8.3 ■ Architecture and planning

The problem under consideration involves extracting information from the source code and reporting it in a formatted way. Adopting the compiler architecture described above, this processing should be performed on the intermediate representation.

Since the result of the documentation is HTML we decide to use a structural representation of HTML as an intermediate representation. The intermediate representation can easily be serialized and converted into an HTML document.

A more general and reusable solution would use the Extensible Markup Language (XML) as intermediate representation language, but this is beyond the scope of this chapter.

Adopting the architectural style described above we can define the architecture depicted in Figure 8.5. It is made up of three components that are responsible for:

■ run time dynamic generation of HTML documents;
■ parsing and formatting of Java code;
■ interaction with the user through a graphical driver interface.

We can see that the HTML DOM component is used by both the language front end and the graphical driver: the former uses it while assembling an in-memory representation of the documentation, the latter uses its serialization capability to generate the documentation. In addition the graphical driver uses the language front end when analysis of source code is needed.

Accordingly we will split the development of the application into three phases, each of which builds upon the previous one.

■ *Prototype 1: Intermediate representation.* During the first phase of development we will build a component that supports an intermediate representation of HTML and its serialization to produce readable HTML code. This will be a fairly generic and reusable component.

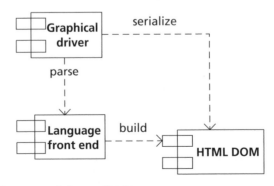

Figure 8.5 Architecture of the application

- *Prototype 2: Code parsing and documentation*. We will develop the analysis and documentation component in the second phase. This module will analyse Java source code and use the previous component to build the documentation.
- *Prototype 3: User interface*. Finally, we will develop a graphical user interface which provides user-friendly access to the application functionality.

8.4 ■ Prototype 1: Intermediate representation

In the first phase we will develop a component that supports a structural representation of HTML documents. This component must provide tools/ methods to build, explore, modify and serialize representation of HTML pages. The idea is to offer an easy to use object-oriented interface for building and manipulating HTML content. This kind of facility is usually called an "object model".

8.4.1 □ Analysis

An example of HTML that should be handled by the component is presented in Figure 8.6. It contains an arbitrary selection of the most common tags found in HTML pages on the internet, i.e.:

- `<HTML>` and `</HTML>` delimit the entire document;
- `<HEAD><TITLE>` and `</TITLE></HEAD>` delimit the document title;
- `<BODY>` and `</BODY>` delimit the document body;
- `<H1>` and `</H1>` delimit a first order titles;
- `<A HREF...>` and `</A>` identify a link to another HTML document,

The structural representation shown in Figure 8.7 corresponds to the object structure of the sample HTML document. This figure shows a UML object diagram; the names of the objects have been defined in order to be

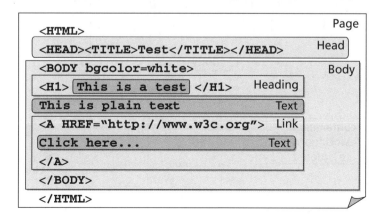

Figure 8.6 Sample HTML

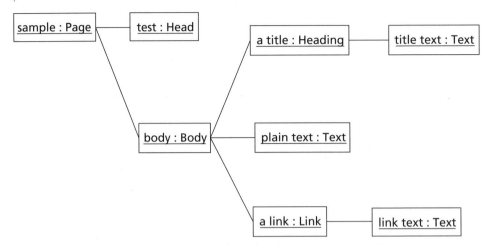

Figure 8.7 Analysis of sample HTML document

as intuitive as possible. The class names correspond to the element types identified above.

The structure of the corresponding class diagram (shown in Figure 8.8 is isomorphic to the static object structure representing the page. Class Page is the class at the root of the containment hierarchy. It can contain directly Head and Body. Class Head is atomic, i.e. it does not contain any other element class. On the other hand, class Body represents a composed element and it has a containment relationship with the other three classes: Heading, Text and Link. Both Heading and Link contain Text. Text is atomic.

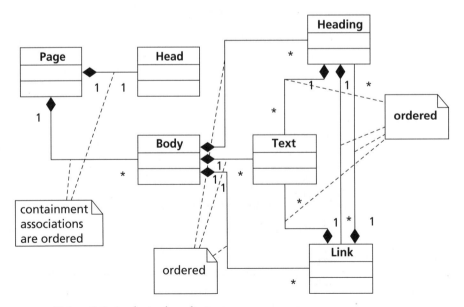

Figure 8.8 Analysis class diagram

The only additions that cannot be directly devised from the static object structure are the each-other containment relationships between Heading and Link; these relationships have been added based on knowledge of the HTML language.

All containment relationships in this class diagram are ordered because the order in which contained elements appear in the container element is important (e.g. the heading of a section should appear before the text that constitutes its content).

Class Page does not contain any specific information. Class Head contains only the title of the HTML page (i.e. Test in the example above). Class Body contains the background colour, which is encoded in the bgcolor parameter inside the <body> tag. Class Text contains the fragment of text it represents. Class Heading contains the text that constitutes the heading. Finally class Link contains the destination URL of the hyperlink. In addition, all classes except Head and Text can contain other elements that are linked to them.

8.4.2 □ Design

We try now to refine the analysis model described so far. First we identify commonalities among different classes and factor them into a common base class connected to the specific classes by inheritance. This is an application of the class generalization idiom presented in Chapter 6. Three main characteristics can be identified as common to the elements of the analysis model.

1 Most elements have a string associated with them, which represents the content of the element or some other parameter. The information associated with the various elements may be very different; the common characteristic is that it can be stored in a string. Examples of such information are the background colour of the tag body, or the text that constitutes a document fragment.
2 All elements must provide an opening tag and a closing one.
3 Most elements must provide mechanisms to iterate on the contained elements for exploring the page elements and for serializing the page contents.

The main differences among these elements are related to the mechanisms used to iterate on the document structure. Each class must provide specific methods for accessing its content; for instance class Page should provide a method for accessing the Head component and another method for accessing its Body component.

Decision point

Document elements must implement iteration mechanisms.

Iteration can be implemented using two different approaches: using element specific methods or using generic methods.

The first approach consists in defining specific document iteration methods for each class. This approach is straightforward but difficult to implement. In fact, some elements (e.g. Body) contain a set of heterogeneous components (e.g. Text and Link). In order to iterate among them, the container class must recognize their type. This can be done using the reflection capability of the Java language. Unfortunately the use of reflection often results in inelegant code.

The second approach consists in defining an abstract container class (e.g. Element) and to derive a concrete subclass for each element (see Figure 8.9). The abstract container class defines a set of generic methods for document iteration. This solution has been adopted by the World Wide Web Consortium (W3C 2004c). For iteration on elements of an HTML page two methods are defined in the common base class:

- first Child, invoked on the container element, returns the first component;
- nextSibling, invoked on a component element, returns the next component inside the same container.

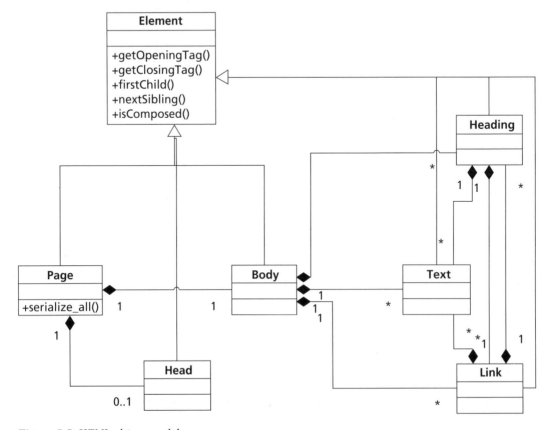

Figure 8.9 HTML object model

A straightforward implementation of these two methods requires that the container holds a reference to the first component, and each component has a reference to the next element. In addition it is useful to have a method to test whether a given element is composite or not; this will make the code that iterates on the elements simpler.

Decision point

How do elements serialize their HTML representation?

The problem is to transform a two-dimensional representation (the tree structure of the objects) into a mono-dimensional or serialized represent-ation (the sequence of characters that form an HTML document). Most of the elements in HTML have an opening and a closing tag; in their serialized form they are represented by putting the children between the opening tag and the closing tag. The object structure can be serialized by means of revisiting the tree.

Two methods should be provided to read the opening and closing tags: getOpeningTag() and getClosingTag(). In the case of Text, both methods should return an empty string. This solution can be combined with the iteration in order to obtain a straightforward serialization method.

The Page class defines a serialization method that is able to serialize the entire web page. The serialization procedure is fairly simple thanks to the methods provided by class Element. For each element the serialization should start by printing the opening tag and terminate by printing the closing tag. In between, if the element is composed, the procedure should iterate on all the contained elements and print them. Since each contained element should be printed using the same procedure, a recursive procedure fits our needs very well. The pseudocode for such a method is the following:

```
serialize_all (Element current ){
  print( current.getOpeningTag() );
  if( current.isComposite() ){
    Element child = firstSibling;
    while(child!=null){
      serialize (child);
      child=child.nextSibling();
    }
  }
  print( current.getClosingTag() )
}
```

This solution would work fine for all elements except Text: it has neither an opening nor a closing tag, but it has a different kind of information that needs to be serialized. A simple and smart solution to this problem is to make the getOpeningTag() method of the class Text return the content of the element. When the serialize_all() method is invoked with a Text as argument it would print the content, then will skip the iteration code (since Text is not composed), finally the getClosingTag() method would return an empty string, thus not affecting the output at all.

Decision point

We want to define a better serialization procedure that does not violate the information hiding principle.

The solution provided above for serialization has some defects; in particular it partly violates the information hiding principle. In fact it accesses the internal structure of each element in order to serialize its children.

A better solution consists in decentralizing the serialization algorithm and delegating each element to serialize itself. Since all the objects are (indirect) instances of Element, and since the algorithm is symmetric, the decentralized algorithm can be defined in Element. Therefore all the objects of the document graph will execute the same algorithm. An improved version of the serialize method of Element can be written as follows:

```
serialize(){
  print( this.getOpeningTag() );
  if( this.isComposite() ){
   Element child = firstSibling;
   while(child!=null){
     child.serialize();
     child=child.nextSibling();
   }
  }
  println( this.getClosingTag() );
}
```

The structure of the method is practically the same as the serialize_all() method. The signature of the method has changed since the previous argument has become implicit, i.e. it is the object on which the method is invoked (this).

Decision point

How can we capture the common characteristics of the elements?

While two elements (Text and Head) are simple elements, the others can contain other elements. This common feature can be captured introducing a new class, Composite.

Each composite object can contain elements, therefore we add an association from Composite to Element. But a composite can be contained within other composites, i.e. it behaves like an element, therefore class Composite inherits from class Element. The new classes are shown in Figure 8.10.

There are several advantages with this solution. The atomic elements and the composite elements are clearly distinguished in the class diagram. The class structure is less complex and easier to understand than the previous one. Finally, the methods to compose elements and serialize composite elements are written once in Composite.

Other elements can be added to the class structure easily, i.e. the elements Ul and Li representing a bulleted list and the items of a list respectively.

The main difference between this design solution and the previous design class diagram is that, based on the semantics of inheritance and aggregation, any composite object can (in principle) contain any other composite or component object. Consequently, containment constraints need to be graphically documented by means of notes attached to the classes in the class diagram.

8.4.3 □ Implementation

Here we present the implementation of the classes that have been defined for this prototype. All the classes that implement the HTML object model are in the package HtmlDOM:

```
package HtmlDOM;
```

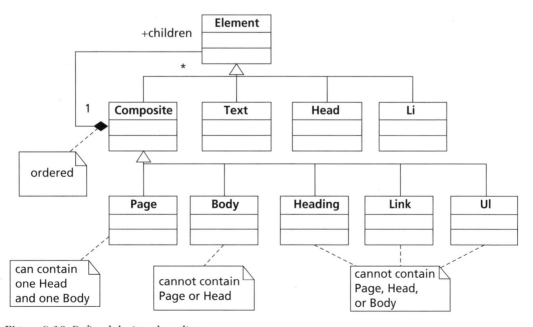

Figure 8.10 Refined design class diagram

The central class in our design is Element, which represents the generic element of an HTML page. It offers methods for iteration and serialization: getOpeningTag(), getClosingTag() and serialize(). This class, together with Composite forms an instance of the *Composite* pattern. The attribute `info` contains generic information, whose specific semantics are defined in each concrete derived class. The attribute `tag` contains the name of the tag, (e.g. BODY, H1).

The one-to-many association children between Composite and Element is implemented by decomposing it into two associations: a child one-to-one association from Composite to Element and a sibling recursive association on Element (see idiom *One-to-many association decomposition* in Chapter 4 (p. 84)). The latter is implemented by attribute sibling.

```java
public abstract class Element {
    protected String info;
    protected String tag;
    Element sibling;
    Element(String p_info, String p_tag){
        info = p_info;
        tag = p_tag;
    }
    public String getOpeningTag() { return "<" + tag + ">"; }
    public String getClosingTag() { return ""; }
    public void serialize(PrintWriter os){
        os.print(getOpeningTag());
        os.print(" ");
    }
    public boolean isComposite() { return false; }
    public boolean hasNext() { return sibling != null; }
    public Element nextSibling() { return sibling; }
    void addSibling(Element newSibling){
        sibling = newSibling;
    }
}
```

The other class that forms the core of the composite pattern is Composite, which represents the composite HTML element. This class redefines the isComposite() method to always return true. It also redefines the serialize() method to iterate over the components. Two new methods are added: addChild() to add a new component and firstChild() to navigate the first semi-association resulting from the split of the children association.

```java
public abstract class Composite extends Element {
    Element child;
    Composite(String info, String tag){
        super(info, tag);
    }
```

```java
  public boolean isComposite() { return true; }
  public Element firstChild() { return child; }
  public void addChild(Element newChild) {
    if(child == null)
      child = newChild;
    else {
      Element currentChild;
      currentChild = child;
      while(currentChild.hasNext())
        currentChild = currentChild.nextSibling();
      currentChild.addSibling(newChild);
    }
  }
  public String getClosingTag() { return "</" + tag + ">"; }
  public void serialize(PrintWriter os){
    os.print(getOpeningTag());
    Element currentChild;
    CurrentChild = firstChild();
    while(currentChild! = null){
      currentChild.serialize(os);
      currentChild=currentChild.nextSibling();
    }
    os.println(getClosingTag());
  }
}
```

The remaining classes extend either **Element** or **Component**. They represent concrete elements that appear in HTML pages.

```java
public class Br extends Element {
  public Br(){
    super(null, "BR"); }
}
public class Link extends Composite {
  public Link(String href){
    super(href,"A");
  }
  public String getOpeningTag() {
    return "<" + tag + " href=\"" + info + "\" >"; }
}
public class Ul extends Composite {
  public Ul(){
    super(null,"UL");
  }
}
public class Head extends Element {
  public Head(String title){
    super(title, "HEAD");
  }
```

```
      public String getOpeningTag() {
        return "<head><title>" + info + "</title></head>"; }
      public String getClosingTag() { return ""; }
   }
   public class Heading extends Composite {
      public Heading(){
        super(null,"H1");
      }
   }
   public class Li extends Composite {
      public Li(){
        super(null,"LI");
      }
   }
   public class Body extends Composite {
      public Body(String bgcolor){
        super(bgcolor,"BODY");
      }
      public String getOpeningTag() {
        return "<" + tag + " bgcolor=\"" + info + "\" >";
      }
   }
   public class Text extends Element {
      public Text(String text){
        super(text,null);
      }
      public String getOpeningTag() { return info; }
   }
   public class Font extends Composite {
      public Font(String size, String color, String face){
        super(null,"FONT");
        String param = "";
        if(size != null)
          param = param + " size=\"" + size + "\"";
        if(color != null)
          param = param + " color=\"" + color + "\"";
        if(face != null)
          param = param + " face=\"" + face + "\"";
        info = param;
      }
      public String getOpeningTag() {
        return "<" + tag + info + " >";
      }
   }
   public class Page extends Composite {
      public Page(){
        super(null, "HTML");
   }}
```

8.4.4 □ Test

To test the intermediate representation we have to check the correctness of both the internal static representation and the serialized form. The simplified test class TestDOM performs these two checks for the specific case of the page described in Figure 8.6. The test method testStaticStructure() checks if the structure of the internal representation conforms to the structure presented in Figure 8.7. The test method testSerialize() checks if the result of the serialization is as expected; it verifies the presence of given substrings in the output (as done in Chapter 6 for the calculator).

```java
public class TestDOM extends TestCase {
  public void testStaticStructure() {
    Page P = new Page();
    Head T = new Head("Test");
    Body B = new Body("white");
    P.addChild(T);
    P.addChild(B);
    Heading H = new Heading();
    Text T1 = new Text("This is a test");
    H.addChild(T1);
    B.addChild(H);
    Text T2 = new Text("This is plain text");
    B.addChild(T2);
    Link L = new Link("http://www.w3.org");
    Text T3 = new Text("Click here...");
    L.addChild(T3);
    B.addChild(L);
    assertEquals(T,P.firstChild());
    assertEquals(B,P.firstChild().nextSibling());
    assertEquals(H,B.firstChild());
    assertEquals(T1,H.firstChild());
  }
  public void testSerialize() {
    Page P = new Page();
    Head T = new Head("Test");
    Body B = new Body("white");
    P.addChild(T);
    P.addChild(B);
    Heading H = new Heading();
    Text T1 = new Text("This is a test");
    H.addChild(T1);
    B.addChild(H);
    Text T2 = new Text("This is plain text");
    B.addChild(T2);
    Link L = new Link("http://www.w3c.org");
    Text T3 = new Text("Click here...");
```

```
          L.addChild(T3);
          B.addChild(L);
          ByteArrayOutputStream buffer =
                                    new ByteArrayOutputStream();
          P.serialize(new PrintStream(buffer));
          String[] expected= {
            "<HTML>", "<HEAD><TITLE>Test</TITLE></HEAD>",
            "<BODY","bgcolor=\"white\"",
            "<H1>","This is a test","</H1>",
            "This is plain text",
            "<A HREF=\"http://www.w3c.org\"", "Click here...",
            "</A>", "</BODY>", "</HTML>"
          };
          System.out.println(buffer.toString());
          assertContainsInOrder(buffer.toString(),expected);
        }
      protected  void assertContainsInOrder(String output,
                                        String[] strings){
        int lastIndex = -1;
        int currentIndex = -1;
        output = output.toUpperCase();
        for (int i = 0; i < strings.length; i++) {
          currentIndex = output.indexOf(strings[i].
                                toUpperCase(),lastIndex+1);
          assertTrue("Couldn't find [" + i + "]:"+ strings[i]
                                      ,currentIndex>-1);
          lastIndex = currentIndex;
        }
      }
    }
```

8.5 ■ Prototype 2: Language front end

The analysis and design of the language front end component will be carried
out for the sample documentation case laid out in the specification section.

8.5.1 ☐ Analysis

The front-end module has the purpose of parsing the source code of a Java
class and to generate the corresponding HTML documentation.

Looking at Figure 8.11, the parsing task consists of finding out the name
of the class and then, inside the class, identifying the declarations of the
public members. Since we are interested only in the signature of methods
and of variables, the parser must extract only a part of the members. In
particular, all the text following the "public" keyword and preceding either a

```
// this is a test class...
class TestClass {
  String an_attribute;
  public int a_public_attribute;
  public void a_method(int a_parameter){
    String s;
    s = "string content"; }
  abstract private int another_method();
}
```

Figure 8.11 Parsing of Java source code

";", a "{", or an "=". Once the relevant fragments of the Java class have been extracted, the generation of the documentation consists in inserting these pieces of information inside a fixed framework of HTML code.

8.5.2 □ Design

We can identify three main features of the front-end module:

■ it must parse the code recognizing the relevant parts;
■ it must interact with the HTML object model to generate documentation;
■ it must be customizable for parsing different programming language and for generating documentation with different styles and formats.

Decision point

> The front-end component must enforce separation of concerns between the parsing and documenting functionalities.

We generalize the problem and define the abstract class Parser and the interface Documenter. The parser provides the methods to parse source code and identify its elements; the documenter is responsible for generating the documentation for each element identified by the parser.

The parser and the documenter interact according to the pattern *Observer* (Gamma *et al.* 1995) using the event notification mechanism supported by the java.util package (see Sidebar 8.1). The documenter plays the role of the observer that receives notification of new elements found by the parser. The parser plays the role of the observable that generates events.

The adopted solution is described in Figure 8.12. Class JavaLanguage extends Parser and implements the abstract method parse to identify the Java language elements and notify them to the documenter. Class SimpleDocumenter receives the notifications from the parser and builds an intermediate representation of the documentation. The information on the language elements are enclosed in JavaParseEvent objects.

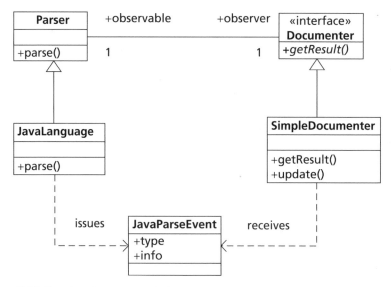

Figure 8.12 Front-end component classes

Class JavaParseEvent carries two pieces of information: the type of event (e.g. the start of parsing, class found ...) and additional information specific for the event (e.g. the name of the class found). The complete list of event types and their related information is given in Table 8.1.

8.5.3 ☐ Implementation

All the classes in the front-end component are in the same package frontend. Class Parser extends class Observable and defines the abstract method parse() that takes as argument one StringTokenizer. In addition it provides another parse() method that adapts the previous to use a string containing the code to be parsed.

```
public abstract class Parser extends Observable {
    public final void parse(String code){
        StringTokenizer scanner = new StringTokenizer(code);
        parse(scanner);
    }
    public abstract void parse(StringTokenizer scanner);
}
```

Table 8.1 Java parse event types

Event type	Description	Specific information
BEGIN_PARSING	The parser is about to begin parsing	
FOUND_CLASS	A class has been found	The name of the class
FOUND_MEMBER	A member of the class has been found	The signature of the member
END_PARSING	The parse has finished parsing	

Sidebar 8.1 Observer/observable

Java provides the java.util.Observable class and the java.util.Observer interface for implementing the event notification mechanism. The Observable is the broadcaster object that provides information to a set of listener objects (Observers). The underlying architectural model is known as Model–View–Controller and has been documented as pattern *Observer*.

Class Observable offers method notifyObservers() to inform observer objects that some data have changed. When this occurs, observers update their state to reflect the new data. State transitions are defined in the update() method that every subclass of interface Observer must implement.

The call to notifyObservers() results in a call to the update() method of each Observer. This means that the Observable object remains blocked until all of the Observer objects have completed the execution of their update() methods.

The code below implements an example, where the Equipment class plays the role of the observable that changes state at random time instants. Class Controller plays the role of the observer that is notified of the observable's state changes. Class Monitor initializes the communication between Equipmet and Controller by adding Controller in the Equipment's list of observer objects.

```java
import java.util.*;
public class Equipment extends Observable implements Runnable {
  int counter = 0;
  public void run() {
    while(true) {
      try {
        System.out.println("Equipment: state change :
                                              " + (++counter));
        this.setChanged();
        this.notifyObservers(new Integer(counter));
        Thread.sleep(Math.round(Math.random()*2000.0 + 500.0));
      }
      catch(InterruptedException i.e.) {}
    }
  }
}
public class Controller implements Observer{
  public void update(Observable observable, Object object) {
    Integer value = (Integer) object;
    if(Math.IEEEremainder(value.intValue(), 2.0) == 0.0)
      System.out.println("Even value " + value.intValue());
    else
      System.out.println("Odd value " + value.intValue());
  }
}
public class Monitor {
  public static void main(String[] args) {
    Equipment equipment = new Equipment();
    Controller controller = new Controller();
    equipment.addObserver(controller);
    Thread thread = new Thread(equipment);
    thread.start();
  }
}
```

The specific parser for the Java language is implemented by JavaLanguage. This class implements the method parse(). It is a very simple parser that recognizes the name of the class and the signatures of the public members. Whenever the parser method recognizes an entity, it notifies the documenter using a new JavaParseEvent object. To make the code more compact the notification is performed by the two methods doNotify().

```java
public class JavaLanguage extends Parser {
  public void parse(StringTokenizer scanner){
    doNotify(JavaParseEvent.BEGIN_PARSING);
    // define and initialize flags
    boolean classNameFound = false;
    boolean nextIsName = false;
    boolean publicMember = false;
    StringBuffer member = null;
    while(scanner.hasMoreTokens()){
      String token = scanner.nextToken();
      // Initially seek for the name of the class
      if(!classNameFound){
        if(token.equals("class"))
          nextIsName = true;
        else if(nextIsName){
          doNotify(JavaParseEvent.FOUND_CLASS,token);
          nextIsName = false;
          classNameFound = true;
        }
      }else // then starts looking for public members
      if(token.equals("public")){
        publicMember = true;
        member = new StringBuffer();
      }else if(publicMember){
        if(token.indexOf(";")>=0){
          member.append(token.substring(0,token.indexOf
                                                 (";")));
          doNotify(JavaParseEvent.FOUND_MEMBER,
                                      member.toString());
          publicMember = false;
        }else  if(token.indexOf("{")>=0){
          member.append(token.substring(0,token.indexOf
                                                 ("{")));
          doNotify(JavaParseEvent.FOUND_MEMBER,
                                      member.toString());
          publicMember = false;
        }else{
          member.append(token);
          member.append(" ");
        }
      }
    }
  }
  doNotify(JavaParseEvent.END_PARSING);
}
```

```java
private void doNotify(int type, String info){
    setChanged();
    notifyObservers(new JavaParseEvent(type,info));
}
private void doNotify(int type){
    setChanged();
    notifyObservers(new JavaParseEvent(type));
}}
```

Class JavaParseEvent contains the information about the events that occurs during parsing. There are four types of events (as defined in Table 8.1). The additional information is specific for each type of event and consists of a string.

```java
public class JavaParseEvent {
    public static final int BEGIN_PARSING = 0;
    public static final int FOUND_CLASS = 1;
    public static final int FOUND_MEMBER = 2;
    public static final int END_PARSING = 3;
    public int type;
    public String info;
    public JavaParseEvent(int type, String info){
        this.type = type;
        this.info = info;
    }
    public JavaParseEvent(int type){
        this.type = type;
        this.info = null;
    }
}
```

The interface Documenter represent a generic documenter, it extends the Observer interface and defines the method getResult() that returns the element containing the generated documentation.

```java
public interface Documenter extends Observer {
    Element getResult();
}
```

The last class in this component is SimpleDocumenter. This class implements the Documenter interface providing implementation of the abstract method in that class. The constructor initializes some attributes that represent the colours of the background, title and information text.

```java
public class SimpleDocumenter implements Documenter {
    // These attributes define the colour schema.
    private String bgColor, titleColor, infoColor;
    // Initializes the documenter, the parameters define the
    // colour schema that will be used in the HTML page.
```

```
public SimpleDocumenter( String p_bgColor,
                String p_titleColor,
                                String p_infoColor) {
  bgColor = p_bgColor;
  titleColor = p_titleColor;
  infoColor = p_infoColor;
}
// The three elements (placeholders) that will be set up by
// the setupFramework method and filled in during parsing
// by the appropriate methods
// Container that will contain the text representing the
// title of the HTML page, i.e. the name of the class
private Composite titlePlaceholder;
// Container that will contain the list of public members
private Composite membersPlaceholder;
// The head of the page, will contain the name of the
// class
private Head head;
// contains the overall structure of the page
private Body body;
// contains the result at the end of the parsing
Page page;
//  Creates the overall structure of the page, which is
//  independent of the specific information. Inside this
//  generic structure some placeholders are inserted that
//  will be filled in during parsing
private void setupFramework() {
  head = null;
  body = new Body(bgColor);
  // create the title placeholder and insert it into the
  // body
  Heading title = new Heading();
  Composite titleFont = new Font("+2", titleColor,
                                        "Tahoma");
  title.addChild(titleFont);
  body.addChild(title);
  titlePlaceholder = titleFont;
  // add a short introductory text that say that a list of
  // public members follows
  Composite introduction = new Font("+2", titleColor,
                                        "Arial");
  introduction.addChild(new Text("Public members:"));
  body.addChild(introduction);
  body.addChild(new Br());
  // create the public members list placeholder and insert
  // it into the body
```

```
    Composite listFormatting = new Font("+2", infoColor,
                                        "Courier New");
    Ul list = new Ul();
    listFormatting.addChild(list);
    body.addChild(listFormatting);
    membersPlaceholder = list;
    // add a small embellishment: a link to Java homepage at
    // Sun
    Composite link = new Link("http://java.sun.com");
    link.addChild(new Text("Java &copy; Sun"));
    body.addChild(link);
}
// handle the name of the class by filling in the title
// of the HTML page and the heading at the top of the page
private void gotClassName(String className) {
    titlePlaceholder.addChild(new Text(className));
    head = new Head("Class: " + className);
}
// handle a public member: put the member inside a LI
// element, then add this element in the placeholder for
// the public elements
private void gotMember(String member) {
    // creates a new LI item
    Li item = new Li();
    // add the last chunk to the list item
    item.addChild(new Text(member));
    // putting a line break at the end
    item.addChild(new Br());
    // add the item to the placeholder
    membersPlaceholder.addChild(item);
}
// compose the components into a single page at the end
// of the parsing
private void composePage() {
    page = new Page();
    if (head != null)
        page.addChild(head);
    page.addChild(body);
}
// receives the notification of parsing events and calls
// the appropriate helper method
public void update(Observable observable, Object arg) {
    JavaParseEvent event = (JavaParseEvent) arg;
    if (event.type == JavaParseEvent.BEGIN_PARSING)
        setupFramework();
```

```
        if (event.type == JavaParseEvent.FOUND_CLASS)
          getClassName(event.info);
        if (event.type == JavaParseEvent.FOUND_MEMBER)
          getMember(event.info);
        if (event.type == JavaParseEvent.END_PARSING)
          composePage();
      }
      // return the resulting page
      public Element getResult() {
        return page;
      }
    }
```

8.5.4 □ Test

To test the front end component we provide the source code of a class and observe the documentation produced. The test class **TestParse** uses the class described in Section 8.4.4. The result produced by the documenter is checked using the same technique adopted in the previous prototype, i.e. by checking the presence of a set of substrings in a given order.

The expected strings are a little tricky: when we want to match a tag we have to take into account that some of them can contain parameters. Thus if we expect a simple tag (e.g. "<BODY>") and the output contains that tag with parameters (e.g. "<BODY bgcolor="white">") the match fails. To solve this problem we include in the expected strings only the opening character of the tag and its name omitting the closing character of the tag (e.g. "<BODY").

```
public class TestParse extends TestCase {
  public void testSimple(){
    String source =
      "//          this is a test class...\n" +
      "class TestClass {\n" +
      "  String an_attribute;\n" +
      "  public int a_public_attribute;\n" +
      "  public void a_method(int a_parameter){\n" +
      "    String s;\n" +
      "    s = \"string content\";  }\n" +
      "  private int another_method() { return 0; }\n" +
      "}\n";
    Parser parser = new JavaLanguage();
    SimpleDocumenter doc = new SimpleDocumenter
                                ("cyan","navy","green");
    parser.addObserver(doc);
    parser.parse(source);
    Element page = doc.getResult();
    assertTrue(page!=null);
```

```
ByteArrayOutputStream buffer = new
                                    ByteArrayOutputStream();
page.serialize(new PrintStream(buffer));
System.out.println(buffer.toString());
String[] expected = {
  "<HTML>",
  "<head><title>Class: TestClass</title></head>",
  "<BODY","<H1>",
  "<FONT","color=\"navy\"","TestClass","</FONT>",
  "</H1>",
  "<FONT","color=\"navy\"","Public members:","</FONT>",
  "<FONT","color=\"green\"",
  "<UL>","<LI>","int a_public_attribute",
  "<LI>","void a_method(int a_parameter)","</UL>",
  "</FONT>",
  "</BODY>",
  "</HTML>"};
assertContainsInOrder(buffer.toString(),expected);
  }
}
```

8.6 ■ Prototype 3: Graphical driver

The core functionality of the application is provided by the HTML object model component and the front-end component, which were developed in the previous phases. To use the application, and possibly test it, a user interface is needed. The user interface must draw the core components and route input and outputs. We have chosen to provide a graphical user interface for several reasons:

■ it is a common practice to have a user interface even for the simplest application;
■ it is easier to use and to understand;
■ it allows the resulting HTML to be shown;
■ the user can easily play with the application by dropping Java code and observe the documentation generated by the application.

8.6.1 □ Analysis

Since the specification gives no details about the user interface, we are free to use whatever solution we prefer. We will opt for the simplest solution that allows:

■ visualizing the documentation;
■ easily inserting and modifying Java classes to be documented; and
■ activating the documentation process.

The minimal user interface that satisfies these requirements is a window containing three components:

■ an HTML panel;
■ a text panel with editing capabilities; and
■ a button for triggering the documentation process.

An example of such an interface is shown in Figure 8.13.

8.6.2 □ Design

Using the Java UI classes, in particular the Swing set of components, makes the realization of the above-described interface fairly simple.

The graphical component classes that we will use are:

■ JeditorPane, which is able to display HTML content;
■ JtextArea, which is a text area with editing capabilities;
■ Jbutton, which is a button.

The whole window can be realized by means of a class that extends the JFrame class.

In order to make the JEditorPane and the JTextArea scrollable they have to be embellished by the JScrollPane class. The description of further details concerning the implementation of the user interface is beyond the scope of this chapter.

8.6.3 □ Implementation

The graphical driver consists of a single class, TestFrame, which extends that Swing class JFrame. It contains three visual components: a text area, an HTML panel and a button. The text area contains the source code of a Java class. Pressing the button fills the HTML panel with the documentation of the class. This class also implements the interfaces ActionListener and HyperlinkListener which define the methods that handle a click on the button and a click on a link in the HTML pane respectively.

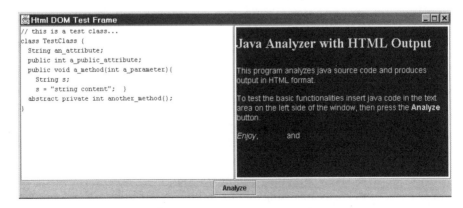

Figure 8.13 The user interface

```java
import HtmlDOM.Element;
import FrontEnd.SampleDocumenter;
import javax.swing.*;
import javax.swing.text.*;
import java.awt.*;              //for layout managers
import java.awt.event.*;        //for action and window events
import javax.swing.event.*;
import javax.swing.text.html.*;  // for HyperlinkListener
import java.net.URL;
import java.io.*;
class TestFrame extends JFrame implements
ActionListener, HyperlinkListener {
  private final static String htmlMessage =
    "<html><head>" +
    "<body bgcolor=navy text=yellow>" +
    "<h1>Java Analyzer with HTML Output</h1>" +
    "<font face=\"Arial,Helvetica\">" +
    "<p>This program analyzes java source code and +
    " produces output in HTML format.</p>"  +
    "<p>To test the basic functionalities insert java " +
    "code in the text area on the left side of the " +
    "window, then press the <b>Analyze</b> button.</p>" +
    "<p><i>Enjoy</i>, " +
    "<a href=\"http://thalia.unibg.it/~brugali/\"> " +
    "Davide</a></font> and " +
    "<a href=\"http://www.idi.ntnu.no/~marco/\">" +
    "Marco</a></font>" +
    "</body>" +
    "</html>" ;
  private final static String javaCode =
    "// this is a test class...\n" +
    "class TestClass {\n" +
    "  String an_attribute;\n" +
    "  public int a_public_attribute;\n" +
    "  public void a_method(int a_parameter){\n" +
    "    String s;\n" +
    "    s = \"string content\";\n" +
    "  }\n" +
    "  abstract private int another_method();\n" +
    "}\n" ;
  // the HTML panel visual component
  private JEditorPane htmlPane;
  // the text is a visual component
```

```java
private JTextArea sourceArea;
// the button visual component
private JButton button;
// the constructor assembles the visual components and
// sets up the event handling
public TestFrame(){
  super("Html DOM Test Frame");
  //Create a text area.
  sourceArea = new JTextArea(javaCode);
  sourceArea.setFont(new Font("Courier", 0, 12));
  sourceArea.setLineWrap(false);
  JScrollPane areaScrollPane = new JScrollPane
                                          (sourceArea);
  // create the HTML visualization pane
  htmlPane = new JEditorPane();
  htmlPane.setEditable(false);
  htmlPane.addHyperlinkListener(this);
  JScrollPane editorScrollPane = new JScrollPane
                                          (htmlPane);
  htmlPane.setContentType("text/html");
  htmlPane.setText(htmlMessage);
  // create the button
  button = new JButton("Analyze");
  button.setActionCommand("Analyze");
  button.addActionListener(this);
  // define the frame layout
  GridBagLayout gridbag = new GridBagLayout();
  GridBagConstraints c = new GridBagConstraints();
  Container frame = getContentPane();
  frame.setLayout(gridbag);
  // add components to frame
  c.gridx = 0;
  c.gridy = 0;
  c.weightx = 1;
  c.weighty = 1;
  c.fill = GridBagConstraints.BOTH;
  gridbag.setConstraints(areaScrollPane,c);
  frame.add(areaScrollPane);
  c.gridx = 1;
  gridbag.setConstraints(editorScrollPane,c);
  frame.add(editorScrollPane);
  c.gridx = 0;
  c.gridy = 1;
  c.fill = GridBagConstraints.NONE;
  c.anchor = GridBagConstraints.CENTER;
  c.gridwidth = 2;
```

```java
        c.weighty = 0;
        gridbag.setConstraints(button,c);
        frame.add(button);
        pack();
        this.setSize(800,600);
        // add listener for window closing event
        addWindowListener(new WindowAdapter() {
                public void windowClosing(WindowEvent e) {
                System.exit(0);
            }
        });
    }
    // Event handler for the button.
    // It creates the documentation for the source code
    // contained in the text area and puts the result into
    // the HTML panel.
    public void actionPerformed(ActionEvent e){
        Parser parser = new JavaLanguage();
        Documenter printer=new SimpleDocumenter
                                        ("cyan","navy","green");
        parser.addObserver(printer);
        parser.parse(sourceArea.getText());
        Element page=printer.getResult();
        ByteArrayOutputStream buffer =
                                    new ByteArrayOutputStream();
        page.serialize(new PrintStream(buffer));
        htmlPane.setText(buffer.toString());
    }
    // event handler for hyperlinks activation in the HTML
    // panel
    public void hyperlinkUpdate(HyperlinkEvent e) {
        if (e.getEventType() ==
                            HyperlinkEvent.EventType.ACTIVATED) {
            JEditorPane pane = (JEditorPane) e.getSource();
            try {
                pane.setPage(e.getURL());
            } catch (Throwable t) { t.printStackTrace(); }
        }
    }
    //  main program for the application:
    //  it just creates the window.
    public static void main(String [] args){
        TestFrame frame = new TestFrame();
        frame.setVisible(true);
    }
}
```

8.6.4 □ Test

The test of a graphical user interface is a very complex subject; here we describe a simple approach. The test class **TestGUI** contains the test method **testSimple()** that applies the same test case used in the previous prototype. The test checks the text in the HTML pane using the same techniques as the previous prototypes. Since the **JEditorPane** can modify the text introducing or removing spaces, special care must be devoted to avoid spaces in the expected substrings.

```java
public class TestGUI extends TestCase {
  //...
  public void testSimple(){
    String source =
      "//        this is a test class...\n" +
      "class TestClass {\n" +
      "  String an_attribute;\n" +
      "  public int a_public_attribute;\n" +
      "  public void a_method(int a_parameter){\n" +
      "    String s;\n" +
      "    s = \"string content\";  }\n" +
      "  private int another_method() { return 0; }\n" +
      "}\n";
    // creates the window
    TestFrame window = new TestFrame();
    // activate it
    window.setVisible(true);
    // set the source code
    window.sourceArea.setText(source);
    // simulate a click on the button
    window.button.doClick();
    // get the text from the htmlPane
    String result = window.htmlPane.getText();
    // destroy the window
    window.dispose();
    String[] expected = {
      "<HTML>",
      "<head>","<title>","Class: TestClass",
      "</title>","</head>",
      "<BODY>","<H1>",
      "<FONT","color=\"navy\"","TestClass","</FONT>",
      "</H1>",
      "<FONT","color=\"navy\"","Public members:","</FONT>",
      "<UL>",
      "<LI>","<FONT","color=\"green\"",
      "int","a_public_attribute",
      "</FONT>",
```

```
            "<LI>","<FONT","color=\"green\"",
            "void","a_method(","int","a_parameter)",
            "</FONT>",
            "</UL>",
            "</BODY>",
            "</HTML>"};
        assertContainsInOrder(result,expected);
    }
}
```

8.7 ■ Extension

The HtmlDOM, as it is implemented now, does not check the semantic correctness of composition; for instance it is possible to add a Page into a Link, which is clearly wrong. To enforce semantic correctness of composition try to convert the notes in Figure 8.10 into code that checks the correctness of the structure of the HTML page. This can be performed in two ways: first by writing methods that statically verify whether the structure of the page conforms to the constraints; second by modifying the existing methods in order to check dynamically if any operation violates some constraints (hint: in this case the add() operation is the only one that can perform violations).

8.8 ■ Assessment

Architectural style. The application is built around the internal representation of an HTML page. This is a typical example of data-centred architectural style. A component (HTML DOM) is devoted to contain the data, while the other components produce, modify and consume the data.

Generic component. The model that resulted from the analysis of the problem, based on an example, was too specific. We derived a more generic solution by using several patterns.

Communication mechanism. The communication between the components is based on the method invocation.

Concurrency. Since the application performs a unique functionality, we did not need any concurrency; the components work one at a time.

During the design phase of the first prototype we used several patterns: the *Class generalization* and *Delegation* idioms, and the *Composite* design pattern. These patterns are widely used in many similar cases. They should be part of the everyday vocabulary of both system designers and programmers.

The implementation of the first prototype made use of the *One-to-many association* idiom. The solution adopted in the design of the language front end is an application of the pattern *Observer*. The architecture of the system is simple because of the choice to adopt an internal representation that is isomorphic to the output format.

Idiom	Delegation
Context	An operation is to be performed involving many interconnected objects. Even if a few interactions with each single object are required, if several objects are involved the complexity rises quickly. We require an algorithm that can be performed ideally based only on local information. In practice it will be based on as little global information as possible.
Problem	A centralized algorithm performed on an interconnected graph of objects involves a large number of interactions.
Forces or tradeoffs	The algorithm is centralized and can be located externally to the object graph or in a node of it. The algorithm involves visiting all or most of the objects of the graph. As a result, a lot of, possibly complex, interactions take place with the objects that form the graph. The classes of the nodes of the graph feature low encapsulation, since the algorithm needs to access the information in all the nodes. There is high coupling between the class that hosts the algorithm and all the other classes: any change may cause a ripple effect of related changes.
Solution	A divide and conquer technique can be applied. Each object part of the graph is responsible for a small part of the overall task. The algorithm needs to be transformed from a centralized to a decentralized form. Each object will be responsible for operating on itself and will reduce the interaction to direct neighbours.
Force resolution	The algorithm is decentralized and the duties are distributed among the nodes of the object graph. Each object accesses its own information. This increases encapsulation and lowers coupling. The complexity of interaction is reduced drastically.
Design rationale	Since we have an algorithm that operates on local information, we leverage this characteristic and break up the algorithm. Each node of the object graph will execute a part of the task.

Pattern	Composite
Context	A tree structure contains different objects. Some objects are leaves, others intermediate. Both leaves and intermediate nodes can have different types.
Problem	Application needs to manipulate a hierarchical collection of primitive and composite objects.

Forces or tradeoffs	Composite can also be a component. Different kinds of nodes. Ordering of different kinds of nodes is difficult. Nodes should be seen uniformly. Visiting of nodes can require many special cases.
Solution	The following structure of classes should be adopted.

	All the concrete leaves can be subclasses of Leaf while all concrete composites can be subclasses of Composite. If there is only one leaf (composite) class then the Leaf (Composite) class can be substituted by this class.
Force resolution	It is possible to visit all the nodes of the hierarchy seamlessly. Node classes must conform to the common interface. It is easy to add new kinds of nodes. It is much easier to understand.
Design rationale	This pattern results from the application of two idioms: class generalization and relationship factoring. It minimizes redundancy and provides a simpler and more uniform interface to the structure.

8.9 ■ References

Gamma, E., Helm, R., Johnson, R. and Vlissides, J. (1995) *Design Patterns: Elements of Reusable Object-Oriented Software*, Addison-Wesley.

W3C (2004a) *HyperText Markup Language (HTML)*, http://www.w3.org/MarkUp/.

W3C (2004b) *Extensible Markup Language (XML)*, http://www.w3.org/XML/.

W3C (2004c) Document Object Model (DOM), http://www.w3.org/DOM/.

Manufacturing work cell

9

Synthesis

Any complex application requires prototyping and simulation. Simulation is typically used in three different situations:

- When part of the application's functionality is in time-consuming computations, or is not ready yet.
- When the application is a distributed system and needs to be tested locally on a single computer.
- When the application interacts with real devices, which cannot be used for testing and debugging.

A typical example is a manufacturing work cell made up of a number of physical devices (robots, machines, transporters) and a work cell controller, which coordinates and synchronizes the concurrent activities of the work cell system (e.g. moving piece, machining, loading). The prototype that simulates the work cell system is an executable specification on a single processor of the naturally concurrent reality. This chapter addresses the problem of building a discrete event simulation environment for testing the correct behaviour of a work cell controller.

- Focus: the emphasis is on the software architecture of the simulator that is general enough to be applied in a variety of application scenarios.
- OO techniques: finite state automata to model the components' dynamics.
- Java features: information hiding and inheritance.
- Background: the chapter refers to well-known domain models for event communication, synchronization and time simulation.

9.1 ■ Specifications

A manufacturing work cell is a control system at the shopfloor level of a factory. It is made up of a certain number of machine tools, stores and automatic transportation systems, which concurrently process pieces in lots. Each piece undergoes a sequence of operations that implements the manufacturing process. For simplicity, each machine can perform only one type of operation. The processing time depends on the type of operation.

Let's consider the case of a work cell for machining and assembling bolts. The cell is made up of two numerically controlled machines for machining nuts (the drill) and screws (the cutter), a machine for assembling bolts (the assembler), and an automatic guided vehicle system (AGV) for moving pieces between machines. Each machine has an input buffer for raw pieces and an output buffer for finished pieces. The buffers have finite capacities. The machines can execute only one task at a time (machining a nut or a screw and assembling a nut with a screw). The AGV can transport only one piece at a time. An automated inventory system supplies raw pieces to and collects finished pieces from the work cell.

Pieces are taken sequentially, at random instants of time, from the inventory system and placed in the input buffer of the machine where the first operation is performed (the drill or the cutter). The machines are able to pick up one piece at a time from their input buffers and to place them in the operation position. As soon as one operation is finished, the piece is evacuated from the machine and dropped in the output buffer. When the input buffer is empty or the output buffer is full, the machine stops.

The AGV transports semi-finished pieces (nuts and screws) from the drill and cutter to the assembler. It is equipped with a robotic arm that unloads pieces from the drill and cutter output buffers and loads pieces onto the assembler input buffer. For the sake of simplicity, we assume that the AGV transports only one piece at a time. The inventory system picks up bolts from the assembler output buffer at random instants of time.

The work cell controller, with a real-time dispatcher, assigns pieces to the machines as soon as they become idle, and issues requests for missions to the AGV system. The objective of this case study is to develop a prototype of the work cell controller in order to test the correct behaviour of the real-time dispatcher before installation in the real work cell controller.

9.1.1 □ Operations synchronization

The task of the real-time dispatcher is to synchronize the machines' activities. For this purpose, the following considerations should be taken into account.

- The drill and the cutter need raw pieces to produce nuts and screws. As long as raw pieces are available in their input buffers, the drill and the cutter continue the production of nuts and screws.
- The assembler needs a nut and a screw to produce a bolt. As long as nut and screw pairs are available in its input buffer, the assembler continues the production of bolts.
- If the three machines never fail, if they have the same processing time τ, if the automated inventory systems supplies raw pieces and consumes bolts with the same frequency η and if the following relation holds: $\eta = 1/\tau$, then the machines' buffers never get empty or full, the machines never stop, and the throughput is equal to η.
- In any other situation, when the machines are unreliable, or the machine processing times and the inventory supply and consumption frequency differ, the buffers might get full or empty and the machines might need to stop and restart.

9.1.2 □ **The simulator**

The work cell controller is a software application that runs on a workstation interconnected with the physical devices through specialized networks. The physical devices are reactive systems that receive stimuli from the work cell controller (e.g. "start the next operation on a new piece") and responds to them by updating their state ("machine working") and giving feedback ("work done"). The dynamic of the physical devices is modelled as a sequence of states, which they visit during a period of observation.

Event-driven systems are special kinds of reactive systems, where the interaction with the external world (stimuli and feedback) takes place through events. An event is characterized by two parameters: *type* (what happened) and *time* (when did the event happen). State transitions are triggered by occurrences of discrete events at given time instants. The behaviour of the entire work cell system emerges from the exchange of events between the physical devices and the work cell controller.

We want to develop an event-driven simulator that models and executes the behaviour of the physical devices and of the work cell controller. The simulation consists of the evolution of the work cell state from an initial configuration that defines the levels of the input and output buffers. The evolution is caused by the occurrence of discrete events and terminates after a predefined number of state transitions or when there are no enabled events.

9.2 ■ **Problem analysis**

The work cell simulator is an event-driven system that models and executes the concurrent behaviour of a number of interconnected subsystems (machine, AGV, inventory system, etc.).

The dynamic of each subsystem comprises short-lived actions such as picking up a piece from the input buffer, or moving the AGV to the target station. Groups of these actions, which are triggered by events, are present inside a sequential process (e.g. piece machining, piece assembly and piece transporting).

Each process is a finite state automaton that offers the protected environment to short-lived actions and hides the local state from other processes.

The processes synchronize with each other through shared resources and event communication. In the work cell, the input and output buffers play the role of shared resources between the machines, the assembler and the AGV.

9.2.1 □ **The production cycle**

Three types of operation characterize the manufacturing process under consideration: piece machining, bolt assembling and piece moving. Each operation consists of a sequence of actions.

Piece machining (nut drilling and screw cutting) operations consist of the following sequence of actions:

- The machine picks up a piece from the input buffer. If the input buffer is empty, it waits for a piece.
- The machine manufactures the piece and produces a nut (screw). The operation duration is known.
- The machine drops the nut (screw) in the output buffer, if it is not full; otherwise it waits for a position available in the output buffer.
- The machine performs the above steps sequentially and repeats the sequence until the program halts.

Bolt assembling operations consist of the following sequence of actions:

- The assembler picks up either a nut or a screw from the input buffer. If the input buffer is empty, it waits for a piece.
- The assembler picks up a second piece (nut or screw), which must be different from the first one. If the piece is not available, the assembler waits for that piece.
- The assembler assembles a nut and a screw and produces a bolt. The operation duration is known.
- The assembler drops the bolt in the output buffer, if it is not full; otherwise it waits for a position available in the output buffer.
- The assembler repeats the above sequence of steps until the control program halts.

Piece moving operations consist of the following sequence of actions:

- The AGV elaborates the next operation, if any. Otherwise, it waits for the next operation.
- The AGV moves to the unloading station.
- The AGV unloads a piece from a machine output buffer.
- The AGV moves to the loading station.
- The AGV unloads the piece in the assembler input buffer.
- The AGV repeats the above sequence of steps until the control program halts.

The automated inventory system feeds the drill and cutter input buffers with new raw pieces at random instants of time. Similarly, it extracts finished pieces from the assembler output buffer at random instants of time. We are now able to formally specify the behaviour of each component of the work cell. This is an important step towards the definition of the simulation model. The complexity of this modelling activity lies in the difficulty of enumerating all the admissible combinations of the basic ingredients: states, events and transitions.

9.2.2 □ The drill and cutter finite state automata

The drill and cutter machine are made up of an input buffer, a production unit and an output buffer (see Figure 9.1). The input and output buffers have

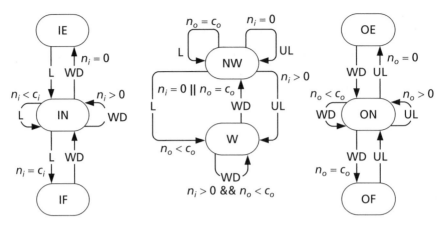

Figure 9.1 The automata of the input buffer, the production unit and the output
buffer

finite capacity. Parameters c_i and c_o represent their capacity, while n_i and
n_o represent the current number of pieces respectively. The model of the
production unit has two states, WORKING (W) and NOT WORKING (NW); the
model of the input buffer has three states, EMPTY (IE), NOT EMPTY NOT FULL
(IN), and FULL (IF); similarly, the model of the output buffer has three states
(OE, ON and OF).

Three events determine the dynamics of these automata:

- WORKDONE (WD) is notified when the production unit completes the
  machining of a piece and places it in the output buffer. If the input buffer
  is empty or the output buffer is full, the production unit enters the NW
  state.
- LOADED (L) is notified when a new piece is loaded from the inventory to
  the input buffer. This event may fire the transition of the production unit
  from the NW to the W state.
- UNLOADED (UL) is notified when a piece is unloaded from the output
  buffer to the AGV. This event may fire the transition of the production
  unit from the NW to the W state.

At any instant of time the machine current state is the union of the
current states of the three automata depicted in Figure 9.1. If we compute
the Cartesian product of these states, we come up with a new automaton
characterized by eighteen states, three events and a large number of possible
state transitions. In reality, five out of those eighteen states are inadmissible
because they represent situations like:

- The machine is working when the output buffer is full.
- The machine is not working when the output buffer is not full.

Note that the state (IN – W – OF) is inadmissible because it corresponds to
the situation where the production unit is machining a piece but there is no
room in the output buffer to place it when the work is done. Of course, it

may happen that the output buffer gets unloaded before the production unit completes the work, but if this does not happen the WD event cannot be raised when the work is done.

Table 9.1 lists the states that describe the machine behaviour. It identifies the enabled events for each admissible state. The resulting automaton comprises eleven states.

9.2.3 □ The assembler finite state automaton

The assembler automaton comprises four states (see Figure 9.2):

- E: the input buffer is empty.
- N: the input buffer contains only nuts.
- S: the input buffer contains only screws.
- W: the assembler is working.

Three events determine state transitions:

- SL: a screw has been loaded in the input buffer.
- NL: a nut has been loaded in the input buffer.
- WD: a bolt has been assembled.

The x and y state variables represent the number of nuts and screws in the input buffer. The automaton depicted in Figure 9.2 does not take into account the possibility that the input and output buffers get full and therefore the assembler cannot work. Similarly, it does not model the BROKEN and REPAIRED states.

Table 9.1 The list of states of the machine and the enabled events

States				Enabled events	
INPUT FULL	WORKING	OUTPUT FULL		*Inadmissible*	
INPUT FULL	WORKING	OUTPUT NOT FULL		WORKDONE	UNLOADED
INPUT FULL	WORKING	OUTPUT EMPTY		WORKDONE	
INPUT FULL	NOT WORKING	OUTPUT FULL			UNLOADED
INPUT FULL	NOT WORKING	OUTPUT NOT FULL		*Inadmissible*	
INPUT FULL	NOT WORKING	OUTPUT EMPTY		*Inadmissible*	
INPUT NOT FULL	WORKING	OUTPUT FULL		*Inadmissible*	
INPUT NOT FULL	WORKING	OUTPUT NOT FULL	LOADED	WORKDONE	UNLOADED
INPUT NOT FULL	WORKING	OUTPUT EMPTY	LOADED	WORKDONE	
INPUT NOT FULL	NOT WORKING	OUTPUT FULL	LOADED		UNLOADED
INPUT NOT FULL	NOT WORKING	OUTPUT NOT FULL		*Inadmissible*	
INPUT NOT FULL	NOT WORKING	OUTPUT EMPTY		*Inadmissible*	
INPUT EMPTY	WORKING	OUTPUT FULL		*Inadmissible*	
INPUT EMPTY	WORKING	OUTPUT NOT FULL	LOADED	WORKDONE	UNLOADED
INPUT EMPTY	WORKING	OUTPUT EMPTY	LOADED	WORKDONE	
INPUT EMPTY	NOT WORKING	OUTPUT FULL	LOADED		UNLOADED
INPUT EMPTY	NOT WORKING	OUTPUT NOT FULL	LOADED		UNLOADED
INPUT EMPTY	NOT WORKING	OUTPUT EMPTY	LOADED		

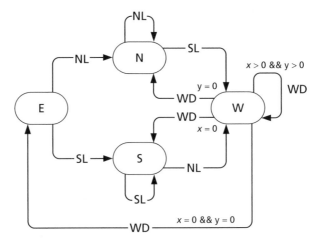

Figure 9.2 The assembler automaton

9.2.4 □ The AGV finite state automaton

The AGV executes operations on demand. The drill and the cutter machines issue requests of piece transfer from their output buffers to the assembler's input buffer as soon as they complete manufacturing operations. The AGV records the requests of operations and executes them one at a time. Four basic states characterize the AGV behaviour: it is waiting at a station or it is moving towards a station; it is empty or it is full (carrying a piece). In order to represent the correct sequence of operations, it is necessary to determine whether the AGV is waiting at the unloading stations (the drill and the cutter machines) or at the loading station (the assembler). In fact, different events are enabled in these situations. Accordingly, Figure 9.3 depicts the AGV automaton that comprises five states. The state variable x represents the number of mission requests still pending.

■ WE_LS: the AGV is empty and is waiting at the loading station of its last mission. This state corresponds to the situation when it has completed all the requested missions.
■ ME: the AGV has started a new mission and it is moving towards the unloading station. The AGV records any new mission request that is issued meanwhile.
■ WE_US: the AGV has arrived at the unloading station. It is ready to unload a new piece from the drill or the cutter machines.
■ MF: the AGV has unloaded a piece from the machine and is carrying it at the assembler.
■ WF: the AGV has arrived at the assembler station and is loading the piece in its input buffer.

Four events determine state transitions:

■ WD: a machine has completed an operation and issues a new mission request.

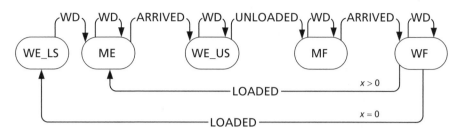

Figure 9.3 The AGV automaton

- ARRIVED: the AGV has arrived at the next loading/unloading station.
- UNLOADED: a piece has been unloaded from a machine output buffer to the AGV.
- LOADED: a piece has been loaded from the AGV buffer to the assembler input buffer.

9.2.5 ☐ The inventory finite state automaton

The automated inventory system supplies raw pieces to the work cell at random instants of time. The arrival frequency might correspond, for example, to the production rate of an upstream work cell of the same shopfloor that supplies raw pieces. Similarly, finished pieces leave the work cell at random instants of time according to the production rate of a downstream work cell that consumes them.

Figure 9.4 depicts two automata that model the behaviour of the automated inventory system. They each comprise two states. The automaton at the left-hand side of the picture models the piece feeding into the drill or cutter input buffers. The other automaton models the extraction of finished pieces from the assembler output buffer. The state variable x represents the number of raw pieces in the drill and cutter input buffers, while y represents the number of finished pieces in the assembler output buffer.

- W: the automated inventory system is working, i.e. it is loading raw pieces into the drill and cutter input buffer or unloading finished pieces from the assembler output buffer.

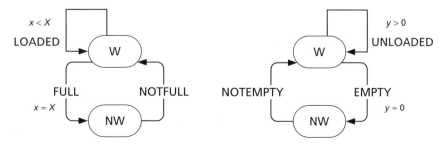

Figure 9.4 The automated inventory system automaton

■ NW: the automated inventory system is not working either because the drill or cutter input buffers are full, or because the assembler output buffer is empty.

Six events determine state transitions:

■ LOADED: the inventory system has loaded a piece into the drill or cutter input buffer.
■ UNLOADED: the inventory system has unloaded a piece from the assembler output buffer.
■ FULL: the drill or cutter input buffer is full.
■ NOTFULL: the drill or cutter input buffer is not full.
■ EMPTY: the assembler output buffer is empty.
■ NOTEMPTY: the assembler output buffer is not empty any more.

9.2.6 □ Domain models

The work cell system is a typical example of production line that produces high volumes of a specific type of product (e.g. bolts). Work pieces follow a predefined sequence of operations and thus the production line is called a *flow line* (see Figure 9.5).

A number of simulation models have been proposed in the literature, such as continuous or discrete, synchronous or asynchronous, deterministic or stochastic, etc. The flow line described in this chapter is a typical discrete, asynchronous and stochastic production line. The manufacturing process is simulated piece by piece. An infinite source of raw parts feeds the first machine and an infinite sink collects finished products at the end of the line.

The simulation of a discrete event dynamic system consists of modelling the permanence of the system in a state as the interval time between the occurrences of two subsequent discrete events. For example, the execution of the screw cutting operation corresponds to the permanence of the cutter in the WORKING state. When a LOADED event is notified the cutter enters the WORKING state and activates the WORKDONE event, whose lifetime is equal to the duration of the cutting operation. The cutter leaves the WORKING state when the WORKDONE event is notified.

When the system is made up of a number of interacting subsystems, event notification must refer to the same simulation time. Thus, the simulation

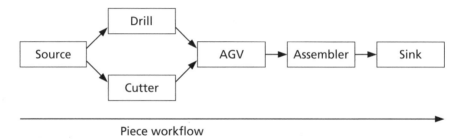

Piece workflow

Figure 9.5 A flow line

clock is centralized and shared among all the subsystems of the production line. When an event is notified, the affected subsystems trigger state transitions and update their current states. A new event might be activated. Then the simulation clock is advanced to the time of the next event to be notified. This procedure is repeated until the end of the simulation.

9.2.7 □ Main features

We are now able to summarize all the main features that have emerged from the problem analysis.

- *Event-driven architecture*. The simulator enforces a strict separation of concerns between the components (discrete processes) that model finite state automata and the components that execute them.
- *Work cell simulation*. The finite state automata that model the behaviour of each work cell subsystem: the drill, the cutter, the assembler, the AGV and the Inventory. The behaviour of the whole system will emerge from the interactions between the subsystems.
- *Graphical user interface*. The step-by-step evolution of the simulation is under the control of the user who fires the next scheduled event with a simple mouse click. The graphical representation of the work cell physical structure depicts the components and displays the last event that has been fired and depicts the current state of the work cell system (the position of the AGV, which machines are working, etc.).

9.2.8 □ Test

In order to verify the correct behaviour of the simulator, we need to test the behaviour of each single automaton and the interactions among them, and in particular:

- The conservative behaviour of the system: the number of pieces in the system should always be equal to the difference between the number of pieces that entered and exited the system.
- The correct order of the scheduled events.

9.3 ■ Architecture and planning

The architecture of the discrete event simulator is structured according to the simulation model described in the previous section. The basic components are the event clock, the subsystems of the production line (inventory system, machines, transport and assembler), and the graphical user interface (see Figure 9.6).

The development process of the work cell simulator is organized into three phases that produce three prototypes. The first phase focuses on the

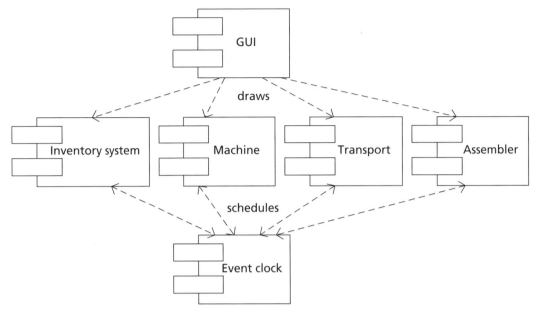

Figure 9.6 The system architecture

simulator architecture, the second phase on the manufacturing processes implementation, and the last phase on the system integration.

- *Prototype 1: Event-based simulation*. This consists of a simple application that exemplifies the event-based simulation mechanisms. The simulation is limited to the automated inventory system. Simulation data are shown in a textual user interface.
- *Prototype 2: Work cell simulator*. This adds a graphical user interface to Prototype 1 and extends the simulator with all the work cell components.

9.4 ■ Prototype 1: Event-based simulation

The first prototype exemplifies the functioning principles of the event-based simulator. The test-bed consists in simulating the behaviour of the automated inventory system that supplies raw pieces to the drill and cutter machines.

9.4.1 □ Analysis

The simulator is a single-threaded application that runs on a PC. It is made up of a collection of finite state automata and a centralized clock, which schedules and fires events. Figure 9.7 depicts the analysis model described hereafter.

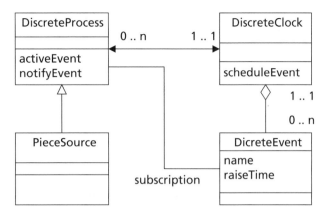

Figure 9.7 The analysis diagram of the first prototype

DiscreteEvent is the basic entity that records the name of an event (e.g. WORKDONE) and its raise time. DiscreteProcess represents the generic finite state automaton and has two main functionalities:

■ To update the automaton current state when an enabled event is notified.
■ To activate events when a state transition occurs.

DiscreteClock represents the centralized clock and has two main functionalities:

■ To schedule events. It is the bookkeeper of the current time and of the scheduled events. It knows what event is next to be raised and when. It also knows which processes are listening to which event.
■ To raise events when their lifetime has expired. It notifies the processes that are listening to them.

PieceSource represents the automated inventory system that feeds the drill and cutter input buffers with raw pieces. It generates LOADED events at random time instants.

The resulting application has a graphical user interface that displays the sequence of events that are fired from the beginning to the end of the simulation. For each event, the interface shows the event name, the raise time and the name of the process that is broadcasting the event.

9.4.2 □ Design

We need the class WorkCell to represent the entire manufacturing work cell. It encapsulates the discrete processes embedding the dynamics of the work cell subsystems (see Figure 9.8). This class listens to all the events raised by the work cell subsystems and manages the graphical user interface that displays the state of the sequential processes every time a state transition occurs. WorkCell encapsulates the global clock that synchronizes the event-based communication between the discrete processes.

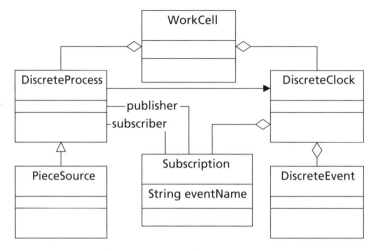

Figure 9.8 The class diagram of the first prototype

Class EventObject has been part of the java.util package since version 1.1 of the Java 2 Platform. This is the root class of a deep hierarchy of classes for handling event-based communication between the components of any graphical user interface. The event model of the work cell simulator is substantially different from the event model of the java.util package. Thus, we decide to introduce the new class DiscreteEvent, which records the following information:

■ the name of the event;
■ the raise time;
■ the data associated with the event;
■ the name of the process that activates this event.

The clock maintains a sorted collection of events that is updated whenever a new event is activated. The first event is the event that will be raised next, that is the event with the shortest time residue. The current time is always equal to the raise time of the last fired event, which is triggered by the user who controls the simulation. When an event is raised, the clock notifies the event to all the subscribed processes.

Decision point

How does a process activate events?

When a state transition is triggered, the process undertakes some activities that will be completed after a given time period. The end of these activities corresponds to the notification of a corresponding event. For example, when the AGV receives a request of mission, a state transition is triggered that sets the current state to MOVING EMPTY and activates the ARRIVED event. The lifetime of this event is set equal to the duration of the move operation.

The process activates the ARRIVED event by adding it to the clock's list of scheduled events. Similarly, PieceSource activates a LOADED event to notify the drill and cutter that a piece has been loaded into their input buffers. PieceSource listens to its own events. When a LOADED event is notified, a state transition activates the next LOADED event.

Figure 9.9 shows the object interaction diagram representing the operations that class PieceSource executes when it is initialized. First it attaches itself to the LOADED event. Then it activates the first LOADED event that will be raised after a random time period.

Decision point

How does the clock notify events?

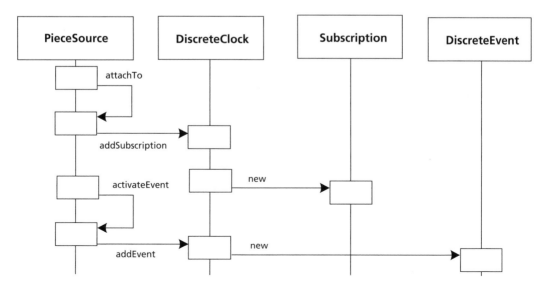

Figure 9.9 The initialization of the automated inventory system

Each process has a unique name that distinguishes it from the other processes. The DiscreteEvent class records the name of the process that activated the event. This information is used to distinguish events that can be raised by different processes but have the same name. For instance, the drill, the cutter and the assembler all activate WORKDONE events, but the AGV is listening only to those raised by the drill and the cutter.

In some cases the event name and the owner name are not enough to distinguish events. For example, the AGV raises the UNLOADED event when a nut or a screw is unloaded from a machine. The drill and the cutter are listening to this event and they should be able to recognize when a piece is unloaded from their output buffers. Thus the UNLOADED event carries the information about the type of piece that has been unloaded.

Class Subscription records the association between the event name, the publisher (the process that broadcasts the event) and the listener (the process that is listening to the event). Before the simulation starts, processes should subscribe to the events they are listening to. The clock maintains a collection of event/listener subscriptions.

Every process implements a callback function that the clock invokes when an event is raised. This function implements the finite state machine that models the process behaviour. It determines which state transition should be triggered when a given event is notified.

The clock implements an iterative procedure (see Figure 9.10) that consists of three steps:

- Whenever a process activates a new event, the clock re-schedules the list of events.
- It waits for the user's command to process the event with the shortest time residue.
- The clock notifies the event to all the subscribed processes (e.g. the PieceSource itself).

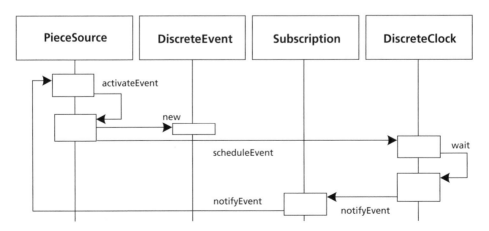

Figure 9.10 The iterative event activation/notification cycle

9.4.3 □ Implementation

Class DiscreteEvent is the basic component of the architecture. It implements the Comparable interface in order to define a natural sorting criterion for event objects. The clock's list of events will use the compareTo() method to insert event objects in their ordered position.

```java
package workcell;
public class DiscreteEvent implements Comparable {
  String name;              // the name of the event
  long raiseTime;           // the absolut raise time
  Object value;             // the data associated to the event
  String ownerName;         // the process that activates this
                            // event
  public DiscreteEvent(String name, long raiseTime,
                       String ownerName, Object value){
    this.name = name;
    this.raiseTime = raiseTime;
    this.ownerName = ownerName;
    this.value = value;
  }
  public int compareTo(Object obj) {
    if(this.raiseTime < ((DiscreteEvent) obj).raiseTime)
      return -1;
    if(this.raiseTime > ((DiscreteEvent) obj).raiseTime)
      return 1;
    return 0;
  }
}
```

Class DiscreteProcess is the parent class of every sequential process. It is abstract since every subclass needs to redefine the notifyEvent() method that implements the specific finite state automaton. The attachTo() method registers this instance of DiscreteProcess in the clock's subscription list. The activateEvent() method creates inserts a new instance of DiscreteEvent in the clock's list of active events.

```java
package workcell;
public abstract class DiscreteProcess {
  String name;                // the name of this process
  DiscreteClock clock;        // a reference to the global clock
  public DiscreteProcess(String name, DiscreteClock clock) {
    this.name = name;
    this.clock = clock;
  }
  public void attachTo(String eventName,
                            DiscreteProcess publisher) {
    clock.subscribe(this, eventName, publisher);
  }
```

```
   protected void activateEvent(String eventName,
                            long lifetime, Object value) {
     clock.activate(this, eventName, lifetime, value);
   }
   protected abstract void notifyEvent(DiscreteEvent event);
}
```

Class DiscreteClock implements the event clock. The inner class Subscription records the association among an event, a subscriber process and a publisher process. The clock maintains a list of subscriptions and offers the subscribe() method to register new subscriptions. It also maintains a list of events and offers the activate() method to schedule a new event.

```
import java.util.ArrayList;
import java.util.Collections;
public class DiscreteClock {
  // definition of the class Subscription.
  class Subscription {
    String eventName;           // the name of an event
    DiscreteProcess subscriber; // the process listening to
                                // the event
    DiscreteProcess publisher;  // the process that
                                // broadcast the event
    public Subscription(DiscreteProcess s, String event,
                        DiscreteProcess p) {
      this.subscriber = s;
      this.eventName = event;
      this.publisher = p;
    }
    public void notifyEvent(DiscreteEvent event) {
      // Verifies if "subscriber" is listening to "event".
      // If event name is equal to "any","subscriber" is
      // listening to all the events raised by "publisher"
      if( (eventName.equals(event.name) ||
          eventName.equals("any")) &&
          publisher.name.equals(event.ownerName) )
        subscriber.notifyEvent(event);
    }
  } // end of class Subscription
  ArrayList subscriptions = new ArrayList();
  // list of process subscriptions
  ArrayList eventQueue = new ArrayList();
                                  // list of active events
  public long currentTime = 0;    // the current global time
  public DiscreteClock() {}       // the constructor
```

```
public void subscribe(DiscreteProcess s, String event,
                      DiscreteProcess p) {
  // Process "s" subscribes only to events activated
  // after this subscription
  subscriptions.add(new Subscription(s, event, p));
}
public void activate(DiscreteProcess p, String event,
                     long lifetime, Object obj){
  // Publisher "p" activates "event" that will be raised
  // after "lifeTime" seconds
  eventQueue.add(new DiscreteEvent(event,
               currentTime+lifetime, p.name, obj));
  Collections.sort(eventQueue);
}
public void next() {
  // the GUI invokes this method to process the next event
  while(eventQueue.size() > 0) {
    DiscreteEvent mostRecentEvent =
                 (DiscreteEvent) eventQueue.remove(0);
    currentTime = mostRecentEvent.raiseTime;
    for(int i=0; i < subscriptions.size(); i++)
      ((Subscription) subscriptions.get(i)).
                         notifyEvent(mostRecentEvent);
  }
}
}
```

Class **PieceSource** implements the finite state machine of the inventory system that loads raw pieces into the machines' input buffers. The current version does not deal with the situation when the input buffers get full. It generates new **LOADED** events at random time instants. The constructor initializes the process name, the piece type and the loading rate, that is the maximum number of pieces loaded per minute. The minimum rate is set to half of the maximum rate. The actual rate is computed as a random number between the minimum and maximum rate. An event's lifetime is computed as the inverse of the actual loading rate.

```
package workcell;
public class PieceSource extends DiscreteProcess  {
  int numPieces = 0;      // the total number of loaded pieces
  String pieceType;       // type of piece (nut or screw)
  double maxRate;         // max number of pieces per minute
                          // (in millisecs)
  public PieceSource(String name, String type,
                   DiscreteClock clock, double rate) {
    super(name, clock);
    this.pieceType = type;
```

```
    this.maxRate = rate / 60000;
    attachTo("LOADED", this);
                            // it listens to its LOADED event
    long lifetime = Math.round( (1.0 + 0.5*Math.random()) /
                                                    maxRate);
    // activates the first event
    activateEvent("LOADED", lifetime, pieceType);
  }
  protected void notifyEvent(DiscreteEvent event) {
    // when a "LOADED" event is notified, it activates
    //the next "LOADED" event.
    if(event.name.equals("LOADED")) {
      numPieces++;
      long lifetime = Math.round( (1.0 + 0.5*Math.random()) /
                                                    maxRate);
      this.activateEvent("LOADED", lifetime, pieceType);
    }
  }
}
```

Class **WorkCell** creates two processes that generate nut and screw pieces.

```
package workcell;
public class WorkCell{
  PieceSource nutSource;
          // a reference to the source of pieces for nuts
  PieceSource screwSource;
          // a reference to the source of pieces for screws
  public WorkCell(String name, DiscreteClock clock) {
    nutSource = new PieceSource("NutSource","Nut",clock,30);
    screwSource = new PieceSource("ScrewSource", "Screw",
                                              clock, 50);
  }
}
```

9.4.4 □ **Test**

The test case consists in the visualization of the sequence of events that the nut source and the screw source generate during the simulation. The maximum rate of generated pieces is set to 30 for the nut source and to 50 for the screw source.

We consider two situations:

■ The lifetime of a **LOADED** event (e.g. the delay between two generated pieces) is constant and proportional to the maximum rate. Accordingly, the delay between two nut pieces is equal to 2000 milliseconds, while the delay between two screw pieces is equal to 1200 milliseconds. Table 9.2 (left side) lists the sequence of events corresponding to the generation of nut and screw pieces.

Table 9.2 Constant and random delay

Constant delay		Random delay	
Piece	**Time**	**Piece**	**Time**
Screw	1 200	Screw	1 398
Nut	2 000	Nut	2 860
Screw	2 400	Screw	3 026
Screw	3 600	Screw	4 585
Nut	4 000	Nut	4 936
Screw	4 800	Screw	6 137
Nut	6 000	Nut	7 614
Screw	6 000	Screw	7 839
Screw	7 200	Screw	9 090
Nut	8 000	Nut	10 477
Screw	8 400	Screw	10 807

■ The event lifetime is random and is evaluated according to the expression coded in class PieceSource. The delay between two nut pieces is between 2000 and 3000 milliseconds, while the delay between two screw pieces is between 1200 and 1800 milliseconds (see Table 9.2 right side).

9.5 ■ Prototype 2: Work cell simulator

The second prototype implements the finite state automata that describe the behaviour of all the work cell subsystems. We will not implement the full set of requirements specified in Section 9.1. In fact, we will leave a few synchronization aspects out of this prototype in order to give the reader the opportunity to complete them as exercises. This prototype visualizes the evolution of the simulation in a graphical user interface.

9.5.1 □ Analysis

As described in Section 9.2, the work cell is composed of the inventory system, the drill, the cutter, the transport and the assembler. We model the inventory system with three distinct processes: two sources of pieces that supply nuts and screws to the machines' input buffers and a sink that consumes bolts from the assembler's output buffer. Every work cell subsystem behaves as a finite state machine. The AGV has deterministic transport and load times, while the other subsystems have stochastic processing times that can range in a given interval (e.g. between the maximum value and half of it).

The work cell subsystems synchronize their activities by exchanging events. Table 9.3 lists the event types that the work cell subsystems can raise and listen to.

Table 9.3 List of event subscriptions

Event	Broadcaster	Listener
WORKDONE	Drill	Drill, AGV
FULL	Drill	Inventory
NOTFULL	Drill	Inventory
WORKDONE	Cutter	Cutter, AGV
FULL	Cutter	Inventory
NOTFULL	Cutter	Inventory
WORKDONE	Assembler	Assembler
EMPTY	Assembler	Inventory
NOTEMPTY	Assembler	Inventory
ARRIVED	AGV	AGV
UNLOADED	AGV	AGV, Drill, Cutter
LOADED	AGV	AGV, Assembler
UNLOADED	Inventory	Inventory, Assembler
LOADED	Inventory	Inventory, Drill, Cutter

Interactions occur as exchanges of events between two or more sub-systems. Each subsystem can play two roles: that of event broadcaster or event listener. The event broadcaster raises an event at random time instants (e.g. the inventory system generates a new raw piece for the drill machine) or owing to a state transition (e.g. the drill notifies the completion of its current operation). One or more subsystems might be listening to events. For example, the automated inventory system is listening to the events raised by the drill in order to know when its input buffer gets full or starts getting empty.

Subsystems might play both roles simultaneously. In particular, a subsystem might be listening to events raised by itself. For example, the drill raises the WORKDONE event when the current operation gets completed. The same event triggers a state transition that starts a new operation.

9.5.2 □ Design

The work cell subsystems are specializations of class DiscreteProcess (see Figure 9.11). Every subclass needs to redefine the notifyEvent() method in order to implement the state transitions of the corresponding finite state automaton.

Decision point

How do we implement finite state automata?

Sidebar 5.2 (see page 99) describes a procedure to translate a subset of UML statecharts into Java code. It consists of a sequence of steps starting

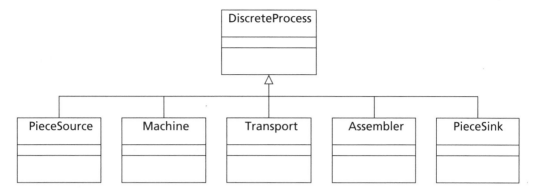

Figure 9.11 The classes that implement the work cell subsystems

with the enumeration of all the automaton states. Then it identifies, for each state, the enabled events and indicates, for each of them, how to implement the transition to the next state.

The finite state automata presented in this case study have more states than events. Thus, we follow the dual approach, i.e. we list the events that the automaton is listening to, and for each event we determine the state transition from the current state to the next.

Decision point

How does the graphical user interface interact with the simulator?

The graphical user interface is represented by class WorkCellGUI (see Figure 9.12), which extends class javax.swing.JFrame. It implements the main() method and initializes the clock and the work cell simulator. Class Workcell extends class DiscreteProcess in order to listen to all the events raised by each subsystem. When an event is notified, the work cell invokes method repaint() of class WorkCellGUI, which refreshes the graphical layout. This method accesses through class WorkCell the state of the work cell components in order to animate the simulation.

9.5.3 □ Implementation

This new implementation of class PieceSource includes the definition of the state transitions triggered by the FULL and NOTFULL events. The working variable is set to true when the drill (or cutter) input buffer is not full. Otherwise it is set to false. It might happen that the input buffer gets full when a new LOADED event has already been activated. Since we do not want to manage event deactivation, we assume that the drill and the cutter raise the FULL event when their input buffers have still one place available.

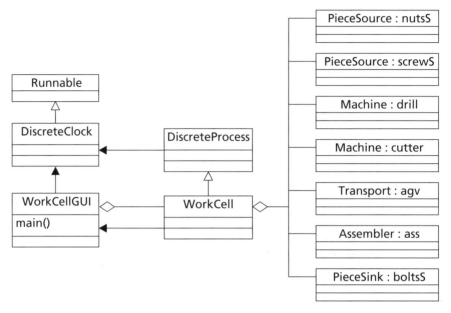

Figure 9.12 The relationships between the work cell simulator and the graphical user interface

```
package workcell;
public class PieceSource extends DiscreteProcess  {
  int numPieces = 0;
                  // the total number of loaded pieces
  String pieceType;
                  // type of piece (nut or screw)
  double maxRate;
                  // maximum number of pieces per minute
  boolean working = true;
                  // true if it is generating new pieces
  public PieceSource(String name, String type,
                  DiscreteClock clock, double rate) {
    super(name, clock);
    this.pieceType = type;
    this.maxRate = rate/60000;
                  // the rate is expressed in milliseconds
    attachTo("LOADED", this);
                  // it listens to its LOADED event
    long lifetime = Math.round( (1.0 + 0.5*Math.random()) /
                                maxRate);
    // activates the first event
    activateEvent("LOADED", lifetime, pieceType);
  }
```

```
protected void notifyEvent(DiscreteEvent event) {
  if(event.name.equals("LOADED")) {
    numPieces++;
    if(working) {
      // the inventory can prepare a new piece to be
      // loaded in the input buffer
      long lifetime = Math.round((1.0 + 0.5*Math.random()) /
                                         maxRate);
      this.activateEvent("LOADED", lifetime, pieceType);
    }
  }
  else if(event.name.equals("FULL")) {
    // the machine's input buffer is full (only one
    // place available)
    working = false;
  }
  else if(event.name.equals("NOTFULL")) {
// the machine's input buffer is not full
    working = true;
    long lifetime = Math.round( (1.0 + 0.5*Math.random()) /
                                         maxRate);
    this.activateEvent("LOADED", lifetime, pieceType);
  }
 }
}
```

Class **Machine** extends the **DiscreteProcess** class and implements the state transitions triggered by the events LOADED, WORKDONE and UNLOADED. The current state is represented by three Boolean variables working, inputFull and outputFull and by the current number of pieces in the input buffer. Both the drill and the cutter listen to the UNLOADED event that the AGV raises when it unloads a piece from their output buffers. In order to distinguish whether the AGV is unloading a piece from the drill or from the cutter, the UNLOADED event carries a datum (the value field) that records the name of the machine. The machine activates the events FULL and NOTFULL that **PieceSource** is listening to and the event WORKDONE that the machine itself is listening to.

```
package workcell;
import java.util.ArrayList;
public class Machine extends DiscreteProcess {
  ArrayList inputBuffer = new ArrayList();
  ArrayList outputBuffer = new ArrayList();
  double maxRate;           // maximum number of pieces per
                            // minute (in milliseconds)
  int inputSize;            // the size of the input buffer
  int outputSize;           // the size of the output buffer
```

```java
    boolean working = false;
                    // true when the machine is working
    boolean inputFull = false;
                    // true when the input buffer is full
    boolean outputFull = false;
                    // true when the output buffer is full
    public Machine(String name, DiscreteClock clock,
                double rate, int in, int out) {
      super(name, clock);
      this.maxRate = rate / 60000;
      this.inputSize = in;
      this.outputSize = out;
      attachTo("WORKDONE", this);
    }
    protected void notifyEvent(DiscreteEvent event) {
      if(event.name.equals("LOADED")) {
        // a raw piece has been loaded in the input buffer
        inputBuffer.add(event);
        // if the machine is not working and the output buffer
        // is not full it starts a new manufacturing operation
        if(! working && ! outputFull) {
          // extracts a raw piece from the input buffer and
          // starts an operation
          inputBuffer.remove(0);
          working = true;
          // the WORKDONE event will notify the completion of
          // this operation
          long processingTime = Math.round( (1.0 +
                        0.5 * Math.random()) / maxRate);
          this.activateEvent("WORKDONE", processingTime,
                                            this.name);
        }
        if(inputBuffer.size() == inputSize-1) {
          // The machine notifies that the input buffer is
          // full when only one position remains available.
          // In fact, it might happen that the piece
          // source has already activated a new LOADED event
          // and we do not want to disable it.
inputFull = true;
          activateEvent("FULL", 0, null);
        }
      }
      else if(event.name.equals("WORKDONE")) {
        // the current operation has been completed
        // it drops the piece in the output buffer
        outputBuffer.add(event);
```

```
if(outputBuffer.size() == outputSize) {
  // if the output buffer is full the machine is
  // not working
  outputFull = true;
  working = false;
}
else if(inputBuffer.size() > 0) {
  // the input buffer is not empty, thus the machine
  // starts a new operation
  working = true;
  inputBuffer.remove(0);
  long processingTime = Math.round( (1.0 +
                        0.5 * Math.random()) / maxRate);
  this.activateEvent("WORKDONE", processingTime,
                                        this.name);
  if(inputFull && inputBuffer.size() < inputSize-2) {
    // notifies the NOTFULL event only if it notified
    // the FULL event before
    inputFull = false;
    activateEvent("NOTFULL", 0, null);
  }
}
else
  // the input buffer is empty
  working = false;
}
else if(event.name.equals("UNLOADED") &&
        event.value.equals(this.name)) {
  // a piece has been unloaded from the output buffer
  // of this machine
  outputBuffer.remove(0);
  // the buffer is not full any more
  outputFull = false;
  if(! working && inputBuffer.size() > 0) {
   // if the machine is not working and the input buffer
   // is not full it starts a new manufacturing operation
   working = true;
   inputBuffer.remove(0);
   long processingTime = Math.round( (1.0 +
                         0.5 * Math.random()) / maxRate);
   this.activateEvent("WORKDONE", processingTime,
                                         this.name);
   if(inputFull && inputBuffer.size() < inputSize-2) {
     // notifies the NOTFULL event only if it notified
     // the FULL event before
     inputFull = false;
```

```
                activateEvent("NOTFULL", 0, null);
            }
        }
    }
  }
}
```

Class Transport extends the DiscreteProcess class and implements the state transitions triggered by the events WORKDONE, ARRIVED, UNLOADED and LOADED. The first event is raised by the drill or cutter, while the other three events are raised by the AGV itself. The current state is represented by two variables: working is true when the transport is executing a mission; loaded is true when the transport is carrying a piece. This implementation of class Transport does not manage the synchronization with the assembler. In fact, it might happen that the assembler's input buffer gets full. In this case the AGV should suspend the execution of its missions until the input buffer starts emptying.

```java
package workcell;
import java.util.ArrayList;
public class Transport extends DiscreteProcess {
  ArrayList missions = new ArrayList();
                                    // the list of missions
  long moveTime; // travel time between two stations
  long loadTime; // duration of loading/unloading operations
  String loadStation = "Assembler"; // the assembler station
  String unloadStation;   // the drill or cutter station
  String currentPosition; // the AGV's current position
  boolean working = false;
                          // true if it is executing a mission
  boolean loaded = false; // true if it is carrying a piece
  public Transport(String name, DiscreteClock clock,
                          long moveTime, long loadTime){
    super(name, clock);
    this.moveTime = moveTime;
    this.loadTime = loadTime;
    this.currentPosition = loadStation;
    attachTo("LOADED", this);
    attachTo("UNLOADED", this);
    attachTo("ARRIVED", this);
  }
  protected void notifyEvent(DiscreteEvent event) {
    if(event.name.equals("WORKDONE")) {
      // drill or cutter have completed a manufacturing
      // operation. This event notification corresponds
      // to a mission request to the AGV
      missions.add(event);
```

```java
    if(! working) {
      // if the AGV is not executing a mission,
      // it leaves its current position
      // and moves to the unloading station
      working = true;
      DiscreteEvent mission = (DiscreteEvent)
                                    missions.remove(0);
      unloadStation = (String) mission.value;
      // activates the event that notifies its arrival
      // at the unloading station
      activateEvent("ARRIVED", moveTime, unloadStation);
    }
}
else if(event.name.equals("ARRIVED")) {
  currentPosition = (String) event.value;
  if(currentPosition.equals(loadStation))
    // the AGV is arrived at the drill (cutter) station
    // and unloads a piece; when the unloading operation
    // has been completed it notifies the machine
    activateEvent("LOADED", loadTime, unloadStation);
  else
    // the AGV is arrived at the assembler station and
    // starts loading a piece; when the loading operation
    // has been completed, it notifies the assembler
    activateEvent("UNLOADED", loadTime, unloadStation);
}
else if(event.name.equals("UNLOADED")) {
  // the AGV has completed the unload operation at
  // the drill or cutter station
  currentPosition = unloadStation;
  loaded = true;
  // the AGV moves towards the assembler station
  activateEvent("ARRIVED", moveTime, loadStation);
}
else if(event.name.equals("LOADED")) {
  // the AGV has loaded a nut or a screw in the
  // assembler input buffer
  currentPosition = loadStation;
  loaded = false;
  // it starts a new mission if there is a request.
  if(missions.size() > 0) {
    DiscreteEvent mission = (DiscreteEvent)
                                  missions.remove(0);
    unloadStation = (String) mission.value;
    // activates the event that notifies its arrival
    // at the unloading station
```

```
        activateEvent("ARRIVED", moveTime, unloadStation);
      }
    else
      working = false;
    }
  }
}
```

Class **Assembler** extends the **DiscreteProcess** class and implements the state transitions triggered by the events **WORKDONE**, **LOADED** and **UNLOADED**. The first event is raised by the assembler, the second by the AGV and the third by the inventory. The current state is represented by two variables: working is true when the assembler is executing an assembling operation; outputEmpty is true when the assembler's output buffer is empty. This implementation of class **Transport** does not manage the synchronization with the transport since it does not activate the events **FULL** and **NOTFULL** that notify the state of the input buffer. It also does not verify if the output buffer is getting full.

```
package workcell;
import java.util.ArrayList;
public class Assembler extends DiscreteProcess {
  ArrayList nutBuffer = new ArrayList();
  ArrayList screwBuffer = new ArrayList();
  ArrayList boltBuffer = new ArrayList();
  double maxRate; // maximum number of pieces per minute
  int inputSize;  // the size of the input buffer
  int outputSize; // the size of the output buffer
  boolean working = false;
  boolean outputEmpty = true;
  public Assembler(String name, DiscreteClock clock,
                            double rate, int in, int out){
    super(name, clock);
    this.maxRate = rate / 60000;
    this.inputSize = in;
    this.outputSize = out;
    attachTo("WORKDONE", this);
  }
  protected void notifyEvent(DiscreteEvent event) {
    if(event.name.equals("LOADED")) {
      // a nut or a screw has been loaded in the input buffer
      if(event.value.equals("Drill"))
        nutBuffer.add(event);
      else if(event.value.equals("Cutter"))
        screwBuffer.add(event);
      // if the machine is not working and there is at least
      // a nut and a screw it starts a new manufacturing
      // operation
```

```
      if(! working && nutBuffer.size() > 0 &&
         screwBuffer.size() > 0) {
    working = true;
    nutBuffer.remove(0);
    screwBuffer.remove(0);
    // the WORKDONE event will notify the completion of
    // this operation
    long processingTime = Math.round( (1.0 +
                          0.5 * Math.random()) / maxRate);
    this.activateEvent("WORKDONE", processingTime, null);
  }
}
else if(event.name.equals("WORKDONE")) {
  // the current operation has been completed
  // it drops the bolt in the output buffer
  boltBuffer.add(event);
  if(outputEmpty && boltBuffer.size() > 2) {
    // the output buffer is not empty
    outputEmpty = false;
    activateEvent("NOTEMPTY", 0, null);
  }
  if(nutBuffer.size() > 0 && screwBuffer.size() > 0) {
    // if the input buffer is not empty the machine
    // starts a new operation
    working = true;
    nutBuffer.remove(0);
    screwBuffer.remove(0);
    long processingTime = Math.round( (1.0 +
                          0.5 * Math.random()) / maxRate);
    this.activateEvent("WORKDONE", processingTime, null);
  }
  else
    // one of the input buffers is empty
    working = false;
}
else if(event.name.equals("UNLOADED")) {
  // a bolt has been unloaded from the output buffer
  boltBuffer.remove(0);
  if(boltBuffer.size() <= 1) {
    // the output buffer is empty
    outputEmpty = true;
    activateEvent("EMPTY", 0, null);
  }
}
    }
  }
}
```

Class **PieceSink** represents the automated inventory system that picks up bolts from the assembler's output buffer. It extends the **DiscreteProcess** class and implements the state transitions triggered by the events UNLOADED, EMPTY and NOTEMPTY. The first event is raised by the inventory itself, while the other two are raised by the assembler. The current state is represented by the variable **working** that is true when the inventory is consuming bolts from the assembler output buffer.

```
package workcell;
public class PieceSink extends DiscreteProcess {
  int numPieces = 0; // the number of pieces unloaded
                     // from the assembler's buffer
  double maxRate;    // maximum number of pieces per minute
  boolean working = false; // true if the sink is working
  public PieceSink(String name, DiscreteClock clock,
                                            double rate) {
    super(name, clock);
    this.maxRate = rate / 60000;
    attachTo("UNLOADED", this);
  }
  protected void notifyEvent(DiscreteEvent event) {
    if(! working && event.name.equals("NOTEMPTY")) {
      // the assembler's output buffer is not empty
      working = true;
      // activates the event that notifies the completion
      // of an unload operation
      long unloadTime = Math.round( (1.0 +
                        0.5 * Math.random()) / maxRate);
      this.activateEvent("UNLOADED", unloadTime, null);
    }
    else if(working && event.name.equals("UNLOADED")) {
      // it has completed an unload operation;
      // activates the next UNLOADED event
      numPieces++;
      long unloadTime = Math.round( (1.0 +
                        0.5 * Math.random()) / maxRate);
      this.activateEvent("UNLOADED", unloadTime, null);
    }
    else if(working && event.name.equals("EMPTY")) {
      // the assembler output buffer is empty
      // (it contains only one piece)
      working = false;
    }
    else if(! working && event.name.equals("UNLOADED")) {
      // it unloads the last piece from the assembler's
      // output buffer
```

```
        numPieces++;
      }
    }
  }
```

Class **WorkCell** creates and initializes all the subsystems. For the sake of simplicity, the process data characterizing the subsystems' behaviour (transport time, processing time, etc.) are hard coded in the current implementation. The work cell listens to all the events raised by the subsystems in order to refresh the graphical user interface that displays the evolution of the simulation every time an event is broadcast.

```java
package workcell;
public class WorkCell extends DiscreteProcess {
  WorkCellGUI gui;
  PieceSource nutSource;
  PieceSource screwSource;
  Machine drill;
  Machine cutter;
  Assembler assembler;
  Transport transport;
  PieceSink sink;
  public WorkCell(String name, DiscreteClock clock,
                  WorkCellGUI gui) {
    super(name, clock);
    this.gui = gui;
    // creates the work cell subsystems
    nutSource   = new PieceSource("NutSource", "Nut",
                                              clock, 80);
    screwSource = new PieceSource("ScrewSource", "Screw",
                                              clock, 70);
    drill       = new Machine("Drill", clock, 40, 4, 4);
    cutter      = new Machine("Cutter", clock, 30, 4, 4);
    transport   = new Transport("AGV", clock, 650, 300);
    assembler   = new Assembler("Assembler",
                                        clock, 35, 4, 4);
    sink        = new PieceSink("Sink", clock, 50);
    // attaches the listeners to the events raised by the
    // broadcasters
    drill.attachTo("LOADED", nutSource);
    drill.attachTo("UNLOADED", transport);
    cutter.attachTo("LOADED", screwSource);
    cutter.attachTo("UNLOADED", transport);
    assembler.attachTo("LOADED", transport);
    assembler.attachTo("UNLOADED", sink);
    transport.attachTo("WORKDONE", drill);
    transport.attachTo("WORKDONE", cutter);
```

```
        nutSource.attachTo("FULL", drill);
        nutSource.attachTo("NOTFULL", drill);
        screwSource.attachTo("FULL", cutter);
        screwSource.attachTo("NOTFULL", cutter);
        sink.attachTo("EMPTY", assembler);
        sink.attachTo("NOTEMPTY", assembler);
        // the work cell attaches itself to all the events
        // raised by the subsystems
        attachTo("any", nutSource);
        attachTo("any", screwSource);
        attachTo("any", drill);
        attachTo("any", cutter);
        attachTo("any", transport);
        attachTo("any", assembler);
        attachTo("any", sink);
    }
    // the work cell delegates the GUI to display the event
    // raised by the subsystems
    protected void notifyEvent(DiscreteEvent event) {
      gui.display(event);
    }
}
```

9.5.4 □ Test

The test case consists of the simulation of the work cell behaviour in a variety of possible configurations. Every configuration differs in the values of the process data of each subsystem and is characterized by the presence of a bottleneck corresponding to the slowest subsystem. Table 9.4 reports the process data of a configuration where the cutter is the slowest subsystem. The rates are expressed in number of pieces per minute while the move and load times are expressed in number of milliseconds. Accordingly, Table 9.5 reports two consecutive sequences of events and two GUI screen shots corresponding to the event raised at instant 3909 and at instant 6109 (both expressed in number of milliseconds since the simulation's start).

Table 9.4 The subsystems process data of a possible configuration

Nut source	Screw source	Drill	Cutter	AGV		Assembler	Bolt sink
Max rate	Max rate	Max rate	Max rate	Move time	Load time	Max rate	Max rate
80	70	40	30	650	300	35	50

Table 9.5 The sequence of events generated during the simulation and two GUI screen shots

Broadcaster	Event	Value	Time
NutSource	LOADED	Nut	809
ScrewSource	LOADED	Screw	1461
NutSource	LOADED	Nut	1694
Drill	WORKDONE	Drill	2309
ScrewSource	LOADED	Screw	2807
AGV	ARRIVED	Drill	2959
NutSource	LOADED	Nut	3181
AGV	UNLOADED	Drill	3259
Cutter	WORKDONE	Cutter	3261
Drill	WORKDONE	Drill	3809
AGV	ARRIVED	Assembler	3909

Broadcaster	Event	Value	Time
ScrewSource	LOADED	Screw	4101
NutSource	LOADED	Nut	4108
AGV	LOADED	Drill	4209
AGV	ARRIVED	Cutter	4859
ScrewSource	LOADED	Screw	4964
Cutter	WORKDONE	Cutter	5061
NutSource	LOADED	Nut	5124
AGV	UNLOADED	Cutter	5159
Drill	WORKDONE	Drill	5309
AGV	ARRIVED	Assembler	5809
AGV	LOADED	Cutter	6109

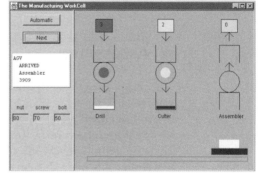

9.6 ■ Extension

A number of functional requirements have not been taken into consideration in Prototype 2. The reader might want to develop a new prototype of the work cell system that solves the design problems that have not been addressed so far. Here is a list of possible extensions.

- Class Assembler should implement the notification of the events FULL and NOTFULL to inform the AGV that the input buffer is full or is getting empty.
- Class Assembler should manage two distinct input buffers for nuts and screws; in fact if we model a single input buffer for both types of piece, it might happen that the input buffer gets full of nuts (or screws). This situation causes a deadlock, because the assembler extracts only pairs of nuts and screws from the input buffer. Thus, if the buffer contains only pieces of the same type, it will never start getting empty and there will never be positions available for pieces of the other type.

■ Class **Transport** should implement the state transitions triggered by the assembler's **FULL** and **NOTFULL** events.

■ Class **Machine** should extend the finite state automaton to consider the possibility of a machine breaking down at random time instants and getting repaired after a certain time period.

■ Class **DiscreteProcess** should offer the possibility of removing an event from the list of active events. If this functionality is available, the implementation of its subclasses should be revised.

■ Class **Piece** could be introduced to represent different types of piece with different processing times and different sequences of manufacturing operations. For example, a piece might need two sequential operations by the same machine.

■ The simulator should elaborate statistical data describing the work cell behaviour in a given time frame. For example, it might report the work cell throughput, the total processing time of each machine, the total number of bolts produced, and the number of times the buffers got full or empty.

9.7 ■ Assessment

The case study exemplified the development of a simulated work cell controller.

Architectural style. The problem specification clearly sketched the physical architecture of the work cell system in terms of physical devices, their individual behaviour and their functional dependencies. The work cell controller has been designed as a virtual machine that simulates the event-driven dynamic of the physical devices.

Generic components. In order to promote software reuse, the design of the work cell simulator defined an architecture that clearly factorizes the basic simulation mechanisms (e.g. the event clock) of any event-driven system from the specific description of the work cell components' dynamics.

Communication. From an implementation point of view, the simulator architecture builds on the model of asynchronous communication between objects.

Concurrency. The behaviour of the work cell components has been formalized by means of finite state automata. This choice appeared particularly appropriate for an event-driven system since a finite state automaton models components in terms of states (the possible configurations of their attributes), transitions (the rules to change the current state), and events (the stimuli that fire transitions). Event-driven systems can be found in a variety of application domains: factory automation, telecommunications, traffic forecasting and control, robotics, video games, simulation of physics principles, etc.

Architecture	Event-driven simulation
Context	Event-driven control systems are special kinds of reactive system, where the interaction with the external world (stimuli and feedback) takes place through events. The external world may assume two distinct forms in a control program: it may be either a reference to an external object, or a wrapper of a physical device.
Problem	Any complex control system requires prototyping and simulation. Simulating the external world can make testing and debugging of the application much easier. A complex control system is characterized by the presence of many different activities being executed concurrently. The behaviour of the whole system emerges from the interaction among independent activities. Interaction requires synchronization.
Forces or tradeoffs	A prototype of the external world and its physical implementation are two distinct aspects of the same concept. Often both are present at the same time during development. A seamless evolution from the simulation to the final implementation should be ensured.
Solution	The control system is made up of a collection of control modules that map external entities. A control module's behaviour is modelled as a finite state automaton. Its dynamic is modelled as a sequence of states, which the control module visits during a period of observation. Control modules interact through event exchange. Events are triggered when a state transition occurs and indicates the start or end of a control module's activities. A centralized event clock manages synchronization. It is the bookkeeper of the current time and of the scheduled events. It knows what event is next to be raised and when.
Force resolution	The interaction between control modules is limited to events exchange. Every control module behaves as a reactive event-driven system. It is easy to substitute the prototype of an external component with the wrapper of its physical implementation.
Design rationale	Prototype and reality have the same event-based interface.

Idiom	Broadcaster–listener
Context	Asynchronous communication between objects.
Problem	A set of dependant objects ("listeners") should be informed of state changes in one or more observed ("broadcaster") objects.

Forces or tradeoffs	The state of a broadcaster object changes according to its own dynamic behaviour. When a state transition occurs, the broadcaster object raises an event. One or more listener objects observe state changes in the broadcaster object. In order to enforce reusability, the broadcaster object does not know which objects are observing its state changes. Listener objects might change over time.
Solution	Event notification is centralized. Broadcaster objects post their events at the centralized clock. Listener objects subscribe to event notification. When a broadcaster object posts an event, the centralized clock notifies the subscribed listeners.
Force resolution	Broadcaster objects post events whenever a state transition occurs using a method of the centralized clock. Listener objects implement a common interface that includes a notification method. When an event is posted, the clock invokes the notification method of each listener. The clock implements methods for event subscription and unsubscription.
Design rationale	In Chapter 8 the broadcaster–listener model has been presented in the context of Pattern *Observer*. Sidebar 8.1 Observer/observable (page 181) describes the classes of the java.util library that implement this communication model.

9.8 ■ Reference

Kouikogloui, V. S. and Phillis, Y. A. (2001) *Hybrid Simulation Models of Production Networks*, Kluwer Academic/Plenum Publishers.

Mobile robot exploration

10

Synthesis

A mobile robot is a complex system that integrates sensors (sonar, laser, etc.), actuators (motors) and processing units (onboard computer and remote control station) and carries on complex tasks (obstacle avoidance, navigation, exploration, etc.) autonomously.

This chapter addresses the problem of developing a software application that simulates the behaviour of the robot system and of its basic components. The emphasis is on the simulator's architecture that is multithreaded and allows plug-and-play integration of software components for the simulation of robotics devices. The synchronous and asynchronous communication between the robot and the remote workstation is simulated using the pipe mechanism. The robot environment is described in XML files and is represented graphically in a user interface.

- Focus: this case study exemplifies the development of a multithreaded application.
- OO techniques: active objects and pipe communication.
- Java features: Java Threads.
- Background: the reader is required to know the basic concepts of concurrency and synchronization and of the XML mark-up language.

10.1 ■ Specifications

Several new applications, such as planetary navigation, construction, toxic waste clean-up and even office automation employ autonomous mobile robots to reduce the need for human intervention in many dangerous or repetitive activities. These applications require the mobile robot to be able to operate in unstructured environments with little *a priori* information. To achieve this ability the robot must exhibit high degrees of autonomy by being able to recover robust and consistent descriptions of its surroundings using sensory information; this kind of task is commonly called exploration of an unknown environment. This means that the robot should exhibit several important functionalities:

- Ability to move in the environment, avoiding obstacles.
- Ability to manage a variety of sensors; a single sensor is rarely enough to acquire useful information from the environment.

■ Ability to record sensor information and build a representation of the environment.

The autonomous robot is made up of a mobile platform, a set of sensors and an onboard computer which elaborates commands and coordinates the robot's devices. A remote control station maintains a description of the robot environment, elaborates exploration strategies and communicates with the onboard computer in order to receive sensory data and submit commands to the robot. The robot control system is thus structured as a master–slave system.

10.1.1 □ Mobile platform

The mobile platform is a four-wheeled rectangular base. The rear wheels are mounted on a common axis controlled by separate motors (differential drive), while the front wheels are castor wheels. The robot motion is determined by controlling the velocities of the two independent motors. Each wheel is connected to a sensor (encoder) that measures the exact number of rotation degrees. Figure 10.1 shows the top and side view of a typical mobile platform. The robot's pose (x, y) and orientation (θ) are represented by a Cartesian reference frame whose origin coincides with the middle point of the rear axis.

The onboard computer implements high-level commands that determine the movements of the mobile platform. Table 10.1 lists the supported commands.

10.1.2 □ Sensors

Autonomous robots are usually equipped with a variety of sensors that guarantee that the robot will perceive useful information in different environmental conditions. The accuracy of the sensory measurements depends on the sensor resolution (the minimum perceived value), the sensor position (e.g. orthogonal to an obstacle), and the physical characteristics of the environment (e.g. the obstacle surface is opaque). For example, lasers are not able to detect opaque surfaces, sonars are not able to detect smooth surfaces, and video cameras require good light conditions. In this case study

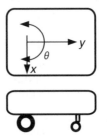

Figure 10.1 The mobile platform structure

Table 10.1 The mobile platform commands

Command	Description
MOVEFW [dist]	Move the robot forward for "dist" millimetres on a straight path
MOVEBW [dist]	Move the robot backwards for "dist" millimetres on a straight path
ROTATELEFT [deg]	Rotate the robot counterclockwise for "deg" degrees
ROTATERIGHT [deg]	Rotate the robot clockwise for "deg" degrees

we consider a robot equipped with a telemeter device and a ring of ultrasonic devices.

A telemeter device is composed of a laser range finder and a tower that rotates the laser around a vertical axis. Each telemetric reading measures the distance to the nearest obstacle in front of the telemeter device (see Figure 10.2). The laser range finder is highly precise (let's say a precision of 1 millimetre) but the perception range is usually short (e.g. 1 metre). Similarly, the rotary tower is highly precise (one-tenth of a degree) but usually slow (10 degrees per second).

Combining the orientation of the rotary tower with the distance to the obstacle in front of the laser it is possible to calculate the Cartesian coordinates of a 2D point belonging to the obstacle surface. These point coordinates are related to the robot reference frame (see Figure 10.2). A sequence of consecutive measures acquired while the tower is rotating allows the robot to track the edges of the obstacles that fall within the laser's range of action.

The onboard computer supports the high-level commands listed in Table 10.2.

A sonar device is a sensor that emits ultrasonic signals and listens to their echo. The distance to the obstacle that reflects the signal is proportional to the signal flight time. Sensor devices are quite cheap and thus it is common to equip a robot with a ring of twelve, sixteen or twenty-four sonars that cover the entire working area around the mobile platform (see Figure 10.3). Sonar measures have a very poor accuracy: the sonar beam propagates from the device as a cone whose width is usually 30 degrees. If the sonar measures a distance equal to 1 metre, the front of the sonar beam is approximately equal to half a metre. This means that the position of the detected obstacle

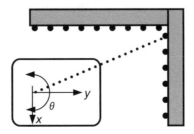

Figure 10.2 The telemeter device installed on the mobile platform and its measurements

Table 10.2 The telemeter device commands

Command	Description
ROTATETO [dir]	Positions the rotary tower at the dir direction (in degrees)
READ	Reads the distance to the nearest obstacle in front of the laser device
SCAN	Gets a distance measure every single degree while the rotary tower is rotating clockwise for 360 degrees
	Returns the set of measures (degree–distance). The distance is set to 0 if the obstacle is too far
DETECT	Scans the area in front of the robot between −45 and +45 degrees. It repeats the scan until it detects an obstacle

can be estimated with a resolution of half a metre. The sonar devices have the advantage of covering a wide area around the robot and of reading measures quickly (one per second). The onboard computer supports the high-level commands listed in Table 10.3.

10.1.3 ☐ Onboard computer

The autonomous mobile robot is equipped with an onboard computer that communicates with the remote control station using a serial or wireless connection. The computer hosts the software application that controls the robot's motion and sensing activities. The control application waits for commands from the remote station (e.g. read a laser measure) and returns responses (e.g. the distance to the nearest obstacle). It manages the robot's devices independently. For example, the laser detects obstacles while the mobile platform is moving forward. The control application has an open architecture that allows the plug-and-play configuration of new sensors on the robot.

10.1.4 ☐ Remote control station

The remote control station coordinates the robot's activities, builds a representation of the explored environment and visualizes the graphical user interface. The exploration strategy is based on the Move → Sense →

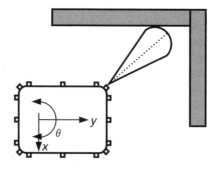

Figure 10.3 The sonar ring structure

Table 10.3 The sonar ring commands

Command	Description
READ	Reads the distance to the nearest obstacles around the robot. Returns the set of measures (sonar id–distance). The distance is set to 0 if the obstacle is too far
DETECT	Measures the area around the robot. It repeats the measurement until it detects an obstacle

Update → Plan cycle. Initially the environment might be completely or partially unknown. The robot moves in the environment, avoiding obstacles. When the robot stops at a place, it acquires distance measures to the surrounding obstacles. We assume that the environment is static, that is the obstacles do not change their position and shape. The robot records the sensory information and updates its internal representation of the operational environment. According to this representation, the robot plans its next move in order to reach new places from which to acquire useful information. The exploration is concluded when the operational environment is completely known or the human operator stops the robot.

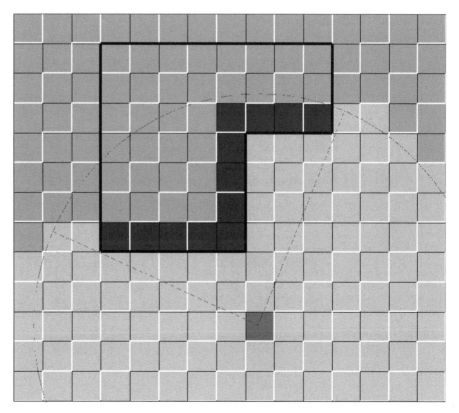

Figure 10.4 The spatial lattice that records the internal representation of the operational environment

The robot maintains an internal representation of the operational environment in the form of a spatial lattice as depicted in Figure 10.4. In the robotics literature this is called an "occupancy grid" and consists of a matrix of cells, where each cell stores the state of a corresponding rectangular area of the environment. A cell could be occupied by an obstacle (shown in black), free of obstacles (light grey), or not yet explored (dark grey). Figure 10.4 represents the case of an obstacle (the polygon with black boundaries) partially seen by the laser range finder. The black cells represent the obstacle's boundary sensed by the laser.

It is easy to update this representation with sensory measures acquired by a laser range finder or a set of sonars. The main drawback is the poor resolution of the obstacle description. The width of each cell is the result of a tradeoff between precision and computational complexity. We assume that each cell has a width of 10 cm. The robot uses its internal representation of the operational environment to plan its next moves. It always plans paths that avoid the known obstacles. It chooses the next position within the known region in such a way that it can sense the presence of obstacles in the unknown region.

10.1.5 □ Simulation

The aim of this case study is to develop a software application that simulates the behaviour of the mobile robot and its interaction with the external

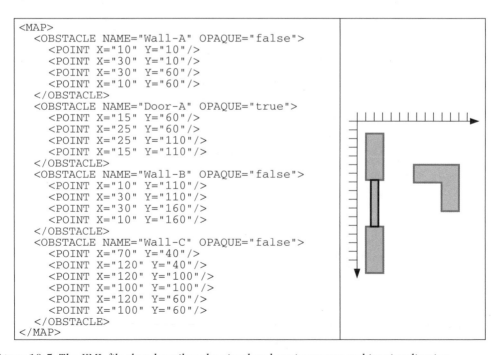

```
<MAP>
  <OBSTACLE NAME="Wall-A" OPAQUE="false">
    <POINT X="10" Y="10"/>
    <POINT X="30" Y="10"/>
    <POINT X="30" Y="60"/>
    <POINT X="10" Y="60"/>
  </OBSTACLE>
  <OBSTACLE NAME="Door-A" OPAQUE="true">
    <POINT X="15" Y="60"/>
    <POINT X="25" Y="60"/>
    <POINT X="25" Y="110"/>
    <POINT X="15" Y="110"/>
  </OBSTACLE>
  <OBSTACLE NAME="Wall-B" OPAQUE="false">
    <POINT X="10" Y="110"/>
    <POINT X="30" Y="110"/>
    <POINT X="30" Y="160"/>
    <POINT X="10" Y="160"/>
  </OBSTACLE>
  <OBSTACLE NAME="Wall-C" OPAQUE="false">
    <POINT X="70" Y="40"/>
    <POINT X="120" Y="40"/>
    <POINT X="120" Y="100"/>
    <POINT X="100" Y="100"/>
    <POINT X="120" Y="60"/>
    <POINT X="100" Y="60"/>
  </OBSTACLE>
</MAP>
```

Figure 10.5 The XML file that describes the simulated environment and its visualization

environment. The simulation consists in the exploration of an indoor environment described by a geometric representation of obstacles. Each obstacle is a polygon, whose corners are identified by Cartesian coordinates related to a global reference frame.

The description of the simulated environment is loaded from a file that is structured using the XML language. Figure 10.5 shows an example of such a file. It is important to note that obstacle might be opaque or shiny and that the laser range finder is not able to sense opaque obstacles.

The robot controller does not have access to the XML description of the environment, i.e. the robot does not use the information in this representation to plan its exploration activity. Only the robot's sensors access the obstacles' descriptions to simulate the interaction with the external environment.

10.2 ■ Problem analysis

The robot simulator is a software application structured as a master–slave application. The control program that runs on the remote station (the remote controller) plays the role of master, while the control program that runs on the onboard computer (the onboard controller) plays the role of slave.

The first requirement of the onboard controller is to manage several independent activities: the robot mobility in the operational environment and the acquisition of sensor information from the laser range scanner and from the sonar sensors. A second requirement is to offer concurrency: the robot should be able to sense the environment while moving in order to avoid obstacles. Another requirement is hiding the internal architecture of the robot from the remote controller and supporting plug-and-play configuration of the robot's components. The last requirement is managing the geometric representation of the simulated environment.

The sensors and the mobile platform are the basic components that simulate the interaction of the robot with the environment. The onboard controller delegates to these components the execution of sensing and moving commands. For standardization purposes these components have a common representation that enforces reusability and facilitates the robot customization with additional devices.

The remote controller has the responsibility of keeping the representation of the operational environment up to date using the sensor information that the robot acquires during the exploration. The interaction between the onboard and remote controllers is a feedback control loop that consists in an iterative exchange of commands and sensor data. The remote controller sends commands to the robot that change its position and thus its interaction with the surrounding environment. As a consequence, the robot acquires new sensory data that the remote controller uses to plan its next exploration step. The communication between the remote and the onboard controllers is message-based. Commands and responses are in textual format.

10.2.1 □ Domain models

The most traditional robot control architecture is structured in layers of functional modules as depicted in Figure 10.6. There is a straightforward transformation of sensor data (perception) in environment representation (modelling), decision-making (planning), task decomposition (execution), and elementary commands (motor control).

Several robot control architectures have been derived as refinements or extensions of this control–feedback loop and have been documented in the literature.

Reactive architectures minimize the role of modelling and planning activities in order to cope with real time requirements of the robot controller. The controller reacts to external stimuli, such as the presence of an obstacle along its path, by exhibiting elementary behaviours, such as stopping the motors or turning the robot in the opposite direction.

Deliberative architectures rely on a detailed description of the surrounding environment in order to enable the robot to plan its activities and carry out useful tasks. Tasks are described in terms of goals that the robot has to achieve, such as transporting an object from one place to another (e.g. two rooms in a building).

Hybrid architectures split the control activity into a number of independent behaviours that enforce the robot's reactivity to external stimuli and goal directedness. Typically they are decentralized architectures, i.e. they are made up of a collection of autonomous and collaborating control modules.

Subsumption architectures are special types of hybrid architectures, where reactive behaviours (such as landmark detection or obstacle avoidance) and deliberative behaviours (such as map building and navigation) use sensor data independently and asynchronously to produce control commands. Reactive and deliberative behaviours have the ability to inhibit or suppress the control commands of other behaviours.

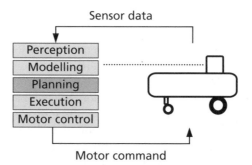

Figure 10.6 Traditional robot control feedback loop

10.2.2 ☐ **Main features**

We are now able to summarize all the main features that have emerged from the problem analysis.

- *Robot software architecture*. The robot architecture should be highly configurable and should allow the robot customization to have a variety of sensors and actuators.
- *Environment representation*. The simulator should maintain two different descriptions of the surrounding environment: a 2D geometric map of the simulated environment and the robot's internal representation as occupancy map.
- *Robot control*. The onboard controller coordinates the robot's devices concurrently. The remote controller is a sequential program that sends commands to the onboard controller and receives sensor information. The communication between onboard and remote controllers is message-based.

10.2.3 ☐ **Test**

Three main functionalities need to be tested carefully.

- The interaction between the robot and the simulated environment. The test consists of placing the robot in various positions with regard to the simulated environment and verifying the distances to the surrounding objects measured by the sensors. Some objects should not be visible by the sensors.
- The concurrent execution of the robot's activities. The test consists in sending sequences of commands to the onboard controller and verifying the correct behaviour of sensors and actuators.
- The construction of the occupancy map. The test consists of comparing the result of an exploration session with the geometric representation of the simulated environment.

10.3 ■ **Architecture and planning**

The system architecture is made up of five main components as described in Figure 10.7. The remote controller builds the occupancy map using the sensor data of the robot that interacts with the simulated environment. The graphical user interface paints the occupancy map and the simulated environment in two separate windows. The robot shape is visualized within the simulated environment.

The development process of the work cell simulator is organized in three phases that produce three prototypes.

- *Prototype 1: Simulated environment*. This consists of a graphical application that exemplifies the robot–environment interaction. It defines the

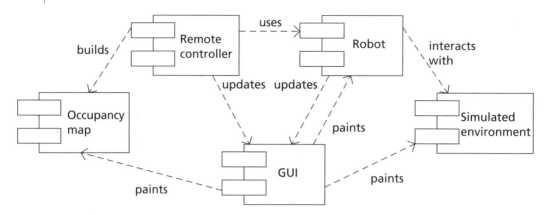

Figure 10.7 The system architecture

robot software architecture and provides the basic implementation of the robot components, the XML representation and the geometric visualization of the simulated environment.

■ *Prototype 2: Dynamic behaviour.* It extends Prototype 1 in order to simulate the dynamic behaviour of the robot. It deals with concurrency and synchronization of sensors and actuators and with the dynamic interaction between robot and environment.

■ *Prototype 3: Map building.* A graphical application that exemplifies the exploration of an indoor environment and the construction of an occupancy map.

10.4 ■ Prototype 1: Simulated environment

The first prototype develops the basic components of the robot's architecture and implements their interaction with the simulated environment.

10.4.1 □ Analysis

According to the problem specification the environment is described as a limited area (e.g. a hall in a building) occupied by a set of obstacles (walls, doors, etc.) and the robot. Thus we introduce the following classes (see Figure 10.8).

Class Environment represents the robot operational field and is characterized by its dimensions and the list of obstacles. We model the operational field as a rectangular area whose dimensions are expressed with regard to a Cartesian reference frame. We assume that the origin of the reference frame coincides with a vertex of the rectangular area.

Class Obstacle represents a physical obstacle that is characterized by a geometric shape and a position in the environment. We describe an obstacle's shape as an ordered list of vertices whose position in the environment is

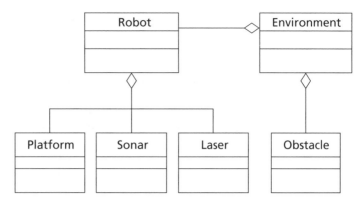

Figure 10.8 The analysis diagram

expressed by a pair of x, y Cartesian coordinates related to the environment's reference frame. The description of each obstacle is loaded from an XML file.

At this stage we are mainly interested in the geometric representation of the robot, not in its dynamic behaviour and control. The robot is made up of a mobile platform, a telemeter device and a ring of sonar devices. For each component we define a class. Class **Robot** plays the role of integrator of the robot's devices.

Class **Platform** represents the mobile platform that is made up of a rectangular base, four wheels and two motors. For the sake of simplicity we do not model the individual components. The mobile platform occupies a place in the environment and can change its position. This requires defining a geometric shape that delimits the robot's physical boundaries. We introduce a robot reference frame that is co-located with the robot. The origin of this reference frame coincides with the middle point of the rear wheels' axis (see right-hand side of Figure 10.9). The x-axis coincides with the forward movement direction. Thus, the robot's position in the environment is described

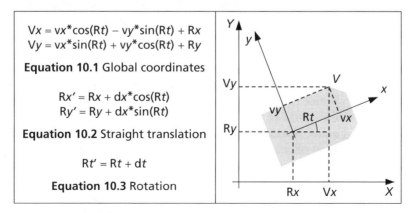

Figure 10.9 The geometric relations between the robot and the environment reference frames

by three parameters (Rx, Ry and Rt) representing the coordinates of the origin of the robot reference frame and its rotation with respect to the environment reference frame. As for the obstacles, we describe the robot's shape as an ordered list of vertices related to the robot's reference frame. In order to calculate the position of the robot shape in the environment, we need to roto-translate its vertices with regard to the environment's reference frame. The left-hand side of Figure 10.9 sets out Equation 10.1 which expresses the correspondence between the coordinates of a vertex in the robot reference frame (vx, vy) and its coordinates in the environment reference frame (Vx, Vy). When the platform changes its position, the origin of the robot reference frame needs to be updated. Equations 10.2 and 10.3 express the new origin coordinates and rotation in the case of straight translation (dx, dy represent the Cartesian components of the displacement) and rotation (represented by the angle dt) around the vertical axis.

Class Laser represents the telemeter device that is the combination of the laser range finder and the rotary tower. Thus, class Laser has the responsibility of measuring the distance to the surrounding obstacles and rotating the laser with respect to the robot. The laser is mounted on the robot in a given position, thus we define a laser reference frame whose origin is expressed by a pair of x, y Cartesian coordinates in the robot reference frame. The laser reference frame can simply rotate with respect to the robot reference frame. The laser beam is modelled as a segment coincident with the laser's x-axis whose length is equal to the laser's range of action. In order to measure the distance between the laser and the obstacles surrounding the robot, we need to express the laser beam position with regard to the environment reference frame using Equation 10.1. A laser measurement is computed as the distance between the origin of the laser reference frame and the point of intersection between the laser beam and the boundary of the nearest obstacle in front of the telemeter device.

Class Sonar is similar to class Laser and thus we leave its description to the reader. The sonar ring is modelled as a set of Sonar objects whose positions on the robot are known. The sonars do not have the ability to rotate, but they are positioned in different orientations.

10.4.2 ☐ Design

The transition from analysis to design is quite straightforward and only a few issues need to be addressed. We can observe that the robot's components have similar characteristics: they have a physical shape, they visualize their shape on a graphical user interface, they interact with the environment and they offer services on demand. One of the basic requirements of the robot architecture is the plug-and-play configuration of its components. Thus, we decide to define the abstract class Device that generalizes the definition of the robot's components (see Figure 10.10). In the following we do not address the design and implementation of class Sonar; that we leave to the reader as a further extension of the robot simulator.

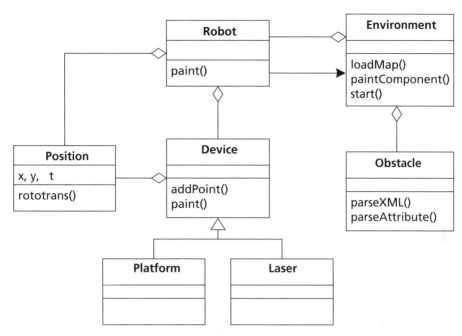

Figure 10.10 The class diagram that depicts the relationships between the components of the architecture

Decision point

How do we record the position of the robot and its components in the environment?

We introduce class Position that encapsulates the Cartesian coordinates (x and y) of the origin of a reference frame and the direction (θ) of this reference frame with regard to a global reference frame. Class Position offers the rototrans() method that implements the mathematical relations to rotate and translate the reference frame. Both the robot and its components encapsulate an instance of this class.

Decision point

How do we implement the robot–environment interaction?

Class Environment is designed as a collection of Obstacle objects and has a reference to an instance of class Robot. When the environment description is loaded from the XML file, class Environment passes to the Robot object a reference to the obstacles list. Similarly, the robot passes this reference to its component devices. Thus, every device knows its position with regard to the reference frame of the simulated environment and has access to its description. A laser measurement is simulated as depicted in Figure 10.11. Coordinates Lx and Ly represent the laser position in the environment's reference frame. Variable θ indicates the global orientation of the rotary tower (equal to the sum of the robot's orientation and the laser's orientation with regard to the robot's reference frame). V1 and V2 indicate the end points of the segment that represents the edge of an obstacle. Segment LF represents the laser beam. Its length corresponds to a laser distance measurement.

According to the problem specification, the operational environment is assumed to be static; this means that the obstacles do not change their size, shape and position in the environment during the robot exploration. The interaction between the robot and the environment is dynamic because, during exploration, the robot and the sensors change their position with regard to the environment. Real robot actuators have a limited resolution that adds uncertainty to the exact entity of the robot displacement. We assume that the execution of movement commands is not affected by uncertainty. As described in Section 10.1.1 the laser device and the rotary tower are highly precise. The simulation of a laser scan consists of a sequence of fine-grained rotation steps (e.g. one degree) and, for each step, the acquisition of a distance measure.

It might happen that the laser acquires distance measures while the robot is moving. The simulation of the robot movements must consist of sequences of fine-grained displacement steps. For sake of simplicity, we assume that the robot displacements consist of forward and backward translation or clockwise and anticlockwise rotations around the origin of its reference frame. In Section 10.1.2 we have pointed out that the laser needs to know the current position of the robot in the environment in order to simulate distance measurements and to detect the surrounding obstacles. This can be modelled by giving the laser access to the current position of the mobile platform.

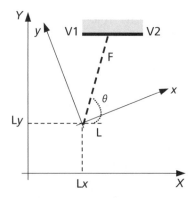

Figure 10.11 Simulation of a laser measurement

10.4.3 □ Implementation

Class Position represents 2D Cartesian reference frames.

```java
package moro;
import java.awt.geom.*;
public class Position {
  double x, y, t; // the coordinates and direction of the
                  // reference frame
  public Position(double x, double y, double t) {
    this.x = x;   this.y = y;   this.t = t;
  }
  // executes the roto-translation of this reference frame
  public void rototrans(double da, double db, double dt) {
    this.x += da * Math.cos(this.t) - db * Math.sin(this.t);
    this.y += da * Math.sin(this.t) + db * Math.cos(this.t);
    this.t += Math.toRadians(dt);
  }
  // executes the roto-translation of a point
  public void rototrans(Point2D point) {
    double px = point.getX() * Math.cos(t) -
                point.getY() * Math.sin(t) + x;
    double py = point.getX() * Math.sin(t) +
                point.getY() * Math.cos(t) + y;
    point.setLocation(px, py);
  }
  // copies this position into the parameter
  public void copyTo(Position position) {
    position.x = this.x;
    position.y = this.y;
    position.t = this.t;
  }
  // the getX(), getY(), and getT() methods
}
```

Class Device is the abstract class that generalizes the robot's components. It records the device's position and orientation with regard to the global reference frame and the robot's reference frame. The geometric shape is implemented using class Polygon of the Java AWT framework. It has a reference to the environment in order to give the device access to the obstacles list.

```java
package moro;
import java.awt.*;
import java.awt.geom.Point2D;
public abstract class Device {
  String name;                    // the name of this device
  Environment environment;
                                  // a reference to the environment
```

```
Polygon shape = new Polygon();
                    // the device's shape in local coords
Robot robot;        // a reference to the robot
Position robotPos = new Position();
                    // the robot's current position
Position localPos;
                    // the device position on the robot
public Device(String name, Robot robot,
            Position local, Environment env) {
  this.name = name;
  this.robot = robot;
  robot.readPosition(this.robotPos);
  this.localPos = local;
  this.environment = env;
}
// this method is invoked when the geometric shape of the
// device is defined
public void addPoint(int x, int y) {
  shape.addPoint(x, y);
}
// draws the device's geometric shape on the graphical
// interface
public void paint(Graphics g) {
  // reads the robot's current position
  robot.readPosition(robotPos);
  // draws the shape
  Polygon globalShape = new Polygon();
  Point2D point = new Point2D.Double();
  for(int i=0; i < shape.npoints; i++) {
    point.setLocation(shape.xpoints[i], shape.ypoints[i]);
    // calculates the coordinates of the point
    // according to the local position
    localPos.rototras(point);
    // calculates the coordinates of the point
    // according to the robot position
    robotPos.rototras(point);
    // adds the point to the global shape
    globalShape.addPoint((int)Math.round(point.getX()),
                         (int)Math.round(point.getY()));
  }
  ((Graphics2D) g).drawPolygon(globalShape);
}
}
```

Class **Platform** inherits from the abstract class **Device** and defines the shape of the robot's platform. Its local position is set to zero since the platform's reference frame coincides with the robot's reference frame.

```
public class Platform extends Device {
  public Platform(String name, Robot robot, Environment env){
    super(name, robot, new Position(0.0, 0.0, 0.0), env);
    this.addPoint(20, 20);    this.addPoint(30, 10);
    this.addPoint(30, -10);   this.addPoint(20, -20);
    this.addPoint(-20, -20);  this.addPoint(-20, 20);
  }
}
```

Class **Laser** inherits from the abstract class **Device** and implements the read() method that measures the distance from the laser to the nearest obstacles around the robot. The inner class **Measure** records a laser measurement in terms of distance from a point on an obstacle's boundary and of current direction of the rotary tower.

```
package moro;
import java.awt.*;
import java.awt.geom.*;
import java.util.*;
public class Laser extends Device{
  class Measure {
    double distance = 0.0;  // distance from an obstacle
    double direction = 0.0;
                        // current direction of the rotary tower
  }
  ArrayList scanMeasures = new ArrayList();
                                        // list of measures
  int range = 100;  // maximum range in centimetres
  public Laser(String name, Robot robot,
            Position local, Environment env) {
    super(name, robot, local, env);
    this.addPoint(0, 2);       this.addPoint(100, 2);
    this.addPoint(100, -2);    this.addPoint(0, -2);
  }
  // if first is true, returns the distance to the first
  // obstacle encountered otherwise it returns the distance
  // to the nearest obstacle
  public double read(boolean first) {
    Point2D centre = new Point2D.Double(localPos.getX(),
                                    localPos.getY());
    Point2D front = new Point2D.Double(localPos.getX()+
                    range * Math.cos(localPos.getT()),
                    localPos.getY() +
                    range *Math.sin(localPos.getT()));
    // reads the robot's position
    robot.readPosition(robotPos);
    // centre's coordinates according to the robot position
```

```
      robotPos.rototras(centre);
      // front's coordinates according to the robot position
      robotPos.rototras(front);
      // intersects the laser beam with the obstacles'
      // boundaries
      for(int i=0; i < environment.obstacles.size(); i++)
        ...
   }
}
```

Class **Robot** is the container of the robot's devices. It maintains a **Position** variable that records the current robot position with regard to the global reference frame. This variable is modified by the mobile platform and is passed to all the robot's devices to keep track of their position in the environment.

```
package moro;
import java.util.*;
import java.awt.*;
public class Robot {
  String name;  // the robot name
  Position position;
          // the robot position in the global reference frame
  Environment environment;
          // a reference to the environment
  Platform platform;
          // a reference to the mobile platform
  ArrayList sensors = new ArrayList();
          // the list of sensor devices
  public Robot(String name, double x, double y,
              double t, Environment env) {
    this.name = name;
    this.environment = env;
    position = new Position(x, y, Math.toRadians(t));
    platform = new Platform("P1", this, env);
    sensors.add(new Laser("L1", this,
              new Position(20.0, 0.0, 0.0), env));
  }
  public void paint(Graphics g) {
    platform.paint(g);     // paints all the mobile platform
    ...                    // paints the sensor devices
  }
}
```

Class **Obstacle** encapsulates an object of class **Polygon** and implements the methods for parsing the obstacle description from the XML input file and for visualizing its geometric shape.

```
package moro;
import java.io.*;
import java.awt.*;
public class Obstacle {
  String name;
  boolean opaque;
  Polygon polygon = new Polygon();
  public Obstacle() { }
  // parses a line of the XML input file
  public boolean parseXML(String line,
                          BufferedReader lineReader) { ...}
  public void paint(Graphics g) {
    // paints this obstacle
    ((Graphics2D) g).fillPolygon(polygon);
  }
}
```

Class **Environment** extends the **JPanel** class of the Java Swing framework to implement the graphical window that displays the robot's operational

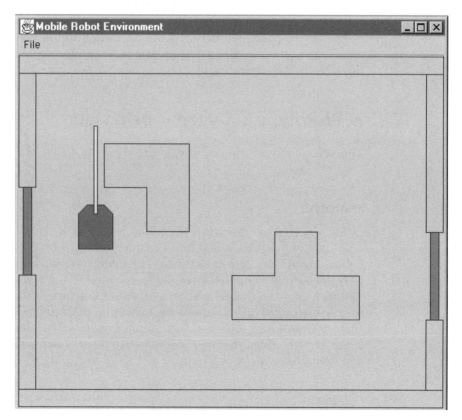

Figure 10.12 The graphical representation of the simulated environment.

environment. It maintains the list of obstacles and implements the methods to load their description from the XML input file.

```
package moro;
import java.util.*;
import java.awt.*;
public class Environment extends JPanel {
  ArrayList obstacles = new ArrayList();
  Robot robot;
  // Construct the application
  public Environment() {
    robot = new Robot(50, 350, 270, this);
  }
  public boolean loadMap(File mapFile) {}
  public void paintComponent(Graphics g) {}
}
```

10.4.4 □ Test

The test case consists in the visualization of the operational environment in the graphical user interface (see Figure 10.12). The test should verify the correct correspondence between the XML description and the geometric representation of the simulated environment and the correct positioning of the robot in the environment.

10.5 ■ Prototype 2: Dynamic behaviour

The second prototype deals with the dynamic behaviour of the robot's components.

10.5.1 □ Analysis

In Section 10.2 we described the robot system as a slave component that offers mobility and sensing services to the remote controller. We identify the onboard controller with class Robot. The robot receives commands from the remote controller and delegates their execution to the appropriate devices. The laser and the mobile platform execute their tasks autonomously. The remote controller might request the execution of a sequence of commands, such as translation and rotation commands to move the robot along a complex path. Thus, the robot's devices should maintain a list of commands and execute them one at a time.

10.5.2 □ Design

In the previous chapter we saw an example of a discrete event dynamic system. The event-based model is well suited to the simulation of the work cell system, whose behaviour is characterized by a number of macro events (e.g. **WORKDONE**) that trigger transitions between macro states (e.g. **WORKING** and **NOT WORKING**). The work cell simulator does not animate the execution of manufacturing operations but simply represents their start and completion times. The behaviour of the robot system, however, is characterized by a few macro states (e.g. **PLATFORM ARRIVED**) and a large number of micro states (e.g. every single rotation step).

Decision point

How do we model the micro and macro behaviours of the robot system?

We can generalize the macro behaviour of a robot's device with the finite state machine described in Figure 10.13 (left-hand side). This is characterized by two states, **RUNNING** (device is executing a task) and **NOT RUNNING** (the device has completed the last task and there are no more tasks to execute), and two events, **NEW TASK** (NT) and **TASK COMPLETED** (TC). As soon as a new command is issued it is executed immediately if the device is not running, or it is inserted in a command list if the device is running. As soon as a task gets completed a new one is started unless the command list is empty.

When the device is running the simulator animates the micro steps that discretize the task execution. The number of steps depends on the device precision. For example, if the platform has a resolution of one degree, the complete rotation around the vertical axis is simulated with 360 micro rotation steps. The duration of each micro step depends on the device speed. We model the execution of a task with the finite state machine depicted in Figure 10.13 (right-hand side). It has only the **TICK** event and three states: the **INITIAL** state, the **FINAL** state and the **WAITING** state. The device is in the waiting state for the entire duration of a micro step, which is executed when the tick event is raised.

Decision point

Which execution model is best suited to simulate the robot system?

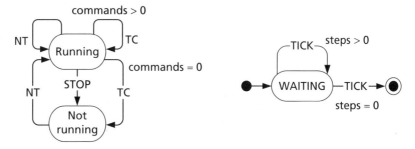

Figure 10.13 The finite state machine describing a device's behaviour

The centralized event-scheduling model presented in the previous chapter is not well suited to the simulation of the robot system. The robot system is highly decentralized: the devices are autonomous and their interactions are very limited.

There is no need for event synchronization among the device activities. The robot devices share only the data structures that represent the position of the robot in the environment. The event-based model provides features to model complex finite state machines, whereas a very simple finite state machine can describe the behaviour of every robot device.

Thus, we choose to adopt the process-based model that consists of implementing every robot device as a thread (see Sidebar 10.1 for a description of Java threads). The definition of class Device needs to be extended to implement the run() method of the Runnable interface. This method is common to every concrete device and implements the finite state machines depicted in Figure 10.13. Class Device defines two abstract methods that every subclass must implement. Method executeCommand() initializes the device state in order to execute a new command when the device is not running. Method nextStep() performs a micro state transition that executes a new micro step. This solution corresponds to the implementation of pattern *Template method* described in Gamma *et al.* (1995). Figure 10.14 depicts the interaction diagram between class Device and class Laser. Method println(command) specifies which command should be executed.

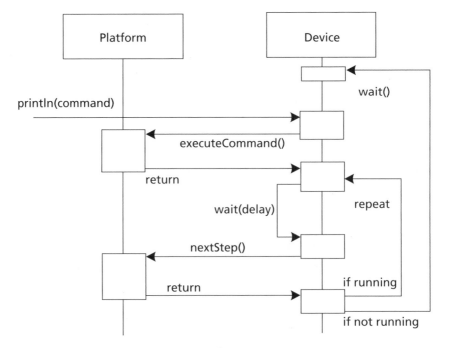

Figure 10.14 The interaction diagram of the run() method

Sidebar 10.1 Java threads

Multithreading is a powerful programming tool that is native in the Java language. It builds on the concept of "thread", an execution flow that processes a sequence of programming instructions.

Traditional programming environments are single-threaded, i.e. a program consists in a single execution flow. In a multithreaded environment, several execution flows are active simultaneously. An application might run several threads that execute the same sequence of instructions or different sequences of instructions simultaneously. The thread mechanism abstracts from the single-processor nature of the computer hardware and allows the creation of an undefined number of virtual processors that share the computer's CPU. The operating system schedules the allocation of the CPU to the active threads transparently. When a thread is created, it is initialized with the code to execute and the data to process. Code and data are passed to the thread in the form of a class instance. The programmer builds the simplest multithreaded application in three steps:

- Implement the class that defines data and code to be executed (e.g. class Clock). This class should implement the Runnable interface that requires the programmer to write the code for the run() method. For example, the run() method increments a counter every second and displays its current value on the screen.
- Define the main class (e.g. class WatchMaker) that represents the whole application and implements the main() method.
- In the main() method, create instances of class Thread and initialize each of them with a different instance of class Clock. Then, for each Thread instance invoke method start().

A thread's execution can be suspended for a predefined time period using the sleep() method or for an undefined time period using the wait() method. The execution can be resumed explicitly using the notify() method. For more details on Java threads and synchronization refer to a Java reference manual.

```java
public class Clock implements Runnable {
  long delay;
  int tick = 0;
  String name;
  public Clock(String n, long d) {
    name = n;
    delay = d;
  }
  public void run() {
    while(true)
      try {
        tick++;
        System.out.println(name + " : " + tick);
        Thread.sleep(delay);
      } catch(InterruptedException ie){}
  }
}
public class Application {
  public static void main(String[] args) {
    Thread t1 = new Thread(new Clock("Clock A", 100));
    Thread t2 = new Thread(new Clock("Clock B", 500));
    t1.start();
    t2.start();
  }
}
```

The execution model is not pre-emptive. Every new command is inserted in a command list. The device thread extracts commands from this list one at a time. Only special commands (e.g. STOP) are executed immediately and cause the interruption of other commands.

Do the robot's devices need to synchronize their activities?

The mobile platform and the sensors share a reference to the robot's current position. The platform modifies the robot position (the x, y coordinates and the direction), while the sensors use its value to simulate distance measurements. This is a typical one-writer–multiple-readers situation that requires synchronized access to the shared resource: when the platform is updating the current position no sensor should be allowed to read the position; all the sensors should be allowed to read the position simultaneously after it has been updated.

It might happen that the platform needs to update the robot position while the sensors are reading the old value. We choose the simplest solution that forces the platform to wait for the sensors to complete their reading operation. This might cause a random delay between two consecutive movement steps of the mobile platform. Since position updating requires writing the values of three primitive variables, we decide not to worry about this problem.

Decision point

How does the remote controller request services from the robot and get the result of a task?

Every device behaves as an autonomous slave component that offers services on demand. Thus class Device implements two methods for receiving commands from the master and for writing out the result. The current prototype does not deal with the synchronization between robot and controller. Thus, for simplicity, every device prints the result of a task on the standard output using method writeOut().

Since the robot's devices are encapsulated within the robot's shell, the remote controller is not allowed to access the device's services directly. Thus the remote controller submits commands to the robot according to the following format:

<device name>.<command>

For example, the remote controller requests platform "P1" to move forward sending the command:

P1.MOVEFW 50

and requests laser "L1" to scan the obstacles with the command:

L1.SCAN

The robot itself can provide services. For example, robot "R1" returns the current position when the master submits the following command:

R1.GETPOS

The interested reader might extend the robot's functionalities by implementing more complex behaviours that combine the services of several devices. For example, the robot might be able to follow the middle line of a corridor autonomously maintaining the same distance from two parallel walls.

10.5.3 ☐ Implementation

Class **Robot** represents the entire robot system as it encapsulates the robot's components and offers a single point of access to the controller. It is in charge of synchronizing the read and write operations on the robot's position and of dispatching the controller's commands to the appropriate device. The structure of the robot system (type and position of each device) would be conveniently defined in a configuration file that class **Robot** read at the initialization phase. This functionality is not supported by the following implementation and is left to the reader as an exercise.

```java
public class Robot {
  String name;
  Position position; // absolute robot position
  Environment environment; // reference to the environment
  // representation used for simulating the interaction with
  // the robot sensors
  Platform platform; // reference to the platform device
  ArrayList sensors = new ArrayList();
  // list of installed sensors
  public Robot(String name, double x, double y, double t,
               Environment environment) {
    this.name = name;
    this.environment = environment;
    position = new Position(x, y, Math.toRadians(t));
    // configures the robot's devices. A better
    // implementation would read this information from a
    // configuration file
    platform = new Platform("P1", this, environment);
    sensors.add(new Laser("L1", this,
                          new Position(20.0, 0.0, 0.0),
                          environment));
  }
  // The writeOut() method is invoked by the device when it
  // has to communicate the result of a command's execution.
```

```java
// The current implementation displays the result on the
// standard output
protected synchronized void writeOut(String data) {
  System.out.println(data);
}
// the following two methods synchronize the read and
// write operations of the robot's position performed by
// the robot's devices
public void readPosition(Position position) {
  synchronized(this.position) {
    this.position.copyTo(position);
  }
}
public void writePosition(Position position) {
  synchronized(this.position) {
    position.copyTo(this.position);
  }
}
// starts the robot's devices
public void start() {
  platform.start();
  for(int i=0; i < sensors.size(); i++) {
    Device sensor = (Device) sensors.get(i);
    sensor.start();
  }
}
// The println() method parses a string that specifies a
// command according to the following format :
//          "<deviceName>.<command> <parameter>".
// It invokes the println() method of that device. Returns
// false if the device name is incorrect
public boolean println(String p_command) {
  int indexInit = p_command.indexOf(".");
  if(indexInit < 0)
    return false;
  String deviceName = p_command.substring(0, indexInit);
  String command = p_command.substring(indexInit+1);
  if(deviceName.equals(this.name)
              && command.equalsIgnoreCase("GETPOS")) {
    writeOut("GETPOS X=" + position.getX() +
                " Y=" + position.getY() + " DIR=" +
                Math.toDegrees(position.getT())));
  }
  else if(deviceName.equals(platform.name))
    return platform.println(command);
```

```
      else
        for(int i=0; i < sensors.size(); i++) {
          Device sensor = (Device) sensors.get(i);
          if(deviceName.equals(sensor.name))
            return sensor.println(command);
        }
        return false;
  }
}
```

Class **Device** implements the concurrency mechanisms that handle the dynamics of the robot's components. It encapsulates the list of commands that the device receives from the controller and implements the run() method of the **Runnable** interface to process these commands.

```
public abstract class Device implements Runnable{
  protected ArrayList commands = new ArrayList();
                  // the list of commands
  protected Thread thread;
                  // the reference to a Thread object
  protected long delay = 20;
                  // the delay between two steps in millisecs
  protected boolean alive = false;
                  // true when the thread is started
  protected boolean running = false;
                  // true when it is executing a command
  protected Object lock = new Object();
                  // a lock for thread synchronization
      ...
  public Device(String name, Position global,
                  Position local, Environment env) {
      ...
    thread = new Thread(this);
  }
  // Inserts a new command in the command list and notifies
  // the thread
  public boolean println(String message) {
    commands.add(command);
                  // inserts the command in the commands' list
    synchronized(lock) { lock.notify();}
                  // notifies the thread
    return true;
  }
  protected synchronized void writeOut(String data) {
    System.out.println(data);
  }
  // The start() method activates the thread that executes
  // this device
```

```
  public synchronized void start() {
    if(! alive) {
      alive = true;
      thread.start();
    }
  }
  // The run() method implements the finite state machine
  // that manages the commands' execution
  public void run() {
    do {
      try {
        if(running) // pause before the next step
          synchronized(this) { wait(delay); }
        else if(commands.size() > 0) {
          // extracts the the next command and executes it
          String command = (String) commands.remove(0);
          executeCommand(command);
        }
        else // waits for a new command
          synchronized(lock) { lock.wait();   }
        // processes the next step of the current command
        nextStep();
      } catch (InterruptedException ie) {continue;}
    } while(alive);
  }
  // These abstract methods must be implemented in every
  // subclass of Device
  public abstract void executeCommand(String command);
  public abstract void nextStep();
}
```

Class **Platform** extends class **Device** to implement the dynamics of the mobile platform device.

```
public class Platform extends Device {
  int orientation = 1;      // 1: clockwise  -1: otherwise
  double rotStep = 1.0;     // one degree
  double moveStep = 1.0;    // one centimetre
  double numRotSteps = 0;
                  // number of steps to complete the rotation
  double numMoveSteps = 0;
                  // number of steps to complete the movement
  public Platform(String name, Position global,
                Position local, Environment env){ ... }
  // This method parses the command string and initializes
  // the state variables
  public void executeCommand(String command) {
```

```java
if(command.indexOf("ROTATERIGHT") > -1) {
  double angle = Math.abs(Double.parseDouble(
                 command.trim().substring(12).trim()));
  numRotSteps = angle / rotStep;
  orientation = 1;
  running = true;
}
else if(command.indexOf("ROTATELEFT") > -1) {
  double angle = Math.abs(Double.parseDouble(
                 command.trim().substring(11).trim()));
  numRotSteps = angle / rotStep;
  orientation = -1;
  running = true;
}
else if(command.indexOf("MOVEFW") > -1) {
  double distance = Math.abs(Double.parseDouble(
                 command.trim().substring(7).trim()));
  numMoveSteps = distance / moveStep;
  orientation = 1;
  running = true;
}
else if(command.indexOf("MOVEBW") > -1) {
  double distance = Math.abs(Double.parseDouble(
                 command.trim().substring(7).trim()));
  numMoveSteps = distance / moveStep;
  orientation = -1;
}
else
  writeOut("DECLINED");     // invalid command
}
// The nextStep() method implements the elemental steps of
// each command
public void nextStep() {
  if(! running) return;
  if(numRotSteps > 0.0) {
    // executes a rotation step
    if(numRotSteps < 1.0)
      robotPos.rototrans(0.0, 0.0,
                   numRotSteps*orientation*rotStep);
    else
      robotPos.rototrans(0.0, 0.0, orientation*rotStep);
    // updates the robot's position
    robot.writePosition(robotPos);
    // repaints the graphical interface
    environment.repaint();
    numRotSteps-=1.0;
  }
```

```
      else if(numMoveSteps > 0.0) {
        // executes a movement step
        if(numMoveSteps < 1.0)
          robotPos.rototrans(numMoveSteps*moveStep*orientation,
                             0.0, 0.0);
        else
          robotPos.rototrans(moveStep*orientation, 0.0, 0.0);
        // updates the robot's position
        robot.writePosition(robotPos);
        // repaints the graphical interface
        environment.repaint();
        numMoveSteps-=1.0;
      }
      else {
        // the task has been fulfilled
        running = false;
        writeOut("PLATFORM ARRIVED");
      }
    }
  }
}
```

Class **Laser** extends class **Device** to implement the dynamics of the tele-meter device. It executes four tasks: (1) positions the rotary tower at a given direction; (2) reads a single distance measure; (3) detects obstacles in front of the robot; (4) scans the surrounding environment and returns the list of distance measures.

```
public class Laser extends Device{
  int orientation = 1;      // 1: clockwise  -1: otherwise
  double rotStep = 1.0;     // one degree
  double numSteps = 0;      // number of rotation steps
  boolean detect = false;
               // true if the laser executes a detect task
  boolean scan = false;
               // true if the laser executes a scan task
  Measure detectMeasure = null;
  public void executeCommand(String command) {
    if(command.indexOf("ROTATETO") > -1) {
      rotStep = 4.0;
      double direction = Math.abs(Double.parseDouble(
                    command.trim().substring(9).trim()));
      while(direction < 0.0)
        direction+=360.0;
      while(direction > 360.0)
        direction-=360.0;
      double dirDiff = direction - Math.toDegrees
                                   (localPos.getT());
```

```java
  if(dirDiff >= 0.0 && dirDiff <= 180.0) {
    numSteps = dirDiff / rotStep;
    orientation = 1;
  }
  else if(dirDiff >= 0.0 && dirDiff > 180.0) {
    numSteps = (360.0 - dirDiff) / rotStep;
    orientation = -1;
  }
  else if(dirDiff < 0.0 && -dirDiff <= 180.0) {
    numSteps = -dirDiff / rotStep;
    orientation = -1;
  }
  else if(dirDiff < 0.0 && -dirDiff > 180.0) {
    numSteps = (360.0 + dirDiff) / rotStep;
    orientation = 1;
  }
  running = true;
}
else if(command.equalsIgnoreCase("READ")) {
  writeOut("t=" + Double.toString(this.localPos.getT()) +
           " d=" + Double.toString(this.read(true)));
}
else if(command.equalsIgnoreCase("SCAN")) {
  rotStep = 1.0;
  scanMeasures.removeAll(scanMeasures);
  numSteps = 360.0 / rotStep;
  orientation = 1;
  scan = true;
  // send the list of measures
  commands.add("GETMEASURES");
  running = true;
}
else if(command.equalsIgnoreCase("GETMEASURES")) {
  Measure measure = null;
  String measures = "SCAN";
  for(int i=0; i < scanMeasures.size(); i++) {
    measure = (Measure) scanMeasures.get(i);
    measures += " d=" + measure.distance +
                " t=" + measure.direction;
  }
  writeOut(measures);
}
else if(command.equalsIgnoreCase("DETECT")) {
  detect = true;
  rotStep = 8.0;
```

```
      if(detectMeasure != null) {
        writeOut("LASER DETECT d=" + detectMeasure.distance +
                          " t=" + detectMeasure.direction);
        detectMeasure = null;
      }
      else if(localPos.getT() == Math.toRadians(45.0)) {
        // move the laser to the left position
        commands.add("ROTATETO 315");
        // repeats this command
        commands.add("DETECT");
      }
      else if(localPos.getT() == Math.toRadians(315.0)) {
        // move the laser to the right position
        commands.add("ROTATETO 45");
        // repeats this command
        commands.add("DETECT");
      }
      else {
        // move the laser to the right position
        commands.add("ROTATETO 45");
        // repeats this command
        commands.add("DETECT");
      }
    }
    else
      writeOut("DECLINED");
  }
  public void nextStep() {
    if(running && numSteps > 0.0) {
      if(numSteps < 1.0)
        local.rototrans
                  (0.0, 0.0, orientation*numSteps*rotStep);
      else
        local.rototrans(0.0, 0.0, orientation*rotStep);
      environment.repaint();
      numSteps-=1.0;
      running = true;
    }
    else if(running) {
      running = false;
      if(!detect && !scan) writeOut("LASER ARRIVED");
    }
    if(detect) {
      double distance = this.read(true);
      if(distance > -1.0) {
        if(detectMeasure == null)
          detectMeasure = new Measure
                                  (distance, localPos.getT());
```

```
      else if(detectMeasure.distance > distance)
        detectMeasure.set(distance, localPos.getT());
    }
  }
  else if(scan) {
    double distance = this.read(false);
    if(distance > -1.0)
      scanMeasures.add
                  (new Measure(distance, local.getT()));
  }
  }
}
```

10.5.4 □ Test

The test case consists of a laser scan from a given robot position. Table 10.4 reports the sequence of measurements related to the environment depicted in Figure 10.11. The laser rotates clockwise from the initial direction along the robot's *x*-axis. It encounters the polygonal obstacle in front of the robot when the laser direction is equal to 0.13962 radians (8 degrees). The distance is equal to 71.8529 centimetres.

The laser continues to detect the obstacle until the direction is equal to 1.88495 radians (108 degrees). The distance is equal to 63.0877 centimetres. Then the laser does not perceive the presence of other obstacles until it reaches the direction of 3.92699 radians (225 degrees) where it measures a distance equal to 98.9949 centimetres.

Table 10.4 The distance measures of a laser scan

Distance/Direction	Distance/Direction	Distance/Direction	Distance/Direction
d=71.8529	d=39.1622	d=63.0877	d=61.8368
t=0.13962	t=0.69813	t=1.25663	t=1.81514
d=63.9245	d=39.7503	d=62.7415	d=62.1165
t=0.15707	t=0.71558	t=1.27409	t=1.83259
d=57.5877	d=40.3689	d=62.4179	d=62.4179
t=0.17453	t=0.73303	t=1.29154	t=1.85004
d=52.4084	d=41.0198	d=62.1165	d=62.7415
t=0.19198	t=0.75049	t=1.30899	t=1.86750
d=48.0973	d=41.7049	d=61.8368	d=63.0877
t=0.20943	t=0.76794	t=1.32645	t=1.88495
d=44.4541	d=42.4264	d=61.5782	d=98.9949
t=0.22689	t=0.78539	t=1.34390	t=3.92699
d=41.3356	d=43.1866	d=61.3404	d=92.1466
t=0.24434	t=0.80285	t=1.36135	t=5.04400
d=38.6370	d=43.9883	d=61.1230	d=87.7141
t=0.26179	t=0.82030	t=1.37881	t=5.06145
d=36.2795	d=44.8342	d=60.9255	d=83.7128

continued

Table 10.4 (*continued*)

Distance/Direction	Distance/Direction	Distance/Direction	Distance/Direction
t=0.27925	t=0.83775	t=1.39626	t=5.07890
d=34.2030	d=45.7275	d=60.7479	d=80.0840
t=0.29670	t=0.85521	t=1.41371	t=5.09636
d=32.3606	d=46.6717	d=60.5896	d=76.7791
t=0.31415	t=0.87266	t=1.43116	t=5.11381
d=31.7286	d=47.6704	d=60.4505	d=76.6245
t=0.33161	t=0.89011	t=1.44862	t=5.13126
d=31.9253	d=48.7280	d=60.3304	d=77.2364
t=0.34906	t=0.90757	t=1.46607	t=5.14872
d=32.1343	d=49.8492	d=60.2291	d=77.8821
t=0.36651	t=0.92502	t=1.48352	t=5.16617
d=32.3560	d=51.0390	d=60.1465	d=78.5628
t=0.38397	t=0.94247	t=1.50098	t=5.18362
d=32.5908	d=52.3034	d=60.0823	d=79.2799
t=0.40142	t=0.95993	t=1.51843	t=5.20108
d=32.8390	d=53.6487	d=60.0365	d=80.0347
t=0.41887	t=0.97738	t=1.53588	t=5.21853
d=33.1013	d=55.0823	d=60.0091	d=80.8290
t=0.43633	t=0.99483	t=1.55334	t=5.23598
d=33.3780	d=56.6123	d=60.0000	d=81.6643
t=0.45378	t=1.01229	t=1.57079	t=5.25344
d=33.6697	d=58.2481	d=60.0091	d=82.5424
t=0.47123	t=1.02974	t=1.58824	t=5.27089
d=33.9771	d=60.0000	d=60.0365	d=83.4654
t=0.48869	t=1.04719	t=1.60570	t=5.28834
d=34.3006	d=61.8799	d=60.0823	d=84.4352
t=0.50614	t=1.06465	t=1.62315	t=5.30580
d=34.6410	d=63.9016	d=60.1465	d=85.4542
t=0.52359	t=1.08210	t=1.64060	t=5.32325
d=34.9990	d=66.0806	d=60.2291	d=86.5247
t=0.54105	t=1.09955	t=1.65806	t=5.34070
d=35.3753	d=66.7561	d=60.3304	d=87.6494
t=0.55850	t=1.11701	t=1.67551	t=5.35816
d=35.7708	d=66.2026	d=60.4505	d=88.8312
t=0.57595	t=1.13446	t=1.69296	t=5.37561
d=36.1865	d=65.6781	d=60.5896	d=90.0731
t=0.59341	t=1.15191	t=1.71042	t=5.39306
d=36.6232	d=65.1816	d=60.7479	d=91.3785
t=0.61086	t=1.16937	t=1.72787	t=5.41052
d=37.0820	d=64.7120	d=60.9255	d=92.7509
t=0.62831	t=1.18682	t=1.74532	t=5.42797
d=37.5640	d=64.2686	d=61.1230	d=94.1942
t=0.64577	t=1.20427	t=1.76278	t=5.44542
d=38.0705	d=63.8506	d=61.3404	d=95.7129
t=0.66322	t=1.22173	t=1.78023	t=5.46288
d=38.6027	d=63.4572	d=61.5782	d=97.3114
t=0.68067	t=1.23918	t=1.79768	t=5.48033

This measurement is related to the left doorpost of the window. Finally, the laser perceives part of the left-hand side wall from the direction of 5.044 radians (289 degrees) up to 5.48033 radians (314 degrees).

10.6 ■ Prototype 3: Map building

The third prototype addresses two main problems: the communication and synchronization mechanisms between the remote controller and the robot and the construction of the occupancy map of the environment.

10.6.1 □ Analysis

The robot and the remote controller are two independent processes that communicate and synchronize by exchanging messages. The controller sends commands to the robot, which replies with task results. This kind of communication is direct and symmetric, that is the robot and the controller send messages over the same communication medium (e.g. a serial cable).

Since the robot's devices are autonomous, the controller might send a sequence of commands to different devices and wait for the first reply from any of those devices. For example, the controller might activate the laser detection behaviour and request the mobile platform to move forward a given distance. The laser scans the area in front of the robot continuously while the robot is moving towards the next destination and returns the distance to the first obstacle encountered. The communication between the controller and the robot is asynchronous. We assume that the serial port has a buffer and that messages are cached until the controller reads them. For example, the controller is waiting for a reply from the platform ("Platform arrived") and from the laser ("Obstacle detected"), but it does not know which message will arrive first. If the laser detects an obstacle, the controller might request the mobile platform to halt; on the other hand, the controller might request the laser to abort the detection behaviour when the platform has arrived at its destination. When a device communicates a result, it must specify its name in order to allow the controller to identify the sender.

As described in Section 10.1.2, the remote controller uses sensor data to build the occupancy map that describes the robot's surroundings. The environment has been completely explored when the robot has updated the value of all the cells of the occupancy map that correspond to visible areas of the environment. The internal part of an obstacle is not a visible area. The robot controller can implement several exploration strategies. For example, it might move randomly in the environment looking for unexplored areas. A more sophisticated strategy might try to minimize the travel path or the number of laser scans.

10.6.2 □ **Design**

Class Controller represents the remote controller that interacts with the robot system (see Figure 10.15). It implements the run() method of the Runnable interface according to the Move → Sense → Update → Plan exploration cycle. After each robot movement, the controller requests the laser to acquire new distance measures, updates the internal representation of the environment and plans the next move.

The controller communicates with the robot using the pipe mechanisms of the Java language (see Sidebar 10.2). It supports asynchronous direct and symmetric communication between two independent threads. Accordingly, the implementation of method writeOut() of class Device needs to be modified.

We introduce class OccupancyMap to manage the internal representation of the robot's environment. The controller requests the robot to scan the environment and updates the map with the laser measurements. This class can be easily extended to elaborate sensor measurements acquired from sonar devices or other sensors and to support the exploration strategies of the controller, giving indications about the unexplored areas.

10.6.3 □ **Implementation**

Class OccupancyMap records the matrix of cells that correspond to square areas of the environment. The width and height of each area are equal to 10 centimetres.

```
package moro;
import java.awt.*;
import javax.swing.*;
public class OccupancyMap extends JPanel {
    int cellDim = 10;      // the cell dimension in centimetre
    int width = 510;       // the map width (number of cells)
    int height = 460;      // the map height (number of cells)
```

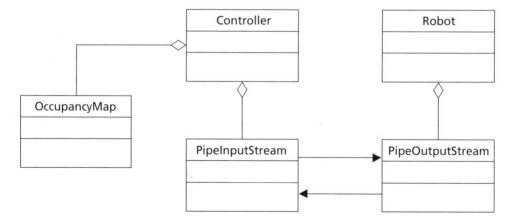

Figure 10.15 The class diagram representing the interaction between the controller and the robot

Sidebar 10.2 Pipe communication

Java Pipe is a mechanism for thread communication. A pipe is a unidirectional channel that connects two threads. One thread writes streams of data into the pipe and the other thread reads them. The pipe has a buffer that stores data until a thread reads them. Reading operations are blocking. When a thread wants to read data from the pipe, it suspends its execution if the pipe is empty and resumes its execution when another thread writes new data into the pipe. Thus, the pipe mechanism can be used for thread synchronization. The code below implements a simple application that uses the pipe mechanism. An instance of class Writer sends an integer value through the pipe. An instance of class Reader waits for an integer value from the pipe. Both classes, Writer and Reader, implement the Runnable interface. Class Communication creates the input and output ends of the pipe and initializes the writer and reader threads.

```java
import java.io.*;
public class Writer implements Runnable {
  PipeOutputStream output;
  int counter = 0;
  public Writer(PipeOutputStream o) {this.output = o; }
  public void run() {
    while(true)
      try {
        counter++;
        System.out.println("Sending " + counter);
        output.write(counter);
        Thread.sleep(Math.round(Math.random()*2000.0 + 500.0));
      } catch(Exception e) {}
  } }
public class Reader implements Runnable {
  PipeInputStream input;
  public Reader(PipeInputStream i) { this.input = i; }
  public void run() {
    while(true)
      try {
      int value = (int) input.read();
        System.out.println("Receiving " + value);
        Thread.sleep(Math.round(Math.random()*2000.0 + 500.0));
      } catch(Exception e) {}
  } }
public class Communication {
  public static void main(String[] args) throws Exception {
    PipeInputStream input = new PipeInputStream();
    PipeOutputStream output = new PipeOutputStream(input);
    Thread writer = new Thread(new Writer(output));
    Thread reader = new Thread(new Reader(input));
    writer.start();
    reader.start();
  } }
```

```
char grid[][] = new char[width/cellDim][height/cellDim];
public OccupancyMap() {
  // initializes the occupancy map
  for(int i=0; i < width/cellDim; i++)
    for(int j=0; j < height/cellDim; j++)
      grid[i][j] = 'n';
                        // the cell has not been explored yet
  this.repaint();        // repaints the window
}
// draws the map
public void paintComponent(Graphics g) {  }
// updates the map with the laser measures
public void drawLaserScan(double position[],
                                    double measures[]) {

}
}
```

Class **Device** implements the slave side mechanisms of the pipe communication between the robot and the controller. Each concrete device invokes
the writeOut() method to send a response to the controller. The controller
initializes the communication with the robot by invoking the setOutput()
method of class **Robot**, which initializes the **output** member of each device.

```
public abstract class Device implements Runnable{
  ...
  // the reference to the output pipe
  protected PrintWriter output = null;
  public void setOutput(PrintWriter o)
                                    { this.output = output; }
  // concrete devices invoke writeOut()to send a response
  // to the controller
  protected synchronized void writeOut(String data) {
    if(output != null)
      output.println(data);
    else
      System.out.println
                    (this.name + " output not initialized");
  }
}
```

Class **Controller** implements the exploration strategy, plans the robot
activities and send commands to the robot's devices. For the sake of
simplicity, this implementation defines a hard-coded sequence of commands that guarantee an obstacle-free path. In every new position the robot
acquires laser measures and updates the map.

```
package moro;
import java.util.*;
```

```java
import java.io.*;
public class Controller implements Runnable{
  Robot robot;     // a reference to the robot
  Thread thread = new Thread(this, "Controller");
                                      // a thread object
  OccupancyMap map = new OccupancyMap();
                                      // the occupancy map
  // the constructor
  public Controller(Robot robot) {
    this.robot = robot;
   }
  // starts the robot thread and the controller thread
  public void start() {
    robot.start();
    thread.start();
  }
  public void run() {
    String result;  // the string that records a task result
    double position[] = new double[3];
                          // the robot position
    double measures[] = new double[360];
                          // the array of laser measures
    int numMeasures = 0;  // the number of laser measures
    try {
      // initializes the communication with the robot
      PipeInputStream pipeIn = new PipeInputStream();
      BufferedReader input = new BufferedReader(
          new InputStreamReader(pipeIn));
      PrintWriter output = new PrintWriter(
          new PipeOutputStream(pipeIn), true);
      robot.setOutput(output);
      // requests the current robot position
      robot.println("R1.GETPOS");
      result = input.readLine();
      parsePosition(result, position);
      // requests a laser scan
      robot.println("L1.SCAN");
      result = input.readLine();
      parseMeasures(result, measures);
      drawLaserScan(position, measures);
      this.repaint();
      // requests a backward translation of the robot
      robot.println("P1.MOVEBW 60");
      result = input.readLine();
    }
    catch(IOException ioe) {ioe.printStackTrace();}
  }
```

```
private void parsePosition(String value,
                           double position[]) {}
private void parseMeasures(String value,
                           double measures[]) {}}
```

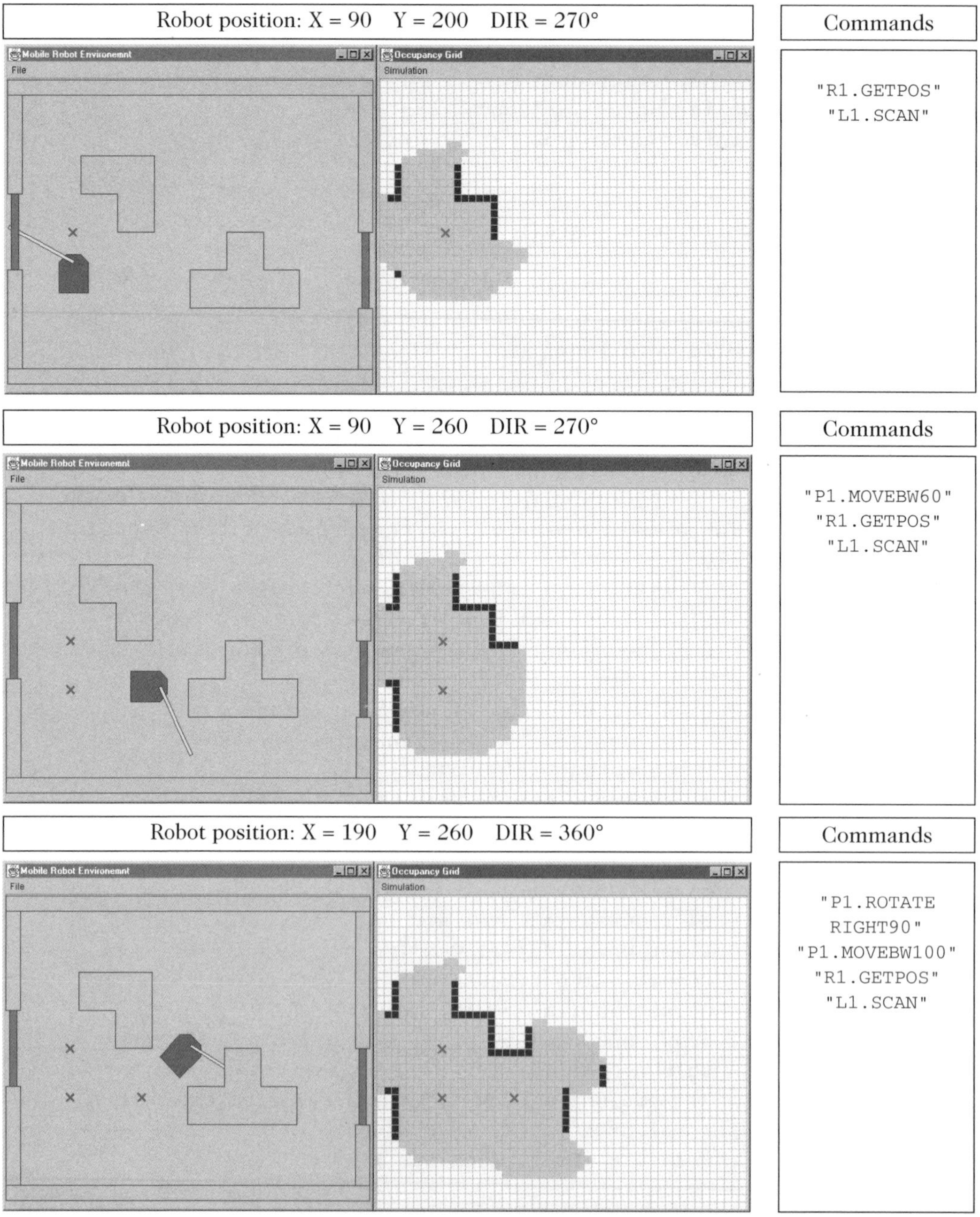
Robot position: X = 90 Y = 200 DIR = 270°
Commands
Mobile Robot Environemnt
File
Occupancy Grid
Simulation
"R1.GETPOS"
"L1.SCAN"
Robot position: X = 90 Y = 260 DIR = 270°
Commands
Mobile Robot Environemnt
File
Occupancy Grid
Simulation
"P1.MOVEBW60"
"R1.GETPOS"
"L1.SCAN"
Robot position: X = 190 Y = 260 DIR = 360°
Commands
Mobile Robot Environemnt
File
Occupancy Grid
Simulation
"P1.ROTATE RIGHT90"
"P1.MOVEBW100"
"R1.GETPOS"
"L1.SCAN"

Figure 10.16 A sequence of laser scans from different positions.

10.6.4 ☐ **Test**

The test case consists of a series of laser scans from different robot positions. Figure 10.16 reports the sequence of updates of the occupancy map (right-hand side). The small crosses indicate the robot positions during the laser scan. Please note that the origin of the robot's reference frame coincides with the middle point of the rear axis. The robot's shape (left-hand side) is depicted in the next position while acquiring new laser measurements.

10.7 ■ Extension

The reader can extend the robot simulator in several ways:

- Design and implement the sonar device.
- Review the robotics literature in order to get specifications of real devices such as video cameras and bumpers, and dead reckoning systems (odometer, global positioning system, etc.).
- Add uncertainty to the robot movements and to the sensor measurements.
- Extend the simulated environment in order to include moving obstacles (e.g. human beings). The remote controller should be able to update the occupancy map accordingly.
- Implement complex robot commands such as tracking a moving object.
- Define more complex exploration strategies that minimize the exploration time and the number of sensor measurements.

10.8 ■ Assessment

The case study exemplified the development of a robot control system for indoor exploration.

As described in the problem specification, the robot is equipped with a variety of sensors and actuators. Each sensor provides information about the surrounding environment that the robot uses to build an internal map-based representation.

Architectural style. The problem analysis emphasized the composite nature of a robotic system. Sensors and actuators are standard devices that can be installed on the robot in order to extend its sensing and moving capabilities when more complex tasks should be performed autonomously. Consequently, from the analysis it emerged that the robot control system should be structured according to the master–slave architecture. This kind of architecture was originally conceived for the control of electronic devices interconnected through an information bus.

Concurrency. The sensors and the mobile platform behave as independent processes that execute tasks independently. The robot controller sends commands to the devices and waits for results.

Communication. The communication between the robot devices and the robot controller is asynchronous and message-based. The physical inter-action between the robot and the environment is simulated by means of a predefined geometric map that represents the robot and the obstacles with regard to the same Cartesian reference frame.

Generic components. From an implementation point of view, each device is implemented according to the pattern *Template method* (Gamma *et al.* 1995): class Device defines method run() which invokes the abstract methods executeCommand() and nextStep(). Every concrete device has to override these abstract methods in order to implement specific behaviours in response to external commands. The communication among the robot controller and the devices is implemented using the pipe mechanism.

Architecture	Master–slave architecture
Context	Decentralized systems made up of several functional units with independent capabilities. Some units process data on behalf of other units.
Problem	Functional units communicate using a common information bus. No centralized clock is used to coordinate data transfers between functional units.
Forces or tradeoffs	Functional units have no means of starting the communication without a risk of collision.
Solution	Some units play the role of master; other units play the role of slave. Master units request slave units to process input data and to return output data. The communication is direct, bidirectional, and asynchronous. Each slave unit has a unique address and responds only to commands addressed to its address. The responding slave decodes the address and reads the command. The slave never starts the communication. The master periodically polls all connected slave units for return values.
Examples	The robot devices play the role of slave; the remote controller plays the role of master.
Force resolution	The master unit assigns the "right to transmit" to slave units. Assignment is done centrally via pooling, where the master unit periodically asks all slaves whether they have data to transmit. If so, the questioned station sends the data immediately; otherwise, it does not reply.

Idiom	Message-based communication
Context	Asynchronous communication between components, applications, systems.
Problem	Two or more functional units need to communicate regardless of their underlying technology. Different units might be implemented in different programming languages, on different platforms, according to different execution models, etc.
Forces or tradeoffs	Communicating complex data structure requires serialization. Communication among functional units occurs not only at a syntactical level (where they commonly agree on a set of data structure definitions and on the meaning of the operations on those structures), but also at a semantic level: functional units communicate in terms of knowledge transfer instead of data transfer.
Solution	Functional units have a message-based interface, which is defined in terms of the set of messages that the unit can interpret. Messages are structured according to a declarative communication language made up of (1) a communication primitive, called performative, that corresponds to a specific linguistic action (e.g. query, answer, assert, define), and (2) the content. The content of a message is a sequence of declarative statements; it is an expression built using a knowledge representation language and formed from words defined in a shared ontology. Each functional unit implements a parser that interprets incoming messages.
Examples	The robot and the remote controller communicate by exchanging textual messages over a serial cable.
Force resolution	Functional units adopt a standard message-based interface that abstracts from their specific implementations.
Design rationale	The main design objective behind this architecture is to achieve a plug-and-play mechanism for reusable components that can be automatically plugged into a host system.

Pattern	Template method
Context	Abstract methods and method redefinition.
Problem	Two or more components have similar data structures and functionalities. The implementation of some methods may differ, but their external behaviour is similar.
Forces or tradeoffs	When the behaviour of a method is complex and its implementations in a variety of components are slightly different, loading of the entire method may be too heavy.
Solution	Define the skeleton of the common method and separate common operation steps from the variable ones. Substitute the code implementing the variable steps with invocations to abstract methods. Implement the abstract methods in subclasses.
Examples	
Force resolution	The pattern supports the reuse of the structure of a complex method and requires only the redefinition (customization) of the variable parts.
Design rationale	The *Template method* design pattern defines hook operations that permit behaviour extension of a complex method only at specific points.

10.9 ■ References

Gamma, E., Helm, R., Johnson, R. and Vlissides, J. (1995) *Design Patterns: Elements of Reusable Object-Oriented Software*, Addison-Wesley.

Nehmzow, U. (2000) *Mobile Robotics: A Practical Introduction*, Springer-Verlag.

Car parking

11

Synthesis

This chapter deals with simulation and animation of an access control system for car parking.

This case study exemplifies the development of a multithreaded and event-based software architecture. The system is organized into a client–server hierarchy of control modules. The clients send commands to the servers according to the caller–provider paradigm. The servers notify state changes by raising events.

- Focus: hierarchical control architecture.
- OO techniques: encapsulation, abstract classes and inheritance.
- Java features: the observer–observable mechanism offered by the java.util package.
- Background: patterns and mechanisms discussed in Chapters 8, 9 and 10.

11.1 ■ Specifications

Access control systems are employed when the flow of people or vehicles must be regulated. Typical examples are museums, motorway toll stations and car parking.

Let us consider Figure 11.1. It depicts the access zone to car parking. Only one car at a time can be in the access zone. When a car arrives, the driver should withdraw the ticket and then proceed into the parking area.

The car flow is regulated by an access control system that is made up of the following devices:

- SEM is a semaphore. When it is red the car should stop. When it is green the car can proceed towards the ticket dispenser.
- IN_PhC is a photocell positioned at the beginning of the access zone. It detects the arrival of a car.
- TD is a ticket dispenser that delivers one ticket at a time.
- SB is a stopping bar that prevents the car from proceeding.
- OUT_PhC is a photocell positioned at the end of the access zone. It detects the entrance of a car inside the parking area.

A computer is connected to the devices with a field bus. It transmits signals from the devices to the computer and commands from the computer

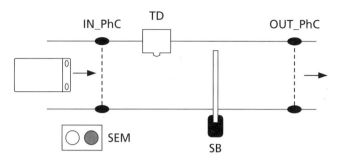

Figure 11.1 The car parking system

to the devices. The computer executes a control program that coordinates the physical devices in order to prevent cars entering the parking area without a ticket.

11.1.1 □ **The physical devices**

The semaphore is a standard two-colour traffic light. It behaves as a finite state machine that has two states, RED and GREEN, and two state transitions between them.

A photocell is a simple device made up of an optical sensor that detects the light beam of a transmitter. The sensor and the transmitter are positioned at the opposite sides of the access lane. When a car enters the sensor zone, it interrupts the light beam. When the car leaves the sensor zone, the sensor detects the light beam. Thus, a photocell behaves as a finite state machine that has two states, CLEARED and OCCUPIED, and two state transitions between them. Whenever a state transition occurs, the device sends a signal to the computer. We assume that a photocell is a reliable device that always behaves according to these specifications.

The ticket dispenser is a machine that delivers a ticket when it receives a command from the controller. The dispenser delivers only one ticket at a time. When the driver withdraws the ticket, the dispenser is ready to deliver a new one. It can be modelled as a finite state machine with two states, DELIVERED and WITHDRAWN, and two transitions between them. When a state transition occurs, the machine sends a signal to the computer.

The stopping bar receives two commands from the controller, raise and lower and signals the controller when it reaches the UP and DOWN positions. We assume that the stopping bar is an unreliable device that might be unavailable for certain periods of time when the intervention of the operator is required.

11.1.2 □ **The car and the driver**

The car represents the external world that sends stimuli to the access control system and receives feedback from it. The car sends stimuli to the photocells, when it occupies and clears the sensor zones, and to the ticket dispenser, when the driver withdraws a ticket. The driver watches the semaphore, the ticket dispenser and the stopping bar to ascertain when it is time to proceed and to withdraw the ticket.

11.1.3 □ The control program

The controller imposes a behaviour on the access control system consisting of the following sequence of phases.

- Phase 1: The controller is waiting for a car to occupy the area of the first photocell.
- Phase 2: The car is proceeding towards the ticket dispenser. The controller waits for the car to clear the first photocell. The controller sets the semaphore to red and sends the command to deliver a ticket. If a new car arrives, it must wait for the semaphore to become green.
- Phase 3: Both the car and the controller are waiting for the ticket to be delivered.
- Phase 4: The ticket dispenser delivers the ticket. The controller waits for the car driver to withdraw the ticket. When the driver withdraws the ticket, the controller sends the command to raise the stopping bar.
- Phase 5: Both the car and the controller wait for the stopping bar to be up.
- Phase 6: The stopping bar is up. The car proceeds into the parking area. The controller waits for the car to occupy the second photocell.
- Phase 7: The car has occupied the second photocell. The controller waits for the car to clear the second photocell. When the car has cleared the second photocell, the controller sends the command to lower the stopping bar
- Phase 8: The controller waits for the stopping bar to be down. When the stopping bar is down the controller sets the semaphore to green. A new car can proceed along the access lane.

The control program should be highly reconfigurable: the programmer might implement control programs that handle new scenarios. For example, the behaviour of the access control system is different in the case of malfunctioning (e.g. the dispenser needs maintenance) or emergency (e.g. a fire engine is not required to obtain a ticket).

11.1.4 □ The simulator

The simulator is a program that animates the access area depicted in Figure 11.1.

- It visualizes the car while it is proceeding along the access lane. The car should be represented graphically in a sequence of consecutive positions every 100 milliseconds.
- It visualizes the light beam of the photocells with a dashed red line that crosses the access lane. When the car occupies the photocells, the red line is not displayed.

- When a ticket has been delivered, it visualizes the ticket outside the dispenser. The ticket dispenser simulates the printing operation with a delay of 700 milliseconds.
- It visualizes the stopping bar while it is raising and lowering step by step every 100 milliseconds. The bar is down when it is in the horizontal position (0 degrees). The bar is up when it is in the vertical position (90 degrees). Every step corresponds to 9 degrees.

11.2 ■ Problem analysis

The access control system is a typical reactive system: its dynamic is governed by stimuli received from the external world. In this scenario, the external world is represented by the car that proceeds on the access lane and interacts with the physical devices. This case study shows several similarities with those discussed in Chapter 9 and Chapter 10.

The work cell (Chapter 9) is an example of a discrete event dynamic system: the dynamic behaviour is described with a set of finite state machines that synchronize their activities by exchanging events. The work cell system is characterized by a number of different macro events that notify the start and completion time of the components' activities. When state transitions occur, physical devices generate events, which in turn trigger state transitions in other devices. In terms of simulation, we were interested in testing the correct interaction between the work cell components and thus we disregarded the animation of the physical devices.

The mobile robot (Chapter 10) is an example of process-based dynamic system: the dynamic behaviour emerges from the exchange of service requests between autonomous components and the use of shared resources. The system is characterized by frequent fine-grained interactions between the environment and the robot's devices. We simulated the behaviour of the laser and the mobile platform with independent threads that animate the robot during the exploration. The robot controller was modelled as an independent thread that interacts with the robot's components according to the communication and synchronization patterns of client–server software architectures.

The specification of the access control system indicates four fundamental requirements:

- At most, two cars can be present within the system simultaneously: one car is proceeding along the access lane; another car is waiting for the semaphore to go green.
- The simulator should animate the behaviour of the cars and of the physical devices.
- The control logic should be encapsulated in a control module, which must be easily reprogrammable without affecting the rest of the system.
- The cars, the controller and the devices synchronize themselves by exchanging events.

According to these requirements, the access control system resembles a typical event-driven client–server control architecture.

11.2.1 □ Domain models

Typically the evolution of a software control system is bottom-up. Very often, control applications are built by integrating existing components, which have been developed without any prior knowledge of the environment in which they will be embedded.

The architecture of software control systems usually consists in a hierarchy of component layers (Aarsten *et al.* 1996). A higher-level component (e.g. the controller of the access control system), acting as a client, integrates lower-level components, which act as servers (e.g. the photocells, the ticket dispenser and the stopping bar.) In such systems, lower-level components are more stable than higher-level components, which undergo frequent reconfigurations according to rapidly evolving functional requirements.

In complex control systems, some components might play both the role of clients of lower-level components and the role of servers of higher-level components. A major issue is the design of the software glue that integrates the components and allows them to communicate. Communication requires that some sort of visibility must exist among the components. Visibility implies dependency with respect to changes, and hence it has consequences for the entire system's design. In hierarchical software architectures it is better to avoid visibility loops between components at different layers. This is achieved by offering the components two communication mechanisms where visibility and flow of information move in the same direction and in the opposite direction with respect to the communicating components.

The first mechanism, known as caller–provider and deeply rooted in object-oriented programming, is involved when an object invokes another object's method. In hierarchical software architectures, it is convenient that higher-level components (more volatile) have visibility of lower-level components (more stable) but not vice versa. A client requests services from a server by invoking the methods of its interface. For example, the controller requests the ticket dispenser to deliver a ticket. Thus, both visibility and flow of information move from the client to the server.

The second mechanism, the broadcaster–listener mechanism, consists in giving the components the ability to both broadcast and listen to events. The broadcaster does not know the identity of its listeners, which might change over time. Conversely, the components that want to be notified when an event is raised must know the identity of the component that broadcasts that event. In hierarchical software architectures it is convenient that lower-level components communicate with the higher-level ones by broadcasting events. Thus, visibility and flow of information move in the opposite direction: the client knows the server that broadcasts events of interest.

11.2.2 □ **Main features**

Three main features characterize the development of the car parking system: the control system architecture, the interaction between the access control system and the car, and the graphical animation.

- *Control system architecture.* The simulator is a concurrent software application structured as a hierarchical client–server system. The system components synchronize by exchange of events.
- *Car–system interaction.* The application should simulate the physical interaction between the car and the photocells and between the car driver, the ticket dispenser and the stopping bar.
- *Graphical animation.* The simulator should animate the cars and the physical devices.

11.2.3 □ **Test**

Two main functionalities need to be tested carefully: the communication and synchronization mechanisms between the system components, and the correct behaviour of the car, the physical devices and the controller.

11.3 ■ Architecture and planning

The system architecture is organized into three control layers (see Figure 11.2). The lower layer includes the physical devices that make up the access lane. The middle layer includes the car and the controller that interact with the access lane. The upper layer is made up of the graphical user interface that visualizes the cars moving within the access lane.

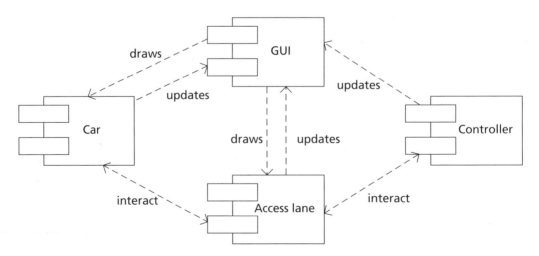

Figure 11.2 The system architecture

The development of the access control system is organized into three phases that produce two prototypes.

■ *Prototype 1: Event-based communication*. A simple client–server application that tests the correct functioning of the communication and synchronization mechanisms: broadcaster–listener and caller–provider.

■ *Prototype 2: Graphical animation*. The graphical application that animates the access control system. Only one car is running within the system.

11.4 ■ Prototype 1: Event-based communication

The first prototype identifies the functional requirements of the access control system and the interaction patterns among the system components. The goal is to identify, develop and test a standard architecture that can then be customized for this case study and for its possible extensions.

11.4.1 □ Analysis

The components of the access control system can be classified into two categories:

■ Photocell, ticket dispenser and stopping bar play the role of servers. They receive stimuli from the car and controller and notify state transitions by raising events. Their dynamic behaviour consists in the graphical animation of the physical devices.

■ The car and controller play the role of clients. They submit stimuli to the physical devices and wait for the event they raise. The car's dynamic simulates the behaviour of the driver, who conducts the car along the access lane. His or her behaviour can be completely automated or can respond to the command that the user submits through the graphical interface. The controller dynamics implement the sequence of phases described in Section 11.1.3.

Two cars might be present in the system simultaneously. In reality, we can assume that outside the access lane there is a queue of cars waiting to enter into the car parking area. Let's consider three cars arriving at the area: a red car, a green car and a blue car. The behaviour of the queue is as follows:

■ When the red car arrives, the semaphore is green. The car proceeds within the access lane and the semaphore goes red.

■ When the green car arrives, the semaphore is red. It waits for the semaphore to go green.

■ When the blue car arrives, the green car is in front of it. The blue car waits for the green car to proceed.

■ When the red car enters the car parking area, the semaphore goes green, the green car proceeds and notifies the blue car.

■ In order to run the simulation indefinitely, the red car is queued again after the blue car.

■ This procedure repeats until the user stops the simulation.

Tables 11.1 and 11.2 report component interactions according to the caller–provider and broadcaster–listener communication mechanisms.

It is interesting to note that the car plays both the role of broadcaster and listener. In fact, an object of class Car broadcasts event PROCEEDING when it enters the access lane. Objects representing cars waiting in the queue listen to this event to know when they can proceed. This mechanisms simulates the visual interactions between the car driver and the car in front of him or her.

11.4.2 □ Design

In the previous two case studies we discussed two examples of dynamic systems. For the work cell system we chose a centralized event-based architecture. For the mobile robot system we chose a decentralized process-based architecture. The access control system shows characteristics common to the previous two case studies.

Decision point

Which execution model supports the caller–provider interaction pattern?

To animate the dynamics of the car and the physical devices requires the implementation of the system components as independent threads of execution. The physical devices notify the car and the controller that a state transition has occurred by raising events. Thus, we choose to implement every system component as an event-based process.

We introduce the abstract class EventProcess to implement the concurrency and synchronization mechanisms that are common to all the system components. Class EventProcess inherits from the Runnable interface (see Sidebar 10.1, p. 255) but leaves the implementation of the run() method

Table 11.1 The list of stimuli exchanged between callers and providers

Caller	Stimulus	Provider
Controller	setRed	Semaphore
Controller	setGreen	Semaphore
Car	occupy	Photocell
Car	clear	Photocell
Controller	deliver	Ticket dispenser
Car	withdraw	Ticket dispenser
Controller	raise	Stopping bar
Controller	lower	Stopping bar

Table 11.2 The list of events exchanged among broadcasters and listeners

Broadcaster	Event	Listener
Photocell	OCCUPIED	Controller
Photocell	CLEARED	Controller
Ticket dispenser	DELIVERED	Car, controller
Ticket dispenser	WITHDRAWN	Controller
Stopping bar	UP	Car, controller
Stopping bar	DOWN	Controller
Car	PROCEEDING	Car

to its concrete subclasses. Class EventProcess encapsulates an instance of class Thread that executes the run() method of its concrete subclasses. Clients and servers extend class EventProcess adding data structures and implementing the control logic in the run() method.

Servers implement specific methods to handle requests of services from the clients and to start the execution tasks. They can handle only one request at a time and remain idle until a client invokes an interface method.

Decision point

Which communication mechanisms support the broadcaster–listener interaction pattern?

Since clients and servers encapsulate independent threads that govern their dynamics, event scheduling cannot be centralized. In contrast to the solution adopted for the work cell system, events are not scheduled in advance to simulate the duration of an operation and to determine its completion. Instead, server threads suspend their execution for the amount of time corresponding to the duration of their operations (see the sleep() primitive in Sidebar 10.1, p. 255) and raise an event that notifies the completion of that operation.

Clients synchronize with servers by suspending their execution until the server notifies a given event. An example is the car waiting for the ticket dispenser to deliver a ticket. The package java.util offers class Observable and interface Observer to implement the server side and client side respectively of the broadcaster–listener interaction pattern (see Sidebar 8.1, p. 181). Class EventProcess inherits from both of them. In this way, every subclass of EventProcess can play both the roles of client and server.

Class EventProcess implements method waitEvent() in order to allow clients to wait for specific events. Accordingly, class EventProcess implements method update() of interface Observer in order to notify clients of the events they are waiting for. This solution offers two main advantages. First, it allow clients to use a standard implementation of method update() that does not block the server thread for unspecified amounts of time (see Sidebar 8.1, p. 181, for this issue). Second, it does not prevent clients from redefining their own **update()** methods to handle specific situations. Figure 11.3 depicts the class diagram that defines class **EventProcess**.

11.4.3 □ Implementation

Class **EventProcess** implements the abstract component that represents the generic control module of a client–server architecture. Every concrete control module must implement the run() method. The **attachTo()** method can be invoked by the object itself or by an external object that holds a reference to this object. Clients wait for an event and suspend their execution by invoking method **waitEvent()**. Servers notify their state transitions by notifying events with method **notifyObservers()**.

```java
package parking;
import java.util.Observable;
import java.util.Observer;
public class EventProcess extends Observable implements
                                    Observer, Runnable{
  String name;            // the name of this EventProcess
  Thread thread;
              // the thread that executes the run() method
  boolean alive = false; // true when the thread is running
  String observable = ""; // the name of an observable object
  String event = "";
                  // the event this object is waiting for
  public EventProcess(String name) {
    this.name = name;
  }
  // the invoker of attachTo() is an Observer; the parameter
  // is an Observable; it adds this object to the list of
  // observers of "process";
```

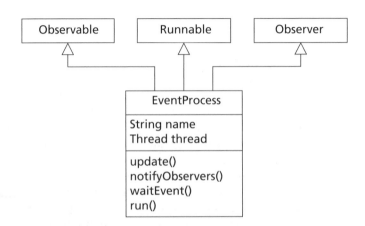

Figure 11.3 The class diagram

```java
public void attachTo(EventProcess process) {
  process.addObserver(this);
}
// notifies this process that "observable" raised "event"
public synchronized void update(Observable observable,
                                             Object event) {
  // records the name of the observable and of the event
  // in member variable;
  this.observable = observable.toString();
  this.event = (String) event;
  // wakes up the thread that is waiting for an event
  notify();
}
// the waitEvent() method is invoked by an Observer
// object; it suspends this thread until process
// "p_observable" raises event "p_event"
public synchronized void waitEvent(Observable observable,
                                             String event) {
  // verifies that the event has been raised
  while(! (this.observable.equals(observable.toString()) &&
           this.event.equals(event)))
    try {
      // the thread suspends its execution until the
      // notify() method has been invoked
      this.wait();
    }
    catch(InterruptedException ie)
                                    { ie.printStackTrace();}
  // reset the event; this allows the process to wait for
  // a new event of the same type
  this.event = "";
}
// this method is called by an Observable object;
// it notifies the observers that its state has changed
public void notifyObservers(String event) {
  this.setChanged();
  super.notifyObservers(event);
}
// starts this process
public void start() {
  // creates a thread object and starts it
  thread = new Thread(this);
  if(! alive) {
    alive = true;
    thread.start();
  }
}
```

```java
    // this method should be overridden in every subclass
    public void run() { }
    // returns the name of this process
    public String toString() {
      return this.name;
    }
    // notifies the graphical user interface
    public void repaint() {
      this.notifyObservers("REPAINT");
    }
  }
```

11.4.4 □ Test

The test case consists of the implementation of a simple client–server application. Class **Server** extends class **EventProcess** adding a reference to the graphical interface (the **frame** member variable). Clients invoke method doService() to start the execution of a task. A task behaviour is implemented in method run() and simply consists of switching the value of a Boolean variable. When the task starts, the server raises the **DOSERVICE** event. When it is completed, the server raises the **WORKDONE** event.

```java
package parking;
public class Server extends EventProcess {
  boolean working = false;    // true when the server is
                              // working the constructor
  public Server(String name) {
    super(name);
  }
  // The Client invoke this method to request the execution
  // of a Server task.
  public void doService() {
    synchronized(this) { this.notify(); }
  }
  // this method implements the Server behaviour
  public void run() {
    while(alive)
    try {
      // waits for a request of execution from a Client
      synchronized(this) { this.wait();  }
      working = true;
      // notifies the Client that the task has been started
      this.notifyObservers("DOSERVICE");
      this.repaint();
      // The Server receives a request of task execution.
      // It simulates the task duration by suspending the
      // thread for 1000 milliseconds
```

```
      thread.sleep(1000);
      working = false;
      this.repaint();
      // notifies the Client that the task has been completed
      this.notifyObservers("WORKDONE");
    }
    catch(InterruptedException ie) { ie.printStackTrace(); }
  }
}
```

Class **Client** extends class **EventProcess**. It holds a reference to the server object and implements the run() method. Every 1500 milliseconds the client sends a request to the Server to execute a task and visualizes string DOSERVICE in the graphical user interface.

```
package parking;
public class Client extends EventProcess {
  Server server;          // a reference to the Server object
  public Client(String name, Server server) {
    super(name);
    this.server = server;
    this.attachTo(server); // attaches itself to the event
                           // raised by the Server
  }
  // this method implements the client's behaviour
  public void run() {
    while(alive)
    try {
      server.doService();
      this.waitEvent(server, "WORKDONE");
      thread.sleep(1500);
    }
    catch(InterruptedException ie) { ie.printStackTrace(); }
  }
}
```

11.5 ■ Prototype 2: Graphical animation

The second prototype simulates the behaviour of the physical devices, the controller and the car and animates them in a graphical user interface.

11.5.1 □ Analysis

Let's consider the dynamic of each subsystem. Figure 11.4 depicts the finite state automata of PhotoCell, TicketDispenser and StoppingBar respectively. Ovals represent states, while rectangles represent state transitions. State names are in bold upper case. Two labels describe state transitions. The

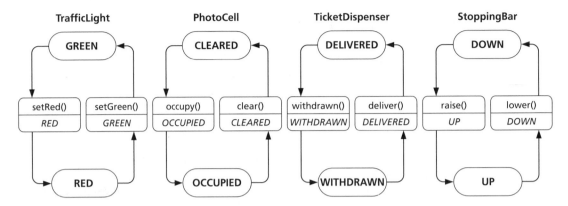

Figure 11.4 Finite state automata of traffic light, photocell, ticket dispenser and stopping bar

upper label indicates the condition that triggers the transition. For example, occupy() is the method of PhotoCell that triggers the transition from CLEARED to OCCUPIED. The lower label indicates the action that is performed during state transition. For example, PhotoCell notifies event *OCCUPIED*. Event names are in italic upper case.

Figure 11.5 depicts the controller's finite state automaton. It is made up of eight states that represent the phases described in Section 11.1.3.

Figure 11.6 depicts the car's finite state automaton. For the sake of simplicity, we assume that only one car is present in the system at any time; that is, in this prototype we do not model the queue of waiting cars.

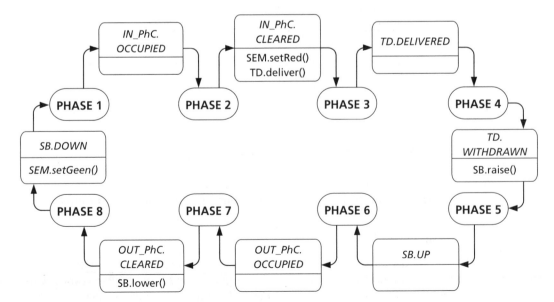

Figure 11.5 Finite state automaton of controller

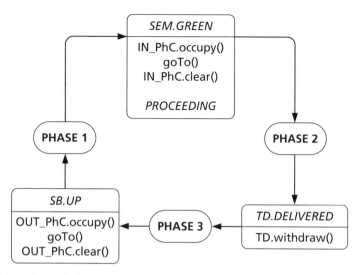

Figure 11.6 The car's finite state automaton

The car repeats a sequence of three phases indefinitely. In the first phase, it waits for the semaphore to go green. Then it proceeds to the ticket dispenser and, in phase 2, it waits for the ticket to be delivered. Finally, in phase 3, the car waits for the stopping bar to be raised. When the car enters the parking area, it starts this sequence again.

The last component to consider is the graphical user interface, which animates the physical devices and the cars. It should observe the event raised by each component and react to them by redrawing the scene accordingly. The layout should look like the diagram shown in Figure 11.1. The user will watch the cars proceeding and crossing the photocell, the stopping bar raising and lowering, and the dispenser delivering the ticket.

11.5.2 □ Design

The physical devices, the car and the controller extend the abstract class EventProcess (see Figure 11.7). Every subclass overrides method run() in order to implement the finite state automata described in the previous section. The classes representing the physical devices implement specific methods that trigger their state transitions.

Figure 11.8 depicts the interaction diagram that shows the exchange of messages between the subsystems. Labels in lower case correspond to method invocations according to the caller–provider schema. Labels in upper case correspond to event notifications according to the broadcaster–listener schema.

The graphical user interface is supported by three classes as depicted in Figure 11.9. Class GUIParkingArea is a panel that represents the layout of the access lane. Class GUIMessages displays events of interests raised by the components. Class GUIFrame is the top class and implements the Observer

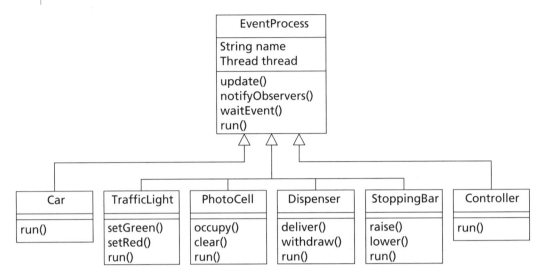

Figure 11.7 The class diagram

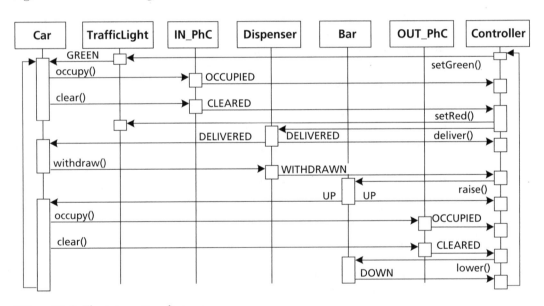

Figure 11.8 The interaction diagram

interface. It initializes all the components of the car parking system and listens to the events they raise.

11.5.3 ☐ Implementation

The following code implements class TrafficLight, class PhotoCell, class TicketDispenser and class StoppingBar. The state of each is represented by a unique Boolean variable. Two methods trigger state transitions that change

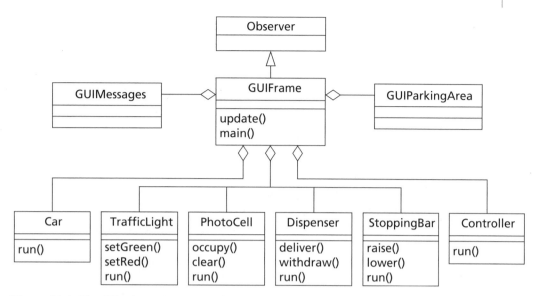

Figure 11.9 The GUI classes

the value of the state variable and wake up the thread. The run() method notifies state transitions.

```java
package parking;
public class TrafficLight extends EventProcess {
  public boolean stop = false;
            // true if the light is red, false if green
  String eventName;
            // the name of an event that will be broadcast
  public TrafficLight(String name) {
    super(name);
  }
// sets the state to "RED", if it is "GREEN";
// then it notifies the thread
  public void setRed() {
    if(stop) return;
    eventName = "RED";
    stop = true;
    synchronized(this) { notify(); }
  }
// sets the state to "GREEN", if it is "RED";
// then it notifies the thread
  public void setGreen() {
    if(!stop) return;
    eventName = "GREEN";
    stop = false;
    synchronized(this) { notify(); }
  }
```

```
                // repaints the GUI when the state changes
            public void run() {
              while(alive)
              try {
                synchronized(this) { wait(); }
                this.repaint();
                this.notifyObservers(eventName);
              } catch(InterruptedException ie) {ie.printStackTrace();}
            }
          }
          package parking;
          public class PhotoCell extends EventProcess {
            public boolean cleared = true;
                                   // true if the photocell is cleared
            String eventName;
            public PhotoCell(String name) {
              super(name);
            }
            // sets the state to "OCCUPIED"
            public void occupy() {
              if(! cleared) return;
              eventName = "OCCUPIED";
              cleared = false;
              synchronized(this) { notify(); }
            }
            // sets the state to "CLEARED"
            public void clear() {
              if(cleared) return;
              eventName = "CLEARED";
              cleared = true;
              synchronized(this) { notify(); }
            }
            // repaints the GUI when the state changes
            public void run() {
              while(alive)
              try {
                synchronized(this) { wait(); }
                this.repaint();
                this.notifyObservers(eventName);
              } catch(InterruptedException ie) {ie.printStackTrace();}
            }
          }
          package parking;
          public class TicketDispenser extends EventProcess {
            boolean delivered = false;
                                // true if the ticket has been delivered
            String eventName;
```

```
  long delay;
    // the duration of a delivering or withdrawing operation
  public TicketDispenser(String name) {
    super(name);
  }
  // sets the state to "DELIVERED"
  public void deliver() {
    if(delivered) return;
    eventName = "DELIVERED";
    delay = 700;
    delivered = true;
    synchronized(this) { notify(); }
  }
  // sets the state to "WITHDRAWN"
  public void withdraw() {
    if(! delivered) return;
    eventName = "WITHDRAWN";
    delay = 200;
    delivered = false;
    synchronized(this) { notify(); }
  }
  // repaints the GUI when the state changes
  public void run() {
    while(alive)
    try {
      synchronized(this) { wait(); }
      thread.sleep(delay);
      delivered = ! delivered;
      this.repaint();
      this.notifyObservers(eventName);
    } catch(InterruptedException ie)
                          { ie.printStackTrace(); }
  }
}
package parking;
public class StoppingBar extends EventProcess {
  double angle = 0.0;    // 0.0 : horizontal, PI/2 : vertical
  double direction = 1.0; // 1.0 : bottom-up, -1.0 : top-down
  String eventName;
  public StoppingBar(String name) {
    super(name);
  }
  // raises the bar and notifies the "UP" event
  public void raise() {
    if(angle == Math.PI / 2.0)
      return;
```

```
      direction = 1.0;
      eventName = "UP";
      synchronized(this) { notify(); }
    }
    // lowers the bar and notifies the "DOWN" event
    public void lower() {
      if(angle == 0.0)
        return;
      direction = -1.0;
      eventName = "DOWN";
      synchronized(this) { notify(); }
    }
    public void run() {
      while(alive)
      try {
        synchronized(this) { wait(); }
        // repaints the stopping bar every 9 degrees
        for(int i=0; i<10; i++) {
          angle += direction * Math.PI / 20.0;
          this.repaint();
          thread.sleep(200);
        }
        this.notifyObservers(eventName);
      } catch(InterruptedException ie)
                                  { ie.printStackTrace(); }

    }
  }
```

Class **Controller** has a reference to all the physical devices of the access control system. It listens to the events raised by the photocells, the ticket dispenser and the stopping bar. Method run() implements the finite state machine depicted in Figure 11.5.

```
package parking;
public class Controller extends EventProcess {
  TrafficLight trafficLight;
                      // a reference to the traffic light
  PhotoCell inPhotoCell;
                      // a reference to the first photocell
  PhotoCell outPhotoCell;
                      // a reference to the second photocell
  StoppingBar stoppingBar;
                      // a reference to the stopping bar
  TicketDispenser ticketDispenser;
                      // a reference to the ticket dispenser
  int phase = 1;      // the counter of the current phase
                      // the constructor
```

```java
public Controller(String name, TrafficLight tLight,
        PhotoCell inPhC, PhotoCell outPhC, StoppingBar
        bar, TicketDispenser dispenser) {
  super(name);
  trafficLight = tLight;
  inPhotoCell = inPhC;
  outPhotoCell = outPhC;
  stoppingBar = bar;
  ticketDispenser = dispenser;
  // attaches to the events raised by the physical devices
  this.attachTo(inPhC);
  this.attachTo(outPhC);
  this.attachTo(bar);
  this.attachTo(dispenser);
}
public void run() {
  trafficLight.setGreen();
  while(alive) {
    switch(phase) {
    case 1:
      // waits for a new car to cross the first photocell
      waitEvent(inPhotoCell, "OCCUPIED");
      phase = 2; break;
    case 2:
      // waits for a new car to clear the first photocell
      waitEvent(inPhotoCell, "CLEARED");
      // set the trafficLight to red
      trafficLight.setRed();
      // a new car proceeds to the ticket dispenser
      ticketDispenser.deliver();
      phase = 3; break;
    case 3:
      // waits for the ticket dispenser to deliver the
      // ticket
      waitEvent(ticketDispenser, "DELIVERED");
      phase = 4; break;
    case 4:
      // waits for the car to withdraw the ticket
      waitEvent(ticketDispenser, "WITHDRAWN");
      // the car has withdrawn the ticket; it raises the
      // stopping bar
      stoppingBar.raise();
      phase = 5; break;
    case 5:
      // the controller waits for the stopping bar to be up
```

```
        waitEvent(stoppingBar, "UP");
        phase = 6; break;
    case 6:
        // waits for the car to cross the second photocell
        waitEvent(outPhotoCell, "OCCUPIED");
        phase = 7; break;
    case 7:
        // the car has crossed the second photocell
        waitEvent(outPhotoCell, "CLEARED");
        // the car has cleared the second photocell;
        // lowers the stopping bar
        stoppingBar.lower();
        phase = 8; break;
    case 8:
        // the controller waits for the stopping bar to be
        // down
        waitEvent(stoppingBar, "DOWN");
        // set the trafficLight to green
        trafficLight.setGreen();
        phase = 1; break;
    }
  }
}
```

Class **Car** animates the car moving along the access lane. Method run()
implements the finite state machine depicted in Figure 11.6.

```
package parking;
public class Car extends EventProcess {
  TrafficLight trafficLight;
                    // a reference to the traffic light
  PhotoCell inPhotoCell;
                    // a reference to the first photocell
  PhotoCell outPhotoCell;
                    // a reference to the second photocell
  StoppingBar stoppingBar;
                    // a reference to the stopping bar
  TicketDispenser ticketDispenser;
                    // a reference to the ticket dispenser
  int phase = 1;
                    // the counter of the current phase
  int distance = 0;
                    // the position along the access lane
                    // the constructor
  public Car(String name, TrafficLight tLight,
            PhotoCell inPhC, PhotoCell outPhC,StoppingBar
            bar, TicketDispenser dispenser) {
```

```java
    super(name);
    trafficLight = tLight;
    inPhotoCell = inPhC;
    outPhotoCell = outPhC;
    stoppingBar = bar;
    ticketDispenser = dispenser;
    // attaches to the events raised by the physical devices
    this.attachTo(tLight);
    this.attachTo(dispenser);
    this.attachTo(bar);
  }
  public void run() {
    while(alive)
    try {
      switch(phase) {
      case 1:
        // waits for the traffic light
        waitEvent(trafficLight, "GREEN");
        // a new car proceeds to the ticket dispenser
        thread.sleep(500);
        goTo(20);
        inPhotoCell.occupy();
        goTo(170);
        inPhotoCell.clear();
        this.notifyObservers("PROCEEDING");
        goTo(320);
        phase = 2; break;
      case 2:
        // waits for the ticket
        waitEvent(ticketDispenser, "DELIVERED");
        // withdraws the ticket
        thread.sleep(1500);
        ticketDispenser.withdraw();
        phase = 3; break;
      case 3:
        // waits for the stopping bar to be raised
        waitEvent(stoppingBar, "UP");
        // proceeds through the second photocell
        goTo(470);
        outPhotoCell.occupy();
        goTo(650);
        outPhotoCell.clear();
        // enters the car park
        goTo(750);
        inside = false;
        distance = 0;
```

```
                    phase = 1; break;
                }
            } catch(InterruptedException ioe)
                                    { ioe.printStackTrace(); }
        }
        // the GUI paints the car in the position corresponding to
        // the value of "distance"
        private void goTo(int pos) {
          while(distance < pos) {
            distance +=10;
            this.repaint();
            try{
              thread.sleep(100);
            } catch(InterruptedException ie)
                                    { ioe.printStackTrace(); }
          }
        }}
```

11.5.4 □ Test

The test case consists of the visualization of the access lane in the graphical user interface (see Figure 11.10). The test should verify the correct

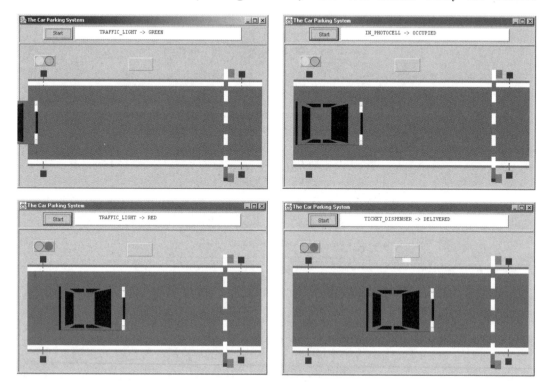

Figure 11.10 The sequence of snapshots that show the car proceeding along the access lane

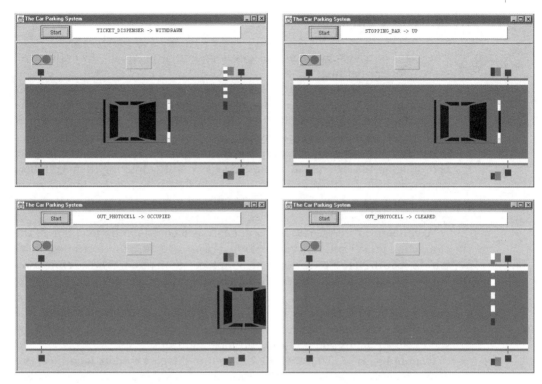

Figure 11.10 (*continued*).

correspondence between the state of the system and the events generated by each component.

11.6 ■ Extension

The second prototype does not simulate the situation where a queue of cars is waiting outside the parking access lane. Typically, while a car is proceeding along the access lane, another car is waiting for the traffic light to go green. The simulator can be extended in such a way that three cars (red, green, blue) are active in the system. For example, at a given time instant, the red car is withdrawing the ticket, the green car is waiting the traffic light to go green, and the blue car is outside the access lane waiting for the green car to proceed. When the red car completes the access procedure, the green car proceeds along the access lane and the blue car stops at the traffic light. In order to animate the simulation repeatedly, cars go to the end of the waiting queue when they exit the access lane. The controller might implement a variety of alternative behaviours. For example, when a fire engine needs to get into the parking area, the ticket is not delivered and the stopping bar goes up immediately.

11.7 ■ Assessment

The case study exemplified the development of a typical access control system for car parking.

Generic components. The problem specification clearly addresses features that have already been discussed in the previous two case studies. In fact, the car parking system is described in terms of the physical components it is made up of. As in the work cell system presented in Chapter 9, these devices behave as finite state machines. The access control system is in charge of coordinating the behaviour of the devices and of animating their graphical representation. In Chapter 10 we have seen how to animate a mobile robot for indoor exploration. Thus, the car parking system has been designed by generalizing the solutions identified in the previous two case studies.

Architectural styles. The problem analysis focused on the selection of the simulation model and thus on the software architecture that better supports both event-driven simulation and graphical animation. The architecture has been designed as a hierarchy of control layers: at the lower layer, the physical devices play the role of servers that receive stimuli from the environment (the car) and the system controller; at the higher layer, the controller supervises the correct behaviour of the physical devices by sending commands and receiving notification events.

Communication. The analysis of existing domain models identified two communication mechanisms (i.e. the caller–provider and the broadcaster–listener) that cope with inter-component visibility issues typically encountered in the development of software control systems.

Concurrency. The implementation builds on the Java mechanism for concurrency presented in Chapter 10 and for event-based communication presented in Chapter 8.

Architecture	Hierarchy of control layers
Context	Large control systems perform multiple concurrent activities.
Problem	How can the system be organized and divided into parts in order to cope with its complexity?
Forces or tradeoffs	Typically the evolution of a software control system is bottom-up. Control applications are built by integrating existing components, which have been developed without any prior knowledge of the environment in which they have to be embedded.
Solution	The different functionalities of the systems should be encapsulated into control modules with precise responsibilities. The representation of control modules has to be standardized in order to facilitate reuse and architectural unity. Generally, a control module has the following characteristics:

- autonomous decision-making capabilities;
- a series of available services;
- a pool of controlled resources.

Control modules should be organized into a hierarchy of control layers, so that higher-level control modules, playing the role of clients, coordinate the control modules below them, which play the role of servers.

Force resolution	Control modules have a standard communication interface. They can play both the role of server of higher-level control modules and the role of client of lower-level control modules.

Pattern	Visibility between control modules
Context	Control modules in the hierarchy need to communicate with one another. Communication requires that some sort of visibility must exist among components.
Problem	In such systems lower-level components are more stable than higher-level components, which undergo frequent reconfigurations according to rapidly evolving functional requirements. How can the right visibility relationships between the control modules be established?
Forces or tradeoffs	Visibility implies dependency with respect to changes, and hence it has consequences for the entire system's design. In hierarchical software architectures it is better to avoid visibility loops between components at different layers.
Solution	This is achieved by offering the components two communication mechanisms. The first mechanism, known as caller–provider and deeply rooted in object-oriented programming, is involved when an object invokes another object's method. In hierarchical software architectures, it is convenient that higher-level components (more volatile) have visibility of lower-level components (more stable) but not vice versa. A client requests services from a server by invoking the methods of its interface. The second mechanism, the broadcaster–listener mechanism, consists in giving the components the ability to broadcast and listen to events. The broadcaster does not know the identity of its listeners, which might change over time. Conversely, the components that want to be notified when an event is raised must know the identity of the component that broadcasts that event. In hierarchical software architectures it is convenient that lower-level components communicate with the higher-level ones by broadcasting events.

Force resolution	According to the communication mechanism that is used, visibility and flow of information move in the same direction and in the opposite direction with respect to the communicating components. Using the caller–provider mechanism, both visibility and flow of information move from the client to the server. Using the broadcaster–listener mechanism, visibility and flow of information move in the opposite direction: the client knows the server that broadcasts events of interest.

11.8 ■ Reference

Aarsten, A., Brugali, D. and Menga, G. (1996) "Designing Concurrent and Distributed Control Systems", *Communications of the ACM*, October.

Distributed Architectures

Distributed architectures

12

Synthesis

Distributed computing can be described as the effort to unify multiple networked machines in such a way that information or other resources can be shared by all of these connected computers (Sun Microsystems 2002).

Developing large distributed architectures is complex. It usually requires decomposition into subsystems, which have to communicate in complex patterns in order to express a fruitful global behaviour. In this context, the object-oriented technology plays an important role, since it offers techniques for creating powerful reference models and scalable architectures.

Middleware infrastructures are a promising technology for reifying proven software designs and implementations in order to reduce the cost and improve the quality of software (*CACM* 1997). They consist of integrated sets of service components that allow distributed systems to operate together. Examples are the java.net package for TCP/IP socket-based communication, the java.security package for cryptography and resource access control, the org.xml.sax and org.w3c.dom packages for XML parsing and object serialization, and the java.jni package for interoperability with applications written in different languages.

The third part of this book is dedicated to the exemplification of middleware-based distributed system development.

12.1 ■ Reuse-based development

Using a middleware framework consists in developing end-user applications by delegating the execution of common functionalities to reusable middleware components.

The software reuse approach improves software development by reducing the amount of code that has to be written by the application designer. In particular, assembling previously existing components greatly reduces time to test new applications. When a component is used in a large number of systems by different developers, the knowledge about the component usage, robustness and efficiency is available in the user community. The more a component is used the less it costs.

The reverse side of the coin is that reusing a middleware component instead of developing it from scratch leaves the user dependent upon the component provider. Components available on the market undergo frequent upgrading in response to error reports. Replacing an old component with its new version usually requires rewriting part of the integrating code and probably replacing other components which are not compatible with the new one.

Choosing to follow the mainstream of reuse-based software development requires the application developer to answer the question of whether to exploit an existing middleware framework or to build everything from scratch. Usually, the answer lies between the two extremes. In order to answer this question, the application developer should identify existing middleware frameworks and compare their specifications against the requirements of the application at hand.

From the application developer's viewpoint, the user requirements specification should be analysed by having in mind which components are already available for reuse, what integration effort they require, and whether to reuse them as they are or to build new components from scratch.

According to Boehm (1995), "in the old process, system requirements drove capabilities. In the new process, capabilities will drive system requirements ... it is not a requirement if you can't afford it".

For distributed system development, the application developer should evaluate the middleware against the specific architectural model and distribution paradigm it supports.

12.2 ■ Distributed architecture models

The architecture of a distributed system is described in terms of identified system components (the applications or parts of them), how they are connected (the relationships among the components), and the nature of the connections (the mechanisms used to establish the relationships). Three architectural models are described in the following.

12.2.1 □ The client–server model

In OO programming, interactions between two objects are implemented as operations on one of the two: the object that performs the operations is called the "server", while the object that requests an operation and uses its results is called the "client" (Lewandowsky 1998). When both the client and the server reside in the same address space (i.e. they are part of the same single program), the client holds a reference to the server (its memory address) to invoke its operations. When the client and the server reside on remote computers, a middleware infrastructure allows them to exchange data and services through the network.

12.2.2 □ The three-tier model

Designing a client–server system requires the system's functionality to be split between the clients and the servers. The question is whether to have fat servers (the server manages both the data and the processing) or fat clients (the server manages only the data). It is a matter of how many clients share common data and operations on them and has implications for the system scalability, portability and efficiency.

An evolution of the client–server model is the three-tier model (Shan and Earle 1998). The main difference is that the system functionality is completely separated from the user interface management (the client) and from the data persistence management (the database server) and resides in a middle layer called the application server. The resulting application is easily scalable. As the client is lightweight, moderate computing power is required, and it can be customized and ported to other platforms. The system functionality can be upgraded by replacing or modifying the application server without affecting the clients. The data persistence management can easily be ported to other platforms, since it is clearly separated from the application server.

12.2.3 □ The broker-based model

Due to advances in networking technology, increasingly heterogeneous distributed computing resources are becoming available on the internet. A broker represents a mediation level between clients and servers. According to the information that it manages, the broker acts as a domain name server (it knows the name and internet location of a group of server objects), matchmaker (it knows the service offered by the server objects), facilitator (it knows the policies and protocols to access the services of the server objects) or mediator (it offers new services as a composite of other servers' services).

12.3 ■ Distributed computing paradigms

Information sharing across a network assumes several forms at different levels of abstraction. In this context, abstraction means the capability of accessing distributed resources in a transparent way with regard to their physical location, data format, structure, implementation language and execution support.

12.3.1 □ The stub–skeleton paradigm

This distribution paradigm consists in implementing a distributed address space where client and server objects can exchange messages, i.e. method invocations and return values. This is accomplished by means of two ancillary objects called the "stub" and the "skeleton". The stub is a surrogate (proxy) of the server and resides in the client's address space. It offers the same set of operations (called the "interface") as the remote server. The client invokes the stub's operations as if it were the server itself. The stub is in charge of marshalling the client's request and transmitting it through the network. The skeleton resides in the server's address space and is in charge of receiving and unmarshalling the client's request and of invoking the corresponding server's operation. Similarly, the matched pair stub–skeleton is used to transmit the result of a server's operation to the client through the network. The matched pair stub–skeleton is automatically generated at compile time or at run time by the middleware used to network the client and the server.

The *Remote Method Invocation* (RMI) is the Java mechanism for remote object communication based on the stub–skeleton approach. The client can invoke remote server methods by passing object arguments to the server's stub and receiving object values from it. Thanks to RMI the client can pass objects belonging to subclasses of the arguments supported by the server's methods. If the server does not know the class, it downloads its code dynamically.

12.3.2 □ The mobile code paradigm

In most distributed object systems, the information that can be passed between the client and the server is limited to a small number of primitive data types, or references to other distributed objects, or structures made up of these types and references. It seems natural to expect clients and servers to be able to exchange fully-fledged objects carrying over both the data and the code that manipulates them. This is possible using a different approach from distributed computing, i.e. code mobility. Code mobility can be defined as the capability to dynamically change the bindings between objects and the location where they are executed.

The *Java Applet* technology supports code mobility in the form of *code on demand*, where the client is a standard web browser and the server is a web server.

The programmer implements specific applets on the server side. When a remote user accesses a web page containing a reference to an applet, the applet's code is downloaded from the website and executed inside the browser. The applet is not allowed to access the local resources on the client side (e.g. its file system), but it sends data and commands to the remote server (e.g. via RMI).

12.3.3 □ The declarative communication paradigm

Both the stub–skeleton and the mobile code paradigms require the client and the server to commonly agree on a set of data structure definitions and on the meaning of the operations on those structures. This is a strong requirement that limits the possibility of integrating heterogeneous (e.g. legacy) systems. An alternative approach has emerged from the distributed artificial intelligence field: the definition of standard application-level communication languages and protocols.

Distributed applications can cooperate since they share the same communication language and a common vocabulary, which contains words appropriate to common application areas and whose meaning is defined in a shared ontology. A declarative communication language is a messaging protocol, where a message is a textual expression composed of (1) a communication primitive, called performative, that corresponds to a specific linguistic action (e.g. query, answer, assert, define), and (2) the content, i.e. a sequence of declarative statements built using a knowledge representation language. The implementation of the declarative communication paradigm does not call for the use of the stub–skeleton mechanism, or a common execution environment as code mobility does. Each distributed component relies on a parser component that interprets the incoming messages.

Java applications supporting the declarative communication paradigm use the Java Socket mechanism to exchange messages over the network or the Java Servlet API.

Servlets are small applications that run within a web server. The programmer implements specific servlets on the server side and gives them network names in the same way as is done for standard web pages. A remote user connects to a servlet's URL using a web browser. A servlet can receive multiple connection requests from different browsers simultaneously and can return entire web pages containing images, sounds and text resulting from a query to the server's database. The user can send data and commands to a remote servlet by means of a HTML form or an applet. *Java Server Pages* (JSP) are an extension of servlet technology that provide a declarative method of developing servlets.

12.4 ■ Part overview

The third part of this book exemplifies the development of distributed software architectures addressing the architectural models and distribution paradigms discussed above (see Table 12.1).

Chapter 13 (Supervisory control and data acquisition system) exemplifies the development of a simple supervisory control and data acquisition (SCADA) system for car surface painting. The emphasis is on the design of the distributed client–server architecture, and the Java RMI mechanism is used to interconnect distributed components such as the work cell simulator, the colour tank controllers and the supervisory station.

Chapter 14 (Supermarket operation support system) deals with the design of a typical information system supporting the activities of a supermarket.

Table 12.1 Architectural models, distribution paradigms and technologies adopted in each case study

Case study	Architecture model	Paradigm	Technology
13 SCADA	Client–server	Stub–skeleton	RMI
14 Supermarket	Three-tier	Declarative	Socket
15 GIS	Three-tier	Mobile code	Applet
16 Ubiquitous email	Broker-based	Declarative	JSP

It exemplifies the separation of concerns between user interface, communication and back-end computation. The information system is structured according to the three-tier architecture. The user interface at the supermarket counter consists of a touch screen and a bar code reader; information on the products' prices and stock levels are kept in a separate server machine. The server machine centralizes most of the computing activities and allows monitoring of the ongoing activities by the sales manager.

Chapter 15 (Geographic information system) presents the development of a simple geographic information system (GIS). The goal is to exemplify the process of integrating disparate technologies and, in particular, data storage in a database, data transmission using sockets and data visualization through Java Applets.

Chapter 16 (Ubiquitous email) addresses the problem of developing an email server which provides nomadic access to the email of its users by supporting several communication channels and communication media, such as wired and wireless internet. The ubiquitous email server can therefore be considered a sort of mediator broker, which offers mediation support between a standard mail server and its users by enhanced mail access with advanced functionalities.

12.5 ■ References

Boehm, B. (1995) "A Technical Perspective on Systems Integration", in *Proceedings of the SEI/MCC Symposium on the Use of COTS in Systems Integration*, A.W. Brow, D.J. Carney, M.D. McFalls (eds), SEI Special Report CMU/SEI-95-SR-007, Software Engineering Institute, Pittsburgh PA.

Communication of the ACM (1997) Special Issue on Object-Oriented Application Frameworks, No. 10, October.

Lewandowsky, S.M. (1998) "Frameworks for Component-based Client/Server Computing", *ACM Computing Surveys*, Vol. 30, No. 1.

Shan, Y-P. and Earle, R.H. (1998) *Enterprise Computing with Objects. From Client/Server Environments to the Internet*, Addison-Wesley.

Sun Microsystems (2002) *A New Approach to Distributed Computing* (white paper), http://java.sun.com/products/javaspaces/whitepapers/dcpaper.pdf.

Thai T. and Lam, H. (2001) *.NET Framework Essentials*, O'Reilly, June.

Vinoski, S. (1997) "CORBA: Integrating Diverse Applications within Distributed Heterogeneous Environments", *IEEE Communications Magazine*, Vol. 14, No. 2, February.

Supervisory control and data acquisition system

13

Synthesis

A typical distributed subsystem that integrates data and functionalities within a factory work cell is represented by the SCADA (supervisory control and data acquisition) system. It collects process data from hardware devices (e.g. temperatures, speeds, forces, etc.), stores relevant data in a central database, processes data in order to identify anomalous situations, generates reports and alarms, and allows the operator to send commands to the hardware devices in order to control the manufacturing process. This case study exemplifies the development of a very simple SCADA system for car surface painting.

- Focus: the emphasis is on the system architecture and the mechanisms used to interconnect distributed components such as the work cell simulator, the colour tank controllers and the supervisory station.
- OO techniques: distributed components.
- Java features: Remote Method Invocation (RMI).
- Background: Chapters 9, 10 and 11 presented three simulation models that are taken into consideration in this case study as a starting point for analysis and design.

13.1 ■ Specifications

Increasingly, automotive manufacturers recognize that vehicle paint appearance is strongly representative of the quality of the product as a whole and makes an important contribution to customer product satisfaction. The main problem the measurement of paint appearance. Since there has been no point so far in attempting to automatically correlate process data with customer perception coherently, feedback process control is based on online adjustments of process parameters performed by responsible technicians. Currently, there are SCADA systems available for measuring process parameters such as pressure, flow and spray booth data that are plotted on attribute charts.

We want to develop a SCADA system for the remote control of a car painting work cell. The work cell is made up of three paint tanks (one for each fundamental colour) and a mixture tank that receives paint flows from them (see Figure 13.1). The colour tanks behave as finite capacity buffers that

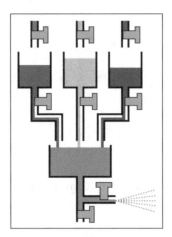

Figure 13.1 The car painting equipment

receive paint flows from outside the work cell and supply paint flows to the mixture tank through pipes.

Every tank has input and output pumps that generate the paint flows. The mixture tank outputs mixed paint through a spray pump. A drain pump is used to empty the mixture tank when necessary. The colour and mixture tanks are equipped with sensors that measure the current paint level.

The SCADA system is made up of a network of distributed software controllers that regulate the paint level of the colour tanks, the paint tonality of the mixture tank, and the output flow of the spray pump under the supervision of a responsible technician.

13.1.1 □ Programmable logic controllers

Colour tank controllers are software applications that emulate classical programmable logic controllers (PLCs) and offer two functionalities:

- They open and close the output pump in order to guarantee a given output flow.
- They open and close the input pump in order to guarantee that the tank gets neither full nor empty. For this purpose the controller reads sensor measures that indicate the current paint level in the tank.

The mixture tank controller is a PLC that offers two additional functionalities:

- It communicates with the tank controllers in order to pump the desired flow of paint into the mixture tank.
- It determines the percentage of paint volume for each fundamental colour in order to get the desired colour mixture. When a new tonality is required and the mixture tank is not empty, the controller should take into account the current volume and tonality of paint in the mixture tank.

13.1.2 ☐ **Local consoles**

The responsible technician can take control over the automatic controller in order to operate the input and output pumps directly. For this purpose, each PLC has a graphical console that displays the current status of each pump and allows the technician to modify the paint flow.

13.1.3 ☐ **Supervisory console**

The supervisory console is a graphical interface that displays the tonality of paint in the mixture tank. The responsible technician can select a new colour by varying the percentage of the three fundamental colours. For the sake of simplicity, we use the RGB palette although this is not appropriate to represent the behaviour of real paints. Using the RGB palette, a generic colour is obtained as the sum of light emissions of the three RGB components. The RGB palette is meant for display on monitors. A generic colour of real paint is obtained as the sum of light absorption of three fundamental paint colours (i.e. magenta, cyan, yellow). Once the new colour has been mixed in the mixture tank, the technician can open the spray pump. The supervisory console regulates the output flow.

13.1.4 ☐ **Simulation**

The painting work cell is simulated by a software application that has a graphical interface depicting the system as in Figure 13.1 and showing its dynamic evolution.

The SCADA system is physically distributed over a wide area. The colour tanks and the mixture tank may be quite far from each other; the supervisory station may be outside the work cell. The design of the SCADA system should favour a seamless transition from the simulated work cell to the interconnection with the real system.

13.2 ■ **Problem analysis**

The SCADA system is a distributed system made up of six main components: the plant simulator, the four PLCs and the supervisory console.

The first requirement of the system components is to manage independent activities.

- The simulator manages a graphical interface that displays the paint levels within the tanks and the paint flows of the input and output pumps. It animates the car painting process by updating the current status of tanks and pumps continuously. It interacts with the controllers in order to receive commands and give feedback.
- The PLCs implement the control logic that keeps the physical equipment in a coherent state. They interact with the simulator and the supervisory

station by exchanging commands and feedback data. A graphical user interface represents the PLC's local console.

- The supervisory station has a graphical user interface that allows the technician to control the car painting process.

The second requirement deals with system distribution. Distribution spans two dimensions: the work cell equipment and the control system.

- The real car painting work cell is made up of physically distributed colour tanks connected to each other through pipes and pumps, which control the paint flow from one tank to another. The simulator behaviour must enforce the physical constraints that characterize the work cell's equipment, that is, the paint level of two connected tanks should decrease and increase consistently without dissipation.
- The real work cell area may be very wide, up to thousands of square metres. The supervisory station might reside in a control cabin that jointly supervises several work cells. The SCADA system consists in a local area network or even in a wide area network of workstations.

Finally, it is important to guarantee a seamless transition of the SCADA system from the computer simulation to its deployment in a real work cell. For this purpose we need to evaluate how many control workstations are needed, how they are interconnected with the work cell simulator and the supervisory station, and which communication mechanisms are best suited.

13.2.1 □ Domain models

Traditionally, SCADA systems use dedicated high-bandwidth networks to interconnect physical devices such as sensors and actuators, a central database of process data, and computational resources such as the supervisory station.

A new generation of virtual SCADA systems builds on internet technology. The current trend, "embedding the Internet" (Estrin *et al.* 2000), pursues the interconnection of any kind of physical and virtual device through the internet. Strictly speaking, from the point of view of automation, the most challenging opportunity offered by the new web technology is to achieve tight dynamical interaction over the internet (i.e. real time monitoring and control).

Figure 13.2 represents the distributed architecture of a virtual SCADA system. The rectangular boxes indicate the typical control modules of a SCADA system. The communication infrastructure is logically structured as an information bus (Brugali and Menga 2002), i.e. a flat interconnection of autonomous and decentralized control modules that manage local resources, support decision making by formulating problem-solving plans, carry out these plans through querying and exchanging information with other control modules, and delegate to them the execution of specific services.

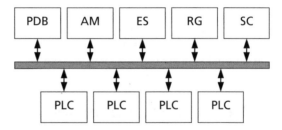

Figure 13.2 The functional modules of a SCADA system

The programmable logic controllers (PLCs) are simple hardware/software devices that operate the manufacturing equipment (e.g. pumps and tanks) by exchanging signal data through a dedicated link, such as a serial cable. In the virtual SCADA the PLCs are replaced by common PCs that emulate the control logic of the PLCs. The database of process data (PDB) stores relevant data from the physical devices and keeps track of the interventions of the responsible technician. The alarm manager (AM) allows the technician to program which events should fire an alarm. The expert system (ES) formulates hypotheses to manage exceptional situations and gives decision support to the responsible technician. The report generator (RG) generates trends that report on the evolution of the manufacturing process. The supervisory console (SC) is the input/output graphical interface that allows the operator to read process data from the database and to send commands to the CDs.

13.2.2 □ **Main features**

We can now summarize the main features that characterize the development of the SCADA system.

- It is important to choose the right simulation model taking into account the tradeoffs between discrete time and continuous time simulation.
- The SCADA components communicate remotely by exchanging sensor data and commands. Visibility dependencies should be identified carefully along with synchronization mechanisms.

13.2.3 □ **Test**

Two main functionalities need to be tested carefully.

- The simulator should enforce the physical constraints of the work cell equipment. For this purpose, test programs should be developed to verify that the pumps behave correctly according to the chosen simulation model, that is, they pull and push the same amount of paint that is to be transferred between two tanks. Exceptional conditions should be checked for: it is not possible to pull out paint from an empty tank or to push paint into a full tank.

■ The supervisory console should visualize the paint tonality in accordance with the paint composition of the mixture tank. The output flow and volume of the spray pump should be consistent with the values set by the technician in the supervisory console.

13.3 ■ Architecture and planning

The system architecture is made up of four main subsystems as described in Figure 13.3. The simulator component models the physical equipment of the work cell and enforces the physical consistency constraints.

The tank controller and mixture controller components monitor the paint level in the tanks and control the input and output pumps in order to regulate the paint level. The mixture controller sends commands to the tank controller in order to regulate the composition of fundamental colours in the mixture tank. Every controller has a local console that allows the technician to operate the equipment directly.

The supervisory component implements the supervisory console that displays the tonality of the paint in the mixture tank and allows the technician to change the colour composition and to regulate the output flow and volume of the spray pump.

The development process of the SCADA system is organized into three phases that produce three prototypes.

■ *Prototype 1: Work cell simulation.* A standalone application that simulates the physical work cell. A graphical user interface depicts the equipment as in Figure 13.1 and allows the user to open and close the pumps manually.

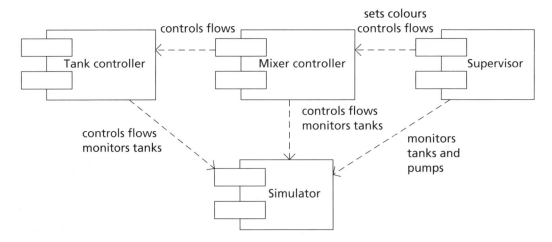

Figure 13.3 The system architecture

■ *Prototype 2: Tank controllers*. A distributed application that interconnects the simulator with the colour tank controllers. The controllers regulate the level of paint in the tanks.

■ *Prototype 3: The supervisory station*. The fully distributed system which interconnect the mixture tank controller with the colour tank controllers and the remote supervisory station.

13.4 ■ Prototype 1: Work cell simulation

This section identifies the functional requirements of the car painting work cell, defines the architecture of the work cell simulator and implements its basic components. The result is a standalone application that animates the behaviour of the physical devices (tanks and pumps) under the control of the responsible technician.

13.4.1 □ Analysis

The main entities found in the problem specification are colour tank, mixture tank, input pump, output pump and pipes. The colour tanks and the mixture tank differ only in their functionality: the colour tanks behave such as buffers that can guarante a continuous output flow. The mixture tank receives paint quantities of different tonalities and mixes them in order to obtain a homogeneous paint tonality. The problem specification does not indicate any detail about the mixing process. Thus, the simulator can abstract from the real mixing process; the new tonality is obtained from the sum of the fundamental colours' tonality weighted by their corresponding paint volumes. Some functional requirements should be taken into account:

■ The simulator architecture should promote a seamless transition from the prototype to the real system in such a way that the rest of the SCADA system will not be affected by the transition.

■ Consistency of physical constraints must be enforced: the pumps and the pipes guarantee that the same volume of paint is pulled from an upstream tank and pushed into the downstream tank.

■ The responsible technician should be allowed to monitor the variations of pump flow and tank level in real time and can operate the pump manually from a local console.

13.4.2 □ Design

According to the SCADA model described in Section 13.2.1 physical devices such as tanks and pumps are equipped with sensors and actuators that are connected to the PLCs through dedicated communication links such as serial cables. We can assume that the communication protocol and the data format are standard, i.e. every physical device is a blackbox component that

TankInterface	PumpInterface
int getLevel()	void setOutputFlow(int percent)

Figure 13.4 The interfaces of two physical devices

has a well-defined communication interface. Similarly, we simulate the behaviour of the physical devices by implementing objects that export well-defined interfaces. Basically, a PLC needs to access the value of the current level of paint in a tank and to set the output flow of a pump. Figure 13.4 shows the UML definition of the tank and pump interfaces.

The equipment of the car painting work cell is physically distributed over a wide area. Groups of closely connected devices (e.g. a tank and the input/output pumps) are controlled by dedicated PLCs that run on networked computers physically located in proximity to the equipment. In order to facilitate the transition from the simulated prototype to the real system, the design of the simulator's architecture must take into account the distributed nature of the manufacturing work cell.

Decision point

Simulator architecture: centralized or distributed?

A first design solution consists in simulating the behaviour of each device or group of devices as part of the behaviour of the PLC that controls their functioning (Figure 13.5). This solution has a major drawback: the physical constraints that characterize the paint flow between two tanks should be enforced through the exchange of data between the corresponding PLCs. This approach requires defining two different implementations of each PLC for the control of the simulated work cell and of the real work cell, making the results of the test cases performed in simulation useless.

A second design solution consists in simulating each physical device or group of devices as independent applications that run on dedicated computers connected to the PLCs through the network. The result is a fully distributed simulator.

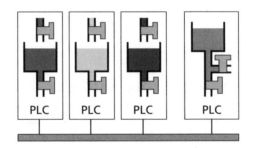

Figure 13.5 The symbiosis between simulated devices and PLCs

Once the SCADA system has been completely tested, the network connection between the PLCs and the simulated devices is replaced with the serial connection with the physical devices. The rest of the SCADA system remains unaffected by this substitution. Even this solution has a major drawback. The physical links between any two tanks (i.e. the pipes) are simulated as the interconnection of two software applications that run on remote computers (see Figure 13.6). Synchronization problems may arise when two networked simulated devices need to enforce consistency constraints. The transfer of a certain amount of paint between two tanks must result in the simultaneous update of paint level in both tanks. We know that communication over the internet is affected by unpredictable delays. This might cause the situation where a pump transfers a certain volume of paint from an empty tank or to a full tank.

An alternative design solution consists in simulating each physical device as a component of an application that runs on a single networked computer. The PLCs will have visibility of each individual component as a remote object (see Figure 13.7). The second prototype will address this issue and will introduce the Java mechanisms for the invocation of public methods on remote objects. According to these mechanisms it is completely immaterial whether the physical devices are simulated by components that run on a single computer or on different networked computers. The transition from the simulated prototype to the physical system will require the simple substitution of the network connection between each PLC and the work cell simulator with the serial connection between each PLC and the controlled group of physical devices.

Decision point

Simulation model: discrete events or thread-based simulation?

According to the discrete events model (see the Chapter 9 case study "Manufacturing work cell"), the behaviour of each physical device is

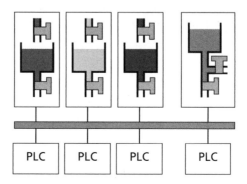

Figure 13.6 The structure of the fully distributed simulator

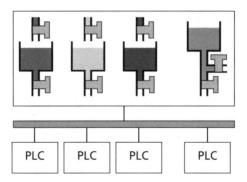

Figure 13.7 The interconnection of the centralized simulator with the PLCs

modelled as a finite state automaton. For example, the pump behaviour is characterized by two states (**OPENED, CLOSED**) and two transitions (**open, close**). Similarly, the tank behaviour is characterized by at least three states (**EMPTY, NOTEMPTY, FULL**) and two transitions (**pull, push**). This model does not seem appropriate for simulating the car painting work cell for two reasons:

1 We need to model a pump's output flow explicitly as a parameter that can assume a set of values within the range 0 to the maximum flow value.
2 We need to animate a tank's level variations in such a way that the user has the impression that the input and output paint flows are continuous as in the real work cell.

Thus, we choose the thread-based simulation model (see the Chapter 10 case study "Mobile robot exploration"). Accordingly, the paint flow between two tanks is modelled as a sequence of micro-volumes that are continuously pulled from the upstream tank and pushed into the downstream tank.

The flow intensity is proportional to the section of the pump's valve that links the two tanks and to the speed of the paint flow. We assume that the flow speed is constant and thus we stipulate that the transfer frequency of micro-volumes of paint is constant. Let $x[t_k]$ be the paint level in a tank at time instant t_k, $u[t_k]$ the input micro-volume at t_k, $y[t_k]$ the output micro-volume at t_k, $\phi_I(t_k)$ and $\phi_O(t_k)$ the input and output paint flows of a tank, $S(t_k)$ the section of a pump valve, v the constant flow speed, and ΔT the constant time interval between two subsequent micro-volume transfers. The following relations hold.

$$\phi(t_k) = S(t_k) * v \qquad S(t_k) = p(t_k) * S_{Max} \qquad p(t_k) = 0, ..., 100$$
$$u(t_k) = \phi_I(t_k) * \Delta T \qquad y(t_k) = \phi_O(t_k) * \Delta T$$
$$x(t_{k+1}) = x(t_k) + u(t_k) - y(t_k) \qquad t_{k+1} = t_k + \Delta T$$

Decision point

Execution model: single thread or multithreads?

As in previous case studies the simulation is characterized by the presence of multiple concurrent activities. In the "Manufacturing work cell" case study (Chapter 9) we adopted a single-thread execution model, where the evolution of the simulation is caused by the occurrence of discrete events (ticks) generated by a centralized clock that synchronizes all the activities. The multithread model is adequate to simulate activities characterized by different temporal evolutions, as in the case of the robot sensors and actuators in Chapter 10 and in the case of the car parking devices in Chapter 11. In these case studies every concurrent activity is executed by an independent thread of control.

For the car painting work cell we adopt the single-thread execution model. The simulator repeatedly invokes the method flush() of each pump every ΔT milliseconds. The flush() method pulls a micro-volume of paint from the upstream tank and pushes the same micro-volume into the downstream tank. We assume that the pump has an automatic mechanism that inhibits the paint transfer when the upstream tank is empty or the downstream tank is full.

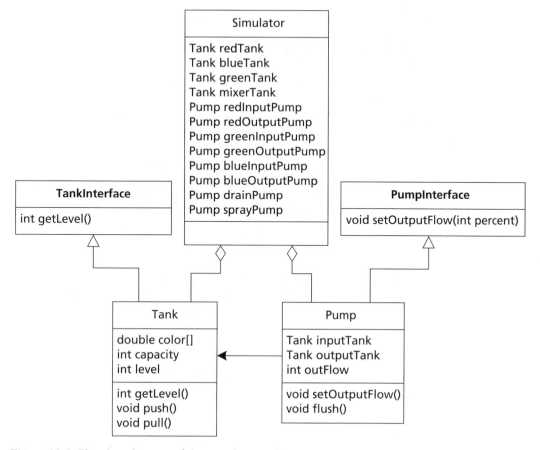

Figure 13.8 The class diagram of the simulator and its components

A graphical user interface allows the responsible technician to open and close every single pump using a slider button. The value of the slider is automatically set to zero when the paint transfer is inhibited. The class diagram of the car painting work cell simulator is reported in Figure 13.8.

13.4.3 □ Implementation

Class Tank simulates the behaviour of a colour tank. It implements five public methods:

- void push(int microVol, double c[]) receives a certain amount of paint of a given colour and updates the current level and tonality of the paint in the tank. The colour is expressed as a vector of double values in order to maintain good precision of the colour tonality after mixing with a different colour. This method is invoked by the input pump.
- void pull(int microVol) updates the current paint level in the tank by subtracting the micro-volume indicated as argument. This method is invoked by the output pump.
- public int getLevel(), public int getResidue() and public double[] getColor() return the current paint level in the tank, the difference between the tank capacity and the current level, and the paint colour. The first two methods are used by the pump to determine if the upstream tank is empty or the downstream tank is full.

```
package scada.simulator;
public class Tank {
  private double[] color = {0.0, 0.0, 0.0};
                              // colour tonality in RGB scale
  private int capacity = 100000;
                              // tank capacity in millilitres
  private int level;          // current level in millilitres
  public Tank(int color[], int percentLevel){
    for(int i=0; i<3; i++)
      this.color[i] = color[i];
    this.level = capacity / 100 * percentLevel;
  }
  public int getLevel() { return level; }
  public int getResidue() { return capacity-level; }
  public double[] getColor() { return color; }
  // the push() method receives a quantity of paint of a
  // given colour and updates the current level and colour
  // tonality
  public void push(int microVol, double c[]) {
    if(c != null) {
      // the amount of paint in the tank for each tonality
      double qr = color[0]*level/(color[0]+color[1]+color[2]);
      double qg = color[1]*level/(color[0]+color[1]+color[2]);
```

```
      double qb = color[2]*level/(color[0]+color[1]+color[2]);
        // quantity of paint received from the pump for each
        // tonality
        double tqr = c[0] * microVol / (c[0] + c[1] + c[2]);
        double tqg = c[1] * microVol / (c[0] + c[1] + c[2]);
        double tqb = c[2] * microVol / (c[0] + c[1] + c[2]);
        // the resulting tonality of the mixed paint
        double maxColor = Math.max( qr+tqr,qg+tqg );
        maxColor = Math.max(maxColor,qb+tqb);
        color[0] = 255 * (qr + tqr) / maxColor;
        color[1] = 255 * (qg + tqg) / maxColor;
        color[2] = 255 * (qb + tqb) / maxColor;
      }
      level += microVol;
    }
    // the pull method updates the current paint level in the
    // tank
    public void pull(int microVol) { level -= microVol; }
  }
```

Class **Pump** simulates the behaviour of a pump. It exports three methods:

- public void setOutputFlow(int percent) sets the pump output flow.
- public int getOutputFlow() gets the current pump output flow.
- void flush(int DT) transfers a micro-volume of paint from the upstream tank to the downstream tank. The micro-volume is proportional to the pump's current output flow and to the time interval DT. The micro-volume is equal or less than the current volume in the upstream tank and the residue volume in the downstream tank. This constraint ensures that the pump never flushes paint from an empty tank or into a full tank.

```
package scada.simulator;
public class Pump {
  private Tank upstreamTank = null;
                  // reference to the upstream tank
  private Tank downstreamTank = null;
                  // referece to the downstream tank
  private int MAXFLOW = 10000;
                  // max output flow (millilitres/second)
  private int outputFlow = 0;
                  // current output flow (millilitres/second)
  public Pump(Tank upstream, Tank downstream) {
    upstreamTank = upstream; downstreamTank = downstream;
  }
  // this method opens the pump's valve
  public void setOutputFlow(int percent) {
    outputFlow = MAXFLOW / 100 * percent;
  }
```

```
public int getOutputFlow() { return outputFlow; }
// this method transfers a micro-volume of paint from the
// upstream tank to the downstream tank
public void flush(int DT) {    // interval in milliseconds
  int microVol;      // volume in millilitres
  if(outputFlow == 0 ||
     (upstreamTank == null && downstreamTank == null))
    return;
  else if(upstreamTank != null && downstreamTank != null) {
    // the case of a pump connecting an upstream tank and a
    // downstream tank: the output quantity is equal to the
    // minimum of the current level of upstream tank, the
    // residue of the downstream tank and the output volume
    microVol = (int) Math.min( upstreamTank.getLevel(),
                          downstreamTank.getResidue() );
    microVol = (int)Math.min(microVol,
                                 DT * outputFlow / 1000);
    upstreamTank.pull(microVol);
    downstreamTank.push(microVol, upstreamTank.getColor());
    outputFlow = microVol * 1000 / DT;
  }
  else if(upstreamTank != null) {
    // this is the case of a pump that doesn't have a
    // downstream tank (e.g. the spray pump and the drain
    // pump of the mixture tank)
    microVol = (int) Math.min( upstreamTank.getLevel(),
                          DT * outputFlow / 1000);
    upstreamTank.pull(microVol);
    outputFlow = microVol * 1000 / DT;
  }
  else {
    // this is the case of a pump that doesn't have an
    // upstream tank (e.g. the input pump of the colour
    // tanks)
    microVol =
      (int) Math.min( downstreamTank.getResidue(),
                    DT*outputFlow/1000 );
    downstreamTank.push(microVol, null);
    outputFlow = microVol * 1000 / DT;
  }
}
}
```

Class Simulator implements the main application class of the car painting work cell simulator. It has two main functionalities:

■ It creates the tank and pump components, initializes their interconnections, and creates a thread object that invokes the flush method of each pump every 100 milliseconds.

■ It updates the graphical user interface every 100 milliseconds. In particular, it updates the paint level of each tank and the slider buttons that open and close the pumps.

```java
package scada.simulator;
public class Simulator extends JFrame implements Runnable{
  Tank redTank, greenTank, blueTank, mixerTank; // the tanks
  Pump redInputPump, redOutputPump;              // the pumps
  Pump greenInputPump, greenOutputPump;
  Pump blueInputPump, blueOutputPump;
  Pump drainPump, sprayPump;
  private int DT = 100;  // interval in milliseconds (0.1 s)
  Thread thread = new Thread(this);
  public Simulator() {  // initializes tanks and pumps
    // Note that the initial values of paint level are
    // hard-coded. It is easy to modify this constructor in
    // such a way that the values are read from a
    // configuration file.
    redTank = new Tank(colorRed, 20);
    greenTank = new Tank(colorGreen, 50);
    blueTank = new Tank(colorBlue, 40);
    mixerTank = new Tank(colorWhite, 10);
    redInputPump = new Pump(null, redTank);
    redOutputPump = new Pump(redTank, mixerTank);
    greenInputPump = new Pump(null, greenTank);
    greenOutputPump = new Pump(greenTank, mixerTank);
    blueInputPump = new Pump(null, blueTank);
    blueOutputPump = new Pump(blueTank, mixerTank);
    drainPump = new Pump(mixerTank, null);
    sprayPump = new Pump(mixerTank, null);
    initGUI(); // initializes the graphical user interface
  }
  public void run() {
    while(true)
    try {
      thread.sleep(DT);        // sleeps for DT milleseconds
      // requests the pumps to flush a micro-volume of paint
      // according to their output flow
      redInputPump.flush(DT);      redOutputPump.flush(DT);
      greenInputPump.flush(DT);    greenOutputPump.flush(DT);
      blueInputPump.flush(DT);     blueOutputPump.flush(DT);
      drainPump.flush(DT);         sprayPump.flush(DT);
      this.repaint();    // repaints the graphical interface
    } catch(InterruptedException ie) {ie.printStackTrace();}
  }
```

13.4.4 □ **Test**

The following test cases can be performed to verify the correct behaviour of the simulator using the simulator GUI depicted in Figure 13.9.

- Open the input pump of a colour tank and verify that:
  – the paint level increases and the speed is proportional to the pump's output flow;
  – the input pump is closed automatically when the tank gets full.
- Open the output pump of a tank or the spray and drain pumps of the mixture tank and verify that:
  – the paint level increases and the speed is proportional to the pump's output flow;
  – the output pump is closed automatically when the tank gets empty. For this test it is necessary that in the meantime the downstream tank does not get full.
- Open all the output pumps of the three colour tanks and verify that:
  – they are closed when the mixture tank is full and the drain and spray pumps are closed;

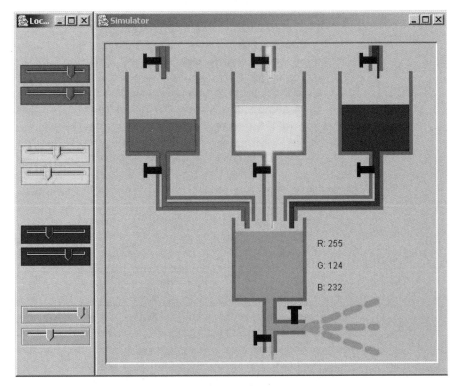

Figure 13.9 The graphical representation of the simulated plant.

– the sum of their output flow is equal to the sum of the output flows of the spray and drain pump when the mixture tank is full.

13.5 ■ Prototype 2: Tank controllers

This prototype implements the automatic controllers that regulate the flow of paint between the tanks. The result is a distributed system that animates the behaviour of tanks and pumps under the control of the automatic controllers and the responsible technician.

13.5.1 □ Analysis

According to the domain model discussed in Section 13.2.1, the SCADA architecture is organized as a flat interconnection of autonomous and decentralized control modules that implement specific functionalities, e.g. they implement the control logic of a PLC. In a real car painting system, every PLC would be connected to the sensors and actuators of a physical device through dedicated communication media, such as a serial cable. The PLCs communicate with each other through the internet.

In Section 13.4 we have designed the work cell simulator as a standalone application that animates the behaviour of all the physical devices. Figure 13.7 shows the distributed structure of the SCADA system after the introduction of the work cell simulator. The PLCs are no longer connected to the physical devices directly. Instead, they communicate with the work cell simulator through the internet. Thus, the first requirement that we have to deal with is the possibility of interconnecting the simulator with the PLCs through the internet.

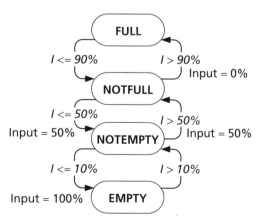

Figure 13.10 The PLC's finite state automaton

The second requirement is the establishment of a local control loop between the PLCs and the simulated devices and a remote control loop among the PLCs.

The third requirement is the definition of the PLC behaviours as finite state automata. The tank controller should measure the current level of paint in the tank and control the input and output pump in order to maintain the paint level between given thresholds. Figure 13.10 shows the finite state automaton that describes the control logic of the PLC controlling a colour tank. It is made up of four states: FULL, NOTFULL, NOTEMPTY and EMPTY. The state transitions fire when the paint level of the tank reaches the values of predefined thresholds. In correspondence to some state transitions, the controller opens or closes the input pump.

13.5.2 □ **Design**

In Prototype 1 we introduced interfaces TankInterface and PumpInterface. They define the public methods implemented in class Tank and class Pump that can be invoked by other components such as the local console. In Prototype 2 these methods are invoked by the remote PLCs to impose the desired behaviour on the work cell equipment.

Decision point

Which distribution mechanism is best suited to the interconnection of the SCADA subsystems?

The choice is between Java Sockets and Java RMI (see Sidebar 13.1). Since RMI builds on the Sockets mechanism, the rationale of choosing one technology or the other relies on the opportunity to have a more abstract view of the communication mechanism or a more fine-grained control of it.

In Prototype 2 we have two different situations that require the use of distribution mechanisms: the interconnection of the controllers to the work cell equipment and the interconnection between the mixer controller and the colour tank controllers. The first type of interconnection is meant to be completely reimplemented when the simulated devices are replaced by the real devices. Thus, using Sockets or RMI for the interconnection of the simulated devices does not seem to matter. The second type of interconnection is not affected by the transition from the prototype to the real application. Thus, the communication mechanism should be selected carefully.

Remote controllers basically exchange a low-traffic stream of commands and signals according to highly specific data formats. Thus, we argue that the RMI mechanism is more appropriate because the software developer can take advantage of compile-time type checking of data structures to avoid data type mismatch in commands and signals. The Socket mechanism

Sidebar 13.1 Java RMI

Java RMI is a middleware framework that allows a client application to invoke a method of an object residing in a different address space, i.e. that is a remote object. Let's consider the example depicted in the figure below. Classes Naming, Remote and UnicastRemoteObject are provided by the Java RMI package. Classes SumStub and SumSkeleton are automatically generated by the RMI compiler. The other classes are defined by the programmer.

The Client object and the Server objects reside on two different networked computers, each one being identified by a unique IP address. The Server creates an object of class SumImplementation that exports the int sum(int a, int b) method defined in interface SumInterface. The RMI framework allows a Client to invoke the sum method on a SumImplementation object by passing its actual parameters and getting the result.

This is accomplished by means of two ancillary objects called the SumStub and the SumSkeleton. The Stub is a surrogate (proxy) of the remote object and resides in the client's address space. It offers the same set of operations as the remote object, i.e. the sum method. The Stub is in charge of marshalling the client's request and transmitting it through the network. The Skeleton resides in the Server address space and is in charge of receiving and unmarshalling the client's request and of invoking the corresponding operation of the SumImplementation object. The matched pair Stub/Skeleton is automatically generated at compile time from the definition of SumInterface.

In order to make the SumImplementation object accessible from a remote application, the Server must register it with a symbolic name using the Naming class's bind method. Once a remote object is registered on the local host, clients on a remote host can look up the remote object by name using the Naming class's lookup() method, obtain its reference and then invoke remote methods on the object.

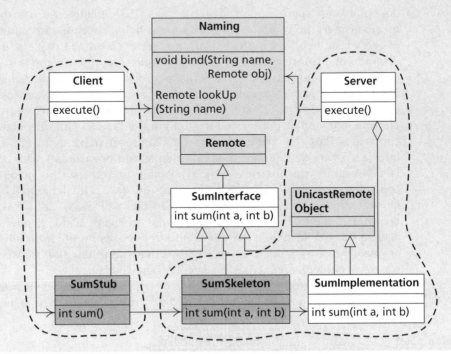

```
import java.rmi.*;
import java.rmi.server.*;
public interface SumInterface extends java.rmi.Remote {
    public int sum( int a, int b ) throws java.rmi.RemoteException;
}
public class SumImplementation extends UnicastRemoteObject
                               implements SumInterface {
    public int sum( int a, int b ) {return a + b;}
}
public class Server {
    public void execute() {
        SumImplementation  sumImpl  = new SumImplementation();
        Naming.bind( "Adder", sumImpl );
    }
}
public class Client {
    String serverIP = "193.211.32.3";
    String adderUrl = "//"+serverIP+"/Adder" ;
    public void execute() {
        SumInterface  adder  = (SumInterface) Naming.lookup( adderUrl );
        int result = adder.sum(5, 8);
    }
}
```

does not offer such support. For the sake of simplicity, we use the RMI mechanism as the common distribution mechanism for the interconnection of every remote object in the SCADA system. Figure 13.11 depicts the class diagram of Prototype 2. Class TankController represents the PLCs that control the colour tanks. It invokes the methods of class Pump and class Tank defined in PumpInterface and TankInterface using the RMI mechanism.

Class MixerController extends class TankController, since it controls the mixture tank and its pumps and in addition it interacts with the colour tank controllers. For this purpose, class TankController implements the remote interface ControllerInterface that exports method openPump(). This method is invoked by the mixture tank controller to request the colour tank controllers to supply paint flows. The same interface is implemented by class MixerController, as the supervisory console will need to invoke the openPump() method to open the spray pump. In Figure 13.11 we have drawn dashed lines to highlight the distribution of classes on different sites. The arrows that cross a dashed line indicate that the interaction between two classes is implemented using the Java RMI mechanism.

Both TankController and MixerController implement interface Runnable as they manage an independent thread of control that executes their behaviours.

Decision point

How do PLCs and work cell devices handle synchronization of their behaviours?

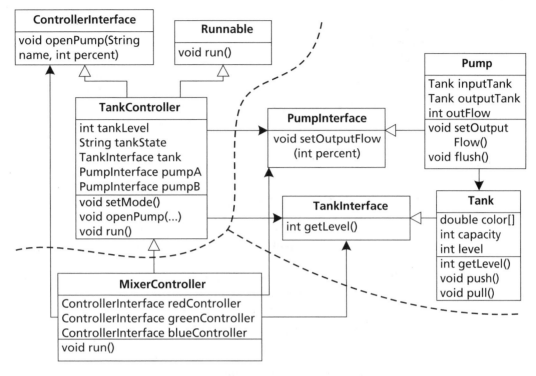

Figure 13.11 The class diagram of Prototype 2

As we have described in the previous section, the PLCs behave like finite state automata, whose state transitions fire when the paint level of a colour tank or mixer tank reaches the values of predefined thresholds. This means that the PLCs should measure the current paint level of the tanks continuously. This approach is consistent with the mechanism used to get state information from a physical device.

13.5.3 □ Implementation

The implementation of the second prototype requires the transformation of the work cell simulator into a remote application in order to allow the PLCs to exchange data and commands with the simulated devices via the internet. Since we decided to use Java RMI for the interconnection of remote objects, we have to define the interfaces exported by the Tank and the Pump classes, i.e. TankInterface and PumpInterface. These interfaces indicate which methods can be invoked by a remote application. Then, we modify the declaration of class Tank and class Pump so as to extend the basic class UnicastRemoteObject. Their constructors should declare that they throw java.rmi.RemoteException. Finally, class Simulator registers the device objects with unique names using the java.rmi.Naming class.

```java
package scada.simulator;
import java.rmi.*;
import java.rmi.server.*;
public interface TankInterface extends java.rmi.Remote{
  public int getLevel() throws java.rmi.RemoteException;
}
public class Tank extends UnicastRemoteObject
                   implements TankInterface {
  public Tank(int color[], int percentLevel)
                   throws RemoteException { . . . }
    . . .
}
public interface PumpInterface
                   extends java.rmi.Remote {
  public void setOutputFlow(int percent)
                   throws java.rmi.RemoteException;
}
public class Pump extends UnicastRemoteObject
                   implements PumpInterface {
  public Pump(Tank upstream, Tank downstream)
                   throws RemoteException { . . . }
    . . .
}
public class Simulator extends JFrame
                   implements Runnable{
  public Simulator() {
    try {
      // Registers the tanks and the pumps
      Naming.rebind("RedTank", redTank);
      Naming.rebind("GreenTank", greenTank);
      Naming.rebind("BlueTank", blueTank);
      Naming.rebind("MixerTank", mixerTank);
      Naming.rebind("RedPumpA", redInputPump);
      Naming.rebind("RedPumpB", redOutputPump);
      Naming.rebind("GreenPumpA", greenInputPump);
      Naming.rebind("GreenPumpB", greenOutputPump);
      Naming.rebind("BluePumpA", blueInputPump);
      Naming.rebind("BluePumpB", blueOutputPump);
      Naming.rebind("MixerPumpA", sprayPump);
      Naming.rebind("MixerPumpB", drainPump);
    } catch (Exception e) { e.printStackTrace(); }
      . . .
  }
}
```

The PLCs are implemented as finite state automata (see Figure 13.10) with class TankController. Every 100 milliseconds (this is the default sampling time) each PLC measures the current paint level in the controlled tank.

For this purpose the PLCs request a reference to the remote tank objects using the RMI lookup mechanism. They just need the IP address of the networked computer that runs the work cell simulator. In correspondence to predefined threshold values (minimum, medium, maximum paint level) the PLC updates its current state and sends commands to the remote pump objects. Here, the colour tank PLCs and the mixture tank PLC have slightly different behaviours. Thus, we implement class MixerController as an extension of TankController.

Class TankController controls the paint level in the remote colour tank by invoking the setOutputFlow() method of its input pump. In contrast, class MixerController controls the paint level in the mixture tank by sending commands to the three colour tank controllers. For this purpose, the tank controllers are implemented as remote objects that allow the remote invocation of their public methods. In particular, they export the method openPump() defined in interface ControllerInterface.

Both TankController and MixerController use class LocalConsole to build a graphical user interface that allows the technician responsible to disable the PLC and operate the work cell equipment manually.

```java
package scada.controller;
import scada.simulator.*;
import java.rmi.*;
import java.rmi.server.*;
public interface ControllerInterface extends java.rmi.Remote {
  public void openPump(String name, int percent)
            throws java.rmi.RemoteException;
}
public class TankController extends UnicastRemoteObject
                implements Runnable, ControllerInterface {
  protected String name;  // name of this controller
  protected String tankState; // controller's state
  protected final static String FULL="FULL"; // state values
  protected final static String NOTFULL="NOTFULL";
  protected final static String NOTEMPTY="NOTEMPTY";
  protected final static String EMPTY="EMPTY";
  protected int tankLevel = 0; // paint level in the tank
  protected final static int MINIMUM = 10000;
                                // level thresholds
  protected final static int MEDIUM  = 50000;
  protected final static int MAXIMUM = 90000;
  protected final static long SAMPLING = 100;
                                // milliseconds
  protected TankInterface tank = null;
                                // interface to the tank
  protected PumpInterface pumpA = null;
                                // interface to the pumps
  protected PumpInterface pumpB = null;
```

```java
    protected boolean automatic = false;
    protected LocalConsole console;
                                    // reference to the GUI console
    public TankController(String name, String simAdd)
            throws RemoteException {
      this.name = name;
      try {
        // Registers the controller
        Naming.rebind( name+"TankController", this );
        // links the controller to the corresponding pumps
        pumpA = (PumpInterface)
                Naming.lookup("//"+simAdd+"/"+name+"PumpA");
        pumpB = (PumpInterface)
                Naming.lookup("//"+simAdd+"/"+name+"PumpB");
        // links the tank to the controller
        tank = (TankInterface)
                Naming.lookup("//"+simAdd+"/"+name+"Tank");
      } catch (Exception e) {e.printStackTrace();}
    }
    // opens one of the two pumps and updates the buttons
    // of the local GUI console
    public void openPump(String name, int percent) {
      try {
        if(name.equals("PumpA")) {
          pumpA.setOutputFlow(percent);
          console.pumpASlider.setValue(percent);
        }
        else if(name.equals("PumpB")) {
          pumpB.setOutputFlow(percent);
          console.pumpBSlider.setValue(percent);
        }
      } catch(RemoteException re) { re.printStackTrace(); }
    }
    // implements the control logic
    public void run() {
      try {
        // initializes the state according to the initial
        // paint level
        tankLevel = tank.getLevel();
        if(tankLevel <= MINIMUM)
          tankState = EMPTY;
        else if(tankLevel <= MEDIUM)
          tankState = NOTEMPTY;
        else if(tankLevel <= MAXIMUM)
          tankState = NOTFULL;
        else
          tankState = FULL;
```

```java
while(true) {
  Thread.sleep(SAMPLING);
  tankLevel = tank.getLevel();
  // states transitions
  if(tankState.equals(EMPTY) && tankLevel > MINIMUM) {
    tankState = NOTEMPTY;
  }
  else if(tankState.equals(NOTEMPTY)
                              && tankLevel > MEDIUM) {
    tankState = NOTFULL;
    if(automatic) {
      // opens the input pump in order to fill the tank
      pumpA.setOutputFlow(50);
      console.pumpASlider.setValue(50);
    }
  }
  else if(tankState.equals(NOTFULL)
                              && tankLevel > MAXIMUM) {
    tankState = FULL;
    // closes the input pump
    pumpA.setOutputFlow(0);
    console.pumpASlider.setValue(0);
  }
  else if(tankState.equals(FULL)
                              && tankLevel <= MAXIMUM) {
    tankState = NOTFULL;
  }
  else if(tankState.equals(NOTFULL)
                              && tankLevel <= MEDIUM) {
    tankState = NOTEMPTY;
    if(automatic) {
      // opens the input pump in order to fill the tank
      pumpA.setOutputFlow(50);
      console.pumpASlider.setValue(50);
    }
  }
  else if(tankState.equals(NOTEMPTY)
                              && tankLevel <= MINIMUM) {
    tankState = EMPTY;
    if(automatic)
            { // opens the input pump (maximum flow)
      // in order to fill the tank
      pumpA.setOutputFlow(100);
      console.pumpASlider.setValue(100);
    }
  }
}
```

```
      } catch (Exception e) { e.printStackTrace(); }
    }
    // the main method
    public static void main(String[] args) {. . . }
}
public class MixerController extends TankController
              implements Runnable, ControllerInterface {
  // interfaces to the tank controller
  private ControllerInterface redController = null;
  private ControllerInterface greenController = null;
  private ControllerInterface blueController = null;
  public MixerController(String simAdd, String redContrAdd,
              String greenContrAdd, String blueContrAdd)
              throws RemoteException {
    super("Mixer", simAdd);
    try {
      // links the controller to the TankControllers
      redController = (ControllerInterface)
          Naming.lookup
                  ("//"+redContrAdd+"/RedTankController");
      greenController = (ControllerInterface)
          Naming.lookup
                  ("//"+greenContrAdd+"/GreenTankController");
      blueController = (ControllerInterface)
          Naming.lookup
                  ("//"+blueContrAdd+"/BlueTankController");
    } catch (Exception e) { e.printStackTrace(); }
  }
  // implements the control logic
  public void run() {
    try {
      // initializes the state according to the initial
      // paint level
      tankLevel = tank.getLevel();
      if(tankLevel == 0) tankState = EMPTY;
      else if(tankLevel <= MEDIUM) tankState = NOTEMPTY;
      else if(tankLevel <= MAXIMUM) tankState = NOTFULL;
      else tankState = FULL;
      while(true) {
        Thread.sleep(100);
        tankLevel = tank.getLevel();
        // states transitions
        if(tankState.equals(EMPTY) && tankLevel > MINIMUM) {
          tankState = NOTEMPTY;
        }
        else if(tankState.equals(NOTEMPTY)
                                    && tankLevel > MEDIUM) {
```

```
                    tankState = NOTFULL;
            }
            else if(tankState.equals(NOTFULL)
                                    && tankLevel > MAXIMUM) {
                tankState = FULL;
                // closes the output pumps of the colour tanks
                redController.openPump("PumpB", 0);
                greenController.openPump("PumpB", 0);
                blueController.openPump("PumpB", 0);
            }
            else if(tankState.equals(FULL)
                                    && tankLevel <= MAXIMUM) {
                tankState = NOTFULL;
            }
            else if(tankState.equals(NOTFULL)
                                    && tankLevel <= MEDIUM) {
                tankState = NOTEMPTY;
            }
            else if(tankState.equals(NOTEMPTY)
                                    && tankLevel <= 0) {
                tankState = EMPTY;
                // closes both the output pumps
                pumpA.setOutputFlow(0);
                pumpB.setOutputFlow(0);
                console.pumpASlider.setValue(0);
                console.pumpBSlider.setValue(0);
            }
        }
    } catch(Exception e) { e.printStackTrace(); }
  }
}
```

13.5.4 □ Test

The test case is very similar to that for the first prototype. In addition, we need to verify the correct behaviour of the PLCs when automatic control is enabled. This means verifying that the input and output pumps are opened and closed when the paint level in the tanks reaches the predefined threshold values. Specific behaviours to verify are the following:

■ When the output flow from the colour tanks is high (>50 per cent of the maximum value), the paint level varies between the minimum and medium thresholds.
■ When the output flow from the colour tanks is low (<50 per cent of the maximum value), the paint level varies between the medium and maximum thresholds.

■ The colour tank controllers close the output pumps when the mixture tank reaches the maximum threshold.

13.6 ■ Prototype 3: The supervisory station

The third prototype deals with the interconnection of the supervisory station with the PLCs. The result is the fully distributed SCADA system that allows the technician responsible to control the car painting process from a desktop console.

13.6.1 □ Analysis

The supervisory console is a graphical user interface that runs on a networked computer, displays relevant process data and events, and provides the technician with tools to operate the car painting work cell. Prototype 3 implements a simplified version of a real-world supervisory console. In particular, the console allows the technician to select a paint tonality and the output flow of the spray pump. The console is directly interconnected with the PLC that controls the mixture tank (i.e. Prototype 3 does not use a central database for the exchange of process data between the distributed components of the SCADA system).

13.6.2 □ Design

The mixer controller is in charge of controlling the paint mixing in order to obtain the desired colour tonalities as specified by the technician responsible through the graphical interface of the supervisory console. Therefore, the mixer controller must export two new methods that are invoked by the remote supervisory console, that is void setColor (int r, int g, int b) and boolean colorReady (). The first method sets the values of the three fundamental colours corresponding to the desired tonality. The other method returns the value "true" when the mixing process has been completed and the new colour is ready. The class diagram in Figure 13.12 includes the new interface MixerInterface that extends ControllerInterface and is implemented by class MixerController.

Class Supervisor obtains a remote reference to the MixerController using the RMI mechanism.

13.6.3 □ Implementation

The first step towards the interconnection of the mixture tank controller with the supervisory console is the extension of class MixerController with the implementation of methods setColor() and colorReady(). Since both methods are invoked by the remote supervisory console, they need to be declared in a remote interface. Thus, we introduce interface MixerInterface that extends

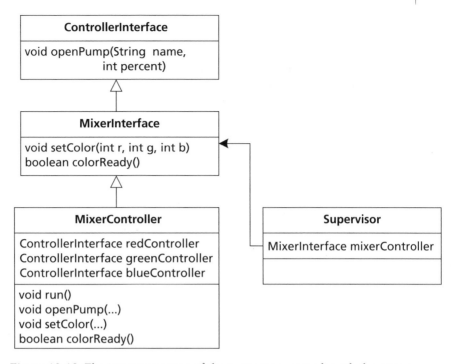

Figure 13.12 The interconnection of the supervisory console with the mixer controller

ControllerInterface. Accordingly, class MixerController should be declared to implement MixerInterface instead of ControllerInterface.

The setColor() method first closes the input pumps and the spray pump of the mixture tank. Then it opens the drain pump and evaluates the paint flows from the colour tanks. When the run() method enters the EMPTY state, the mixer controller requests the colour tank controllers to open their output pumps to provide the evaluated paint flow. The mixer controller guarantees that the mixture tank never gets empty until a new setColor() request is received.

The colorReady() method returns the value "false" only when the drain pump is open.

```
package scada.controller;
import java.rmi.*;
public interface MixerInterface extends ControllerInterface {
    public void setColor(int rc, int gc, int bc)
            throws java.rmi.RemoteException;
    public boolean colorReady() throws java.rmi.RemoteException;
}
import scada.simulator.*;
public class MixerController extends TankController
        implements Runnable, MixerInterface {
```

```java
private boolean mixing = false;
                            // true when mixing is in process
private int redColorFlow = 0;
private int greenColorFlow = 0;
private int blueColorFlow = 0;
public void setColor(int rc, int gc, int bc){
  try {
    // closes the output pumps of the colour tanks
    redController.openPump("PumpB", 0);
    greenController.openPump("PumpB", 0);
    blueController.openPump("PumpB", 0);
    // closes the spray pump
    pumpA.setOutputFlow(0);
    console.pumpASlider.setValue(0);
    // opens the drain pump
    pumpB.setOutputFlow(100);
    console.pumpBSlider.setValue(100);
    // evaluates the needed paint flows from the colour
    // tanks
    redColorFlow = (int) Math.round(rc*100.0 / 255.0);
    greenColorFlow = (int) Math.round(gc*100.0 / 255.0);
    blueColorFlow = (int) Math.round(bc*100.0 / 255.0);
    // the drain pump is open
    mixing = true;
  } catch(RemoteException re) {re.printStackTrace();}
}
// return false only if the drain pump is open
public boolean colorReady() { return ! mixing; }
// implements the finite state automaton
public void run() {
  try { . . .
    while(true) { ... // states transitions
      if(tankState.equals(EMPTY)
                            && tankLevel > MINIMUM) {...}
      else if(tankState.equals(NOTEMPTY)
                              && tankLevel > MEDIUM) {
        tankState = NOTFULL;
        // the superviswory console is now allowed
        // to open the spray pump
        if(mixing) mixing = false;
      }
      else if(tankState.equals(NOTFULL)
                              && tankLevel > MAXIMUM) {
        ...
      }
```

```
      else if(tankState.equals(FULL)
                             && tankLevel <= MAXIMUM) {
         ...
      }
      else if(tankState.equals(NOTFULL)
                             && tankLevel <= MEDIUM) {
        tankState = NOTEMPTY;
        if(automatic && ! mixing) {
          // opens the colour tank pumps in order
          // to refill the mixture tank
          redController.openPump("PumpB", redColorFlow);
          greenController.openPump
                            ("PumpB", greenColorFlow);
          blueController.openPump("PumpB", blueColorFlow);
        }
      }
      else if(tankState.equals(NOTEMPTY)
                             && tankLevel <= 0) { ...
        if(mixing) {
          // the mixture tank is now empty; opens the
          // color tank pumps in order to fill the mixture
          // tank
          redController.openPump("PumpB", redColorFlow);
          greenController.openPump
                            ("PumpB", greenColorFlow);
          blueController.openPump("PumpB", blueColorFlow);
        }
      }
    }
  } catch(Exception ex) { ex.printStackTrace(); }
}
```

Class **Supervisor** implements the supervisory console. It is simply a graphical user interface that allows the technician to set the desired paint tonality and to open the spray pump.

```
package scada.supervisor;
import scada.controller.MixerInterface;
import java.awt.*;
import java.rmi.*;
public class Supervisor extends JFrame {
  private MixerInterface mixerController = null;
  // the graphical components
  ColorPanel colorPanel = new ColorPanel();
     . . .
  public Supervisor(String mixerAddress) {
```

```
    try {
      // links the supervisor to the MixerController
      mixerController = (MixerInterface)
          Naming.lookup
                  ("//"+mixerAddress+"/MixerTankController");
    } catch (Exception e) { e.printStackTrace(); }
    initGUI();
  }
  // the methods used to set the paint tonality
  void redSlider_stateChanged(ChangeEvent e) {
    colorPanel.setColor('r', redSlider.getValue());
  }

      ...
  // the method used to open the spray pump
  void setButton_actionPerformed(ActionEvent e) {
    try {
      flowSlider.setValue(0);
      mixerController.setColor(colorPanel.color[0],
          colorPanel.color[1], colorPanel.color[2]);
      // waits for the drain pump to close
      while(! mixerController.colorReady())
        Thread.sleep(100);
    } catch(Exception ex) { ex.printStackTrace(); }
  }
  void flowSlider_mouseReleased(MouseEvent e) {
    try {
      mixerController.openPump
                            ("PumpA", flowSlider.getValue());
    } catch(RemoteException re) { re.printStackTrace(); }
  }
}
```

13.6.4 □ Test

The last test case verifies the functionalities of the supervisory console and of the mixer controller using the simulator GUI (see Figure 13.13), and in particular:

- Colour selection. The selected colour should correspond to the tonality of the paint in the mixture tank.
- Paint mixing. When the "Set Color" button is pressed, the mixture tank should first be emptied and then filled with paint corresponding to the selected colour. During this phase, the technician is not allowed to change colour or to open the spray pump.
- Spraying. The output flow of the spray pump should be proportional to the state value of the "Flow" slider button. When the mixture tank starts

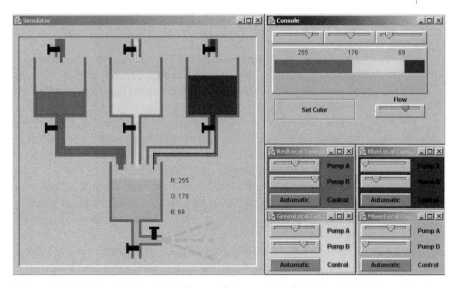

Figure 13.13 The graphical interfaces of the entire SCADA system.

getting empty, the colour tanks should supply paint flows according to the selected colour.

13.7 ■ Extension

The reader can extend the SCADA system in several ways:

- The main limitation of the third prototype is the waste of paint when the technician changes the colour tonality. In fact the mixture needs to be emptied before the new paint flows start filling the tank. A better solution would be to mix the current paint in the tank with new paint flows from the fundamental colour tanks. This would require the evaluation of the exact quantity of paint already present in the tank for each fundamental colour and the quantity of colour to be added to get the desired tonality. In some cases, this approach may still require draining a certain amount of paint from the mixture tank.
- The synchronization between the PLCs and the simulator is handled with the polling mechanism. Think about the possibility of using the event notification mechanism. This is critical if we want the PLCs to be able to deal with exceptional conditions. For example, it might happen that the input pumps of the tank controllers are disabled because there is no more paint supply from outside the work cell.
- Real SCADA systems are structured around a central database. Its introduction may require the redefinition of the system architecture in terms of interconnection between the distributed components.

13.8 ■ Assessment

This case study has presented the development process of a distributed control system in the factory automation domain. Such a system is characterized by a variety of concurrent activities that need to be controlled and supervised.

The analysis of the problem emphasized a typical issue that affects distributed systems, i.e. the consistency problem. The network introduces unpredictable time delays in the communication between remote components that prejudice the correct behaviour of the entire system.

Architecture model. The consistency issue has been addressed in the design phase, where a centralized architecture for the plant simulator and a distributed client–server architecture for the control modules and the supervisor station were chosen.

Distribution paradigm. Since the simulator's architecture is highly structured and the fundamental components (tank and pump) are reusable building blocks with well-defined interfaces, it has been judged appropriate to expose these interfaces to remote clients according to the stub–skeleton paradigm.

Middleware technology. The resulting system is structured as a distributed client–server system that builds on the Java RMI mechanism for remote component communication.

Architecture	Decentralized control
Context	Computer integrated manufacturing (CIM) systems build on large client–server control architectures and factory-wide information systems. They are created by integrating multi-vendor, heterogeneous and ad hoc subsystems, and their development spans a relatively long period of time.
Problem	A manufacturing control system accomplishes the production process without human assistance. Large, distributed control systems are difficult to design and manage. The presence of multiple concurrent activities increases the difficulty further. The design of a control system must enforce functional requirements and non-functional requirements (such as optimum performance, high dependability, etc.).
Forces or tradeoffs	Optimum performance of the entire production system is achieved by having a centralized controller that receives input data from the manufacturing facilities, equipment and physical devices, maintains the global state information, computes the global optimum and commands the remote peripheries accordingly. However, centralized architectures are highly sensitive to system failures, since the whole system depends on the availability of the single decision-making component. Furthermore, the design of centralized control systems tends to be hard and expensive as the physical systems are by their nature geographically distributed: even when technologically feasible, a centralized decision point might require prohibitive hardware and software costs, especially for large systems. In addition, centralized control problems have to be solved with ad hoc techniques. Every new problem must be solved from scratch.

Solution	It is necessary to organize the control system following a hierarchical decentralized architecture. A control module with precise responsibilities should be made for each component of the system. Control modules should be assigned to the different levels in the hierarchy so that a higher-level control module coordinates the control modules below it. Every control module is an autonomous decision maker that maintains its local state, processes input data from physical devices or other control modules, elaborates commands and cooperates with higher-level control modules.
Force resolution	Decentralized control enhances system reliability and modularity. New system components can be easily integrated within the control architecture when system functionality must be updated or faulty components replaced.

13.9 ■ References

Brugali, D. and Menga, G. (2002) "Architectural Models for Global Automation Systems", *IEEE Transactions on Robotics and Automation*, Vol. 18, No. 4, August, 487–493.

Estrin, D., Govindan, R. and Heidemann, J. (eds) (2000), Special Issue on "Embedding the Internet," *Communications of the ACM*, Vol. 43, No. 5.

Supermarket operation support system

14

Synthesis

We want to develop an information system to support the counter activities in a supermarket. The system must also support the back-end activities, such as statistics on the sales performed by the employees and on the products bought by the customers.

A typical interface at the supermarket counter consists of a touch screen and a bar code reader, information on product prices and stock levels are kept in a separate server machine. The server machine centralizes most of the computing activities and allows monitoring of the ongoing activities by the sales manager.

- Focus: this case study exemplifies the separation of concerns between data presentation, data processing and data persistence, introducing the three-tier architecture.
- OO techniques: proxy objects are used to make the communication among components transparent.
- Java features: sockets are used as a communication means; the JDBC technology is used to access a relational database.

14.1 ■ Specifications

The activities performed in a supermarket are mainly located at the counters (or points of sale) where the customers present the products they want to buy to an employee, who registers the products and accepts the payments. These activities involve accessing the product database in order to retrieve prices and to update their quantities.

Each counter is equipped with a terminal. Terminals are low-cost PCs with cheap processors and limited memory and an LCD touch screen. The touch screen emulates the functionalities of a mouse; this simplifies the interface and eliminates the need for a keyboard. A central server computer performs all the operations and interacts with a database containing all the information about products, employees and customers. The supermarket has a local area network connecting all the terminals and the central server.

The typical usage scenario takes place at the counter. At the beginning of his/her shift, the employee activates the counter. The counter remains active until the end of the shift when the employee deactivates it. The employee sitting at the counter welcomes the customer and asks for the customer's loyalty card. The card has a bar code identifying the customer. Once the bar code is read, the system checks for the code and displays the name of the customer on the screen.

All the products that the customer wants to buy are read through the bar code reader. For each product it is possible to insert the quantity to speed up the activity when several items of the same product are present. In case of problems the employee can type in the product code, for instance when the bar code is scratched or unreadable. When all the items have been read, the receipt can be printed with the sum to be paid by the customer. This closes the transaction with the current customer, and the next customer in line can be served.

The market manager must be able to look at the statistics regarding the sales by day, by employee and by customer. In addition it must be possible to associate the customers with the products they bought to study their preferences.

14.2 ■ Problem analysis

The main feature of the system is supporting the employee activities at the counters. These activities are described by three use cases as depicted in Figure 14.1. Acquisition involves the employee and the customer, but only the employee interacts with the system. Connect and Disconnect are performed by each employee at the beginning and end of each shift.

The system manages information related to three main entities: employee, customer and product. Information about sales must be recorded to keep track of the sales and to update the quantity of products available in the store.

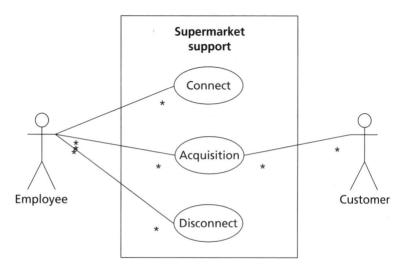

Figure 14.1 Main use cases

The employees are identified by a code and a name, in addition they have a password to enable their authentication when they activate a terminal in the Connect use case. The customers are identified only by a code and a name, since they do not interact directly with the system. Products are described by a code, a name, a price and the available quantity in the store.

The physical structure of the system can be described with the deployment diagram shown in Figure 14.2. Each counter terminal is connected to a bar code reader. Terminals are linked to the central server through an ethernet LAN, the usual standard network protocol for this kind of network is TCP/IP. The central server accesses information stored in a database.

Since the all the counter terminals share the same network connection to the central server, the application level protocol for the interaction between the terminals and the central server must be as simple and lightweight as possible. In addition the protocol must be implemented with low computing resource demands. This is due to the fact that low-cost PCs are used as counter terminals.

14.2.1 □ Domain models

An important issue in a large distributed system such as this supermarket operation support system is its scalability. It is crucial to know the maximum number of terminals that can be added to the system without degrading its performance. On the central server side the problem can be solved (to a certain extent) by upgrading the hardware. The performance bottleneck in this case is the shared network connection between the terminals and the server. Thus it is important to analyse the characteristics of the communication protocol and the influence it has on the data throughput.

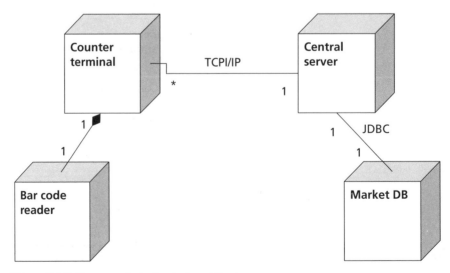

Figure 14.2 Supermarket physical architecture

Using a simplified and conservative approach, the relationship between the network throughput and the protocol characteristics can be described by Equation 14.1:

$$AT > NM * T * (PL + NO)$$

Equation 14.1 Throughput and protocol characteristics

AT is the actual throughput available on the network measured in bytes per second, NM is the maximum number of packets exchanged per second between a terminal and the central server, T is the number of terminals, PL is the size in bytes of the protocol payload per packet, NO is the total network protocol overhead (e.g. the TCP header size) measured in bytes.

We can assume that the time between the scan of two consecutive products by the bar code reader is about 1 second. Therefore this is the time required to exchange all the information about the product and signal quantity of products acquired. The nominal throughput of an ethernet LAN is 10 Mbit/s, but in the case of several nodes and heavy traffic we can consider an actual throughput of 1 Mbit/s–120 KB/s. The overhead per packet caused by TCP/IP and the ethernet protocol is about 80 bytes including the acknowledge packet (Huston 2000). We assume that each message will require only one TCP packet. Considering the extreme case where the available throughput is entirely consumed by communication, we can rewrite Equation 14.1 as follows, expressing the number of supported terminals as a function of the other factors.

$$T = AT/(NM * (PL + NO))$$

Equation 14.2 Number of terminals

We can estimate the relationship between the payload and the maximum number of terminals supported by the protocol. NM is a consequence of the particular application protocol adopted. The graphical representation of this relationship is shown in Figure 14.3. We consider three types of application protocol that require the number of messages to buy a product to be 4, 6 and 8. In the case of a supermarket with 60 counters, if the number of messages required by the application protocol to buy a product is 6, then the payload limit is 180 bytes per message.

14.2.2 □ Main features

The supermarket operation support system exhibits four main features:

- *Counter terminal.* This provides a simple interface integrated with specific devices such as bar code readers.
- *Central server.* This hosts the main computations and interacts with a database containing all the required information.
- *Remote communication.* The terminals and the server communicate though a simple and lightweight interaction protocol.
- *Monitoring.* The sales manager should be able to check the current status of the store and active counters.

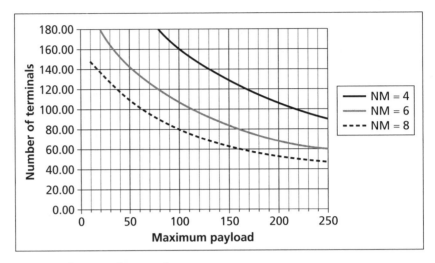

Figure 14.3 Supported terminals

14.2.3 □ Test

The tests of the system should address the typical usage scenario of the system, i.e. the employee connecting to the system, execution of a sequence of acquisition and, finally, disconnecting. The results of these operations could be observed from three perspectives:

- the effects of the single operations on the user interface;
- the effects of the operations on the database, and
- the information exchanged through the communication protocol between the terminals and the server.

14.3 ■ Architecture and planning

The application falls into the large category of client–server systems operating over a network. Typically the functionalities of this kind of system are organized into three layers or tiers; they are dubbed as three-tier architectures. The first tier has the purpose of interacting with the users (the employees in this case); the middle tier focuses on the computationally intensive tasks; and the third layer carries out the interaction with persistent storage.

Modularity can improve system scalability as well as system maintenance: with a modular approach it is possible to upgrade the UI or the database easily. Since the system is intrinsically distributed, it is important to identify a "cut" within the architecture where the communication takes place. The communication must be as simple as possible, and separated from the other features of the system.

The main components of the architecture are shown in Figure 14.4. The Counter UI and Counter components address the first feature and form the

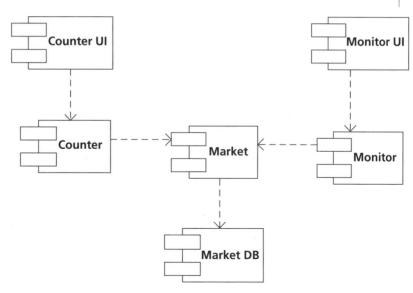

Figure 14.4 Components of the system

first layer of the architecture: the former implements the graphical user interface, while the second embeds the problem of the interaction with the rest of the system. The Market component performs all the computational activities. In its operation it makes use of the Market DB component that embeds all the interactions with the persistent storage. This module simplifies database upgrades.

The development process of the supermarket operation support system is organized into four phases that produce the following prototypes.

- *Prototype 1: Counter terminal*. A system is developed to test the counter user interface. This is a dummy interface detached from any server.
- *Prototype 2: Centralized system*. A full working system is developed in a centralized fashion; all the components reside in the same process. There is no persistent storage of the database and the communication is implemented through direct method invocation.
- *Prototype 3: Distributed system*. The fully distributed system is implemented; the communication takes places through a TCP/IP-based protocol.
- *Prototype 4: Data persistence*. A persistent database is introduced; an SQL DBMS is used to hold the static data and to store the information about the transactions.

14.4 ■ Prototype 1: Counter terminal

This section identifies both the functional and non-functional requirements of the counter terminal user interface. The functional requirements are related to the main use cases: connect, disconnect, acquisition. The non-functional requirements address the interaction mode: the use of a touch screen and the presence of a bar code reader.

14.4.1 □ Analysis

Three use cases describe the functionalities of the terminal user interface as shown in Figure 14.5. They are:

- Connect: when the employee at the counter starts working, he or she connects to the central server. The initial state of the user interfaces should provide only the option of connecting to the server: the connection requires the input of the employee identifier and the related password.
- Acquisition: when a customer arrives at the counter with the products he or she wants to buy, the employee performs three basic operations, as shown in Figure 14.5:
  - Set customer: when a known customer comes to the counter the fact can be registered, so that all the products bought are linked to the customer identifier. The customer is identified by a code: the terminal shows the name of the customer to the employee.
  - Buy product: all the products bought are registered together with their quantities. The employee must insert the product code and (in case more than one item is present) the quantity.
  - End transaction: after the last product has been recorded, the transaction is ended, the sum is computed and the bill is produced. The employee is ready to serve the next customer.

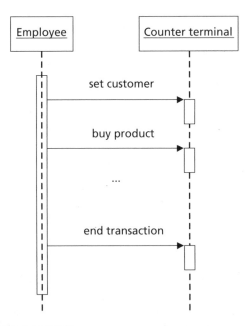

Figure 14.5 Acquisition scenario

- Disconnect: at the end of his or her shift, the employee disconnects from the central server, thus deactivating the counter terminal and returning it to the initial state. The terminal is ready to be used by another employee.

The non-functional requirements are defined by two constraints:

- The interaction takes place through a touch screen.
- The codes of products and customers can be entered through a bar code reader.

As a consequence of the first constraint we must assume that a keyboard is not available. Since the touch screen operates as a mouse, all the input

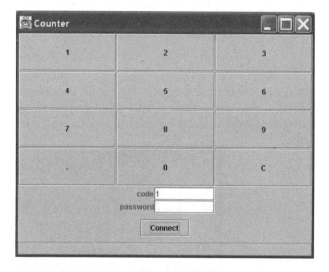

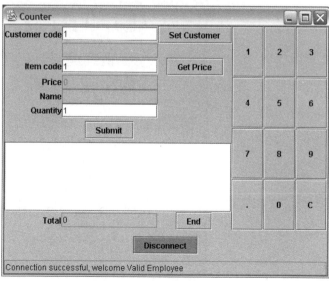

Figure 14.6 Initial and acquisition screen. Copyright © 2005 Sun Microsystems, Inc. All rights reserved. Reproduced by permission of Sun Microsystems, Inc.

must be available though buttons on the screen. The input characters required in the use cases are all decimal digits. Thus the graphical interface shall have a section with buttons corresponding to the numbers, plus a comma and a delete button.

The initial screen that allows connection to the server should look like Figure 14.6 (top). After connection, the layout of the screen is reconfigured to support the operations performed during the acquisition use case. The screen should appear as in Figure 14.6 (bottom).

The second non-functional requirement is the presence of a bar code reader. It can read both product codes and customer codes. The prototype we develop will emulate the bar code reader in a separate window, shown in Figure 14.7. The pressure on a button simulates the scanning of a bar code from the reader.

14.4.2 ☐ Design

The design of the interface is very simple. It consists of two main classes that represent the two windows identified in the analysis above: the counter terminal interface and the bar code reader emulation window.

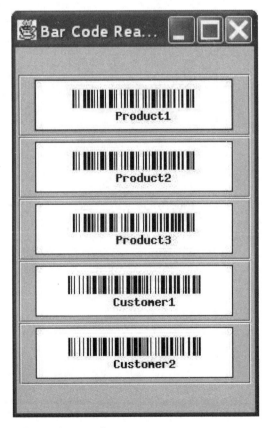

Figure 14.7 Bar code reader window.

How do we make the bar code reader and the terminal communicate?

We adopt the *Observer* pattern (see Sidebar 8.1, page 181); the observer interface is BarCodeListener, which is implemented by class CounterFrame. The observable is the class BarCodeReader, which generates an event of class BarCodeReaderEvent that contains all the information related to the bar code read. Such an approach is similar, but simpler, to the solution adopted by the Java for Retail POS Committee (Java POS Committee 2001). The classes are described in Figure 14.8. This design decouples the counter window and the bar code reader window making it easier to replace the emulation window with the actual device.

The appearance of the terminal GUI must be reconfigured upon a successful login. The login layout shown in Figure 14.6 (top) must be transformed into the normal operation layout shown in Figure 14.6 (bottom).

How to reconfigure the graphical layout of the terminal user interface?

The reconfiguration of the user interface can be achieved in two alternative ways: first by using several windows, second by modifying the contents of a single window. The latter option is made possible by dynamically reconfigurable layouts such as the grid bag layout. It has the advantage of being simpler and more lightweight. The grid bag layout is one of the standard layout managers of the Java AWT.

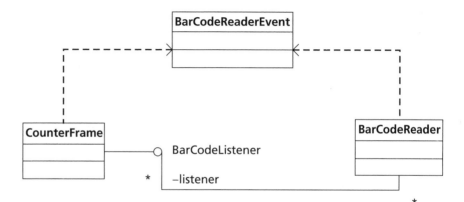

Figure 14.8 Counter terminal user interface class diagram

Decision point

How to use the onscreen keypad to insert values into text fields?

The basic idea is to let the user click on the buttons of the keypad to insert the values into the fields. This is equivalent to touching the keys on the touch screen that will equip the real counter terminal. This solution has a practical problem. The insertion of data into a field on a user interface is based on the concept of the currently active element: the last element clicked by the user is the active element that will receive the user input. Both the simulated keypad and the fields are part of the same graphical user interface and there can be only one active element at a time; thus, the active element is either on the simulated keypad or on the main user interface. To solve this problem we have to explicitly keep track of the last active element (i.e. the one that was active before the current one) and send to it the input from the keypad.

14.4.3 ☐ Implementation

The main class of the user interface is CounterFrame, it defines the main elements of the counter user interface. It includes the input fields and the keypad. In addition this class implements the BarCodeListener interfaces, so it is able to receive events from the (simulated) bar code reader.

The method input_focusGained() is invoked whenever one of the input fields gets the focus (i.e. becomes the active element of the GUI); it stores a reference to the input field in the attribute lastInputField. A click on one of the buttons of the keypad triggers the execution of method keypad_action Performed(), which sends a key to the last active input field (i.e. lastInputField).

```
package CounterUI;
import java.awt.*;
import javax.swing.*;
import java.awt.event.*;

public class CounterFrame extends JFrame
implements BarCodeListener {
  private JTextField lastInputField = null;
  void input_focusGained(FocusEvent e) {
    lastInputField = (JTextField)e.getComponent();
    System.out.println(e.getComponent().getName() +
                                  " got focus");
  }
  void keypad_actionPerformed(ActionEvent e) {
    String cmd=e.getActionCommand();
```

```
          System.out.println(e.getActionCommand() +
                                " action performed");
      if(lastInputField!=null){
        String text = lastInputField.getText();
        if(cmd.equals("C")){
          if(text.length()>0){
            lastInputField.setText(text.
                    substring(0,text.length()-1));
          }
        }else{
          lastInputField.setText(text+cmd);
        }
        lastInputField.requestFocus();
      }
    }
  }
}
```

The BarCodeListener interface is quite simple; it contains one method that is called when a new bar code is read.

```
package CounterUI;
public interface BarCodeListener {
  void readValue(BarCodeReaderEvent event);
}
```

The information relating to a new bar code read is stored in BarCode ReaderEvent objects. In our case the only information is represented by the code.

```
package CounterUI;
public class BarCodeReaderEvent {
  String code;
  BarCodeReaderEvent(String code){
    this.code = code;
  }
  String getCode() { return code; }
}
```

The simulated bar code reader is implemented as a frame: BarCode ReaderUI. Each bar code is an image stored on the hard disk and used as an icon for a button. When a button is pressed the listener is notified that the corresponding code has been read.

```
package CounterUI;
import java.awt.*;
import javax.swing.*;
import java.awt.event.*;
public class BarCodeReaderUI extends JFrame {
  private JButton btProduct1 = new JButton();
```

```
    private ImageIcon iconProduct1 =
                new ImageIcon("Product1.jpg");
    private GridBagLayout gridBagLayout1 =
                new GridBagLayout();
    //...
    private BarCodeListener listener;
    public void setListener(BarCodeListener newListener){
       listener = newListener;
    }
    void readCode_actionPerformed(ActionEvent e) {
       if(listener!=null){
          String cmd = e.getActionCommand();
          listener.readValue(new BarCodeReaderEvent(cmd));
       }
    }
  }
}
```

14.4.4 □ Test

The test on the user interface consists of a set of operations that correspond to user touches on the terminal screen. The sequence of operations and expected effects on the user interface are:

■ Run the terminal program:
  – The terminal starts with the initial screen (Figure 14.6, top).
■ Select the "code" field and type "1" on the keypad.
■ Select the "password" field and type "111" on the keypad.
■ Click on the "Connect" button:
  – the terminal switches to the Acquisition screen (Figure 14.6, bottom);
  – the bar code reader emulation window appears.
■ Simulate the reading of the code of a customer by clicking on one of the customer bar codes:
  – the terminal window shows the name of the customer.
■ Simulate the reading of a product code:
  – the terminal window shows the name and the price of the product.
■ Simulate the reading of another product code:
  – the "Check" area contains the first product with quantity equal to 1;
  – the total is incremented by the price of product 1;
  – the terminal window shows the name and the price of the second product;
■ Select the "Quantity" field, type on the "C" button of the keypad and then on the "2" button.
■ Click on the "End" button:
  – the "Check" area contains the list of the two products with the relative quantities and the total;
  – the customer name has been erased;
  – the total has been reset to 0.

The sequence presented above is one of many possible sequences; in addition, it is important to test abnormal conditions such as invalid codes for employee, customer and product.

14.5 ■ Prototype 2: Centralized system

In this prototype we develop a centralized version of the system running in a single process. This system has a non-persistent database that resides in memory.

14.5.1 □ Analysis

There are two main aspects of this prototype that should be considered: first the behaviour of the system, second the information handled by the system. The behaviour concerns the support of the operations of the employees at the counter.

The information deals with three main entities: products, customers and employees. They are related to each other as depicted in Figure 14.9. Item

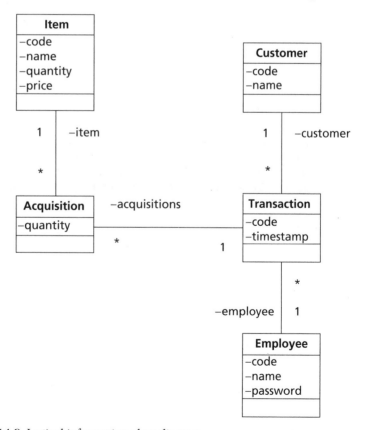

Figure 14.9 Logical information class diagram

describes products present either on the shelves or in the stockroom. **Employee** represents the employee sitting at the counter, who requires a password to access the system. **Customer** represents a customer, who has no password because it has no direct access to the system. **Transaction** represents a set of acquisitions performed by a customer, at a certain time with a given employee at the counter.

The transaction and acquisition entities can be used to compute statistics on customer data (e.g. the best selling products or the preferred products of particular customers) in order to improve sales. This data makes it possible to conduct market analyses through data mining techniques.

14.5.2 □ **Design**

The main issue in this prototype is to achieve a modular design that can be easily extended. For this purpose this prototype is structured into four packages as shown in Figure 14.10. The packages correspond to and implement the homonymous components of the architecture (see Figure 14.4).

Decision point

How to keep the packages loosely coupled?

Since the dependencies between packages form a chain, low coupling is achieved by ensuring that any interaction takes places through a limited set of interfaces. Because the interactions are quite simple we define an interface for each package.

There are three interfaces that regulate the interactions between the packages. The package **CounterUI** communicates with the package **Counter** through its interface **MarketProxy**. The interface **Market** mediates the interactions between the package **Counter** and the package **Market**. Finally the

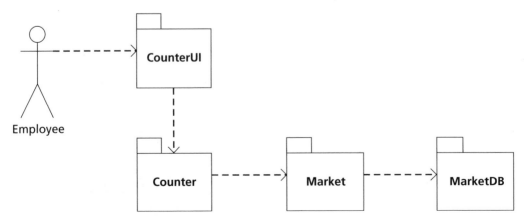

Figure 14.10 Package structure

interface DBManager conveys requests from the package Market to package MarketDB.

The complete class diagram is shown in Figure 14.11. The classes belonging to different packages are separated by a dashed line. All the packages contain a limited set of classes. The best package is MarketDB: it contains the BManager interface, the VolatileDB interface that implements an in-memory database, and four data classes: Item, Employee, Customer and Transaction The data classes do not perform any operations; they only contain the information relative to an entity stored in the database.

Each operation of the employee on the graphical user interface triggers a sequence of interactions that span all four packages. As an example we can examine in detail the scenario related to the Connect use case, which is shown in Figure 14.12.

When the employee at the counter pushes the "Connect" button (after filling in the code and password fields) the graphical user interface invokes the btConnect_actionPerformed method. This method takes the values of code and password and calls the LocalProxy, through the MarketProxy interface. The local proxy asks the server for authentication (through the Market interface) which takes place in two stages: first the employee information is

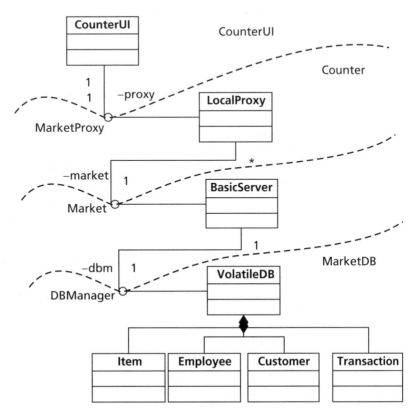

Figure 14.11 Complete class diagram

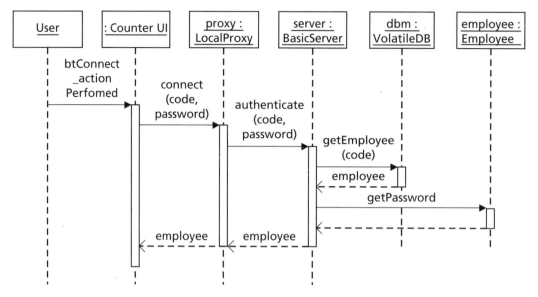

Figure 14.12 Connect scenario

obtained through the **DBManager** interface from the database, then the provided password is compared with the one stored in the database.

14.5.3 ☐ Implementation

The interface **MarketProxy** defines all the operations that are available to the counter terminal.

```
package Counter;
public interface MarketProxy {
  // connect() and disconnect () implement the login/logout
  // scenario
  public String connect(long employee, String password)
                                          throws Exception;
  public void disconnect();
  // define the current customer and get its name
  public String getCustomer(long code) throws Exception;
  // information about a product consists of name and price
  public String getName(long item) throws Exception ;
  public double getPrice(long item) throws Exception ;
  // notify that the given quantity of a product has been
  // bought
  public void buy(long item, long quantity) throws Exception;
  // terminate the transaction and produces the sum of the
  // check
  public void endTransaction() throws Exception;
}
```

The class LocalProxy implements the MarketProxy interface for the single process prototype. It has a few private attributes to keep track of the codes of the currently connected employee, the current customer and the current transaction. In addition the server attribute implements the association to the Market interface.

This class implements all the methods of the interface. It ensures that the normal operations are performed only after a connection has been made (method assertConnected()). In addition it initiates a new transaction when the first product is bought by a new customer.

```java
package Counter;
import Market.Market;
public class LocalProxy implements MarketProxy {
  // code of the currently logged employee
  private long employee;
  // information about the ongoing transaction
  private long customer;
  private long transaction;
  // the actual server that carries on the processing
  private Market server;
  // constructor
  public LocalProxy(Market server) {
    this.server = server;
    employee = 0;
    customer = 0;
    transaction = 0;
  }
  // connects a terminal to the server and stores
  // the code of the employee
  public String connect(long employee, String password)
            throws Exception{
    String employeeName = server.authenticate(employee
                                          ,password);
    if(employeeName==null) return null;
    this.employee = employee;
    return employeeName;
  }
  public void disconnect() {
    employee = 0;
    customer = 0;
    transaction = 0;
  }
  // verify that a connection has been succesfully
  // completed, otherwise throw an exception
  private void assertConnected() throws Exception {
    if(employee==0)
      throw new Exception("Not connected");
  }
```

```java
  public String getName(long item) throws Exception {
    assertConnected();
    return server.getName(item);
  }
  public double getPrice(long item) throws Exception {
    assertConnected();
    return server.getPrice(item);
  }
  public String getCustomer(long code) throws Exception{
    assertConnected();
    String customerName = server.getCustomer(code);
    if(customerName==null) return null;
    customer = code;
    return customerName;
  }
  public void buy(long item, long quantity)
                                    throws Exception{
    assertConnected();
    // if no transaction has been started, start a new one
    if(transaction==0){
      transaction = server.
           startTransaction(customer,employee);
    }
    server.buy(item,quantity,transaction);
  }
  public void endTransaction() throws Exception {
    assertConnected();
    server.endTransaction(transaction);
    transaction = 0;
  }
}
```

The interface Market defines all the operations provided by the market server. They are closely related to those available in the MarketProxy interface.

```java
package Market;
public interface Market {
  // authenticate an employee,
  // return null in case of failure
  public String authenticate(long employee,
                             String password);
  // return the name of a customer,
  // null if it doesn't exist
  public String getCustomer(long customer);
  // return the name of an item,
  // null if it doesn't exist
  public String getName(long item);
```

```
// return the price of an item,
// 0.0 if it doesn't exist
public double getPrice(long item);
// start a new transaction
public long startTransaction(long customer,
                            long employee)
        throws Exception;
// buy a given quantity of a product
// in a transaction
public void buy(long item, long quantity,
                long transaction)
            throws Exception;
// terminate the transaction
public void endTransaction(long transaction)
            throws Exception;
}
```

The class **BasicServer** implements the market interface and manages the requests coming from a client. The methods are very simple: they forward the requests to the database and extract the required information from the data provided by the database.

```
package Market;
import MarketDB.*;
public class BasicServer
implements Market {
  private DBManager dbm;
  public BasicServer(DBManager db) {
    dbm = db;
  }
  public String authenticate(long code, String password){
    Employee employee=dbm.getEmployee(code);
    if(employee != null &&
            employee.password.equals(password)){
      return employee.name;
    }
    return null;
  }
  public String getCustomer(long code){
    Customer customer = dbm.getCustomer(code);
    if(customer==null) return null;
    return customer.name;
  }
  public String getName(long code){
    Item it = dbm.getItem(code);
    if(it==null) return null;
    return it.name;
  }
```

```
   public double getPrice(long code){
      Item it = dbm.getItem(code);
      if(it==null) return -1;
      return it.price;
   }
   public long startTransaction(long customer,
                                    long employee)
                throws Exception {
      return dbm.startTransaction(customer, employee);
   }
   public void buy(long item, long quantity,
                    long transaction)
            throws Exception {
      dbm.buy(item,quantity,transaction);
   }
   public void endTransaction(long transaction)
                throws Exception  {
      dbm.closeTransaction(transaction);
   }
}
```

The interface **DBManager** defines the operations offered by a database. It is similar to the **Market** interface but is more data oriented.

```
package MarketDB;
public interface DBManager {
   // return information about an employee
   Employee getEmployee(long code);
   // return information about a customer
   Customer getCustomer(long code);
   // return information about a product
   Item getItem(long code);
   // start a new transaction and return its code
   long startTransaction(long customer, long employee)
            throws Exception;
   // record the acquisition of a product
   // in a transaction
   void buy(long item, long quantity, long transaction)
            throws Exception;
   // close a transaction
   void endTransaction(long code) throws Exception;
}
```

The information stored in the database is handled through four data classes: Item, Customer, Employee, Transaction. These classes hold information in public attributes.

```
package MarketDB;
public class Item {
```

```java
  public long code;
  public String name;
  public double price;
  public long quantity;
  Item(long code, String name,
            double price, long quantity){
    this.code = code;
    this.name = name;
    this.price = price;
    this.quantity = quantity;
  }
}
public class Customer {
  public long code;
  public String name;
  Customer(long code, String name){
    this.code = code;
    this.name = name;
  }
}
public class Employee {
  public long code;
  public String name;
  public String password;
  Employee(long code, String name, String password){
    this.code = code;
    this.name = name;
    this.password = password;
  }
}
public class Acquisition {
  public long quantity;
  public Item item;
  Acquisition(Item item, long quantity){
    this.item = item;
    this.quantity=quantity;
  }
}
import java.util.Vector;
public class Transaction {
  public long code;
  public Employee employee;
  public Customer customer;
  public boolean open;
  public Vector acquisitions = new Vector();
  Transaction(long code, Employee employee,
                    Customer customer){
```

```
      this.code = code;
      this.employee = employee;
      this.customer = customer;
      open = true;
  }
}
```

The VolatileDB class implements the functionalities defined by the interface DBManager. It implements a non-persistent database. The database is initialized with the same data whenever the application starts. Four vectors (items, employees, customers and transactions) hold the data. The methods are very simple because they perform an indexed access to the vectors. Only the method buy() is slightly more complex: it recovers the information on the current transaction, if existent, then gets the required item and updates its quantity.

```java
package MarketDB;
import java.util.Vector;
public class VolatileDB implements DBManager {
  static Vector items = new Vector();
  static Vector employees = new Vector();
  static Vector customers = new Vector();
  static Vector transactions = new Vector();
  public VolatileDB() {
    items.add(new Item(1,"Beer",1.5,1000));
    items.add(new Item(2,"Peanuts",0.5,1000));
    items.add(new Item(3,"Cookies",2.2,500));
    employees.add(new Employee(1,"Yee Emplo","111"));
    customers.add(new Customer(1,"John Doe"));
    customers.add(new Customer(1,"Jane Doe"));
  }
  public Employee getEmployee(long code) {
    return (Employee)employees.get((int)code-1);
  }
  public Customer getCustomer(long code) {
    return (Customer)customers.get((int)code-1);
  }
  public Item getItem(long code) {
    return (Item)items.get((int)code-1);
  }
  public long startTransaction(long customer,
                               long employee)
                  throws Exception {
    Customer cust=getCustomer(customer);
    if(cust == null) throw
              new Exception("Customer non existent");
    Employee emp = getEmployee(employee);
```

```
    if(emp == null) throw
               new Exception("Employee non existent");

    Transaction t = new Transaction(transactions.size()+1,
                                emp,cust);
    transactions.add(t);
    return t.code;
  }
 public void buy(long item, long quantity,
                           long transaction)
    throws Exception {
    Transaction t;
    try{
      t = (Transaction)transactions.
                elementAt((int)transaction-1);
    }catch(Exception e){
      throw new Exception("Transaction non existent");
    }
    Item it = getItem(item);
    if(it == null){ throw
                new Exception("Non existent item");}
    t.acquisitions.add(new Acquisition(it,quantity));
  }
 public void endTransaction(long code)
                throws Exception {
    Transaction t = (Transaction)transactions.
                       elementAt((int)code-1);
    if(t == null) throw
            new Exception("Transaction non existent");
    if(!t.open) throw
            new Exception("Transaction already closed");
    t.open = false;
  }
}
```

The main program instantiates all the components of the system in the correct order. In addition it creates the bar code reader simulator.

```
import CounterUI.*;
import Market.BasicServer;
import Counter.LocalProxy;
import MarketDB.VolatileDB;
public class TestLocal {
  public static void main(String [] args) {
    BasicServer server = new BasicServer(
                                new VolatileDB());
    LocalProxy proxy = new LocalProxy(server);
```

```
            CounterFrame counter = new CounterFrame(proxy);
            counter.show();
            BarCodeReaderUI reader = new BarCodeReaderUI();
            reader.setLocation(100300);
            reader.show();
            reader.setListener(counter);
        }
    }
```

14.5.4 ☐ Test

The test consists of a sequence of steps similar to those performed in the previous prototype. In addition the acquisition of all the products (with codes 1 through 3) should be simulated. To pass the test we need to check the coherence between the types of products, the quantity and the total of the check.

14.6 ■ Prototype 3: Distributed system

This prototype addresses a new concern: the distribution of the system. There are several counter terminal devices that are separated from the central server. A simple protocol is designed to support the interactions between each terminal and the server.

14.6.1 ☐ Analysis

The functional requirement for the communication protocol between the counter terminals and the central server is to support the basic operations of the counter user interface, which are codified by the MarketProxy interface defined in the previous prototype. In particular the operations are: connect, product info, set customer, acquire product, end transaction and disconnect.

The main constraint for the communication protocol is to occupy a limited network band. The size of the messages exchanged by the protocol is limited by Equation 14.1.

14.6.2 ☐ Design

The design of this prototype is divided into two main parts: the design of the data exchange protocol and the design of the software infrastructure. The former is developed from scratch while the latter builds on the previous prototype.

Decision point

What protocol do we use?

There is no standard protocol for this type of application. Therefore, we have to develop our own protocol. We decide to use a synchronous protocol, because it is simpler to implement than an asynchronous one. To perform any of the required operations the terminal software sends a request message to the server and waits for the reply. The messages that constitute the protocol are described in Table 14.1.

If a request succeeds, the reply message starts with the string OK followed by a parameter that contains additional information specific to each request. If the request fails, then the server's reply starts with the string ERROR followed by a description of the cause of failure.

The acquisition of a product requires three interactions as shown in Figure 14.13. Therefore six messages are required. The longest message is a reply containing the name of the product, which can be 20 characters long; the payload in this case is 25 bytes. According to Equation 14.2, the maximum number of supported terminals for this protocol is 60.

Decision point

How do we introduce the data exchange protocol into the system?

To implement the client–server interaction through the protocol a modification of the structure of the previous prototype is required. On the counter terminal side the class LocalProxy is substituted by the class SocketProxy, shown on the left side of Figure 14.14. This class implements the MarketProxy interface as well but, instead of invoking directly the Market interface, exchanges messages according to the protocol described above.

On the central server side two new classes are required as shown on the right side of Figure 14.14. The class MarketStub is the counterpart of the SocketProxy as far as the communication protocol is concerned. This class mediates, through the communication protocol, the access of the Socket Proxy class to the Market interface. The class StubFactory accepts connections from the terminals; whenever a terminal establishes a connection a new MarketStub object is created to handle the communication.

Table 14.1 Protocol messages

Request	Reply	Description
AUTH <employee code> <password>	OK <employee name>	Log in the employee; if successful return the name of the employee
GET_CUSTOMER <customer code>	OK <customer name>	Set the current customer and return the name
GET_NAME <product code>	OK <product name>	Get the name of a product
GET_PRICE <product code>	OK <product price>	Get the price of a product
BUY <product code> <quantity>	OK	Buy a quantity of product
END	OK	Terminate the transaction
QUIT		Close the socket connection

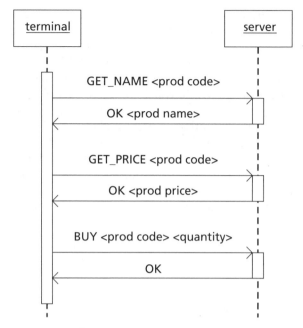

Figure 14.13 Acquisition of a product

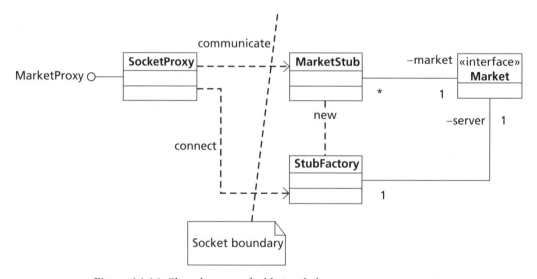

Figure 14.14 Class diagram of additional classes

14.6.3 □ Implementation

The implementation of the increment of this prototype with respect to the previous one consists of communication via sockets (for further details see Sidebar 14.1).

Sidebar 14.1 Sockets

Sockets are the standard tool used for communicating over a computer network. Sockets are a flexible tool and support a large spectrum of communication protocols, the most common being those in the TCP/IP framework.

We will focus on the TCP protocol. There are two classes that are used to establish and carry out normal TCP connections: ServerSocket and Socket. For simple connections between a client and a server they are likely to be sufficient.

ServerSocket represents the socket on a server that waits and listens for requests for service from a client. Socket represents the endpoints for communication between a server and a client. When a server gets a request for service, it creates a Socket for communication with the client and continues to listen for other requests on the ServerSocket. The client also creates a Socket for communication with the server. The sequence is shown below in Figure 14.15 (from the Sun Java Networking Overview).

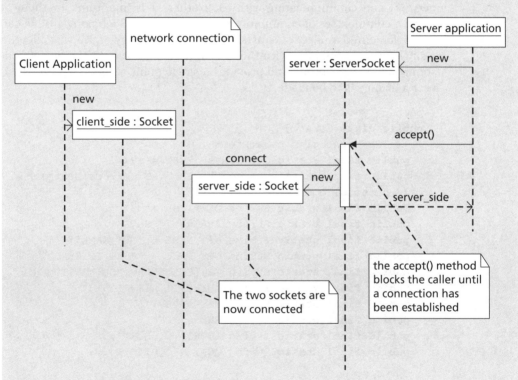

Figure 14.15 Setup of a socket connection

Once the connection is established, getInputStream() and getOutputSteam() may be used in communication between the sockets. A sample server program is the following:

```
ServerSocket server= new ServerSocket(SERVER_PORT);
Socket socket = server.accept();
InputStream in = socket. getInputStream();
OutputStream out = socket. getOutputStream();
```

The constant SERVER_PORT identifies a port on the server to which the clients must make the connection. For instance, the port for the HTTP protocol is 80. If a server must serve more than one client at once, it creates a new thread for each connection. Typically a server has a loop that accepts new connections and then creates a new thread.

The client program that connects to the server is as follows:

```
Socket socket = new Socket(SERVER_HOST,SERVER_PORT);
InputStream in = socket. getInputStream();
OutputStream out = socket. getOutputStream();
```

The constant SERVER_HOST is the name (e.g. www.polito.it) or IP address of the server and the SERVER_PORT specifies the address to which it is connected.

Since there are several components residing on distributed nodes of the network and communicating with each other, it is important for them to share a common set of communication conventions. Such conventions can be implemented as a set of constants that for simplicity of use we collect in a single class. Compared with the use of immediate values, the use of constants is less error prone and provides a single point of modification whenever a change is to be made.

```
package Market;
public class Const {
    // TCP connection parameters
    public final static int SERVER_PORT = 1971;
    public final static String SERVER_HOST = "localhost";
    // protocol commands
    public final static String OK = "OK";
    public final static String ERROR = "ERROR";
    public final static String GET_NAME = "GET_NAME";
    public final static String GET_PRICE = "GET_PRICE";
    public final static String GET_CUSTOMER= "GET_CUSTOMER";
    public final static String AUTHENTICATE= "AUTH";
    public final static String BUY = "BUY";
    public final static String END = "END";
    public final static String ABORT = "ABORT";
    public final static String QUIT = "QUIT";
}
```

Class SocketProxy implements the terminal side of the communication protocol. All the messages are sent through the method sendMessage() that receives the message to be sent as an argument and returns the reply received from the server. Since the protocol is synchronous this method sends the message and waits for the reply.

```
package Counter;
import Market.Const;
import java.net.Socket;
import java.io.InputStream;
```

```java
import java.io.OutputStream;
public class SocketProxy
implements MarketProxy {
  // the socket and the associated in and out streams
  private Socket socket;
  private InputStream in;
  private OutputStream out;
  // the name of the host where the market server runs
  private String host;
  public SocketProxy(String host){
    this.host = host;
  }
  // send a synchronous message to the market
  // server and returns the reply
  private String sendMessage(String request)
                  throws Exception {
    out.write((request+"\n").getBytes());
    out.flush();
    byte [] buffer=new byte[1024];
    int en;
    len = in.read(buffer);
    String reply = new String(buffer,0,len);
    return reply;
  }
  // connect to the market server providing the employee
  // code and pwd the server authenticates the employee
  public String connect(long employee, String password)
                  throws Exception{
    socket = new Socket(host,Const.SERVER_PORT);
    in = socket.getInputStream();
    out = socket.getOutputStream();

    String reply = sendMessage(Const.AUTHENTICATE + " " +
                            employee + " " + password);
    if(reply.startsWith(Const.OK)){
      return reply.substring(Const.OK.length());
    }else{
      return null;
    }
  }
  // return the name of a product given the code
  public String getName(long item) throws Exception {
    String reply = sendMessage(Const.GET_NAME + " "
                                + item);
    if(reply.startsWith(Const.OK)){
      return reply.substring(Const.OK.length());
    }else{
```

```java
      return reply.substring(Const.ERROR.length());
    }
  }
  // return the price of a product given the code
  public double getPrice(long item) throws Exception{
    String reply = sendMessage(Const.GET_PRICE + " "
                                        + item);
    if(reply.startsWith(Const.OK)
      return Double.parseDouble(reply.
                      substring(Const.OK.length())));
    else
      return Double.parseDouble(reply.
                      substring(Const.ERROR.length())));
  }
  // returns the name of the customer given the code
  public String getCustomer(long code) throws Exception{
    String reply = sendMessage(Const.GET_CUSTOMER + " "
                                        + code);
    if(reply.startsWith(Const.OK))
      return reply.substring(Const.OK.length());
    else
      return reply.substring(Const.ERROR.length());
  }
  // communicate a new purchase for the current customer
  public void buy(long item, long quantity)
            throws Exception {
    String reply = sendMessage(Const.BUY + " " + item
                                      + " " + quantity);
    if(reply.startsWith(Const.ERROR))
      throw new Exception(reply
                  .substring(Const.ERROR.length())));
  }
  // terminates the transaction
  public void endTransaction() throws Exception {
    String reply = sendMessage(Const.END);
    if(reply.startsWith(Const.ERROR))
      throw new Exception(reply.
                  substring(Const.ERROR.length())));
  }
  // disconnect the terminal from the market server
  public void disconnect() {
    try{
      out.write((Const.QUIT + "\n").getBytes(
      out.flush();
    }catch(Exception e){ }
    socket = null;
```

```
      in = null;
      out = null;
  }
}
```

The class MarketStub implements the other end of the communication protocol. A new instance of this class is created every time a terminal connects to the server. This class is run in a separate thread, the method run() consists of a long message loop that waits for a message, performs the required operation and sends the reply containing the result.

```java
package Market;
import java.net.Socket;
import java.io.InputStream;
import java.io.OutputStream;
import java.util.StringTokenizer;

public class MarketStub
implements Runnable {
  Socket socket;
  Market market;
  MarketStub(Socket sk, Market mk){
    socket = sk;
    market = mk;
  }
  // messages from the counter terminal are handled by
  // the message loop that is executed in a
  // separate thread
  public void run(){
    try{
      InputStream in = socket.getInputStream();
      OutputStream out = socket.getOutputStream();
      byte [] buffer=new byte[1024];
      long customer=0;
      long transaction=0;
      long employee=0;
      while(( int len=in.read(buffer)) != -1){
        String request = new String(buffer,0,len);
        System.out.println(">" + request);
        StringTokenizer parser =
                       new StringTokenizer(request);
        String command = parser.nextToken();
        String param="";
        String response;
        if(parser.hasMoreTokens())
          param = parser.nextToken();
        try{
```

```java
        if(command.equals(Const.GET_NAME)){
          String result = market.getName(
                            Long.parseLong(param));
          if(result==null)
            response = Const.ERROR + " Item not found";
          else
            response = Const.OK + " " + result;
        }else if(command.equals(Const.GET_PRICE)){
          double result = market.getPrice(
                            Long.parseLong(param));
          if(result < 0 )
            response = Const.ERROR + " Item not found";
          else
            response = Const.OK + " " + result;
        }else if(command.equals(Const.GET_CUSTOMER)){
          customer = Long.parseLong(param);
          String result = market.getCustomer(customer);
          if(result==null)
            response=Const.ERROR + " Customer not found";
          else
            response = Const.OK + " " + result;
        }else if(command.equals(Const.AUTHENTICATE)){
          String password = parser.nextToken();
          employee = Long.parseLong(param);
          String result = market.
                    authenticate(employee,password);
          if(result==null)
            response = Const.ERROR +
                        " Wrong employee or password";
          else
            response = Const.OK + " " + result;
        }else if(command.equals(Const.BUY)){
          String quantity = parser.nextToken();
          if(transaction == 0)
            transaction = market.
                startTransaction(customer,employee);
          market.buy(Long.parseLong(param),
              Long.parseLong(quantity),transaction);
          response = Const.OK;
        }else if(command.equals(Const.END)){
          market.endTransaction(transaction);
          transaction = 0;
          response = Const.OK;
        }else if(command.equals(Const.ABORT)){
          market.abortTransaction(transaction);
          transaction = 0;
          response = Const.OK;
```

```
      }else if(command.equals(Const.QUIT))
        break;
      else
        response = Const.ERROR + " Unknown command";
      }catch(Exception e){
        response = Const.ERROR + " " + e.getMessage();
      }
      System.out.println("<" + response);
      out.write((response).getBytes());
      out.flush();
    }
  }catch(Exception ex)
  { } // do nothing, just jump out of the loop
 }
}
```

The class **StubFactory** waits for a connection from a terminal, creates a new **ServerStub** object, and assigns it to serve the new socket. It is a runnable class; its run() method contains an infinite loop that accepts connections.

```
package Market;
import java.net.ServerSocket;
import java.net.Socket;
public class StubFactory
implements Runnable {
  private Market market;
  public StubFactory(Market market){
    this.market = market;
  }
  // this thread accepts connections from the counter
  // terminals and for each connection creates a market
  // stub to handle it
  public void run(){
    try{
      ServerSocket ss = new ServerSocket(Const.SERVER_PORT);
      while(true){
        Socket sk = ss.accept();
        MarketStub stub = new MarketStub(sk,market);
        (new Thread(stub)).start();
      }
    }catch(Exception ex){ ex.printStackTrace() }
  }
}
```

14.6.4 ☐ Test

The test of this prototype is the same as the previous one because no functionality was added. Only the internal communication mechanism has changed.

It is possible to run a simplified test running both the client and the server on the same machine. In this case a single application contains all the components:

```
import Counter.SocketProxy;
import CounterUI.*;
import Market.StubFactory;
import Market.BasicServer;
import MarketDB.VolatileDB;
public class TestSocket {
  public static void main(String[] args) {
    // instantiate the server components
    BasicServer server = new BasicServer(new VolatileDB());
    StubFactory factory = new StubFactory(server);
    (new Thread(factory)).start();
    // instantiate the client components
    CounterFrame counter = new CounterFrame(
                    new SocketProxy("localhost"));
    counter.show();
    BarCodeReaderUI reader = new BarCodeReaderUI();
    reader.setLocation(100300);
    reader.show();
    reader.setListener(counter);
}}
```

14.7 ■ Prototype 4: Data persistence

This prototype addresses the last concern: the persistence of data. Information on product availability and history of acquisitions must be kept permanently. The former information is required so that new supplies can be ordered, the latter so that statistical analyses can be performed.

14.7.1 □ Analysis

The main issue in this prototype is the selection of the information that has to be made persistent. The pertinent information has been identified in Section 14.5.1 and described in Figure 14.9; we don't need to add anything.

The persistence solution to be adopted must guarantee ease of access to specific information. For instance, given a key we should be able to access the corresponding employee. In addition it should be possible to store the associations between product data.

14.7.2 □ Design

Decision point

What kind of persistent storage do we use?

To make the data persistent we choose to use a relational database, because it allows immediate access to information given its key, and it supports associations between product data. An alternative solution could be a file, the main drawback being the lack of support for direct data access.

Decision point

How do we connect to and access the persistent storage?

The persistence layer of the supermarket system makes use of a set of standard technologies to support independence from the DBMS. In particular we will use JDBC (see Sidebar 14.2) as the connectivity technology and SQL as the data management language. In our implementation we will use the Cloudscape DB, because it bundles with the J2EE distribution.

Decision point

What is the structure of the persistent data tier?

The structure of the data we want to store in the database has been defined in the previous iterations. The database structure will follow the same structure as the logical information presented in Figure 14.9.

Each class will be implemented as a separate table and the many-to-one associations will be implemented with external keys on the many side (Date 2000).

14.7.3 ☐ Implementation

To build the database we can use an SQL script *CreateTables.sql* that contains the commands to create the tables. For each table we define a primary key that is a long integer. This file can be used from the Cloudscape interactive SQL environment (activated with the command cloudscape – isql) with the command run 'CreateTables.sql'.

```
CREATE TABLE item (
  ID LONGINT CONSTRAINT pk_item PRIMARY KEY,
  name VARCHAR(30),
  price DOUBLE PRECISION,
  quantity INT
);
CREATE TABLE customer (
  ID LONGINT CONSTRAINT pk_customer PRIMARY KEY,
  name VARCHAR(30)
);
```

Sidebar 14.2 JDBC

JDBC is the standard Java protocol for accessing a database that is compliant with the SQL92 standard. To use the JDBC API with a particular database management system, you need a JDBC technology-based driver to mediate between JDBC technology and the database.

The connection to the database is represented by a **Connection** object. It is possible to operate on the database through a **Statement** object, which offers methods to update and query the database. The rows resulting from a query are stored in a **ResultSet** object.

We take as an example the steps to be performed in order to use the Cloudscape database that is bundled with the J2EE distribution. The following example shows how to list the content of the Item table.

```java
// load the cloudscape driver
Class.forName("COM.cloudscape.core.RmiJdbcDriver");
// define the connection string
String connection = "jdbc:rmi:jdbc:cloudscape:Supermarket;create=true";
// ask the driver manager to create a connection
Connection conn = DriverManager.getConnection(connection);
// create a statement
Statement stmt = conn.createStatement();
// define a query
String query = "SELECT * FROM ITEM";
// execute a query
ResultSet rs = stmt.executeQuery(query);
// loop over the rows in the result set
while(rs.next()){
  // get the long field ID
  long id = rs.getLong("ID");
  // get the String field Name
  String name = rs.getString("Name");
  // prints the values
  System.out.println("ID=" + id + "; Name=" + name);
}
```

```sql
CREATE TABLE employee (
  ID LONGINT CONSTRAINT pk_employee PRIMARY KEY,
  name VARCHAR(30),
  password VARCHAR(15)
);
CREATE TABLE trans (
  ID LONGINT CONSTRAINT pk_transaction PRIMARY KEY,
  employee INT,
  customer INT,
  is_open INT
);
CREATE TABLE acquisition (
  ID LONGINT CONSTRAINT pk_acquisition PRIMARY KEY,
  trans INT,
  item INT,
  quantity INT
);
```

The class **PersistentDB** implements the DBManager interface. It accesses a SQL database by means of the JDBC technology (see Sidebar 14.2). There is only one attribute, connection, that contains the connection string. The program that instantiates the DB manager is responsible for loading the appropriate driver.

The class has a set of methods, getItem(), getEmployee() and getCustomer(), that retrieve the information from a database in the form of an object. In addition there are the methods that operate on the transaction and a method to store a new acquisition.

The methods startTransaction() and buy() are synchronized because they need exclusive access to the database in order to assign a unique ID to the new row.

```java
package MarketDB;
import java.sql.*;
import javax.sql.*;
import java.util.Vector;
import java.util.List;
public class PersistentDB implements DBManager {
  private String connection;
  // creates the db manager storing the connection string
  public PersistentDB(String connection){
          this.connection = connection;}
  // utility method to simplify the execution of queries
  ResultSet select(String query) throws SQLException {
    Connection conn = DriverManager
                            .getConnection(connection);
    Statement stmt = conn.createStatement(
                    ResultSet.TYPE_FORWARD_ONLY,
                    ResultSet.CONCUR_READ_ONLY);
    return stmt.executeQuery(query);
  }
  // creates an Item object from the table ITEM
  public Item getItem(long code) {
    try{
      ResultSet rs =select("SELECT * FROM ITEM WHERE ID="
                                    + code);
      if(rs.next()) return new Item(rs);
    }catch(SQLException e){ }
    return null;
  }
  // creates an Employee object from the table EMPLOYEE
  public Employee getEmployee(long code) { ... }
  // creates a Customer object from the table CUSTOMER
  public Customer getCustomer(long code) { ... }
  // starts a customer transaction
```

```java
public synchronized long startTransaction(long customer,
                                          long employee)
        throws Exception {
  Connection conn = DriverManager.getConnection
                                        (connection);
  Statement stmt = conn.createStatement();
  ResultSet rs = stmt.executeQuery(
              "SELECT MAX(ID) AS M FROM TRANS");
  long code;
  if(rs.next())
    code = rs.getLong("M")+1;
  else
    code = 1;
  stmt.executeUpdate("INSERT INTO TRANS " +
                     "(ID,employee,customer,is_open)"
                  + " VALUES ( "+ code + ", "
                        + employee + "," +
                        customer + ", 1)");
  return code;
}
public void closeTransaction(long code)
              throws Exception {
  Connection conn = DriverManager
                        .getConnection(connection);
  Statement stmt = conn.createStatement();
  ResultSet rs = stmt.executeQuery(
          "SELECT * FROM TRANS WHERE ID=" + code);
  Transaction trans=null;
  if(rs.next()) trans = new Transaction(rs);
  if(trans==null) throw new Exception(
                     "Transaction non existent");
  if(!trans.open) throw new Exception(
                     "Transaction is closed");
  stmt.executeUpdate("UPDATE TRANS SET is_open=0 " +
                     "WHERE ID=" + code);
}
public synchronized void buy(long code, long quantity,
                             long transaction)
                    throws Exception {
  Connection conn = DriverManager
                        .getConnection(connection);
  Statement stmt = conn.createStatement();
  ResultSet rs;
  Transaction t;
  try{
    rs=stmt.executeQuery("SELECT * FROM TRANS WHERE ID="
                                    + transaction);
```

```
    if(rs.next())  t = new Transaction(rs);
    else throw new Exception(
                    "Transaction non existent");
    Item item;
    rs=select("SELECT * FROM ITEM WHERE ID=" + code);
    if(rs.next()) item = new Item(rs);
    else throw new Exception("Item non existent");
    item.quantity -= quantity;
    rs = stmt.executeQuery(
        "SELECT MAX(ID) AS M FROM ACQUISITION");
    long acq_code;
    if(rs.next())
      acq_code = rs.getLong("M") + 1;
    else
      acq_code = 1;
    rs.close();
    stmt.executeUpdate(
      "INSERT INTO ACQUISITION (ID,TRANS,ITEM,QUANTITY)"
      + " VALUES ( " + acq_code + ", " + transaction +
      ", " + item.code + ", " + quantity +")");
    stmt.executeUpdate("UPDATE ITEM SET QUANTITY=" +
                    item.quantity +
                    " WHERE ID=" + code);
  }catch(Exception e){ throw e; }
  }
 }
```

14.7.4 □ Test

To test the introduction of the database, we can conduct a test in a local context, i.e. by instantiating all the components of the system in a single process.

```
import CounterUI.*;
import Market.BasicServer;
import Market.MarketServer;
import Counter.SocketProxy;
import MarketDB.PersistentDB;
public class TestPersistent {
  public static void main(String [] args) {
    // instantiate the server components
    try{
      Class.forName("COM.cloudscape.core.RmiJdbcDriver");
    }
    catch(Exception e){e.printStackTrace();}
    String connection =
      "jdbc:rmi:jdbc:cloudscape:Supermarket;create=true";
```

```
        BasicServer server = new BasicServer(
                            new PersistentDB(conneciton));
        StubFactory factory=new StubFactory(server);
        (new Thread(factory)).start();
        // instantiate the client components
        CounterFrame counter = new CounterFrame(
                            new SocketProxy("localhost"));
        counter.show();
        BarCodeReaderUI reader = new BarCodeReaderUI();
        reader.setLocation(100300);
        reader.show();
        reader.setListener(counter);
    }
}
```

14.8 ■ Extension

The reader can extend the supermarket support system in several ways:

■ Add the monitoring interface to the supermarket server.
■ Adapt the system to a web-based interface, consider the increment in network traffic and the scalability limits.
■ Use RMI instead of sockets as a communication medium.

14.9 ■ Assessment

Architectural model. Since the nodes are client, server and database, the architecture selected for the application is a three-tier model.

Paradigm. The components that represent the three tiers of the architecture should be loosely coupled. This suggested an approach based on a declarative communication paradigm. The communication between the client and the server tiers is based upon an application-specific protocol, which has been designed ad hoc. The interaction between the server and the database uses the JDBC standard protocol.

Technology. The application-specific protocol uses the socket technology. It is based on a TCP/IP connection between client and server; this type of connection guarantees the delivery of packets, thus relieving the application protocol of this issue. Access to the database is based on JDBC, which is a standard protocol supported by classes in the standard Java library.

Architecture	Three-tier architecture
Context	Client–server systems, with a complex client user interface. Most processing can be performed on the server side. There is a significant part of data that is persistent.
Problem	The presentation of the information on the client side is complex and the client cannot perform all the processing. The server carries on computation and persistence tasks. Changes to any feature of the system are likely to make an impact on several components.
Forces or tradeoffs	The client side has too many tasks to carry out. The server side could carry out some computations. Presentation and processing of data are mixed in the client. Processing and persistence features are mixed in the server.
Solution	We split the system into three layers or tiers, each one with well-defined responsibilities: 1 Client tier. 2 Server tier. 3 Data tier. The client tier is responsible for presentation and carries out only the simplest data validation checks. The server tier performs all the processing and ignores both presentation and persistence issues. Finally the data tier encapsulates all the details concerning the persistence of data. The transformation of a simple client–server system into a three-tier system is described in the following figure.

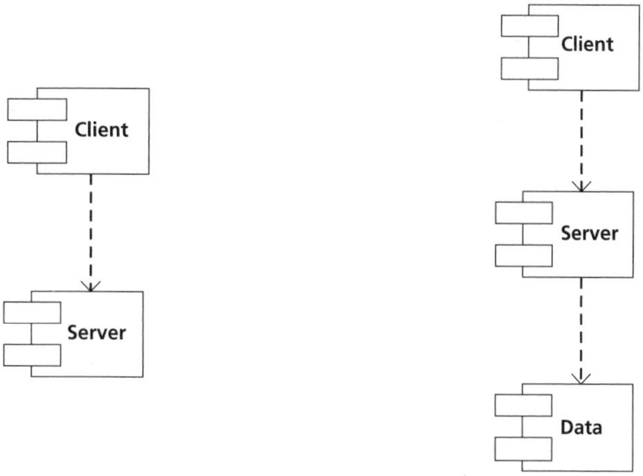

Examples	The supermarket operation support system is an example of a three-tier system. The client component (user interface + communication) is concerned only with presentation issues; the market server performs all the processing; the market DB encapsulates all the details of data persistence.

Force resolution	The client side focuses only on presentation issues, and is relieved of computationally intensive tasks. The server side carries out all the processing. Presentation and processing are kept separate, the former on the client tier the latter on the server tier. Processing and persistence are kept separate, the former on the server side, the latter on the data side.
Design rationale	This strict separation of concerns gives rise to several benefits. A lower processing power is required on the client side; it has only to support the graphical user inteface. All the processing is concentrated in the server tier, allowing for a simpler design. The server design is further simplified because it does not care about persistence, which is the data tier's responsibility. The user interface can be changed with a reduced impact on the processing component. Different persistence solutions can be adopted within the data tier which are transparent to the rest of the system.

14.10 ■ References

Date, J. (2000) *Design and Implementation of Database Systems*, Addison-Wesley.

Huston, G. (2000), "TCP Performance", *The Internet Protocol Journal*, Cisco Systems, Vol. 3, No. 2, July, 2–24.

Java POS Committee (2001) *Java for Retail POS – Programming Guide*, Version 1.6.

Geographic information system

15

Synthesis

This case study presents the development of a simple geographic information system (GIS). The target context is archaeology with examples of geographic information related to the Roman civilization in Italy.

- Focus: this case study exemplifies the process of integrating disparate technologies and, in particular, data storage in a database, data transmission using sockets and data visualization through Java Applets.
- OO techniques: inclusion and inheritance.
- Java features: JDBC, Sockets, Applets, XML.
- Background: the reader is required to know the basic concepts of relational databases and of the Standard Query Language (SQL), as well as of computer networking, such as network address and protocol.

15.1 ■ Specifications

A geographic information system is a system of computer software, hardware and data that grants people web access to geographical information, i.e. information that is tied to spatial location.

GIS is useful in a variety of business and social contexts, such as:

- Logistic: efficient transportation of materials and people requires real time information about roads, traffic and weather conditions. This information comes from disparate sources and can be easily integrated using GIS.
- Environment monitoring: environmental data are heterogeneous in format, temporal validity, volume, scale, etc. GIS supports the dynamic visualization and traceability of these data.
- Education and leisure: GIS is a powerful tool for computer-based teaching of a number of disciplines in relation to their geographic context: history, economy, politics, archaeology, arts, etc.

A GIS offers two basic functionalities: image visualization and data browsing. Image visualization is the ability to display complex 2D or 3D images representing cartographic maps and to allow the user to elaborate them, i.e. zoom, rotate, change perspective, etc. For the purpose of this case study, we limit the GIS functionalities to simple visualization of 2D images available on the file system in standard formats (jpg, gif, etc.). Data browsing is the ability to retrieve geographical information associated with relevant features of the image being visualized (e.g. cities, roads, parks, etc.). This functionality requires graphical interaction between the user and the image. Typically, the user selects a geographic feature (e.g. the city of Rome) and obtains a display of some information (e.g. the foundation date, i.e. 756 BC). Geographic features are conveniently classified into three categories:

- Sites are circumscribed regions whose extent on the image is not relevant for data browsing. Sites indicate cities or locations represented at a coarse-grained resolution and are visualized as small circles.
- Links represent linear geographic regions such as roads, rivers and boundaries and are visualized as polygonal lines made up of rectilinear segments.
- Areas indicate bi-dimensional geographic regions such as parks, mountains, agglomerates, and areas homogeneous for some specific characteristic (population, agriculture, etc.). They are visualized as polygonal shapes.

Geographic information is alphanumeric data, such as numbers or short textual descriptions. They are stored in a relational database as attribute-value pairs. For example, for the city of Rome we would find in the GIS database the pairs [foundation, "756 BC"], [founder, "Romulus"], [nickname, "caput mundi"].

Geographic features should be clearly recognizable on the cartographic map and organized in layers that are homogeneous for the semantic of the associated information. For example, a layer may encompass sites, links and areas that are related to archaeology in Italy during the Augustan age (see the example below). It must be possible to display several layers simultaneously on the same image, but only one layer is active at a time, that is the user can browse only information associated with the active layer.

The GIS is a distributed system that offers its functionalities to the user through the web by connecting to the GIS server where the cartographic maps and the related information are stored. The GIS includes a suite of software tools to create cartographic maps and to link data to their geographic features.

15.1.1 □ **An example**

We are the web managers of the Historic Archive in Rome, and we want to implement a new service that provides high school students with an opportunity to learn the history of the ancient world interactively. The idea is to build a virtual cartographic map that represents the evolution of the Roman settlements in the Italian peninsula from the foundation of Rome (756 BC) up to the peak of the Roman Empire's expansion (circa 336 AD). The virtual map is organized into temporal layers that correspond to different historic ages: the reign of the seven kings, the republican period, the civil war, the first emperors, the advent and achievement of Christianity. For every historic age we are interested in offering a comprehensive view of the settlements in terms of cities founded by the Romans, main communication routes in the Italian peninsula, and the regions occupied by "barbarians", i.e. not yet under Roman control. Students should be allowed to select a specific historic age and interactively browse the information associated with each settlement's indicator (e.g. cities, routes, regions). Typical pieces of information are the following:

- A city is described in terms of the year of its foundation or occupation year, name given by the Romans, number of inhabitants, extent, size of the military settlement, etc.
- A route lists the linked cities, indicates the distance of each city from the origin, the name of the council or emperor that ordered its construction, the year of construction, etc.
- A region is associated with information about the culture of the people who were occupying it before the advent of the Roman civilization, i.e. the name, the religion, the language, etc.

Figure 15.1 shows an example of a cartographic map that indicates the cities and roads in the Italian peninsula during the age of the first emperors.

The interactive web service should also offer the possibility of displaying for each temporal age only a subset of the settlement indicators, i.e. only

The network of Roman roads was set up in Republican times when the oldest road, Via Appia (330 BC), was built. It links (still today) Rome with Brindisi on the Adriatic Sea via Capua, Benevento and Bari. In the same period were built the Via Aurelia (241 BC) from Rome to Genoa and subsequently up to Arles in Provence, the Via Flaminia (232 BC) from Rome to Rimini through the Umbria region, and the Via Emilia (109 BC) from Rimini to Milan through Bologna. A number of roads linked the Italian network to the provinces. The incredible network of 100,000 km of road (more than seven times the equatorial circumference of the Earth) was completely paved in order to allow fast transfer of military troops and to facilitate commercial exchanges. The average pace was around 35 km per day. The network stretched over the entire Mediterranean basin and into a large part of Europe, and was implemented during the Empire. Augustus completed the Italian network. Tiberius created the African network, Trajan built the Balkan network and Hadrian worked towards the creation of the British network.

Figure 15.1 A cartographic map that shows the Roman roads in the Italian peninsula

cities and roads, or regions, etc. It should also allow the simultaneous visualization of a settlement's indicators belonging to different temporal ages.

The interactive web service should be highly customizable. New cartographic maps can be easily created by choosing a different geographic image, defining the relevant spatial features, and associating historic information with them. For example, we can choose an image that depicts the topography of ancient Rome, and represents the location of relevant sites (e.g. the Colosseum), links (e.g. the watercourses of the old aqueducts and sewers), and areas (e.g. the squares, markets, parade grounds). Historic information can report on the lifestyle of Roman citizens in terms of entertainments, health and social relations.

15.2 ■ Problem analysis

The GIS is made up of three applications: the graphical editor, the data linker and the GIS browser.

The graphical editor is a standalone application that enables the creation of cartographic maps and supports the following functions:

■ Load an image from a file system and visualize it on the editor's main window.
■ Create a new layer and assign it a unique name.
■ Select the geographic feature to add to the layer (e.g. links).
■ Draw one or more instances of the selected geographic feature.
■ Save the description of the cartographic map and of its geographic features in a file.
■ Open the file of a cartographic map and add new layers and feature instances.

The data linker is a standalone application that allows the GIS manager to associate information stored in persistent storage with the geographic features of a cartographic map. It supports the following functions:

■ Load a cartographic map from file.
■ Select the active layer.
■ Select a geographic feature.
■ Select information from persistent storage and link it to the selected feature.
■ Save the association between information and feature instances in a file that can be subsequently edited.

The GIS browser is a web-based distributed application that grants users remote access to the GIS server where the cartographic maps and the associated information are stored. It supports the following functions:

■ Connect to the GIS web server and get the home page displayed in a standard web browser.

- Select a cartographic map from a list and display it in the browser.
- Select one or more layers from a list and display them on the cartographic map.
- Select one or more geographic features to be displayed (sites, links, areas).
- Select the active layer and the active feature.
- Browse the information associated with the geographic features by selecting specific instances on the cartographic map (e.g. the site corresponding to the city of Rome).

15.2.1 ☐ Domain models

GIS services are usually built using a set of commercial tools that encompass software and hardware systems to acquire and elaborate aerial images, professional CAD environments for drawing accurate geometric figures, efficient database management systems to store large amounts of information, and a suite of programming tools and libraries to create customer-specific graphical interfaces for interactive browsing of spatial data. The interoperability of all these tools is ensured by the adoption of standard data interchange formats.

The core of a GIS is the data model used to record the spatial objects that represent the active features of a cartographic map (DeMers 2002). Spatial objects react to user events by performing different actions, such as displaying a list of properties when the left mouse button is pressed or opening a personalization window when the right mouse button is pressed.

The architecture of a GIS is organized according to the three-tier model (see Section 11.1.2), where the client tier is a standard web browser. Several solutions exist for the data persistence manager. The most common makes use of a standard relational database to store only alphanumeric information and of the file system to save images and cartographic maps. More complex databases allow storage of images and spatial objects.

15.2.2 ☐ Main features

We can now summarize the main features that characterize the GIS under development.

- Graphical editing of figures superimposed on a user-selected image to create a cartographic map.
- Association handling between the geographic features of a user-defined cartographic map and the data stored in a relational database.
- Remote access to cartographic maps and associated data from a standard web browser.

15.2.3 ☐ Test

The test cases developed for the editor and linker tools should verify that all the possible interaction patterns with the user show correct behaviour and that the data model is always in a consistent state. The web access to the GIS should support multiple concurrent user sessions.

15.3 ■ Architecture and planning

The system architecture is made up of four main subsystems as described in Figure 15.2. Three of them correspond to the applications that allow the user to create the cartographic map (the editor), to associate information to the geographic features (the linker), and to browse spatial data with a standard web browser (the browser). These three applications share a common data model that encompasses the geometric elements of the cartographic map and their association with data stored in a relational database. By factoring the three applications it appears convenient to condense the data model management into a separate component (the data manager).

The development process of the GIS is organized into three phases that produce three prototypes.

- *Prototype 1: The graphical editor.* A standalone application that offers the functionalities of a graphical editor. It allows the user to load an image of a geographic area from a file and to define a set of geometric regions that can be selected using the mouse. The description of the geometric regions is saved in a file that can be reloaded and updated subsequently. We call "map" the association between an image and a set of geometric regions defined over it.
- *Prototype 2: The data linker.* A standalone application that offers the functionalities of a data linker. It allows the user to load the description of a map and to record associations between its geometric regions and the data stored in a database.
- *Prototype 3: The web browser.* A web-based distributed map browser that allows a user to visualize a map, select its geometric regions and browse data retrieved from a remote database.

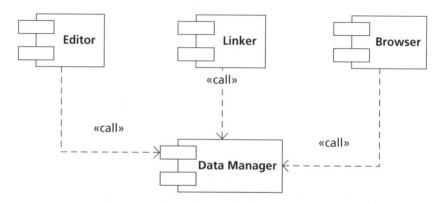

Figure 15.2 The main components of the GIS suite of tools

15.4 ■ Prototype 1: The graphical editor

This section defines the architectural building blocks that will be first used for the development of the graphical editor and then reused for the implementation of the data linker and the web browser. The analysis phase identifies the basic elements of a cartographic map and the functionalities of the graphical editor. The design phase transforms these entities into reusable classes by isolating the specific functionalities of the graphical editor from the generic architecture of the cartographic model.

15.4.1 □ Analysis

The problem specification indicates three types of geographic features that build up a cartographic map as detailed in Section 15.2.1. Accordingly, we identify the following basic entities:

- MapSite represents a geometric figure (a point or a small circle) that visualizes the position of a site on a cartographic map, e.g. a city or generically a location.
- MapLink represents a geometric path constructed from straight lines. It visualizes the layout of a link, e.g. a route or a boundary.
- MapArea represents an arbitrarily shaped geometric area that visualizes the boundaries of a region, e.g. a park or a country.

Map entities have four basic properties:

- *Visibility*: entities are visualized in a graphical window and overlap a cartographic image. The user can choose which types of entities are actually visible.
- *Connection*: associations can be set between map entities and spatial information stored in a database.
- *Selection*: the user can select entities using the mouse pointer in order to browse related information.
- *Persistence*: entities' descriptions are saved in persistent storage so that they may be retrieved subsequently.

Instances of map entities are grouped in layers, i.e. sets of geographic features associated with semantically homogeneous information (e.g. they correspond to the same historic age). We introduce entity MapLayer to represent them. A cartographic map may be made up of multiple layers. Only one layer at a time can be active, i.e. its map entities can be selected using the mouse pointer. Entity MapLayer has three basic properties:

- *Visibility*: it should be possible to select which layers are visible simultaneously.
- *Selection*: the entities of only one layer at a time can be selected.
- *Persistence*: the layer composition is saved in persistent storage.

A set of layers overlapping the same image form a cartographic map that is represented by the entity CartographicMap. It has one basic property:

■ *Persistence*: the association between the image and the overlapping layers is saved in persistent storage.

Finally, entity Editor represents the graphical editor to build cartographic maps. It is a standalone application made up of a graphical user interface that maps user events to actions on the cartographic entities defined above.

15.4.2 □ Design

Entities MapSite, MapLink and MapArea share the same functionalities and differ only in their geometric representation. Thus, we decide to introduce class MapEntity that is the abstract superclass of all the three cartographic entities. This generalization enables the exploitation of polymorphism more than reuse of data structures which are specific for every subclass. Common methods will be defined in class MapEntity. Some of them need to be implemented in every subclass.

Decision point

How is entity visibility handled?

The user can select which types of geographic entity are visible in a cartographic map. For example, one may select only sites and links, while areas remain hidden. We have two possibilities for managing entity visibility. The first solution consists in defining attribute visible in class MapEntity. When the user wants to set an entity type visible, the attribute visible of all the instances of that entity type in all the visible layers is set to true. The second solution consists in grouping entities according to their type. Thus, each layer is made up of three sets of entities, one for sites, one for links and one for areas. In order to make a given type of entity visible or hidden, only the visibility attribute of the corresponding entity set needs to be set to true or false. This solution improves the performance of the graphical editor and of the other two GIS tools. It requires the introduction of the new class MapEntitySet.

Figure 15.3 represents the class diagram of the GIS cartographic model. It includes classes MapLayer and CartographicMap, which correspond to the entities identified in the previous section. In particular, it shows that a cartographic map has a reference to an Image object and is made up of a collection of map layers that overlap the map image. Each map layer is made up of a collection of map entities.

Decision point

How is entity selection handled?

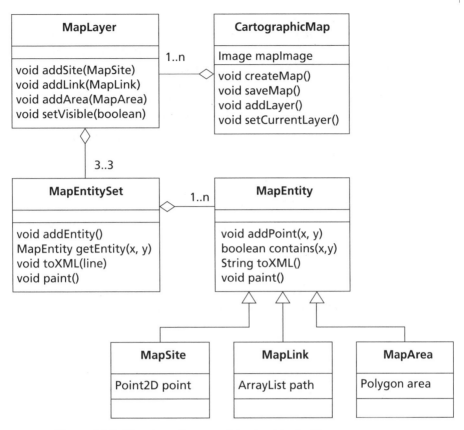

Figure 15.3 The class diagram of the graphical editor

Every subclass of MapEntity adopts a specific data structure for the definition of the corresponding geometric figure (circles, lines, polygons). Each figure is represented in 2D Cartesian coordinates related to the image reference frame. Even the position of the mouse pointer is expressed in 2D coordinates related to the same reference frame. When the user clicks the left button of the mouse, the graphical editor (or one of the other GIS tools) grabs the coordinates of the point that corresponds to the mouse position on the screen and searches for the entity that includes it within its boundary or is close enough to it. This is achieved by defining method contains() in class MapEntity and implementing it specifically in every concrete subclass. We assume that geometric figures of entities belonging to the same layer do not overlap.

Decision point

How is entity persistence handled?

As we did in previous chapters, we choose XML to structure the information that will be made persistent in a file. Every subclass of MapEntity has the responsibility to serialize the content of its data structure. Similarly, classes MapEntitySet, MapLayer and CartographicMap make their data persistent using XML. When the user creates a cartographic map, he or she is requested to choose the name of a file that will then be saved on the local file system. The following tags are used to structure the file as shown in Figure 15.4.

- POINT indicates the coordinates of a 2D point belonging to the boundary of a geometric figure.
- ENTITY delimits a list of point tags describing the geometric figure of a map entity.
- SET groups entities of the same type.
- LAYER groups several set sections.
- GISMAP records the name of the cartographic map and the location of the image file.

15.4.3 □ Implementation

The implementation of the object model is quite simple. Class MapEntity defines three abstract methods that are implemented in every subclass in order to handle the construction of the entity's geometric figure (method

```
<GISMAP MAPNAME="Imperial Rome" FILENAME="C:\GIS\images\Rome.jpg"/>
  <LAYER NAME="Settlements" COLOR="Blue">
    <SET TYPE="SITE" >
      <ENTITY>
        <POINT X="119" Y="89"/>
      </ENTITY>
    </SET>
    <SET TYPE="LINK">
      <ENTITY>
        <POINT X="286" Y="236"/>
        <POINT X="269" Y="252"/>
        <POINT X="263" Y="260"/>
      </ENTITY>
    </SET>
    <SET TYPE="AREA">
      <ENTITY>
        <POINT X="327" Y="265"/>
        <POINT X="355" Y="266"/>
        <POINT X="350" Y="274"/>
      </ENTITY>
    </SET>
  </LAYER>
</GISMAP>
```

Figure 15.4 An XML file that records the geometric description of a cartographic map

addPoint(int x, int y)), the entity selection (method contains(int x, int y)), the entity representation in XML format (method toXML()), and the entity visualization (method paint()).

```java
package gis.model;
import java.awt.*;
import java.util.*;
public abstract class MapEntity {
  // variable "closed" is used to set the entity's endpoint
  protected boolean closed = false;
  public MapEntity(){}
  public void close() { this.closed = true; }
  public abstract void paint(Graphics2D g, Color color);
  // these methods should be implemented in every subclass
  public abstract void addPoint(int x, int y);
  public abstract boolean contains(int x, int y);
  public abstract String toXML();
}


public class MapSite extends MapEntity {
  private Point2D point = null; // the site's 2D location
  private static int DIST = 4; // the site's radius in pixel
  public MapSite(){}
  // sets the site's coordinates
  public void addPoint(int x, int y) {
    point = new Point2D.Double(x, y);
  }
  // returns true if point x,y is inside the site's circle
  public boolean contains(double x, double y) {
    double dist = point.distance(x, y);
    if(dist <= DIST) return true;
    return false;
  }
  // converts the site's data to XML format
  public String toXML() {
    StringBuffer stream = new StringBuffer();
    stream.append("\n      <ENTITY>");
    stream.append("\n         <POINT X=" + '"' +
      (int)Math.round(point.getX()) + '"' + " Y=" + '"' +
      (int)Math.round(point.getY()) + '"'+ "/>");
    stream.append("\n      </ENTITY>");
    return stream.toString();
  }
  public void paint(Graphics2D g, Color color) { . . . }
}
public class MapLink extends MapEntity {
  private static int DIST = 4;// link's surrounding in pixel
```

```java
  private ArrayList path = new ArrayList(); // the vertices
  public MapLink() {}
  public void addPoint(int x, int y) {
    path.add(new Point2D.Double(x, y));
  }
  public boolean contains(double x, double y) {
    Point2D p1 = (Point2D) path.get(0);
    for(int i=1; i < path.size(); i++) {
      //measures the distance between point x,y and the path
      Point2D p2 = (Point2D) path.get(i);
      double dist = Line2D.ptSegDist(p1.getX(),p1.getY(),
                               p2.getX(),p2.getY(),x, y);
      if(dist <= DIST) return true;
      p1 = p2;
    }
    return false;
  }
  public String toXML() { . . . }
  public void paint(Graphics2D g, Color color) { . . . }
}

public class MapArea extends MapEntity {
  private Polygon area = new Polygon();
  public MapArea() {}
  public void addPoint(int x, int y) { area.addPoint(x, y);}
  public boolean contains(double x, double y) {
    if(area.contains(x, y)) return true;
    return false;
  }
  public void paint(Graphics2D g, Color color) { . . . }
  public String toXML() { . . . }
}
```

Classes MapEntitySet, MapLayer and CartographicMap implement the data structures defined in Figure 15.3 and a set of methods to create the GIS object model, to select entities, to record their description in XML format, and to set the visibility of entities and layers. Class CartographicMap extends class JPanel and represents the main component of the graphical editor. It implements methods to create, open and save a cartographic map.

```java
public class MapEntitySet {
  // the list of geographic entities
  private ArrayList entityList = new ArrayList();
  private boolean visible = false;
  public void setVisible(boolean visible) {
    this.visible = visible;
  }
```

```java
  public void addEntity(MapEntity entity) {
    entityList.add(entity);
  }
  // gets the entity found in location posX,posY
  public MapEntity getEntity(int posX, int posY) {
    Iterator iterator = entityList.iterator();
    while(iterator.hasNext()) {
      MapEntity entity = (MapEntity) iterator.next();
      if(entity.contains(posX, posY))
        return entity;
    }
    return null;
  }
  public void paint(Graphics2D g, Color color) { . . . }
  // converts the list of entities in XML format
  public String toXML(String entityType) {
    StringBuffer stream = new StringBuffer();
    stream.append("\n    <LIST TYPE="    + '"' +
                  entityType + '"' + ">");
    Iterator iterator = entityList.iterator();
    while(iterator.hasNext())
      stream.append(((MapEntity) iterator.next()).toXML());
    stream.append("\n    </LIST>");
    return stream.toString();
  }
}
public class MapLayer {
  // name of the layer; "xxx" when not initialized
  private String name = "xxx";
  private String colorName = ""; // colour of the entities
  private Color color = null;
  private boolean visible = false;
  private MapEntitySet siteSet = new MapEntitySet();
  private MapEntitySet linkSet = new MapEntitySet();
  private MapEntitySet areaSet = new MapEntitySet();
  // this constructor is invoked when a new layer is created
  public MapLayer(String name, String colorName) {
    this.name = name;
    this.colorName = colorName;
  }
  // this constructor is used to load a layer from file
  public MapLayer(String line, BufferedReader lineReader) {
    // extracts the name of the layer
    String docLine = line;
    int indexInit = docLine.indexOf("NAME=");
    docLine = docLine.substring(indexInit+6);
```

```java
      int indexEnd = docLine.indexOf('"');
      this.name = docLine.substring(0, indexEnd);
      try {
        String entityType = "";
        while ((docLine = lineReader.readLine())!=null) {
          if((indexInit = docLine.indexOf("</LAYER")) > -1)
            return; // end of this layer description
          else if((indexInit=docLine.indexOf("<LIST")) > -1) {
            // extracts the type of entity list
            indexInit = docLine.indexOf("TYPE=");
               . . .
          }
               . . .
        }
      } catch(IOException ioe) { ioe.printStackTrace(); }
    }
    // sets the visibility of the entire layer
    public void setVisible(boolean visible) {
      this.visible = visible;
    }
    // sets the visibility of the entities' type
    public void setEntityVisibility(String t, boolean v) {
      if(t.equalsIgnoreCase("SITE"))
        siteSet.setVisible(v);
         . . .
    }
    public void paint(Graphics2D g, boolean sites,
                         boolean links, boolean areas) { ...}
    public String toXML() {
      StringBuffer stream = new StringBuffer();
      stream.append("  <LAYER NAME=" + '"' + name + '"' +
                    " COLOR=" + '"' + colorName + '"' + ">");
      stream.append(siteSet.toXML("SITE"));
         . . .
    }
    public void addSite(MapSite s) { siteSet.addEntity(s); }
    public void addLink(MapLink l) { linkSet.addEntity(l); }
    public void addArea(MapArea a) { areaSet.addEntity(a); }
    // gets the entity of a given type located at x,y
    public MapEntity getEntity(String type, int x, int y) {
      if(type.equalsIgnoreCase("SITE"))
        return siteSet.getEntity(x, y);
         . . .
      return null;
    }
}
```

```
public class CartographicMap extends JPanel {
  private ArrayList layerList = new ArrayList();
  private MapLayer currentLayer = null; // selected layer
  private Image mapImage = null;
  private String fileName = null;
  private String mapName = null;
  private boolean sitesVisible = true; // true for entities
  private boolean linksVisible = true; // to be displayed
  private boolean areasVisible = true; // on the map image
  public void createMap(String fileName, String mapName) { }
  private void showMap() { }
  public void saveMap(String mapName) { }
  public void openMap(InputStream inStream) { }
  public void addLayer(String layerName, String colorName) {
    currentLayer = new MapLayer(layerName, colorName);
    layerList.add(currentLayer);
  }
  public String[] getLayerList() { }
  public void setCurrentLayer(String layerName) { . . . }
  public MapLayer getCurrentLayer() { return currentLayer; }
  public void setLayerVisibility(String name, boolean v) { }
  public void setEntityVisibility(boolean sites,
                        boolean links, boolean areas) { }
}
```

Class Editor is the main class of the graphical editor. It builds on the graphical components of the java.awt.* and javax.swing.* packages that implement the menu and the mouse handlers used to create and edit a cartographic map and to select its entities. We do not show the code, since it is quite standard and could be created using any commercial CASE tool.

15.4.4 □ Test

The test cases should verify the correct behaviour of the graphical interface and the correspondence between data inserted by the user through the interface, the data displayed on the screen, and the data saved on the XML file. In particular it is necessary to verify that:

- The creation of new maps, new layers and new entities is handled properly.
- Layer visibility and entity visibility are handled properly through the menus of the graphical interface.
- Only one layer and one type of entity are active at a time during the editing process.
- The vertices of the entities' shapes correspond to the selected mouse positions.
- For each map the user can save the list of layers and entities on an XML file.

Figure 15.5 Different views of a cartographic map: sites (upper left), links (upper right) and areas (lower)

- The user can load the description of a cartographic map from a previously generated XML file.

Figure 15.5 shows three views of a cartographic map. The first view shows only the sites of the map, the second view only the links, and the last view only the areas.

15.5 ■ Prototype 2: The data linker

This section analyses the requirements of the data browsing functionality needed to build the GIS data model. The second prototype implements the data linker as a standalone application that allows the user to select graphical features in the cartographic map and associate information stored in a relational database.

15.5.1 □ Analysis

The power of a GIS is its versatility. As we have seen in the previous section, we can build a cartographic map by simply selecting a picture of a geographic area (e.g. an aerial photograph) and overlapping geometric features that represent active portions of that picture. The last step consists of associating each geometric feature with thematic information (e.g. historical events) retrieved from persistent storage. In this case, versatility means that the GIS does not impose strong constraints on the origin of the data (where they are stored) and their format. For the sake of simplicity, we make a few assumptions.

- *Data origin*. We assume that thematic information is stored in relational databases. This is the most general and common type of persistent storage and the most efficient for large amounts of data. Geographic features belonging to the same cartographic map may be associated with information stored in a multitude of databases.
- *Data format*. Typically, thematic information assumes the form of textual description (e.g. a bibliographic reference) or simple data, such as strings (e.g. the name of a Consular route), integers (the population of Rome), or dates (e.g. the murder of Julius Caesar).

We can suppose that the GIS manager is able to generate query tables, i.e. new tables that record a synthesis of a table or a set of tables in a database. Let's consider the GIS service described in Section 15.2.1. The Historic Archive of Rome manages two databases: "Historic Geography" and "Ancient People". The former stores information related to the historical evolution of human settlements in Italy and has three main query tables: Cities, Routes and Ports. The latter records information related to the people that were native to the Italian peninsula or occupied it in different historical periods. It has two main query tables: Native and Barbarians. The attributes

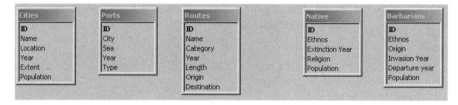

Figure 15.6 An example of thematic database

of these five tables are shown in Figure 15.6 while an example of data in table Routes is shown in Table 15.1.

Geographic features are linked to information extracted from a relational database using the data linker tool. According to the requirements identified in Section 15.3, it consists of a graphical user interface that provides the GIS manager with the following functionalities:

- Open the XML file that stores the geometric description of a cartographic map.
- Select the active layer (e.g. Archaeology) from a menu and one of the feature types (sites, links, areas).
- Select an active feature using the mouse.
- Select the data origin (database name) from a menu and one of its tables.
- Select a record of the chosen table and link its key value to the active feature.
- Record in an XML file the association between geographic features and thematic information.

Two additional requirements should be taken into account in order to enhance the tool's usability:

- Graphically distinguish geographic features associated with thematic information from features still unbound.
- Allow the iterative update of the cartographic map with new geographic features and with new associations between features and thematic information.

15.5.2 □ Design

The essence of the data linker functionalities is to produce an XML file that records the association between the geographic features described in the cartographic map (i.e. in the XML file that stores it) and the thematic

Table 15.1 Data stored in table Routes

ID	Name	Category	Year	Length	Origin	Destination
1	Via Appia	Consular route	330 BC	600 km	Rome	Brindisi
2	Via Aurelia	Consular route	241 BC	550 km	Rome	Genoa
3	Via Flaminia	Consular route	232 BC	350 km	Rome	Rimini

information extracted from one or several databases. We argue that it is not efficient to maintain two distinct XML files, one for the geometric description of the features and one for the association between features and information. In fact, successful commercial products adopt the unique file solution, which stores the association as attributes of the geometric features. The adoption of this approach gives rise to a number of design problems that concern how the GIS data model and XML model should be revised and extended to keep track of the feature–information associations during the construction of a GIS map.

Decision point

How is thematic information extracted from the databases?

Thematic information can be retrieved from several relational databases. We assume that all of these databases are accessible directly from the GIS server, i.e. we do not consider distributed databases. Every database has a unique logical name and is made up of a number of tables. Every table may store thousands of records and every record may have tens of attributes.

Typically, only a subset of the entire volume of data is relevant for a specific GIS service. Thus, it is worthwhile to find an approach to reduce the dimension and number of tables and records that need to be considered. We have to take into consideration the following issues:

- Only a subset of the number of GIS databases needs to be considered.
- For each GIS database, only a subset of its tables stores relevant information for that service.
- For each table, only a subset of its records and attributes are relevant for the service.
- We should adopt the less intrusive approach that does not require restructuring the databases.

The simplest approach consists in building a new database (the GIS database) that maintains only the index of the available thematic databases and of the tables that store relevant information. Figure 15.7 depicts the table's layout of the GIS database.

Table **Databases** (see Table 15.2) records the logical name (**Name**) and description (**Description**) of a set of databases that store information useful for the GIS service at hand. Every database is uniquely identified with the values of the **ID** attribute. For each database, **Tables** records the list of the tables relevant for the GIS service (see Table 15.3). Each table is described with six attributes: a unique identifier (**ID**), a reference to the database it is part of (**IDDataBase**), its name (**Name**), a textual description of the table (**Description**), the name of the attribute that plays the role of key (**Key**), and the name of the attribute that plays the role of label (**Label**). Figure 15.8 shows the contents of these two tables for the example described above.

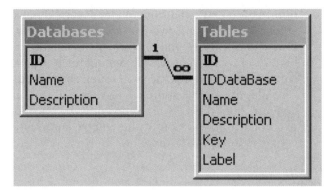

Figure 15.7 The structure of the GIS database

We need to find the right balance between flexibility and usability. At one extreme, we could decide to associate single geographic features (e.g. the city of Naples or the Via Appia) with data records extracted from different tables and databases. This approach is extremely flexible, but does not guarantee semantic consistency. The user expects to get similar information (e.g. people) when he or she browses the same type of geographic features (e.g. cities). At the other extreme, we could associate an entire cartographic map to a single data record. This approach makes the GIS almost useless.

We adopt an intermediate solution. For each map layer, every entity set can be associated with only one table of a given database. For example, the set of links in layer "Imperial Rome" of map "Roman History", is associated with table Routes in database GIS.HistoricGeography. The key of this table is attribute ID and the label is attribute Name. Every feature instance is

Table 15.2 An example of content description of table Databases

ID	Name	Description
1	GIS.HistoricGeography	Historical evolution of human settlements in Italy
2	GIS.AncientPeople	People that occupied the Italian peninsula in different ages

Table 15.3 An example of content description of table Tables

ID	ID_DB	Name	Description	Key	Label
1	1	Cities	Main cities	ID	Name
2	1	Routes	Connection routes	ID	Name
3	1	Ports	Seaports	ID	City
4	2	Native	Native people of the Italian peninsula	ID	Ethnos
5	2	Barbarians	People that invaded the Italian peninsula	ID	Ethnos

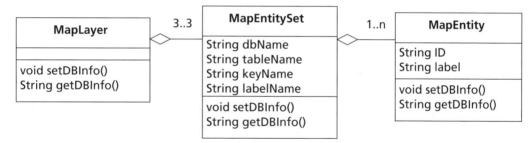

Figure 15.8 The revised GIS class diagram

associated with only one record of the selected table. For example, the path that links Rome to Brindisi is associated with the record whose ID is "1" and name is "Via Appia".

Decision point

How should the object model and XML model be revised?

The class diagram in Figure 15.8 shows the three classes that record the references to information in the GIS database. Class MapEntitySet has four fields: the name of a database, the name of a table, the name of the attribute that plays the role of table key and the name of the attribute that plays the role of label. Similarly, class MapEntity has two fields that store the key attribute's value of a specific table record and the value of the corresponding label attribute. The three classes offer public methods to set and get the values of their fields.

According to this object model, the associations between geographic features and information extracted from the thematic databases are saved in XML files as described in the example reported in Figure 15.9.

```
<GISMAP MAPNAME="Roman History" FILENAME=".\Rome.jpg"/>
  <LAYER NAME="Imperial Rome" COLOR="Blue">
    <SET TYPE="LINK" DBNAME="GIS.HistoricGeography"
         DBTABLE="Roads" DBKEY="ID" DBLABEL="Name">
      <ENTITY ID="1" LABEL="Via Appia">
        <POINT X="286" Y="236"/>
        <POINT X="269" Y="252"/>
        <POINT X="263" Y="260"/>
      </ENTITY>
    </SET>
  </LAYER>
</GISMAP>
```

Figure 15.9 The revised XML file of a cartographic map

Class DBConnector (see Figure 15.10) plays the role of database proxy. It implements a persistent layer that loads into memory the contents of the GIS database and provides the data linker with access to the contents of the thematic databases. It makes use of three ancillary classes. Class DBListRecord stores the values of a record extracted from tables Databases, i.e. the description of a thematic database (e.g. GIS.HistoricGeography). Class DBTableRecord stores the values of a record extracted from table Tables, i.e. the description of a table (e.g. Routes) belonging to the selected thematic database. Class DBValueRecord stores the values of a record extracted from the table identified by DBTableRecord, i.e. the description of route Via Appia.

15.5.3 ☐ Implementation

Classes MapEntity, MapEntitySet and MapLayer are extended with the data structures that record the references to the tables and records in the thematic databases and with the methods to store these references in an XML file.

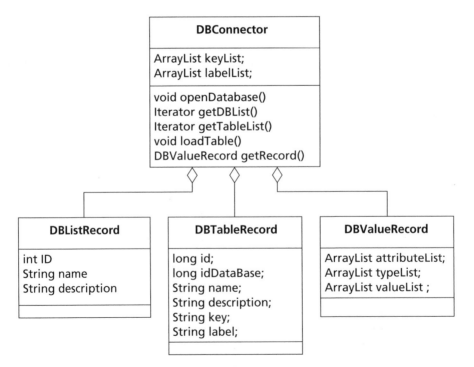

Figure 15.10 The class diagram of the persistent layer

```java
public abstract class MapEntity {
  protected String[] dbInfo = {
    "xxx",     // ID
    "xxx"      // label
    };
  public MapEntity(String line) {
    String docLine = line;
    // extracts the ID of the link
    int indexInit = docLine.indexOf("ID=");
    docLine = docLine.substring(indexInit+4);
    int indexEnd = docLine.indexOf('"');
    dbInfo[0] = docLine.substring(0, indexEnd);
    // extracts the label of the link
      . . .

  }
}


public class MapEntitySet {
  private String[] dbInfo = {
    "xxx",     // db name
    "xxx",     // table name
    "xxx",     // key name
    "xxx"      // label name
    };
  public String toXML(String entityType) {
    StringBuffer stream = new StringBuffer();
    stream.append("\n    <LIST TYPE=" + '"'+entityType+'"' +
                  " DBNAME="  + '"' + dbInfo[0] + '"' +
                  " DBTABLE=" + '"' + dbInfo[1] + '"' +
                  " DBKEY="   + '"' + dbInfo[2] + '"' +
                  " DBLABEL=" + '"' + dbInfo[3] + '"' +">");
    Iterator iterator = entityList.iterator();
    while(iterator.hasNext())
      stream.append(((MapEntity) iterator.next()).toXML());
    stream.append("\n    </LIST>");
    return stream.toString();
  }
}
public class MapLayer {  }
  public String toXML() {
    StringBuffer stream = new StringBuffer();
    stream.append("  <LAYER NAME=" + '"' + name + '"' +
                  " COLOR=" + '"' + colorName + '"' + ">");
    stream.append(siteSet.toXML("SITE"));
    stream.append(linkSet.toXML("LINK"));
    stream.append(areaSet.toXML("AREA"));
```

```
      stream.append("\n  </LAYER>");
      return stream.toString();
   }
}
```

Class **DBConnector** loads the list of thematic databases and the list of available tables from the GIS database. It offers methods to iterate through these lists and to retrieve selected records from the thematic databases. It uses class **DBListRecord**, class **DBTableRecord** and class **DBValueRecord** (see Figure 15.11 on p. 417) to store a record extracted from the list of databases, the list of tables and the selected thematic table respectively.

```
import java.sql.*;
import java.util.*;
public class DBConnector {
   // records extracted from "Databases" and from "Tables"
   private static ArrayList dbList = new ArrayList();
   private static ArrayList tableList = new ArrayList();
   public static void openDataBase() {
     try {
       // Load the jdbc-odbc bridge driver
       Class.forName ("sun.jdbc.odbc.JdbcOdbcDriver");
       String dbName = "jdbc:odbc:Gis";
       Connection con = DriverManager.getConnection (dbName);
       // Create a Statement object so we can submit
       // SQL statements to the driver
       Statement stmt = con.createStatement ();
       // Extract the information about available databases
       String query = "SELECT ID, Name, Description"+
                      "FROM Databases";
       ResultSet rs = stmt.executeQuery (query);
       // Load data, fetching until end of the result set
       dbList.removeAll(dbList);
       while (rs.next())
         // Loop through each column, getting the column data
         dbList.add(new DBListRecord(rs.getLong("ID"),
           rs.getString("Name"),rs.getString("Description")));
       // Close the result set
       rs.close();
       // Extract the information about available tables
       query = "SELECT ID, IDDataBase, Name, Description, " +
                      "Key, Label FROM Tables";
       rs = stmt.executeQuery (query);
       // Load data, fetching until end of the result set
       tableList.removeAll(tableList);
       while (rs.next())
         // Loop through each column, getting the column data
```

```
        tableList.add(new DBTableRecord(rs.getLong("ID"),
          rs.getLong("IDDataBase"), rs.getString("Name"),
          rs.getString("Description"), rs.getString("Key"),
          rs.getString("Label")));
      rs.close(); stmt.close(); con.close();
    } catch (Exception e) { e.printStackTrace();}
}
// returns an iterator of the list of thematic databases
public static Iterator getDBListIterator() {
  return dbList.iterator();
}
// returns the list of tables in database "dbName"
public static Iterator getTableListIterator(String name){
  ArrayList selectedTableInfo = new ArrayList();
  long idDataBase = 0;
  Iterator iterator = dbList.iterator();
  while(iterator.hasNext()) {
    DBListRecord dbRecord =(DBListRecord) iterator.next();
    if(dbRecord.name.equals(name)) {
      idDataBase = dbRecord.id;
      break;
    }
  }
  iterator = tableList.iterator();
  while(iterator.hasNext()) {
    DBTableRecord tableRecord =
                      (DBTableRecord) iterator.next();
    if(tableRecord.idDataBase == idDataBase)
      selectedTableInfo.add(tableRecord);
  }
  return selectedTableInfo.iterator();
}
public static DBValueRecord getRecord(String dbInfo[],
                                      String keyValue) {
  try {
    // Load the jdbc-odbc bridge driver
    Class.forName ("sun.jdbc.odbc.JdbcOdbcDriver");
    String dbName = "jdbc:odbc:"+dbInfo[0];
    Connection con = DriverManager.getConnection(dbName);
    Statement st = con.createStatement ();
    // Extract the record related to the selected key
    String query = "SELECT * FROM " + dbInfo[1] +
                   " WHERE (" + dbInfo[2] +
                   " = " + keyValue + ')';
    ResultSet rs = st.executeQuery (query);
    // parses the record
```

```
                ResultSetMetaData rsmd = rs.getMetaData();
                String name = "";
                String type = "";
                String value = "";
                DBValueRecord record = new DBValueRecord();
                if(rs.next())
                for(int i=1; i <= rsmd.getColumnCount(); i++) {
                  name = rsmd.getColumnName(i);
                  type = rsmd.getColumnTypeName(i);
                  if(type.equals("COUNTER"))
                    value = ""+rs.getLong(name);
                  else if(type.equals("VARCHAR"))
                    value = rs.getString(name);
                  record.addElement(name, type, value);
                }
                return record;
              } catch (Exception e) {e.printStackTrace();}
              return null;
          }
        }
```

15.5.4 □ Test

The test cases should verify two fundamental requirements, namely correctness and completeness of data retrieval from the GIS database and from the thematic databases. The data linker behaves correctly when it allows an association of a geographic entity with a selected record extracted from a thematic database. The data linker should therefore allow the user to browse the GIS database and all the available thematic databases.

The associations between geographic entities and data records are recorded in an XML file. The test cases should verify that the data linker saves the XML file correctly and that it allows the user to load a cartographic map from a previously created XML file.

15.6 ■ Prototype 3: The web browser

The third prototype implements of the web-based data browser. This section analyses non-functional requirements of the distributed system and builds the design of the data browser taking into account the available domain models and the data model defined for the previous prototypes.

15.6.1 □ Analysis

As we have discussed so far, a GIS service allows the user to interact with a cartographic map by selecting geographic entities with the mouse and having the associated information displayed on the screen. In a web scenario, users access GIS services using a standard web browser that shows the cartographic map within an HTML page. The information is retrieved from the remote GIS database and displayed on the same web browser. The Java world offers two main technologies to implement web-based dynamic access to remote data, namely Java Servlets and Java Applets.

Servlets are small programs that run on a web server handling requests coming from HTTP clients such as a web browser. Their job is to elaborate the incoming data, retrieve information from a database, format the result inside an HTML document, and send the document back to the client (see upper part of Figure 15.11). Multimedia data, such as images, can be embedded in the resulting HTML document. Java Servlets are an efficient technology to build dynamic web pages, i.e. documents whose content depends on the specific client's request. Although it is possible, it is not recommended to allow the servlet to retrieve the needed information from the database directly. For security reasons it is preferable to get confidential data from an application server using secure socket communication.

Java Applets (see Sidebar 15.1) are small programs with a graphical user interface that run on a web browser. They reside on the file system of the web server as byte code files. When a remote HTTP client connects to a web page embedding a reference to an applet, the applet's code is uploaded and executed inside the client's browser. The applet is not allowed to access the local resources on the client side (e.g. its file system), but it communicates

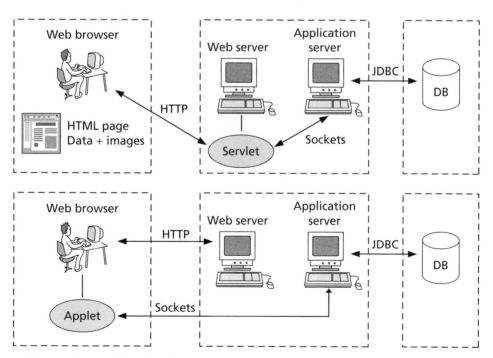

Figure 15.11 Web-based distributed systems that use servlet (upper) or applet (lower) technology

with the remote application server using sockets (see lower part of Figure 15.11).

Sidebar 15.1 Java Applet

An applet is implemented by specializing class java.applet.Applet or javax.swing. JApplet. These classes offer four basic methods, namely init(), start(), paint() and destroy(). The applet lifecycle is depicted in the figure below. These methods are overridden in every concrete subclass.

Applet classes do not have a main method, since they are created by the browser and do not stand alone. They also do not have a constructor, which is replaced by method init().

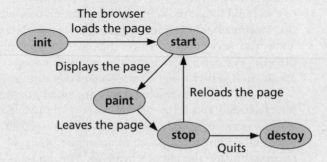

The code below exemplifies the implementation of a simple applet.

```
package example;
import java.applet.*
public class Simple extends Applet {
 . public void init()
    {System.out.println("initializing...."); }
  public void start()
    {System.out.println("starting... "); }
  public void paint(Graphics g)
    {System.out.println("painting...."); }
  public void stop()
    {System.out.println("stopping... "); }
  public void destroy()
    {System.out.println("unloading...."); }
}
```

Once the code has been compiled, the applet is embedded in a web page as shown in the following HTML code.

```
<html><body>
<APPLET CODE="example.Simple.class" CODEBASE="." WIDTH="700"
 HEIGHT="600">
<PARAM NAME = MAPLIST VALUE = "value" >
</APPLET>
</body></html>
```

15.6.2 □ **Design**

Both technologies can be exploited to build GIS services. What should be carefully evaluated is their different impact on performance, i.e. on the network traffic that they generate when the client selects a geographic feature and waits for the associated information to be displayed.

Decision point

Java Servlets or Java Applets?

The central point of a GIS service implementation is display of the cartographic map on the web browser. If we choose the servlet technology, a cartographic map is encoded as a jpg image (or another standard format) and embedded in an HTML page. Whenever the user selects a new map or wants a different layer to be displayed on it, the servlet encodes a new jpg image and sends it to the client's web browser. The selection of geographic features on the cartographic map is handled by the web browser itself, since it is able to get the coordinates of the mouse pointer on the image and send them to the remote servlet. Using these coordinates, the servlet can identify the selected feature and compose a new HTML page with the associated information. It is clear that the transmission of images through the internet may cause appreciable delays in the transition from the visualization of a map layer or map entity to another one.

An applet does not have this disadvantage, since it behaves like a standard graphical user interface that is able to draw graphics and display images locally. When the user selects a cartographic map, the applet retrieves from the application server the map's XML description and instantiates in the client's PC memory the objects corresponding to all the map layers and map entities. No further communication is required between the applet and the remote application server when the user wants a new layer or entity to be visualized on the map. The applet manages the entity selection in the same way as the graphical editor and the data linker. It sends the identifier of the selected entity to the remote application server which queries the database and sends the associated information back to the applet. From the point of view of network traffic and user interaction, the applet solution is more convenient and user friendly.

Decision point

How are the GIS functionalities partitioned in the three-tier architecture?

The GIS application server acts as a middle layer between the applet and the database. As such, it basically extends the functionalities of class DBConnector to handle multiple client requests at any one time (see

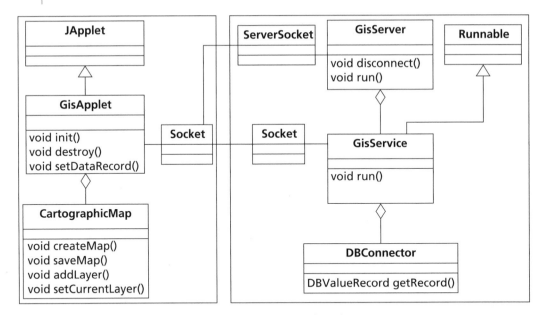

Figure 15.12 The class diagram of the applet-based distributed system

Figure 15.12). The main class is GisServer which listens to incoming requests on a socket port. When a connection request is received, it instantiates an object of class GisService in order to handle the socket communication with the remote applet. Both the GisServer class and the GisService class implement the Runnable interface. The GisService receives from the applet the reference to a database record, i.e. the name of the database, the name of a table, the name of the key attribute and a value of the key. It queries the database with this information, serializes the retrieved record and sends the resulting data stream back to the applet.

The GisApplet is basically a graphical user interface that builds on class CartographicMap. It allows the user to load a cartographic map from a list of available maps that is initialized when the applet is loaded on the web browser. The XML file of the selected map is retrieved directly from the file system on the GIS web server and parsed by the applet. When the applet is started, a socket connection is established with the GIS server. This creates a dedicated GIS service. The applet listens to the user's mouse events to acquire the coordinates of the selected geographic entities. The database references bound to these entities are serialized and sent to the GIS service in order to retrieve the associated geographic information.

15.6.3 □ Implementation

Classes GisServer and GisService implement the multithreaded application server that listens to incoming requests from the remote applet, extracts the selected record from a thematic database and sends the associated information back to the applet.

```java
Import java.net.*;
import java.io.*;
import java.util.*;
import gis.model.*;
public class GisServer implements Runnable {
  // server socket listening to incoming requests on PORT
  private ServerSocket serverSocket;
  private static final int PORT = 2002;
  // the list of active services
  private ArrayList serviceList = new ArrayList();
  private Thread thread = null;
  public GisServer() {
    try {
      serverSocket = new ServerSocket(PORT);
    }catch(Exception e) {e.printStackTrace();}
    DBConnector.openDataBase();   // opens the GIS database
    thread = new Thread(this);
    thread.start();
  }
  public void run() {
    while(true)
    try {
      // the server socket is waiting for incoming requests
      Socket socket = serverSocket.accept();
      // creates the service that interacts with the applet
      serviceList.add(new GisService(socket, this));
    }catch(IOException e){ e.printStackTrace();}
  }
  public void disconnect(GisService service) {
    serviceList.remove(service);
  }
  public static void main(String[] args) {
    GisServer gisServer = new GisServer();
  }
}

public class GisService implements Runnable {
  private static String PATH = "gis//";
  private Socket socket = null;
  private GisServer server = null;
  private Thread thread;
  public GisService(Socket socket, GisServer server) {
    this.socket = socket;
    this.server = server;
    thread = new Thread(this);
    thread.start();
  }
```

```
public void run() {
  try {
    // Initializes input and output streams
    BufferedReader  input = new BufferedReader(
      new InputStreamReader(socket.getInputStream()));
    PrintWriter output = new PrintWriter(
      new BufferedOutputStream(socket.getOutputStream()),
                                              false);

    while(true) {
      // waiting for a request
      String message = input.readLine();
      if(message == null) continue;
      if(message.equals("Bye.")) break;
      else if(message.equals("GETRECORD")) {
        String dbInfo[] = new String[3];
        dbInfo[0] = input.readLine();        // db name
        dbInfo[1] = input.readLine();        // table name
        dbInfo[2] = input.readLine();        // key name
        String keyValue = input.readLine(); // key value
        // extracts a record from the selected database
        DBValueRecord record =
                  DBConnector.getRecord(dbInfo, keyValue);
        // serializes the record's attributes
        output.println("" + record.getSize());
        for(int i=0; i < record.getSize(); i++)
          output.println(record.getAttribute(i) + " " +
          record.getValue(i));
        output.flush();
      }
    }
    input.close(); output.close(); socket.close();
    server.disconnect(this);
  }
  catch(Exception e){ server.disconnect(this); }
  }
}
```

Class GisApplet implements the applet that displays the cartographic map within the user's browser. The list of available cartographic maps is loaded from the HTML file that embeds the applet as shown in the HTML code in Figure 15.13.

When the applet is loaded within the web browser, it creates a socket to establish a connection with the remote application server in order to retrieve data records associated with the selected geographic features.

```
public class GisApplet extends JApplet {
  Socket socket;
  // the IP address of the remote application server is set
```

```
<html>
<head><title>GisApplet</title></head>
<body BGCOLOR="#ffffff"">
<APPLET CODE="gis.client.GisApplet.class" CODEBASE="."
        WIDTH="700" HEIGHT="600">
<PARAM NAME = MAPLIST
 VALUE = "RomanItaly|RomeEurope|RomeMediterraneum" >
</APPLET>
</body>
</html>
```

Figure 15.13 The HTML code that embeds the GIS Applet

```
// equal to the localhost for test purposes
String HOST = "127.0.0.1";
int PORT = 2002;
boolean connected = false;
BufferedReader input = null;
PrintWriter output = null;
CartographicMap mapWindow = new CartographicMap ();
DataWindow dataWindow = null;

public synchronized void init() {
  // loads the list of available maps from the HTML file
  ArrayList mapList = new ArrayList();
  String mapNameList = getParameter("MAPLIST");
  if(mapNameList == null) return;
  StringTokenizer tokenizer =
              new StringTokenizer(mapNameList, "|");
  while(tokenizer.hasMoreTokens()) {
    String mapName = tokenizer.nextToken();
    mapList.add(mapName);
  }
  // connect to the remote server
  try {
    socket = new Socket(HOST, PORT);
    input = new BufferedReader(
        new InputStreamReader(socket.getInputStream()));
    output = new PrintWriter(socket.getOutputStream(),
                                                    false);
  } catch(Exception e) {
    e.printStackTrace();
    return;
  }
  // the list of available cartographic maps is shown in a
  // menu of the graphical interface; when an item is
  // selected, the following method is executed
```

```java
public void mapItem_actionPerformed(ActionEvent e) {
  String mapName = e.getActionCommand();
  // loads the image file and map file
  URL mapUrl = null;
  URL imageUrl = null;
  try {
    mapUrl = new URL(this.getCodeBase(), mapName+".map");
    String imageFile = mapWindow.openMap(
                                  mapUrl.openStream());
    StringTokenizer tokenizer =
                    new StringTokenizer(imageFile, "\\");
    String fname = "";
    while(tokenizer.hasMoreElements())
      fname = tokenizer.nextToken();
    imageUrl = new URL(this.getCodeBase(), fname);
    Image image = (new ImageIcon(imageUrl)).getImage();
    mapWindow.setImage(image);
  } catch (Exception ex) {return; }
  // loads the list of layers for the selected map
  String layerList[] = mapWindow.getLayerList();
    . . .
}
// invoked by the Web browser to kill the Applet
public void destroy() {
  output.println("Bye.");
}
// this method is invoked by the mouse handler when a
// geometric entity is selected
public void setDataRecords(String dbInfo[], String key) {
  dataWindow.resetRecords();
  output.println("GETRECORD");
  output.println(dbInfo[0]);
  output.println(dbInfo[1]);
  output.println(dbInfo[2]);
  output.println(key);
  output.flush();
  // shows the record values in the data window
  try {
    int size = Integer.parseInt(this.input.readLine());
    for(int i=0; i < size; i++) {
      StringTokenizer tokenizer =
            new StringTokenizer(input.readLine(), " ");
      String attribute = tokenizer.nextToken();
      String value = tokenizer.nextToken();
      dataWindow.addRecord(attribute, value);
    }
  }
```

```
    catch(IOException ioe) { ioe.printStackTrace(); }
    dataWindow.redraw();
  }
}
```

15.6.4 □ Test

The test cases of the third prototype require installing the GIS application server on a desktop PC that runs a web server and starting a web browser on another networked computer. The test should verify that the applet is downloaded from the web server and started by the web browser correctly and that the applet and the application server communicate correctly. The following steps illustrate how to install the GIS.

- On the server side:
  - Create the GIS database and insert the references to the available thematic databases and tables.
  - Create the ODBC logical links to the GIS database and to the thematic databases.
  - Copy the byte code of class GisApplet and the HTML file shown in Figure 15.13 in the home directory of the web server or in one of its subdirectories.
  - Start the application server, i.e. run class GisServer.
- On the client side:
  - From a web browser connect to the HTML file that embeds the GIS applet.
  - Once the applet has been loaded in the web browser, its graphical interface should appear as shown in Figure 15.5.

15.7 ■ Extension

In Section 15.6.1 we assumed that the GIS manager is able to generate query tables within the thematic databases in order to circumscribe the data that can be linked to a cartographic map. Prototype 2 allows the user to associate geographic entities with single records of a query table. A more flexible solution would allow the user to associate an entity with the SQL query that generates a record from a set of tables.

The GIS applet allows the user to select only one geographic entity at a time and to browse the associated data. When entities belonging to different layers overlap, it would be nice to visualize the union of the data associated with those entities.

15.8 ■ Assessment

This case study has shown how to develop a set of tools for building geographic information systems: a map editor, a data-map linker and a map-based data browser.

Architecture model. One crucial issue that has been discussed is the definition of a highly modular three-tier architecture where the middle-tier acts as a software glue between the relational database and the object-oriented data structures of the suite of local editing and remote browsing tool.

Distribution paradigm. An accurate analysis has been conducted in order to identify the distribution paradigm best suited to support the remote visualization of cartographic maps in a web browser. The alternative choices were the declarative paradigm of Java Servlets and the mobile code paradigm of Java Applets. The latter was chosen because it better supports graphical user interactivity.

Middleware technology. Multiple disparate technologies combine in the development of an internet-based geographic information system: data storage in a relational database, data transmission using sockets and data visualization through Java Applets.

Idiom	Data exchange format
Context	Distributed systems integrate applications and resources that are heterogeneous and not able to interoperate. They are usually implemented using different technologies, different languages and for different operating platforms.
Problem	While indeed any application can pass any data to any other application, each distributed application has its own semantics which define the specific usage constraints on shared data, the specific transformations that can occur and the relationship of those transformations to particular types of messages.
Forces or tradeoffs	In the past, EDI technology has been proposed as a mechanism to allow heterogeneous applications to exchange multi-format documents. Its limit is the excessive rigidity of the standard format. In the opposite direction, a different solution consists of managing multiple and evolving classifications of terms and concepts structured in specialization/generalization hierarchies.
Solution	The extensible mark-up language (XML) is a uniform data exchange format among distributed applications. XML documents are semi-structured, as they have a flexible syntactic structure based on tag (mark up) nesting, which may contain unstructured information. Following the original spirit of the W3C recommendation (www.w3c.org) that introduced XML, a generic XML processor should be able to process a generic XML document.

Force resolution	The structure of an XML document is defined by a DTD (Document Type Definition), an XML specification based on suitable meta-tags; a document that respects a specific DTD is said to be valid. Consequently, a DTD induces a class of documents, i.e. the class of all valid documents with regard to the specific DTD.
Design rationale	Distributed applications share the same DTD schema.

15.9 ■ Reference

DeMers, M.N. (2002) *Fundamentals of GIS*, 2nd edn, John Wiley & Sons.

Ubiquitous email

16

Synthesis

The diffusion of 3G communication networks and mobile computing together with the massive use of computer-based systems and applications represent a strong motivation for ubiquitous access to such applications. An example of a widely diffused application is email. We want to be able to access our email from everywhere and through a wide range of media.

The purpose of this case study is to develop the UbiMail application, which provides ubiquitous access to email though several media and devices: HTML browsers running on PCs and connecting to the wired internet, WML browsers running on high-end mobile phones and connecting through the wireless internet, and text messages on GSM mobile phones and connecting through the GSM network.

- Focus: this application exemplifies the use of Java to develop simple web applications and the use of multiple user interfaces.
- Java features: Java Server Pages and Java Mail classes.
- Used knowledge: the reader should be familiar with the basics of web standards such as HTML and HTTP.

16.1 ■ Specifications

The UbiMail system should provide access to email via the most diffuse types of devices that can connect to the internet, i.e. personal computers and cell phones. It must adapt the presentation of email to the device capabilities; for instance controlling the number of characters shown on a cell phone.

The user should be able to switch from one to the other medium of access seamlessly. For instance, reading the mail from a PC in the office and continuing to look at the email on a WAP (Wireless Access Protocol) phone while out of the office.

The system must be able to access different types of mail servers, using several kinds of mail access protocol such as POP3 (Post Office Protocol 3) and IMAP (Internet Mail Access Protocol).

When such flexible devices as PCs and WAP phones are not available a limited service must be available. It must be able to notify new messages by means of GSM (Global System for Mobile Communications) SMS (Short

Message Service). There are two main problems with this service: first, the typical email user receives a large number of spam messages in his or her mailbox; second, not all messages are so urgent as to require a message on the GSM phone. Consequently a mechanism to notify only the selected emails is required.

16.1.1 □ Problem analysis

The UbiMail system must essentially provide nomadic access to the email of its users by supporting several communication channels and media.

The basic functions of the UbiMail system are summarized in the use case diagram presented in Figure 16.1.

UbiMail must present a compact list of mail present on the mail server. On demand the user can access the full email contents. In particular the two main access channels are:

- the web browser (HTML); and
- WAP devices (WML).

In addition the system must periodically check the mail server and notify the user when new messages have arrived. This notification consists of an SMS message sent to the user's GSM mobile phone. It must be possible to filter the messages for which a notification is required to avoid a flood of messages.

The system must be configurable and allow setting of the user preferences and the mail server parameters. All the information about a user forms the user profile.

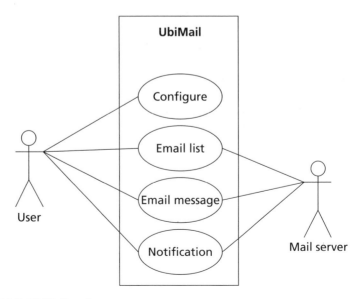

Figure 16.1 UbiMail main use cases

16.1.2 □ **Domain models**

The Post Office Protocol – Version 3 (POP3) defined in RFC-1939 (Network Working Group 1996) is intended to permit a workstation to dynamically access a maildrop on a server host in a useful fashion. Usually, this means that the POP3 protocol is used to allow a workstation to retrieve mail that the server is holding for it.

Initially, the server host starts the POP3 service by listening on TCP port 110. When a client host wishes to make use of the service, it establishes a TCP connection with the server host. When the connection is established, the POP3 server sends a greeting. The client and POP3 server then exchange commands and responses (respectively) until the connection is closed or aborted.

Commands in POP3 consist of a case-insensitive keyword, possibly followed by one or more arguments. Keywords and arguments consist of printable ASCII characters. Keywords and arguments are each separated by a space. Keywords are three or four characters long. Each argument may be up to 40 characters long. Responses in POP3 consist of a status indicator and a keyword possibly followed by additional information. The server states and the commands' specification can be found in the RFC.

The Wireless Access Protocol (WAP) is a suite of standards to provide access to the internet over wireless communication networks (see WAP Forum Specification).

The Wireless Application Environment (WAE) is part of the WAP Forum specification of an application framework for wireless terminals such as mobile phones, pagers and PDAs. The contents are structured according to the Wireless Markup Language (WML) that is homologous to HTML. WML is identified by the MIME type "text/vnd.wap.wml". The WAP content can be provided either directly to the mobile network or on the internet; in the latter case a suitable WAP gateway takes care of protocol conversion. For further details see WAP Forum Specification.

GSM was born as a standard for digital mobile voice communications. Currently, second-generation GSM networks deliver high quality and secure mobile voice and data services (such as SMS/text messaging) with full roaming capabilities in several parts of the world. The SMS are short text messages that can be sent though the GSM network to any user; if the user is not connected to the network the message is queued for a certain time and delivered to the user as soon as he or she connects to the GSM network. GSM phones can be connected to a PC and act as interfaces to the GSM network; in particular they can be used to send SMS messages. The interface to interact with a GSM phone is described in (ETSI 1996).

16.1.3 □ **Main features**

The UbiMail system exhibits the following main features:

■ *Access to mail server*. It must be able to connect to existing mail servers and fetch mail from them.

- *Presentation in HTML.* The system provides an HTML-based interface to read email.
- *Presentation in WML.* It provides a limited version of HTML, one tailored for the limited capabilities of WAP phones.
- *GSM notification.* The system must notify the arrival of certain messages through SMS.
- *Profile management.* The system must store a profile for each user containing all the relevant information.

16.1.4 □ Test

The test cases will focus on two main aspects of the UbiMail system: the user interface and the communication among the nodes of the system.

To test the UI functionalities we have to check if the email messages are displayed correctly and if the navigation through the pages is correct (i.e. the links are named correctly, there are no dead links, etc.). When dealing with multiple presentations we must check that the transition from one to another is as seamless and coherent as possible (the messages must be the same, and the information shown in different media must be consistent).

To test the communication between the nodes we have to send a message to the mail server and observe it through the HTML and WAP interfaces. In addition we must check the delay between the message send time and the notification through SMS.

16.2 ■ Architecture and planning

The system provides access through several different communication channels and media. The physical structure of the system is fairly complex and is presented in Figure 16.2.

The main node is the AppServer where all the software system resides. It accesses the GSM equipment to send the SMS messages through a serial connection. The GSM equipment is a GSM cellular phone that is connected to the GSM network and is able to send and receive messages. The information about the users of the system and their preferences is stored in a database residing on the DB server that is accessed by means of JDBC.

Outside the system boundary the UbiMail must communicate with a WAP device through the WAP protocol, with a web browser over the HTTP protocol, and with a mail server over the POP protocol. Finally the server must be able to send SMS messages to GSM mobile phones over the GSM network.

Since the system is complex and has to interact with other systems through several protocols, it will build on as many off-the-shelf components as possible.

The system is formed by four main components as shown in Figure 16.3. The main component is the presentation, which uses the email component and the profile management. The email component accesses the information

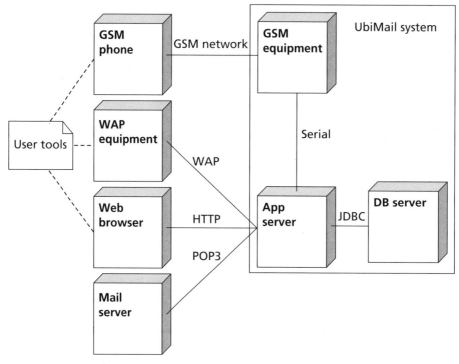

Figure 16.2 Physical architecture of the system

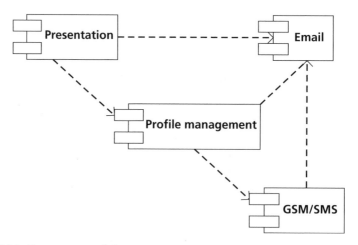

Figure 16.3 Components of the system

on the mail server. The profile management handles the profiles of the users and takes care of the notification. To perform the notification it uses the email component.

The development process of the UbiMail system is organized into four phases that produce the following prototypes:

- *Prototype 1: Mail access*. A system providing basic email access to an external server through a web/HTML-based interface.
- *Prototype 2: User profiles*. The system adds the definition of user profiles that are stored and can be reused.
- *Prototype 3: WAP access*. The access through WAP/WML interface is added, which can be used as an alternative to the web interface.
- *Prototype 4: Mail notification*. A new mail notification service through SMS/GSM is integrated into the system.

16.3 ■ Prototype 1: Mail access

This prototype focuses on providing a basic web interface to access a mail server that implements the POP protocol. The prototype is based on the Java technology for the web, i.e. Java Server Pages.

16.3.1 □ Analysis

The system must provide access to a mail server through the POP3 protocol (Network Working Group 1996). The purpose of the system is to seamlessly adapt the low-level POP protocol to an HTML-based interface that can be used through a web browser.

The user interface consists of a set of HTML pages that contain the list of the messages received by the user and the content of each message.

The parameters to connect to the mail server must be provided by the user, since in this prototype there is no persistent storage of user profiles. In addition, to improve the friendliness of the user interface the user should be able to provide a name, which will be used by the system to address him more directly (e.g. "Welcome John"). The user can interact with the system depending on the current state of UbiMail. The states and the transitions between them are represented as a statechart in Figure 16.4.

When the user enters the UbiMail system, he is in the state Begin in which he is expected to provide his name. After this the user is logged in and can provide the parameters for the connection to the mail server (i.e. the name

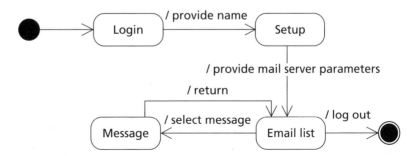

Figure 16.4 Flow of states

of the server, the username and the password). With this information, UbiMail can show a list of the messages received by the user, who can select one of the messages to look at its content.

The UbiMail system must also interact with the user's mail server. The system specification defines the protocol to be supported, i.e. the standard Post Office Protocol (POP). UbiMail must be able to access the list of messages received by the server (in state Email List) and to retrieve the contents of each of them (in state Message). In addition to correctly displaying the contents of email messages the system must be able to deal with standards to embed complex contents in email messages, such as MIME.

16.3.2 □ **Design**

This prototype of the UbiMail system behaves like a gateway that converts the low-level unfriendly POP protocol to a high-level user-friendly HTML interface. The design can be divided into three parts: the interaction with the mail server (back end), the interaction with the user (front end), the conversion and adaptation among the two.

Decision point

How do we implement the back-end mail component?

The implementation of the POP protocol is not difficult but becomes fairly complex if we want to support the MIME standard as well. For the back end we decide to use the standard Java extension package javax.mail (see Sidebar 16.1). This avoids both unnecessary work and possible implementation mistakes.

Decision point

How do we implement the user interface component?

The user interface consists of a series of linked HTML pages. For each state in Figure 16.4 there will be one or more pages. The content of the pages depends on the user and on the information provided by the mail server. Therefore the pages must be generated dynamically every time they are requested.

Java supports several methods for dynamic web page generation. The two most common technologies are Java Servlets and Java Server Pages (JSP) (Bodoff *et al.* 2002). Most implementations of these standards internally convert JSPs into servlets. Thus they can be considered mostly equivalent, the main difference being the syntax.

Sidebar 16.1 Java Mail

Java Mail is part of the Java Enterprise Edition and contains the classes modelling a mail system. The javax.mail package defines classes that are common to all mail systems (see http://developer.java.sun.com/developer/onlineTraining/JavaMail/).

The main class is Session which behaves like a factory (see the Class Factory pattern (see Gamma *et al.* 1995)) for the mail stores (class Store) and transport protocols (class Transport).

The first step in using Java Mail is to create a session object specifying some default properties:

```
Properties props = new Properties();
props.setProperty("mail.store.protocol","pop3");
Session ms = Session.getInstance(props);
```

Then it is possible to create a mail store and connect it to the server, the mail store is a proxy (see the Proxy pattern (see Gamma *et al.* 1995)) of the server:

```
Store pop = ms.getStore("pop3");
pop.connect(popServer,popUser,popPass);
```

The mail stored on a mail store can be browsed through the class Folder. Folder is an abstract class that represents a folder for mail messages. The case-insensitive folder name INBOX is reserved to mean the "primary folder for this user on this server".

```
Folder folder = pop.getFolder("INBOX");
folder.open(Folder.READ_ONLY);
```

The Message objects within the Folder represent the email messages.

```
Message msg = folder.getMessage(1);
System.out.println("Subject: " + msg.getSubject());
```

The messages implement the Part interface, and its contents can be either simple or composed of multiple parts.

```
Multipart multi = (Multipart)msg.getContent();
BodyPart part = multi.getBodyPart(0);
System.out.println("Type: " + part.getContentType());
System.out.println("Content: " +  part.getContent());
```

Because of its easier syntax we opt for the JSP technology. Each HTML page with dynamic contents corresponds to a JSP (see Sidebar 16.2). We design the structure of JSPs in accordance with the state flow presented in Figure 16.4. We represent the web pages (both static HTML and dynamic JSPs) as classes; the links between them are represented as associations with the stereotype «link». Figure 16.5 shows the class diagram describing the structure of the prototype's user interface.

Decision point

How do we convert the information on the mail server into HTML pages?

Sidebar 16.2 Java web applications

The Java 2 Enterprise Edition includes several technologies to build web applications (Bodoff *et al.* 2002). We are interested in web components, i.e. those items that provide dynamic content when a web client (e.g. a web browser) connects to the application.

J2EE provides two main technologies to develop web components: Java Servlets and Java Server Pages (JSPs). They are equivalent and can be used interchangeably. Servlets are best suited to managing the control functions of an application, such as dispatching requests and handling non-textual data. JSPs are more appropriate for generating text-based markup such as HTML, WML and XML.

Servlets are Java classes that implement the Servlet (or HttpServlet) interface. JSP are text-based documents that contain two types of text: static template data (e.g. HTML elements) and JSP elements. The JSP elements are enclosed within "**<%**" and "**%>**".

The web components are Java classes that are contained in an application called "web container". The web container receives HTTP requests and dispatches them to the appropriate web component. We prefer not to go into details about web components here. The reader can find more information in, for example, Bodoff *et al.* (2002).

The web components can maintain information about a user session. The session can contain several attributes that are associated with a user; in JSP it is accessible through the object "session". In addition it is possible to store information that is shared by all sessions of the application. This is the web context and is accessible in JSP though the object "application".

Web applications run inside a container. Thus, in order to run, the applications must be deployed to the container. The deployment of Java web applications is based on a standard directory structure:

- / : the root directory contains the static pages and the JSPs.
- /WEB-INF : contains the application descriptor in the file web.xml.
- /WEB-INF/classes : contains all the classes required by the application, including the servlet classes.
- /WEB-INF/lib : contains the libraries in the form of .jar files.

The method of deployment can vary according to the web container. Using the Tomcat container the deployment consists of copying the deployment structure into a new directory under the webapps directory of the Tomcat installation location.

The initial page (index) is a static HTML page, it contains a form where the user can specify his name, and this information is processed by the JSP login, which presents to the user a form to specify all the mail server parameters. Then the JSP main provides a list of the email messages contained in the user's mailbox. Each message can be read in detail by means of the JSP message that shows the contents of a given message. Both main and message make use of the javax.mail package to access the information stored on the mail server. Finally the JSP logout closes the connection.

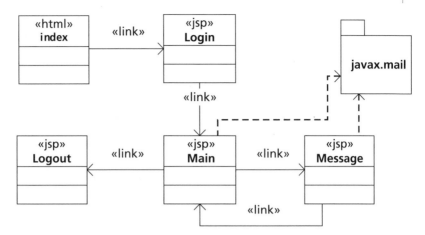

Figure 16.5 Design of the basic access system

16.3.3 □ Implementation

The initial page is a static HTML page, index.html; it contains a form to input the name of the user. The form data is submitted to the JSP login.jsp.

```
<html><head><title>Ubi Mail Login</title></head>
<body><h1>UbiMail</h1>
Ubiquitous E-Mail System
<p><hr>
<table>
<tr><td align="center">
<form method="POST" action="login.jsp">
User: <input type=text name="login" size="15"/>
<br><input type=submit value="Login">
</form>
</td></tr>
</table>
<hr>
<i>Your email everywhere!</i>
</body></html>
```

The first JSP of the system, login.jsp, takes the information about the user and asks for the parameters to connect to the mail server. It gets the value of the data login entered in the index page and stores it in the session attribute user. The session contains all the information shared by the JSPs that make up the application; in this case the information consists of the username and the objects that represent the mail server.

```
<%@ page contentType="text/html" language="java" %>
<%
    String user = request.getParameter("login");
    session.setAttribute("user",user);
%>
```

```
<html><head><title>UbiMail -
                        <%=user%>'s details</title></head>
<body><h1>UbiMail</h1>
Hello <%=user%>.
<hr>
<h2>User details</h2>
Please provide the details for your POP server.
<form method="POST" action="main.jsp">
<table>
<tr><td>POP server:
<td><input type=text name="popServer" size=30>
<tr><td>POP user:
<td><input type=text name="popUser" size=30>
<tr><td>POP password:
<td><input type=password name="popPass" size=30>
<tr><td colspan=2 align=center>
                        <input type=submit value="Enter">
</table>
</form>
<hr>
<i>UbiMail - Ubiquitous e-mail system</i>
</body></html>
```

The core of the application is main.jsp. If this is the first invocation of this JSP in the session, it starts a new mail session, connects to the server and opens the default message folder. Otherwise it recovers the mail objects stored in the session attributes. This page builds a table and for each message in the folder adds a row containing the subject, the sender and the date of the message. Each message has a number that is a link to the JSP that shows the contents; the URL has an additional ?index=n where *n* is the number of the message. This is the standard way of passing parameters. To make reading a long list of messages easier the rows alternate a light blue and a pink background.

```
<%@ page contentType="text/html" language="java" %>
<%@ page import="javax.mail.*, java.util.Properties,
                        java.util.Enumeration" %>
<%  if(session.isNew()){
        response.sendRedirect("index.html");
        return;
    }
    String user = (String) session.getAttribute("user");
    Folder folder = (Folder) session.getAttribute("folder");
%>
<html><head><title>UbiMail -
                        <%=user%>'s mailbox</title></head>
<body>
```

```
<%  try{
        if(folder == null){ // i.e. coming from login
          // get the server parameters
          String popServer=request.getParameter("popServer");
          String popUser=request.getParameter("popUser");
          String popPass=request.getParameter("popPass");
          // set the default protocol
          Properties props=new Properties();
          props.setProperty("mail.store.protocol","pop3");
          // open a mail session
          Session ms = Session.getInstance(props);
          // connect to the server using the POP protocol
          Store pop = ms.getStore("pop3");
          pop.connect(popServer,popUser,popPass);
          // get the default folder
          folder = pop.getFolder("INBOX");
          folder.open(Folder.READ_ONLY);
          // store the folder in the session
          session.setAttribute("folder",folder);
        }
        int n = folder.getMessageCount();
%>
<h1>UbiMail</h1>
Hello <%=user%>.
<hr>
<a href="logout.jsp">Logout</a>.
<h2>Your Mailbox</h2>
Contains <%=n%> messages.
<table  width="100%">
<tr><th>#<th>Subject<th>Sender<th>Date</tr>
<%      for(int i=0; i<n; ++i){
          Message msg = folder.getMessage(i+1);
          // even messages are shown with a light blue
          // background, odd ones have a pink background
          %><tr bgcolor="<%=(i%2==0?"#FFE0E0":"E0E0FF")%>">
            <td><a href="message.jsp?index=<%=i+1%>">
                                          <%=(i+1)%></a>
            <td><%=msg.getSubject()%>
            <td><%=msg.getFrom()[0]%>
            <td><%=msg.getSentDate()%>
<%      }%>
</table>
<%  }catch(Exception e){ %>
UbiMail encountered an error while accessing your mailbox.
<p><tt><%=e%></tt>
<%  }%>
```

```
<hr><a href="logout.jsp">Logout</a>.
<hr><i>UbiMail - Ubiquitous e-mail system</i>
</body></html>
```

The JSP message.jsp displays the contents of a message, which is identified by the parameter index that is provided by mail.jsp. The body of the email message can be in different formats: in the most common case it is a string, otherwise it is formatted as a multipart content. If it is multipart, each of the parts must be shown. For the sake of simplicity in this prototype we decided to show only the textual parts (either plain text or HTML) and to provide the indication of the MIME type of the remaining parts.

```
<%@ page contentType="text/html" language="java" %>
<%@ page import="javax.mail.*, javax.mail.internet.
                                    InternetAddress" %>
<%
  if(session.isNew()){
    response.sendRedirect("index.html");
    return;
  }
  String user = (String) session.getAttribute("user");
  Folder folder = (Folder) session.getAttribute("folder");
  int index=Integer.parseInt((String)request.
                                getParameter("index"));
%>
<html><head><title>UbiMail -
                    <%=user%>'s mailbox</title></head>
<body>
...
<h2>Message # <%=index%></h2>
<%try{
    Message msg = folder.getMessage(index);
    InternetAddress addr=(InternetAddress)msg.getFrom()[0];
%>
    <table border=1 width="100%">
    <tr><td bgcolor="#FFE0E0">Subject
        <td bgcolor="#E0E0FF"><%=msg.getSubject()%>
    <tr><td bgcolor="#FFE0E0">From<td bgcolor="#E0E0FF">
      <tt><a href="mailto:<%=addr.getAddress()%>">
                            <%=addr.getPersonal()%>
      &lt;<%=addr.getAddress()%>&gt;</tt>
      <tr><td bgcolor="#FFE0E0">Date
          <td bgcolor="#E0E0FF"><%=msg.getSentDate()%>
      <%
      Object content = msg.getContent();
      if( content instanceof String){
        %>
```

```
    <tr><td colspan=2><pre><%=content%></pre>
    <%
  }else{
    Multipart multi = (Multipart)content;
    for(int j=0; j<multi.getCount(); ++j){
      BodyPart part = multi.getBodyPart(j);
      String type = part.getContentType();
      content = part.getContent();
      if( content instanceof String){
      %>
        <tr><td><%=j%><td><pre><%=content%></pre>
      <%
      }else{
      %>
        <tr><td><%=j%><td><%=type%>
      <%
  } } }
  %>
  </table>
<%}catch(Exception e){ %>
    UbiMail encountered an error while accessing your
                                                    mailbox.
    <p><tt><%=e%></tt>
<%}  %>
...
</body></html>
```

The end of the interaction with the system is carried out by logout.jsp. It invalidates the session, with all the attributes it contains.

```
<%@ page contentType="text/html" language="java" %>
<%  session.invalidate(); %>
<html><head><title>UbiMail - Goodbye!</title></head>
<body><h1>UbiMail</h1>
You just logged out!
<br>To login again go to the <a href="index.html">login
                                                    page</a>.
<hr><i>UbiMail - Ubiquitous e-mail system</i>
</body></html>
```

16.3.4 ☐ Test

The test must check the main area of usage and some typical error conditions. It is important to have a mail server that supports the POP protocol with some email messages stored on it.

The main scenario to test is the following:

■ Open the index.html page.

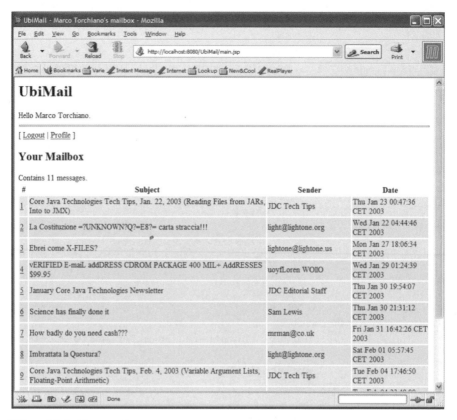

Figure 16.6 Message list

- Provide a name, e.g. "TestUser" and click login. The browser shows the login.jsp page, that asks "TestUser" to provide data.
- Provide server name, username, password for the mail server. The browser shows the main.jsp page containing a list of the messages on the server, similar to Figure 16.6; the rows have an alternate colour background to facilitate reading.
- Click on the number of a message. The browser shows the contents of the selected message.
- Click on the link to return to the message list. The browser shows the list of messages again.
- Click the logout link. The browser shows the logout.jsp page that confirms that the user has logged out.

16.4 ■ Prototype 2: User profiles

In this prototype we develop a web mail system that keeps track of the profiles of the users in persistent storage. The users who are registered with the system can provide the server parameters once and have the system record them.

16.4.1 □ Analysis

The increment to be developed in this prototype is the persistence of user information. The main information to be kept consists of the mail server parameters: the server name, the username and the password. They must be provided once, when the user is registered with the system, without the need to repeat them at each connection as in the previous prototype.

In addition, since the mail is private, we need to add some security. The users need to authenticate themselves with the system to use the stored information. For this application we use a simple security scheme: users authenticate with a username and password.

In addition to providing a user-friendly application we need to store the user's full name, since the username can be just a given name.

All the information concerning a user forms the user profile that is made up of the following items:

- server parameters;
- username and password;
- full name.

The user interface must provide the ability to register new users with the system and to modify the profile of an existing user.

16.4.2 □ Design

The structure of this prototype is far more complex than the previous one. The user interface should allow the registration of new users and the modification of profiles. The profiles are persistent; therefore they must be stored in a database.

In the previous prototype we noticed that some sections of code are repeated in several places; an example is the code that deals with the mail server. In addition, to avoid larger repetitions, we store the folder in the session context. This is inefficient because it keeps a connection to the mail server open, thus consuming resources. This can be a threat to the scalability of the system. We need to factor the common code to avoid repetitions and improve efficiency.

Decision point

How do we factor the common code?

We introduce a new package, UbiMail, that contains the classes where we put the common code. This package forms a sort of layer that simplifies the development of the user interface. The classes in this layer and their relationship to the session and application context are shown in Figure 16.7.

Class **Manager** is a singleton that provides access to the persistent storage. It hides all the details of the access to the database through JDBC, in particular all the SQL queries are inside this class, thus making the JSPs simpler and cleaner. When the JSP container starts, an instance of **Manager** is created and a reference to it is stored in the web context (that is accessible through the variable "application" in JSP). Class **ContextListener** is responsible for this initialization (it opens a database connection). On demand the manager can load the user profiles from the database. The **User** class represents the user profiles and is responsible for opening and closing the connection to the mail server.

Decision point

How do we structure the user interface in order to allow the registration of new users?

The structure is an extension of the one defined in the previous prototype. The JSPs that make up the interface use the classes **Manager** and **User** to simplify their operation. The structure of the user interface is presented in Figure 16.8.

The upper two elements provide the tools to register a new user. **Register. html** shows a form with all the details of the profile. **Add.jsp** validates the submitted information and creates a new user profile in the database. This mechanism allows anyone to create a profile on the UbiMail system. If required, these elements can be modified to limit or regulate the subscriptions to UbiMail.

The login, main and message pages work exactly as in the previous prototype. Two new pages are used to edit the profile: **setup** and **update**. The former shows the user profile and allows its modification, the latter takes the modified profile and updates the database.

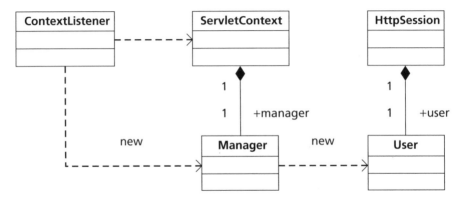

Figure 16.7 Basic access layer

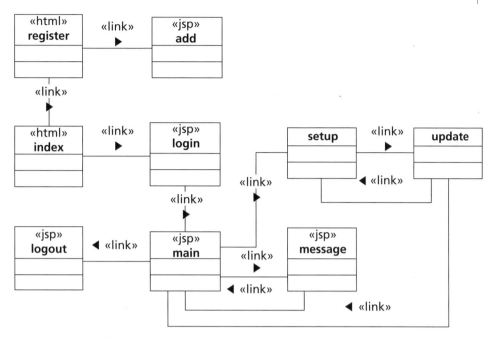

Figure 16.8 User interface structure

Decision point

What is the structure of the database?

The database must store the user profiles, which contain the information shown in Table 16.1. The database consists of a single table that stores the profile information.

16.4.3 ☐ Implementation

Class **Manager** is the main entry point to access the profiles. Its constructor receives a **Connection** to the database that contains the profiles. It provides

Table 16.1 UbiMail user profile

Field	Type	Description
Username	VARCHAR(15) PRIMARY KEY	The name used to identify the user at login
Pass	VARCHAR(20),	The password to authenticate the user
Firstname	VARCHAR(25),	The first name of the user
Lastname	VARCHAR(25),	The last name of the user
Popserver	VARCHAR(50),	The mail server name
Popuser	VARCHAR(20),	The user name used to access the mail server
Poppass	VARCHAR(20)	The password to access the mail server

the method authenticate() to verify usernames and passwords. New profiles can be created by means of the createUser() method.

```java
package UbiMail;
import java.sql.*;
public class Manager {
  private Connection connection;
  private Statement stmt;
  private String lastError=null;
  // create a mail manager using a connection to a database
  public Manager(Connection p_connection) {
    try{
      connection = p_connection;
      stmt = connection.createStatement();
    }catch(Exception e){ lastError = e.getMessage(); }
  }
  // authenticate a pair (username,password),
  // on success return the corresponding User object
  public User authenticate(String username, String password){
    User user=null;
    try{
      String query= "SELECT * FROM ubimailuser" +
                    "WHERE username='" + username +
                    "' AND pass='" + password + "'";
      ResultSet rs=stmt.executeQuery(query);
      if(rs.next())
        user = new User(rs);
      rs.close();
    }catch(Exception e){ lastError = e.getMessage(); }
    return user;
  }
  // creates a new user in the database if the username is
  // not yet in use
  public User createUser(String name){
    User user=null;
    try{
      String query = "SELECT * FROM ubimailuser" +
                     "WHERE username='" + name + "'");
      ResultSet rs=stmt.executeQuery(query) ;
      if(rs.next()){
        lastError = "User '" + name + "' already present";
      }else{
        user = new User(name);
        user.create(stmt);
      }
    }catch(Exception e){ lastError = e.getMessage(); }
    return user;
  }
```

```
  // return the description of the last error
  public String getError(){ return lastError; }
  // update the user profile
  public boolean update(User user){
    return user.update(stmt);
  }
}
```

Class User embeds the profile information; it provides two methods to open and close a connection to the mail server: openPopServer() and closePopServer(). In addition it provides getter and setter methods to access the profile parameters.

Several methods have package visibility. The constructors can load the information from a row of the database represented by a ResultSet object, or create a brand new profile with only the name.

```
package UbiMail;
import java.sql.*;
import javax.mail.*;
import java.util.Properties;
// represents a user profile
public class User {
  // profile information
  private String username;
  private String pass;
  private String firstname;
  private String lastname;
  private String popserver;
  private String popuser;
  private String poppass;
  // error message
  private String lastError;
  // mail server connection
  private Session ms;
  private Store pop;
  private Folder folder;
  // creates a user from a row in the database
  User(ResultSet rs) throws SQLException {
    username = rs.getString("username");
    pass = rs.getString("pass");
    firstname = rs.getString("firstname");
    lastname = rs.getString("lastname");
    popserver = rs.getString("popserver");
    popuser = rs.getString("popuser");
    poppass = rs.getString("poppass");
    Properties props = new Properties();
    props.setProperty("mail.store.protocol","pop3");
    ms = Session.getInstance(props);
  }
```

```
// creates a new user with a given username
User(String p_username){
  username = p_username;
  Properties props=new Properties();
  props.setProperty("mail.store.protocol","pop3");
  ms = Session.getInstance(props);
}
// updated the user profile in the database
boolean update(Statement stmt){
  try{
    stmt.executeUpdate("UPDATE ubimailuser
    SET pass='"+ pass + "'," + " firstname='" + firstname
    + "'," + " lastname='" + lastname + "',"
    + " popserver='" + popserver + "'," + " popuser='"
    + popuser + "',"       + " poppass='" + poppass + "'"
    + " WHERE username='" + username  + "'");
    return true;
  }catch(Exception e){
    lastError = e.getMessage();
    return false;
  }
}
// create a new user in the database
boolean create(Statement stmt){
  try{
    stmt.executeUpdate("INSERT INTO ubimailuser
    (username, pass, " + " firstname, lastname, popserver,
    popuser, poppass)" + " VALUES ('" + username + "',"
     + " '" + pass + "'," + " '" + firstname + "'," + " '"
     + lastname + "'," + " '" + popserver + "'," + " '"
     + popuser + "'," + " '" + poppass + "')");
    return true;
  }catch(Exception e){
    lastError = e.getMessage();
    return false;
  }
}
// open a connection to the POP server defined in the
// profile and return the default mailbox folder
public Folder openPopServer(){
  folder = null;
  try{
    pop = ms.getStore("pop3");
    pop.connect(popserver,popuser,poppass);
    folder = pop.getFolder("INBOX");
    folder.open(Folder.READ_ONLY);
```

```
    }catch(Exception e){ lastError = e.getMessage(); }
    return folder;
  }
  // close the connection with the POP server
  public void closePopServer() {
    try{
      folder.close(true);
      pop.close();
    }catch(Exception e){ }
    folder = null;
    pop = null;
  }
  // return the last error message
  public String getError(){ return lastError; }
  // getters
  public String userName(){ return username;  }
  public String firstName(){ return firstname; }
  public String lastName(){ return lastname; }
  public String popServer(){ return popserver; }
  public String popUser(){ return popuser; }
  public String popPass(){ return poppass; }
  // setters
  public void setPass(String newValue){ pass=newValue; }
  public void setFirstName(String newValue)
                                    { firstname=newValue; }
  public void setLastName(String newValue)
                                    { lastname=newValue; }
  public void setPopServer(String newValue)
                                    { popserver=newValue; }
  public void setPopUser(String newValue)
                                    { popuser=newValue; }
  public void setPopPass(String newValue)
                                    { poppass=newValue; }
}
```

Class **ContextListener** implements the **ServletContextListener** interface. This class is registered with the JSP container and is invoked whenever the application context is created or destroyed.

```
import UbiMail.*;
import javax.naming.InitialContext;
import javax.sql.*;
import java.sql.*;
import javax.servlet.*;
import java.io.IOException;
public final class ContextListener
implements ServletContextListener {
```

```
public void contextInitialized(ServletContextEvent event) {
    System.out.println("Initializing UbiMail context...");
    ServletContext context = event.getServletContext();
    try{
        InitialContext initial=new InitialContext();
        DataSource ds =(DataSource)
         initial.lookup("java:comp/env/jdbc/CloudscapeDB");
        Connection con =ds.getConnection();
        Manager mgr = new Manager(con);
        context.setAttribute("manager",mgr);
        if(mgr.getError()!=null){
          System.out.println("Manager error:"
                                      + mgr.getError());
        }
    }catch(Exception e){ e.printStackTrace(); }
    System.out.println("Completed.");
}
public void contextDestroyed(ServletContextEvent event) {
    System.out.println("UbiMail destroyed.");
}}
```

The use of a database from JSP requires some setup steps as described in Sidebar 16.3.

The application descriptor is the *web.xml* file, located in the WEB-INF folder. It provides a name for the application, then declares the Context Listener class as a listener for the application. Then it defines "index.html" as the welcome file. Finally it declares the database resource that is used to connect to the database. The welcome file is the file that is sent to the user if no specific file is requested (e.g. with the URL: http://server:8080/ UbiMail/).

```
<?xml version="1.0" encoding="ISO-8859-1"?>
<!DOCTYPE web-app
    PUBLIC "-//Sun Microsystems, Inc.//DTD Web
                                     Application 2.3//EN"
    "http://java.sun.com/dtd/web-app_2_3.dtd">
<web-app>
    <display-name>UbiMail - Ubiquitous Email</display-name>
    <listener>
      <listener-class>ContextListener</listener-class>
    </listener>
    <welcome-file-list>
      <welcome-file>index.html</welcome-file>
    </welcome-file-list>
    <resource-ref>
      <res-ref-name>jdbc/CloudscapeDB</res-ref-name>
      <res-type>javax.sql.DataSource</res-type>
      <res-auth>Container</res-auth>
    </resource-ref>
</web-app>
```

Sidebar 16.3 Database resources in JSP

The use of a database from a Java web application is more complex than the use of a JDBC connection from a normal Java program. It requires setting up a resource that will be used by the web application.

The exact configuration depends on the container and database. Here we assume the use of the Tomcat servlet and JSP container, an open source that is freely available from the Jakarta Project, http://jakarta.apache.org/. The database we use is the Cloudscape DB that is bundled with the Java 2 SKD Enterprise Edition.

First, we need to make the database jar files available to the web container. In our case we have to copy the cloudscape.jar and the RmiJdbc.jar files to the common/lib directory of Tomcat.

Then we need to declare a DataSource in the configuration of the JSP container. In our case we need to add the following fragment to the server.xml file:

```
<Resource name="jdbc/CloudscapeDB" auth="Container"
                type="javax.sql.DataSource" scope="Shareable"/>
<ResourceParams name="jdbc/CloudscapeDB">
  <parameter><name>user</name><value></value></parameter>
  <parameter><name>password</name><value></value></parameter>
  <parameter><name>driverClassName</name>
    <value>COM.cloudscape.core.RmiJdbcDriver</value></parameter>
  <parameter><name>driverName</name>
    <value>jdbc:rmi:jdbc:cloudscape:CloudscapeDB</value>
                        </parameter></ResourceParams>
```

Finally the descriptor of the application must include a reference to the resource declared in the container configuration. The web.xml file of the application contains an entry like this:

```
<resource-ref>
  <res-ref-name>
    jdbc/CloudscapeDB
  </res-ref-name>
  <res-type>
    javax.sql.DataSource
  </res-type>
  <res-auth>
    Container
  </res-auth>
</resource-ref>
```

The Cloudscape DB is based on the RmiJdbc connector, thus the database runs as a separate process. Before starting the server we need to start the Cloudscape DB with the cloudscape -start command from the bin/ directory of the J2SDKEE.

The JSP login authenticates the user and, in the case of success, redirects the user's browser to the main page; the authentication is performed by the object manager of class Manager that is registered in the application context. If the authentication is successful the user object is registered in the session context.

```
<%@ page contentType="text/html" language="java" %>
<%@ page import="UbiMail.*" %>
<%

    Manager manager = (Manager)application.getAttribute
                                              ("manager");
    String name = request.getParameter("login");
    String pass = request.getParameter("pass");
    // authenticate the user
    User user = manager.authenticate(name,pass);
    if(user!=null){
      // register the user in the session context
      session.setAttribute("user",user);
      // redirect the browser to the main page
      response.sendRedirect("main.jsp");
    }else{
      // close the session and show an error message
      session.invalidate();
      %>
      <html>
      <head><title>UbiMail - failed login</title></head>
      <body><h1>UbiMail</h1>
      Sorry user not existent or password incorrect.
      <br><i><%=manager.getError()%></i>
      <p>To try again go to <a href="index.html">
                                      login page</a>.
      </body></html>
  <%}%>
```

The JSP main displays a list of the messages, exactly as in the previous prototype. The difference lies in the way this page gets access to the mail server. In this prototype the User class mediates the access to the server and returns the main folder. As a result the JSP is much simpler. We present here only the parts that are different from the previous version.

```
<%@ page contentType="text/html" language="java" %>
<%@ page import="javax.mail.*, java.util.Properties,
                             java.util.Enumeration" %>
<%@ page import="UbiMail.*" %>
<%
    User user = (User)session.getAttribute("user");
    if(session.isNew() || user==null){
      response.sendRedirect("index.html");
      return;
    }
%>
<html>
<head><title>UbiMail - <%=user.firstName()%>
              <%=user.lastName()%>'s mailbox</title></head>
```

```
<body><h1>UbiMail</h1>
Hello <%=user.firstName()%> <%=user.lastName()%>.
<hr>[ <a href="logout.jsp">Logout</a> |
                       <a href="setup.jsp">Profile</a> ]
<h2>Your Mailbox</h2><%
  try{
      Folder folder = user.openPopServer();
      if(folder==null) throw new Exception(user.getError());
      int n = folder.getMessageCount();
      %>Contains <%=n%> messages.
      ...
      <%
      user.closePopServer();
  }catch(Exception e){
      %>UbiMail encountered an error while accessing your
                                               mailbox.
      <p><tt><%=e%></tt><%
  }
  %>
  ...
</body></html>
```

16.4.4 □ Test

The test for this prototype extends the test of the previous one with the test of the registration part.

The scenario to test is when the system is first deployed and the database contains no user profile:

■ Open the initial page and follow the link to the registration page. The browser shows the registration page that asks for the information of the user profile

■ Fill the form and click the register button. The browser shows the page that confirms the correct registration of the user

■ Go to the login page and perform the same test as in the previous prototype with the difference that this time, provided that the username and password are defined in the registration, the system already knows the profile.

16.5 ■ Prototype 3: WAP access

In this prototype an additional channel is enabled: the WAP protocol. It sits alongside the HTML interface and provides access through WAP-enabled mobile phones.

16.5.1 □ Analysis

The UbiMail system must provide access to the email messages through channels alternative to the web. The Wireless Access Protocol (WAP) is one of these. Since the WAP is intended for mobile phones the interface must show the amount of information that fits into the limited displays of these devices.

An example of the login screen on a WAP phone emulator is shown in Figure 16.9. It is the initial page; from this example the limitations of the phone screen appear evident.

The WAP interface should present the list of email messages. For each message the required information is the sender, the date and the subject.

The WAP and the HTML interfaces must be integrated seamlessly and they should share the same access point URL. Both the web and WAP browsers should be pointed to a URL such as http://my.server.com/UbiMail. This makes the setup operations on the user side as simple as possible.

16.5.2 □ Design

This prototype extends the previous one with a WAP user interface that works in parallel with the web interface. The information presented though this interface is similar, though reduced, to those offered by the previous one.

Decision point

How to integrate the WAP interface with the web interface?

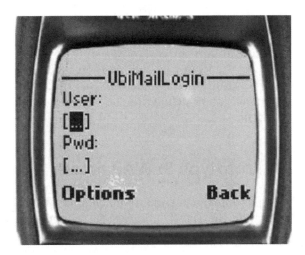

Figure 16.9 Example of WAP page

It is possible to use JSPs to generate WML content, using the content type "text/vnd.wap.wml". It is possible to use two different applications or to put all the JSPs, both for the web and for WAP, in the same application. The latter solution has the advantage of simplicity.

To have a single point of access (e.g. http://server.com/UbiMail) we need to recognize which type of browser is connected and then address it to the correct interface. We introduce a new JSP, Accept, that is responsible for recognizing the browser type. The Accept JSP then redirects the user to the web or WAP interface as shown in Figure 16.10. To identify the type of browser (HTML or WML) the Accept JSP looks into the "accept" header of the HTTP request. If the accepted content types include "text/vnd.wap.wml" we deduce that there is a WML browser, otherwise we assume it is an HTML browser.

The WAP version of the UbiMail interface is made up of pages written in WML. The initial page, index.wml, is a static page that asks the user for username and password. This information is sent to the wap_login JSP that authenticates the user, as the Login JSP in the web interface. The wap_main JSP presents the user with a list of the messages on the mail server.

16.5.3 □ Implementation

The entry point of the WAP interface is the index.wml file. It is a static WML page that prompts the user for username and password and gives control to the WAP login JSP.

```
<?xml version="1.0"?>
<!DOCTYPE wml PUBLIC "-//WAPFORUM//DTD WML 1.3//EN"
    "http://www.wapforum.org/DTD/wml13.dtd">
<wml>
  <template>
    <do type="prev"><prev/></do>
  </template>
  <card id="login" title="UbiMailLogin">
    <do type="unknown" label="Login">
```

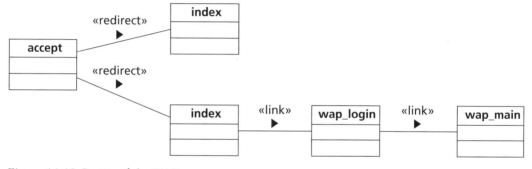

Figure 16.10 Design of the WAP access

```
        <go href="wap_login.jsp" method="post">
          <postfield name="login" value="$login" />
          <postfield name="pass" value="$pass" />
        </go>
      </do>
      <p>
        User: <input type="text" name="login"/>
        Pwd: <input type="password" name="pass"/>
      </p>
    </card>
  </wml>
```

The JSP wap_login is:

```
<%@ page contentType="text/vnd.wap.wml" language="java" %>
<%@ page import="UbiMail.*, javax.mail.*" %>
<?xml version="1.0"?>
<!DOCTYPE wml PUBLIC "-//WAPFORUM//DTD WML 1.3//EN"
      "http://www.wapforum.org/DTD/wml13.dtd">
<wml>
  <template>
    <do type="prev"><prev/></do>
  </template>
<%
    String name = request.getParameter("login");
    String pass = request.getParameter("pass");
    Manager manager = (Manager)application.getAttribute
                                                 ("manager");
    User user = manager.authenticate(name,pass);
    if(user!=null){
       session.setAttribute("user",user);
       Folder folder=user.openPopServer();
%>
  <card id="hello" title="Welcome">
    <do type="unknown" label="Messages">
      <go href="<%=response.encodeURL("wap_main.jsp")%>">
      </go>
    </do>
    <p>
      Hello <%=user.firstName()%> <%=user.lastName()%>.
    </p>
    <p align="center">
<%
      if(folder==null){
%>
    <em>Problems in contacting you mail server!</em>
<%    }else{    %>
      <%=folder.getMessageCount()%> messages in you mailbox.
```

```
<%      }
        user.closePopServer();
%>
  </p>
  </card>
<%
      }else{
        session.invalidate();
%>
  <card id="hello" title="UbiMail">
    <p>
      Sorry the user name or the password is incorrect.
    </p>
  </card>
<%}%>
</wml>
```

To provide a single point of access to both the web and WAP user interfaces we define the accept.jsp that analyses the request from the browser and redirects the browser to the correct initial page. The type of browser is identified by looking at the "accept" header.

```
<%
    String accept = request.getHeader("accept");
    if(accept.indexOf("text/html") >=0 ){
      response.sendRedirect("index.html");
      return;
    }else
    if(accept.indexOf("text/vnd.wap.wml") >=0 ){
      response.sendRedirect("index.wml");
      return;
    }
%>
Cannot serve any of the accepted formats: <%=accept%>
```

The previous JSP must be set as the welcome file in the application descriptor web.xml.

```
<web-app>
...
<welcome-file-list>
<welcome-file>accept.jsp</welcome-file>
</welcome-file-list>
</web-app>
```

16.5.4 ☐ Test

To test the system it is important to access the system via a WAP emulator (e.g. the Nokia Mobile toolkit) and possibly via a WAP phone. If the WAP emulator is installed on the same machine as the JSP container the URL to start the system is http://localhost:8080/UbiMail .

16.6 ■ Prototype 4: Mail notification

This prototype adds a new functionality to the UbiMail system: the notification of new messages via GSM Short Message Service (SMS).

16.6.1 □ Analysis

The UbiMail system must be able to notify users of the arrival of new email messages. The notification must be asynchronous, i.e. without the explicit intervention of the user.

When a new message arrives for a registered user, the UbiMail system sends an SMS message to the user mobile phone. This service is available on the GSM network. The user must provide the number of the mobile phone that will receive the notification messages.

Since the SMS messages have a cost, to keep the overall expense of notification as low as possible it is important to allow the user to select the messages of which he wishes to receive notification. The user can define a filter that selects the messages.

16.6.2 □ Design

The POP protocol does not allow asynchronous notification therefore we need to implement a mechanism to periodically check the presence of new messages on the mail server. In addition we need a class to interact with the GSM equipment.

The structure of the classes is presented in Figure 16.11. The class Notify implements the Runnable interface and runs in a separate thread; it periodically checks the email status of users that have enabled the SMS notification, and for each new message that has arrived the filter is applied. If the message is selected then it sends an SMS message to the user's mobile.

The class SMSSender takes care of interacting with the GSM equipment (see Sidebar 16.4). To communicate over the serial connection it uses the Java Comm extension that is in the javax.comm package.

The notification of new email messages requires new information to be added to the user profiles. Table 16.2 summarizes the new elements of the user profile. These fields ought to be added to the database table that store the user preferences.

16.6.3 □ Implementation

The class Notify is responsible for periodically checking the mail folders and notifying the users via SMS. It implements the Runnable interface and the

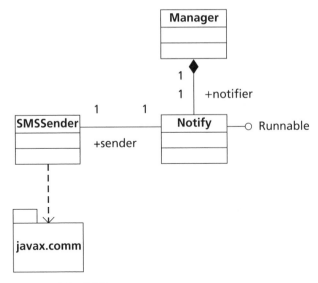

Figure 16.11 Design of the WAP access

Sidebar 16.4 GSM equipment

There are two main alternatives for interacting with the GSM network. The first option is to use a GSM mobile phone that is connected to a provider's network; the second is to use a mobile phone connected to a computer. While the first is more scalable and dependable, the second is simpler and cheaper.

Most medium- to high-level GSM phones include a modem and the ability to connect to a computer. A GSM mobile phone can be embedded in a PCMCIA card or can be connected to the computer via a serial connection (either an infrared link or a cable) or a wireless connection such as Bluetooth.

Here we will focus on the serial connection because it is relatively easy to manage and there are Java classes that encapsulate the low-level implementation details.

Java Comm is an extension to the Java runtime environment. It is designed to handle low-level communication through serial and parallel ports. It provides support for asynchronous communication. At the time of writing, the Java Comm is not yet a standard extension.

To interact with a serial port using Java Comm we need a method to write to the port and a method that handles the events issued by the port, a typical event being the availability of data.

The communication with the GSM modem is based on the AT command structure, in particular the message-sending commands are defined by the GSM 07.05 technical specification standard (ETSI 1996).

Table 16.2 Notification profile data

Name	Type	Description
sms	VARCHAR(1)	Enables/disables the notification via SMS
mobile	VARCHAR(15)	Number of mobile phones that will receive the notification
filter	VARCHAR(50)	String that must be contained in the subject or in the sender to trigger the notification

operations performed by the new thread are defined in the run() method. It creates an SMSSender object that encapsulates the details of SMS message sending. The constructor of the notifier requires a Connection to the database and the mail server sampling interval.

```java
package UbiMail;
import java.sql.*;
import javax.mail.*;
import sms.SMSSender;
class Notify implements Runnable {
  Connection conn;
  long interval;
  SMSSender sender;
  public Notify(Connection connection, long p_interval) {
    conn = connection;
    interval = (p_interval<1000?1000:p_interval);
    // too low an interval would consume all the server
    // resources
    try{
      // creates an SMSSender object used to send SMS
      // messages
      SMSSender sender = new SMSSender();
    }catch(Exception ex){
      System.out.println("UbiMail notifier,
                          Error: " + ex.getMessage());
    }
  }
  public void run(){
    try{
      while(sender!=null){ // notification loop
        Thread.sleep(interval);
        try{
         Statement stmt = conn.createStatement();
         ResultSet rs=stmt.executeQuery(
            "SELECT * FROM ubimailuser WHERE sms='Y'");
         sender.open();
         while(rs.next()){
           User user=new User(rs);
           Folder folder=user.openPopServer();
           if(folder==null) throw
            new Exception("Cannot connect to mail server.");
           int n = folder.getMessageCount();
           int newCount = folder.getNewMessageCount();
           for(int i=n-newCount; i<n; ++i){
             Message msg = folder.getMessage(i+1);
             String from = msg.getFrom()[0].toString();
             String subject = msg.getSubject();
```

```
                        if( user.filter==null || user.filter.length()==0 ||
                            from.indexOf(user.filter)>=0 ||
                            subject.indexOf(user.filter)>=0){
                          String sms = from + "> " + subject + ": ";
                          if(msg.getContentType().startsWith
                                                  ("text/plain"))
                            sms += (String)msg.getContent();
                          else
                            sms += "type: " + msg.getContentType();
                          sender.send(user.mobile,sms);
                        }
                      }
                    }
                    sender.close();
                  }catch(Exception dbe){
                    System.out.println("UbiMail notifier, Error: "
                                        + dbe.getMessage());
                  }
                  if(Thread.interrupted()) break;
                } // end notification loop
              }catch(InterruptedException e){
                // do nothing. An interrupted exception makes the
                // execution exit the loop
              }
              try{
                conn.close();
              }catch(Exception e){}
            }
          }
```

The class **Manager** instantiates a notifier object in its constructor and creates a thread that executes the notifier.

```
public class Manager {
  // ...
  public Manager(DataSource p_dataSource, long interval) {
    dataSource = p_dataSource;
    try{
      Connection conn = dataSource.getConnection();
      Statement stmt = conn.createStatement();
      Notify nf = new Notify(conn,interval);
      notifier = new Thread(nf,"UbiMailNotifier");
      notifier.start();
    }catch(Exception e){
      lastError = e.getMessage();
    }
  }
  // ...
}
```

The sampling interval for the notifier is taken by the ContextListener class from the application context.

```java
public final class ContextListener
implements ServletContextListener {
  public void contextInitialized(ServletContextEvent event) {
    ...
        Long interval =(Long)initial.lookup
                               ("java:comp/env/interval");
        Manager mgr = new Manager(ds,interval.longValue());
    ...
  }
}
```

The value of the interval attribute of the application context is set in the application descriptor contained in the web.xml file.

```xml
<web-app>
...
<env-entry>
  <env-entry-name>interval</env-entry-name>
  <env-entry-value>10000</env-entry-value>
  <env-entry-type>java.lang.Long</env-entry-type>
</env-entry>
</web-app>
```

The notification is based on the SMSSender class. It has a constructor that tries to find a serial port connected to a GSM modem. To send a message we need first to open the connection with the open() method, then to send one or more messages using the send() method, and finally close the connection with the close() method.

The communication with the modem is carried out by the method sendCmdNoCR(). This method writes to the serial port and then blocks for a given delay. In the meantime the modem sends a reply; the presence of data coming from the modem is notified asynchronously via the serialEvent() method, which reads the available data and puts it into the buffer answer. When the serialEvent() method recognizes the end of a reply or the timeout has expired the sendCmdNoCR() method is woken up and returns the content of the answer buffer.

```java
package sms;
import java.io.*;
import java.util.*;
import javax.comm.*;
// SMSSender is a class that can be used to send SMS messages
// through a mobile phone connected to a serial port.
public class SMSSender implements SerialPortEventListener {
  InputStream inputStream;
  OutputStream outputStream;
  SerialPort serialPort;
```

```java
CommPortIdentifier portId;
// bind to the first serial port attached to a GSM enabled
// modem.
public SMSSender() throws Exception {
  super();
  portId = getMobilePort();
  if(portId!=null)
    System.out.println("GSM equipment found: "
                                  + portId.getName());

  else
    throw new Exception("No mobile modem available");
}
public void finalize(){
  close();
}
// Open the connection to the mobile.
public void open() throws Exception {
  serialPort = (SerialPort) portId.open
                                  ("SMSSender", 2000);
  serialPort.setSerialPortParams(19200,
    SerialPort.DATABITS_8,
    SerialPort.STOPBITS_1,
    SerialPort.PARITY_NONE);
  inputStream = serialPort.getInputStream();
  outputStream = serialPort.getOutputStream();
  serialPort.addEventListener(this);
  serialPort.notifyOnDataAvailable(true);
}
// Close the connection to the mobile.
public void close(){
  try{
  if(serialPort != null){
    serialPort.removeEventListener();
    inputStream.close();
    outputStream.close();
    serialPort.close();
  }
  }catch(Exception e){}
  serialPort = null;
}
// Look for a serial port attached to a GSM-enable device
CommPortIdentifier getMobilePort() throws Exception {
  Enumeration portList = CommPortIdentifier.
                                  getPortIdentifiers();
  while (portList.hasMoreElements()) {
    portId = (CommPortIdentifier) portList.nextElement();
```

```java
      if (portId.getPortType() ==
                        CommPortIdentifier.PORT_SERIAL) {
        try{
          open();
          boolean result = isMobile();
          close();
          if(result){
            return portId;
          }
        }catch(Exception e){}
      }
    }
    return null;
  }
  // Check if the CE connected to the current port is GSM
  // enabled
  synchronized boolean isMobile(){
    String reply;
    sendCmd("ATV1",500); // verbose result
    sendCmd("ATQ0",500); // enables result codes
    reply = sendCmd("AT",500);
    if(reply.endsWith("OK\r\n")){ // there's an AT enabled
                                 // modem
      sendCmd("ATE0",500);
      reply = sendCmd("AT+CSMS=?",500);
                              // check for SMS capabilities
      if(reply.endsWith("OK\r\n") ||
                        reply.endsWith("+CSMS: (0,1)\r\n"))
          return true;
    }
    return false;
  }

  // Send an SMS. Method open() must have been called before.
  // @parameter dest destination address (tlf #)
  // @parameter msg the text of the message
  // (at most 160 chars)
  public synchronized String send(String dest, String msg){
    String reply;
    try {
      reply=sendCmd("AT+CSMS=0");
      //System.out.print(reply);
      reply=sendCmd("AT+CMGF=1");
      //System.out.print(reply);
      if(msg.length() > 160){
        msg = msg.substring(0,160);
      }
```

```java
      reply=sendCmd("AT+CMGS=\"" + dest + "\"",200);
      //System.out.print(reply);
      if(reply.endsWith("\r\n> ")){
        reply=sendCmdNoCR(msg + (char)27,5000);
        System.out.print(reply);
      }
      reply=sendCmd("AT+CGMI");
      System.out.print(reply);
    } catch (Exception e) {
      reply = e.getMessage();
      e.printStackTrace();
    }
    return reply;
}


// Send a command to the modem with the predefined timeout
String sendCmd(String cmd){ return sendCmd(cmd,2000);   }
// Send a command to the modem
String sendCmd(String cmd,long timeout){
    return sendCmdNoCR(cmd+"\r",timeout);}
// Send a command to the modem, and wait for the given
// timeout.
synchronized String sendCmdNoCR(String cmd, long timeout){
    String reply="";
    try{
      readAnswer=true;
      outputStream.write((cmd+"\r").getBytes());
      this.wait(timeout);
      reply=answer.toString();
      if(readAnswer){ // i.e. timed out
        readAnswer=false;
      }
      answer= new StringBuffer();
    }catch(Exception e){}
    return reply;
}
private StringBuffer answer= new StringBuffer();
private boolean readAnswer=false;

// Receive events from the serial port
public synchronized void serialEvent
                                (SerialPortEvent event) {
    switch(event.getEventType()) {
      case SerialPortEvent.DATA_AVAILABLE:
        try {
          char ch=0;
          // read the available data
```

```
        while(inputStream.available()>0)
          answer.append(ch=(char)inputStream.read());
        // check if the buffer contains a full reply..
        if(readAnswer && ch=='\n'){
          String res=answer.toString();
          if(res.endsWith("OK\r\n") ||
                              res.endsWith("ERROR\r\n") ||
          res.indexOf("+CME ERROR: ")>(res.length()-20) ||
          res.indexOf("+CMS ERROR: ")>(res.length()-20) ){
          // ..wake up sendCmdNoCR if a full reply is
          // present
              readAnswer=false;
              notify();
          }
        }
      } catch (IOException e) {}
      break;
    }
  }
}
```

16.6.4 □ Test

To test the notification we need to connect a mobile phone to the computer via a serial connection. Then we have to set up a profile with a valid mobile number and with the SMS notification enabled. At this point, sending an email message to the user should trigger the sending of an SMS message. The delay between the sending of the email and reception of the notification is given by the sum of three delays: delay of reception by the mail server, sampling interval of the notifier and delay of SMS delivery from the GSM network.

16.7 ■ Extension

The reader can extend the UbiMail system in several ways:

■ Improve the notification filter. Currently the system checks if either the sender or the subject contains a given string. This mechanism could be extended, defining multiple criteria to create more flexibility. In addition, criteria could be used to approve or to reject the notification of a message. Finally, regular expressions could be used to obtain better message matching.

■ Improve the presentation of messages. Currently only text and HTML parts of messages are shown. It should be possible to handle the other formats of multipart messages; this includes attachments that the system should allow to be downloaded.

■ Implement other internet mail protocols. Currently POP3 is the only protocol that can be used to access mail servers. It is important to be able to use the IMAP protocol as well.

16.8 ■ Assessment

Architectural model. The ubiquitous email system facilitates the access to the mail server. It is an example of broker-based architecture, where the UbiMail application plays the role of broker. It adapts the POP3 protocol, which is mail-specific and computer-oriented, to the HTML/HTTP protocol, which is general purpose and human-oriented.

Paradigm. The communication between the system and both the mail server and the clients is based on well-defined protocols. It is an example of declarative communication.

Technology. The interaction with the client through HTML/HTTP is implemented by means of the JSP technology. The interaction with the mail server through POP3 is based on the classes in the Java standard extension library.

Architecture	Multiple presentations
Context	Distributed computing. Multiple access devices.
Problem	We need access to the same information through different media and devices. As the user changes device he/she must be offered the same service according to the device's capabilities.
Forces or tradeoffs	The same service must be presented through different channels. Each device has different capabilities. The detail that can be presented depends heavily on the device capability.
Solution	Add a presentation layer for each specific device and let it select the features that can be shown on the device and organize the contents in the most suitable way. All the versions of the user interface are based on the same back-end component; they only adapt the information in the back end to specific languages/devices. In addition we need an entry point that can redirect the user to the most suitable presentation on the basis of the user's device capabilities.
Examples	As an example, using JSP to provide access to devices using different languages would yield the following structure:

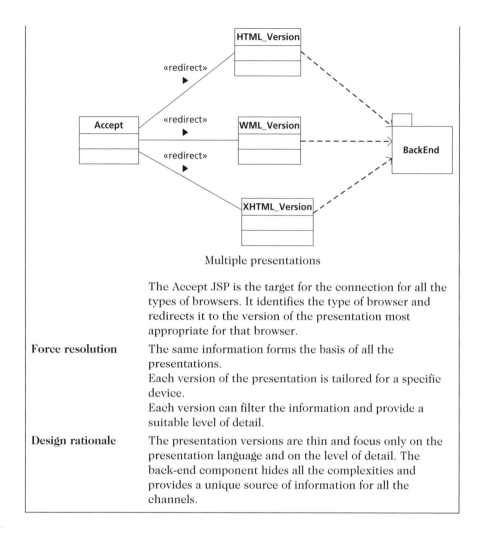

Multiple presentations

	The Accept JSP is the target for the connection for all the types of browsers. It identifies the type of browser and redirects it to the version of the presentation most appropriate for that browser.
Force resolution	The same information forms the basis of all the presentations. Each version of the presentation is tailored for a specific device. Each version can filter the information and provide a suitable level of detail.
Design rationale	The presentation versions are thin and focus only on the presentation language and on the level of detail. The back-end component hides all the complexities and provides a unique source of information for all the channels.

16.9 ■ References

Bodoff, S., Green, J. and Haase, K. (2002) *The J2EE Tutorial*, Addison-Wesley.

ETSI (1996) "GSM 07.05: Digital cellular telecommunications system (Phase 2+); Use of Data Terminal Equipment–Data Circuit Terminating Equipment (DTE–DCE) interface for Short Message Service (SMS) and Cell Broadcast Service (CBS)", July.

Gamma, E., Helm, R., Johnson, R. and Vlissides, J. (1995) *Design Patterns: Elements of Reusable Object-Oriented Software*, Addison-Wesley.

Network Working Group (1996) RFC-1939: Post Office Protocol – Version 3, May.

Nokia (2002) "AT Command Set for Nokia GSM Products", Version 1.0. May 8.

Sun Microsystems, *"Fundamentals of the JavaMail API"*, available at http://developer.java.sun.com/developer/onlineTraining/JavaMail/.

WAP Forum Specification, available at http://www.wapforum.org/what/technical.htm.

Object Frameworks

Object frameworks

17

Synthesis

Complex applications are rarely built from scratch. They are usually derived from the reuse of similar applications or parts of them. Object-oriented technology supports the concept of the object-oriented framework for the development of families of similar applications.

A framework indicates, in the software community, an integrated set of domain-specific software components (Coplien and Schmidt 1995), which can be reused to create applications, the most common examples being graphical user interfaces (Weinand and Gamma 1994).

A framework is more than a library of software components: it defines the common architecture underlying the concrete applications built on the framework (Fayad, Schmidt and Johnson 1999). Frameworks are a powerful development approach as they consist of both reusable code (the component library) and reusable design (the architecture). The interpretation of "framework" ranges from structures of classes of cooperating objects that provide, through extension, reusable basic designs for a family of similar applications (Johnson and Foot 1988), to the more restrictive view (Schmid 1995) of complete high-level components which, through customization, directly result in specific applications for a certain domain.

The fourth part of this book is dedicated to the exemplification of application framework development. This is the natural continuation of Part III where the reader has learnt how to exploit system-level reusable artifacts. Here the focus is on how to develop such artifacts.

17.1 ■ Reuse-oriented development

Systematic reuse is generally recognized as a key technology to improve the software process (Mili *et al.* 1995). In many cases object-oriented technology (OOT) is seen as an essential enabler for reuse (Kain 1994) while others argue that OOT alone does not guarantee reuse (Griss 1995).

The failure of class-library reuse is partly due to the fact that class libraries commonly restrict polymorphism to work on objects which are specializations of a class supplied with that library, and that each library provides a different, incompatible version of this top-level class. More importantly, however, the size and complexity of projects had grown significantly since the introduction of subroutine libraries, so that the design and architecture of a software program represented a large part of the development effort, and systematic reuse of design and architecture was not supported in any way.

Such reuse is more difficult than code-level reuse, since a design is not worth much in itself as a reusable artifact; the design, with its tradeoffs and consequences, must be understood by the application developer so that the necessary adaptations and changes can be performed. The challenge, therefore, was to find a good way of representing not only the design, but also the design knowledge and expertise that led to that design. This has become possible with the introduction of design patterns and application frameworks in software engineering.

An application framework may be roughly defined as a set of interacting objects that, together, realize a set of functions. The set of functions defines the area of "expertise" or "competencies" of the framework; we refer to it as the domain of the framework. A *domain* may be either a subset of the *business domain* (the problem space), or a subset of the *computing domain* (the solution space). A banking application framework, for example, implements functions with the business domain of banking. The Model–View–Controller (MVC) framework, developed for the Smalltalk language, covers a subset of the *computing domain*, and more specifically, the design domain. It does so by addressing the problem of connecting business logic with graphical user interface (GUI) logic in a way that minimizes the dependencies between the two. Other computing domain frameworks address architectural issues, and include artifacts such as middleware frameworks (e.g. CORBA, EJB and COM).

Developing frameworks for a specific application domain requires a careful requirements analysis, in order to recognize the stable entities and relationships that can be captured by reusable assets. Two complementary approaches are commonly followed by analysts: domain analysis and legacy analysis. Domain analysis consists in identifying the enduring-business themes (EBT) and processes that characterize a given business domain. Typically, an EBT is concerned with a business issue; namely, "what is being done", not "how it is being done" (Fayad, Hamu and Brugali 2000). For example, in the transportation industry, the EBT is concerned with moving material from one location to another. Legacy analysis consists in identifying common functional, architectural and implementation aspects in a family of already existing software products that have been developed in the past for the same application domain, but independently from each other. This is obtained by insulating the homogeneous parts of the those software products with regard to the driving factors of changes. The homogeneous software modules become the core components of the framework. Those changes that are required by every specific application built on the framework will then be in the periphery, since the core was based on something that has remained, and will remain, stable. Therefore, only these small external modules need to be engineered.

Although framework requirements are generally defined by an independent standards body (e.g. CORBA), a software vendor (e.g. Microsoft's MFC, COM and DCOM, FASTech's FACTORYworks, IBM's San Francisco Project, Philips' New York Project) or a systems engineering group (e.g. Motorola's CIM Baseline), at one time or other, every developer or development team has created a framework. Such frameworks often manifest themselves as undocumented or loosely documented standards for developing an application (or applications).

17.2 ■ Framework scope

Although the design principles underlying frameworks are largely independent of the application domain, we have found it useful to classify frameworks by their scope as follows:

- *Service frameworks* are plug-and-play software components that offer domain-independent functionalities such as service discovery, service configuration and data filtering. They can be easily customized for a very specific application.
- *Middleware integration frameworks* (Bernstein 1996) enhance the ability of software developers to modularize, reuse and extend their system infrastructure to work seamlessly in a distributed and heterogeneous environment where application interoperability is a major concern. Common examples include message-oriented middleware and ORB frameworks.
- *Enterprise application frameworks* (Fayad, Hamu and Brugali 2000) are structured collections of software components conceived for specific application domains: they solve most of the design and implementation problems common to the applications in that domain and are frequently built on top of a middleware framework. They address broad application domains (such as telecommunications, manufacturing, avionics and financial engineering) and are the cornerstone of enterprise business activities.

17.3 ■ Framework customization

Frameworks can be classified by the techniques used to customize them in concrete applications, which range along a continuum from white-box, grey-box to black-box frameworks.

White-box frameworks rely heavily on OO language features such as inheritance and dynamic binding in order to achieve extensibility. Existing functionality is reused and extended by (1) inheriting from framework base classes and (2) overriding predefined hook methods using design patterns such as the *Template Method* (Gamma *et al.* 1995).

Black-box frameworks support extensibility by defining interfaces for components that can be plugged into the framework via object composition. Existing functionality is reused by defining components that conform to a particular interface and integrating these components into the framework.

Grey-box frameworks avoid the disadvantages of both white-box and black-box frameworks since they have enough flexibility and extensibility, and hide unnecessary information from the application developer.

Any application framework follows an evolution in time, which is called the framework life span (Brugali, Menga and Aarsten 1997). In this life span, the basic architectural elements, which are independent from any specific application, are implemented first. Then, by generalizing from concrete applications, as stated in Roberts and Johnson (1997), the framework evolves. This evolution means that in its early stages, the framework is mainly conceived as a white-box framework (Johnson and Foot 1988). However, through its adoption in an increasing number of applications, the framework matures: more concrete components which provide black-box solutions for the difficult problems, as well as high-level objects which represent the major abstractions found in the problem domain, become available within the framework.

The components of a framework offer different levels of abstraction from the design needs found in the application domain. They are classified as elemental, basic design and domain-dependent components (Brugali, Menga and Aarsten 1999). The classification also reflects the different stages of the framework life span in which they are introduced.

- Elemental components, such as mechanisms for logical communication and concurrency, determine the language (elements of the architecture) in which the whole application will be written.
- Basic components are intermediary classes, which are fairly application independent, although they have been conceived bearing in mind a specific application domain.
- The others are domain dependent and are usually specializations of the basic components. They are the result of the adoption of the framework for the development of more and more applications and in some cases they become pluggable black boxes.

17.4 ■ Part overview

The fourth part of this book is organized into four case studies that present object frameworks characterized by different scope and customization techniques (see Table 17.1).

Chapter 18 (Recoverable applications) addresses the development of a simple framework that enables the automatic recovery of an application after a crash and the undo/redo operations of relevant state transitions. The framework is an example of service component that sits between the generic

Table 17.1 Frameworks classification based on their scope and customization
techniques

Case study	Requirements analysis	Framework scope	Framework customization
18 RECAP	Domain	Service framework	Black-box
19 MMI	Legacy	Middleware framework	White-box
20 Negotiation	Domain	Service framework	Grey-box
21 Workflow	Domain	Enterprise framework	Grey-box

software application and the file system where application states and state
changes are recorded in log files.

Chapter 19 (Multi-modal interaction framework) presents a middleware
framework that supports the development of large concurrent and distributed systems. This case study abstracts the common features that characterize distributed systems developed in Part III of this book with the aim of
building a software infrastructure that provides mechanisms and abstract
classes for remote service creation, allocation and execution.

Chapter 20 (Negotiation-based service configuration) exemplifies the
development of an agent-based service framework that enables automated
negotiation of service execution contracts between service providers and
service customers. The framework extends the multi-modal interaction
framework presented in Chapter 19.

Chapter 21 (Workflow management system) deals with the development
of a workflow management system (WMS). A WMS is an example of grey-box
enterprise framework that enacts application-specific business processes.
Customization is performed using a suitable process definition language.
Enactment consists of assigning the right task to the right person at the
right time and ensuring that it is carried out within the required deadline.
A standard interface for monitoring and controlling processes is adopted. A
proof-of-concept interface is developed making use of web-based techniques.

17.5 ■ References

Bernstein, P.A. (1996) "Middleware: A Model for Distributed System Services",
Communications of the ACM, Vol. 39, No. 2, February.

Brugali, D., Menga, G. and Aarsten, A. (1997) "The Framework Life Span", in
Communication of the ACM, October.

Brugali, D., Menga, G. and Aarsten, A. (1999) "A Case Study for Flexible Manufacturing
Systems", in *Domain-Specific Application Frameworks: Manufacturing, Net-
working, Distributed Systems, and Software Development*, Fayad, Johnson,
Schmidt (eds), John Wiley & Sons.

Coplien, J.O. and Schmidt, D.C. (1995) "Frameworks and Components", in *Pattern
Languages of Program Design*, 1–5, Addison-Wesley.

Fayad, M.E., Hamu, D. and Brugali, D. (2000) "Enterprise Frameworks Characteristics,
Criteria, and Challenges", *Communications of the ACM*, Vol. 43, No. 10, October.

Fayad, M.E., Schmidt, D. and Johnson R. (1999) *Building Application Frameworks: Object-Oriented Foundations of Framework Design*, John Wiley & Sons.

Gamma, E., Helm, R., Johnson, R. and Vlissides J. (1995) *Design Patterns: Elements of Reusable Object Oriented Software*. Addison-Wesley.

Griss, M. (1995) "Software Reuse: Objects and Frameworks are not Enough", *Object Magazine*, February.

Johnson, R.E. and Foote, B. (1988) "Designing Reusable Classes", *Journal of Object-Oriented Programming*, June.

Kain, J.B. (1994) "Making Reuse Cost Effective", *Object Magazine*, Vol. 4 No. 3, June, 48–54.

Mili, H., Mili, F. and Mili, A. (1995) "Reusing Software: Issues and Research Directions", in *IEEE Transactions on Software Engineering*, Vol. 21, No. 6, June.

Roberts, D. and Johnson, R. (1997) "Evolve Frameworks into Domain-Specific Languages", *Pattern Languages of Program Design 3*, Addison-Wesley.

Schmid, H.A. (1995) "Creating the Architecture of a Manufacturing Framework by Design Patterns", in *Proceedings of OOPSLA '95*, SIGPLAN, ACM.

Weinand, A. and Gamma, E. (1994) "ET++ – a Portable, Homogenous Class Library and Application Framework", in *Proceedings of the UBILAB '94 Conference*, Zurich.

Recoverable applications

18

Synthesis

This case study addresses the development of a simple framework that enables the automatic recovery of an application after a crash and the undo/redo operations of relevant state transitions.

The framework is an example of a service framework that sits between the generic software application and the file system where application state and state changes are recorded in log files.

The peculiarity of this case study is that the framework and the applications using it are designed independently and not influenced by each other.

- Focus: development of service components with domain-independent functionalities.
- OO techniques: reflection.
- Java features: static methods, file I/O.
- Background: basic OO design principles.

18.1 ■ Specifications

Software applications may be very complex, encompassing a number of state changes, which may finally lead to a completion state. Tracking all state changes produced by an arbitrarily complex software application during its execution may be useful for several purposes. For instance, consider the following scenarios:

- A failure occurs during the application execution. In this case, a record of all state transitions would allow restarting the computation from a stable state and recovering some of the completed steps, without having to redo parts of the work already completed.
- Part of the transition sequence has to be undone, e.g. because some external condition has changed (the user revises some input data). In this context, a record of all relevant state transitions would allow undoing or redoing specific parts of the execution.

The first scenario outlines a classical application of recovery after a failure, while the second scenario identifies the requirement of reconstructing parts of a task.

We want to develop a software framework, called RECAP, for tracking application executions that enables the design and implementation of recoverable applications, i.e. applications in which relevant state transitions may be undone or redone upon request or in case of system failures.

Since tracking all state changes produced by an arbitrarily complex application may become significantly time-consuming, thus wasting useful computation resources, our recovery framework requires the software designer to define explicitly the recoverable domain of the application to be tracked, i.e. the set of classes whose state is significant and has to be recoverable. After the recoverable domain has been defined, all operations which cause a state transition for registered classes are recorded in sequence. Hence, the evolution of an application is modelled as a continuous stream of modification operations on registered classes.

The RECAP framework should provide a variety of explicit undo/redo primitives which can be invoked explicitly by the application or under the user's control.

18.2 ■ Problem analysis

Tracking takes place only for a subset of all the objects manipulated by a software application. In particular, we call *trackable* a class whose state changes are tracked by the system, hence making it possible to undo or redo its state transitions.

State changes are usually caused by the invocation of methods, which may perform complex operations affecting several classes of the application.

The framework should offer a set of classes and interfaces that implement simple mechanisms for recording state transitions occurring in a software application. The use of these mechanisms must not affect the design of the recoverable application. Nevertheless, the use of the tracking mechanisms might affect the application's performance.

18.2.1 □ Domain models

The problem of recovering from a failure has been traditionally addressed in the field of database management systems and transaction managers. In the context of traditional transaction processing, a transaction is defined as an atomic unit of work, i.e. a sequence of database modification operations (state transitions) that have to be executed completely or not at all. If the final state in the sequence is not reached, the DBMS restores its last state before the beginning of the sequence. The atomicity property is guaranteed by appropriately registering in a log file (Hulse and Dearle 1998) the sequence of state transitions (old state–new state) caused by application data modification requests. The recovery functionality of these systems is based on the fact that all modification operations (store a value, update a value, delete a value) can be registered in a log file, by storing (in a compact form) the page containing the old and new states for each updated datum. This mechanism (called *physical recording*) guarantees that each single operation can be undone and that the pair of do/undo operations is idempotent, i.e. if needed, can be re-executed an arbitrary number of times without changing the final database state.

Physical recording is managed by reducing operations of arbitrary complexity to simple operations, i.e. operations on objects of a single class that may cause a simple state transition for a single object in the class. This recording technique is efficient when (possibly complex) computations usually cause limited changes in the system's state. If, on the other hand, quite simple operations can cause significant changes in the system's state (i.e. require recording a huge number of old state/new state pairs), this recording mechanism turns out to be inadequate.

A different approach (see, for example, Alvisi and Marzullo (1998)) to the problem of saving computation states and recovering after a failure is called *logical recording*. It mainly consists in a different way of representing complex operations, which are expressed in terms of the external events that trigger the state transition (the cause of an operation), thus reducing the need to store large amounts of information when significant changes take place in the system's state. Complex operations are recorded by simply describing how they are invoked, i.e. they are represented by their name, together with the set of actual parameters in the invocation of the operation, and a reference to the object on which the operation is invoked.

The undo and redo functions must be idempotent, i.e. the same operation can be undone or redone an arbitrary number of times, always producing the same correct state (i.e. the state before or after the operation was executed). This property is especially important in case the recovery process fails: it allows the repetition of the restart procedure an arbitrary number of times without affecting its final outcome.

18.2.2 □ Main features

The following features characterize the RECAP framework:

- *Physical recording* of an application's stable states.
- *Physical* and *logical recording* of state transitions.
- State recovers after a crash.
- Undo/redo of operations that cause state transitions.

18.2.3 □ Test

The test application implements the classical Tower of Hanoi puzzle. We are given three pegs, let's call them *source, auxiliary* and *destination*. Initially, a number of discs (usually 8 or 10) are stacked in decreasing size on the *source* peg, giving it a tower.

The objective is to transfer the entire tower to peg *destination*, moving only one disc at a time and never a larger one onto a smaller. Discs can be moved temporarily to peg *auxiliary* or back to peg *source*. The goal is to transfer all the discs using the smallest number of moves possible.

The test application displays the puzzle in a graphical user interface and allows the user to click and drag one disc at a time with the mouse in order to move it from one peg to another. The application must be recoverable, i.e. it should be possible to save its state (the position of every disc) and any state change (the user's moves), and to reconstruct the current state after a restart.

According to mythology, in the distant past, there were three pegs in Hanoi. In the very beginning, there were 64 discs of different sizes stacked on the peg *source*. By the time that all 64 discs are moved to peg *destination*, the world will end.

18.3 ■ Architecture and planning

At this stage we envisage the RECAP framework as a service component that sits between the recoverable application and persistent storage, e.g. the file system. The component offers methods to record the application's state and the sequence of state changes of the file system. In the case of application recovery, the service component loads the saved information from the file system and rebuilds the last image of the application state before the crash.

The system architecture is made up of three main subsystems as shown in Figure 18.1.

- *Application*. This represents the generic application that needs to be recoverable. It maintains the state of the application and implements the control and information flow.
- *Tracker*. This is an application-independent component and represents the core of the RECAP framework. It offers functionalities that allow the software developer to make applications recoverable.
- *Console*. This is an application-independent graphical user interface that allows the user to manage application recovery and undo/redo operations.

The development process of the RECAP framework is organized into two phases that produce two prototypes.

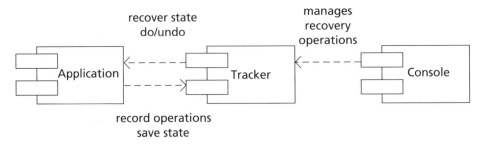

Figure 18.1 The main components of a recoverable application

- *Prototype 1: Physical recording*. The framework components implementing functionalities for state logging, state recovering, physical recording of both single and complex operations, and managing undo/redo of simple operations.
- *Prototype 2: Logical recording*. The framework components implementing functionalities for logical recording of state transitions.

18.4 ■ Prototype 1: Physical recording

The focus of this prototype is on the framework's mechanisms for physical recording of the application's state and of state changes.

18.4.1 □ Analysis

All the operations on recoverable classes taking place during the evolution of the tracked application are recorded in a journal, which is called *tracking log*, or simply log, of the application. This journal is written in a sequential fashion and records all information that may be necessary for undoing or redoing operations.

For physically recorded operations, the actual states of the affected object(s) before and after the operation are directly available in the log, hence idempotence is easily guaranteed.

These operations are considered as elementary operations, meaning that they cannot be further decomposed into simpler components. A *complex operation* or *macro operation* is a sequence of simple operations on a set of recoverable classes. Complex operations may be arbitrarily nested, hence defining a hierarchy of nested complex operations. Nesting of complex operations and interleaving of simple and complex operations is depicted in Figure 18.2, where the horizontal axis represents increasing time and the origin is the beginning of the tracked application. Simple operations are represented as × and dashed boxes delimit the boundaries of complex operations.

It may be useful periodically to define stable states, i.e. frozen states before which we are not interested in going backwards in the computation. Saving a stable state means taking a snapshot of the current state of the recoverable classes. This state becomes the initial state from which undo or redo operations may take place.

For the sake of simplicity, we limit our analysis to user interactive applications, where the evolution is determined by the sequence of external events corresponding to user stimuli as in the test application described in

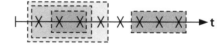

Figure 18.2 Graphical representation of simple and complex operations

Section 18.2.3. Accordingly, the definition of stable states is under the user's control and the initial state corresponds to the initial configuration of the application when no user stimuli have yet been generated. This makes the application recovery quite easy. After the application restart, any logged state change is applied starting from the initial state or the last saved stable state.

18.4.2 □ Design

The main framework component is represented by class Tracker. It acts as an intermediate layer between the recoverable application and the persistent storage. Complex applications are made up of a large number of classes that might need to be recoverable. For this kind of application it is not feasible to pass the reference to an instance of class Tracker throughout the entire application hierarchy of nested classes.

For this reason it is convenient to implement class Tracker as a container of global functions. This approach is similar to the implementation of class System of package java.lang.

Decision point

How does the tracker save the state of an application?

The java.io package offers interface Serializable. Every class implementing this interface can have its state serialized automatically, i.e. converted to a form suitable for external storage. Persistent storage of objects of serializable classes can be accomplished by passing the objects to an output stream, e.g. using a file (named trackerState.log) for the stream. Thus, every recoverable class must implement the Serializable interface.

Since an application may be made up of several recoverable classes, saving the state of the entire application means serializing all of the objects that are instances of recoverable classes. For this purpose, we need to find a way of keeping track of all the recoverable objects being created during the application's life span.

We adopt a solution that is similar to the naming mechanism of Java RMI. The Tracker class provides methods for storing and obtaining references to objects in an object registry and methods to save the state of the entire set of registered objects in persistent storage. See, for example, the following code fragment, where Target is a recoverable class.

```
public Application() {
  try {
    target = new Target();
    Tracker.bind(target, "target");
  }
  catch(Exception e) { e.printStackTrace(); }
}
```

How does the tracker restore the state of an object after a crash?

A new object is registered in the tracker registry by invoking method bind() of class Tracker. This method accepts two parameters: a reference to a trackable object and a label that identifies the object univocally. This label is always the same every time the application is restarted. When the application state is saved in a persistent storage, the state of every registered object is saved along with its associated label.

Restoring the last saved state of a recovered application is as simple as copying in every registered object the state loaded from the persistent storage associated to the same object label. For this purpose, every trackable object must implement interface Trackable which defines method restore().

How does the tracker log state changes (physical recording)?

Every method that causes a state transition in a recoverable object must invoke method record() of class Tracker before and after the state change. Method record() saves the object's current state in a log file named trackerPhysical.log. The method accepts three parameters: a reference to the recoverable object, a string that corresponds to the name of the method causing the state transition, and a label that indicates whether the state has been saved before or after the state transition. See, for example, the following code fragment, where increment() is a method of a recoverable class that modifies the value of state variable sum.

```
public void increment(int num) {
    Tracker.record(this, "increment", Tracker.BEFORE);
    sum += num;
    Tracker.record(this, "increment", Tracker.AFTER);
}
```

How does the tracker restore the application's state corresponding to the last state transition (physical recording)?

When a system crash occurs, the application needs to be restarted appropriately, by recovering the state previously reached during its execution. This is achieved by performing the following steps:

- Build the application.

- Read from the persistent storage (file **trackerState.log**) the last stable state of the application.
- Read forward the state changes log (file **trackerPhysical.log**) and redo all operations from the last stable point to the end of the log (i.e. the point where the crash occurred). At the end of this step, the correct state before the system crash is rebuilt.

Redoing an operation requires getting reference to the object that has performed the operation using its associated label and copying the state saved after the operation's execution.

The log file can be read forwards and backwards in order to perform undo and redo of single operations. For this purpose, the framework offers class TrackingConsole implementing a simple graphical interface that allows the user to move forwards and backwards the application's current state.

Decision point

How does the tracker record complex operations (physical recording)?

A recoverable class might aggregate objects of other recoverable classes. Thus, operations on the composite class (called "complex operations") might cause the execution of operations on the component objects. Tracking state changes caused by complex operations is performed in the same way as for simple operations. From a performance point of view, saving the state of a composite class is partially redundant because it includes the state of each component object.

18.4.3 □ Implementation

Interface Trackable defines two methods that every concrete subclass must implement. Method cloneTarget() instantiates a new object of the same class and initializes its state. It is used to create a copy of a trackable object when a state transition is saved. Method restore() is used to undo or redo an operation: it restores an object's *before* or *after* state.

```java
package recap;
import java.io.*;
import java.util.*;
public interface Trackable extends Serializable {
  public Trackable cloneTarget();
  public void restore(Trackable obj);
}
```

Class Entry represents the data structure used to record an object's before or after state when an operation is performed.

```java
public class Entry implements Serializable {
```

```
private Trackable target = null;
            // a copy of a recoverable object
private String targetRef;
            // the label identifying a recoverable object
private String methodName; // the name of a method
private String when;
            // a label assuming values "before" and "after"
public Entry(Trackable target, String methodName,
                                            String when) {
  this.target = target.cloneTarget();
  this.targetRef = Tracker.getObjectRef(target);
  this.methodName = methodName;
  this.when = when;
}
public Trackable getTarget() { return target; }
public String getTargetRef() { return targetRef; }
public String toString() {
  return targetRef + "." + methodName +"() - " + when;
}
}
```

Class Tracker is the service component that implements the functionalities for managing application recovery. It uses two distinct files to save stable states and state changes. The first is opened when a stable state is saved, the second when method startTracking() is invoked, i.e. when the application is started and when a new stable state is saved.

Member variable recording assumes the value true when Tracker is recording state changes and false when Tracker is redoing operations. Member variable objectList is a hash table that records the references to all the trackable objects that have been registered with method bind() along with their unique string identifiers. Member variable entrytList records the list of Entity objects loaded from the log file when the application is restarted or its operations are undone or redone.

```
public final class Tracker {
  private static int currentEntry = 0;
  private static FileOutputStream outputFile = null;
  private static ObjectOutputStream outputObject = null;
  private static Hashtable objectList = new Hashtable();
  private static ArrayList entryList = new ArrayList();
  public static final String BEFORE="before";
  public static final String AFTER="after";

  public static void startTracking() {
    try {
      outputFile = new FileOutputStream
                                  ("trackerPhysical.log");
```

```java
      outputObject = new ObjectOutputStream(outputFile);
    } catch(IOException ioe) { ioe.printStackTrace(); }
  }

  public static void bind(Trackable target, String key)
        throws Exception{
    if(objectList.containsValue(target))
      throw new RuntimeException("Object already bound");
    else if(objectList.containsKey(key))
      throw new RuntimeException("Key already in use");
    else
      objectList.put(key, target);
  }

  public static void record(Trackable target,
                      String methodName, String when){
    try {
      Entry entry = new Entry(target, methodName, when);
      outputObject.writeObject(entry);
    } catch(IOException ioe) { ioe.printStackTrace(); }
  }

  public static void saveStablePoint() {
    Tracker.startTracking();
    entryList.removeAll(entryList);
    try {
      // save the state of every registered object in the
      // log file
      FileOutputStream outputFile =
              new FileOutputStream("trackerState.log");
      ObjectOutputStream outputObject =
              new ObjectOutputStream(outputFile);
      outputObject.writeObject(objectList);
      outputObject.close();
      outputFile.close();
      currentEntry = 0;
    } catch(IOException ioe) { ioe.printStackTrace();  }
  }

  public static void restore()    {
    try {
      // loads the last saved stable point
      FileInputStream inputFile =
              new FileInputStream("trackerState.log");
      ObjectInputStream inputObject =
              new ObjectInputStream(inputFile);
```

```
        Hashtable temp = (Hashtable) inputObject.readObject();
        Iterator iterator = temp.entrySet().iterator();
        while(iterator.hasNext()) {
          Map.Entry entry = (Map.Entry) iterator.next();
          Trackable target =
                ((Trackable)objectList.get(entry.getKey()));
          target.restore((Trackable)entry.getValue());
        }
        inputObject.close();
        inputFile.close();
        // loads the saved sequence of entries
        inputFile = new FileInputStream
                                  ("trackerPhysical.log");
        inputObject = new ObjectInputStream(inputFile);
        entryList.removeAll(entryList);
        Entry entry = null;

        // builds the list of Entry objects
        while((entry = (Entry)inputObject.readObject()) != null)
          entryList.add(entry);
        inputObject.close();
        inputFile.close();
    }
    catch(Exception e) {
      System.out.println("*** end of file ***");
      currentEntry = 0;
    }
}

public static void redoUntil(int entryID) {
  if(entryID == currentEntry || entryID > entryList.size())
    return;
  // in the case of undo operation, the application state
  // is restored to the last saved stable state;
  if(entryID < currentEntry)
    restore()
  // it redos all of the operations loaded from the log
  // file up to the current entry
  while(entryID > currentEntry){
    Entry entry = (Entry) entryList.get(currentEntry);
    Trackable target = (Trackable) objectList.get
                                  (entry.getTargetRef());
    target.restore(entry.getTarget());
    currentEntry++;
  }
}
```

```
    // looks for a registered object in objectList and
    // returns its label identifier
    public static String getObjectRef(Object obj) {
      Iterator iterator = objectList.entrySet().iterator();
      Map.Entry entry = null;
      while(iterator.hasNext()) {
        entry = (Map.Entry) iterator.next();
        if(entry.getValue().equals(obj))
          return (String) entry.getKey();
      }
      return null;
    }
    // this method is used to display the list of registered
    // operations
    public static String[] getEntryList() {
      String list[] = new String[entryList.size()];
      Entry entry;
      for(int i=0; i < entryList.size(); i++) {
        entry = (Entry) entryList.get(i);
        list[i] = entry.toString();
      }
      return list;
    }
  }
```

18.4.4 □ Test

The test case described in Section 18.3.3 is implemented by three classes:
class **Tower**, class **Hanoi** and class **Game**. Class **Tower** represents the simplest
recoverable objects of the applications, i.e. the three pegs with the stacked
discs. It implements methods pull() and push() that remove and add a single
disc from and to the peg respectively and the methods defined in interface
Trackable.

```
  package hanoi;
  import recap.*;
  import java.io.*;
  public class Tower implements Trackable {
    public static int DIM = 10; // the total number of disks
    int queue[] = new int[DIM];
                        // the set of discs stacked on the peg
    int first = 0;
                        // the first free position on the peg.
    DrawingArea drawingArea = null;
                        // the reference to the GUI
    public void init(int numBlocks) {
      if(numBlocks > DIM)
        numBlocks = DIM;
```

```java
    for(int i=0; i < numBlocks; i++)
      queue[i] = numBlocks - i;
    first = numBlocks;
  }
  public void setGUI(DrawingArea drawingArea){
    this.drawingArea = drawingArea;
  }
  int getBlock(int pos) {
    if(pos > DIM || pos <= 0) return 0;
    return queue[pos-1];
  }
  int sizeOfFirst() {
    if(first == 0) return 0;
    return queue[first-1];
  }
  public Integer pull() {
    // records the state of this tower before the execution
    // of method pull()
    Tracker.record(this, "pull", Tracker.BEFORE);
    // pull the first disc from the peg.
    if(first == 0) return new Integer(0);
    int size = queue[first-1];
    queue[first-1] = 0;
    first - ;
    drawingArea.drawingPanel.repaint();
    // records the state of this tower after the execution
    // of method pull()
    Tracker.record(this, "pull", Tracker.AFTER);
    return new Integer(size);
  }
  public void push(Integer size) {
    // records the state of this tower before the execution
    // of method push()
    Tracker.record(this, "push", Tracker.BEFORE);
    // push a disc on top of the first disc
    if(first == DIM) return;
    queue[first] = size.intValue();
    first++;
    drawingArea.drawingPanel.repaint();
    // records the state of this tower after the execution
    // of method push()
    Tracker.record(this, "push", Tracker.AFTER);
  }
  public void restore(Trackable obj) {
    this.first = ((Tower) obj).first;
    for(int i=0; i < DIM; i++)
      this.queue[i] = ((Tower) obj).queue[i];
  }
```

```java
    public Trackable cloneTarget() {
      Tower clone = new Tower();
      clone.restore(this);
      return clone;
    }
    public String toString() {
      String result = "";
      for(int i=0; i < 10; i++)
        result += queue[i]+" ";
      return result;
    }
  }
```

Class Hanoi represents a complex recoverable object, i.e. the container of the three Tower objects. Method move() causes a state transition and thus its invocations must be registered.

```java
  public class Hanoi implements Trackable {
    Tower[] towers = new Tower[3];
    DrawingArea drawingArea = null;
    public void init() {
      try {
        towers[0] = new Tower();
        towers[1] = new Tower();
        towers[2] = new Tower();
        towers[0].init(10);
        // registers the three Tower objects with three
        // different labels
        Tracker.bind(towers[0], "tower_1");
        Tracker.bind(towers[1], "tower_2");
        Tracker.bind(towers[2], "tower_3");
      }
      catch(Exception e) { e.printStackTrace(); }
    }
    // moves a disc between two pegs
    public void move(String from, String to) {
      int f = towers[Integer.parseInt(from)].sizeOfFirst();
      int t = towers[Integer.parseInt(to)].sizeOfFirst();
      if(f >= t && t != 0)
        return;
      // records the state of this object before
      // the execution of method move()
      Tracker.record(this, "move", Tracker.BEFORE);
      towers[Integer.parseInt(to)].push(
            towers[Integer.parseInt(from)].pull() );
      drawingArea.drawingPanel.repaint();
      // records the state of this object after
      // the execution of method move()
      Tracker.record(this, "move", Tracker.AFTER);
    }
```

```
  public void restore(Trackable obj) {
    for(int i=0; i < 3; i++)
      towers[i].restore( ((Hanoi)obj).towers[i] );
  }
  public Trackable cloneTarget() {
    Hanoi clone = new Hanoi();
    clone.towers[0] = new Tower();
    clone.towers[1] = new Tower();
    clone.towers[2] = new Tower();
    clone.restore(this);
    return clone;
  }
}
```

Class **Game** represents the application's top level. It creates and initializes the test application and activates the tracking process.

```
public class Game {
  TrackingConsole console = null;
  DrawingArea drawingArea = null;
  Hanoi hanoi = null;
  public Game() {
    try {
      // activates the tracking process
      Tracker.startTracking();
      console = new TrackingConsole();
      hanoi = new Hanoi();
      // registers the Hanoi instance
      Tracker.bind(hanoi, "hanoi");
      hanoi.init();
      drawingArea = new DrawingArea(hanoi);
    }
    catch(Exception e) { e.printStackTrace(); }
  }
  /**Main method*/
  public static void main(String[] args) {
    new Game();
  }
}
```

Figures 18.3(a, b, c) show three snapshots of the graphical user interface during the tracking process. The right-hand side of each image depicts the tracking console that allows the user to save a stable state, to restore a saved stable state, and to redo and undo single operations.

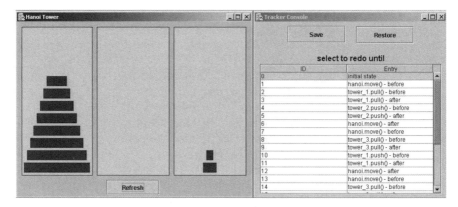

Figure 18.3(a) The Tower of Hanoi configuration corresponding to a saved stable state

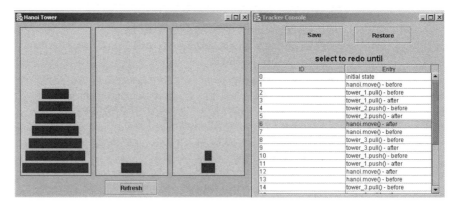

Figure 18.3(b) The Tower of Hanoi after the first re-execution of complex operation move()

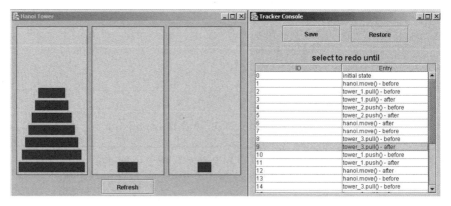

Figure 18.3(c) The Tower of Hanoi after the re-execution of simple operation pull(). Count the number of discs!

18.5 ■ **Prototype 2: Logical recording**

The focus of this prototype is on the framework's mechanisms for logical recording of application state changes.

18.5.1 ☐ **Analysis**

For logical recording, only the characteristics of the invocation of the operation are recorded. This mechanism is extremely efficient because does not require storing the object state before and after the operation execution, but it prevents a straightforward cancellation or repetition of the last operation.

Undo/redo will then require the reconstruction of a stable state of the application from which to proceed forward, reconstructing operations by re-executing them. In this case, provided that the recoverable domain represents in a complete way the execution environment of the application, idempotence is guaranteed, since we always undo/redo starting from the same stable state. If instead the recoverable domain only represents a portion of the execution environment of the application, the idempotence property is lost.

Periodically defining stable states is particularly important for logical recording, since it allows the definition of reference points from which logical operations can be re-executed.

18.5.2 ☐ **Design**

We simply need to add more functionalities to class Tracker in the form of new methods that handle state changes, transitions and recovey.

Decision point

How does the tracker log state changes (logical recording)?

Every operation that causes a state transition in a recoverable object must invoke, only once during its execution, method record() of class Tracker. Method record() saves the operation's signature in a log file named trackerLogical.log, i.e. the label of the recoverable object, the name of the method that causes the state transition, the list of parameter types and the list of argument values. For this purpose, we need to assume that all of the argument values are instances of serializable classes.

See, for example, the following code fragment, where increment() is a method of a recoverable class that modifies the value of state variable sum.

```
public void increment(Integer num) {
   Tracker.record(this, "increment", Class[]
{Integer.class},
                  new Object[] {num});
   sum += num.intValue();
}
```

Decision point

How does the tracker restore the application's state corresponding to the last state transition (logical recording)?

As for physical recording, the last stable state is restored and all the subsequent state transitions re-applied, i.e. all the operations that cause the state transitions are redone. This is achieved using the reflection mechanism. Reflection exploits the information stored in the log file to generate the same external events (method invocations) that caused state transitions in the objects of the recoverable domain.

It is important to note that the tracking process needs to be disabled during the recovery phase. In fact, when logical tracking is performed, the redo of an operation causes the re-execution of the entire method and, therefore, the recording of its invocation. Actually, transactional systems do record undo and redo operations in the log file but, for the sake of simplicity, we prefer to disregard this functionality.

Decision point

How does the tracker record complex operations (logical recording)?

Every operation of a recoverable class can be tracked using the logical recording mechanism, but for every specific recoverable application the program developer should choose whether to track complex or simple operations. In fact, tracking a complex operation and its component simple operations makes the undo and redo operations non-idempotent. During the normal evolution of an application, the execution of a complex execution causes the execution of all the nested simple or complex operations. Thus, tracking the top-level complex operation is enough to re-execute it and its component operations during the recovery phase. Conversely, tracking all complex and simple operations causes multiple re-executions of the same operation, making the application's state inconsistent.

18.5.3 □ Implementation

The implementation of the second prototype requires the extensions of class Entry and class Tracker in order to support operations' logical recording. In particular, array "parameters" and "arguments" are added to the definition of class Entry in order to store all the information that defines a method invocation. Method invoke() uses reflection to re-execute the saved operation.

```
package recap;
import java.io.*;
import java.lang.reflect.*;
public class Entry implements Serializable {
  private Trackable target = null;
                    // a copy of a recoverable object
  private String targetRef;
                    // the label of a recoverable object
  private String methodName;
```

```
  private String when = null; // "before" or "after"
  private Class[] parameters=null;
                              // the list of parameter types
  private Object[] arguments=null;
                              // the list of argument values
      . . .
  public Entry(Trackable target, String methodName,
                  Class[] parameters, Object[] arguments) {
    this.methodName = methodName;
    this.targetRef = Tracker.getObjectRef(target);
    this.parameters = parameters;
    this.arguments = arguments;
  }
  // use reflection to invoke a method on a target object
  public Object invoke(Object target) {
    Object result = null;
    try {
      Class c = target.getClass();
      Method m = c.getMethod
                          (this.methodName, this.parameters);
      result = m.invoke(target, this.arguments);
    } catch (Exception e) { System.out.println(e); }
    return result;
  }
}
```

Class Tracker has two new member variables that are used to enable and disable the tracking process and to select the tracking type (logical or physical).

```
public final class Tracker {
      . . .
  private static boolean tracking = false;
  private static boolean logicalRecording = false;
  public static void setLogicalRecording(boolean logical) {
    logicalRecording = logical;
  }
  public static boolean isLogicalRecording() {
    return logicalRecording;
  }
  // opens the tracking log
  public static void startTracking() {
    try {
      if(logicalRecording)
        outputFile = new FileOutputStream
                                    ("trackerLogical.log");
```

```java
    else
      outputFile = new FileOutputStream
                              ("trackerPhysical.log");
    outputObject = new ObjectOutputStream(outputFile);
    tracking = true;
  } catch(IOException ioe) { ioe.printStackTrace(); }
}
// records the signature of a method causing a state change
public static void record(Trackable target,
                 String methodName, Class[] parameters,
                 Object[] arguments) {
  if( ! tracking)
    return;
  try {
    Entry entry = new Entry(target, methodName,
                           parameters, arguments);
    outputObject.writeObject(entry);
  } catch(IOException ioe) { ioe.printStackTrace(); }
}
// loads the last saved stable point and the sequence of
// operations
public static void restore()    {
  try {
        ...
    if(logicalRecording)
      inputFile = new FileInputStream
                              ("trackerLogical.log");
    else
      inputFile = new FileInputStream
                              ("trackerPhysical.log");
    inputObject = new ObjectInputStream(inputFile);
    entryList.removeAll(entryList);
    Entry entry = null;
    while((entry = (Entry) inputObject.readObject())
                                              != null)
      entryList.add(entry);
  } catch(Exception e) {
    System.out.println("*** end of file ***");
    currentEntry = 0;
  }
}
// applies state changes until the execution of operation
// "entryID"
public static void redoUntil(int entryID) {
  if(entryID == currentEntry || entryID > entryList.size())
    return;
```

```
    if(entryID < currentEntry)
      restore();  // restores the last saved stable state
    tracking = false;  // disables the tracking process
    while(entryID > currentEntry){
      Entry entry = (Entry) entryList.get(currentEntry);
      Target target = (Trackable)
                     objectList.get(entry.getTargetRef());
      if(logicalRecording)
        entry.invoke(target);
      else
        target.restore(entry.getTarget());
      currentEntry++;
    }
    tracking = true; // enables the tracking process
  }
}
```

18.5.4 □ Test

We need to test the logical recording functionalities in two scenarios: logical recording of simple operations and logical recording of complex operations.

Figure 18.4 shows a snapshot of the puzzle application, where the tracking console displays the sequence of simple operations performed on the three instances of class Tower. The code below exemplifies logical recording of pull() and push() methods invocation of class Tower.

```
package hanoi;
import recap.*;
import java.io.*;
public class Tower implements Trackable {
       . . .
  public Tower() { }
```

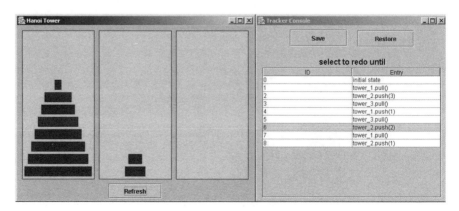

Figure 18.4 The Tower of Hanoi after the re-execution of simple operation push().

```
  public Integer pull() {
    Tracker.record(this, "pull", null, null);
    if(first == 0)
      return new Integer(0);
    int size = queue[first-1];
    queue[first-1] = 0;
    first - ;
    drawingArea.drawingPanel.repaint();
    return new Integer(size);
  }
public void push(Integer size) {
    Tracker.record(this, "push", new Class[] {Integer.class},
                  new Object[] {size});
    if(first == DIM)
      return;
    queue[first] = size.intValue();
    first++;
    drawingArea.drawingPanel.repaint();
  }
}
```

The second scenario tests logical recording of complex operations, i.e. of method move() in class Hanoi. Figure 18.5 shows the list of performed operations.

```
public class Hanoi implements Trackable {
  . . .
  public Hanoi() { }
  public void move(String from, String to) {
    int f = towers[Integer.parseInt(from)].sizeOfFirst();
    int t = towers[Integer.parseInt(to)].sizeOfFirst();
    if(f >= t && t != 0)
      return;
```

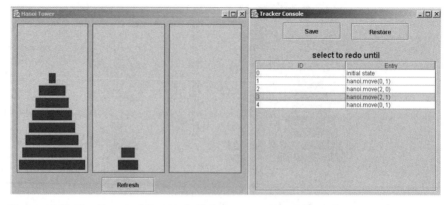

Figure 18.5 The Tower of Hanoi after the re-execution of simple operation move()

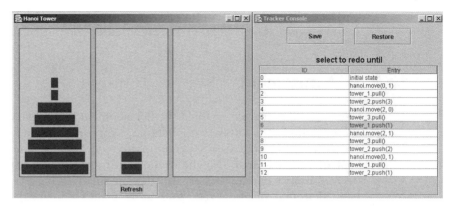

Figure 18.6 The Tower of Hanoi in an inconsistent state.

```
Tracker.record(this, "move", new Class[] {String.class,
               String.class}, new Object[] {from, to});
towers[Integer.parseInt(to)].push(
               towers[Integer.parseInt(from)].pull() );
drawingArea.drawingPanel.repaint();
  }
}
```

Figure 18.6 shows an inconsistent configuration of the Tower of Hanoi puzzle resulting from the re-execution of operations recorded in the log file when logical recording of both complex and simple operations is enabled.

18.6 ■ Extension

The reader can extend the framework in several ways:

- Consider the problem of tracking operations that return a value. Is it necessary to log the return value?
- Add more sophisticated and efficient undo/redo functionalities. Is it necessary to recover from the last saved stable state in order to undo operations in the case of physical recording? Is it possible to undo a few operations and then continue normal execution? Should the log file record that some operations have been undone?
- Address not only user interactive applications, but also autonomously running applications. This requires the definition of more complex recovery procedures: when the application restarts, it must recover the last stable state, reapply all the subsequent state changes, and then continue its execution autonomously.
- Address concurrent applications. This requires solving synchronization problems for concurrent read and write operations on the log file.
- Adopt the framework to make recoverable some of the case studies discussed in previous chapters, such as Chapter 3 (Scheduler), Chapter 4

(Classifier), Chapter 9 (Manufacturing work cell), Chapter 10 (Mobile robot exploration), Chapter 14 (Supermarket operation support system).

18.7 ■ Assessment

The case study has exemplified the development of a framework that tracks the evolution of a software application, supports the undo and redo of its state transitions, and allows its automatic recovery after a crash.

Requirements analysis. The framework requirements have mainly been derived from a careful analysis of the domain. Two basic approaches have been identified: *physical recording* and *logical recording*.

Framework scope. The RECAP framework is a typical example of a service framework. It offers functionalities that are not tailored to any specific application domain, but instead support the development of any application that requires recovering functionalities.

Framework customization. The framework is offered in the form of black-box component that does not need to be customized. Any application developed with the RECAP framework simply delegates to it the recording of execution states and transitions.

Idiom	Global functions
Context	Service components are software modules that simplify the access to and the exploitation of global resources, such as a file system, a database, the network.
Problem	Complex software applications are usually structured as hierarchies of components and subcomponents. Service components offer functionalities that cut across this inclusion hierarchy. The problem is that of implementing interactions between a service component and a large number of an application's components.
Forces or tradeoffs	Information hiding simplifies software development and enhances maintenance and reuse. Objects interact only through their interfaces, which make functionalities visible and hide data structures and implementation. When objects at different levels of the inclusion hierarchy need to access the same resource or functionality, the reference to the component offering it must be passed to all of the objects across the inclusion reference.
Solution	Implement service components as classes with static methods and static member variables. Such methods and variables belong to the class itself, rather than to specific objects. Static methods may be simply accessed through the class name, thus preventing the need to pass a reference to a class instance throughout the application's inclusion hierarchy.

Examples	The following code shows the implementation of three classes. Class Service represents a service component that offers static method execute(). Class Father and Child make a simple inclusion hierarchy.

```java
public class Counter {
  private static int value = 0;
  public static void increment() { value++; }
}
public class Child {
  public void doService() {
    Counter.increment();
    . . .
  }
}
public class Father {
  private Child child;
  public void doService() {
    child.doService();
    . . .
    Counter.increment();
  }
}
```

Force resolution	Static methods behave like global functions. They are accessible from every level of an application's inclusion hierarchy. Information hiding is enforced since they modify data confined in a single class.
Design rationale	The relationship between the service component and the components that use it is implemented as the relation between a class definition and a set of objects.

18.8 ■ References

Alvisi, L. and Marzullo K. (1998) "Message Logging: Pessimistic, Optimistic, Causal, and Optimal", *IEEE Transactions on Software Engineering*, Vol. 24, No. 2, February, 149–159.

Hulse, D. and Dearle A. (1998) "Lumberjack: A Log-structured Persistent Store", in *Proc. of Eighth Int. Workshop on Persistent Object Systems (POS-8)*, Tiburon, California, 187–198.

Multi-modal interaction framework

19

Synthesis

This case presents a middleware framework that supports the development of large concurrent and distributed systems.

In Part II, Part III and Part IV of this book we have developed a number of software applications that simulate or are structured as distributed systems. They address two typical application domains, i.e. control systems (Chapters 9, 10, 11 and 13) and information systems (Chapters 14, 15 and 16) and are usually structured as client–server systems: server components offer services to remote client components.

This case study abstracts the common features that characterize those distributed systems with the aim of building a software infrastructure that provides mechanisms for remote service creation, allocation and execution.

- Focus: separation of commonalties and variabilities in a family of similar applications; factorization of common functionalities and features; design of a reusable framework.
- OO techniques: abstraction, generalization, inheritance.
- Java features: Sockets, Remote Method Invocation.
- Background: the requirements analysis builds on the specifications of most of the previous case studies.

19.1 ■ Specifications

Distributed systems are networks of distributed software components (in the literature they are sometimes referred to as "agents", but we prefer to call them "control modules") that manage local resources (such as manufacturing equipments, knowledge bases, computational facilities, etc.), carry out problem-solving plans autonomously, exchange information with other control modules, and delegate to them the execution of specific services.

Internet-based distributed systems are large open systems that can dynamically scale up when new services (e.g. web-control of a mobile robot for outdoor surveillance) and new interconnections (e.g. business relationships across enterprise boundaries) become available. In this scenario, hand-held devices, such as personal digital assistants (PDAs), smart phones, and car navigators, are likely to replace traditional desktop computers as the preferential access point to internet services.

While developing distributed systems, our experience is that many design problems are recurrent and have similar solutions in different applications. Basically, distributed systems development requires decomposition into subsystems or control modules, which share resources and communicate in complex patterns of interaction in order to achieve a common objective.

The case studies addressed in previous chapters represent our past design experience and domain knowledge. Our goal now is to reuse that experience and knowledge in order to build an internet-based software framework. The framework is intended to simplify the development of open distributed systems by providing mechanisms, abstract classes and customizable building blocks to support the interconnection of distributed resources. It must enforce well-known (de facto) standards for data visualization (HTML, WML), communication protocols (TCP/IP, HTTP, WAP), and inter-process communication (Remote Procedure Call, Sockets). We call it the "multi-modal interaction" (MMI) framework.

19.2 ■ Problem analysis

The MMI framework is a typical system infrastructure that consists of well-defined software architecture and a library of reusable software components. The key feature of the MMI framework is the distributed object model, which defines how the generic component controls local resources and how it interacts with remote resources.

Three main aspects characterize the distributed object model of the MMI framework:

- Control modules are active objects that perform multiple activities simultaneously and manage concurrent access to shared resources.
- Control modules are collaborative objects that synchronize their activities with those of other control modules.
- Control modules are distributed objects that interact with one another by exchanging information through the internet.

19.2.1 □ Multi-task execution

In Chapters 9, 10 and 11 we developed three applications that simulate real control systems. All of them exemplify control applications that build on one of two basic execution models or on a mix of them, namely the event-based and the process-based execution models.

In Chapter 9 (Manufacturing work cell) the AGV uses a finite capacity buffer to transport semi-finished pieces and executes transport missions on demand. Requests for transport services are received asynchronously, but the AGV can execute only one mission at a time. When the AGV is busy, mission requests are queued.

In Chapter 10 (Mobile robot exploration) the onboard controller coordinates the activities of the physical devices in order to perform complex tasks such as obstacle avoidance. It receives commands from the remote controller, decomposes complex tasks into sub-tasks, and delegates their execution to the robot's devices. Each device performs its tasks autonomously.

In Chapter 11 (Car parking) the ticket dispenser interacts with both the car and the controller by receiving commands and raising events.

Another case study that is relevant for our analysis was described in Chapter 15 (Geographic information system). The data browser manages the simultaneous access of multiple users to the same set of databases.

19.2.2 □ Multi-mode synchronization

Autonomous control modules communicate with one another in order to cooperate. The need to cooperate induces synchronization requirements among their activities.

In OO programming interactions between two objects are implemented as operations on one of the two: the object that performs the operations is called the "server", while the object that requests an operation and uses its results is called the "client". The case studies described in previous chapters exemplify a variety of interaction patterns among control modules playing the role of server and those playing the role of client. We can classify client–server interactions in three categories: *synchronous*, *asynchronous* and *deferred synchronous interactions*.

In Chapter 13 (Supervisory control and data acquisition system) the supervisory console allows the user to change the paint colour. When the user sets the new tonality, the supervisory console issues a command to the mixer controller, which performs a sequence of operations (e.g. close the spray pump, open the drain pump, open the colour pumps, etc.). The supervisory console is synchronized with the mixer controller since it remains in the tonality setting state until the mixing process is completed. Similar examples can be found in Chapter 14 (Supermarket operation support system) and Chapter 15 (Geographic information system).

In Chapter 11 (Car parking) we structured the access control system as a collection of software modules organized in a hierarchy of control layers. A higher-level control module (the car, the controller), acting as a client, integrates lower control modules, which act as servers (the physical devices). In order to avoid visibility loops between control modules at different layers, clients and servers communicate using two different mechanisms: the clients send commands to the servers according to the caller–provider paradigm; the servers notify clients of state changes according to the broadcaster–listener paradigm. This is an example of asynchronous interaction: the controller issues the command that requests the stopping bar to rise and continues its execution; when the stopping bar notifies that its current state is "up", the controller may be performing some other activities. A similar example can be found in Chapter 9 (Manufacturing work cell).

In Chapter 10 (Mobile robot exploration) the remote controller issues a sequence of commands to the onboard controller and subsequently verifies that they have been executed or some anomalous situation occurred. This is an example of deferred synchronous interaction.

19.2.3 ☐ **Multi-protocol communication**

As the computational resources provided in user devices (e.g. mobile phones) can vary considerably and may not satisfy the resource requirements of complex communication platforms like Java RMI, the MMI framework should enable the development of control modules that support the most appropriate communication mechanisms and protocols from a number of alternatives such as TCP Sockets and HTTP connections. In previous case studies all of these communication protocols were exploited to build distributed systems.

In Chapter 13 (Supervisory control and data acquisition system) the control modules and the supervisory console use Java RMI to invoke methods on remote objects.

In Chapter 14 (Supermarket operation support system) the counter terminals and the central server communicate using TCP Sockets.

In Chapters 15 (Geographic information system) the client is an applet that communicates with the GIS application server through a TCP Socket connection.

In Chapters 16 (Ubiquitous email) HTTP users read their emails using a variety of client devices connected to the remote server through the internet. Depending on the type of device, different communication protocols are used (e.g. HTTP or WAP).

19.2.4 ☐ **Domain models**

A middleware framework for distributed computing consists of an integrated set of service components that allow distributed systems to operate together. Typically, middleware frameworks offer at least the following services:

- Distributed event management supports dynamic notification of events raised by remote objects.
- Location-transparent access to remote objects allows distributed objects to cooperate regardless of their network location, of the operating platforms where they are executed, and possibly of their implementation language.
- Distributed object location allows client objects to determine at run time which server objects offer the functionality they need. Client and server objects can appear and disappear on the network dynamically.
- Persistency and transaction management supports persistent storage, access to distributed data, data replication and data consistency.

Using a middleware framework consists in developing end-user applications by delegating the execution of common functionalities to middleware services. The following middleware frameworks are commonly used to build large-scale distributed systems.

Java 2 Enterprise Edition (J2EE) (Sun Microsystems 2000) is a middleware framework specifically designed for developing enterprise applications. It builds on the *Enterprise Java Beans* (EJB) component-based technology, whose basic concept is the EJB Container, a database management application that provides persistence and transaction services to the enterprise beans. There are two types of enterprise beans. Session beans offer services on demand to the container's clients and are usually stateless. Entity beans represent data maintained in a database and are persistent. The J2EE platform is structured as three-tier architecture. In reality, the middle tier is made up of two distinct but tightly coupled tiers: the web tier and the business tier.

- The client tier typically consists of a web browser or a standalone application that displays information and collects data from the users. Web clients interact through the HTTP protocol with the web tier exchanging XML data, while standalone clients interact with the EJB containers of the business tier through the RMI mechanism.
- The web tier manages the dynamic content creation of the web pages available to the web clients. Servlets map JavaBeans components to the HTML presentation format.
- The business tier hosts the EJB components that implement application-specific business logic. It represents the core J2EE infrastructure implementing system-level services such as transaction management, concurrency control and security.
- The server tier builds on the J2EE Connector Architecture, which is the bridge between the business tier and heterogeneous enterprise information systems such as enterprise resource planning, mainframe transaction processing and database systems.

The *Common Object Request Broker Architecture* (CORBA) (Vinoski 1997) is a standard for distributed middleware defined by the Object Management Group (OMG) (www.omg.org), a consortium of more than 700 organizations including software industry leaders such as Sun, HP, IBM, Microsoft and Rational. This architecture has reached a good level of maturity and is now implemented in more than ten commercial products.

The basic component of the architecture is the object request broker (ORB), which should be installed on each connected host. The ORB uses the stub–skeleton mechanism for remote communication between client and server objects. The stub and the skeleton of a server object are generated at compile time from a declarative specification of the server's interface in the language-neutral interface definition language (IDL). The interface describes which methods the server object supports, which events the object can trigger, and which exceptions the object raises. The server object can be implemented in any programming language (C, C++, Java, etc.). The ORB installed on the server side is in charge of translating the incoming IDL service requests from remote clients into the server's method invocations.

The IDL supports the declaration of only basic type arguments, which have to be passed to a remote server. The connection between the stub and the skeleton is established using the remote procedure call (RPC) mechanism.

The ORB supports location transparency, as it provides the client with a reference to the server object regardless of its network location. The client-side ORB dispatches service requests to the server-side ORB transparently. Since CORBA can be implemented using different technologies, the Internet Inter-ORB Protocol (IIOP) defines the standard communication protocol for inter-vendor ORB compatibility.

The ORB supports the control of the threading policy used by the servers, such as one-thread-per-request and one-thread-per-object. This threading capability is at the basis of recent CORBA extensions towards a real-time ORB.

Microsoft.NET (Thai and Lam 2001) is a new technology for developing distributed systems. It borrows many successful concepts from the Java world and from CORBA in order to achieve interoperability of heterogeneous applications. The following four aspects characterize the .NET framework:

- The Common Type System (CTS) is an object model that extends the previous COM and DCOM models with the goal of supporting multiple language software development.
- The Intermediate Language (IL) is an object-oriented language that conforms to the CTS. Various Microsoft and third-party language compilers (for C++, Java, etc.) generate code in the IL language (e.g. Microsoft VisualStudio.NET).
- The Common Language Infrastructure (CLI) is a run time environment (similar to the Java Virtual Machine) that executes code compiled in the IL language.
- The .NET Software Development Kit (SDK) is an object-oriented collection of reusable components. It provides run time hosts for the CLI for a variety of execution platforms. Internet Explorer is an example of a run time host. It also supports the development of customer run time hosts.

The essence of the Microsoft proposal is the possibility of compiling existing code and new code written in the programmer's preferred language. The resulting applications can interoperate with class libraries and components written in different languages using the .NET run time environment. The *.NET Remoting* service allows applications to interact over the internet using binary encoding where performance is critical, or XML encoding where interoperability with heterogeneous applications is essential. Similar to Java RMI, it is based on the stub–skeleton model: the stub (called proxy) is created at run time using the metadata published by the server.

19.2.5 ☐ **Main features**

The following features characterize the MMI framework:

- *Reusability*: the framework offers a library of reusable components to build autonomous control modules, which are the building blocks of a distributed system.

■ *Flexibility*: control modules execute multiple concurrent tasks and offer services to other control modules. They interact with each other according to a variety of synchronization modes and communication protocols.

■ *Maintainability*: the framework allows the incremental development of control modules, whose capabilities can be extended by adding new types of task and communication protocols.

19.2.6 □ Test

We need to develop a test application using the library components of the MMI framework. For the sake of simplicity, the test application is a small client–server system that demonstrates the correct behaviour of the framework components with regard to the main features described above.

■ The client is a graphical user interface that displays a jogging track. The track is made up of a graph of lay-bys where the runner can rest. The user can select the path that the runner will follow repeatedly and the runner's speed. A path is a sequence of adjacent lay-bys.

■ The server is the manager of the jogging track. Since many runners can be on the track simultaneously, it guarantees that every lay-by is occupied by only one runner at a time. When a runner is going to move towards a lay-by that is currently occupied, the server stops the runner until the lay-by is free.

The client can be a standard application or an applet, or even an HTML page that offers a textual representation of the jogging track and of the position of each runner.

19.3 ■ Architecture and planning

The system architecture is made up of three main subsystems as described in Figure 19.1. Control module is the basic component of the MMI framework that is specialized for each distributed system in a collection of server components and a collection of client components. Clients and servers inherit all the mechanisms and features to handle multiple tasks concurrently, to synchronize their activities and to communicate through the internet.

The development process of the MMI framework is organized into three phases that produce three prototypes.

■ *Prototype 1: Synchronous communication*. The components library enables the development of multi-task control modules and allows them to interoperate using Java RMI. The test application exemplifies synchronous and deferred-synchronous communication between client and server.

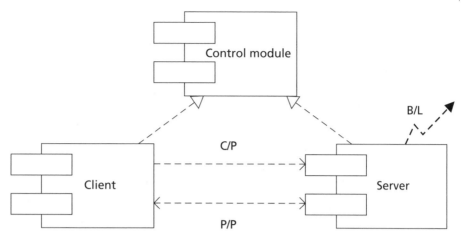

Figure 19.1 The system architecture

- *Prototype 2: Asynchronous communication.* The interaction between client and server is asynchronous. The server notifies the client of relevant events.
- *Prototype 3: Web communication.* The library of components implements the mechanisms that allow client and server to interoperate using sockets. The client side of the test application is an applet or a servlet that supports remote access to the server from a web browser.

19.4 ■ Prototype 1: Synchronous communication

The focus of this prototype is on the multi-task execution model and on the synchronous and deferred-synchronous communication models. Remote control modules communicate via Java RMI.

19.4.1 □ Analysis

The central component of the MMI framework is the autonomous control module that executes multiple tasks concurrently, coordinates access to shared resources, and allows remote clients to exploit its services through the internet.

Similar requirements were analysed in previous case studies. In particular, Prototype 3 of Chapter 15 (Geographical information system) deals with multi-clients' remote access to a shared collection of thematic databases, while Prototype 2 of Chapter 13 (Supervisory control and data acquisition system) exemplifies the use of Java RMI for the interconnection of remote control modules. Chapter 10 (Mobile robot exploration) and Chapter 11 (Car parking) present two different execution models.

19.4.2 □ **Design**

Control module architecture is inspired by the EJB model, which introduces the distinction between component (the Java Bean) and container (the component server). We have already adopted this solution in Prototype 3 of Chapter 15 where we had to manage the concurrent access of remote clients to the GIS databases.

Decision point

How does the control module manage the execution of multiple concurrent tasks?

The framework offers two abstract classes to support multiple concurrent tasks: DActivity and DProcess. A DActivity object represents an independent sequential thread of execution belonging to a unique DProcess owner, embeds the dynamic specification of its task, and has internal data.

The DActivity class has to be redefined for every concrete specification that implements the logic of a control service. DProcess is the base class of every control module. It encapsulates a collection of DActivity objects and has to be redefined in order to encapsulate specific resources. Figure 19.2 shows the class diagram that depicts the architecture of the control module. The right-hand side of the figure indicates the framework classes, while the left-hand side indicates their customization for a given application.

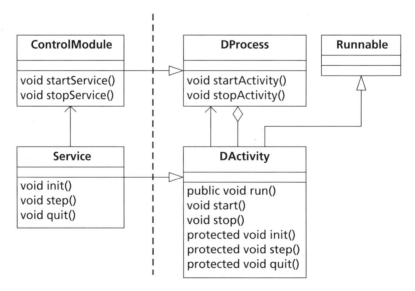

Figure 19.2 The basic architecture of a control module

Decision point

How does the control module support multiple synchronization modes?

Concrete control modules extend class DProcess by implementing specific interface methods that clients can invoke to request an activity's execution. If the communication between the client and the control module is synchronous, the client invokes a method that returns only when the activity is terminated. This situation is represented in Figure 19.3 (left-hand side). The remote interaction between supervisory console and mixer controller described in Prototype 3 of Chapter 13 is an example of synchronous communication.

If the communication is deferred synchronous, when the client requests an activity's execution it immediately receives back a reference to the activity object and uses it for subsequent interactions with the activity (see Figure 19.3 right-hand side).

We will deal with asynchronous communication in Prototype 2.

Decision point

How do remote control modules communicate and cooperate?

The MMI framework implements the client–server communication paradigm between remote control modules using the RMI mechanism.

Class DActivity and DProcess extend java.rmi.UnicastRemoteObject to give remote access to their methods. Every subclass of DActivity implements application-specific interfaces that client objects use to handle service execution. Figure 19.4 shows class MyService that specializes class DActivity and implements method doMyService() of interface MyServiceInterface. Similarly, class MyServer extends DProcess and implements method startMyService() of

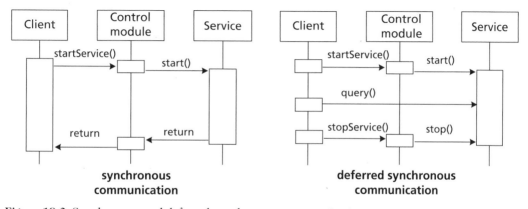

Figure 19.3 Synchronous and deferred synchronous communication

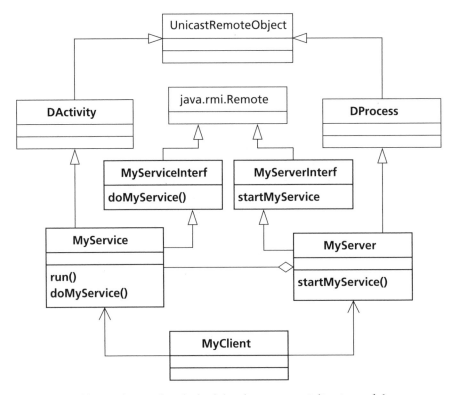

Figure 19.4 Classes depicted with thick borders are specializations of the framework classes

interface MyServerInterface. Both interfaces extend interface java.rmi. Remote. When a remote client invokes this method, an instance of MyService is created within MyServer and is registered as a remote object with the Naming.bind() mechanism of RMI. The URL of MyService object is returned to the client that uses it to get a reference to the remote service.

19.4.3 □ Implementation

Class DActivity is the superclass of every remote control service. It implements methods to set and get the URL of the service, to start and stop it and to execute it as an independent thread of control. Every concrete service should implement three basic methods: init() is invoked when the service is created, step() is invoked repeatedly while the service is running, quit() is invoked before the service terminates its execution.

```
package mmi;
import java.rmi.*;
import java.rmi.server.*;
import java.util.*;
public abstract class DActivity
```

```
                extends UnicastRemoteObject
                implements Runnable {
protected String name = "";
                // this name is assigned by DProcess
protected String address = "";
                // the IP address of the hosting machine
protected DProcess process;
protected Thread thread;
private boolean alive = false;
public DActivity(DProcess process)
                throws java.rmi.RemoteException {
  this.process = process;
}
// this method is invoked by class DProcess
// when the activity is started
void setURL(String name, String address) {
  this.name = name;
  this.address = address;
}
// returns the URL of this activity
public String getURL()
                { return "//" + address + "/" + name; }
// repeats the invocation of method step
public void run() {
  init();
  while(alive)
    step();
  quit();
}
// starts the thread of this activity
public void start() {
  if(alive) return;
  thread = new Thread(this);
  alive = true;
  thread.start();
}
// stops the thread of this activity
public void stop() {
  if(! alive) return;
  alive = false; // stops the thread
  try {
    if(Thread.currentThread() != thread)
      // this activity is not stopping itself
      // thus waits for thread to die
      thread.join();
  } catch(InterruptedException ie) { ie.printStackTrace();
}
```

```
        }
        // the following methods should be overriden in every
        // subclass
        public void init() {}
                        // executed when the activity is started
        public void step() {}
                        // executed while the thread is alive
        public void quit() {}
                        // executed before the activity is stopped
    }
```

Class DProcess is the superclass of every control module. It implements methods to register the control module in the RMI registry and methods to start and stop control services. Every concrete control module will have its own specific resources and will implement methods to allow its activities to access them concurrently.

```
public class DProcess extends UnicastRemoteObject {
    private String name;     // name of this process
    private String address;  // IP address of the host
    private int ID = 0;      // used for activity identifiers
    // list of running activities
    private ArrayList activityList = new ArrayList();
    public DProcess(String address, String name)
                    throws java.rmi.RemoteException {
        this.address = address;
        this.name = name;
        try { // Registers the process with RMI
            Naming.rebind(name, ((DProcess)this) );
        } catch(Exception e) { e.printStackTrace(); }
    }
    // This method can be invoked only by subclasses of
    // DProcess, which implement specific methods for the
    // creation and execution of their activities. It returns
    // the activity's URL in the case of succesful activation,
    // null otherwise
    protected String startActivity(DActivity activity) {
        try {
            activityList.add(activity);
            activity.setURL(this.name + "_A" + (++ID), address);
            // Registers the activity
            Naming.rebind( activity.name, activity );
            activity.start();
            return activity.getURL();
        } catch(Exception e) { e.printStackTrace(); }
        return null;
    }
```

```
// This method can be invoked only by subclasses of
// DProcess, which implement specific methods for the
// termination of their activities.
protected void stopActivity(String activityURL) {
  Iterator iterator = activityList.iterator();
  while(iterator.hasNext()) {
    DActivity activity = (DActivity) iterator.next();
    if(activity.getURL().equals(activityURL)) {
      try {
        activity.stop();
        activityList.remove(activity);
        Naming.unbind(activity.name);
      } catch(Exception e) { e.printStackTrace();}
      return;
    }
  }
}
```

19.4.4 ☐ Test

In order to test the functionalities of the framework classes, we implement a simple client–server distributed application that exemplifies multi-client interaction. Figure 19.5 shows a screenshot of the graphical interface and of the command line. The server manages the representation of a jogging park made up of lay-bys connected via tracks. A client application is a graphical interface that allows the user to select a path, i.e. a sequence of lay-bys, and that animates a runner on that path. Each lay-by can be occupied by only one runner at a time. The server manages the concurrent access to shared lay-bys.

The server and the client applications (instances of class Server and Client in Figure 19.6) are implemented as control modules that run on different hosts and communicate through the internet.

Figure 19.5 A screen shot during the test case execution. Copyright © 2005 Sun Microsystems, Inc. All rights reserved. Reproduced by permission of Sun Microsystems, Inc.

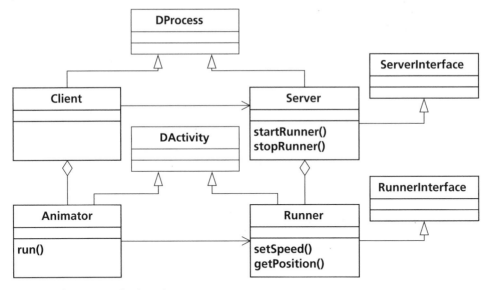

Figure 19.6 The test case's class diagram

Every client control module executes a single activity (instance of class Animator in Figure 19.6) that animates one runner. This is not a limitation of the framework. In fact, it is possible to have a single client control module that executes several activities simultaneously. The server is a control module that executes one activity (instance of class Runner in Figure 19.6) for each remote user who wants to go jogging in the park.

The communication between client activities and server activities is deferred synchronous. When a new instance of class Animator is created it gets an RMI reference to a new instance of class Runner. The Runner object is initialized with the path and speed selected by the user. Repeatedly it moves the runner's position forward along its path. When the next lay-by is occupied it waits until it is empty. The Animator object queries the Runner object at fixed intervals of time in order to get the runner's current position and visualize it on the graphical interface.

```
package jogging.server;
import java.rmi.*;
import mmi.*;


public interface ServerInterface
                    extends java.rmi.Remote {
  public String startRunner(int path[])
                throws java.rmi.RemoteException;
  public void stopRunner(String activityURL)
                throws java.rmi.RemoteException;
}
```

```
public class Server extends DProcess
                    implements ServerInterface{
  private String cells[] = {"", "", "", "", "", "", "", ""};
  public Server(String address, String name)
                throws java.rmi.RemoteException {
    super(address, name);
  }
  // moves the position of runner "id" to the cell number
  // "pos" when it is empty
  public synchronized void next(String id, int pos) {
    try {
      while(! cells[pos].equals(""))
        wait(); // the cell is not empty
      for(int i=0; i<cells.length; i++)
        if(cells[i].equals(id)) {
          cells[i] = "";
          break;
        }
      cells[pos] = id;
      notifyAll(); // wakes up the activities moving toward
                   // this cell
    } catch(InterruptedException ie) {}
  }
  // overrides method stopActivity in class DProcess
  public void stopActivity(String activityURL) {
    super.stopActivity(activityURL);
    // removes from path the id of activity
    for(int i=0; i < cells.length; i++)
      if(cells[i].equals(activityURL)) {
        cells[i] = "";
        break;
      }
  }
  public String startRunner(int path[])
        throws java.rmi.RemoteException{
    return startActivity(new Runner(this, path));
  }
  public void stopRunner(String activityURL)
        throws java.rmi.RemoteException {
    stopActivity(activityURL);
  }
public interface RunnerInterface
        extends java.rmi.Remote {
  public void setSpeed(int percent)
        throws java.rmi.RemoteException;
  public int getPosition()
        throws java.rmi.RemoteException;
}
```

```
public class Runner extends DActivity
                    implements RunnerInterface {
  private int path[];
                // the set of lay-bys on the runner's track
  private long delay; // one step's duration
  private long maxDelay = 1000;
                                // one step's maximum duration
  private int currentPosition = 0;
  private int currentStep = 0;
  public Runner(DProcess server, int path[])
         throws java.rmi.RemoteException {
    super(server);
    this.path = path;
    this.delay = maxDelay;
  }
  // every "delay" milliseconds the runner moves to the next
  // cell
  public void step() {
    try {
      Thread.sleep(delay);
      ((Server) process).next(this.getURL(),
                                      path[currentStep]);
      currentPosition = path[currentStep];
      currentStep++;
      if(currentStep == path.length) currentStep = 0;
    } catch(InterruptedException ie) { ie.printStackTrace(); }
  }
  // sets the duration of a transition between two cells
  public void setSpeed(int percent)
         throws java.rmi.RemoteException {
    this.delay = maxDelay - 80 * percent;
  }
  // returns the ID of the cell currently occupied by the
  // runner
  public int getPosition() throws java.rmi.RemoteException {
    return currentPosition;
  }
}
package jogging.client;
import mmi.*;
import jogging.server.*;
public interface ClientInterface extends java.rmi.Remote {}
public class Client extends DProcess
                    implements ClientInterface {
  public ServerInterface server;
                            // reference to the remote server
```

```java
  public Client(int path[], String address, String name,
                                          String serverURL)
              throws java.rmi.RemoteException {
    super(address, name);
    try {
      // gets a reference to the remote server and
      // starts an Animator service
      server = (ServerInterface) Naming.lookup(serverURL);
      startActivity(new Animator(this, path));
    } catch(Exception e) { e.printStackTrace(); }
  }
}
public interface AnimatorInterface extends java.rmi.Remote {}
public class Animator extends DActivity
                      implements AnimatorInterface {
  private PathFrame pathFrame = new PathFrame(this);
                          // the GUI
  private ServerInterface server;
                          // reference to the remote server
  private RunnerInterface runner;
                          // reference to the remote service
  private String runnerURL = null;
                          // URL of the remote service
  private int path[];
                          // runner's sequence of lay-bys
  private long refresh = 100;
                          // refresh interval in milliseconds
  public Animator(Client c, int path[])
                      throws java.rmi.RemoteException{
    super(c);
    this.path = path;
  }
  // this method requests the remote server to start a
  // "runner" service; it gets the service's URL which is
  // used to create a reference to the remote service
  public void init() {
    try {
      runnerURL = ((Client) process).server.startRunner(path);
      runner = (RunnerInterface) Naming.lookup(runnerURL);
    } catch(Exception e) { e.printStackTrace(); }
  }
  // this is invoked by the run() method of class DActivity
  // repeatedly; every "refresh" milliseconds it gets the
  // runner's current position from the remote service
  // "runner" and displays it in the graphical interface.
```

```
  public void step() {
    try {
      pathFrame.setPosition(runner.getPosition());
      thread.sleep(refresh);
    } catch(Exception e) {e.printStackTrace(); }
  }
  // requests the remote server to terminate the "runner"
  // service
  public void quit() {
    try {
      ((Client) process).server.stopRunner(runnerURL);
    } catch(RemoteException re) { re.printStackTrace(); }
  }
  // requests the remote server to change the runner's speed
  public void setSpeed(int percent) {
    try {
      runner.setSpeed(percent);
    } catch(RemoteException re) {re.printStackTrace();}
  }
}
```

19.5 ■ Prototype 2: Asynchronous communication

The focus of this prototype is on the asynchronous communication between remote control modules.

19.5.1 □ Analysis

In open distributed systems the communication between remote control modules is often structured according to the broadcaster–listeners (B–L) paradigm (see Section 8.8), which gives control modules the ability to broadcast and listen to events. The broadcaster does not know the identity of its listeners, which might change over time. Conversely, the clients that want to be notified when an event is raised must know the identity of the server that broadcasts that event.

In previous case studies we developed a few event-driven systems, such as the manufacturing work cell (Chapter 9) and the car parking control system (Chapter 11). In particular, Prototype 2 of Chapter 11 shows how to use class Observable and interface Observer of package java.util (see Sidebar 8.1, page 181) to build a standalone application that implements the B–L paradigm.

Now our goal is to extend the MMI framework in order to support the B–L paradigm in a distributed setting, i.e. to allow autonomous control modules to exchange events through the internet.

19.5.2 □ **Design**

CORBA supports two distinct approaches called the "push model" and the "pull model". The push model gives the broadcaster the responsibility of notifying the remote listeners when an event is raised. The pull model gives the listener the responsibility of pulling events from the broadcasters periodically.

We want the MMI framework to support the push model, since it is the seamless evolution in a distributed setting of the Observer–Observable model described in Sidebar 8.1 (page 181).

Decision point

How does the control module support asynchronous communication?

The MMI framework uses the Java RMI mechanism to implement the B–L communication paradigm. This is achieved by implementing new classes and interfaces that resemble those described in Sidebar 8.1. Figure 19.7 shows the new interfaces DObservable and Observer, which extend the java. rmi.Remote interface, class DEvent, which implements the java.io.Serializable interface in order to allow distributed clients and servers to exchange events over the internet, and class DSubscription, which records the association between a remote observer of an activity and an event that the activity may notify.

Interface DObservable defines the addObserver() method which is implemented in class DActivity. Remote clients register themselves as observers of a DActivity object by passing their own URL address to addObserver() along

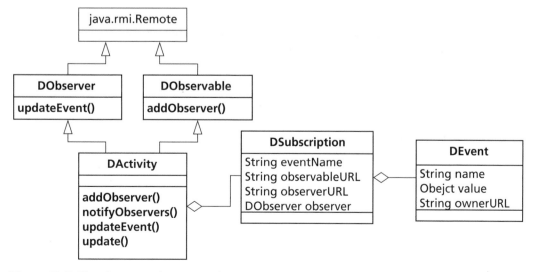

Figure 19.7 The classes implementing the B–L communication paradigm

with the name of the event they want to listen to. This method creates a new instance of class DSubscription and inserts it into the list of observers. In order to be registered as observers, remote clients must implement the updateEvent() method of interface DObserver.

Observable servers notify events to their remote observer clients according to the push model by invoking method notifyObservers() of class DActivity. This method looks for registered observers in its DSubscription list and invokes their remote method updateEvent().

Since DActivity objects can play the roles of both observable and observer, we extend class DActivity in order provide a standard implementation of method updateEvent(): it creates a temporary thread that invokes the abstract method update(), which should be implemented in every subclass of DActivity.

Please note how important is to use a temporary thread in method updateEvent(). This approach decouples the remote observable service from the actual execution of the observer's update() method. In fact, the update() method might be a complex and time-consuming procedure that must be executed by the observer's thread of execution. If we did not follow this approach, the update() method of every registered observer would be executed by the observable service itself.

19.5.3 □ Implementation

The implementation of the class diagram depicted in Figure 19.7 reuses part of the code written for Prototype 1 of Chapter 9 (Manufacturing work cell) and for Prototype 1 of Chapter 11 (Car parking).

Class DEvent represents the generic event that is notified by a distributed control module to its observers. The broadcaster control module is the owner of the event and is identified by its URL.

Class DSubscription records the association between an event, an observer and an observable. The observer's URL is used to obtain an RMI reference of the observer control module.

Class DActivity is extended in order to implement the methods defined in interface DObserver and interface Observable.

```java
package mmi;
import java.io.*;
import java.rmi.*;


public class DEvent implements Serializable{
  public String name;  // the name of the event
  public Object value; // the data associated with the event
  public String ownerURL;
                    // the process that activates this event
  public DEvent(String name, String ownerURL, Object value) {
    this.name = name;
    this.ownerURL = ownerURL;
```

```java
      this.value = value;
  }
}
class DSubscription {
  private String eventName;
                    // the name of the observed event
  private String observableURL;
                    // the URL of the observable activity
  private String observerURL;
                    // the URL of the observer activity
  private DObserver observer;
                    // a reference to the observer activity
  public DSubscription(String observerURL, String eventName,
                    String observableURL){
    this.observerURL = observerURL;
    this.eventName = eventName;
    this.observableURL = observableURL;
    try { // gets a reference to the remote observer
      this.observer = (DObserver) Naming.lookup(observerURL);
    } catch (Exception e) {  e.printStackTrace(); }
  }
  // notifies the remote observer
  public void notifyObservers(DEvent event) {
    if( (eventName.equals(event.name) ||
        eventName.equals("any")) &&
        observableURL.equals(event.ownerURL) )
      try {
        observer.updateEvent(event);
      } catch(RemoteException re) { re.printStackTrace(); }
  }
}
public interface DObservable extends java.rmi.Remote {
  public void addObserver
                    (String observerURL, String eventName)
        throws java.rmi.RemoteException;
}
public interface DObserver extends java.rmi.Remote {
  public void updateEvent(DEvent event)
        throws java.rmi.RemoteException;
}

public abstract class DActivity extends UnicastRemoteObject
        implements Runnable, DObservable, DObserver {
        . . .
  // the list of subscriptions
  private ArrayList subscriptions = new ArrayList();
```

. . .

```
    public void addObserver(String observerURL,
                                          String eventName)
        throws java.rmi.RemoteException {
      subscriptions.add(new DSubscription(observerURL,
                      eventName, this.getURL()));
    }
    // This method is invoked by subclasses of DActivity when
    // state transitions occur
    public void notifyEvent(DEvent event) {
      for(int i=0; i < subscriptions.size(); i++)
        ((DSubscription) subscriptions.get(i)).
                                          notifyEvent(event);
    }
    // This method is invoked by remote observable activities
    // to notify events
    public void updateEvent(final DEvent event)
          throws java.rmi.RemoteException {
      Thread thread = new Thread() {
        public void run() {  update(event);   }
      };
      thread.start();
    }
    // this is executed when an observed activity raises an
    // event; it should be overridden in every subclass
    public void update(DEvent event){}
  }
```

19.5.4 □ Test

Class Runner and class Animator must be extended in order to test the implementation of the distributed B–L paradigm described above. In particular, method step() of class Runner invokes method notifyObservers() of class DActivity to notify event NEXT whenever the runner changes position, while method update() of class Animator wakes up the thread when event NEXT is notified. Method init() of class Animator subscribes to event NEXT of the remote Runner activity to be notified of any new position.

```
import mmi.*;
// public interface RunnerInterface extends java.rmi.Remote {
public interface RunnerInterface extends DObservable {
  public void setSpeed(int percent)
                            throws java.rmi.RemoteException;
  public int getPosition() throws java.rmi.RemoteException;
}
```

```java
public class Runner extends DActivity implements
RunnerInterface {
    . . .
  // every "delay" milliseconds the runner moves forward to
  // the next cell and notifies the remote observers the new
  // position
  public void step() {
    try {
      . . .
      this.notifyObservers(new DEvent("NEXT", this.getURL(),
                           new Integer(currentPosition)));
    } catch(InterruptedException ie) { ie.printStackTrace(); }
  }
}

public interface AnimatorInterface extends DObserver {}

public class Animator extends DActivity
                      implements AnimatorInterface {
  private Object lock = new Object();
  private DEvent lastEvent = null;
    . . .
  public void init() {
    try {
      // gets a reference to the remote activity and
      // subscribes to event "NEXT"
      runnerURL = ((Client) process).
                                      server.startRunner(path);
      runner = (RunnerInterface) Naming.lookup(runnerURL);
      runner.addObserver(this.getURL(), "NEXT");
    } catch(Exception e) { e.printStackTrace(); }
  }
  public void update(DEvent event){
    lastEvent = event;
    synchronized(lock) {
      // notifies activities that have invoked the
      // waitEvent() method
      lock.notify();
    }
  }
  public void step() {
    try { // sleeps until the new position is notified
      synchronized(lock) {
        lock.wait();
      }
      pathFrame.setPosition(((Integer)lastEvent.value).
                                              intValue());
```

```
        } catch(Exception e) { e.printStackTrace(); }
    }
}
```

19.6 ■ Prototype 3: Web communication

The focus of this prototype is on the extension of the control module model in order to provide support for multi-protocol communication.

19.6.1 □ Analysis

Client applications might use different technologies to access the services of a remote control module. Web browsers use applets or active HTML pages, mobile phones use midlets or WML pages, desktop applications visualize data in complex graphical interfaces.

The MMI framework should allow the development of control modules that support a variety of communication mechanisms and protocols such as TCP Sockets and HTTP connections. The goal is to improve reusability and versatility of control modules in order to avoid the need to implement multiple versions of the same service for different types of client application.

19.6.2 □ Design

We basically need to find a way to implement the synchronous and asynchronous communication paradigms using different communication mechanisms instead of Java RMI.

Decision point

How does the control module support socket-based communication?

The new solution should not affect the way control modules implement and execute services or synchronize with remote clients. The simplest solution requires implementing a specific activity that acts as a bridge between the RMI mechanism used by the control modules and the Socket mechanism used by remote clients. Figure 19.8 depicts the class diagram that describes two new framework components: class DSocketListener, class DParserInterface, and class DParser. Class MyParser extends DParser

Class DSocketListener extends DActivity and is in charge of listening to incoming service requests on a specific port. Every control module should activate an instance of this service in order to provide clients with a socket access to its services. When a connection request is received, the DSocketListener object creates an instance of class DSocketActivity, which implements method update() of the DObserver interface. It delegates a

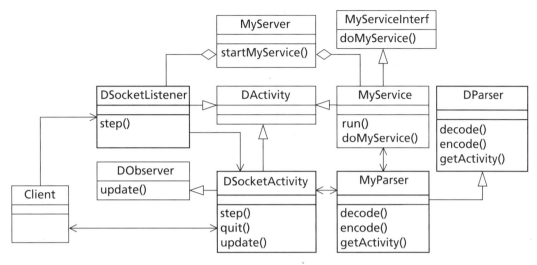

Figure 19.8 The framework components needed to access remote services through Sockets

concrete implementation of class DParser (e.g. MyParser) to translate incoming socket messages into service method invocations and to serialize service events. Simple clients like applets running inside a browser can thus access remote services using Sockets.

Figure 19.9 shows the interaction diagram that illustrates three phases of the socket-based communication between a control module and its remote clients.

■ Phase 1: Client sends a request for socket connection to DSocketListener, which creates a DSocketActivity instance that will manage the socket-based

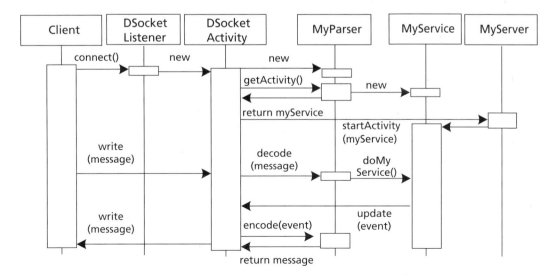

Figure 19.9 The interaction diagram that illustrates the socket-based communication

communication between Client and MyServer. In particular, DSocketActivity receives a message with the name of a requested service, creates the corresponding DParser object, which decodes the message and starts MyService.

■ Phase 2: Client writes a message on the socket including a command to MyService. DSocketActivity receives the message, decodes the command and invokes the corresponding method of MyService.

■ Phase 3: DSocketActivity is listening to events raised by MyService. When it notifies an event, DSocketActivity encodes the event in a socket message and sends it to Client.

Decision point

How does the control module support HTTP-based communication?

Since the HTTP protocol does not support "push" operations, the remote client, i.e. a web browser running on a desktop computer or on a mobile phone, cannot be notified of events raised by the control module. Thus, we need first to extend the MMI framework in order to add support for the pull model of event notification. When Client requests the activation of a service (e.g. MyService) it specifies whether it supports the push model or not. If it does not support this model, class DSocketActivity catches all the events raised by MyService and registers them in an event list. Client is in charge of querying DSocketActivity periodically about registered events.

The bridge between the HTTP communication protocol and the TCP/IP Socket mechanism is implemented using a servlet component that needs to be implemented for each specific client application. The servlet runs inside a web server, implements the basic doPOST() and doGET() methods to interact with the remote web browser, and communicates with DSocketActivity through sockets. Whenever the web browser refreshes the HTTP connection with the web server, the servlet writes a query message on the socket. DSocketActivity parses the message, extracts registered events from the event list, and composes them into a response message that it writes back to the servlet. Finally, the servlet composes a new web page according to the received events and forwards it to the web browser.

19.6.3 ☐ Implementation

The implementation of class DSocketListener, class DSocketActivity and DParser is quite simple. It should be noted that method step() of class DSocketActivity uses reflection to create an instance of the parser associated with the requested service and that the DSocketActivity thread dies when the remote client closes the socket. When this occurs, it catches a SocketException and invokes method stopActivity() of class DProcess. Finally, method quit() of class SocketActivity, closes the socket's input/output buffers and stops the service.

```
package mmi.sockets;
import java.net.*;
import java.io.*;
import java.util.*;
import mmi.*;
public class DSocketListener extends DActivity
                                implements DObserver{
  private ServerSocket serverSocket;
  private static final int PORT = 2002;
  public DSocketListener(DProcess process)
         throws java.rmi.RemoteException {
    super(process);
    try {
      serverSocket = new ServerSocket(PORT);
    } catch(IOException ioe){ ioe.printStackTrace(); }
  }
  public void step() {
    try {
      // SocketListener waiting for a connection request
      System.out.println("DSocketListener waiting" +
                        "for a connection request");
      Socket socket = serverSocket.accept();
      // creates and starts the socket activity that
      // interacts wiht the client
      process.startActivity(new DSocketActivity
                                    (process, socket));
    } catch(IOException e){ e.printStackTrace(); }
  }
}
public class DSocketActivity extends DActivity
                                implements DObserver {
  private Socket socket = null;
                              // created by DSocketListener
  private BufferedReader input = null;
                    // the socket's input buffer
  private PrintWriter output = null;
                    // the socket's output buffer
  private DActivity service = null;
                    // the requested service
  private DParser parser = null;
                    // the parser for the requested service
  private ArrayList eventList = new ArrayList();
                    // list of incoming events
  private boolean pushMode = false;
  DSocketActivity(DProcess process, Socket socket)
                    throws java.rmi.RemoteException{
```

```
            super(process);
            this.socket = socket;
            try {
              input = new BufferedReader(
                     new InputStreamReader
                                     (socket.getInputStream()));
              output = new PrintWriter(
                     new BufferedOutputStream
                                 (socket.getOutputStream()), false);
            } catch(IOException se) { se.printStackTrace(); }
        }
        public void step() {
            try {
              // waiting for a request
              String message = input.readLine();
              if(message != null) {
                // message format :
                // "START PUSH | PULL activityName par1 par2 ... parN"
                if(message.substring(0,5).equals("START")) {
                  // verifies the synchronization mode
                  if( message.substring(6,10).equals("PUSH"))
                    pushMode = true;
                  String str = message.substring(11).trim();
                  // creates a service activity
                  if(str.indexOf(' ') >= 0) {
                    // gets the activity's class name
                    String activityClass = str.substring(0,
                                        str.indexOf(' ')).trim();
                    // gets the service parameters
                    String parameters = str.substring(activityClass.
                                              length()).trim();
                    // uses reflection to create a parser for the
                    // requested activity
                    parser = (DParser)Class.forName(activityClass+
                                        "Parser").newInstance();
                    // initializes the parser with a reference to
                    // the server
                    parser.setProcess(process);
                    // gets an instance of the requested service
                    service = parser.getActivity(parameters);
                    // starts the service
                    process.startActivity(service);
                    // parserActivity listens to the events raised
                    // by the service
                    service.addObserver(this.getURL(), "any");
                  }
                }
```

```java
      else if(message.indexOf("<EVENT>") >= 0) {
        // the client is pulling the events
        for(int i=0; i < eventList.size(); i++)
          output.println("<" +
                          (String)eventList.get(i) + ">" );
        output.println("<NOEVENT>");
        output.flush();
      }
      else if(message.indexOf("MSG:")
                              >= 0 && parser != null) {
        // receives a message with a command from the
        // remote client
        String msg = message.substring(5).trim();
        // decodes the message and executes the command
        parser.decode(msg);
      }
    }
  } catch(SocketException se) {
    // quits this activity
    process.stopActivity(this.getURL());
  } catch(Exception e) { e.printStackTrace();  }
}
public void quit() {
  // closes the sockets
  try {
    input.close();
    output.close();
    socket.close();
  } catch(IOException ioe) { ioe.printStackTrace(); }
  // quits the service
  process.stopActivity(service.getURL());
}
public void update(DEvent event) {
  if(parser == null)
    return;
  // delegates the parser to encode the event
  StringBuffer sb = parser.encode(event);
  if(pushMode) {
    // sends the event to the client
    output.println(sb.toString());
    output.flush();
  }
  else
    eventList.add(sb.toString());
  output.flush();
  }
}
```

```
public abstract class DParser {
  protected DProcess process = null;
                            // a reference to the control module
  public void setProcess(DProcess process) {
    this.process = process;
  }
  public abstract DActivity getActivity(String parameters);
  public abstract void decode(String message);
  public abstract StringBuffer encode(DEvent event);
}
```

19.6.4 □ Test

The test case develops the web-based version of the client–server application presented in the previous prototypes. The client is represented by class JoggingApplet, which is an applet embedded in the HTML page reported in Figure 19.10. When the applet is loaded in a web browser, it loads service configuration parameters (server URL, socket port and runner's path) from the HTML file and opens a socket connection with the remote server.

Class **Server** implements method **main()** which creates and starts an instance of **SocketListener**. Class **RunnerParser** extends class **DParser** to encode and decode socket messages.

```
package jogging.server;
import mmi.*;
import mmi.sockets.*;
import java.rmi.RemoteException;
import java.util.*;

public class Server extends DProcess implements
                                        ServerInterface{
  private String cells[] = {"", "", "", "", "", "", "", ""};
  public Server(String address, String name)
              throws java.rmi.RemoteException {
    super(address, name);
  }
```

```
<html><head><title>Jogging Applet</title></head><body>
  <APPLET CODE = "jogging.client.JoggingApplet.class"
              CODEBASE = "." WIDTH = "330" HEIGHT = "330" >
    PARAM NAME = HOST VALUE = "127.0.0.1" >
    PARAM NAME = PORT VALUE = "2002" >
    PARAM NAME = PATH VALUE = "4 3 5 6 7 4 3 0 1 2" >
  </APPLET>
</body></html>
```

Figure 19.10 The HTML code that embeds the applet

```java
    public static void main(String[] args) {
      String address = "127.0.0.1";
      String name = "Server";
      if(args.length > 0) address = args[0];
      if(args.length > 1) name = args[1];
      try {
        Server server = new Server(address, name);
        // creates and starts the socket listener
        DSocketListener socketListener =
                              new DSocketListener(server);
        server.startActivity(socketListener);
      } catch(RemoteException re) { re.printStackTrace(); }
    }
}
public class RunnerParser extends DParser {
  Runner runner = null;  // a reference to the Runner service
  public RunnerParser() {  }
  public DActivity getActivity(String parameters) {
    try {
      // parses the parameters
      StringTokenizer st = new StringTokenizer(parameters);
      int path[] = new int[st.countTokens()];
      int id=0;
      while(st.hasMoreTokens())
        path[id++] = Integer.parseInt(st.nextToken());
      // creates and initializes an instance of the Runner
      // service
      runner = new Runner(process, path);
      return runner;
    } catch(RemoteException re) { re.printStackTrace(); }
    return null;
  }
  public void decode(String message) {
    try {
      if(message.indexOf("SPEED") >= 0) {
        // decodes the speed value
        int speed = Integer.parseInt
                            (message.substring(6).trim());
        runner.setSpeed(speed);
      }
    } catch(RemoteException re) { re.printStackTrace(); }
  }
  public StringBuffer encode(DEvent event) {
    // encodes the event that notifies a new position
    StringBuffer buffer = new StringBuffer();
    buffer.append("EVENT " + event.name + " ");
```

```java
        buffer.append("POSITION " +
                          ((Integer)event.value).intValue());
        return buffer;
    }
}


package jogging.client;
import java.io.*;
import java.net.*;
import java.awt.*;
import javax.swing.event.*;
import javax.swing.*;
public class JoggingApplet extends JApplet
                              implements Runnable {
  private PathPanel pathPanel = new PathPanel();
                              // the graphical panel
  private JSlider speedSlider = new JSlider();
                              // the speed control button
  private BufferedReader input = null;
                              // the socket input buffer
  private PrintWriter output = null;
                              // the socket output buffer
  public synchronized void init() {
    this.getContentPane().add(pathPanel, null);
    speedSlider.addChangeListener(
                  new javax.swing.event.ChangeListener() {
      public void stateChanged(ChangeEvent e) {
        output.println
                ("MSG: SPEED " + speedSlider.getValue());
        output.flush();
      }
    });
    this.getContentPane().add(speedSlider, null);
    // gets connected to the remote server and starts the
    // thread
    try {
      // reads the HOST address and the PORT number
      // from the HTML file that embedds the applet
      String host = getParameter("HOST");
      int port = Integer.parseInt( getParameter("PORT") );
      // creates the socket and the input/output buffers
      Socket socket = new Socket(host, port);
      input = new BufferedReader(
              new InputStreamReader
                            (socket.getInputStream()));
      output = new PrintWriter
                          (socket.getOutputStream(), false);
```

```
      // starts the thread
      Thread thread = new Thread(this);
      thread.start();
      // sends a message to the server to start the Runner
      // service
      String path = getParameter("PATH");
      output.println("START jogging.server.Runner " + path);
      output.flush();
    } catch(Exception e) {  e.printStackTrace(); }
  }
  public void run() {
    while(true)
    try {
      String message = input.readLine();
      String str = message.substring(6).trim();
      String eventName = str.substring(0,
                                  str.indexOf(' ')).trim();
      str = str.substring(str.indexOf("POSITION "));
      str = str.substring(8).trim();
      pathPanel.currentPos = Integer.parseInt(str);
      pathPanel.repaint();
    } catch(IOException ioe) {ioe.printStackTrace();}
  }
  void speedSlider_stateChanged(ChangeEvent e) {
    output.println("MSG: SPEED " + speedSlider.getValue());
    output.flush();
  }
}
```

19.7 ■ Extension

The reader can adopt the MMI framework to develop new versions of the case studies presented in previous chapters. The following extensions are increasingly challenging.

■ Chapter 14 (Supermarket operation support system) and Chapter 15 (Geographic information system): client and server components can be implemented using the framework's classes.
■ Chapter 13 (Supervisory control and data acquisition system): tank controllers and the physical devices (pumps and tanks) can be redesigned in order to support asynchronous communication.
■ Chapter 9 (Manufacturing work cell) and Chapter 11 (Car parking): the simulators can be transformed into fully distributed systems.

19.8 ■ **Assessment**

The case study describes the development of a software framework for distributed system interconnection.

Requirements analysis. The framework has been designed taking into account the requirements of systems and applications presented in previous case studies and generalizing from their common features and functionalities. The framework requirements were compared with the specifications of available commercial technologies, such as Sun J2EE, CORBA and Microsoft.NET.

Framework scope. The framework is a middleware infrastructure that simplifies the development of open and heterogeneous distributed systems. In particular it supports multi-task execution, multi-mode synchronization, and multi-protocol communication.

Framework customization. The framework consists in well-defined software architecture and a library of reusable software components. It provides mechanisms, abstract classes and customizable building blocks to support the interconnection of distributed resources.

Idiom	Abstraction by generalization
Context	Frameworks are software templates that support and simplify the development of a variety of different but similar software artifacts for the same application domain. Building a framework is cost-effective only if it reduces the effort of developing an entire family of new applications.
Problem	Building a reusable framework is usually difficult: it requires a deep understanding of the application domain for which it has been conceived in terms of the entities and relationships that can be captured and reused. The more concrete the framework's components are, the more specific their interactions become, and the less likely they will meet the requirements of future applications.
Forces or tradeoffs	The framework approach builds on the concepts of code reuse and design reuse. Code reuse means reusing an existing class library developed in the past for other applications. The more tightly a class library is developed for the functional requirements of a specific application, the less it is reusable in future applications. Design reuse means taking the architecture of an existing application as the starting point for the design of new applications. Architectural design is usually more reusable than class libraries, but choosing the right architectural model is highly difficult and is one of the key success factors of a software application.

Solution	Building a reusable framework is just a matter of reusing previous experience in developing applications in a given domain (e.g. manufacturing, graphical interfaces, etc.). This is done by analysing previous applications in the same domain, identifying recurrent data structures, functionalities and relationships among common entities, and generalizing them by selectively ignoring their differences. Generalization is the process of formulating general concepts by abstracting common properties of instances.
Force resolution	A framework promotes software reuse as much as it captures the stable elements of an application domain in terms of reusable components and reusable patterns of interactions among the components.
Design rationale	In order to enhance software stability, it is necessary to insulate the homogeneous parts of a software product with regard to the possible driving factors of changes. Keep the distinction between commonalties and variability clear. ■ Which elements of the application domain are more stable? ■ Which standards are available? ■ What kind of evolution does the domain undergo?

19.9 ■ References

Sun Microsystems (2000) *Writing Enterprise Applications with Java 2 SDK Enterprise Edition*, http://java.sun.com/j2ee/white/j2ee.pdf.

Thai, Thuan and Lam, Hoang (2001) *.NET Framework Essentials*, O'Reilly.

Vinoski, S. (1997) "CORBA: Integrating Diverse Applications within Distributed Heterogeneous Environments", *IEEE Communications Magazine*, Vol. 14, No. 2, February.

Negotiation-based service configuration

20

Synthesis

Dynamic client–server interaction in internet distributed scenarios requires the definition of middleware infrastructure that provides some level of intelligence in service mediation. This document describes an approach that builds on client and service profiles and that enables automated negotiation of service execution contracts.

- Focus: this case study exemplifies the development of a reusable negotiation framework and its integration with a distributed framework.
- OO techniques: no new technique.
- Java features: no new feature.
- Used knowledge: the negotiation framework builds on the MMI framework developed in the previous chapter.

20.1 ■ Specifications

The internet is, simply stated, the technical infrastructure that supports the matching process between problems and solutions: the assignment of available business solutions to problems can be viewed as a many-to-many mapping of services to requests that changes over time. Typical internet services are hotel reservations, book purchasing, etc. Service customization is a key factor for this matching process: users express preferences for service characteristics (e.g. room position) that must comply with provider's constraints (e.g. availability, cost).

This case study describes a service negotiation framework that provides some level of intelligence in service configuration. It enables automated negotiation of service execution contracts between service providers and service customers (Huhns and Malhotra 1999). The framework is built around the concept of agent (Brugali and Sycara 1999), which operates either on behalf of the customer, taking into account its preferences, or on behalf of the provider, taking into account its constraints. Agents employ multi-criteria decision mechanisms (Triantaphyllou and Shu 2001) for service preference/constraint specification and evaluation. The framework extends the multi-modal interaction framework presented in Chapter 19.

The framework is service independent and must be customized for each specific service provisioning system. In this case study it is used to develop a reservation system for workstations in a computer laboratory.

20.1.1 □ **Workstation booking**

The responsible technician of a university laboratory is in charge of assigning available computers to the students who make requests for their use. Usually the students pick a day and negotiate with the responsible person to find a computer with given characteristics at a given time.

In practice such a discussion is time consuming and often has an unfair outcome. Demanding students are more likely to see their requests accepted, while shy students never get the PC they want at the time they need. In addition, the distribution of the students over time and over machines is not uniform; there are time ranges where most of the students would like to access the laboratory; top-performing computers are the most desired.

Using the service negotiation framework we have to develop a booking tool that copes with this problem and finds the fairest solution. The students can express their preferences, the responsible technician expresses constraints to make the distribution of students as uniform as possible.

Students can express preferences with respect to the following service configuration parameters:

- the CPU power expressed in terms of operating frequency;
- the size of the RAM; and
- the time when the computer is needed.

The idea is to try to have demand distributed more or less uniformly through all the days of the week, the hours of each day, and the PCs in the laboratory.

20.2 ■ **Problem analysis**

We have to develop a service negotiation framework that can deal with the laboratory reservation problem and similar problems. The framework must support the definition of the problem characteristics, which are the base for the negotiation process.

The laboratory reservation problem is a specific instance of a more generic problem: the offering of services based on limited resources.

There are explicit requirements for the integration of this reservation negotiation system into an already existing education portal. The reservation preferences are specified through the portal. We need to have a separate negotiation server to ensure fairness. Therefore the resulting system is distributed: there is a negotiation server that manages a fair negotiation, and two clients: the student portal and the laboratory server.

20.2.1 □ **Domain models**

The negotiation process is based on a service specification that defines the attributes that can be subject to negotiation and the values they can assume.

An example of service specifications for the computer assignment problem is shown in Table 20.1. In order to simplify the automatic negotiation process, attributes assume discrete values only. For example, the CPU frequency of a computer might assume the following values: 500 MHz, 1 GHz, 2 GHz. The usage period (time) specifies predefined intervals expressed in hours.

The result of a negotiation process is a contract between the service provider and the service consumer, which defines unique values for each service configuration attribute. Table 20.2 provides three examples of possible contracts. The first contract assigns the best computer configuration to a student during the most popular period; this contract satisfies the student's preferences maximally. The second contract assigns the worst computer configuration to a student during a less popular period; this contract satisfies the provider's constraints maximally. The third contract is a fair tradeoff proposed by the automatic negotiation tool.

The negotiation process is carried out by a pair of negotiator agents that act on behalf of the service provider and the service consumer, taking into account their preferences and constraints.

The negotiation is based on the exchange of contract proposals between the parties involved. Each party evaluates proposals it receives according to its own criteria and formulates a counter proposal. The negotiators alternatively evaluate proposals until an agreement is reached or a given number of proposals have been exchanged.

The evaluation of a proposal is based on a table of preferences/constraints such as the one in Table 20.3. The values that are not of interest to the user or not available are excluded from the list of preferences (this is the case of the period before 10, between 12 and 13 and after 15).

Each parameter value is mapped to a numerical value (between 1 and the inverse of the number of values) that corresponds to the rank of the participant for that value, 1 being associated with the best ranked attribute value. For example, the provider might order the CPU frequency values as follows: 2 GHz (0.66), 1 GHz (1.00), 500 MHz (0.33). This means that the preferred CPU frequency (most available) is 1 GHz; a higher frequency is better than

Table 20.1 Attributes and values of the computer allocation service

Attribute	Possible values
CPU	500 MHz, 1 GHz, 2 GHz
Memory	256 MB, 500 MB, 1 GB
Time	8–9, 9–10, 10–11, 11–12, 12–13, 13–14, 14–15, 15–16, 16–17

Table 20.2 Attributes and values of the computer allocation service

Attribute	Value	Attribute	Value	Attribute	Value
CPU	2 GHz	CPU	500 MHz	CPU	1 GHz
Memory	1 GB	Memory	256 MB	Memory	500 MB
Time	10–11	Time	14–15	Time	14–15

Table 20.3 Provider's constraints

Attribute	Weight	Value	Rank
CPU	0.2	2 GHz	0.66
		1 GHz	1.00
		500 MHz	0.33
Memory	0.3	500 MB	1.0
		1 GB	0.66
		256 MB	0.33
Time	0.5	10–11	1.0
		11–12	0.75
		13–14	0.5
		14–15	0.25

a lower. Note that there is not a direct correlation between the value of an attribute and its associated rank. In some cases it might occur that the greater the value, the greater the rank but this is not always the case.

Each attribute is associated with a weight that expresses its relevance in the negotiation process. For example, if the technician responsible for the laboratory can accept a change in computer memory better than a change in the time, then the time has a higher weight than the memory. Attributes with a single admitted value do not have a corresponding weight (i.e. they are not negotiable), because that value is required. Table 20.3 represents a synthetic way of expressing preferences for attribute values. The alternative would be to enumerate all the possible combinations of attributes and values and to order them according to the user preferences.

A contract proposal consists of the selection of a single value for each attribute. Let R_i, (for $i = 1, 2, 3, ...$) be the rank associated to the value that attribute i assumes in the contract proposal during negotiation step k (for $k = 1, 2, 3, ...$), W_i the weight of attribute i, and T_k the total value associated to a contract proposal at step k. The following relations hold:

$$\sum W_i = 1 \qquad T_k = \sum W_i * R_i$$

Equation 20.1 Proposal evaluation

Using Equation 20.1, the proposer can rank every admissible contract and select the best proposal to submit to the reviewer. More sophisticated methods for enumerating and ranking admissible contracts can be found in Triantaphyllou and Shu (2001).

This approach resembles a typical weighted sum multi-criteria model: the entire contract proposal is reduced to a single number – the total value.

The basic negotiation mechanism is contract matching. At the beginning of the negotiation process, the proposer and the reviewer exchange contract proposals that have different values for some or all of the attributes.

During each negotiation step, the reviewer (in our case the laboratory server) evaluates the proposer's contract and formulates a counter-proposal. The simplest approach consists of selecting a contract that reduces the difference for each attribute between the value indicated in the proposer proposal and that in the reviewer counter-proposal.

Let $R_i[k-1]$ be the rank of the attribute i in the last proposal formulated by the reviewer and $R_i[k]$ the rank of the attribute i in the proposal received from the proposer. The negotiator selects the attribute i where:

$$R_i[k-1] - R_i[k] = \text{Max}(\forall j \, R_j[k-1] - R_j[k])$$

Equation 20.2 Selection of the attribute to change

The counter proposal has all the attributes equal to the last proposal formulated but the selected attribute. For this attribute the counter-proposal will have the value that has a rank immediately lower than the previous one.

If there exists more than one user interested in booking the same resource, the negotiation processes can interfere with each other and produce different results based on the duration of each negotiation process and the number of concurrent negotiators. In the case of scarce resources, the negotiators might be competitors: only one will conclude the negotiation process and get the service.

The negotiation process might last hours or days. Each contractor can set the period of time that must separate two negotiation steps, that is how long the proposer wants to wait before submitting a counter-proposal to the reviewer. An anxious proposer will try to get the service by formulating proposals that accommodate the reviewer's counter-proposal as fast as possible.

20.2.2 □ Main features

The laboratory reservation system must exhibit the following features:

- *Problem representation.* The problem that is the object of negotiation must be represented in terms of attributes and their possible values.
- *Negotiation.* Based on the problem description it is possible to carry out the negotiation to reach an agreement.
- *Resource management.* The resources are limited and once booked they are no longer available, this is a further dimension that needs to be added to the negotiation framework.
- *Distribution.* The system runs in a distributed environment where the user nodes are separate from the reservation server and possibly from the negotiation server.

20.2.3 □ Test

The problem description for this application is presented in Table 20.1. It defines the possible values and the available resources corresponding to certain combinations of the possible values; the resource availability is presented in Table 20.4, there are only certain computer types, that are described by a certain combination of the values of the attributes CPU and

Table 20.4 Resource availability

Resource	CPU	Memory	Available
PC1	500 MHz	256 MB	10
PC2	1 GHz	500 MB	10
PC3	1 GHz	1 GB	5
PC4	2 GHz	1 GB	5

memory; initially the availability of the resources is the same at every time.

The server preferences are recomputed periodically on the basis of availability, while the client preferences are defined in Table 20.3

20.3 ■ Architecture and planning

The main constraint in the development of this application is provided by the physical architecture, which is presented in Figure 20.1. The negotiation takes place on the negotiation server that mediates between the student preferences and the service provider's constraints. The service provider component manages resource availability and constraints. Students access the booking system through a standard web server.

The service provider and the student web server do not interact directly; they go through the mediation agent that is in charge of guaranteeing fairness. The connections between the nodes are normal network links, therefore the nodes can communicate using any protocol ranging from plain sockets to rmi.

An important constraint in the development of this application is that the goal is a reusable framework.

The system is partitioned into four components as shown in Figure 20.2. Each component addresses specifically one or more essential features of the system. The negotiation framework component handles the negotiation problems. The resource booking component is a framework that works on top of the negotiation framework and extends it to handle the problem of limited resources.

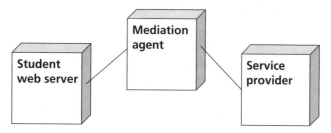

Figure 20.1 Physical structure of the system

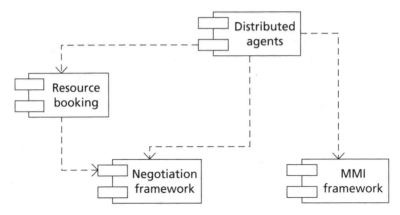

Figure 20.2 Components of the system

The distributed agents component encapsulates the resource booking framework and adapts it to a networked environment. In particular it allows the actors of the negotiation to be distributed over a network. This component uses the MMI framework (see Chapter 19) to provide remote interaction.

The development of the system is broken into three steps:

- *Prototype 1: Negotiation framework.* The kernel of the negotiation framework is developed; it allows the definition of the terms of a negotiation problem.
- *Prototype 2: Resource negotiation.* This prototype builds upon the previous one and allows the negotiation of limited resources.
- *Prototype 3: Distributed negotiation.* A distributed implementation based on the MMI framework.

20.4 ■ Prototype 1: Negotiation framework

The first step develops a generic negotiation framework. A service configuration problem is defined in terms of service configuration attributes, admissible values and the user preferences/constraints specification.

20.4.1 □ Analysis

This prototype solves the problem of negotiating contracts for the provision of a service. The negotiation involves two main roles: the service provider and the service customer. Since the negotiation ought to be fair another role is required: an arbiter or mediator.

We assume, as specified in Section 20.2.1, that the attributes can assume only discrete values. Therefore the problem description defines the set of possible values.

The negotiation takes place by exchanging proposals and counter-proposals. The mediator asks one of the parties for an initial proposal and then asks the other party to evaluate it and to produce a counter-proposal.

The negotiation terminates either when a proposal and the corresponding counter-proposal agree, a given number of iterations have been completed, or the value associated with a proposal descends below a given threshold for one of the negotiators.

Not all the attributes defined in the problem specification are of interest for both parties, therefore the negotiation concerns only the intersection of the relevant attributes for the parties.

The parties must be able to specify some preferences and have their agents use them to carry on the negotiation on their behalf. Preferences are given for each relevant attribute. They are expressed in terms of the weight of each attribute and of a rank for the possible values. The possible values ranked in a preference are a subset of the possible values for the attribute defined in the problem specification.

20.4.2 □ **Design**

The design of the negotiation framework must address three main issues: the problem description, the representation of the information used during the negotiation and the negotiation process.

Decision point

How do we describe the problem?

The problem description is well defined by the existing domain models. The classes used to describe the problems are shown in Figure 20.3. Class Specification is a collection of attributes. The attributes are represented by

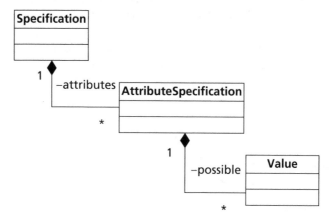

Figure 20.3 Problem description

class AttributeSpecification; each attribute has a weight and contains the collection of the possible values.

There are two issues: first the type of attributes/values, second the range of possible values. We use the interface Value to accommodate several different value types. Since we assume that only discrete values are possible, the range of attribute values is expressed by enumeration.

How do we represent a proposal and the preferences?

As shown in Figure 20.4, the proposals are represented by class Proposal that consists of a collection of attributes. Each attribute is characterized by a value; in addition the attribute has a reference to the set of admissible values from which the value must be picked. Users' preferences are represented by class PreferenceMap; the preferences are defined at the attribute level by means of the class AttributeMap, which assigns a weight to the single attributes and ranks the values of the attribute. The ranking is accomplished by the RankedAttribute class, which adds to the class Attribute the rank for a specific value.

How do we realize the negotiation process?

As shown in Figure 20.5, the negotiation is managed by the mediator that ensures fairness of the process; its task is to drive the proposal exchange between the service provider and service customer. Interface Negotiator represents the two contenders of the negotiation process, the classes that implement it provide a specific negotiation strategy. The negotiation strategies can vary a great deal. We define the basic strategy described in Section 20.2.1, by class BasicNegotiator.

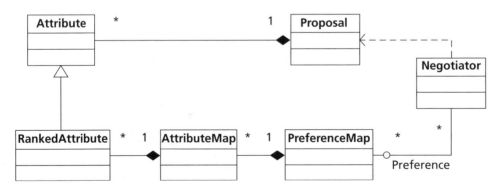

Figure 20.4 Problem representation

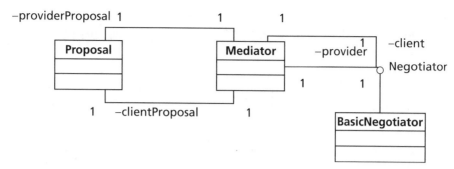

Figure 20.5 Negotiation structure

The negotiation process enacted by the mediator is illustrated by the sequence diagram presented in Figure 20.6. There are two negotiators, the client and the provider, each linked to the relative preferences. Initially the mediator asks both negotiators to provide an initial proposal and to intersect their own proposal with that from the counterpart. This phase ensures that any following proposal will contain only values that are admissible for both parties.

Then the mediator enters a loop where it first asks the client to formulate a counter-proposal, this proposal is passed to the provider which formulates a counter-proposal. The BasicNegotiator formulates the counter-proposal using the preference object to rank the values of the proposal of the other party. The strategy adopted by this class is the simplest one, which is presented in Section 20.2.1.

To ensure fairness only the negotiator has access to its own preferences while the other negotiator and the mediator can only see the proposal formulated.

The negotiation is terminated by the mediator either because an agreement has been reached (i.e. both parties formulated the same proposal) or because the maximum number of iterations have been completed.

20.4.3 □ Implementation

All the framework classes are part of a package named Negotiation. The class Specification provides a definition of the negotiation constraints. It is contains a collection of AttributesSpec objects that define the possible values for each attribute.

```
package Negotiation;
import java.util.*;
public class Specification {
  String name;
  Map attributes = new Hashtable();
  public void add(String name){
    attributes.put(name, new AttributeSpec(name));
  }
```

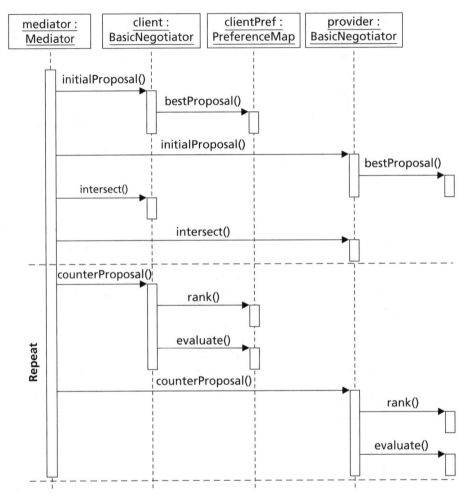

Figure 20.6 Behaviour of the mediator

```java
public void addValue(String name, Value value){
  AttributeSpec attribute = (AttributeSpec)
                                     attributes.get(name);
  attribute.addValue(value);
}
public AttributeSpec attribute(String name){
  return (AttributeSpec)attributes.get(name);
}
public Collection attributes(){
  return attributes.values();
}
public String toString(){
  StringBuffer buffer = new StringBuffer();
  Iterator it = attributes.values().iterator();
```

```
    while(it.hasNext())
      buffer.append(it.next()).append("\n");
    return buffer.toString();
  }
}
```

Interface **Preference** defines the operations offered to the negotiators by the instances of class **PreferenceMap**. Method **attribute()** returns the detail of the preference for an attribute. The **evaluate()** method evaluates a proposal or a single attribute. Method **rank()** returns the rank of an attribute value. The **ensureAdmissible()** method modifies an attribute or a proposal so that is admissible. The **decrease()** method decreases the value of an attribute of a proposal.

```
package Negotiation;
import java.util.*;
public interface Preference {
  public AttributeMap attribute(String name);
  public double evaluate(Proposal proposal);
  public double evaluate(Attribute attribute);
  public double rank(Attribute attribute);
  public double rank(String name, Value value);
  public Proposal bestProposal();
  public void ensureAdmissible(Proposal attribute);
  public void ensureAdmissible(Attribute proposal);
  public Proposal decrease(Attribute attribute,
                                  Proposal proposal);
}
```

Class **PreferenceMap** represents the user preferences. It implements the collection of the attributes as a **Map**, where the attributes are inserted with their names as key. The constructor is based on the **Specification** of the problem. The methods **setWeight()** and **add()** are used to define the preferences in terms of attribute weight and value rank.

The other methods implement the **Preference** interface. The **ensure Admissible()** method checks if an attribute (or all the attributes of a proposal) has an admissible value, i.e. that its value is included in the collection of admissible values for that attribute; in case it is not admissible it replaces the value by an admissible value with the closest ranking.

```
package Negotiation;
public class PreferenceMap implements Preference {
  Map attributes = new Hashtable();
  // build a preference map from the service specification
  public PreferenceMap(Specification spec){
    Iterator it = spec.attributes.values().iterator();
    while(it.hasNext()){
      AttributeSpec attrSpec=(AttributeSpec)it.next();
      // the weight of every attribute is initialized to 0
```

```java
      AttributeMap attribute = new AttributeMap
                                       (attrSpec.name,0.0);
      attributes.put(attribute.name,attribute);
    }
  }
  // set the weight for an attribute
  public void setWeight(String name, double weight){
    AttributeMap attribute = (AttributeMap)
                                        attributes.get(name);
    attribute.weight = weight;
  }
  // define the rank for a value of an attribute
  public void add(String name, Value value, double rank){
    AttributeMap attribute = (AttributeMap)
                                        attributes.get(name);
    attribute.add(value,rank);
  }
  // get the details of the preferences for an attribute
  public AttributeMap attribute(String name){
    return (AttributeMap)attributes.get(name);
  }
  // evaluate a proposal
  public double evaluate(Proposal proposal){
    double value = 0.0;
    Iterator it = attributes.values().iterator();
    while(it.hasNext()){
      AttributeMap attribute=(AttributeMap)it.next();
      value += attribute.eval(proposal);
    }
    return value;
  }
  // evaluate a single attribute of a proposal
  public double evaluate(Attribute attribute){
    AttributeMap map=(AttributeMap)
                            attributes.get(attribute.name);
    if(map==null) return 0.0;
    return map.eval(attribute);
  }
  // returns the rank of the value of an attribute
  public double rank(Attribute attribute){
    return rank(attribute.name,attribute.value);
  }
  public double rank(String name, Value value){
    AttributeMap map=(AttributeMap)attributes.get(name);
    if(map==null) return 0.0;
    return map.rank(value);
  }
```

```
// return the best proposal, that is the one with the
// highest value where every attribute assumes the value
// with the highest rank
public Proposal bestProposal(){
  Proposal best = new Proposal();
  Iterator it=attributes.values().iterator();
  while(it.hasNext()){
    AttributeMap attribute=(AttributeMap)it.next();
    if(attribute.weight>0)
      best.add(attribute.name,attribute.best(),
                                    attribute.values());
  }
  return best;
}
// fix the values of the attributes of a proposal
// so that each attribute is admissible
public void ensureAdmissible(Proposal proposal){
  Iterator it=proposal.getAttributes().iterator();
  while(it.hasNext()){
    Attribute attribute=(Attribute)it.next();
    ensureAdmissible(attribute);
  }
}
public void ensureAdmissible(Attribute attribute){
  // if the current value is admissible there's nothing
  // to do
  if(attribute.admissibleValues.contains(attribute.value))
                                                    return;
  // otherwise find among the admissible values the one
  // having the rank closest to that of the current value.
  // In case of equal difference of ranks, preference is
  // given to values having lower ranks.
  double previousRank = rank(attribute);
  double newRank=-1;
  Value newValue=null;
  Iterator it=attribute.admissibleValues.iterator();
  while(it.hasNext()){
    Value value=(Value)it.next();
    double rank = rank(attribute.name,value);
    if(Math.abs(rank - previousRank)
                      < Math.abs(newRank - previousRank)){
      newRank = rank;
      newValue = value;
    }else
    if(Math.abs(rank - newRank)
                          == Math.abs(rank - previousRank)
```

```
                 && rank < previousRank ){
        newRank = rank;
        newValue = value;
      }
    }
    if(newValue==null)
      System.err.println("Error: no admissible value");
    attribute.value = newValue;
  }
  // substitute the value of an attribute of a proposal with
  // a value with the immediately lower rank
  public Proposal decrease(Attribute attribute,
                                        Proposal proposal){
    AttributeMap map=(AttributeMap)
                          attributes.get(attribute.name);
    if(map==null) return proposal;
    double rank = map.rank(attribute);
    double newRank=0;
    Value newValue=null;
    Iterator it=map.ranks.values().iterator();
    while(it.hasNext()){
      RankedAttribute attr=(RankedAttribute)it.next();
      if(attr.rank > newRank && attr.rank < rank){
        newRank=attr.rank;
        newValue=attr.value;
      }
    }
    if(newRank!=0){
      attribute.value = newValue;
    }
    return proposal;
  }
  public String toString(){
    StringBuffer buffer=new StringBuffer();
    Iterator it=attributes.values().iterator();
    while(it.hasNext()){
      AttributeMap attribute=(AttributeMap)it.next();
      buffer.append(attribute.toString()).append("\n");
    }
    return buffer.toString();
  }
}
```

Interface **Negotiator** defines the possible interactions between the mediator and the negotiators. Method **intersect**() takes a proposal by the negotiator and a proposal from the counterpart and creates a proposal that contains only the attributes that are present in both proposals and, for each attribute, sets as admissible values those that are admissible for both.

```
package Negotiation;
public interface Negotiator {
  public void intersect(Proposal own, Proposal other);
  public Proposal initialProposal();
  public Proposal counterProposal(Proposal received);
  public void completed(boolean success);
  public Proposal finalProposal();
}
```

Class **Mediator** executes the negotiation process. The behaviour is defined in the method startNegotiation() that implements the negotiation process described in Figure 20.6. The constructor receives as a parameter the maximum number of iterations for the negotiation process.

```
package Negotiation;
public class Mediator {
  Proposal providerProposal;
  Proposal clientProposal;
  int maxIterations;
  public Mediator(int max) {
    maxIterations = max;
  }
  // return the last client proposal
  public Proposal getClient() { return clientProposal; }
  // return the last provider proposal
  public Proposal getProvider() { return providerProposal; }
  public boolean startNegotiation(Negotiator client,
                                  Negotiator provider) {
    // ask the negotiators for their first proposal
    providerProposal = provider.initialProposal();
    clientProposal = client.initialProposal();
    // intersect the proposals
    // (only the attributes relevant for both are taken into
    // consideration)
    provider.intersect(providerProposal, clientProposal);
    client.intersect(clientProposal, providerProposal);
    // perform the negotiation repeating the loop for a
    // limited number of times
    for(int i=0; i<maxIterations; ++i){
      clientProposal = client.counterProposal
                                        (providerProposal);
      if(clientProposal.equals(providerProposal)) break;
      providerProposal = provider.counterProposal
                                        (clientProposal);
      if(clientProposal.equals(providerProposal)) break;
    }
```

```
    if(clientProposal.equals(serverProposal)){ // successful
      clientProposal.merge(client.initialProposal());
      serverProposal.merge(server.initialProposal());
      return true;
    }else
      return false;
  }
}
```

Class **BasicNegotiator** implements interface **Negotiator** and defines the maximum number of iterations for the negotiation process. The main method is **counterProposal()** that formulates a new proposal.

```
package Negotiation;
import java.util.*;
public class BasicNegotiator extends Negotiator {
  PreferenceMap preference;
  Proposal lastProposal=null;
  double threshold;
  private Proposal finalProposal;
  public BasicNegotiator(Preference preference) {
    this.preference = preference;
    this.threshold = 0.5;
  }
  public void intersect(Proposal own, Proposal other) {
    own.intersect(other,preference);
  }
  public Proposal initialProposal() {
    try{
      lastProposal = preference.bestProposal();
    }catch(Exception e){
      e.printStackTrace();
    }
    return lastProposal;
  }
  public Proposal counterProposal(Proposal received) {
    if(lastProposal==null){
      return initialProposal();
    }
    // the counter-proposal is equal to the last proposal
    // but..
    Proposal counterProposal = new Proposal(lastProposal);
    // only with the allowed values for the common
    // attributes and..
    counterProposal.intersect(received,preference);
    // the values proposed by the counterpart for the
    // nonrelevant attributes
    counterProposal.merge(received);
```

```
    try{
      double maxGap=0.0;
      Attribute maxGapAttribute=null;
      // search the attribute with the highest gap between
      // the ranking of the value proposed by the
      // counterpart and the last proposed value
      Iterator it=counterProposal.attributes.values().
                                                  iterator();
      while(it.hasNext()){
        Attribute attr=(Attribute)it.next();
        AttributeMap ranking = preference.attribute
                                                (attr.name);
        if(ranking!=null){ // i.e. attribute is relevant
          Attribute rec=received.get(attr.name);
          if(rec!=null){ // i.e. it does matter for the
                          // other too
            double gap=preference.rank(attr)-preference.
                                                  rank(rec);
            if(gap > maxGap){
              maxGap = gap;
              maxGapAttribute = attr;
            }
          }
        }
      }
      if(maxGapAttribute!=null){
        // decrease the value for the attribute with the
        // highest gap
        counterProposal =
              preference.decrease(maxGapAttribute,
                                      counterProposal);
      }
    }catch(Exception e){ e.printStackTrace(); }
    try{
      if(preference.evaluate(counterProposal)>threshold){
        lastProposal = counterProposal;
        return counterProposal;
      }
    }catch(Exception e){ e.printStackTrace(); }
    return lastProposal;
  }
  public Proposal finalProposal() {
    return finalProposal;
  }
  public void completed(boolean success){
    if(success){
```

```
        finalProposal = new Proposal(lastProposal);
        finalProposal.merge(initialProposal());
    }else
        finalProposal = null;
    }
}
```

20.4.4 □ Test

The test can be carried out by running a negotiation. The following code is the driver for the test; it must be completed by writing the following methods:

- the defineSpecification() method creates the specification, e.g. reading it from a file;
- the createClientPref() method creates the preferences for the client;
- the createProviderPref() method creates the preferences for the service provider.

```java
import Negotiation.*;
public class TestDefinition {
  public static final int MAX_ITERATIONS=10;
  public static void main(String []args) throws Exception {
    // define the specification of the problem that consists
    // of attributes and the enumeration of their possible
    // values
    Specification spec = defineSpecification();
    System.out.println(spec);
    // define the preference map of the client
    PreferenceMap clientPref=createClientPref(spec);
    // creates the client negotiator
    Negotiator client = new BasicNegotiator(clientPref);
    // define the preference map of the server
    PreferenceMap providerPref=createProvider Pref(spec);
    // creates the server negotiator
    Negotiator provider = new BasicNegotiator(provider Pref);
    // carry out the negotiation
    Mediator mediator = new Mediator(10);
    // print the result if successful
    if(mediator.startNegotiation(client,provider)){
      System.out.println("Client " +
         mediator.getClient() +
         clientPref.evaluate (mediator.getClient()));
      System.out.println ("Provider " +
         mediator.getProvider() +
         providerPref.evaluate (mediator.getProvider()));
    }
  }
```

20.5 ■ Prototype 2: Resource negotiation

The second prototype extends the negotiation framework to handle the problem of limited resources offered by the service provider.

20.5.1 □ Analysis

We extend the previous prototype in order to take into account that the computer booking service manages scarce resources. In fact, after a successful negotiation there is a computer reservation, which means that the reserved computer is no longer available for other students and thus cannot be considered during subsequent negotiation processes.

Let's consider an example of negotiation. The last proposal formulated by the provider's agent is (time: 10–11, CPU: 1 GHz), the attribute with the highest gap is time, so the negotiator would decrease the value of that attribute proposing (time: 11–12, CPU: 1 GHz). It is possible that there are no more 1 GHz PCs available in the time range 11–12, but plenty of other types; in this case the agent would be formulating a proposal that cannot be supported by the service provider.

This case cannot be handled simply omitting the time range 11–12 from the admissible values because that value is perfectly admissible for another type of PC. This means that constraints on possible values of the attributes become more complex than a simple list of available values for each attribute. There are constraints that involve several attributes.

The main issues we have to address are:

■ resources are limited and each successful negotiation modifies the availability of resources;
■ the preferences of the service provider depend on the availability of resources;
■ after each negotiation the provider's preferences must be computed again based on the new resource condition.

A further problem could arise if multiple negotiations are carried on at the same time. For simplicity we assume that only one negotiation takes place at a time, the requests from the clients are serialized.

20.5.2 □ Design

This prototype must integrate the management of limited resources into the negotiation framework addressing the specific issues raised by this new topic.

Decision point

How do we integrate limited resource management into the negotiation framework?

There are two options: the first consists of creating new classes inside the negotiation framework, the second consists of building on top of the negotiation framework. The advantage of the first solution is a simpler approach that can access the internal classes of the framework and allows ad hoc solutions. The second solution is more generic; it leaves the negotiation framework unmodified and insulates the problem of managing limited resources that can be addressed from several perspectives depending on the problem.

We adopt the second solution and define a new package that contains the classes that extend the framework in order to handle limited resources. The structure of the booking package is described by the class diagram of Figure 20.7. The resources are managed by a ResourceAllocator that conforms to the problem specification expressed by the Specification class of the Negotiation framework. The resources and their availability are represented by class Resource.

Decision point

How do we handle inter-attribute constraints?

Since the class PreferenceMap is too simple to handle the inter-attribute constraints and we do not want to modify the negotiation framework, the only solution is to create a new preference class: ResourcePreference. This class extends PreferenceMap and redefines the methods (decrease() and bestProposal()) that can potentially create proposals that are not valid for the current resource availability status. To verify the validity of the proposals,

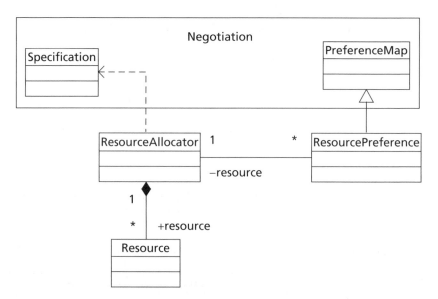

Figure 20.7 Class diagram of the booking package

ResourceReference is linked to the ResourceAllocator that provides all the required information about the resource status.

The booking of the resources after a successful negotiation is not automatically ensured by the framework. Thus when customizing the framework it is mandatory to provide a class that is responsible for booking the resource. Usually such a class is the one that creates the negotiator. This class is responsible for booking the resource with the ResourceAllocator and for recalculating the preferences based on the new availability of the resources.

The preferences are computed with the goal of giving preference to scarcely requested resources in order to distribute reservations as uniformly as possible over the resources.

The rank of a value of an attribute is proportional to the availability of that value. The rank 1 is assigned to the value having the maximum availability. The availability of value v for attribute i is the number of free resources that have the value v for attribute i, that is:

$$availability(i, v) = |\{resource\,|\,free(resource) \wedge resource.attr_i = v\}|$$

Equation 20.3 Availability of a value

The weight of each attribute is proportional to the variance of the availability of the values of each attribute. The weight of attribute i can be computed using Equation 20.4. The rationale for this choice is that higher weight is assigned to attributes that have scarcely available values (where σ^2 is the variance of the availability of attribute i for all the possible values):

$$w_i = \frac{\sigma_i^2}{\sum_j \sigma_j^2}$$

Equation 20.4 Weight of attribute

The sequence diagram in Figure 20.8 shows the evolution of the preferences for limited resources. Initially the ResourceAllocator creates the service provider's preferences for the initial state of the resources. Then the mediator drives the negotiation that must be followed by the booking of a resource (if successful); after the resource is booked the preferences can be recomputed on the basis of the new resource availability.

20.5.3 ☐ Implementation

The package booking contains all the classes that implement the management of limited resources. The class Resource describes the availability of a

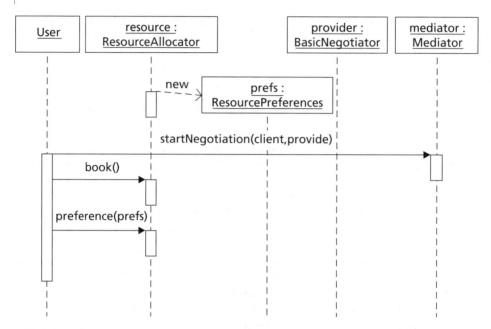

Figure 20.8 Initialization scenario

resource. Each resource is described by the values of the attributes; such values can be seen as coordinates in an n-dimensional space, thus the description of a resource is implemented as a Map that maps the name of the attribute (or dimension) into the value of the attribute (or coordinate). In addition it has two counters that represent the available and the booked items. Method match() matches the coordinates of the resource against a set of values for the attributes.

```java
package booking;
import java.util.*;

class Resource {
    // the description of the resource expressed as
    // coordinates in an n-dimensional space, one dimension
    // for each attribute.
    Map coordinates;
    int available; // number of available resources
    int booked; // number of booked resources
    Resource(Map coordinates, int available){
        this.coordinates = coordinates;
        this.available = available;
        booked = 0;
    }
    // compares the resource coordinates with other
    // coordinates
```

```java
boolean match(Map other){
  Iterator it=coordinates.keySet().iterator();
  while(it.hasNext()){
    Object key=it.next();
    Object otherValue = other.get(key);
    Object value=coordinates.get(key);
    if(otherValue!=null && !otherValue.equals(value))
      return false;
  }
  return true;
}
// compare a single coordinates
boolean match(Object key, Object value){
  Object coord = coordinates.get(key);
  if(coord == null) return false;
  return value.equals(coord);
}
// book a resource, ensuring that the sum of
// available and booked is a constant
synchronized void book() {
  available--;
  booked++;
}
public String toString(){
  StringBuffer buffer = new StringBuffer();
  Iterator it=coordinates.keySet().iterator();
  while(it.hasNext()){
    Object key=it.next();
    Object value=coordinates.get(key);
    buffer.append(key).append("=").append(value).
                                          append(" ");
  }
  return buffer.toString();
}
}
```

Class **ResourceAllocation** manages the resources. Method **preference()** computes the preferences on the basis of the current resource availability. The weights of the attributes are proportional to the variance of the availability of the values. The ranking of the values of an attribute is proportional to the availability of the values.

```java
package booking;
import java.util.*;
import Negotiation.*;

public class ResourceAllocation {
  // the collection of all the resources
```

```
Collection resources=new Vector();
// the specification, defining the attributes
// (i.e. coordinates)
Specification specification;
public ResourceAllocation(Specification specification) {
  this.specification = specification;
}
// define the number of available resources of a given type
// the type is expressed in terms of coordinates
public void setAvailability(Map coordinates,int available){
  Resource res = new Resource(coordinates,available);
  resources.add(res);
}
// book a resource corresponding to a proposal
// this method MUST be invoked at the end of a successful
// negotiation
public void book(Proposal proposal){
  if(proposal==null) return;
  Map coordinates = new Hashtable();
  Iterator it = proposal.getAttributes().iterator();
  while(it.hasNext()){
    Attribute attribute=(Attribute)it.next();
    coordinates.put(attribute.getName(),
                                    attribute.getValue());
  }
  book(coordinates);
}
// book a resource with the given coordinates
private void book(Map coordinates){
  Iterator it=resources.iterator();
  while(it.hasNext()){
    Resource resource=(Resource)it.next();
    if(resource.match(coordinates)){
      resource.book();
      return;
    }
  }
}
// return the preferences
public PreferenceMap preference(){
  PreferenceMap pref=new ResourcePreference
                                    (specification,this);
  return preference(pref);
}
// re-calculate the ranks and weights of the preference
public PreferenceMap preference(PreferenceMap pref){
```

```java
double sum = (double) sumAvailable();
double sigma[] = new double[specification.attributes().
                                                   size()];
double sumSigma = 0.0;
Iterator it_attr = specification.
                                   attributes().iterator();
for(int i=0; it_attr.hasNext(); ++i)
                                    { // for each attribute
  AttributeSpec attribute =
                            (AttributeSpec)it_attr.next();
  sigma[i]=0.0;
  double average= sum / ((double)attribute.getValues().
                                                   size());
  double rank[] = new double[attribute.getValues().
                                                   size()];
  double max = 0;
  Iterator it_val=attribute.getValues().iterator();
  for(int j=0;it_val.hasNext();++j){ // for each value
    Value value=(Value)it_val.next();
    int count = sumAvailable(attribute.getName(),value);
    rank[j] = (double)count;
    if(rank[j]>max) max = rank[j];
    sigma[i] += (count - average)*(count - average);
  }
  sigma[i] /= rank.length;
  sumSigma += sigma[i];
  // the rank is proportional to how close the value
  // is to the value with the highest availability
  // i.e. preference is given to most available values
  Value values[]=new Value[rank.length];
  attribute.getValues().toArray(values);
  for(int j=0; j<rank.length; ++j){
    for(int k=0; k<rank.length-1; k++){
      if(rank[k]<rank[k+1]){
        double temp = rank[k];
        rank[k]=rank[k+1];
        rank[k+1]=temp;
        Value tempVal = values[k];
        values[k]=values[k+1];
        values[k+1]=tempVal;
      }
    }
  }
  double step=1.0/rank.length;
  double rankValue=1.0;
  for(int j=0; j<rank.length; ++j,rankValue-=step){
```

```
                        pref.add(attribute.getName(),values[j],rankValue);
          }
    }
    // the weight of each attribute is proportional to the
    // variance of the availability of the values of each
    // attribute i.e. higher weight to attributes that have
    // scarcely available values
    it_attr = specification.attributes().iterator();
    for(int i=0; it_attr.hasNext(); ++i)
                                      { // for each attribute
      AttributeSpec attribute =
                            (AttributeSpec)it_attr.next();
      pref.setWeight(attribute.getName(),sigma[i]/sumSigma);
    }
    return pref;
  }
  // evaluates the validity of a proposal
  public boolean valid(Proposal proposal){
    if(proposal==null) return false;
    Map coordinates=new Hashtable();
    Iterator it = proposal.getAttributes().iterator();
    while(it.hasNext()){
      Attribute attribute=(Attribute)it.next();
      coordinates.put(attribute.getName(),
                                  attribute.getValue());
    }
    return valid(coordinates);
  }
  public boolean valid(Map coordinates){
    Iterator it=resources.iterator();
    while(it.hasNext()){
      Resource resource=(Resource)it.next();
      if(resource.match(coordinates)
                    && resource.available>0) return true;
    }
    return false;
  }
  // return the number of available resources
  private int sumAvailable(){
    Iterator it=resources.iterator();
    int sum=0;
    while(it.hasNext()){
      Resource resource=(Resource)it.next();
      sum+=resource.available;
    }
    return sum;
  }
```

```
// return the number of available resources that
// have coordinate name equal to value
private int sumAvailable(String name, Object value){
  Iterator it=resources.iterator();
  int sum=0;
  while(it.hasNext()){
    Resource resource=(Resource)it.next();
    if(resource.match(name,value)){
      sum+=resource.available;
    }
  }
  return sum;
}
}
```

The class **ResourcePreference** represents the preferences for limited resources. It inherits most of the methods and attributes of class **PreferenceMap**. In addition there is a link to the **ResourceAllocator**. In particular, the methods **decrease()** and **bestProposal()** are overridden; they call the version defined in the superclass and then they return the closest valid proposal. The key method is **closest()**: it finds the closest valid proposal.

```
package booking;
import Negotiation.*;
import java.util.*;
public class ResourcePreference extends PreferenceMap {
  ResourceAllocation resources;
  Specification spec;
  public ResourcePreference
         (Specification spec,ResourceAllocation resources ){
    super(spec);
    this.resources = resources;
    this.spec = spec;
  }
  // decrease the value of an attribute in the proposal
  // (i.e. substitute the value with the one having rank
  // immediately lower) return the closest valid proposal
  public Proposal decrease
                    (Attribute attribute, Proposal proposal){
    super.decrease(attribute,proposal);
    if(resources.valid(proposal)){
      return proposal;
    }
    Proposal close = closest(proposal);
    return close;
  }
  // return the best valid proposal
```

```java
public Proposal bestProposal(){
  Proposal best = super.bestProposal();
  if(resources.valid(best)) return best;
  return closest(best);
}
// find the closest valid proposal
private Proposal closest(Proposal proposal){
  String[] names=new String[proposal.getAttributes().
                                               size()];
  Iterator it=proposal.getAttributes().iterator();
  Iterator[] values=new Iterator[names.length];
  Proposal candidate = new Proposal(proposal);
  for(int i=0; i<values.length; ++i){
    names[i] = ((Attribute)it.next()).getName();
    AttributeSpec attribute= spec.attribute(names[i]);
    Collection admissibles = attribute.getValues();
    values[i] = admissibles.iterator();
    candidate.add(names[i],(Value)values[i].next(),
                                          admissibles);
  }
  double min = 2;
  double proposed=evaluate(proposal);
  Proposal closest=null;
  while(true){
    if(resources.valid(candidate)){
      double delta = Math.abs(evaluate(candidate)
                                          -proposed);
      if(delta<min){
        min = delta;
        closest = new Proposal(candidate);
      }
    }
    if(!explore(0,names,values,candidate)) break;
  }
  return closest;
}
// explores all the possible combinations of values for
// the attributes of the proposal, each invocation
// modifies the proposal
boolean explore(int i,String[] names, Iterator[] values,
                                          Proposal p){
  if(i==names.length) return false;
  Value value;
  boolean nested=explore(i+1,names,values,p);
  if(nested){
    return nested;
```

```
    }else{
      boolean result;
      if(values[i].hasNext())
        result = true;
      else{
        result = false;
        values[i] =
spec.attribute(names[i]).getValues().iterator();
      }
      value = (Value)values[i].next();
      p.add(names[i],value,spec.attribute(names[i]).
                                        getValues());
      return result;
    }
  }
}
```

20.5.4 □ Test

The test driver is similar to the previous driver. There are two main differences:

- The preferences of the service provider are generated by the Resource Allocator.
- The driver is responsible for booking the resource upon successful negotiation and for recomputing the provider's preferences.

```
import Negotiation.*;
import booking.*;
import java.util.*;
public class TestLocal {
  public static void main(String[] args){
    Specification spec = createSpec();
    System.out.println(spec.toString());
    ResourceAllocation resources=resources(spec);
    // define the preference map of the server
    PreferenceMap providerPref=resources.preference();
    // creates the server negotiator
    Negotiator provider = new BasicNegotiator(providerPref);
    // define the preference map of the client
    PreferenceMap clientPref=createClientPref(spec);
    for(int i=0; i<300; ++i){
      // creates the client negotiator
      Negotiator client = new BasicNegotiator(clientPref);
      // carry out the negotiation
      Mediator mediator=new Mediator(10);
      try{
```

```
        if(mediator.startNegotiation(client,provider)){
        // if successful
          System.out.println ("Client " + i + ":" +
                mediator.getClient() +
                clientPref.evaluate(mediator.getClient()));
          System.out.println ("Server " + i + ":"  +
                mediator.getServer() +
                providerPref.evaluate(mediator.getServer()));
          // book the resource
          resources.book(mediator.getServer());
          //  recompute the provider preferences
          resources.preference(providerPref);
        }else
          System.out.println("Negotiation failed!!");
      }catch(Exception e){ e.printStackTrace(); }
    }
  }
```

20.6 ■ Prototype 3: Distributed negotiation

This prototype extends the negotiation framework in order to distribute service user, service provider and mediator roles on different network nodes.

20.6.1 □ Analysis

The negotiation node should be decoupled from the service provider and service user nodes.

We adopt the MMI framework developed in Chapter 19 to implement the remote interconnection of users, providers and mediator agents. Each agent is an autonomous application that interact with other agents.

20.6.2 □ Design

The design of this prototype does not add new functionalities to the previous prototype. It enables remote access to the negotiation framework.

Decision point

How do we structure the distributed agent system?

The problem we have to face suggests a client–server structure for the distributed agent system. In our system the negotiation server plays the role of server; the service provider and the service user are clients of the negotiation server. The class diagram in Figure 20.9 presents the server-side classes in the top part and the client-side classes in the bottom part.

On the server side the class Server is the access point, it offers a remote interface (ServerInterface) through which it is possible to register a service provider and to start a negotiation on behalf of a service client. The negotiation is managed by a MediationAgent that interacts with NegotiationAgents that encapsulate the classes Mediator and Negotiator respectively; they extend the MMI class DActivity. Thus they can communicate using the MMI framework.

The service provider and client share a common structure that is made up of a Host that extends the MMI class DProcess and a Proxy that extends the MMI class DActivity. The Proxy is a remotely accessible object that can receive events from the NegotiationAgent with information about the progress of the negotiation.

Decision point

How to distribute the responsibilities?

We keep the preferences and the resource state on the service provider side. This choice avoids data duplication and allows to access to up-to-date data. Another advantage is that we keep the negotiation server as simple as possible: it need not know about limited resources and reservations.

A negative effect of this choice is heavy traffic between the negotiation server and the service provider server to access all the preference settings.

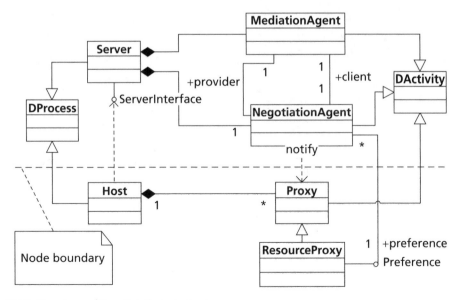

Figure 20.9 Structure of the distributed agents

An alternative choice is to have the negotiation server do all the work and communicate booked resources to the service provider.

The ResourceProxy class extends the class Proxy by implementing the Preference interface. In this way the preferences can be updated in a negotiation. This class is also responsible for making the reservations when the corresponding negotiation agent notifies a successful negotiation.

The typical usage scenario of the distributed negotiation agent framework is illustrated in Figure 20.10. The scenario involves three nodes: the client node on the left side of the figure, the negotiation server node in the middle, and the service provider node on the right side.

Initially the provider process registers the provider preferences with the negotiation server. Upon registration the server creates a negotiation agent that will handle all the negotiations on behalf of the provider.

Then clients can start a negotiation process. When the server receives a negotiation request from a client for a given provider, it locates the appropriate provider agent, then it creates a client negotiation agent that will represent the client, and finally creates a mediation agent that will manage the negotiation process.

The provider agent notifies the provider of the progress and result of the negotiation. On the client side the client agent notifies the client.

20.6.3 □ Implementation

The ServerInterface interface defines the operations that are remotely accessible on the negotiation server. The first operation, registerProvider(), registers a new provider with the server; the second operation allows a client to request a negotiation with a specific provider. This interface extends Remote because it has to be remotely accessible.

```
package agent;
import java.rmi.Remote;
```

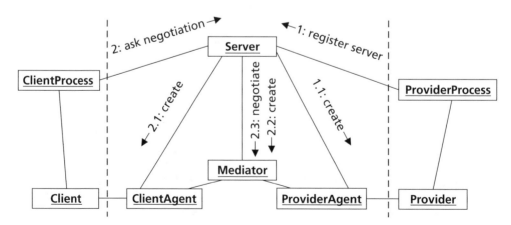

Figure 20.10 Agent negotiation collaboration diagram

```
import java.rmi.RemoteException;
import Negotiation.Preference;
public interface ServerInterface extends java.rmi.Remote {
  public void registerProvider(String providerURL,
            String providerName) throws RemoteException;
  public void negotiate(String clientURL,
            String providerName, Preference preference)
            throws RemoteException;
}
```

The Server class implements the ServerInterface and extends the MMI class DProcess. The constructor specifies the name by which the server will be accessible.

```
package agent;
import mmi.DProcess;
import Negotiation.*;
import java.util.*;
import java.rmi.RemoteException;
import java.rmi.Naming;
public class Server extends DProcess implements
                                        ServerInterface {
  final static String NAME="NegotiationServer";
  private Map providers = new Hashtable();
  public Server(String address) throws RemoteException {
    super(address,NAME);
  }
  public void registerProvider(String providerURL,
                                        String name)
        throws RemoteException{
    try{
      Preference preference = (Preference)Naming.lookup
                                        (providerURL);
      providers.put(name,new NegotiationAgent
                        (this,providerURL,preference));
    }catch(Exception e){ e.printStackTrace(); }
  }
  public void negotiate(String clientURL, String providerName,
            Preference preference) throws RemoteException{
    // find the appropriate provider agent and start it
    NegotiationAgent provider=
            (NegotiationAgent) providers.get(providerName);
    startActivity(provider);
    // create the client negotiation agent and start it
```

```
NegotiationAgent client =
        new NegotiationAgent (this,clientURL,preference);
startActivity(client);
// create a mediation agent and start the negotiation
// process
startActivity(new MediationAgent(this,client,provider));
    }
}
```

The class **NegotiationAgent** is responsible for the interaction with the remote actor, either the client or the provider of the service. It implements the Negotiatior interface. The preference can be either a preference object passed by a client or a reference to a **ProviderPreference** object that is remote. The methods of the **Negotiator** interface are implemented as a delegation to a **BasicNegotiator** object, in addition they send messages to the client to keep it updated about the progress and result of the negotiation. Since the agent must extend class **DActivity** to be remotely visible and Java forbids multiple inheritance we are forced to used delegation.

```
package agent;
import mmi.DActivity;
import mmi.DProcess;
import mmi.DEvent;
import Negotiation.*;
import java.rmi.RemoteException;

public class NegotiationAgent extends DActivity implements
                                        Negotiator {
  // the preference of the negotiator
  // (either the service provider or the service client)
  private Preference preference;
  // the URL of the negotiation client that will be notified
  // about the progress of the negotiation
  private String proxyURL;
  // the negotiator object that is encapsulated by this
  // agent
  private Negotiator negotiator;
  private boolean started;
  public NegotiationAgent(DProcess process, String proxyURL,
                        Preference preference)
                        throws RemoteException{
    super(process);
    this.proxyURL = proxyURL;
    this.preference = preference;
    started = false;
  }
  public void init(){
    negotiator = new BasicNegotiator(preference);
```

```
  try{
    this.addObserver(proxyURL,"any");
    System.out.println(this.getURL() + " started");
  }catch(Exception e){e.printStackTree(); }
}
public synchronized void step(){
  try{
    started=true;
    notifyAll();
    wait();
  }catch(InterruptedException e){}
  stop();
}
public void quit(){ }
public synchronized void completed(boolean s){
  negotiator.completed(s);
  notifyObservers(new Event("COMPLETE", this.getURL(),
                  negotiator.finalProposal()));
  notify();
}
public void intersect(Proposal own, Proposal other){
  negotiator.intersect(own,other);
}
public synchronized Proposal initialProposal(){
  // waits until the DActivity has been started and is
  // therefore remotely visible, otherwise it would not be
  // able to send notifications
  while(!started){
    try{
      wait();
    }catch(Exception e){}
  }
  Proposal initial = negotiator.initialProposal();
  notifyObservers(new DEvent("INITIAL",this.getURL(),
                                              initial));
  return initial;
}
public Proposal counterProposal(Proposal received){
  notifyObservers(new DEvent("RECEIVED",this.getURL(),
                                              received));
  try{
    Proposal sent = negotiator.counterProposal(received);
    notifyObservers(new DEvent("SENT",this.getURL(),sent));
    return sent;
  }catch(Exception e){
    System.err.println("exception in counterproposal!!!");
```

```
        e.printStackTrace();
        return null;
    }
}
public Proposal finalProposal(){
    return negotiator.finalProposal();
}
}
```

20.6.4 □ Test

The test for this application is based on the same test cases as the previous prototype. The only difference is that now three different processes must be started, possibly on different computers connected through a network.

It is important to set the names of the machines in order to allow the MMI framework to find the distributed objects correctly.

20.7 ■ Extension

The previous prototype worked on the assumption that multiple requests from service clients are serialized. In reality this could be too heavy a restriction. Therefore the system should be extended to allow multiple concurrent negotiations to be carried on.

It is important to be able to interrupt or restart a negotiation when another successful negotiation reserves a resource and modifies both the availability and the provider's preferences.

20.8 ■ Assessment

Domain analysis. The need for a general-purpose negotiation service motivated the development of this framework. The analysis of the domain started from the literature using a top-down approach.

Scope. Negotiation is a typical horizontal service that can be used in several domains, ranging from optimization to e-commerce. Domain-specific negotiation services can be developed by customizing the negotiation framework. The scope of this framework can be classified as a service.

Customization. The framework offers two levels of customization. At the first level it is possible to define the domain-specific semantics, which consists of the attributes and their possible values. At a further level it is possible to select specific negotiator classes that implement different negotiation policies. At both levels the customization can be classified as grey box.

Idiom	Cooperative frameworks
Context	There are several interdependent features that ought to be developed in a general way as reusable frameworks.
Problem	How to structure the multiple frameworks that address a possibly wide range of features while maintaining generality and extensibility?
Forces or tradeoffs	The features implemented in the frameworks are interdependent. The frameworks must be flexible and extensible. The merging of the features into a single framework reduces flexibility. A complete separation of the frameworks makes them too complex.
Solution	It is possible to identify a chain of dependency between the features that can be repeated in the frameworks. Therefore we create several layers that correspond to the frameworks; each framework can be extended individually, maintaining flexibility. The upper layers make use of the lower layers, reducing the complexity of the corresponding frameworks.
Examples	The negotiation framework and the booking framework of this prototype are an example of this pattern.
Force resolution	The interdependency is unavoidable but is limited to a chain of dependency instead of a web. The framework layers are largely independent and can be extended separately.
Design rationale	The basic idea is to simplify the dependency graph and keep the frameworks as independent as possible.

20.9 ■ References

Brugali, D. and Sycara, K. (1999) "A Model for Reusable Agent Systems", in *Implementing Application Frameworks: Object Oriented Frameworks at Work*, Fayad, M.E., Johnson, R.E. and Schmidt, D. (eds), John Wiley & Sons. 155–169.

Huhns, M.N. and Malhotra, A.K. (1999) "Negotiating for Goods and Services", *IEEE Internet Computing*, Vol. 3, No. 4, 97–99.

Triantaphyllou, E. and Shu, B. (2001) "On the Maximum Number of Feasible Ranking Sequences in Multi-criteria Decision Making Problems", *European Journal of Operational Research*, No. 130, 665–678.

Workflow management system

21

Synthesis

This chapter deals with the development of a workflow management system. Business processes can be defined using a suitable process definition language; they can be enacted by the system. Enactment consists of assigning the right task to the right person at the right time and ensuring it is carried out within the required deadline. A standard interface for monitoring and controlling processes is adopted. A proof-of-concept interface is developed making use of web-based techniques.

- Focus: the focus is on business processes that consist of long-lived transactions, as opposed to the short transactions that can be found in pure software contexts.
- OO techniques: no specific technique.
- Java features: XML DOM.
- Used knowledge: previous chapters.

21.1 ■ Specifications

The increasing complexity of office procedure has produced, in the last 10 years, an increasing interest in workflow management systems (WfMS) that automate the execution of business processes requiring several participants and a strict sequencing of activities.

We want to develop a WfMS to support the enactment of simple business processes. The system must provide a web-based interface that enables starting and participating in processes. The system operation will be based on a set of process models that can be changed from time to time.

The system must be open to integration with other WfMS applications as well with different types of user interfaces, such as graphical user interfaces and mobile device interfaces (e.g. WAP).

21.1.1 □ Process models

A business process model describes what should be done in order to complete a given task (e.g. to pass an examination). It can be divided into several activities (e.g. attend courses, assign grades, record grades) that should be performed by certain roles (e.g. student, professor, secretary).

A simple process is described by the activity diagram of Figure 21.1 It is a simplified description of a written examination process. There are two roles involved in this process: the teacher and the student. The process is made up of four activities. First the teacher defines the exercise; then the student performs it; after that the teacher corrects the student's work; finally the student can look at the results and grade.

The WfMS does not focus on the definition of process models; it uses a model to enact the process. The WfMS must be able to load a process model. The WfMS maintains a catalogue of process models that can be enacted.

21.1.2 □ Process enactment

The enactment of a process consists in assigning the correct task to the correct participant at the correct time. The rules for this assignment are encoded into the process model.

The same process model can be enacted more than once at the same time. Each instantiation of a process has its own life and evolution. The evolution of a process during its enactment is recorded into the history of the instance. Usually the process evolves in three phases:

- First a participant instantiates a process from the catalogue of available process models.
- Then the workflow participants perform the activities in the sequence required by WfMS.
- Finally after the last activity has been completed the process instance is terminated.

The assignment of activities to the workflow participants is based on matching the roles played by the participants with those required by the process.

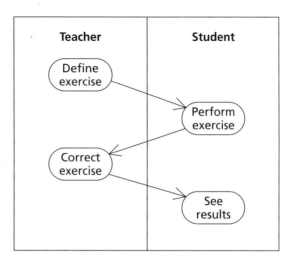

Figure 21.1 Example process

21.1.3 □ **User**

The users of the WfMS are the workflow participants. They are characterized by profiles that match against the roles required by the process models.

Each user connected to the system can see three types of information:

- The work list of pending activities, i.e. the list of activities that the user is required to perform.
- The process list, i.e. the list of processes that the user has started with their status.
- The catalogue, i.e. the list of process models that the user can instantiate and enact.

21.2 ■ **Problem analysis**

A WfMS is the computerized facilitation or automation of a business process, in whole or in part (Hollingsworth 1995). A workflow management system provides procedural automation of a business process by management of the sequence of work activities and the invocation of appropriate human or IT resources associated with the various activity steps.

The enactment of a business process by means of a workflow system can be divided into two phases:

- A build time phase in which the business process is first analysed and then modelled producing a process definition.
- A run time phase during which one or more instances of the business process are enacted requiring interaction with workflow participants.

Workflow participants can be either humans or software components represented by IT tools or specific applications.

The development of a WfMS requires interaction with several types of actors as shown in Figure 21.2. It receives from the process engineers information on the process to enact and interacts with users that can start processes or perform activities.

The specification of the system demands mainly enactment functionalities and the basic monitoring interfaces. Another important interface is the one that enables the definition of processes.

One of the requirements of the system is to be open to integration with other systems. There are standards or proposed standards that cover the above interfaces. We look into them in more detail in the next section.

21.2.1 □ **Domain models**

Since workflow systems are becoming more and more popular, there are several standards or proposed standards. The main standard body is the Workflow Management Coalition (WfMC) (http://www.wfmc.org), which is a consortium of the main vendors of workflow applications.

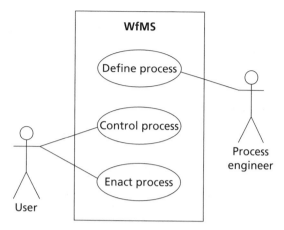

Figure 21.2 WfMS use case

The process definition is covered by a proposal (WfMC 1999). This document proposes a reference model and a grammar for a Workflow Process Definition Language (WPDL). The language is very complex, since it covers all the possible features of a workflow process, thus it is not easy to parse.

The standard Joint Workflow Management Facility – JFlow (OMG 1998) WfMC. JFlow defines the interfaces required at run time for:

- enactment of processes; and
- control of processes.

The standard confronts the issues posed by WfMS and defines a set of CORBA interfaces using the standard IDL language. Such interfaces can be easily converted into classes of any object-oriented programming language (e.g. Java) either manually or with tools (e.g. idlj).

The Java version of the standard interfaces is presented together with their relationships in Figure 21.3.

There are two main enactment interfaces: WfProcess and WfActivity; they represent entities that must perform the common operations defined in the WfExecutionObject interface: state handling (see Figure 21.1), context management and history recording.

A process is created through a WfProcessMgr that encapsulates a process definition. When a process is created it is linked to an object implementing the WfRequester interface, which will receive notifications of the events occurring during the enactment of the process.

A process is made up of steps, i.e. activities, which can either be assigned to a resource that will perform it, or act as a requester and start a subprocess. The resources are required to implement the WfResource interface. Each resource performs the set of assigned activities; the assignments are represented by the interface WfAssignment.

The evolution of the process and its activities is recorded during the enactment and forms the history of the exccution objects. The information contained in these records can be accessed through the WfEventAudit.

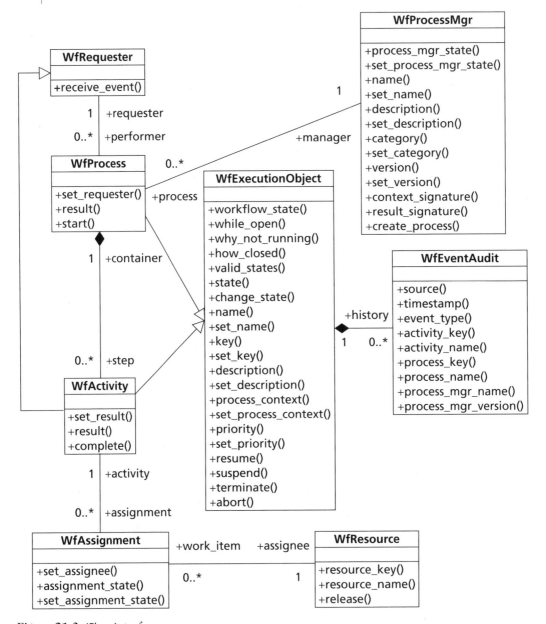

Figure 21.3 JFlow interfaces

The interfaces defined in the JFlow standard do not cover the build time interfaces used for the definition of processes.

The JFlow standard defines the possible states of the execution objects (i.e. processes and activities). Figure 21.4 presents a statechart that describes the process states and their evolution.

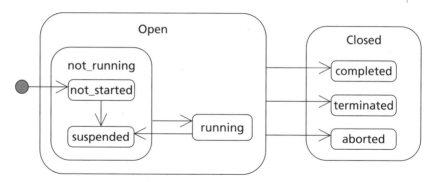

Figure 21.4 Process states

21.2.2 □ Main features

The workflow management system must exhibit the following features:

- *Enactment of processes*. The administrators must be able to activate and monitor the process. The workflow participants interact with the system (e.g. start, advance, close processes).
- *Description of processes*. The managers must be able to describe the processes that will be enacted by the system.
- *Web interface*. The system can be used through a web interface that is accessible using a browser.

21.2.3 □ Test

The test process will focus on the two functional features of the WfMS, i.e. process definition and process enactment. The tests will be carried out directly accessing the available interfaces or through a high-level web interface.

21.3 ■ Architecture and planning

The type of system we want to develop has a strong influence on the logical architecture. Both the selected standards and the literature in the field of workflow are based on a predefined conceptual model, presented in Figure 21.5.

The WfMS must handle two types of information:

- the process definitions provided at build time; and
- the status of the currently enacted processes.

These two pieces of information are closely related since the former constrains how the latter evolves. The processes and activity instances are related to processes and activities definitions that are defined in a process model.

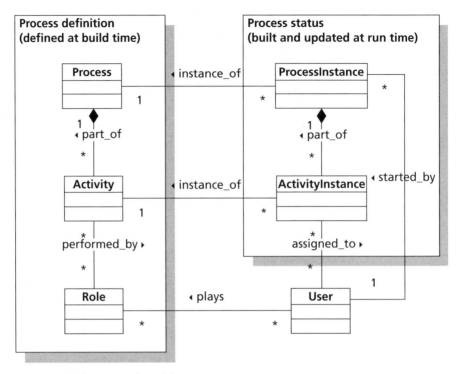

Figure 21.5 Conceptual model

The intrinsic conceptual model inspires the components that form the system. The components and their dependencies are shown in Figure 21.6. A component deals with the process definitions and process models. It is used by the workflow engine that manages the run-time evolution of the process instances. Finally a user interface component provides access to the functionalities of the WfMS.

We split the development into four prototypes, the first three incrementally build the system starting from the lower component (process definition) then adding the workflow engine, and finally providing a user interface.

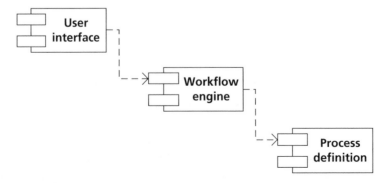

Figure 21.6 Components of the system

The fourth step develops a more complete system.

- *Prototype 1: Process definition*. The first prototype consists of a component that is able to read and manipulate process definitions; it represents the basis for all the following prototypes.
- *Prototype 2: Process enactment*. This prototype is a system that is able to enact processes based on process definitions; it does not include any user interface.
- *Prototype 3: User interface*. At this stage we develop a web-based user interface for accessing the functionalities provided by the previous prototype.
- *Prototype 4: Process data*. The system is extended with the handling of workflow relevant data.

21.4 ■ Prototype 1: Process definition

This prototype focuses on the modelling of business processes. This prototype is able to read a process model from a file and create a corresponding representation that can be accessed by the upper layer of the final WfMS. The process description language is based on the standard WPDL and on XML.

21.4.1 □ Analysis

The main purpose of this component of the WfMS architecture is to load and represent the description of a process in an easily accessible manner.

The definitions of the business processes are stored in a file. They are based on XML; the structure and organization of the description are inspired by the Workflow Process Definition Language (WPDL) described in WfMC (1999). This component must be able to load information from an XML file and provide an easily navigable structure.

The structure of the XML file is based on the description of processes in the WPDL; we ignore most of the information required by that language. The description of a process is made up of three main types of elements:

- activity;
- participant;
- transition.

We adapt the core information of WPDL to the XML syntax. The result is a compact process description language that we name XPDL.

An example of the process that will be used throughout the development of the WfMS is shown in Figure 21.7.

This process describes in XPDL format the process described in Figure 21.1 by means of an activity diagram. The process is made up of four activities described by the <ACTIVITY> tags; they are linked by three transitions

```
<?xml version="1.0" encoding="UTF-8"?>
<WORKFLOW ID="StudentTest" NAME="Student Test" VERSION="1.1" CATEGORY="TEST">
  <DESCRIPTION>
    This is a simple process used for test purposes.
    It describes the process of assigning an exercise to a student.
  </DESCRIPTION>
  <!- Activities ->
  <ACTIVITY ID="define" NAME="Define exercise">
    <IMPLEMENTATION KIND="NO" PERFORMER="professor"/>
  </ACTIVITY>
  <ACTIVITY ID="perform" NAME="Perform exercise">
    <IMPLEMENTATION KIND="NO" PERFORMER="student"/>
  </ACTIVITY>
  <ACTIVITY ID="correct" NAME="Correct exercise">
    <IMPLEMENTATION KIND="NO" PERFORMER="professor"/>
  </ACTIVITY>
  <ACTIVITY ID="feedback" NAME="See results">
    <IMPLEMENTATION KIND="NO" PERFORMER="student"/>
  </ACTIVITY>
  <!- Transitions ->
  <TRANSITION FROM="define" TO="perform"/>
  <TRANSITION FROM="perform" TO="correct"/>
  <TRANSITION FROM="correct" TO="feedback"/>
  <!- Participants ->
  <PARTICIPANT ID="professor" NAME="Professor"/>
  <PARTICIPANT ID="student" NAME="Student"/>
</WORKFLOW>
```

Figure 21.7 XML process description example

represented by the <TRANSITION> tags. The process involves two participants identified by the tag <PARTICIPANT>.

The activity attributes are the ID and the name, in addition there is a subtag – implementation – that tells whether the activity is implemented by some IT application. It specifies the role participant that should perform the activity.

The transitions specify the source and destination activities, identified by their ID. The participants identify the roles and are described by means of a unique ID and a name. The workflow relevant data are characterized by an ID, a meaningful name and the type.

21.4.2 □ Design

This component consists of a set of classes to represent a process model described using XPDL, which was presented above. The main concern we must address is the simplicity that enables seamless access to the process models by the other components of the WfMS.

How do we represent the process model in memory?

Since XPDL is based on XML there are at least two main valid options: the first consists of using the XML DOM (see Sidebar 21.1) to store and access the information, the second is to adopt a custom set of classes designed for this purpose.

The first option has practically zero cost at this moment, but when it comes to the other components that must access the process models we realize that we failed to address the simplicity of access issue. Though the DOM APIs are easy to use they represent an atomic concept, thus they introduce a semantic gap between the access mechanism and the information. This makes accessing the process models clumsy.

The second option provides an easier way to access the process models; it uses the DOM APIs to parse the XML and then stores the information in a simple structure that directly represents the process modelling concepts. The development of such a data structure requires more effort but solves the issue that was not addressed by the previous option; in addition it skips the problem of parsing the XML files.

The classes used to represent the processes described by XPDL are described in Figure 21.8.

The business process is represented by the WfProcessDefinition class. This contains two classes corresponding to the tag types used in XPDL: WfProcess Activity and WfParticipantSpecification.

These classes must be able to load information from an XML file and to generate an XML file conforming to the XPDL format. We decide to operate with the DOM classes defined in the org.w3c.dom package.

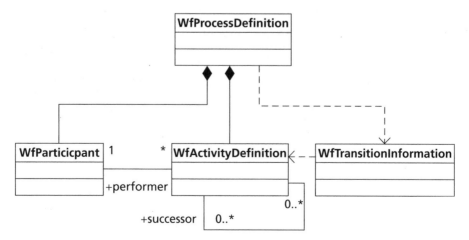

Figure 21.8 Process modelling classes

Sidebar 21.1 Java XML API

The collection of Java APIs for handling XML documents is called JAXP (Java API for XML Processing). There are two alternative strategies to process an XML document. The first consists in building an internal representation, called Document Object Model (DOM), and performing all the processing upon it. This solution and the related classes have been standardized by the W3C (www.w3c.org). The second strategy consists in providing the implementation of an interface whose methods are called when the parser encounters a given XML element; it is supported by the SAX API (Simple API for XML). In this context we will focus on the DOM approach. JAXP is part of the Java Enterprise Edition class libraries.

The main interfaces that make up the DOM API (org.w3c.dom) are represented in Figure 21.9. They are structured according to the composite pattern. The base interface is Node which can contain children nodes and can be parent of other nodes, allowing a hierarchical objects structure.

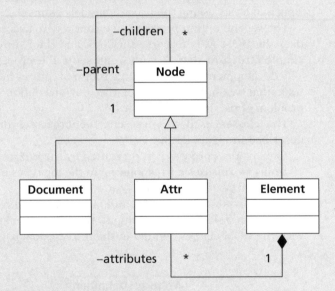

Figure 21.9 Essential XML DOM classes

Interface Document represents a complete XML document, that is the result of parsing an XML file. Interface Element represents any XML element (<TAG... />); its attributes are represented by interface Attr. The relationships are implemented by means of interface NodeList, which is not shown in Figure 21.9.

Given a Node within a document structure, it is easy to navigate to its children and print them, either using the NodeList interface:

```
NodeList children=node.getChildNodes();
for(int i=0; i<children.getLength(); ++i){
  Node child = children.item(i);
  System.out.println(child);
}
```

or using only the Node interface:

```
Node child=node.getFirstChild();
while(child!=null){
  System.out.println(child);
  child = child.getNextSibling();
}
```

Usually the navigation is driven by some criteria. Often we are interested in looking at elements of a given type. For instance, in order to visit all the top-level elements of a document having a given TAG we can use the following fragment of code:

```
Document doc = ... ;
// get the list of elements having tag "TAG"
NodeList elements = doc.getElementsByTagName("TAG");
for(int i=0; i<elements.getLength(); ++i){
  // access the i-th element; since NodeList
  // contains node we need to cast it to Element
  Element element=(Element)elements.item(i);
  // ...
}
```

Elements can contain embedded elements such as any node; in addition they may have attributes that contain string values. Interface Element provides easy access to any attribute value through method getAttribute() that takes the attribute name as parameter.

```
Element element= ... ;
String value = element.getAttribute("NAME");
```

Since JAXP has been designed for genericity, the parsing of an XML documents requires a sequence of steps:

```
// the parsing of XML documents is based on the
// DocumentBuilderFactory class
DocumentBuilderFactory dbf = DocumentBuilderFactory.
                                         newInstance();
// the XML parser is implemented by the DocumentBuilder
// class that is created by the relative factory
DocumentBuilder parser = dbf.newDocumentBuilder();
// the XML document can be obtained by parsing a file
Document doc=parser.parse(new File("test.xml"));
```

21.4.3 □ Implementation

All of the classes that make up this component are in a single package: ProcessDefinition. This simplifies the integration with the other components in the following prototypes.

The main class that is also the entry point to load the process description from an XML file is WfProcessDefinition. The class has a set of getter methods to access the read-only attributes, and the method initialActivities() that returns the activities that have no predecessors, i.e. those to be executed first.

The constructor receives a org.w3c.dom.Element object that contains the parsed description of a business process. It invokes recursively the other classes to build a representation of the process. The method toXML() does the reverse job: it generates the DOM representation of a process.

```java
package ProcessDefinition;
import org.w3c.dom.*;
import java.util.Hashtable;
import java.util.Iterator;
import java.util.Collection;
import java.util.Vector;

public class WfProcessDefinition {
  static final String TAG="WORKFLOW";
  String id;              // attribute id
  String name;            // attribute name
  String description;     // attribute description
  String version;         // attribute version
  String category;        // attribute category
  Hashtable activities=new Hashtable();
                          // the activities of the process
  Hashtable participants=new Hashtable();
                          // the process' participants
  // getter methods for the attributes
  public String getName() { return name; }
  public String getDescription() { return description; }
  public String getVersion() { return version; }
  public String getCategory() { return category; }
  // returns the initial activities
  // i.e. those without a predecessor
  public Collection initialActivities(){
    Iterator it=activities.values().iterator();
    Vector result=new Vector();
    while(it.hasNext()){
      WfActivityDefinition activity=
                      (WfActivityDefinition)it.next();
      if(activity.isStart())
        result.add(activity);
    } return result;
  }
  // return a collection of all the definitions contained
  // in a file
  public static Collection loadDefinitions(Document doc){
    NodeList processes=doc.getElementsByTagName("WORKFLOW");
    Collection definitions = new Vector();
```

```
  for(int i=0; i<processes.getLength(); ++i){
    Element process=(Element)processes.item(i);
    WfProcessDefinition pd = new WfProcessDefinition
                                              (process);
    definitions.add(pd);
  }
  return definitions;
}
// build a process definition from the corresponding XML
// element
public WfProcessDefinition(Element process){
  try{
    // get the process attributes
    id=process.getAttribute("ID");
    name=process.getAttribute("NAME");
    description = Functions.description(process);
    version = process.getAttribute("VERSION");
    category = process.getAttribute("CATEGORY");
    // get the participants
    NodeList parts=process.getElementsByTagName
                                    (WfParticipant.TAG);
    for(int i=0; i<parts.getLength(); ++i){
      Element part=(Element)parts.item(i);
      WfParticipant participant = new WfParticipant(part);
      participants.put(participant.id,participant);
    }
    // get the activities
    // (after the participants are loaded so it is
    //  possible to set up the assignment of activities in
    //  a single pass)
    NodeList acts=process.getElementsByTagName
                              (WfActivityDefinition.TAG);
    for(i=0; i<acts.getLength(); ++i){
      Element act=(Element)acts.item(i);
      WfActivityDefinition activity =
          new WfActivityDefinition(act,participants);
      activities.put(activity.id,activity);
    }
    // get the transitions among activities
    NodeList trans =
        process.getElementsByTagName
                          (WfTransitionInformation.TAG);
    for(i=0; i<trans.getLength(); ++i){
      Element tran=(Element)trans.item(i);
      new WfTransitionInformation(tran,activities);
    }
```

```
      }catch(Exception e){
        e.printStackTrace();
      }
    }
    // generate the XPDL representation of a process
    // description
    public Element toXML(Document doc){
      Element process=doc.createElement(TAG);
      process.setAttribute("ID",id);
      process.setAttribute("NAME",id);
      process.setAttribute("VERSION",version);
      process.setAttribute("CATEGORY",category);
      Element descrE = doc.createElement("DESCRIPTION");
      descrE.appendChild(doc.createTextNode(description));
      process.appendChild(descrE);
      // Activities
      Iterator it=activities.values().iterator();
      while(it.hasNext()){
        WfActivityDefinition activity=
                           (WfActivityDefinition)it.next();
        process.appendChild(activity.toXML(doc));
      }
      // Transitions
      it=activities.values().iterator();
      while(it.hasNext()){
        WfActivityDefinition from =
                           (WfActivityDefinition)it.next();
        Iterator trans=from.out.iterator();
        while(trans.hasNext()){
          WfActivityDefinition to=
                           (WfActivityDefinition)trans.next();
          Element transition=doc.createElement("TRANSITION");
          transition.setAttribute("FROM",from.id);
          transition.setAttribute("TO",to.id);
          process.appendChild(transition);
        }
      }
      // Participants
      it=participants.values().iterator();
      while(it.hasNext()){
        WfParticipant participant=(WfParticipant)it.next();
        process.appendChild(participant.toXML(doc));
      } return process;
    }
  }
```

An exception is the WfTransitionInformation class that does not contain

any information. Its constructor simply adds an outgoing and an incoming
link to the relevant activities.

```
package ProcessDefinition;
import org.w3c.dom.*;
import java.util.Map;

public class WfTransitionInformation {
  static final String TAG="TRANSITION";
  WfTransitionInformation(Element transition,
                                          Map activities){
    // get the object corresponding to the ends of the
    // transition
    WfActivityDefinition to=(WfActivityDefinition)
            activities.get(transition.getAttribute("TO"));
    WfActivityDefinition from=(WfActivityDefinition)
            activities.get(transition.getAttribute("FROM"));
    // add an incoming link to the destination
    to.addInput(from);
    // add an outgoing link to the source
    from.addOutput(to);
  }
```

The other classes in the ProcessDefinition package are similar to (and
usually simpler than) the WfProcessDefinition class. They all have a constructor that loads the information from the XML DOM tree and a toXML()
method that generate the XPDL representation of the process.

21.4.4 ☐ Test

To test the functionalities of the process definition classes we read a process
model from an XML file and write it back to another XML file. The test
succeeds if the contents of the two files are the same, except for the order of
the tags. The test file is the one shown in Figure 21.7.

```
package ProcessDefinition;
import javax.xml.parsers.*;
import org.w3c.dom.*;
import java.io.File;
import org.apache.crimson.tree.XmlDocument;

public class TestClasses {
  public static void main(String[] args) throws Exception {
    // create an XML parser
    DocumentBuilder parser =

DocumentBuilderFactory.newInstance().newDocumentBuilder();
    // parse the document and obtain a dom tree for the
    // document
```

```
Document doc=parser.parse(new File("test.xml"));
// load all the process definitions contained in the file
Collection processes=
              (WfProcessDefinition.loadDefinitions(doc);
// iterates on each process definition
Iterator it=processes.iterator();
Document result=parser.newDocument();
while(it.hasNext()){
  WfProcessDefinition pd=(WfProcessDefinition)it.next();
  // creates the XML corresponding to the process
  // definition
  Element output=pd.toXML(result);
  result.appendChild(output);
}
// use the underlying implementation to print the XML
// file because the standard interfaces do not have a
// pretty printing feature
XmlDocument res = (XmlDocument)result;
res.write(System.out);
res.write(new FileOutputStream(new File("out.xml")));
  }
}
```

21.5 ■ Prototype 2: Process enactment

This prototype focuses on the enactment of the processes. The monitoring and interaction with the processes are carried out through the standard JFlow interfaces.

21.5.1 □ Analysis

We adopt an interface to enact and monitor the evolution of processes conforming to the Joint Workflow Management Facility (OMG 1998), which is described in Section 21.2.1.

The JFlow standard is quite generic therefore we make some simplifying assumptions. First, the execution objects have a process context that should comprise the additional process information; we assume the process context is empty. Second, in general, resources can be anything ranging from a human to an IT application. In our work we make the assumption that resources are only the people that participate in the workflow.

21.5.2 □ Design

The design of the enactment engine is straightforward since it is based on a standard interface. The classes and interfaces are organized into packages as shown in Figure 21.10. The interfaces that are defined by the standard are divided into two packages, WorkflowModel and WfBase. The package WfEngine contains the implementation of the standard interfaces; this package makes use of the ProcessDefinition package that was developed in the previous prototype.

The standard JFlow interfaces have a well-defined structure (shown in Figure 21.3) that constrains the development of the WfEngine package.

Decision point

How do we implement the standard JFlow interfaces?

The problem is how closely we follow the structure of the JFlow interfaces in the WfEngine package. If we want to have more freedom in the development of the engine we can adopt a structure that is loosely related to that of JFlow; this solution requires a set of classes that provide an adaptation layer between the engine and the standard interface. As a result, more freedom requires more effort. On the other hand, if we adopt a structure that is homologous to that of JFlow we are more constrained in the development but we do not need any sort of adaptation. In addition, since the workflow conceptual model is similar to the JFlow structure it is not difficult to conform to both at once.

The structure of the WfEngine package together with the relationships to the ProcessDefinition and WorkflowModel packages are sketched in Figure 21.11. Here only the main classes are shown. In fact there is an implementation class for each JFlow interface, plus the interfaces in the fBase package.

The Catalog class is a singleton that is the access point to select the processes to enact. The process definitions are represented by the class WfProcessMgrImpl that implements the WfProcessMgr interface defined in the WorkflowModel package. A process that is in course of enactment is

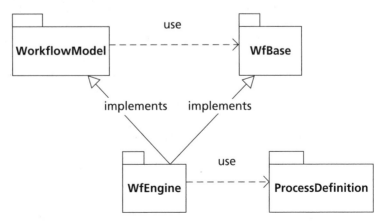

Figure 21.10 Workflow package structure

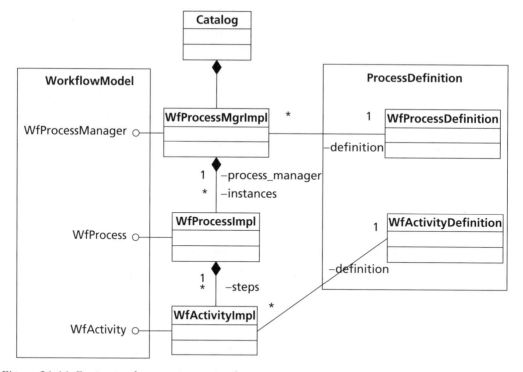

Figure 21.11 Engine implementation main classes

represented by the WfProcessImpl class that implements the WfProcess interface. The activities of the process are described by the WfActivityImpl, which
implements the WfActivity and is driven by a WfActivityDefinition.

The users of the WfMS interact with the system either by starting a process or by performing an activity. The classes involved in starting a process
are those presented above; the main classes involved in the execution of the
activities are presented in Figure 21.12.

The execution of activities requires two main operations: the assignment
of an activity to a user and the performance of the activity by the user.

The users of the WfMS are represented by the Actor class and they are
contained by the class Organization. The actors implement the interface
WfRequester in order to start a process, and they are related to the process
instances that are the performers of the required processes. In addition the
actors implement the WfResource interface so they can become the assignee
of activities, therefore they have a work list made up of work items that
consist of assignments to activities.

The navigation of the data structure is based on the iterator pattern as
shown in the Figure 21.13. The JFlow standard defines a BaseIterator in the
WfBase package that is the base of the specific iterators (e.g. WfProcess Iterator,
WfActivityIterator) defined in the WorkflowModel package. The WfEngine
package provides the implementation of all the iterators; the structure of the
implementation maintains the same structure as that of the JFlow standard.

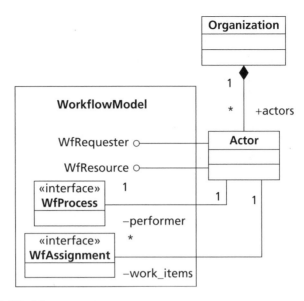

Figure 21.12 Workflow participants

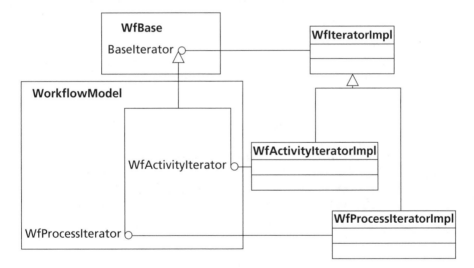

Figure 21.13 Engine iterators

21.5.3 □ Implementation

The workflow engine is divided into three packages: WorkflowModel and WfBase which contain the JFlow interfaces, and WfEngine which contains all the implementation classes.

The entry point of the WfMS is the Catalog class; it contains the collection of available processes that are represented by instances of WfProcessMgrImpl. The catalogue has two methods for browsing the process definitions: getAll() which returns a collection of all available processes, and getProcess() which returns the process manager for a given process. In addition there are two Add() methods to populate the catalogue; they add process definitions or a collections.

```
package WfEngine;
import java.util.*;
import ProcessDefinition.WfProcessDefinition;
import WorkflowModel.WfProcessMgr;
import WfBase.BaseException;
public class Catalog {
  // contains the collection of processes, accessible by name
  private Map processes=new Hashtable();
  // return the collection of all processes
  public Collection getAll(){
    return processes.values();
  }
  // return the manager corresponding to the process with
  // the given name
  public WfProcessMgr getProcess(String name){
    return (WfProcessMgr)processes.get(name);
  }
  // add the manager for the given process definition
  public void Add(WfProcessDefinition process)
                                          throws BaseException {
    WfProcessMgr mgr=new WfProcessMgrImpl(process);
    processes.put(mgr.name(),mgr);
  }
  // add the managers for the collection of process
  // definitions
  public void Add(Collection definitions)
                                          throws BaseException {
    Iterator it=definitions.iterator();
    while(it.hasNext()){
      Add((WfProcessDefinition)it.next());
    }
  }
}
```

The instantiation of processes is mediated by the interface WfProcessMgr through the create_process() method. In addition there are methods to browse all the process instances created by the process manager.

```
package WorkflowModel;
import WfBase.BaseException;
public interface WfProcessMgr {
  int how_many_processes () throws WfBase.BaseException;
  WfProcessIterator get_iterator_process ()
                                          throws BaseException;
```

```
WfProcess[] get_sequence_process (int max_number)
            throws BaseException;
boolean is_member_of_process (WfProcess member)
            throws BaseException;
process_mgr_stateType process_mgr_state ()
            throws BaseException;
void set_process_mgr_state (process_mgr_stateType
                                            new_state)
            throws BaseException, TransitionNotAllowed;
String name () throws BaseException;
void set_name (String new_value) throws BaseException;
String description () throws BaseException;
void set_description (String new_value)
                                    throws BaseException;
String category () throws BaseException;
void set_category (String new_value) throws BaseException;
String version () throws BaseException;
void set_version (String new_value) throws BaseException;
NameValueInfo[] context_signature () throws BaseException;
NameValueInfo[] result_signature () throws BaseException;
WfProcess create_process(WfRequester requester)
            throws BaseException, NotEnabled;
}
```

The **WfPRocessMgrImpl** implements the **WfProcessImpl** interface. The constructor takes a process definition as an argument. All the methods are quite simple since they are getters and setters. Most of the methods defined by JFlow in this and other interfaces are like these.

```
package WfEngine;
...
class WfProcessMgrImpl implements WfProcessMgr {
  private Vector instances;
  private WfProcessDefinition definition;
  private process_mgr_stateType state;
  private String description;

  WfProcessMgrImpl(WfProcessDefinition definition) {
    This.definition = definition;
    state = process_mgr_stateType.enabled;
    instances = new Vector();
  }
  public int how_many_processes() throws BaseException {
    return instances.size();
  }
  public WfProcessIterator get_iterator_process()
                                    throws BaseException {
    return new WfProcessIteratorImpl(instances);
  }
```

```java
public WfProcess[] get_sequence_process(int max_number)
     throws BaseException {
  return (WfProcess[]) instances.subList(0,max_number-1)
                     .toArray(new WfProcess[max_number]);
}
public boolean is_member_of_process(WfProcess member)
                                            throws BaseException {
  return instances.contains(member);
}
public process_mgr_stateType process_mgr_state()
                                            throws BaseException {
  return state;
}
public void set_process_mgr_state (process_mgr_stateType
                                     new_state)
             throws BaseException, TransitionNotAllowed {
  state = new_state;
}
public String name() throws BaseException {
  return definition.getName();
}
public void set_name(String new_value)
                                        throws BaseException {
  throw new WfBase.BaseException
                 ("Cannot change process manager name");
}
public String description() throws BaseException {
  return definition.getDescription();
}
public NameValueInfo[] context_signature()
                                        throws BaseException {
  return null;
}
public synchronized WfProcess create_process(WfRequester
                                  requester)
         throws  BaseException, NotEnabled {
  if( state == process_mgr_stateType.enabled ){
    WfProcess process = new WfProcessImpl (this,
                              definition,requester);
    instances.add(process);
    return process;
  }else{
    throw new NotEnabled();
  }
}
}
```

The state of the manager is represented by the class process_mgr_ stateType. It conforms to the *Enumeration* pattern (see *Enumeration* idiom (McCluskey 2001)). This pattern is used to represent the possible values of the states of the workflow objects.

```
package WorkflowModel;
public class process_mgr_stateType {
  private final String value;
  private process_mgr_stateType(String value)
                                  { this.value = value; }
  public static final process_mgr_stateType enabled=
        new process_mgr_stateType("enabled");
  public static final process_mgr_stateType disabled=
        new process_mgr_stateType("disabled");
  public String toString(){return value;}
}
```

The workflow execution objects (i.e. processes and activities) share several common features that are collected in the WfExecutionObjectImpl class that implements the WfExecutionObject interface. These features include mainly the management of state transitions and the recording of history events. The first feature takes advantage of the WfObjectState class that realizes the *State* pattern (see *State* pattern (Gamma *et al.* 1995)), the second uses the WfEventAuditImpl class that implements the WfEventAudit interface. Here we skip these classes for reasons of space.

The instance of a process is represented by the class WfProcessImpl. The constructor links the instance to its manager, the process definition and the requester. Each instance is assigned a unique identifier; in the presence of a persistent database this id could be generated by the database itself.

The method start() activates the process instance, checks if the process has been started already, then it creates the activities corresponding to the initial activities of the process definition, and finally sends an event to the requester to notify it that the process started (or that some error was encountered).

When an activity of the process is completed, the method completed() is invoked. This method checks whether it was the last activity to be completed. In this case it changes the state of the process to completed. Otherwise it creates the activities corresponding to the successors in the process definition.

```
package WfEngine;
...
public class WfProcessImpl
extends ExecutionObjectImpl
implements WfProcess {
  WfRequester originator;
  WfProcessMgr processManager;
  WfProcessDefinition definition;
```

```
Vector steps=new  Vector();
NameValue[] processResult;
static private long uniqueId=1;
static private String getId(){
  return Long.toString(uniqueId++);
}
WfProcessImpl(WfProcessMgr mgr, WfProcessDefinition def,
                                    WfRequester req) {
  super(def.getName());
  originator = req;
  processManager = mgr;
  definition = def;
  try{
    set_key(getId());
    set_description(def.getDescription());
  }catch(Exception e){ }
}
public void start() throws BaseException, CannotStart,
                                    AlreadyRunning {
  if( state.workflow_state() == workflow_stateType.open){
    if( state.while_open() == while_openType.not_running &&
       state.why_not_running() == why_not_running Type.
                                    not_started ){
      WfEventAudit event;
      try{
        Collection initialActivities =
                         definition.initialActivities();
        Iterator it=initialActivities.iterator();
        while(it.hasNext()){
          WfActivity activity=new WfActivityImpl(this,
                      WfActivityDefinition) it.next());
          steps.add(activity);
        }
        change_state(workflow_stateType.open,
                    while_openType.running, null,null);
        event=new WfEventAuditImpl(this,"process started");
      }catch(Exception e){
        change_state(workflow_stateType.closed,null,null,
                    state.how_closed().aborted);
        event = new WfEventAuditImpl(this,
                "Aborted, reason: " + e.toString());
      }
```

```
        history.add(event);
        originator.receive_event(event);
      }else
        throw new WorkflowModel.AlreadyRunning();
    else
      throw new WorkflowModel.CannotStart();
  }
  void completed(WfActivityImpl current)
                            throws WfBase.BaseException {
    WfEventAudit event=new WfEventAuditImpl
                        (current,"activity completed");
    history.add(event);
    originator.receive_event(event);
    Collection nextActivities = current.definition.
                                        nextActivities();
    if(nextActivities.isEmpty()){
      // When a possible "last" activity has completed,
      //  check if there are other pending (i.e. open)
      //  activities
      WfActivityIterator it=get_iterator_step();
      WfActivity act;
      while((act=it.get_next_object()) != null){
        if(act.workflow_state().equals
                          (workflow_stateType.open)){
          // If an open activity is found then it was not
          // the last activity and nothing is to be done.
          return;
        }
      }
      // Otherwise, it was effectively the last activity,
      // the process then is completed.
      change_state(workflow_stateType.closed, null, null,
                how_closedType.completed);
      event=new WfEventAuditImpl(this,"process completed");
      history.add(event);
      originator.receive_event(event);
      return;
    }
    // creates the successive activities
    Iterator it = nextActivities.iterator();
    while(it.hasNext()){
      WfActivity activity = new WfActivityImpl(this,
                        (WfActivityDefinition)it.next());
      steps.add(activity);
    }
  }
  ...
}
```

The activities are represented by the WfActivityImpl class that implements the WfActivity interface. The constructor has the main task of assigning the activity to some workflow participant.

```
package WfEngine;
...
class WfActivityImpl
extends ExecutionObjectImpl
implements WfActivity {
  WfProcess process;
  WfActivityDefinition definition;
  Vector workItems=new Vector();
  Vector context=new Vector();
  static private long uniqueId=1;
  static private String getId(){
    return Long.toString(uniqueId++);
  }
  public WfActivityImpl(WfProcess proc,
                                    WfActivityDefinition def) {
    super(def.getName());
    process = proc;
    definition = def;
    try{
      set_description(def.getDescription());
      set_key(getId());
    }catch(Exception e){ }
    // set up activity assignments
    WfParticipant performer=def.getPerformer();
    Actor actor=Organization.match(performer.getName());
    WfAssignmentImpl workItem=new WfAssignmentImpl
                                             (this,actor);
    workItems.add(workItem);
    actor.addWorkItem(workItem);
  }
  public void complete() throws BaseException,
                                    CannotComplete {
    if(state.workflow_state() == workflow_stateType.open &&
        state.while_open() == while_openType.running){
      change_state(workflow_stateType.closed, null, null,
              how_closedType.completed);
      history.add(new WfEventAuditImpl(this,"Completed"));
      ((WfProcessImpl)process).completed(this);
    }else{ throw new WorkflowModel.CannotComplete(); }
  }
  ...
  }
```

21.5.4 □ Test

To test the engine and its implementation of the workflow model we need to simulate the enactment of a process. We load the process definitions into the catalogue and create the actors with the profile required by the process.

The file test.xml contains the XPDL description shown in Figure 21.7. We use the **performActivity()** method to simulate a user logging into the system and first starting and then completing the pending activities.

```java
import javax.xml.parsers.*;
import java.io.File;
import org.w3c.dom.*;
import ProcessDefinition.*;
import WfEngine.*;
import WorkflowModel.*;


public class TestEngine {
  public static void main(String[] args) {
    // creates the process catalog and the organization
    WfEngine.Organization org=new WfEngine.Organization();
    WfEngine.Catalog cat = new WfEngine.Catalog();
    try{
        // open a XPDL description file
        DocumentBuilder parser=
            DocumentBuilderFactory.newInstance().
                                        newDocumentBuilder();
        Document doc=parser.parse(new File("web/test.xml"));
        // load the process definitions in the catalog
        cat.Add(WfProcessDefinition.loadDefinitions(doc));
        // define actors that can interact with WFMS
        Actor prof=new Actor("Prof Essor","professor");
        Actor student=new Actor("John Learner","student");
        // and add them to the organization
        org.Add(prof);
        org.Add(student);
        // get the process manager for the test process
        WfProcessMgr mgr=cat.getProcess("Student Test");
        // creates the process
        WfProcess procInst = mgr.create_process(prof);
        prof.addPerformer(procInst);
        // start the process
        procInst.start();
        // loop while the process is open
        while(procInst.workflow_state()==
                                    workflow_stateType.open){
          performActivity(prof);
          performActivity(student);
        }
```

```
      }catch(Exception e){
        System.err.println(e.toString());
        e.printStackTrace();
      }
    }
    // perform all the pending activities on behalf of the
    // actor
    static void performActivity(Actor actor)
                                throws WfBase.BaseException {
      // iterate on all work items of the resource
      WfAssignmentIterator it=actor.get_iterator_work_item();
      WfAssignment workItem;
      while((workItem=it.get_next_object())!=null){
        WfActivity activity=workItem.activity();
        if(activity.workflow_state() ==
                                      workflow_stateType.open){
          if(activity.while_open() == while_openType.running){
            // if the activity is open and running completes it
            activity.complete();
            System.out.println
                            ("Completed: " + activity.name());
          }else
          if(activity.why_not_running() ==
                            why_not_runningType.not_started){
            // if the activity is not started yet,
                                  change its state to running
            activity.change_state(workflow_stateType.open +
                              "." + while_openType.running);
            System.out.println("Started: " + activity.name());
          }
        }
      }
    }
  }
```

21.6 ■ Prototype 3: User interface

This prototype focuses on providing a web-based user interface to the WfMS developed in the previous step. The interface is built with JSP technology (see Sidebar 16.2, page 436), the Java pages use the JFlow interface to monitor and enact the processes.

21.6.1 □ Analysis

The interaction with the WfMS involves two main features:

■ management and monitoring of processes;
■ enactment of processes.

The first feature encompasses operations such as starting processes and observing their state during the enactment. The second feature requires the capability of performing the activities listed in the work list. Since the user interface we want to develop is very simple, we will merge these features together. An example of the interface is shown in Figure 21.14. The figure shows how the page appears in a browser window. The page is divided into three sections:

- Work List: presents the activities that the user should perform.
- Processes: shows the processes that the user started and can monitor.
- Process Catalog: shows a list of available processes the user can start.

The only process available in this case is the StudentTest process that we already developed in the previous prototypes. The user has started two instances of this process; they are both in the state open.running. There are two pending activities in the work list: Define exercise and Correct exercise, they are activities belonging to the instances started by the user (as we can see from the process keys shown in parentheses).

For the sake of simplicity, in this prototype we avoid the use of a database to keep persistent information about users, processes and activities.

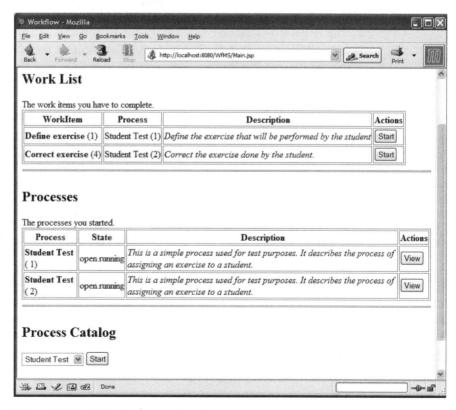

Figure 21.14 Web interface main page

21.6.2 □ **Design**

This prototype consists of a set of JSP classes that give access to the WfMS interfaces. We must keep the information about the users when they are connected to the system, and the information on the state of the processes and activities across the user sessions.

Decision point

How do we keep the state for both the connected user and the processes?

The JSP standard defines two name spaces that can be used to store that information: the context and the session. The former is initialized when the JSP container starts, and destroyed when it shuts down; therefore it is suited for keeping the long-lived information about the process state. The session is associated with an HTTP session and is suited for keeping the information about the user.

The overall structure of the user interface is presented in the class diagram shown in Figure 21.15. The figure is divided into two parts: the upper part shows the classes involved in the context, while the lower part contains the classes involved in the session.

The context is initialized by the ContextListener class that is invoked on startup. It creates an Organization and a Catalog and initializes them, then stores them in the application context that is represented by class ServletContext.

The session contains only one object of class Actor which represents the user. It is created and registered within the session when the user enters the application. The application entry point is represented by the Login page and it is linked to the main page that contains all the useful information. It is possible to start a process through the Instantiate page and monitor its state through the Process page. Likewise, it is possible to access a work item using the WorkItem page and complete the corresponding activity through the Complete page. Finally the Logout page closes the session.

The Main page authenticates the user and creates the corresponding Actor object, then all the pages access the Actor to perform their operations.

21.6.3 □ **Implementation**

The context of the WfMS applications is built up by the ContextListener class, whose method contextInitialized() is invoked when the container starts. This method defines two objects that are part of the context: the organization and the process catalogue.

```
import WfEngine.*;
import ProcessDefinition.*;
import javax.xml.parsers.*;
```

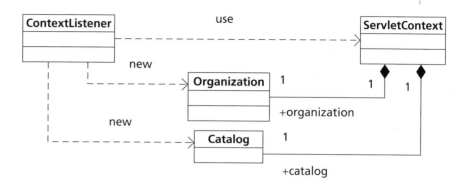

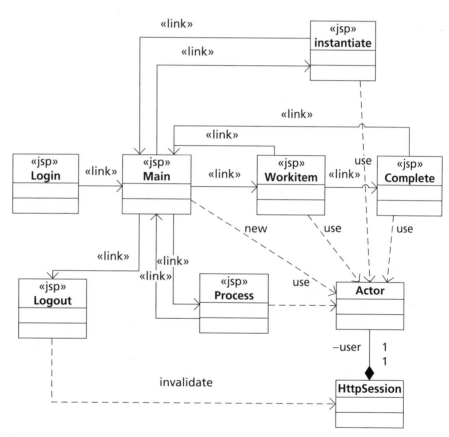

Figure 21.15 Web interface design

```
import org.w3c.dom.*;
import java.io.File;
import javax.servlet.*;
import java.io.IOException;
public final class ContextListener
   implements ServletContextListener {
```

```
public void contextInitialized(ServletContextEvent event) {
   System.out.println("Initializing Workflow context...");
   ServletContext context = event.getServletContext();
   System.out.println("1) Definition of organization");
 try{
   // We define two basic example profiles: professor and
   // student; they are actors that can interact with WFMS
   Actor prof=new Actor("Prof Essor","professor");
   Actor student=new Actor("John Learner","student");
   WfEngine.Organization org=new WfEngine.Organization();
   org.Add(prof);
   org.Add(student);
   context.setAttribute("organization",org);

   System.out.println("2) Load definitions of processes");
   // The processes are loaded from an xml file
   WfEngine.Catalog cat = new WfEngine.Catalog();
   DocumentBuilder parser= DocumentBuilderFactory.
                           newInstance().newDocumentBuilder();
   Document doc = parser.parse(
               context.getResourceAsStream("test.xml"));
   cat.Add(WfProcessDefinition.loadDefinitions(doc));
   context.setAttribute("catalog",cat);
 }catch(Exception e){
   e.printStackTrace();
   e.toString();
 }
 System.out.println("WfMS Initialization Completed.");
 }
 public void contextDestroyed
                       (ServletContextEvent event) {   }
}
```

The initial page is Login.jsp. To simplify the application we ignore all of the security problems and allow the login without any authentication. The Login page presents a list of actors the user can choose to impersonate; they are taken from the actors registered within the organization.

```
<%@ page contentType="text/html" language="java" %>
<%@ page import="WfEngine.*, java.util.Iterator" %>
<% Organization org=(Organization)application.getAttribute
                                     ("organization"); %>
<html><head><title>Workflow</title></head>
<body><h1>Workflow Login</h1>
<table>
<tr><td align="center">
```

```
<form action="Main.jsp" method="POST">
User: <select name="user">
<%Iterator actors=org.getAll().iterator();
  while(actors.hasNext()){
    Actor user=(Actor)actors.next();
    try{
      %><option><%=user.resource_name()%><%
    }catch(WfBase.BaseException e)
                          {%><!-- user with no name  --><%}
  }
%></select>
<br><input type="submit" value="Login">
</form></table>
</body></html>
```

The user interacts with the Main.jsp page. The page first loads the information about the user either from the organization, if the user is arriving from the Login page, or from the session.

The page contains three sections. The first section contains the work list. For each assignment of an open activity there are the summary of the activity and a button to see the details and complete the activity. The second section contains the list of processes started by the user. For each process originated by the user it shows the name (and key), state, description and a link to the detail page. The third section presents a list of the process definitions available in the catalogue.

```
<%t@ page contentType="text/html" language="java" %>
<%@ page import="WfEngine.*, WorkflowModel.*,
                                      java.util.Iterator" %>
<%
  // takes organization and catalog from context
  Organization org=(Organization)application.getAttribute
                                        ("organization");
  WfEngine.Catalog cat=(WfEngine.Catalog)application.
                                  getAttribute("catalog");
  // takes the user name from the request
  String userName = request.getParameter("user");
  Actor user;
  if(userName!=null){ // i.e. arriving from login
    user = org.getActor(userName);
    session.setAttribute("user",user);
  }else{  // returning from other pages
    user = (Actor)session.getAttribute("user");
  }
%>
<html><head><title>Workflow</title></head>
<body>
```

```
<% try{ %>
<h1><%= user.resource_name() %></h1>
<hr><h2>Work List</h2>
The work items you have to complete:
<!--  shows the worklist of the user  -->
<table border=1>
<tr><th>WorkItem<th>Process<th>Description<th>Actions</tr>
<%
    // for each workItem..
    WfAssignmentIterator it=user.get_iterator_work_item();
    WfAssignment workItem;
    while((workItem=it.get_next_object())!=null){
      // ..take the corresponding activity..
      WfActivity activity=workItem.activity();
      // ..and if it is open..
      if(activity.workflow_state() ==
                                 workflow_stateType.open){
      // show a row in the table with the details of the
      // activity
%>
   <tr><td><b> <%= activity.name() %> </b>
                                     (<%= activity.key() %>)
        <td><%=activity.container().name()%>
                         (<%= activity.container().key() %>)
        <td><i> <%=activity.description()%> </i>
        <td><form action="WorkItem.jsp" method="POST">
            <input type=hidden name="workItem"
                                value="<%=activity.key()%>">
        <% if(activity.while_open() ==
                             while_openType.not_running){
          %><input type="submit" value="Start"><%
          }else{
          %><input type="submit" value="View"><%
          }
        %></form><%
        }
      } %>
</table>
<!-- shows the list of processes started by the user -->
<hr><h2>Processes</h2>
The processes you started.
<table border=1>
<tr><th>Process<th>State<th>Description<th>Actions</tr>
<%  // for each process originated by the user..
    WfProcessIterator procs=user.get_iterator_performer();
    WfProcess process;
```

```
            while((process=procs.get_next_object())!=null){
%>
            <!-- ..show name (and key),.. -->
    <tr><td><b> <%=process.name()%> </b> ( <%t=process.key()%>)
              <!-- state,.. -->
        <td> <%=process.state()%>
              <!-- description,..-->
        <td><i><%=process.description()%></i>
              <!-- link to detail page,.. -->
        <td><form action="Process.jsp" method="POST">
            <input type=hidden name="process"
                                    value="<%=process.key()%>">
            <input type="submit" value="View">
            </form><%
        }%>
</table>
<hr>
<!-- shows the catalog of process definitions -->
<h2>Process Catalog</h2>
<form action="Instantiate.jsp" method="post">
<select name="process"><%
    Iterator defs=cat.getAll().iterator();
    while(defs.hasNext()){
      WfProcessMgr mgr=(WfProcessMgr)defs.next();
      %><option><%=mgr.name()%> <%
    }%>
</select>
<input type="submit" value="Start">
</form>
<hr>
<a href="Logout.jsp">Log out</a>
<hr>
<% }catch(WfBase.BaseException e){ %>
  <h1>Error</h1>
  <pre><%=e.toString()%></pre>
<% } %>
</body></html>
```

21.6.4 ☐ Test

It is possible to test the functionalities of the web interface performing the same operations in the test of the underlying workflow engine. The steps are:

- Log in as the professor.
- Start the test process.
- Perform the Define exercise activity.

- Log out.
- Log in as the student.
- Perform the activity **Perform exercise.**
- Log out.
- Log in as the professor.
- Perform the activity **Correct exercise.**
- Log out.
- Log in as the student.
- Perform the activity **See results.**
- Log out.
- Log in as the professor.
- Look at the process details, the process should be in the state **closed. complete.**

21.7 ■ Prototype 4: Process data

This prototype extends the previous one with the capability of handling workflow-relevant data. The data are available in each activity according to the rules defined in the process definition.

21.7.1 □ Analysis

The main enhancement introduced by this prototype is represented by the possibility of defining the data that are manipulated during the enactment of a process. Each piece of data is characterized by a type and the way it can be used in each activity that constitutes the process. The WfMS must handle the data and present them to the user during the enactment.

The first step is the definition of the workflow-relevant data within the process definition. Figure 21.16 shows the **StudentTest** process used in previous prototypes with the addition of the data type declaration and the activity access restrictions.

The XPDL is extended with two tags. The **DATA** tag appears directly inside the **WORKFLOW** element and describes the data manipulated by the process in terms of a name and a type. The **RESTRICT_TO** tag appears within the **ACTIVITY** elements and specifies the access restrictions of the activity to the data.

In principle the workflow can handle a wide range of data types. For the purpose of this prototype we consider only one type: **String.** It is a plain text string that can be easily read and modified by the users.

The access restrictions specify what pieces of data are accessible during the enactment of an activity and how they can be accessed: either read only or read and write. If no **RESTRICT_TO** tag is specified then all the data are accessible in read and write mode. Otherwise the tags specify which pieces of data can be accessed.

Finally the data that are accessible to an activity must be presented to the user by the user interface. When an activity is started the user must see the

```
<?xml version="1.0" encoding="UTF-8"?>
<WORKFLOW ID="StudentTest" NAME="Student Test"
                                    VERSION="1.1" CATEGORY="TEST">
  <DESCRIPTION>
    This is a simple process used for test purposes.
    It describes the process of assigning an exercise to a student.
  </DESCRIPTION>
  <!-- Activities -->
  <ACTIVITY ID="define" NAME="Define exercise">
    <DESCRIPTION> Define the exercise </DESCRIPTION>
    <IMPLEMENTATION KIND="NO" PERFORMER="professor"/>
    <RESTRICT_TO REF="exercise"/>
  </ACTIVITY>
  <ACTIVITY ID="perform" NAME="Perform exercise">
    <DESCRIPTION> Perform the exercise. </DESCRIPTION>
    <IMPLEMENTATION KIND="NO" PERFORMER="student"/>
    <RESTRICT_TO READ_ONLY="Yes" REF="exercise"/>
    <RESTRICT_TO REF="solution"/>
  </ACTIVITY>
  <ACTIVITY ID="correct" NAME="Correct exercise">
    <DESCRIPTION>
          Correct the exercise done by the student.
    </DESCRIPTION>
    <IMPLEMENTATION KIND="NO" PERFORMER="professor"/>
    <RESTRICT_TO READ_ONLY="Yes" REF="exercise"/>
    <RESTRICT_TO READ_ONLY="Yes" REF="solution"/>
    <RESTRICT_TO REF="evaluation"/>
  </ACTIVITY>
  <ACTIVITY ID="feedback" NAME="See results">
    <DESCRIPTION> Look at the correction. </DESCRIPTION>
    <IMPLEMENTATION KIND="NO" PERFORMER="student"/>
    <RESTRICT_TO READ_ONLY="Yes" REF="exercise"/>
    <RESTRICT_TO READ_ONLY="Yes" REF="solution"/>
    <RESTRICT_TO READ_ONLY="Yes" REF="evaluation"/>
  </ACTIVITY>
  <!-- Transitions  -->
  <TRANSITION FROM="define" TO="perform"/>
  <TRANSITION FROM="perform" TO="correct"/>
  <TRANSITION FROM="correct" TO="feedback"/>
  <!-- Participants -->
  <PARTICIPANT ID="professor" NAME="professor"/>
  <PARTICIPANT ID="student" NAME="student"/>
  <!-- Data -->
  <DATA ID="exercise" NAME="Exercise Text" TYPE="String"/>
  <DATA ID="solution" NAME="Exercise Solution" TYPE="String"/>
  <DATA ID="evaluation" NAME="Result" TYPE="String"/>
</WORKFLOW>
```

Figure 21.16 XPDL process definition with workflow data

available data and be able to modify the data and store an updated version or submit the final version and complete the activity.

21.7.2 □ Design

The design of this prototype consists of three increments to the previous one: an extension to the process definition package to load the information about the workflow data, an extension to the engine to handle the data during the enactment, and an extension to the web interface to present the data to the user and allow modification.

The first increment is summarized by the class diagram shown in Figure 21.17. The WfProcessDefinition contains a new class WfDataDefinition, which is linked to the WfActivity class through the WfAccessRestriction class that specifies what data are available, and with what access permission during the activity enactment.

The second increment addresses the classes WfProcessImpl and WfActivityImpl. These two classes should now handle the data. The process must instantiate the data that make up the context when the process is created. The activity must access the data according to the access restrictions defined in the process definition.

Decision point

How do we limit the access to the workflow data in the activities?

We can chose several actors as responsible for complying with the access restrictions provided in the process definition. The three main possibilities are: client code that accesses the JFlow interfaces (e.g. the JSP user interface), the process classes and the activity classes.

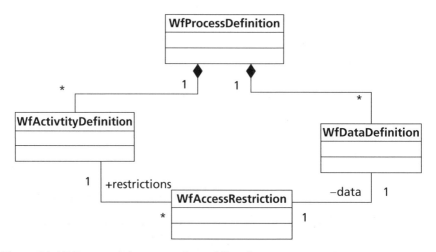

Figure 21.17 Process definition with workflow data

If the client code is responsible there is no guarantee that the access restrictions will be observed and in addition this makes the client code complex. If the WfProcessImpl class is responsible, then all the management of the context is concentrated in that class, but the class is more complex. Finally if the WfActivityImpl class is responsible, the access restrictions that concern an activity are kept together with the rest of the activity-related code. This makes the process class simpler and the activity class more complex. We prefer this last option because we think it best concentrates all the code related to the activities in a single class.

The handling of the workflow data requires only some changes to the JSP developed in the previous prototype. The WorkItem page must present the data visible to the activity while the Complete page must be able either to store an update to the data or to complete the activity.

21.7.3 ☐ Implementation

The class WfProcessDefinition, in addition to the tag already implemented, must be able to load the definitions of the workflow data. This is accomplished by adding a Map object that stores the WfDataDefinition instances and adding a loop that reads all the elements with the DATAtag. An analogous loop is required in the toXML() method to generate the tags.

```
package ProcessDefinition;
...

public class WfProcessDefinition {
  ...
  Map data=new Hashtable();
  // build a process definition from the corresponding XML
  // element
  public WfProcessDefinition(Element process){
    . . .
      //Data
      NodeList dats=process.getElementsByTagName
                                (WfDataDefinition.TAG);
      for(i=0; i<dats.getLength(); ++i){
        Element d=(Element)dats.item(i);
        WfDataDefinition dd=new WfDataDefinition(d);
        data.put(dd.id,dd);
      }
  }
  public Element toXML(Document doc){
    . . .
    // Data
    it=data.values().iterator();
    while(it.hasNext()){
      WfDataDefinition d=(WfDataDefinition)it.next();
      process.appendChild(d.toXML(doc));
    }
```

```
      return process;
    }
  }
```

In addition, class **WfActivityDefinition** must read the access restriction tags in the constructor and generate them in the toXML() method.

```
package ProcessDefinition;
public class WfActivityDefinition {
. . .
  Vector restrictions=new Vector();
  WfActivityDefinition(Element activity, Map participants,
                                            Map data){
  . . .
    // data access restrictions
    restrs=activity.getElementsByTagName("RESTRICT_TO");
    int i;
    for(i=0; i<restrs.getLength(); ++i){
      Element restr = (Element)restrs.item(i);
      WfDataDefinition d=(WfDataDefinition)
                     data.get( restr.getAttribute("REF"));
      WfAccessRestriction restriction =
        new WfAccessRestriction
                     (d,restr.hasAttribute("READ_ONLY"));
      restrictions.add(restriction);
    }
  }
  public Element toXML(Document doc){
    . . .
    Iterator it=restrictions.iterator();
    while(it.hasNext()){
      WfAccessRestriction restriction=
                            (WfAccessRestriction)it.next();
      activity.appendChild(restriction.toXML(doc));
    }
    return activity;
  }
}
```

To use the data during the enactment the class **WfProcessImpl** must create the context on the basis of the workflow data declared in the process definition. Since we do not know in advance the types of the workflow data, we instantiate the values of the context using reflection: we look for a class having the same name as the data type, if no such a class exists then a **String** is instantiated.

```
package WfEngine;
...
public class WfProcessImpl
```

```
extends ExecutionObjectImpl
implements WfProcess {
  ...
  NameValue[] processResult;
  WfProcessImpl(WfProcessMgr mgr, WfProcessDefinition def,
                WfRequester req) {
    ...
    // create context
    Collection data=def.getData();
    NameValue[] ctxt=new NameValue[data.size()];
    // for each data definition..
    Iterator it=data.iterator();
    for(i=0; it.hasNext(); ++i){
      WfDataDefinition dd=(WfDataDefinition)it.next();
      // create an entry in the context..
      ctxt[i]=new NameValue(dd.name,null);
      // instantiate the object type..
      Class cls;
      try{
        cls = Class.forName(dd.type);
      }catch(Exception e){
        String s=new String();
        cls=s.getClass();
      }
      // and put it in the context
      ctxt[i].the_value=cls.newInstance();
    }
    this.set_process_context(ctxt);
    ...
  }
  ...
}
```

The constructor of the class WfActivityImpl builds a copy of the process context that contains only the pieces of data that are accessible to the activity. If there is no access restriction then the entire process context is made available to the activity, otherwise for each restriction an entry is added to the activity context. If the data are accessible in read only mode, a copy of the process context entry is created, otherwise the original entry is used. Two helper methods are used in this task: find() which returns the process context entry corresponding to an access restriction name, and doClone() which creates a duplicate of the value of a process context entry.

```
package WfEngine;
...
class WfActivityImpl
extends ExecutionObjectImpl
```

```
            implements WfActivity {
              . . .
            public WfActivityImpl(WfProcess proc,
                                  WfActivityDefinition def) {
               . . .
              // set up workflow data
              try{
               NameValue[] processContext =
                                      container().process_context();
               //NameValueInfo[] signature=container().manager().
               //context_signature();
               Collection restrictions = def.getRestrictions();
               if(restrictions.size()==0){ // no restriction
                                          // i.e. access to all data
                 set_process_context(processContext);
               }else{ // access only according to restrictions
                 NameValue[] activityContext=new NameValue
                                            [restrictions.size()];
                 Iterator it=restrictions.iterator();
                 for(int i=0; it.hasNext(); ++i){
                   WfAccessRestriction restriction=
                                    (WfAccessRestriction)it.next();
                   NameValue data=find
                              (restriction.data.name,processContext);
                   if(restriction.readOnly){
                     // if read-only make a local copy
                     activityContext[i] = new NameValue(
                         data.the_name,doClone(data.the_value));
                   }else
                     // if read-write user the original data
                     activityContext[i]=data;
                   set_process_context(activityContext);
                 }
               }
              }catch(Exception e){    }
            }
            // find the data given the name
            private static NameValue find
                                    (String name, NameValue[] list){
              for(int i=0; i<list.length; ++i)
                if(name.equals(list[i].the_name))
                  return list[i];
              return null;
            }
            private static Object doClone(Object obj){
              // try using a copy constructor, if it is defined
```

```
try{
  Class cls = obj.getClass();
  Constructor cpyCtor =
              cls.getConstructor(new Class[]{ cls });
  return cpyCtor.newInstance(new Object[]{ obj });
}catch(Exception e){
  // if there's no copy constructor return the string
  // equivalent
  return obj.toString();
}
}
...
}
```

The WorkItem.jsp page now includes a section that contains a text area for each of the data items accessible in the activity. We use the <textarea> tag because in this prototype the only valid data type is String.

```
<%@ page contentType="text/html" language="java" %>
...
<hr><h2>Activity data</h2>
<form action="Complete.jsp" method="POST">
<%
        NameValue[] processContext=activity.
                                    process_context();
        for(int i=0; i<processContext.length; ++i){ %>
          <%=processContext[i].the_name%>:<br>
          <textarea name="<%=processContext[i].the_name%>"
          ><%=processContext[i].the_value%></textarea>
          <p><%
        } %>
<input type="hidden" name="workItem" value="<%=key%>">
<input type="submit" name="action" value="Complete">
<input type="submit" name="action" value="Update">
</form>
...
</html>
```

21.7.4 □ Test

The test procedure is the same as the previous prototype. In addition it is important to test the input of the workflow data for each activity.

21.8 ■ Extension

The workflow management system developed so far did not address two issues that are important for a system that can be used to enact real business processes: handling of complex workflow-relevant data and complex activity sequencing rules. The main extensions are:

■ Introduce the capability of using complex data in the processes; this extension must consider two aspects: the definition of complex data types and the presentation and editing of such data.

■ Add the management of new rules for the sequencing of activities, such as split of thread of control among two (or more) branches that can be executed in parallel or in mutual exclusion (based on some condition), and the join of multiple branches.

21.9 ■ Assessment

Domain analysis. The wide diffusion of workflow and process enactment systems requires a framework to support their development. We started the top-down domain analysis from the reference models defined by international bodies, and from the inter-operation standards. Accordingly we developed a framework that is conformant with the standards.

Scope. The framework provides the infrastructure required to develop workflow systems. It provides the basic mechanisms to enact business processes. The domain comprises the processes, the organization performing such processes and the data manipulated.

Customization. The customization of the framework can be performed by means of definition files that contain the description of both the processes and the data. This file is a sort of script that defines the behaviour of the system. This kind of customization can be classified as grey box.

Architecture	Script extensible framework
Context	Framework development.
Problem	Allow the user to easily customize the framework by adding new functionalities.
Forces or tradeoffs	The concept of the framework requires new classes to customize the framework. The user must not be required to program to customize the framework. The framework must be customizable at run time.
Solution	Define a component (Behavior Specification) that can be used to define the behaviour of the framework. This part of the framework has a meta-functionality because it is used to define an object structure that is interpreted by the core component of the framework. Based on this run-time customization facility it is relatively easy to define a language that is used to script the behaviour definition. A scripting component parses the language and builds a representation using the behaviour specification.

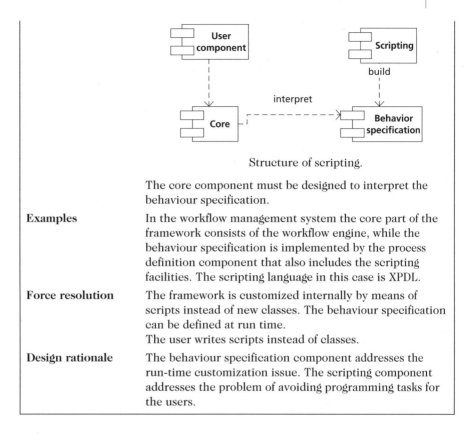

Structure of scripting.

The core component must be designed to interpret the behaviour specification.

Examples
In the workflow management system the core part of the framework consists of the workflow engine, while the behaviour specification is implemented by the process definition component that also includes the scripting facilities. The scripting language in this case is XPDL.

Force resolution
The framework is customized internally by means of scripts instead of new classes. The behaviour specification can be defined at run time.
The user writes scripts instead of classes.

Design rationale
The behaviour specification component addresses the run-time customization issue. The scripting component addresses the problem of avoiding programming tasks for the users.

21.10 ■ References

Gamma, E., Helm, R., Johnson, R. and Vlissides, J. (1995) *Design Patterns: Elements of Reusable Object-Oriented Software*, Addison-Wesley.

Hollingsworth, D. (1995) "The Workflow Reference Model", The Workflow Management Coalition, available at http://www.wfmc.org/standards/docs/tc003v11.pdf.

McCluskey, Glen (2001) "JDC TechTips", 7 August, available at http://java.sun.com/jdc/JDCTechTips/2001/tt0807.html.

OMG (1998) "Joint Workflow Management Facility RFP", available at ftp://ftp.omg.org/pub/docs/bom/98-06-07.pdf.

WfMC (1999) "Interface 1: Process Definition Interchange Process Model", WfMC TC-1016-P, October.

Index